# Presidential Leadership

## *Politics and Policy Making*

### Third Edition

**George C. Edwards III**
*Texas A & M University*

**Stephen J. Wayne**
*Georgetown University*

**St. Martin's Press    New York**

*Executive editor:* Don Reisman
*Manager, publishing services:* Emily Berleth
*Publishing services associate:* Kalea Chapman
*Project management:* Till & Till, Inc.
*Art director:* Sheree Goodman
*Cover photography:* Bill Westheimer

For information, write:
St. Martin's Press, Inc.
175 Fifth Avenue
New York, NY 10010


ISBN: 0-312-07497-2

To Carmella and Cheryl

# Preface

The presidency is a much praised, much damned institution. During the early 1960s it was seen as the major innovative force within the government. People looked to the president to satisfy an increasing number of their demands. Presidential power was thought to be the key to political change.

By the late 1960s and early 1970s, this power was seen as a serious problem. Scholars blamed presidents and their excesses for involvement in the war in Southeast Asia and for Watergate and other scandals. Restrain the "imperial" presidency became the cry.

Presidents Ford and Carter responded to this plea by attempting to deimperialize the office. Ford opened the White House to opposing views; Carter initially reduced the size, status, and perquisites of presidential aides. Both were careful not to exceed their constitutional and statutory powers.

Growing institutional conflict between Congress and the presidency and within the executive branch raised questions about the possibility of effective governance. Worsening economic conditions, increasingly scarce resources, and a series of foreign policy crises produced a desire for more assertive, more directive leadership. The presidency was seen as imperiled; weakness, not strength, its problem. Disappointment in presidential performance replaced fear of presidential abuses.

The Reagan presidency led scholars once again to reevaluate the workings of the system and the role of the president within it. Reagan's ability to achieve some of his major policy goals at the beginning of his administration indicated that stalemate need not paralyze the government. But it also gave rise to fears, particularly after the Iran–Contra affair, of the dangers that improperly exercised power can produce.

During the Bush and Clinton presidencies the issue of divided government, of the need for but difficulty of achieving change, reemerged. The 1992 election campaign focused on how well Bush had done and Clinton and Perot would do in addressing economic, social, and governance issues and providing leadership to deal with them effectively. This book will provide an initial assessment of Clinton's progress in his quest to lead.

Obviously, presidential leadership cuts two ways. It is desirable yet potentially harmful. It is necessary but difficult, perhaps more difficult today than in the past. Even though the president has limited influence over the environment in which he must operate, he is expected to solve most of the major problems that affect a significant portion of the American population. While expectations of the presidency remain as great as ever, the costs of meeting these expectations have increased. To make matters worse, presidents regularly receive more blame and credit for external conditions than they deserve. All of this has complicated the president's leadership task and, at the same time, made that task more critical.

This book, the text's third edition, is about presidential leadership, about the obstacles to that leadership, and about the skills necessary to overcome those obstacles.

In this edition we posit two models of leadership: the president as director of change and the president as facilitator. In the director of change model, presidents lead the nation by dominating other political actors; in the facilitator model, they work, bargaining and pleading, at coalition building to further the attainment of their and their constituency's goals. These models provide the framework within which we assess leadership in the modern presidency and evaluate how individual presidents are doing their job.

We offer no simple formula for success, but we do assess the costs and consequences of presidential leadership in a pluralistic system where separate institutions are forced to share powers. We believe that effective, responsible presidential leadership can play a vital role in providing the coherence, direction, and support necessary to articulate and achieve national policy and political goals.

One of the difficulties we faced in writing this book was trying to make it gender neutral. We have moved away from the conventional male pronoun to represent the president, pluralizing the term where possible. Occasionally, however, pluralizing president is awkward—as is he/she. So in those situations, we revert to the traditional he. We hope we haven't offended anyone by doing so.

We wish to thank our friends at St. Martin's Press, particularly Don Reisman and Mary Hugh Lester, for the help they have provided us in the development, editing, and marketing of the third edition of this work. We wish also to thank Professors Ryan Barilleaux of Miami University, Cary Covington of the University of Iowa, and Delbert Ringquist of Central Michigan University for their insightful critiques. Finally, and most importantly, we want to acknowledge and thank our respective wives, Carmella Edwards and Cheryl Beil, for their patience, encouragement, and help. It is to them we dedicate this book.

*George C. Edwards III*
*Stephen J. Wayne*

# Contents

# 1

# Presidential Leadership: An Introduction

No office within American government, or for that matter most other systems, has commanded the attention, stirred the imagination, and generated the emotions that the presidency has. Considered the first among equals, it has become the dominant institution in a system designed for balanced government, the prime initiator and coordinator among separate and independent institutions, the foremost mobilizer among disparate and, often, competing interests, and the principal communications link from and to a multitude of groups and individuals. It is a many-faceted, dynamic office—with a plethora of responsibilities, a variety of roles, and a large range of powers.

Within it, the president is clearly the chief. Executive officials look to the office for direction, coordination, and general guidance in the implementation of policy; members of Congress look to it for establishing priorities, exerting influence, and providing services; the heads of foreign governments look to it for articulating positions, conducting diplomacy, and flexing muscle; the general public looks to it for enhancing security, solving problems, and exercising symbolic and moral leadership—a big order to be sure.

Unfortunately for most presidents, these expectations often exceed their abilities to meet them. It is not simply a question of skill or personality, although both contribute to the capacity to do the job and to do it well. The problem is the system, particularly its constitutional, institutional, and political structures. The Constitution divides authority; institutions share power; and parties lack cohesion and often a sustained ideological thrust.

Despite the president's position and status, these constraints are difficult to overcome. Expectations cannot easily be ignored or reduced. As a consequence, disappointment is frequent regardless of who occupies the Oval Office.

To some extent, this has always been the case. But in recent times, the gap between expectations and performance seems to have widened. Disenchantment has increased; confidence has declined; the popularity of many presidents has plummeted during the course of their administrations. Effective presidential leadership has thus become more difficult but no less vital if the American system is to work.

This book addresses these problems and the ability of presidents to surmount them. First and foremost, this is a book about presidential leadership, about the capacity of chief executives to fulfill their tasks, to exercise their powers, and to utilize their organizational structures. It is a book about political leadership, about public opinion, group pressures, media coverage, and presidential salesmanship before, during, and after elections. It is also a book about policy leadership, about institutions and processes, about priority setting, coalition building, and governmental implementation. Finally, it is a book about personal leadership, about incumbents in office, about their goals, national needs, and the formal and informal ways of accomplishing their objectives.

In order to understand the problems of contemporary presidential leadership, it is necessary to gain perspective on the institution and its development. The first two parts of this chapter provide that perspective. In them we present an overview of the creation of the office and its evolution. We place particular emphasis on the growth of its policy-making roles, its advisory and administrative structures, and its political and public dimensions. In the third part of the chapter we examine recent changes in the political and policy environment and the impact of those changes on the president's job performance. We assess the sources of the institution's problems and present the dilemmas for contemporary leadership. In the final section we discuss how we will go about exploring these dilemmas.

## THE ORIGINAL PRESIDENCY

### The Creation of the Institution

The contemporary presidency bears little resemblance to the one the framers of the Constitution artfully designed in 1787 in Philadelphia. Their executive had more limited authority, less functional responsibility, and no explicit institutional structure or operating procedures. The times, of course, were different.

Although the Constitution's framers saw the need for an independent executive empowered with its own authority, they did not begin with a consensus on the form this executive should take nor the powers it should possess. At the outset of their deliberations, two basic questions had to be answered: Should the office be entrusted to one person or to several individuals? and What combination of functions, responsibilities, and powers would yield an energetic yet safe executive?

The first of these questions was resolved early in the convention after a short but pointed discussion. James Wilson, delegate from Pennsylvania, had proposed that only a single individual could combine the characteristics of "energy, dispatch, and responsibility." Critics immediately responded that such an executive would be dangerous—"the foetus of monarchy," in the words of Edmund Randolph.

In denying the allegation that what they really wanted was a king, Wilson and James Madison sought to contrast their more limited executive with the powers of a king. As the debate intensified, Madison proposed that the institution's authority be established before the number of executives was decided. This constituted one of the most astute parliamentary moves of the Constitutional Convention. Wilson had previously declared that the prerogatives of the British monarch were not a proper guide for determining the executive's domain. They were too extensive. The American executive, he argued, should possess only executive authority, the power to execute laws and make those appointments that had not otherwise been provided for. The convention accepted Wilson's delineation, a delineation that made it safe to entrust the office to a single individual. This was promptly done. Only later were those powers elaborated.

Wilson was primarily responsible for this elaboration as well. As a member of the committee charged with taking propositions approved by the convention and shaping them into a constitution, he detailed the executive's powers with phraseology taken from the New York and Massachusetts constitutions. Surprisingly, his enumeration engendered little debate. The powers were not particularly controversial. Couching them in the language of two state constitutions made them more palatable to the delegates. Most were quickly and quietly adopted.

Agreement on the checks to secure and restrain the executive was a little more difficult. Abuses of past executives—particularly British monarchs and colonial governors—combined with the excesses of contemporary legislatures made the maintenance of an institutional balance essential. The problem was how to preserve the balance without jeopardizing the independence of the separate branches or impeding the lawful exercise of their authority.

In the end the framers resolved this problem by checking those powers that they believed to be most dangerous, the ones which historically had been subject to greatest abuse (appointments, treaty making, and declarations of war), while protecting the general spheres of authority from encroachment (in the executive's case by a qualified veto). Presidential responsibility was also encouraged by the provisions for reeligibility and a short term of office. Reappointment was the great motive to good behavior. For those executives who flagrantly abused their authority, impeachment was the ultimate recourse.

The traditional weapon to defend executive authority was the veto. Theoretically, it could function to protect those executive prerogatives that were threatened by the legislature. In practice, it had frequently been employed to preclude the enactment of laws that the executive opposed. Herein lay its danger. The compromise was to give the president the veto but allow two-thirds of both houses to override it.

In summary, the relative ease with which the presidency was empowered indicates that a consensus developed on the bounds and substance of executive authority. Not only had certain traditional prerogatives been rejected but others had been readily accepted. In deciding which of these powers should be given to the new institution, the framers turned to the tenets of balanced government as articulated by the French theorist Charles de Montesquieu in his often-quoted treatise, *The Spirit of the Laws,* and practiced to some extent in the states of Massachusetts and New York.[1] Those powers that conformed to the basic division of authority were accepted; those that actually or potentially threatened the institutional balance were rejected.

Fears of potential abuse led to differing opinions on how best to constrain the branches without violating the principle of separate spheres of authority. The majority of the delegates opted for sharing powers, particularly in foreign affairs, and principally with the Senate. Their decision, reached toward the end of the convention when the pressures to compromise were greatest, exacerbated the fears of those who believed that the Senate would come to dominate the president and control the government.

Many of the opponents of the Constitution saw the sharing of powers as far more dangerous than the general grant of executive authority that was specified in Article 2. Although each of the president's powers engendered some objection during the ratification debate, the most sustained criticism was directed at the relationship with the upper chamber. In the end, the proponents of the Constitution prevailed, but the debate over the efficacy of shared powers between executive and legislative branches has continued through the years.

### The Scope of Article 2

In one sense what the framers did is obvious. It is written in Article 2. In another sense, however, their deliberations and decisions have been subject to constant interpretation. Unlike Article 1, where the Constitution detailed the legislative powers that were given to Congress, Article 2 stated executive authority in a more general way: "The executive power shall be vested in a President of the United States of America." For years scholars have debated whether this designation provides presidents with an undefined grant of authority or simply confers on them the title of the office.

Although the answer to this question remains in doubt, the executive portion of the president's responsibilities is relatively clear. The framers charged the president with the administration of government, the task of faithfully executing the law and the capacity to do so by overseeing the executive departments. The departments were not designated by the Constitution. They were established by legislation during the first Congress and later Congresses. The president, however, was to have a hand in choosing the people who ran them.

The need to provide the executive with some discretion to respond to emergency or extraordinary situations was also considered essential. Heading the only institution with continuous tenure and the only one with a national perspective, the president was thought to be able to respond to events more quickly and decisively than the Congress. Traditionally this type of emergency power resided in the executive.

In his *Second Treatise of Civil Government*, the British philosopher John Locke had written of the need for such a power, which he termed a prerogative.[2] The framers agreed. Having themselves experienced under the Articles of Confederation a legislature unable to respond to emergencies, they desired to provide such a capacity in their constitutional arrangement and gave it to the president.

The debate over the war powers illustrates their dilemma as well as their solution. Initially, the Congress was given the authority to make war. Fearing that the word "make" might preclude the executive from responding to an attack if Congress were not in session, the framers agreed to substitute the word "declare." This provided the president with flexibility but did not alter the basic intent—to have Congress decide whether or not to go to war. Even after making that decision, Congress retained powers that affected the conduct of hostilities. These powers serve to limit the president's discretion as commander in chief.

Similarly in foreign affairs, the president was limited in what could be done alone without the approval of the Senate or both houses. The executive did, however, share the treaty-making role with the upper chamber and exercised the initiative. But even here, the wording of the Constitution suggested that the Senate was to have a role in the negotiation of treaties as well as in their ratification.

Although executive powers were expected to expand during emergencies, they were never without limits. The exercise of discretionary powers by the executive was always tied to legislation. Presidents could summon Congress into special session, but they were obligated to report to it on the state of the union; they could recommend necessary and expedient legislation, but it was Congress that in the end had to decide what laws, if any, to enact. Even in the case of the veto, two-thirds of both houses would have the last word.

In short, the relatively general grant of executive authority gave to the office broad discretion in the exercise of its principal responsibility— the execution of the law. Some of its powers were exclusive but others were shared. Some of them were enumerated but that enumeration was not exhaustive. Presidents had considerable freedom to oversee subordinates of their own choosing in their administration of government. On the other hand, their discretion in formulating policy was extremely limited. Congress, not the executive, was expected to assume that role in the normal course of events.

## THE EVOLUTION OF THE PRESIDENCY

### Policy-Making Roles

Although the president's constitutionally designated authority has not been formally amended, the scope of that authority has been expanded by law and precedent. Over the years, the president's policy-making powers have grown dramatically. Chief executives, starting with Washington, set the contours of foreign policy. Beginning with Jefferson, they shaped it to the point of actually defining what the war policy would be. There were other early examples of presidential initiatives in foreign affairs, notably Monroe's famous doctrine that pledged United States protection of the independent states on this side of the Atlantic.

Crisis situations expanded the president's powers still further, as Lincoln's actions during the Civil War demonstrated. Lincoln justified his exercise of power by the gravity of the situation. "Was it possible to lose the nation and yet preserve the Constitution?" he asked. To his own question, he replied, "I felt that measures otherwise unconstitutional might become lawful by becoming indispensable to the preservation of the Constitution through the preservation of the nation."[3]

Lincoln's assertion of power was not checked by Congress during the war, but after it Congress reasserted its authority. Throughout the remainder of the nineteenth century, Congress, not the president, dominated the relationship between the branches. In fact, when, as a professor of politics, Woodrow Wilson wrote his perceptive study on the American political system in the mid-1880s, he titled it *Congressional Government*.

Wilson wrote at the end of an era. By the time he became chief executive, the president's roles in both foreign and domestic affairs had expanded, and Wilson revised his book. Demands for a more activist government had encouraged Presidents McKinley and Theodore Roosevelt to work more closely and harmoniously with Congress to fashion major policy initiatives. Roosevelt was responsible for much of this activity.

Assuming an assertive posture in both foreign and domestic affairs, Roosevelt expanded the president's policy-making roles. He sent the navy halfway around the world (and then requested appropriations from Congress to return it home); he announced a corollary to the Monroe Doctrine, further involving the United States in hemispheric activities; he helped instigate a revolution in Colombia, quickly recognized the independence of insurgents on the Isthmus of Panama, and promptly entered into an agreement with them to build a canal. He was the first president to travel outside of the United States (to Mexico and Panama) and the first to help settle a war, for which he won the Nobel Peace Prize. Within the domestic sphere, Roosevelt busted trusts, crusaded for conservation, and mediated a major coal strike. He was also instrumental in getting Congress to enact important legislation, including the Pure Food and Drug Act, the Meat Inspection Act, and the Hepburn (railroad) Act.

Roosevelt's theory of the presidency justified and accommodated his activism. Writing in his autobiography after his political career had ended, Roosevelt stated:

> My view was that every executive officer, and above all every executive officer in high position, was a steward of the people bound actively and affirmatively to do all he could for the people, and not to content himself with the negative merit of keeping his talents undamaged in a napkin.[4]

In contrast, William Howard Taft, Roosevelt's successor, expressed a much more restrained conception:

> The true view of the executive function is, as I conceive it, that the president can exercise no power which cannot be fairly and reasonably traced to some specific grant of power or justly implied and included within such express grant as proper and necessary to its exercise. Such specific grant must be either in the federal Constitution or in an act of Congress passed in pursuance thereof. There is no undefined residuum of power which he can exercise because it seems to him to be in the public interest.[5]

Roosevelt's *stewardship* theory has prevailed. With the exception of the three Republican presidents of the 1920s, occupants of the Oval Office in the twentieth century have assumed active political and policy-making roles. Woodrow Wilson and Franklin Roosevelt, in particular, expanded Theodore Roosevelt's initiatives in international and domestic matters.

Wilson was the first president to propose a comprehensive legislative program and the first to be involved in summitry. He was the architect of the proposal to establish a League of Nations, although he was unable to persuade the Senate to accept his plan.

Franklin Roosevelt enlarged the president's role in economic affairs. Coming into office in the midst of the Great Depression, he initiated a series of measures to deal with the crisis and succeeded in getting Congress to enact them. He maintained the posture of an international leader, maneuvering the country's entrance into World War II and participating in summit conferences to win the war and plan the peace. He also made the critical decision to develop the atomic bomb.

The modern presidency is said to have begun in the era of Franklin Roosevelt. It is characterized by presidential activism in a variety of policy-making roles. Many of the practices that Roosevelt initiated or continued have been institutionalized by his successors and/or required by Congress.

### Organizational Structure

The structure of the modern presidency also developed during the Roosevelt period. In 1939 the Executive Office of the President was created. Prior to that time presidents had depended largely on their department heads for administration and advice.

The Constitution did not explicitly provide for an administrative structure. It did, however, contain oblique reference to one. There was a provision in Article 2 that the president could demand in writing the opinions of subordinate officials. It was up to the first Congress to establish the executive departments as the principal administrative units of government. It created three departments (Foreign Affairs, Treasury, and War) and appointed an attorney general and a postmaster general. Since then, ten more departments and more than one hundred agencies have been established.

Throughout most of the nineteenth century it was Congress, not the president, who dominated the administration of government. Statutes specified many organizational details of the departments, including their jurisdiction, staffing levels, and even operating procedures. For the most part, there was little oversight from the president.

The autonomy of the departments contributed to the influence of their secretaries, who headed them. Since the department heads were the president's principal advisers, they exercised considerable leverage in helping to design administration goals and in mobilizing congressional support. With the exception of the Jefferson, Jackson, and Lincoln administrations, strong department secretaries and weak presidents characterized executive advisory relationships.

This began to change at the outset of the twentieth century as a consequence of the president's growing influence in Congress. As that increased, the potency of the department secretaries, individually and collectively, began to decline. They lost their privileged position between president and Congress. Their support of administration proposals became less critical than it had been to the president's legislative success.

The concern that Theodore Roosevelt and, particularly, William Howard Taft evidenced toward the organization of government also contributed eventually to the president's enhanced status and power within the executive branch. Taft appointed a Committee on Economy and Efficiency to recommend improvements. Reporting in 1913, the committee urged the creation of a more hierarchical structure with the president assuming a larger administrative role.

Initially, Congress was reluctant to comply. However, sizable budget deficits, inflated by United States involvement in World War I, provided the legislature with a financial (and political) incentive to do so. Unable to control the deficits, Congress turned to the president for help. It enacted the Budget and Accounting Act of 1921, which made it a presidential responsibility to estimate the financial needs of the individual departments and agencies on a yearly basis and provided the president with an institutional mechanism to do so, the Bureau of the Budget.

When Franklin Roosevelt took office and expanded the president's domestic policy role, he needed more information, more expertise, and more staff. At first he depended on personnel provided by the executive departments. When that did not prove satisfactory, he turned to a small group of experts to advise him on how to make the organizational structure of the executive more responsive to his needs. The group, headed by Louis Brownlow, issued a report that said:

> The President needs help. His immediate staff assistance is entirely inadequate. He should be given a small number of executive assistants who would be his direct aides in dealing with the managerial agencies and administrative departments of government.[6]

The Brownlow committee urged the creation of a separate presidential office. In 1939 Congress approved the act that established the Executive Office of the President. Initially the office consisted of five units: the White House, Bureau of the Budget, and three World War II agencies (the National Resources Planning Board, the Liaison Office for Personnel Management, and the Office of Government Reports). Eventually over forty different councils, boards, and offices have been housed at one time or another in this office.

The creation of the Executive Office provided the president with a structure directly responsive to his interests. The White House became his personal office. Presidential aides performed political tasks that were dictated by the president's immediate needs, actions, and goals. Having no constitutional and statutory authority of their own and no political base other than the president's, their influence was dependent on their access to him. They did his calling.

Whereas the White House functioned as a personal extension of the president, the Budget Bureau became an institutional extension of the presidency. It coordinated the policy-making functions of the departments and agencies, imposing a presidential perspective on the executive branch in the process.

During subsequent administrations, the duties of the Executive Office have been expanded and its organizational structure redesigned. Staffed by civil servants and run by political appointees, it continues to perform a variety of critical tasks. It is considered essential for an activist presidency, but its large size, its many roles, and its organizational autonomy make it difficult for the president to oversee, much less to control.

### Public Dimensions

In addition to the development of the presidency as an institution and the growth of its policy-making roles, the public dimension of the office has expanded as well. This too has been a relatively recent phenomenon. Franklin Roosevelt was the first to use the mass media (radio) to communicate directly with the American people on a regular basis. His successors have used television to the same end.

For most of the nineteenth century the presidency was not a particularly visible office, although the president received his share of critical commentary. Jefferson was the first to claim a partisan mandate and Jackson the first to claim a public one.[7]

A variety of factors contributed to a more active public posture by presidents toward the beginning of the twentieth century. The growth of news-gathering organizations and newspaper chains made it possible to communicate with more people more quickly. The advent of yellow journalism combined with the increased activism of government generated more interest in the opinions and behavior of public officials, particularly the president.

Theodore Roosevelt, more than any of his predecessors, took advantage of these developments to focus attention on himself, his policies, and his activities. He was the first president to give reporters a room in the White House and the first to hold regular meetings with the press. Using his position as "a bully pulpit," Roosevelt rallied public support for his positions and proposals.

Roosevelt's presidency prompted Professor Woodrow Wilson to revise his view that the governmental system was dominated by Congress. The president could be as big a man as he wanted, Wilson asserted in 1908. He could use his position as party and national leader to enhance his political power and thereby exert influence on Congress:

> His capacity will set the limit; and if Congress be overborne by him, it will be no fault of the makers of the Constitution—it will be from no lack of constitutional powers on its part, but only because the President has the nation behind him, and Congress has not. He has no means of compelling Congress except through public opinion.[8]

Wilson attempted to heed his own words. The enactment of his legislative program can be attributed in large part to his political leadership and public oratory. His greatest disappointment, however, his inability to persuade the Senate to ratify the Treaty of Versailles ending World War I, stemmed from his failure to exercise these skills successfully. Wilson, who went on a public-speaking tour to build support for his position, overestimated his ability to lead public opinion and underestimated his opponents' capacity to do so.

Although Theodore Roosevelt and Woodrow Wilson used the presidency as a podium, neither of them was as skillful at manipulating the press as was Franklin Roosevelt. In his first term, Franklin Roosevelt held more press conferences than any of his predecessors. Meeting frequently with small groups of reporters in the Oval Office, he used these sessions to articulate his views and float trial balloons. He also made extensive and productive use of radio in his fireside chats.

By the end of the Roosevelt era, the presidency had been permanently altered by the media. It had become the most visible national office. Coverage of the White House was constant. The president was always in the news.

The intensive and extensive media focus on the president has had three principal effects. First, it has permanently added a new role to the president's job, that of communicator in chief, and has required that skills commensurate with this role be exercised. Second, it has heightened public expectations of presidential performance. Advances in communications have enabled organized groups to promote the desires of their membership more effectively. The president has become the focal point for many of these increased demands on government. Third, media coverage has linked public approval more closely to the exercise of presidential power. Now more than ever, presidents need to build support outside of government to gain support within it. Taken together, these factors indicate why increased public exposure for the president has, at best, been a mixed blessing.

## PROBLEMS OF CONTEMPORARY LEADERSHIP

These changes, singularly and together, have created new demands on the president which, as a consequence, have generated new roles and obligations for him and new criteria by which he is to be judged. These new roles and criteria, in turn, have affected perceptions of leadership. In the past, the people did not look to the president to solve most national economic, social, and political problems. Today they do. The president is expected to be a chief policymaker and to exercise a wide range of powers. Ancillary coordination, communication, and co-optation functions have followed from these expanded roles and powers.

Institutional growth has been another consequence of a more activist presidency. The size of the office has increased enormously. Prior to 1939 the president was assisted by a few aides, most of whom were detailed from executive departments and agencies. The total budget for the salaries and expenses of those working for the president was $125,804.98 in 1925. In 1939 when the Executive Office was created, it was about $250,000. Today it is nearing $200 million. The first Executive Office of the President consisted of five agencies, including the White House; fifty-five years later it has twelve agencies and a combined staff of approximately 1,600.

The larger staff has increased the president's capacity to perform added responsibilities and to do so with less dependence on executive departments and agencies. But the enlargement of that staff has also worked to extend the very functions and responsibilities that the staff was designed to serve. This expansion has limited the president's personal influence over what functions are performed and to a lesser extent how the administration is organized to perform them.

Not only has the presidential office grown in size and solidified in organization but its policy processes have become institutionalized. Mechanisms for preparing the budget, formulating a program, building support in Congress, and advising the president whether to sign or veto legislation have developed and continued from administration to administration. These routines have also worked to shape the functions and processes they serve.

There have been significant changes in the public dimensions of the office as well. The selection process has become more individualized. Parties do not organize and mediate between candidates and the voters as they did in the past. Public expectations have increased as a consequence of longer campaigns, more personalized appeals, and many specific promises made to organized groups. Yet, the electoral coalition needed to win no longer provides the basis for governing. New coalitions have to be formed on an issue-by-issue basis.

The national media seemingly are more critical of the president than in the past. Communications from and to the public are more direct and immediate. Such communications enable the White House to measure the pulse of public opinion more accurately, but also condition responses, shorten the time frame, and, ultimately, constrain the president's options.

Interest groups have proliferated and professionalized. They have become more sophisticated at influencing their members and mobilizing them behind specific policy positions. No institution or individual, not the Executive Office of the President, the White House, or even the president, is immune from these pressures.

Lobbying increases the political impact of many presidential decisions. It can force the president's hand, necessitating a compromise for political reasons when an alternative is preferred for policy reasons. The proliferation of professionalized interest groups makes the redistribution of resources more difficult. Over time, it increases levels of dissatisfaction among different sectors of the public. It adversely affects the president's relations with Congress.

Changes within the legislature have reinforced this organized pluralism. Congress has decentralized law making, shifting power to a large number of subcommittee chairs. Ironically, more members of Congress must now be consulted, coordinated, and cajoled at the very time when Congress has involved itself in more issues of executive policy making and policy implementation. Presidents must work harder than in the past to achieve their legislative goals.

Similar constraints are found within the executive branch. The continuing orientation of the bureaucracy to outside groups plus its ongoing relationships with Congress work to limit presidential influence. Most presidential appointees in the departments and agencies soon find themselves with divided loyalties.

And that is not all. External factors within the environment have enlarged policy expectations of the president but at the same time made those expectations less subject to presidential control than they were in the past. The president is expected to manage the economy, but the increasing interdependence of nations limits the ability to do so; the

'Okay, bring in the new guy ...'

scarcity of some natural resources no longer permits unlimited development and forces decisions that have important political consequences; the vulnerability of the United States to nuclear attack shortens the president's reaction time and broadens the effect of national security decisions. It also contributes to the public's psychological dependence on the president and the security needs that the office serves.

Finally, events from the late 1960s to the present—U.S. involvement in Vietnam, the Watergate cover-up, the Iran–Contra affair, and various departmental and congressional scandals—have impugned the motives and integrity of high officials, including the president's. Occupants of the Oval Office no longer enjoy the benefit of the doubt, making it more difficult for them to rally and maintain public support despite the expectation to do so.

## ORIENTATION AND ORGANIZATION OF THIS STUDY

### Thinking about Leadership: Two Perspectives

This book is titled *Presidential Leadership* because it focuses on just that—leadership. The exercise of influence is central to our concept of leadership, as it is to most political scientists. We want to know whether the president can influence the actions and attitudes of others and affect the output of government. It is important to distinguish between attempts to lead and leadership itself. Both are of primary interest in this book, and we devote much of our effort to exploring the relationship between the two.

Presidential leadership typically involves obtaining or maintaining the support of other political actors for the chief executive's political and policy stances. In the American political system, most political actors are free to choose whether or not to follow the chief executive's lead; the president cannot force them to act, presenting a challenge to his political leadership.

Although thinking of leadership in terms of influence is useful for the study of presidential leadership, the concept remains somewhat nebulous. To guide our examination, we consider it useful to refine the concept of leadership by contrasting two broad perspectives on the presidency. In the first the president is the *director* of change, creating opportunities to move in new directions and leading others where they otherwise would not go. In the role of director the president is out in front, establishing goals and encouraging others to follow.

A second perspective is less heroic but nonetheless important. Here the president is primarily a *facilitator* of change, exploiting opportunities to help others go where they want to go anyway. In the role of facilitator the president reflects and perhaps intensifies widely held views, using available resources to achieve his constituency's aspirations.

The director creates a constituency to follow his lead, whereas the facilitator endows his constituency's views with shape and purpose by interpreting and translating them into legislation. The director shapes the contours of the political landscape to pave the way for change, whereas the facilitator exploits opportunities presented by a favorable configuration of political forces.

The director moves mountains and influences many independent actors. This is the more formidable task—establishing the agenda and persuading a perhaps reluctant public or Congress to support administration policies. In contrast, the facilitator works at the margins, influencing a few critical actors and taking advantage of the opportunities for change already present in the environment. In both cases the president exercises leadership, yet the scale of the leadership is clearly different. The range and scope of the director's influence are broad, whereas those of the facilitator are more narrow.

The two perspectives are not neat categories: We employ them simply to aid our understanding of the concept of leadership and its application to the president. The issue is not whether leadership matters, but rather how much and under what conditions. It is not sufficient to conclude, however, that sometimes the environment is receptive to change and at other times not. This viewpoint simply begs the question of whether presidents are able to influence the environment so as to create the opportunity for change. Understanding the possibilities of leadership permits an assessment of the performance of presidents.

The notion of the dominant president who moves the country and the government by means of strong, effective leadership has deep roots in our political culture. Those chief executives whom Americans revere, such as Washington, Jefferson, Jackson, Lincoln, Wilson, and both Roosevelts, have taken on mythic proportions as leaders. Even though the public is frequently disillusioned with the performance of presidents and recognizes that stalemate is common, Americans eagerly accept what appears to be effective presidential leadership, as in the case of Ronald Reagan in 1981, as evidence on which to renew faith in the potential of the presidency. After all, if presidential leadership works some of the time, why not all of the time?

This perception directly influences expectations and evaluations of presidents. If it is reasonable to expect successful leadership from the White House, then failures of leadership must be personal deficiencies. If problems arise because leaders lack the proper will, skills, or understanding, then the solution to the need for leadership is straightforward and simple: Elect presidents willing and able to lead. Because the system is responsive to appropriate leadership, it will function smoothly with the right leaders in the Oval Office. The public can indulge in high expectations of its chief executives and freely criticize them if they fail, for example, to bring around Congress or the public to their point of view. The blame lies clearly in the leader rather than the environment. Americans need not concern themselves with broader forces in American society that may influence presidential leadership. Because these forces are complex and perhaps even intractable, to focus on the individual as leader simplifies analysis and evaluation of the problems of governing.

On the other hand, what if presidential leadership is not preeminent in American government? What if presidential leadership has less potential than holders of the conventional wisdom believe and the president actually operates at the margins in leading the country? What if the national preoccupation with the chief executive is misplaced and belief in the impact of the individual leader is largely a myth—a product of a search for simple solutions in an extremely complex, purposefully inefficient system in which the founders' handiwork in decentralizing power defeats even the most capable leaders?

If this is the case, the public should expect less of its presidents and be less disappointed when they are not successful in leading. In addition, the focus should be less exclusively on the president and more on the context in which the president seeks to lead. Major changes in public policy may then require more than just the "right" person in the job and may not turn on a president's leadership qualities. It does not, of course, follow that failures of presidential leadership may never be attributed to the White House or that presidents have no control over the outcome of their relations with other political actors. It does mean that a better understanding of presidential leadership is necessary to think sensibly about the role of the chief executive in the nation's political system.

### Conceptual Focus

This book will explore the president's leadership problems and the attempts by recent chief executives to overcome them. It will do so by examining multiple facets of the presidency within the context of its political and policy-making roles. Our orientation will be eclectic. Instead of adopting a particular perspective, the book will present several. Instead of imposing a single thesis, it will discuss many of the hypotheses, generalizations, and conclusions that have been advanced by students of the presidency.

The reason for utilizing a variety of approaches and presenting a body of research findings is that there is no one generally accepted theory of the presidency, no one conceptual framework within which to study the office, other than perhaps Richard Neustadt's on presidential power,[9] that has commanded the attention and acceptance of most presidency scholars.

Despite an abundant literature on the presidency, our understanding of how that institution works is not nearly as sophisticated as our understanding of Congress or even the Supreme Court. Much of the presidency still operates behind closed doors.

What factors have conditioned the methodology, shaped the content, and limited the findings of so much of the presidency literature? Three stand out: (1) the view that each president and administration is relatively unique; (2) the difficulty of obtaining first-hand information on the operation of the institution; and (3) the absence of a comprehensive theory. Together these factors have impeded the ability to do rigorous, analytic, empirical research on the presidency.

The personalities of individual presidents and their staffs, the particular events and circumstances of their time in office, and the specific problems and actions of their administrations have led scholars to treat each presidency as if it were unique. Emphasizing the differences between presidencies rather than the similarities between them makes the identification of patterns and relations more difficult and, in turn, makes it harder to generalize. Description rather than analysis and speculation rather than generalization have become the standard fare.

The relatively closed character of the institution has contributed to the problem. The presidency is not easy to observe from a distance. Public pronouncements and actions tell only part of what happens and why it happens—usually the part that the people in power wish to convey. Inside information is difficult to obtain. Decision makers, particularly those at the top of the executive bureaucracy, are not readily accessible. Their busy schedules combined with their natural reluctance to reveal information that may be embarrassing, sensitive, or in other ways controversial often make them unwilling and unresponsive sources.

Nor is dependence on journalistic accounts usually satisfactory. Journalists tend to be event oriented. They do not usually employ a time

frame or perspective that is sufficiently comprehensive to permit generalizations, particularly on the institutional and behavioral aspects of the
office.

The third factor that contributes to the problem is the absence of an
overall theory that explains presidential behavior. Unlike other areas in
political science such as individual voting behavior, in which there is a
body of theory that explains and predicts who votes and why, the presidency literature has not produced an explanation of why presidents do
what they do or what consequences their actions have. Nor has it been
able to predict what they will do or what consequences their actions will
have in the future. There are, however, many prescriptions of what
presidents should do.

The nature of these problems suggests that we should cast our net
as broadly as possible when examining the institution and exploring the
president's leadership opportunities and problems. This is why we have
decided not to focus on a single theme (which might exclude important
information) but to examine a set of critical relationships. These relationships are between the president and those whose support he needs to
do his job.

To function effectively an occupant of the Oval Office must be elected, build and maintain popular support, make decisions, and present,
promote, and implement policies. Each of these requirements involves
reciprocal relationships in which presidents influence and are influenced by others. That is why we must examine both sides of these
relationships rather than focus exclusively on the president.

Relationships provide a conceptual framework for studying presidential leadership. They enable us to explain the behavioral causes and
consequences of presidential activities. By stressing relationships, however, we do not suggest that legal powers, informal roles, institutional
structures, and psychological factors are unimportant. Indeed, we
firmly believe one cannot understand the presidency without an extensive knowledge of these matters, and we provide such a background.
Our point of departure is that we discuss these matters within the context of presidential relationships rather than vice versa. Powers, roles,
structures, and personality should not be viewed as ends in themselves.
They are important to us for what they contribute to the president's
ability to formulate, establish, and implement policies.

### Outline

This book is organized into four broad sections. They deal with
politics and public relations, with the person in the institution, with the
presidency's interaction with the rest of the government, and with the
policy-making process.

The next four chapters concern the relationship between the president and the public. In Chapters 2 and 3 we discuss nomination politics
and the general election. Here we focus on the interaction between

presidential candidates and the electorate. In Chapter 4 we turn to the president in office and his relations with the general public, and in Chapter 5 we examine the communications link between the incumbent and the media. In each of these chapters we explore leadership problems. Obviously, winning electoral support, gaining public approval, and obtaining favorable media coverage are critical to a president's success.

In Chapters 6, 7, and 8 we analyze the relationship between the institution and the people in it. Specifically, we examine the interaction among the president, senior White House advisers, and others who wish to affect presidential decisions. Here attention is directed toward decision making at the presidential level. The institutional environment combined with the incumbent's personal style condition presidential discretion and ultimately presidential choices.

In the third part of the book we turn to the interaction that the president must have with the executive branch, Congress, and the judiciary to achieve policy objectives. Promoting programs in Congress, implementing them in the bureaucracy, and adjudicating them in the courts are necessary if presidential leadership is to be effective.

After scrutinizing presidential relations, we then discuss the formulation of public policy in and by the presidency. Individual chapters concern domestic, budgetary and economic, and foreign and defense policy making. In each chapter we identify and assess expectations of presidential leadership and the resources that are available for meeting these expectations.

Having explored the critical relationships between the president and the public, the president and the presidency, the president and the other branches, and the president and the policy-making process, we end with an appendix that discusses another important but different kind of relationship—that of the president and political science. Our object is to demonstrate how various perspectives on the office and methods of studying it can affect what we know about the president. We conclude where we began. If the presidency is a multifaceted institution (as we claim it is), then it can best be understood only by adopting a variety of approaches and techniques. That is why our orientation is eclectic, why we have introduced a number of themes, and why we have chosen critical presidential relationships as the conceptual framework for this study.

## NOTES

1. Charles de Montesquieu, *The Spirit of the Laws*, vol. 1 (New York: Hafner, 1949).
2. Locke wrote: "Where the legislative and executive power are in distinct hands, as they are in all moderated monarchies and well-framed governments, there the good of the society requires that several things should be left to the discretion of him that has the executive power. For the legislators not being able to foresee and provide by laws for all that may be useful to the community, the executor of the laws, having the power in his hands, has by the common law of Nature a right to make use of it for the good of the

society, in many cases where the municipal law has given no direction, till the legislative can conveniently be assembled to provide for it" (John Locke, "Second Treatise of Civil Government," in Thomas I. Cook, ed., *Two Treatises of Government* [New York: Hafner, 1956], p. 203).

3. Abraham Lincoln, "Letter dated April 8, 1964," reprinted in Harry A. Bailey, Jr., ed., *Classics of the American Presidency* (Oak Park, Ill.: Moore Publishing Co., 1980), p. 34.

4. Theodore Roosevelt, *The Autobiography of Theodore Roosevelt* (New York: Scribner's, 1913), p. 197.

5. William Howard Taft, *Our Chief Magistrate and His Powers* (New York: Columbia University Press, 1916), p. 138.

6. President's Committee on Administrative Management, *Report with Special Studies* (Washington, D.C.: U.S. Government Printing Office, 1937), p. 5.

7. It was during the 1820s that the electorate began to choose presidential electors directly rather than have them selected by state legislatures. This increased the value of obtaining and maintaining public support for the president. Tradition, however, required that this be done in a manner that befitted the dignity of the office. Public addresses were permitted; personal campaigning was discouraged. The party was expected to shoulder the electoral burden for its candidates. Not until William Jennings Bryan's quest for the nation's highest office in 1896 did candidates take to the stump themselves.

8. Woodrow Wilson, *Constitutional Government* (New York: Columbia University Press, 1908), pp. 70–71.

9. Richard E. Neustadt, *Presidential Power* (New York: Free Press, 1990).

## SELECTED READINGS

Cronin, Thomas E., ed. *Inventing the American Presidency.* Lawrence, Kans.: University Press of Kansas, 1989.

Ellis, Richard, and Aaron Wildavsky. *Dilemmas of Presidential Leadership: From Washington through Lincoln.* New Brunswick, N.J.: Transaction Publishers, 1989.

*Federalist Papers,* #67–77 in *The Federalist.* New York: Modern Library.

Neustadt, Richard E. *Presidential Power.* New York: Free Press, 1990.

Pika, Joseph, and Norman Thomas. "The Presidency Since Mid-Century." *Congress and the Presidency* 19 (Spring 1992): 29–49.

Riccards, Michael P. *A Republic, If You Can Keep It.* New York: Greenwood, 1987.

Robinson, Donald L. *"To the Best of My Ability."* New York: W. W. Norton, 1987.

Skowronek, Stephen. *The Politics Presidents Make.* Cambridge, Mass.: Harvard University Press, 1993.

# 2

# The Nomination Process

Every four years there are two presidential selection processes: the first to nominate candidates, the second to choose between them. Both require considerable time, money, and effort.

The nominating system has evolved significantly in recent years. Rules governing delegate selection, laws regulating contributions and spending, communications controlled and uncontrolled by the candidates have all changed dramatically within the last thirty years. These changes have literally revolutionized the nomination process. They have affected the types of candidates who seek their party's nomination, the qualifications they demonstrate as criteria for their selection, and the leadership they are able to exert on their party and, ultimately, as president. Today, aspirants for their party's nomination are more on their own. They have greater opportunity to articulate their own priorities and shape their own issue agenda, to develop their own style, and to build their own political coalitions. In this sense, if successful, they are in a good position to bring new ideas, new people, and new leadership to the presidency.

The nomination process, however, contributes to the difficulty presidential aspirants may encounter in exercising this leadership. This process heightens public expectations but weakens partisan support, usually accentuating divisions within the party. It encourages personality politics by focusing on personal characteristics, a theatrical style, and a "sound-bite mentality," rather than on a more substantive discussion of the critical goals and issues that lie ahead. What it provides to the candidate who wins the nominations is a label, but not necessarily a cohesive organization and coherent policy consensus on which to base a general election campaign and orient a new administration once in office.

In this chapter we will discuss these changes and their impact on those seeking the presidency. The chapter is organized into four parts. First we present a historical overview of the nomination process, describing its evolution from congressional caucus to brokered national conventions to popular selection of the delegates through primaries and caucuses. In the second part we examine the factors that condition that selection: party rules, finance laws, and public relations. Emphasizing the changes that have occurred within each of these areas, we describe their impact on parties and their standard bearers. Next, we turn to the strategy and tactics of seeking the nomination. Here, we discuss the principal components of that strategy for front runners and non–front runners alike. Finally, in the last part of the chapter, we take this quest to the national convention and describe the unofficial and official business of these large, semipublic extravaganzas: drama and staging; rules, credentials, and platforms; and the nominations themselves. We also present a brief characterization of the successful candidates. In conclusion, we summarize changes in this process and their implications for winning the general election and governing the country.

## THE EVOLUTION OF THE SYSTEM

The nominating system began to evolve after the Constitution was written and the first two presidential elections were conducted. The framers had not concerned themselves with nominations because there were no parties to nominate candidates. Assuming that well-qualified individuals would comprise the pool from which the president and vice president would be selected, the convention delegates directed their efforts toward encouraging an independent judgment by the electors. They considered such a judgment essential if the two *most* qualified persons were to be chosen.

Once political parties emerged, however, the notion of making an independent decision was constrained by the party's desire to choose an individual whose views were consistent with its own. This required a mechanism by which the parties could designate their nominees.

In 1796 party leaders met informally to agree on their tickets. Four years later partisan congressional caucuses met for the purposes of recommending candidates. "King Caucus," as it came to be known, constituted the principal mode of nomination until the 1820s, when factions developed within Jefferson's Republican party, the only viable party at the time. These factions eventually led to the demise of the caucus and the development of a more decentralized mode of nomination that was consistent with the increasingly sectional composition of the parties. By the 1830s national nominating conventions became the principal means for brokering those interests and uniting the party for a national campaign.

The first convention was held in 1831 by the Anti-Masons, a small but relatively active third party. Having virtually no congressional representation of its own, this party could not use a caucus of legislators to decide on its candidates. Instead, it organized a general meeting in which delegates from the state parties would choose its nominees as well as determine the party's positions on the important issues of the day. The two major parties followed suit in 1832. Thereafter conventions became the standard method for selecting nominees and for articulating policy positions.

These early conventions were informal and rowdy by contemporary standards. The delegates themselves decided on the procedures for conducting the meetings. Choosing the delegates was left to the state party and, more specifically, to its leadership. In most cases, public participation was minimal.

Nineteenth-century conventions served a number of purposes. They provided a forum for party bosses and constituted a mechanism by which agreements could be negotiated and support mobilized. By brokering interests, they helped unite disparate elements within the party, converting a conglomeration of state organizations into a national coalition for the purpose of electing a president and vice president.

The nominating system buttressed the position of party officials, but it did so at the expense of the rank-and-file party members. The influence of the leadership depended in large part on its ability to deliver the votes. To ensure loyalty, the bosses handpicked their delegations.

Demands for reform began to be heard at the beginning of the twentieth century. A number of states changed their mode of selection to primary elections to permit greater public participation. This movement, however, was short-lived. Low voter turnout in primary states, the costs of holding such an election, and the opposition of party leaders to rank-and-file involvement persuaded several state legislatures to make their primaries advisory or discontinue them entirely. As a consequence, the number of primaries declined after World War I as did the percentage of delegates selected in them (see Table 2-1).

Strong candidates avoided primaries. Running in too many of them was interpreted as a sign of weakness, not strength. It indicated lack of national recognition and/or failure to obtain the support of party leaders.

Those who did enter these public contests did so mainly to test their popularity rather than to win convention votes. Dwight D. Eisenhower in 1952, John F. Kennedy in 1960, and Richard M. Nixon in 1968 had to demonstrate that being a general, a Catholic, or a once-defeated presidential candidate would not be fatal to their chances. In other words, they needed to prove they could win the general election by doing well in some primaries.

With the possible exception of John Kennedy's victories in Wisconsin and West Virginia in 1960 and Barry Goldwater's in California in 1964, primaries were neither crucial nor decisive for winning the nomination until the 1970s.[1] When there was a consensus within the party on a single candidate, primaries helped confirm it; when there was not, primaries were not able to produce it. They had little to do with whether the party was united or divided at the time of the convention.

Table 2-1. Number of Presidential Primaries and Percentage of Convention Delegates from Primary States, by Party, Since 1912

| Year | Democratic | | Republican | |
|------|------------|--|------------|--|
| | Number of Primaries | Percentage of Delegates From Primary States* | Number of Primaries | Percentage of Delegates |
| 1912 | 12 | 32.9% | 13 | 41.7% |
| 1916 | 20 | 53.5 | 20 | 58.9 |
| 1920 | 16 | 44.6 | 20 | 57.8 |
| 1924 | 14 | 35.5 | 17 | 45.3 |
| 1928 | 17 | 42.2 | 16 | 44.9 |
| 1932 | 16 | 40.0 | 14 | 37.7 |
| 1936 | 14 | 36.5 | 12 | 37.5 |
| 1940 | 13 | 35.8 | 13 | 38.8 |
| 1944 | 14 | 36.7 | 13 | 38.7 |
| 1948 | 14 | 36.3 | 12 | 36.0 |
| 1952 | 15 | 38.7 | 13 | 39.0 |
| 1956 | 19 | 42.7 | 19 | 44.8 |
| 1960 | 16 | 38.3 | 15 | 38.6 |
| 1964 | 17 | 45.7 | 17 | 45.6 |
| 1968 | 17 | 37.5 | 16 | 34.3 |
| 1972 | 23 | 60.5 | 22 | 52.7 |
| 1976 | 29* | 72.6 | 28* | 67.9 |
| 1980 | 31* | 74.7 | 35* | 74.3 |
| 1984 | 26 | 62.9 | 30 | 68.2 |
| 1988 | 34 | 66.6 | 35 | 76.9 |
| 1992 | 39 | 78.8 | 38 | 80.4 |

*Does not include Vermont, which holds nonbinding presidential preference votes but chooses delegates in state caucuses and conventions.
†Includes party leaders and elected officials chosen from primary states.
Sources: 1912–1964, F. Christopher Arterton, "Campaign Organizations Face the Mass Media in the 1976 Presidential Nomination Process" (paper delivered at the Annual Meeting of the American Political Science Association, Washington, D.C., September 1–4, 1977); 1968–1976, Austin Ranney, *Participation in American Presidential Nominations, 1976* (Washington, D.C.: American Enterprise Institute, 1977), table 1, p. 6. The figures for 1980 were compiled by Austin Ranney from materials distributed by the Democratic National Committee and the Republican National Committee; figures for elections since 1980 were compiled by the authors from data supplied by the Democratic and Republican National Committees.

## CHANGES IN THE POLITICAL ARENA

### Party Reforms

By the end of the 1960s that situation was to alter dramatically. Largely as a result of the tumultuous Democratic convention of 1968 whose nominee, Hubert Humphrey, had not competed in the primaries, demands for a larger voice for the party's rank and file increased. In response to these demands, the party appointed a series of commissions to examine its rules for delegate selection and to propose changes. The commissions had two basic goals: to encourage greater participation in party activities and to make the convention more representative of typical Democratic voters.

To achieve these objectives, the party in the 1970s attempted to ensure that delegate selection more closely reflected popular sentiment. Delegates had to be chosen in the calendar year of the convention. Three-fourths of them had to be elected in districts no larger than those for members of Congress. Moreover, the allocation of the delegates to candidates had to reflect fairly the popular vote that the candidates received within the state. Previously, the party had permitted delegates to be selected well in advance of the convention, on an at-large basis, and by a winner-take-all method of voting.[2]

In nonprimary states the selection process was reformed as well. Delegates had to be chosen in multistaged caucuses that were well publicized in advance to allow adequate time for campaigning. The old system of proxy voting, whereby a state party leader could cast a large number of votes for the delegates of his or her choice, was abolished.

The other major objective of the reforms was to promote more equal representation of the rank and file in the delegations themselves. To achieve this aim the Democratic party required states to implement affirmative action plans for specific groups that had been subject to discrimination. Beginning in 1980, it also required state delegations be equally divided between men and women.

One consequence of these reforms was to make primaries the preferred method of delegate selection. To avoid having their delegations challenged, many state legislatures simply had the voters choose them (see Table 2-1). A second result was to tie the popular vote more closely to the allocation of convention delegates. This made the process more open and more participatory, and it has continued to be so since the reforms were begun.

In 1992 approximately 20 million people voted in the Democratic primaries and 13 million in the Republican primaries. In 1988 the number was over 23 million for the Democrats and over 12 million for the Republicans. The caucuses of both parties attract additional participants, but the numbers are much smaller.[3] Twenty-four years earlier only 12 million people participated in the entire preconvention nomination process of both parties.

Efforts to make convention delegates more representative of their party as a whole have had mixed results. Demographic representation has improved (see Table 2-2); however, ideological and issue differences between the delegates and the rank and file are still apparent. Those who have attended conventions as delegates have displayed greater ideological consistency than average party voters. Democratic delegates have indicated that they were more liberal and Republican delegates have indicated they were more conservative than the rank-and-file supporters of their respective parties. Table 2-3 presents these ideological differences between delegates and party identifiers in 1992.

In addition to affecting the composition of the delegates, the rules changes had other effects. They lengthened the process and inflated its costs. Candidate fatigue and public boredom increased. The influence of the media also grew, particularly in the early critical stages. The party became more fractionalized with its state and local leadership less able to affect presidential nominations within their own areas. Party leaders were not even guaranteed a place on their own delegations. Initially, the number of party officials attending the national meetings declined.

To offset these unintended results, the Democrats made numerous reforms after their unsuccessful 1980 general election campaign. They tried to shorten the process by tightening the time frame in which the nominating process could occur. Only a few states were given permission to hold their contests prior to the beginning of March. The effect of imposing this "window period" during which states could choose their convention delegates was to compress and frontload the schedule. States moved their contests toward the beginning of the time frame in order to maximize their influence on the results. In 1988 the entire southern region along with eight other states chose to hold their primaries or the initial round of their caucuses during the second week of March, the earliest date permitted that year. In 1992 twenty-four states held Democratic primaries or the first round of their caucus selection process and fifteen states held Republican primaries or caucuses by March 10, the second Tuesday of that month. Approximately one-third of all the Democratic delegates in 1992 and almost 37 percent of all the Republican delegates came from those states that held their contests at the very beginning of the nomination process. There will be even greater frontloading in 1996. Ohio and California have moved their primaries forward to the third and fourth Tuesdays of March, respectively.

Choosing so many delegates so early forces candidates to organize their campaign, raise money, and begin to develop their media strategies even before the year of the election. It gives advantage to better-known candidates who can build a larger organizational and financial base earlier in the campaign.

Democrats also tried to increase the influence of elected and appointed party officials. They allocated each state additional delegates to be selected from its members of Congress and elected and party officials. These delegates, known as superdelegates, cannot be formally committed to a particular candidate. In 1992 they constituted nearly one-fifth of all the Democratic delegates at its convention.

The party has also tried to fine-tune its delegate selection process. Delegates were apportioned to candidates on the basis of the proportion of the vote they received. To receive delegates a candidate had to win at least 15 percent of the total votes cast.[4]

The Democratic party's rules changes in the early and mid-1970s benefited candidates who were outsiders and who appealed to party

**Table 2-2. The Demography of National Convention Delegates, 1968–1992**

| | 1968 | | 1972 | | 1976 | | 1980 | | 1984 | | 1988 | | 1992 | |
|---|---|---|---|---|---|---|---|---|---|---|---|---|---|---|
| | Dem. | Rep. | Dem. | Rep. | Dem. | Rep. | Dem. | Rep. | Dem. | Rep. | Dem. | Rep. | Dem. | Rep. |
| Women | 13% | 16% | 40% | 29% | 33% | 31% | 49% | 29% | 50% | 44% | 48% | 33% | 48% | 43% |
| Blacks | 5 | 2 | 15 | 4 | 11 | | 15 | 3 | 18 | 4 | 23 | 4 | 16 | 4 |
| Under thirty | 3 | 4 | 22 | 8 | 15 | 7 | 11 | 5 | 8 | 4 | 4 | 3 | | 3 |
| Median age (years) | (49) | (49) | (42) | | (43) | (48) | (44) | (49) | (43) | (51) | (46) | (51) | | |
| Lawyers | 28 | 22 | 12 | | 16 | 15 | 13 | 15 | 17 | 14 | 16 | 17 | | 6 |
| Teachers | 8 | 2 | 11 | | | 4 | 15 | 4 | 16 | 6 | 14 | 5 | | 4 |
| Union members | | | 16 | | 21 | 3 | 27 | 4 | 25 | 4 | 25 | 3 | | |
| Attended first convention | 67 | 66 | 83 | 78 | 80 | 78 | 87 | 84 | 74 | 61 | 65 | 68 | 45 | 35 |
| College graduate | 19 | | 21 | | 21 | 27 | 20 | 26 | 20 | 28 | 21 | 32 | 20 | 35 |
| Postgraduate* | 44 | 34 | 36 | | 43 | 38 | 45 | 39 | 51 | 35 | 52 | 34 | 52 | 33 |
| Protestant | | | 42 | | 47 | 73 | 47 | 72 | 49 | 71 | 50 | 69 | 47 | 71 |
| Catholic | | | 26 | | 34 | 18 | 37 | 22 | 29 | 22 | 30 | 22 | 30 | 27 |
| Jewish | | | 9 | | 9 | 3 | 8 | 3 | 8 | 2 | 7 | 2 | 10 | 2 |

*Includes those in the category of college graduates.

Source: CBS News Delegate Surveys, 1968 through 1980. Characteristics of the public are average values from seven CBS News/*New York Times* polls, 1980. Warren J. Mitofsky and Martin Plissner, "The Making of the Delegates, 1968–1980," *Public Opinion* (December–January 1980): 43. Reprinted with permission of American Enterprise Institute. 1984 and 1988 data for delegates and public supplied by CBS News from its delegate surveys and public reprinted with permission of CBS News. 1992 data published in the *New York Times*, July 13, 1992, p. B6 and the *Washington Post*, August 16, 1992, p. A19. This table also appears in Stephen J. Wayne, et al., *The Politics of American Government* (New York: St. Martin's Press, 1994).

**Table 2-3. The Ideology of National Convention Delegates, 1976–1992**

| Ideology | 1976 | | 1980 | | 1984 | | 1988 | | 1992 | | 1992 General Population |
|---|---|---|---|---|---|---|---|---|---|---|---|
| | Dem. | Rep. | Dem. | Rep. | Dem. | Rep. | Dem. | Rep. | Dem. | Rep. | |
| Liberal | 40% | 3% | 46% | 2% | 48% | 1% | 43% | 0% | 47% | 1% | 27% |
| Moderate | 47 | 45 | 42 | 36 | 42 | 35 | 43 | 35 | 44 | 28 | 38 |
| Conservative | 8 | 48 | 6 | 58 | 4 | 60 | 5 | 58 | 5 | 70 | 32 |

Source: CBS News Delegate Surveys, 1976 through 1980. Characteristics of the public are average values from seven CBS News/*News York Times* polls, 1980. Warren J. Mitofsky and Martin Plissner, "The Making of the Delegates, 1968–1980," *Public Opinion* (December–January 1980): 43. Reprinted with permission of American Enterprise Institute. 1984 and 1988 data for delegates and public supplied by CBS News from its delegate surveys and reprinted with permission of CBS News. 1992 data published in the *New York Times*, July 13, 1992, p. B6, and the *Washington Post*, August 16, 1992, p. A19. This table also appears in Wayne, et al., *The Politics of American Government*, cited in Table 2-2.

activists primarily on the basis of their liberal orientation. The exception was Jimmy Carter, who rode a wave of popularism and a promise of good government to the nomination. Since 1980 the rules have favored better-known candidates, who were able to generate a broad, mainstream appeal consistent with the party's traditional economic and social policy positions.

One of the difficulties with the Democratic selection process has been that the beneficiaries of that process often found themselves disadvantaged in the general election because of the length of the nomination campaign and the divisiveness it created within the party and frequently maintained up to and into the convention.[5] The need to appeal to specific groups during the nomination saddled the nominees with images, positions, and affiliations that they could not easily shed. Also, the promises made to different groups to promote unity created additional baggage to carry in the presidential campaign and, if successful, in government. Bill Clinton's promises to lower taxes for the middle class, to end discrimination against homosexuals in the military, and to admit Haitian refugees into the United States all had to be modified or abandoned once in office. In short, the extent of the nomination campaign and what it takes to win it may ultimately weaken a president by hyping performance expectations and generating more discontent when these expectations cannot be achieved.

The Republicans have not been nearly as divided over their rules for choosing delegates. One reason is that the party has been more homogeneous than the Democrats. Another is that the Republicans have not mandated national guidelines on their state parties as the Democrats have. This has generally given Republican candidates an advantage in the general election. Because they have been able to wrap up their nominations earlier than their Democratic counterparts, Republican presidential nominees have led a more united party into their summer convention and fall campaign.[6]

Nonetheless, the Republican party has also been affected by rules changes. The impact on the party has been felt in two ways: through public pressure to broaden participation and improve the representation of minorities and through new state laws, designed to conform to Democratic rules, that affect the scheduling and structure of Republican caucuses and primaries.

States are free to determine how and when nominating elections are to be conducted. However, two Supreme Court decisions, *Cousins* v. *Wigoda* (419 U.S. 477, 1975) and *Democratic Party of the U.S.* v. *La Follette* (449 U.S. 897, 1981), give the party the right to reject delegates to its national convention who are not selected in conformity with its rules. These decisions have put pressure on states, particularly those whose legislature is controlled by the Democrats, to abide by the party's mandatory rules in order to prevent challenges to the state delegation at the national convention.

## Finance Laws

While the reforms in party rules have had a profound effect, they are not the only major changes to affect the nomination process. New finance laws have had a major impact as well. They have altered the way in which money is raised and spent and the amount that is available.

Throughout most of American history candidates of both parties depended almost exclusively on large contributions to finance their campaigns. This dependence, combined with spiraling costs, secret and sometimes illegal contributions, and little public information about giving and spending, raised serious questions about the conduct of elections in a democratic society. Could officials be responsive to national needs as well as to those of their individual benefactors? Had the presidency become an office that only the wealthy could afford or, worse yet, that only those with wealthy "friends" could seek?

In the 1970s Congress began to address some of these issues. It enacted legislation to limit skyrocketing expenses, especially in the media, to control the influence of large contributors, and to bring them out in the open. Limits were placed on the amount of money presidential and vice presidential candidates and their families could contribute to their own campaigns and the amount that could be spent. Other legislation established a fund to subsidize the presidential nomination process and support the general election.[7]

The new law enacted in 1974 provided for public disclosure, contribution ceilings, campaign spending limits, and federal subsidies for the nomination process. Some of its provisions were highly controversial. Opponents of the legislation, who saw the limits on contributions and spending as a violation of the first amendment right to freedom of speech, challenged the law in the landmark case of *Buckley* v. *Valeo* (424 U.S. 1, 1976). In this case the Supreme Court upheld the right of Congress to regulate the contributions and expenditures of campaign organizations but not the independent spending of individuals and groups during the campaign.

The Court's decision forced Congress to pass new legislation in 1976, which it subsequently amended in 1979. The major provisions of this legislation, known as the Federal Election Campaign Act (FECA), provide for public disclosure of all contributions and expenditures over a certain amount (now $200), limits on individual and group contributions (summarized in Table 2-4), and federal subsidies for the nomination process and grants for the general election. These federal subsidies and grants amounted to almost $175 million in 1992 ($42.7 million for matching funds to the candidates for their party's nomination, $21.2 to the Democratic and Republican parties for their conventions, and $110.5 to the Democratic and Republican nominees in the general election).

Candidates who accept public funding are also limited in the

Table 2-4. Contribution Limits

| | To Each Candidate or Candidate Committee per Election | To National Party Committee per Calendar Year | To Any Other Political Committee per Calendar Year | Total per Calendar Year |
|---|---|---|---|---|
| Individual may give | $1,000 | $20,000 | $5,000 | $25,000 |
| Multicandidate committee* may give | 5,000 | 15,000 | 5,000 | No limit |
| Party committees may give | 1,000 or 5,000+ | No limit | 5,000 | No limit |
| Other political committees may give+ | 1,000 | 20,000 | 5,000 | No limit |

*A multicandidate committee is a political action comittee with more than fifty contributors which has been registered for at least six months and, with the exception of state party committees, has made contributions to five or more federal candidates.
+Limit depends on whether or not the party committee is a multicandidate committee.

Source: Federal Election Commission, "The FEC and the Federal Campaign Finance Law" (Washington, D.C.: Government Printing Office, 1978), p. 4.

amount they can spend. During the preconvention period there is an overall ceiling as well as individual state limits. In 1992 the ceiling was $27.62 million. The state limits, based on the size of the voting-age population and a cost-of-living adjustment, ranged from $552,400 in the smaller states to $3.5 million in the largest.[8] Candidates who accept federal funds can only spend $50,000 of their own money in the pre-nomination process.

During the general election, candidates cannot exceed their federal grant. In 1992 Clinton and Bush both received $55.24 million (see Table 2–5). Candidates, however, do not have to accept federal funds, and H. Ross Perot did not in 1992.[9] Not subject to spending limits, Perot spent over $60 million of his own fortune on his campaign.

The 1979 amendments to the FECA, however, do provide a loophole to the spending limits imposed on the presidential candidates in the general election. To encourage voting, the amendments permit an unlimited amount of money to be spent on voluntary efforts by state and local parties to get people out to vote. These expenditures are referred to as "soft money," and political parties have raised substantial amounts of it since 1980. In the 1992 presidential election, the Republicans raised and spent approximately $51.4 million in soft money and the Democrats $36.3 million.[10]

Congress had a number of objectives in enacting campaign finance legislation. It had hoped to reduce the dependence of candidates on large donors, discourage illicit and unreported contributions, broaden the base of public giving, and curtail spiraling costs at the presidential level.

Clearly the law has not achieved all these objectives, but it has had a significant impact on electoral politics. It has substantially reduced secret contributors and unexplained expenses, although it has not eliminated violations, overpayments, and improper reporting procedures. It has severely limited individual and group contributions to candidates but not to political parties. Nor has it constricted the electoral activities of nonparty groups known as political action committees (PACs). They can operate telephone banks, distribute promotional material, hold newsworthy events, and mobilize their membership and sympathizers. All of these activities can have a significant impact on the election, particularly in the early primaries and caucuses when the candidates are not well known and do not have large organizations.

Despite the contributions and activities of PACs, independent ex-

**Table 2-5. Funding Sources for Major Party Nominees, 1988 and 1992 (in millions of dollars)**

|  | 1988 | | 1992 | |
|---|---|---|---|---|
|  | Bush | Dukakis | Bush | Clinton |
| **Primary Elections** | | | | |
| Contributions from Individuals | | | | |
| Less Than $500 | $ 4.9 | $ 7.2 | $ 5.3 | $14.0 |
| $500–$749 | $ 2.7 | $ 4.2 | $ 2.6 | $ 3.8 |
| $750–$1,000 | $15.0 | $ 8.2 | $19.8 | $ 7.6 |
| Contributions from PACs | $ 0.7 | — | — | — |
| Matching Funds | $ 8.4 | $ 9.0 | $10.1 | $12.5 |
| **General Election** | | | | |
| Grant | $46.1 | $46.1 | $55.2 | $55.2 |
| Compliance Fund | $ 6.0 | $ 3.7 | $ 4.3 | $ 6.0 |
| Coordinated Party Expenditures | $ 8.3 | $ 8.3 | $10.2 | $10.2 |
| Independent Expenditures* | $12.8 | $ 0.7 | $ 3.4 | $ 0.5 |
| Partisan Communications† | $ 0.1 | $ 2.0 | — | $ 2.4 |
| Other Funding Sources (in millions of dollars) | | | | |
| Leadership PACs | $11.2 | — | — | — |
| National Party Soft Money† | $22.7 | $25.0 | $36.2 | $31.6 |

*Includes both the expenditures made in support of a candidate and those made against his opponent.

†Partisan communications are reportable only if the communication is primarily devoted to "the election or defeat of a clearly identified candidate" and the "costs exceed $2,000 for any election." 2 U.S.C §431(9)(B)(iii).

†The 1988 figures are estimates. This chart does not include the soft money spent by state party committees. (It should be noted that soft money cannot legally be spent to influence federal elections.)

Source: Federal Election Commission, "The Presidential Public Funding Program," (April 1993), p. 31.

penditures by individuals and groups, and creative ways to circumvent the restrictions of the law, the campaign finance legislation has given lesser-known candidates of the major parties a better opportunity to seek their party's nomination. Candidates lacking national visibility are still at a disadvantage, but as the 1992 campaigns of Democrat Paul Tsongas and Republican Pat Buchanan attest, they have the opportunity to raise money provided they can demonstrate their ability to win elections early in the nomination process.

The negative side to increasing the number of candidates and improving their ability to run in more primaries is that the parties have become more fractionalized and their organizational structure has been subjected to challenge by candidate organizations. Moreover, the proliferation of candidates vying for their party's nomination has significantly increased the amount of money spent in preconvention politics. In 1976 the expenditures of both parties totaled almost $67 million. In 1980 that figure was almost double, $128 million. By 1992 nomination expenditures totaled $117.8 million, with the Democrats spending $64 million, the Republicans $49 million, and the rest by minor party candidates.

### Public Relations

The third major change in the nomination process has been the enlargement of its public dimension. In the past, the quest for the nomination was a relatively private party affair. Candidates made their case primarily to state party leaders. There was little need to discern public attitudes, project public appeals, or build public support. Now, of course, there is.

The cast of characters is also different. In the past, preconvention campaign organizations consisted of a relatively small group of party regulars. Today that organization numbers in the hundreds at its headquarters and in the thousands in the field. Moreover, most of the senior campaign advisers do not hold important party positions but are professional campaign consultants: pollsters, media gurus, grass-roots organizers, direct mailers, accountants, and attorneys, all specializing in electoral politics. No candidate can be without these wizards of modern campaign technology.

Even the demands on the candidates are different. They must be willing to campaign continuously in the public eye through the mass media and primarily on radio and television, often for more than a year. They need to be well versed on a range of issues with relatively well-defined programs designed to appeal to groups within the party's electoral coalition.

To be credible, their programmatic appeals must be in tune with public opinion. The pulse of the voters conditions the message that is presented and the image that is created. Thus, a critical early step for any serious candidate is to have that pulse taken. A pollster must be hired and a private poll commissioned.

POLLS.    John F. Kennedy was the first candidate to engage a pollster in his quest for the nomination. Preconvention surveys conducted by Louis Harris in 1960 indicated that Hubert Humphrey, Kennedy's principal rival, was vulnerable in Wisconsin and West Virginia. On the basis of that information, the Kennedy campaign wisely decided to concentrate time, effort, and money in these states. Victories in both helped demonstrate Kennedy's popularity, thereby improving his chances for the nomination enormously. Similarly, in 1992 it was the reactions of focus groups composed of "average citizens" that enabled Bill Clinton to discern how to respond to the personal attacks that were directed against him in the campaign.

Polls and focus groups are important for several reasons. They provide information about the opinions, beliefs, and attitudes of voters; they identify perceptions people have of the candidates and their positions; they suggest the kinds of appeals that are apt to be most persuasive and the groups to whom these appeals should be made. Armed with this information, media campaigns can be designed and targeted. Polls are important for another reason: They affect media coverage. During the nomination process when the outcome is in doubt, candidates' standings in the polls influence the amount of coverage they receive. In general those who are deemed by the public to be most electable get the most coverage. The coverage in turn increases the ability of candidates to raise money, gain volunteers, and extend their appeal. This produces a situation in which those who cannot gain media attention have great difficulty improving their public standing, and those who cannot improve their public standing cannot gain media attention. Frequently this situation encourages bizarre behavior by candidates who desperately seek the limelight.

MEDIA.    When party leaders exercised the most influence of the nominations, personal contact with party regulars was the most effective method of campaigning. Appearances at rallies, speeches before clubs, and press conferences for local media energized rank-and-file supporters. Before the advent of the electronic media, people received most of their information from newspapers and campaign literature.

All this has changed. The electorate has grown in size and diversity. Primaries and multistage caucuses have proliferated. Today candidates have no choice but to depend on the mass media to reach potential voters.

The use of visual and audio media has revolutionized campaigning. It has made image creation more important, brought public relations specialists into candidate organizations, and siphoned off a relatively large proportion of the campaign budget for television and radio. In 1992 well over half of most candidates' campaign budgets were devoted to television advertising.

The use of media to reach voters has also made the candidates less spontaneous. Fearful that their words and actions might be misinterpreted or misconstrued, they now tend to play it safe. They ad lib less and follow scripts more. In debates, press conferences, and interviews, candidates tend to repeat their "stump" speeches. They sound more and more like their commercials. Even events are staged for home video consumption. During campaign trips, candidates often get no further than the airport tarmac. The purpose of their visits is to get media exposure. Since local television crews will be at the airport, going further is usually unnecessary to receive coverage on the local news. Candidates can also buy satellite time and be interviewed by one station after another in different parts of the country without having to leave the studio.

The media, particularly television, have influenced the nomination process in several other respects. The early contests have become more important because of the attention they are given. New Hampshire, traditionally the first state to hold a presidential primary, produces a lot of media coverage. It usually ranks first in the amount of attention it receives. Naturally, the candidate who does surprisingly well in this primary benefits enormously. Eugene McCarthy in 1968, George McGovern in 1972, Jimmy Carter in 1976, Gary Hart in 1984, and George Bush in 1988 all gained visibility and credibility from their New Hampshire performances, even though none had a majority of the vote. Bill Clinton's strong second place finish in New Hampshire in 1992 against favorite son Paul Tsongas, a former senator from neighboring Massachusetts, enhanced his candidacy, particularly in the light of the personal allegations that had been directed against him prior to the primary.

The news media give disproportionate coverage to these early contests. In 1988 with both parties having contested nominations, there were a total of 601 campaign stories on the three major networks' evening news shows between January 1 and the middle of March; in 1992, there were 424.[11] In comparison there were a total of 1,559 evening news stories on the entire nomination process from January 1, 1992 through the Republican convention on August 21.[12]

Early victories help establish front-runner status. They can provide an important psychological boost. Being declared a winner improves one's standing in the polls, makes fund raising easier, and aids in attracting backers who contribute to later primary success.

But media publicity can have a negative consequence as well, even for the winner. When Bob Dole defeated George Bush in the 1988 Iowa caucus, he jumped 12 percent in tracking polls conducted over the next several days in New Hampshire. His subsequent loss to Bush in that state by only 9 percent of the popular vote was magnified by the exposure accompanying his Iowa victory. Dole was never able to regain the momentum.

Moreover, the media treat front runners more harshly than challengers. There is more investigative reporting and more implicit criticism of their candidacies. Being a front runner guarantees not only greater coverage but also greater scrutiny.[13] Look what happened to Bush and Clinton in 1992. According to an analysis performed by the

Center for Media and Public Affairs of the preconvention period, 78 percent of Bush's coverage on the evening news was negative compared to 59 percent of Clinton's. Bush had twenty-three straight weeks of negative "spin."[14]

Another way in which the media affect delegate selection is in their interpretation of the results of primaries and caucuses. The winners are not necessarily those who do best but those who do better than expected. When performance exceeds expectations or does not meet them, that is news. When performance meets expectations, it is less newsworthy. Candidates therefore tend to underestimate their vote in public in order to be able to claim that they are satisfied with the results. Eugene McCarthy's ability to do this was a key factor in his primary challenge first of Lyndon Johnson and then of Robert Kennedy in 1968. McCarthy contested nine primaries and won two but minimized the impact of his seven losses using this low-prediction posture. Similarly, Jimmy Carter in 1976 purposely kept his predictions low. In the words of his campaign manager Hamilton Jordan:

> It has already been established in the minds of the national press that Mo Udall is going to do well in New Hampshire. He has established that expectation. If he does not win in New Hampshire, I think now by the measuring criteria that the press is going to apply, he will have underperformed. Well, we'd never talk about winning in New Hampshire. We never talk about winning anywhere. We talk about doing well.[15]

Not only is the outcome of the primaries subject to interpretation, but so is the importance attached to particular contests. Generally speaking, the media give primaries more attention than caucuses, close elections more emphasis than one-sided ones, and statewide contests better coverage than district elections. In addition to New Hampshire, the New York primary is traditionally a catalyst, particularly for the Democrats.

Candidates can affect the coverage they receive. The importance they place on individual primaries, for example, especially when a number of them occur on the same day, can affect the impact that those primaries have in the public's eye. Other tactics used to influence the media include the timing and staging of events, the release of information, and even access to the candidate and his senior aides. Major announcements are made in sufficient time to get on the evening news; speeches are scheduled to maximize the viewing audience; quiet periods, such as Saturday, are considered a good time to hold a press conference or schedule interviews. In addition to receiving same-day coverage by television, a Saturday event usually gets prominent treatment in the Sunday papers and may be mentioned on the Sunday morning talk shows.

Access is another valuable commodity. At the beginning of the nomination process, access is cheap, especially for lesser-known candidates who need media attention. As the campaign progresses, access becomes more important and, at the same time, more difficult to obtain because there are greater demands by the media for time with the leading candidates. There is more competition among journalists, the candidates have a more strenuous schedule, and a larger public relations staff stands between the correspondents and the nominees. Granting interviews under these circumstances can do much to affect the quantity and quality of coverage received.

To a large extent those who report the news are dependent on this material. Many news stories come directly from the candidates themselves. A study of the 1980 election by Michael Robinson and Margaret Sheehan reported:

> On UPI, just over 40 percent of the Carter news came directly from Carter, his press office, his staff, or his administration. Fewer than 10 percent came via the investigative route. On CBS, it was the same story, so to speak, only more so. A full two-thirds of the "official" news about Carter came via a Carter-controlled news source.[16]

Advertising is another way to shape and, if need be, change public perceptions. Its principal advantage is the amount of control that can be exercised over it by candidates and their advisers. The messages can be designed to create a certain effect. They also can be aired as often as money permits.

Not only can advertising reach a potentially large population, but it also can be targeted to specific groups within it. Take the appeal to Michigan voters that Bush and Buchanan made in their 1992 nomination fight. Each cast dispersions on their opponent's record of putting America first. Bush's ads said: "Pat Buchanan tells us, America first. But while our auto industry suffers, Pat Buchanan chose to buy a foreign car. A Mercedes-Benz. Pat Buchanan called his American cars . . . lemons."[17] Buchanan replied: "Many of George Bush's top political advisers show up in Justice Department files as foreign agents—Bush strategist Charles R. Black . . . Communications Director James H. Lake . . . Republican chairman Richard N. Bond . . ."[18]

Political ads are not without their limitations, however. Like all commercials, they are blatantly partial, usually expensive, and require the services of skilled personnel to buy time, produce the spot, and act in it. To overcome the problem of partiality, political advertisers have gone to great lengths to project an image of authenticity and spontaneity in their commercials. Ross Perot went so far as to create an "infomercial," a paid program in which he presented information about the country's problems and what he intended to do about them. Perot spent a considerable amount of money on these programs; most candidates, particularly during the preconvention period, do not have Perot's financial resources. To minimize costs, they often concentrate on local, less expensive media. To reach a smaller but specific audience, they use radio. When they appeal to a large, more general population, however, they must employ television.

The increasing importance of the media has had a profound effect on the conduct of campaigns. It has made radio and television the principal communication links between candidates and the voters.

FIELD WORK.    Despite the importance of media, candidates still need to organize at the grass roots. They need advance people to arrange for their appearances and to assemble their crowds, other politicians, and the media. They need schedulers to plan their days and decide which invitations to accept. They need local organizers to run phone banks to identify voters, and they need volunteers to ring doorbells, circulate literature, and get would-be supporters to the polls. Eugene McCarthy and Robert Kennedy recruited thousands of college students to help them in their primary efforts in 1968 as did George McGovern in 1972. Jimmy Carter in 1976, Jesse Jackson in 1984 and 1988, Pat Robertson in 1988, and Jerry Brown in 1992 also had armies of volunteers. In caucus states, these organizations can make a difference, often overwhelming the less effectively organized efforts of those who lack grass-roots support.

## THE QUEST FOR THE NOMINATION

Greater public involvement in the nomination process has changed the strategy and tactics of those seeking the nomination. Campaigns begin much earlier than in the past. They are more broad-based. They require more money up front, an organization in place, and a game plan that targets an appeal and constructs a winning coalition. The game plan in turn is predicated on certain fundamental assumptions about the nomination:

1. That sufficient time and energy be devoted to personal campaigning in the preprimary and early preconvention period. Only an incumbent can remain in the White House and even he can remain there too long.
2. That a strong, in-depth organization for the initial caucuses and primaries be built. Television advertising is important, but it is usually not possible to win by it alone.
3. That a firm financial base be established early and a spending strategy devised. All caucuses and primaries are not equal; the first ones are more important and, hence, require the allocation of greater resources.
4. That the order of events and the rules of the game be understood and, if possible, manipulated. Magnifying victories and minimizing defeats usually require that strong states be isolated and weak ones paired with strong ones.
5. That groups within the party be targeted and appeals to them be made. Over the course of the campaign, however, these appeals must be moderated and broadened. If the overall constituency is

too narrow, it is difficult to win the nomination and even more difficult to win the general election.

The actual strategy that candidates adopt depends on their status at the beginning of the campaign. If they are not well known, their initial goal must be to establish their credibility. Publicly announcing their intentions, creating a campaign headquarters, qualifying for matching funds, and obtaining political endorsements are necessary but not sufficient conditions to do so. At the outset, the key is recognition. Over the long haul, it is momentum and the acquisition of delegates.

Recognition is bestowed by the media on those who do better than expected in the early primaries and caucuses; momentum is achieved by a series of prenomination victories, which increases the amount of delegate support. Together, recognition and momentum compensate for what the non–front runners lack in reputation and appeal. That is why non–front runners concentrate their time, efforts, and resources in the first few contests. They have no choice. Winning will provide them with opportunities later on; losing will confirm their secondary status.

Jimmy Carter's 1976 quest for the Democratic nomination is a good example of a successful non–front-runner approach. Carter began his campaign as a relatively unknown southern governor with limited financial resources and organizational support. He concentrated his efforts in Iowa and New Hampshire with the aim of doing well in these early contests. By attracting media attention, he hoped to establish his credibility as a viable candidate. Early success, he anticipated, would facilitate fund raising, organization building, and continued media coverage. And he was right.

The Carter strategy has become the model for most Democratic aspirants. In 1992 all of them emphasized the early contests although Iowa was less important than in previous years since it was conceded by all candidates to favorite son Senator Tom Harkin.

For the front runners, like Democrat Walter Mondale in 1984 and Republican George Bush in 1988, the task was different. They had to maintain credibility, not establish it. This provided them with a little more flexibility at the outset. Front runners can announce their candidacy later. George Bush waited until December 1991 before formally announcing his candidacy for 1992. Had he not been challenged by Pat Buchanan, it is likely that he would have waited even longer.

Particular primaries and caucuses may be targeted, some can be avoided, but the first ones still have to be contested because of the media attention they receive. However, front runners usually have the resources to plan a broad-based campaign. They still spend most of their money during the early part of the preconvention nomination period in an effort to build an insurmountable lead and discourage their opponents from continuing in the contest.

The principal advantages that front runners have are greater name recognition, a larger resource base, and more political endorsements.

Status and position make it easier for them to raise money and build an organization. This enhances their potential but it also creates expectations that may be difficult to meet. A front runner can overcome a single defeat, but will find it more difficult to survive a string of setbacks.

Ronald Reagan's preconvention campaign in 1980 is a good example of the front-runner approach. He raised and spent a lot of his money in the early primaries and caucuses. He built in-depth organizations in many states, obtained political endorsements, and benefited from a large staff of professionals and volunteers. George Bush followed a similar strategy eight years later. By the beginning of the election year, he had raised over $11 million and built large field organizations in the states that were to hold the first contests. He had a sophisticated media operation already in place. His overwhelming defeat of Senator Bob Dole in the South all but ensured his nomination by the end of the second week in March.

Although Michael Dukakis and Bill Clinton did not begin as front runners, parts of their strategy resembled George Bush's. Like Bush they also had organized effectively and raised funds early. However they did not have the high name recognition and had fewer political endorsements and volunteers than the Bush campaign. They had to pay organizers, earn endorsements, and gain public credibility and national standing by victories in the early contests. Moreover, they had to target their appeals carefully to specific groups within the Democratic party's electoral coalition. Both appealed to moderates within their party, focusing on middle-class, white-collar Democrats. Dukakis also targeted Hispanic voters because of his fluency in Spanish. Clinton did well among African-Americans. In 1992 after Virginia governor Doug Wilder's withdrawal, there was no African-American candidate nor a white liberal with much appeal to this group.

The Jackson campaigns in 1984 and 1988, and to a lesser extent Robertson's in 1988 and Buchanan's in 1992, do not fit the typical strategic models. Lacking a large financial base, they mobilized an army of volunteers in grass-roots efforts that were most effective in states with caucus-type elections or those in which their supporters constituted a significant portion of the electorate.

All three candidates also attracted considerable media attention by virtue of their extreme perspectives, their passionate supporters and detractors, and their effectiveness as speakers and campaigners. All of these qualities play well on television. In each case they used the campaign as their "bully pulpit" to articulate their views, maintain their support, and legitimize their candidacy.

## NATIONAL CONVENTIONS

Theoretically, the party chooses its standard bearers at its national convention in the summer preceding the presidential election. In practice the nominees have usually been decided on well before the convention meets. Since most of the delegates are publicly committed, their decisions are readily predictable. Television networks and wire services provide a running total of the number of delegates pledged to individual candidates throughout the nomination period.

Theoretically, the delegates make policy decisions when formulating their party's platform. In practice, platform decisions have been hammered out by representatives of the principal candidates prior to the convention.

Theoretically, conventions unify the delegates for the forthcoming election. In practice, candidate and policy disagreements are highlighted by the media, perpetuating rather than healing the differences within the party and thereby making a unified appeal in the election that much more difficult to achieve.

What purpose, then, do conventions serve? They are part of American folklore. They ratify decisions of the voters during the primaries and the caucuses. In the event that no candidate emerges with a clear majority, they select the nominee. In the event different groups are unhappy with provisions of the platform, they serve as a vehicle for expressing their dissatisfaction, a court of last resort, and a final arbiter and judge of the party's official doctrine and stands. Finally, they draw attention to the parties and their nominees. They excite the faithful and implore the public to support their candidates in the general election.

It is this public dimension that has gained importance in recent years. From the perspective of the party, the real function of the conventions is to show off its nominees and its policy positions; from the perspective of the candidates, it is to start building a broad-based electoral coalition; from the perspective of organized groups, it is to gain visibility and support for their positions and causes; from the perspective of the media, it is to capture the excitement and ritual of an extravaganza and to spotlight whatever drama and suspense it produces.

### Public Dimensions

Television broadcasting of national conventions began in 1952. Almost immediately, a sizable audience was attracted. According to the Nielsen ratings, 20 to 30 percent of the potential audience watched the conventions between 1952 and 1968, with the number swelling during the most significant events. In 1992 the Nielsen company estimated that between 34 and 35 million people saw each of the acceptance speeches of the presidential nominees on the last night of the conventions.[19]

The large number of viewers is significant because of the potential effect conventions have on those who watch them. The conventions heighten interest, thereby potentially increasing turnout; they arouse latent feelings, thereby raising partisan awareness; and they color perceptions, thereby affecting the public's evaluation of the candidates and their stands.[20]

Party leaders assume that the more unified the convention, the more favorable its impact on the electorate. That is why they take the media, particularly television, into account when planning, staging, and scheduling their national meetings.

Television has changed conventions. They have become faster paced than in the past. Tedious reports and roll calls have been reduced. There are fewer candidates placed in nomination, and the speeches themselves are shorter. The length of the sessions has also been reduced. In 1992 the major networks, with the exception of CNN, carried the sessions only during and after prime time in the East, forcing convention managers to compress their major events into shorter time frames.

Not only do convention planners wish to capture an audience by providing entertainment and a fast-paced meeting, but they also desire to put their candidates and party in the most favorable light. To do this they have scripted the meetings, placing the major unifying events such as the keynote address and acceptance speeches during prime viewing hours and potentially discordant situations such as debates on controversial issues or speeches by people who may be discredited in the eyes of the public or party before or after prime time. Frequently, however, they are forced to provide time for defeated candidates. Both Jerry Brown and Pat Buchanan gave prime-time addresses in 1992 that emphasized their own campaign messages in contrast to those messages which the party and its winning candidates wished to project in the general election.

Although party officials try to present a united front favoring their nominee and platform, the television networks do not. They try to generate interest by emphasizing variety, maximizing suspense, and exaggerating conflict. This attempt often requires them to focus less on the official proceedings and more on other activities, such as demonstrations that may occur outside the convention hall. The vice presidential selection frequently receives much attention, although in recent years, the likely nominee has been identified before the convention has gotten under way. Still, in 1988, Bush's choice of Senator Dan Quayle attracted considerable scrutiny from the media, much of it negative. Information about the senator's background and qualifications counterbalanced some of the favorable coverage Bush received, although it did have the beneficial effect of monopolizing news for the Republican ticket. The media also tend to play up disputes over the rules, delegate credentials, and the party platform, such as the differences over the abortion issue that divided delegates of both parties in 1992.

### Official Business

Conventions still make or at least ratify major decisions. They adopt rules, accept credentials, determine platforms, and choose the standard bearers.

Rules govern the manner in which the meetings are conducted. They can spark heated controversy, particularly if they affect the outcome of the nomination. In 1952, Dwight Eisenhower's supporters at the Republican convention challenged the credentials of a sizable number of delegates for Robert Taft from southern states. Before deciding on the challenges, however, the convention adopted a "fair play" rule that prohibited these contested delegates from voting on any question, including their own credentials. This effectively prevented many Taft delegates from voting and enabled Eisenhower to win the challenges and eventually the nomination.

An even more acrimonious division over party rules occurred in 1980 at the Democratic convention. At issue was a proposed requirement that delegates vote for the candidate to whom they were publicly pledged at the time they were chosen to attend the convention. Trailing Jimmy Carter by about six hundred delegates, Edward Kennedy, who had previously supported the requirement, urged an open convention in which delegates could vote their consciences rather than merely exercise their commitments. This would have required rejection of the pledged delegate rule. Naturally, the Carter organization favored the rule and strenuously lobbied for it. Carter was successful. The vote in support of the rule effectively clinched his nomination. Subsequent rules challenges, including the abolition of this pledged delegate rule, have been decided by the party's National Committee prior to the convention.

Disputes over the credentials of delegates have also divided conventions and influenced their outcomes. In 1912 and again in 1952, grassroots challenges to old-line party leaders generated competing delegate claims at Republican conventions. In each case the result of the challenge affected the outcome of the nomination: William Howard Taft won in the first instance and Dwight Eisenhower in the second. Approximately 7 percent of all Republican delegates were challenged between 1872 and 1956.[21]

The Democrats have also had their share of delegate disputes, particularly in the early 1970s when the party was making major changes in its rules for delegate selection. In recent years there have been fewer credential challenges because so many of the delegates are elected in primaries that are established by state law and have, for the most part, been held in conformity to party rules.

Another function of conventions is to draft a platform. It too has been the subject of considerable controversy. Changes in the selection process seem to have produced more issue-oriented delegates who tend to gravitate to the platform committee and specifically to the subcommittee considering "their" issues. This has tended to exaggerate rather than minimize the policy differences among the delegates. Television has also magnified the problem by providing publicity for platform challenges. As a consequence of these factors, the platform-drafting process has become more open and more divisive. Until recently, the Republicans have suffered less than the Democrats. Being the more homogeneous of the two parties, they have been subjected to fewer and less intense pressures from organized interest groups.

Two often conflicting aims lie at the heart of the platform-drafting process. One has to do with winning the election and the other with pleasing the party's coalition. In order to maximize the vote, platforms cannot alienate. They must permit people to see what they want to see. This is frequently accomplished by increasing the level of vagueness and ambiguity on the most controversial and emotionally charged issues. In 1988 the Democrats went so far as to present a statement of principles in lieu of their usual laundry list of promises for each group comprising their electoral coalition. They reverted to their old approach in 1992.

The Republicans also faced this dilemma in 1992. By adopting a platform that reiterated much of the party's conservative ideology of the Reagan years, the party narrowed its popular appeal and alienated potential voters.

While platforms contain rhetoric and self-praise, they also consist of goals and proposals that differentiate them from one another. In an examination of the Democratic and Republican platforms between 1944 and 1976, Gerald Pomper found that most of the differences were explained by planks made by one party but omitted by the other.[22] Over the years the Republicans have emphasized defense and general governmental matters, while the Democrats have stressed economic issues, particularly those of labor and social welfare. Significant differences have emerged in recent years over the role of government, with the Democrats more supportive of the federal government's involvement in domestic matters than the Republicans who placed more emphasis on the private sector to solve the nation's economic woes. The Republicans have also stressed their support of "family values," which they broadly define as religion, patriotism, and community norms.

Finally, the convention must select the nominees. The decision is usually predictable and generally occurs on the first ballot. Since 1924, when the Democrats took 103 votes before they agreed on John W. Davis, there have been only four conventions (two in each party) in which more than one ballot was needed. For the Republicans this last occurred in 1948, for the Democrats in 1952.

Despite the tendency to develop a consensus well before the convention meets, there have still been attempts to defeat the front runner at the convention itself. Two strategies for doing this have been employed. One is to release polls showing the strength of the non–front runner and the weakness of the convention leader in the general election. The objective here is to play on the delegates' desire to nominate a winner. Republican Nelson Rockefeller tried this in 1968 but to no avail.

A second tactic, one that has been used in more recent conventions, is to create an issue prior to the presidential balloting and win on it, thereby showing the vulnerability of the leader and raising doubts about whether that person can be nominated. If the issue affects rules that have an impact on the vote, so much the better. Ronald Reagan in 1976 and Ted Kennedy in 1980 used this ploy but without success. Their defeats on key votes confirmed their status as also-rans but did not end their campaigns. With the nomination out of reach, both concentrated on the platform. For the most part, the front runners did not accept these platform challenges, choosing instead to concede policy positions in order to obtain their opponents' backing in the forthcoming campaign. Having effectively wrapped up the nomination, they could afford to be magnanimous and were.

### Characteristics of the Nominees

The nomination of small-state governors by the Democrats in 1976, 1988, and 1992 and a former movie actor, ex-California governor by the Republicans in 1980 indicates that changes in the preconvention process have affected the kind of people chosen by their parties. In theory, many are qualified. In practice, a number of informal qualifications limit the pool of potential nominees. Successful candidates have usually been well known prior to the delegate selection process. Most have had promising political careers and have held high government positions.

Of all the positions from which to seek the presidential nomination, the presidency is clearly the best. Only five incumbent presidents (three of whom were vice presidents who succeeded to the office) failed in their quest for the nomination, although it should be noted that several others, including Harry Truman and Lyndon Johnson, were persuaded to retire rather than face tough challenges.

Over the years, there have been a variety of other paths to the White House. When the caucus system was in operation, the position of secretary of state within the administration was regarded as a stepping stone to the nomination if the incumbent chose not to seek another term. When national conventions replaced the congressional caucus, the Senate became the incubator for most successful presidential candidates. After the Civil War, governors emerged as the most likely contenders, particularly for the party that did not control the White House.

In the 1960s Washington-based officials, particularly the vice president and members of the Senate, reemerged as the most viable candidates. They enjoyed the benefit of national media coverage in an age of television and national political experience at a time when the role of the government was greatly expanding. However, the antigovernment, anti-Washington mood of the electorate following the Vietnam War and the Watergate scandals, and continuing throughout much of the period since then, has given outsiders an advantage.

There are other informal criteria, although they have less to do with qualifications for office than with public prejudices. Only white males have ever been nominated by the two major parties for president. Until 1960, no Catholic had been elected, although Governor Al Smith of New York was nominated by the Democrats in 1928. Michael Dukakis, of

Greek ancestry, was the first candidate without a northern European heritage, a surprising commentary on a country that has regarded itself as a melting pot.

Personal matters, such as health, finance, and family life, can also be factors. After George Wallace was crippled by a would-be assassin's bullet, even his own supporters began to question his ability to withstand the rigors of the office. Today, presidential candidates are expected to release medical reports and financial statements. Michael Dukakis's hesitancy to discuss his medical history in 1988 fueled rumors that he had seen a psychiatrist. Both George Bush and Bill Clinton released reports about their health during the 1992 presidential campaign.

Family ties have also affected nominations and elections. There have been only two bachelors elected president, James Buchanan and Grover Cleveland. During the 1884 campaign, Cleveland was accused of fathering an illegitimate child. Taunted by his opponents: "Ma, Ma, Where's my Pa? / Gone to the White House / Ha! Ha! Ha!" Cleveland admitted responsibility for the child, even though he was not certain he was the father.

In more recent times, candidates have been hurt by marital problems and allegations of sexual misconduct. The dissolution of Nelson Rockefeller's marriage and his subsequent remarriage seriously damaged his presidential aspirations in 1964, and Senator Edward Kennedy's marital problems and the Chappaquiddick incident were serious detriments to his presidential candidacy in 1980 and contributed to his decision not to seek his party's nomination in 1984. Reagan's election in 1980, however, suggests that having been divorced is no longer a relevant factor, at least for those who have been happily remarried for some time.

Bill Clinton's election despite the allegations of marital infidelity may render sexual misconduct less of an issue than it was in 1988 when Senator Gary Hart was forced to withdraw from the race after reporters revealed that he had spent the night with a woman who was not his wife.

Most of the characteristics of the presidential nominee apply to the vice presidential candidate as well. However, that choice has also been affected by the perceived need for geographic, ideological, and political balance. Bill Clinton's selection of Senator Albert Gore is an exception. Clinton chose Gore to reenforce rather than balance his own moderate policy perspective, southern political base, and relative youth.

Presidential aspirants have tended to select vice presidential candidates primarily as running mates and only secondarily as governing mates. Despite statements to the contrary, most attention is given to how the prospective nominee would help the ticket. Like the presidential nominee, parties have also insisted that the vice presidential aspirant possess all-American traits, including being of sound mind and body. In 1972 Senator Thomas Eagleton was forced to withdraw as the Democratic vice presidential nominee when his past psychological illness became public. In 1988 the Republican vice presidential nominee, Senator Dan Quayle, was hounded by charges that his father, a wealthy Indiana newspaper publisher, used his influence to get young Quayle into the National Guard and thus reduce his chances of serving on active duty in the Vietnam War.

## CONCLUSION

The nominating process has evolved significantly over the years. Developed initially to enable the parties to influence electoral selection, it now permits the public to affect that selection as well. With broader rank-and-file participation has come expanded activities by candidates, expanded coverage by the mass media, and expanded public appeals by the parties.

When the presidency was created, the nomination of candidates for the office was not distinguished from the election of the president himself. The development of political parties at the turn of the century led to an informal modification of the electoral plan. At first, congressional caucuses performed the nominating function. As the parties acquired a broader, more decentralized base, the caucus system broke down and was replaced by national nominating conventions. These conventions have continued to operate, although power within them has shifted from political leaders within the states to a broader segment of the political party. The growth of primaries, the increasing impact of the mass media, and eventually the changes in party rules, finance laws, and campaign technology accelerated the movement toward more participatory nominating politics in which public support became the critical element.

On balance, these changes in the public dimension of contemporary politics have made the nomination process more democratic. They have encouraged greater rank-and-file participation in the selection of the party's nominees. They have also generated greater sensitivity by the candidates to the desires of groups within the party and to the opinions and attitudes of the general electorate.

But the costs of democracy have been high. They have adversely affected opportunities for winning and governing. Parties have become more fractionalized and exercise less control over who their nominees will be and how they will perform if elected.

Campaigns are also more onerous and more expensive. Candidates have to spend years seeking the nomination. The public is subjected to a barrage of appeals, images, promises, and positions. It is numbed by the campaign.

Not only is it more difficult to win the nomination, but it is also more difficult to govern. Contemporary campaigns hype expectations; they make agendas more expansive and priorities more difficult to define; they also contribute to fragile and more personal alliances; they dispense and ultimately decrease the president's political power while they increase demands on his job. All of this has made strong presidential leadership more difficult to achieve and sustain.

Clinton found this out the hard way at the beginning of his presidency. Seeking to fulfill campaign promises to a variety of constituency groups such as the middle class, homosexuals, small businesses, and urban mayors and their inner-city populations, he was unable to do so and had to alter or abandon many of his initial campaign pledges. The process of publicly promising and then having to back off damaged his reputation, adversely affected his public image, and decreased the political capital he had to achieve his goals. Unfortunately, Clinton's predicament is the rule not the exception for contemporary presidents. It would be nice if new presidents could find their way out of this dilemma, but most of them have not been able to do so.

## NOTES

1. In 1968, however, primaries did provide incentive for Lyndon Johnson to withdraw. In that year, dissent within the Democratic party, as evidenced by Senator Eugene McCarthy's surprisingly strong showing in the New Hampshire primary, indicated that incumbent Lyndon Johnson would have difficulty securing renomination, much less reelection. Johnson chose to step aside and not seek reelection soon after the New Hampshire vote.

2. Since an object of these changes was to make delegate selection more indicative of the preferences of the voters, the party tried to prohibit those who did not consider themselves Democrats from participating in its primaries. It was only partially successful. Because some states did not require or even permit voters to register by party, the Democrats were forced to accept an oral affirmation of party preference, one that permitted independents and even Republicans to cross over and vote in Democratic primaries in certain states.

3. The *Congressional Quarterly* estimates that slightly less than 300,000 people participated in the first round of the eighteen Democratic caucuses (excluding Virginia and Texas) during the party's 1992 nomination process ["Democratic Primary and First-Round Caucus Winners," *Congressional Quarterly* 50 (July 4, 1992):70].

4. In 1984 and again in 1988 exceptions to the proportional voting rule were permitted. These exceptions allowed delegates to be directly elected in districts. This created the possibility of a *winner-take-all* system if all those who were elected supported the same candidate. Another variation of the proportional voting rule gave the candidate who won the most delegates in an electoral district a bonus delegate just for "winning," effectively creating a *winner-take-more* system. Jesse Jackson alleged that these rules were biased against lesser-known and minority candidates. He pointed to discrepancies between his popular vote and the percentage of delegates he received to support his contention. In 1984, for example, Jackson received 18 percent of the popular vote in winner-take-all districts but won only 7 percent of the delegates selected in them. In 1988 it was more of the same. Jackson received 30 percent of the vote in winner-take-all districts but only 14 percent of the delegates. To rectify these inequalities (and gain Jackson's support for the party's presidential ticket in 1988), the Democratic Rules Committee agreed to permit no exceptions to the proportional voting rule in 1992.

5. The proportional voting rule has extended the Democratic nomination process by making it more difficult for candidates to wrap up the nomination as early as Republican candidates have been able to do. Thus, the likely Republican nominees have been better able to coalesce their party and begin planning and even executing their general election

strategy while their likely Democratic opponents are still contending with opposition within their party.

6. Martin P. Wattenberg, *The Rise of Candidate-Centered Politics* (Cambridge, Mass.: Harvard University Press, 1991), p. 65.

7. Under the terms of the original legislation, individuals could designate that $1 of their taxes be placed in the Presidential Election Campaign Fund. Initially more than 25 percent of taxpayers made such a designation. Increased campaign expenditures combined with a decreasing percent of the population designating money for the fund—only 17.7 percent did so in 1991—threatened to create a shortfall of revenue by 1996. Congress responded to this potential problem by raising the amount of money that individuals could designate for the fund. Beginning in 1993, individuals can designate $3 to the fund. The Federal Election Commission estimates that this increased revenue should permit full funding for presidential elections through the year 2004 (Federal Election Commission, "Record," September 1993, pp. 1–2).

8. Fund-raising expenses up to 20 percent of expenditures and accounting and legal fees are exempt from these spending limits.

9. Third and independent party candidates need to receive at least 5 percent of the vote to be eligible for government funds. Having received at least 5 percent of the vote, they are then automatically eligible for a federal grant in the next election. The amount of money they are given is based on the proportion of the vote they received. In 1980 independent candidate John Anderson gained 6.6 percent of the vote and $4.2 million dollars, but he received it after the election. He chose not to run in 1984 although he would have been eligible for government support that year.

10. Federal Election Commission, "Record," February 1993, p. 5.

11. "The Parties Pick Their Candidates: TV News Coverage of the 1992 Presidential Primaries," *Media Monitor* (March 1992), p. 2.

12. "Battle of the Sound Bites: TV News Coverage of the 1992 Presidential Election Campaign," *Media Monitor* (August/September 1992), p. 2.

13. Michael J. Robinson and Margaret A. Sheehan, *Over the Wire and on TV: CBS and UPI in Campaign '80* (New York: Russell Sage Foundation, 1983), p. 243.

14. "The 1992 Elections-Primary Wrap-Up," *Media Monitor* (June/July 1992), p. 5.

15. Hamilton Jordan quoted in F. Christopher Arterton, "Campaign Organizations Face the Mass Media in the 1976 Presidential Nomination Process" (paper delivered at the Annual Meeting of the American Political Science Association, Washington, D.C., September 1–4, 1977), p. 23.

16. Robinson and Sheehan, *Over the Wire and on TV*, p. 184.

17. "30-Second Politics," *Washington Post*, March 14, 1992, p. A12.

18. Ibid.

19. "34 Million View Final Session," *New York Times*, August 22, 1992, p. 6.

20. Thomas E. Patterson, *The Mass Media Election* (New York: Praeger, 1980), pp. 72 and 274.

21. Paul T. David, Ralph M. Goldman, and Richard C. Bain, *The Politics of National Party Conventions* (Washington, D.C.: Brookings Institution, 1960), p. 263.

22. Gerald M. Pomper, "Control and Influence in American Politics," *American Behavioral Scientist* 13 (1969): 223, 228; Gerald M. Pomper with Susan S. Lederman, *Elections in America* (New York: Longman, 1980), p. 161.


## SELECTED READINGS

Baker, Ross K. "Sorting Out and Suiting Up: The Presidential Nominations." In Gerald M. Pomper, ed. *The Election of 1992*. Chatham, N.J.: Chatham House, 1993, pp. 39–73.

Barilleaux, Ryan J., and Randall E. Adkins. "The Nomination Process and Patterns." In Michael Nelson, ed. *The Elections of 1992*. Washington D.C.: Congressional Quarterly, 1993, pp. 21–56.

Bartels, Larry M. *Presidential Primaries and the Dynamics of Public Choice*. Princeton, N.J.: Princeton University Press, 1988.

Caeser, James. *Reforming the Reforms.* Cambridge, Mass.: Ballinger, 1992.

Corrado, Anthony. *Creative Campaigning: Pacs and the Presidential Selection Process.* Boulder, Colo.: Westview Press, 1992.

Orren, Gary R., and Nelson Polsby. *Media and Momentum: The New Hampshire Primary and Nomination Politics.* Chatham, N.J.: Chatham House, 1987.

Smith, Larry David, and Dan Nimmo. *Orchestrating National Party Conventions in the Telepolitical Age.* Westport, Conn.: Praeger, 1991.

Sorauf, Frank J. *Inside Campaign Finance: Myths and Realities.* New Haven, Conn.: Yale University Press, 1992.

Wayne, Stephen J. *The Road To The White House, 1992.* 4th ed. New York: St. Martin's Press, 1992, pp. 3–170.

# 3

# The Presidential Election

Winning the nomination is only half the battle. The real prize comes from being elected. For the candidate the general election campaign is at least as arduous as the nomination struggle. Shorter in length but with a larger and more heterogeneous electorate, it requires similar organizational skills but different strategic plans and public appeals to build a majority coalition. For the party, the quest for the presidency is only one election among many in which it has an interest and an involvement. Like the other elections, however, the campaign is subject to its influence but not to its control. For the voter the effective choice is narrower but the criteria for judgment are more extensive. Personal evaluation alone is not the only factor that affects the decision whether to vote and, if so, for whom.

For the presidency the campaign has significant implications. Not only does it designate which team and what party will direct activities for the next four years, but it highlights the key policy issues at the beginning of the president's term. It provides the contours of the administration's initial agenda and contributes to the components of its governing coalition. Moreover, it sets the tone and indicates the kind of leadership that the public expects and wants. In this sense the campaign defines the president's initial leadership tasks and opportunities, whether that be to direct change or simply facilitate it by keeping the machinery of government working smoothly.

In this chapter we will explore these factors and their implications for our electoral and governing systems. We will do so by examining the strategic environment in which presidential elections occur, the critical factors that must be considered when planning and conducting campaigns, and the meaning of elections for the voters and new administration.

The chapter is organized into three parts. In the first we focus on the environment of the election: the Electoral College, voter attitudes, public financing, and media coverage. We assess the impact of each of these factors on the election. We then turn to the strategy and tactics of the campaign itself. Here we discuss how organizations are constructed, how appeals are designed, projected, and targeted, and how coalitions are built. In the third part we evaluate the election outcome from two perspectives: what it suggests about the moods, opinions, and attitudes of the electorate and what it portends for the president. Does it guide the president, provide a mandate, and increase or decrease the capacity for leadership? To what extent does it enable the president to initiate change or facilitate government?

## THE STRATEGIC ENVIRONMENT

Every election occurs within an environment that shapes its activity and affects its outcome. For the presidency the Electoral College provides the legal framework for this environment, while public attitudes and group loyalties condition the political climate. Money and media constitute the principal resources and instruments by and through which campaign objectives may be achieved. Each of these factors must be considered in the design and conduct of a presidential campaign and in assessing its impact on the election.

### The Electoral College

Of the elements that affect presidential campaigns, only the Electoral College is truly unique. It was designed by the framers of the Constitution to solve one of their most difficult problems: how to protect the president's independence and, at the same time, have a technically sound, politically efficacious system that would be consistent with a republican form of government. Most of the delegates at the Philadelphia convention were sympathetic to a government based on consent but not to direct democracy. They wanted a mechanism that would choose the most qualified person but not necessarily the most popular. And they had no precise model to follow.

Two methods had been proposed originally: selection by the legislature and election by the voters. Each, however, had its drawbacks. Legislative selection posed a potential threat to the institution of the presidency. How could the executive's independence be preserved if election and reelection hinged on the president's popularity with Congress?[1] Popular election was seen as undesirable and impractical. Not only did most of the delegates lack faith in the public's ability to choose the best-qualified candidate, but they also feared that the size of the country and the poor state of its communication and transportation would preclude a national campaign. Sectional distrust and rivalry aggravated this problem, since the states were obligated to oversee the conduct of such an election. A third alternative, some type of indirect election, was proposed a number of times, but it was not until near the end of the convention that election by electors was seriously considered as a possible compromise solution.

According to the terms of the Electoral College compromise, presidential electors were to be chosen by the states in a manner designated by their legislatures. In order to ensure their independence, the electors could not simultaneously hold a federal government position. The number of electors was to equal the number of senators and representatives from each state (see Appendix C). Each elector had two votes but could not cast both of them for inhabitants of his or her own state.[2] At a designated time the electors would vote and send the results to Congress, where they were to be announced in a joint session by the president of the Senate, the vice president. The person who received a majority of votes cast by the Electoral College would be elected president, and the one with the second highest total would be vice president. In the event that no one received a majority, the House of Representatives would choose from among the five candidates with the most electoral votes, with each state delegation casting one vote. The Senate was to determine the vice president in the event that there was a tie for second place.

The new mode of selection was defended on two grounds: (1) it allowed state legislatures to establish the procedures for choosing electors but permitted the House of Representatives to decide if there were no Electoral College majority; and (2) it gave the larger states an advantage in the initial voting for president (in accordance with the principle of majority rule) but provided the smaller states with an equal voice if the electoral vote was not decisive (in accordance with the principle of equal representation for each of the states). These compromises placated sufficient interests to get the proposal adopted and subsequently ratified as part of the Constitution.

EVOLUTION.    Only in the first two elections, when Washington was the unanimous choice, did the electors exercise a nonpartisan and presumably independent judgment. Within ten years from the time the federal government began to operate, the party system had developed and electors became its political captives. Nominated by their party, they were expected to vote for the party's candidates, and they did. In 1800 all of the Republican electors voted for Thomas Jefferson and Aaron Burr. Since the procedure for casting ballots did not permit electors to distinguish between their presidential and vice presidential choices, the result was a tie, which the House of Representatives, controlled by the Federalist party, broke by choosing Jefferson. To avoid such problems in the future, the Constitution was amended in 1804 to provide for separate balloting for president and vice president.

The next nondecisive presidential election occurred in 1824 when four candidates received votes for president: Andrew Jackson (99 votes), John Q. Adams (84), William Crawford (41), and Henry Clay (37). The new amendment required the House of Representatives to choose from among the top three, not the top five as the Constitution had originally prescribed. Eliminated from the competition was Henry Clay, the most powerful member of the House and its Speaker. Clay threw his support to Adams, who won. It was alleged that Clay did so in exchange for appointment as secretary of state, a charge that he vigorously denied. After Adams became president, however, Clay accepted the appointment of secretary of state.

Jackson, the winner of the popular vote, was outraged at the turn of events and urged the abolition of the Electoral College. Although his claim of a popular mandate in 1824 is open to question,[3] opposition to the system mounted, and a gradual democratization of the election process occurred. More and more states began to elect their electors directly on the basis of their partisan leanings. By 1832, only South Carolina retained the practice of having its legislature do the selecting.

There was also a trend toward statewide election of the entire slate of electors. In the past some states had chosen their electors within legislative districts. Choosing the entire slate of electors on the basis of the popular vote produced a bloc of electoral votes. Whichever candidate received the most popular votes in a state got all the electoral votes of that state. This had two principal effects. It maximized the state's voting power, but it also created the possibility of a disparity between the popular and electoral vote in the nation as a whole. It became possible for the candidate with the most popular votes to lose in the Electoral College if that candidate lost the big states by small margins and won the smaller states by large margins.

This occurred in 1876, the next disputed election, when Democrat Samuel J. Tilden received 250,000 more popular votes and nineteen more electoral votes than his Republican rival, Rutherford B. Hayes. However, Tilden was one short of a majority in the Electoral College. Twenty electoral votes were in dispute. Dual returns had been received from three southern states. Charges of fraud and voting irregularities were made by both parties.

Three days before the Electoral College vote was to be officially counted, Congress established a commission to resolve the dilemma. Consisting of eight Republicans and seven Democrats, the commission, by a strictly partisan division, validated all of the Republican claims, thereby giving Hayes a one vote victory. Tilden could have challenged the results in court but chose not to do so.

The only other election in which the popular vote winner was beaten in the Electoral College occurred in 1888. Democrat Grover Cleveland had a plurality of 95,096 popular votes but only 168 electoral votes compared with 233 for the Republican, Benjamin Harrison. Cleveland's loss of Indiana by about 3,000 votes and New York by about 15,000 led to his defeat.

Although all other popular vote leaders have won a majority of electoral votes, shifts of just a few thousand popular votes in a few states could have altered the results in several recent elections. Thomas E. Dewey could have denied Harry S Truman a majority in the Electoral College in 1948 with 12,487 more California votes. In 1960, a change of less than 9,000 votes in Illinois and Missouri would have meant that

John F. Kennedy lacked an Electoral College majority. In 1968, a shift of only 55,000 votes from Richard M. Nixon to Hubert H. Humphrey in three states (New Jersey, Missouri, and New Hampshire) would have thrown the election into a Democratic House of Representatives. In 1976, a shift of only 3,687 in Hawaii and 5,559 in Ohio would have cost Jimmy Carter the election. The potential for the popular will to be thwarted remains.

Not only could the results of these elections have been affected by very small voter shifts in a few states, but in 1948, 1960, 1968, and 1992 there was the further possibility that the Electoral College itself would not be able to choose a winner. In each of these elections, third-party candidates or independent electoral slates threatened to secure enough votes to prevent either of the major candidates from obtaining a majority. In 1948, Henry Wallace (Progressive party) and Strom Thurmond (States' Rights party) received almost five percent of the total popular vote, and Thurmond won 39 electoral votes. In 1960, fourteen unpledged electors were chosen in Alabama and Mississippi. In 1968, Governor George Wallace of Alabama, running on the American Independent party ticket, received almost 10 million popular votes (13.5 percent of the total) and 46 electoral votes. In 1992, H. Ross Perot received 19.7 million votes (19 percent of the total) but no electoral votes. Close competition between the major party candidates and a strong third- or independent party candidacy provides the Electoral College with its most difficult task.

POLITICS.    The Electoral College is not neutral. No system of election can be. In general, it works to the benefit of the very largest states (those with more than fourteen electoral votes) and the very smallest (those with less than four). It helps the largest states not only because of the number of electoral votes they cast but because the votes are normally cast in a bloc. The smallest states are also aided because they are over-represented in the Electoral College. By having three electoral votes, regardless of size, a sparsely populated state such as Alaska will have more of an advantage than it would have in a direct popular vote.

The winner-take-all system also gives an edge to pivotal groups within the larger and more competitive states. Those groups that are geographically concentrated and have cohesive voting patterns derive the most benefit. Part of the opposition to changing the system has been the reluctance of these groups to give up what they perceive as their competitive advantage.

The Electoral College also works to the disadvantage of third and independent parties. The winner-take-all system within states, when combined with the need for a majority within the college, makes it difficult for third parties or independent candidates to accumulate enough votes to win an election. To have any effect, their support must be geographically concentrated, as was George Wallace's in 1968 and Strom Thurmond's in 1948, rather than evenly distributed across the country, as was Henry Wallace's in 1948, John Anderson's in 1980, and H. Ross Perot's in 1992.

Periodically, proposals to alter or abolish the Electoral College have been advanced. Most of these plans would eliminate the office of elector but retain the college. One would allocate a state's electoral vote in proportion to its popular vote; another would determine the state's electoral vote on the basis of separate district and statewide elections. A third, direct election, would abolish the Electoral College entirely. The popular vote winner would be elected provided that person received at least 40 percent of the popular vote. Thus far, Congress has been reluctant to approve any of these changes and seems unlikely to do so until some electoral crisis or unpopular result occurs.

## Political Attitudes and Groupings

As the constitutional framework structures presidential elections, so political attitudes and group loyalties affect the conduct of campaigns. Voters do not come to the election with completely open minds. They come with preexisting views. They do not see and hear the campaign in isolation. They observe it and absorb it as part of their daily lives. In other words, their attitudes and associations affect their perceptions and influence their behavior. This is why it is important for students of presidential elections to examine public attitudes and patterns of social interaction.

Considerable research has been conducted on these subjects.[4] It suggests that people develop political attitudes early in life. Over time these attitudes tend to become more intense and more resistant to change and therefore more important influences on voting behavior. Attitudes affect perceptions of the campaign and evaluations of the parties, the candidates, and the issues.

Of all the factors that contribute to the development of a political attitude, how an individual identifies with a political party is the most important. Party identification operates as a conceptual filter, providing clues for interpreting the issues, for judging the candidates, and for deciding if and how to vote. The stronger this identification, the more compelling the cues. Conversely, the weaker the identification, the less likely it will affect perceptions during the campaign and influence voting.

The amount of information that is known about the candidates also affects the influence of partisanship. In general, the less that is known, the more likely the people will follow their partisan inclinations when voting. Since presidential campaigns normally convey more information than do other elections, the influence of party is apt to be weaker in these higher-visibility contests than in congressional and state elections.

When identification with party is weak or nonexistent, other factors, such as the personalities of the candidates and their issue positions, will be correspondingly more important. In contrast to party identification, which is a long-term stabilizing factor, candidate and issue orientations are short-term, more variable influences that change from election to election. Of the two, the image of the candidate has been more significant.

Candidate images turn on personality and policy dimensions. People tend to form general impressions about candidates on the basis of what is known about their leadership potential, decision-making capabilities, and personal traits. For an incumbent president seeking reelection, accomplishments in office provide much of the criteria for evaluation. People make a retrospective judgment, deciding whether or not to vote for a candidate seeking reelection on the basis of how well they believe that candidate and party have performed during the candidate's term of office.

For the challenger, the criteria are slightly different. Experience, knowledge, confidence, and assertiveness substitute for performance and provide a basis for anticipating how well the candidate might do in office. For both, character issues, such as trustworthiness, integrity, and candor, also affect perceptions, which in turn can affect voting.

Policy positions of the incumbent and challenger are obviously important as well. Knowing how the candidates stand on the issues permits voters to make a judgment on the consequences of electing either candidate. However, the low level of information and awareness that much of the electorate possesses reduces the salience of issues for many people.

To be important, issues must stand out from campaign rhetoric. They must attract attention; they must hit home. Without personal impact, they are unlikely to be primary motivating factors in voting. To the extent that positions on issues are not discernible, personality considerations become more critical.

Ironically, that portion of the electorate that can be more easily persuaded—weak partisans and independents—tends to have the least information. Conversely, the most committed tend to be the most informed. They use their information to support their partisanship.

Since the 1960s, the percentage of the population identifying with a party has declined, as has the intensity of that identification. This has resulted in a more volatile electorate that decides later in the campaign whether and how to vote. In 1992 about two-thirds of the electorate identified with one or the other of the major parties, compared with three-fourths forty years earlier.

TURNOUT.    The weakening of party identification has also contributed to the decline in turnout from 1960 to 1988 by decreasing the partisan motivation for voting. Just slightly over 50 percent of those eligible to vote actually did so in 1988. However, in 1992, that proportion jumped to 55.2 percent. (See Table 3-1.)

The principal explanation for the increase has to do with factors that are not directly related to partisan affiliation. In 1992 people seemed to

Table 3-1. Suffrage and Turnout

| Year | Total Adult Population (including aliens)* | Total Presidential Vote | Percentage of Adult Population Voting |
|------|---------------------|------------------------|--------------------|
| 1824 | 3,964,000 | 363,017 | 9% |
| 1840 | 7,381,000 | 2,412,698 | 33 |
| 1860 | 14,676,000 | 4,692,710 | 32 |
| 1880 | 25,012,000 | 9,219,467 | 37 |
| 1900 | 40,753,000 | 13,974,188 | 35 |
| 1920 | 60,581,000 | 26,768,613 | 44 |
| 1932 | 75,768,000 | 39,732,000 | 52.4 |
| 1940 | 84,728,000 | 49,900,000 | 58.9 |
| 1952 | 99,929,000 | 61,551,000 | 61.6 |
| 1960 | 109,672,000 | 68,838,000 | 62.8 |
| 1964 | 114,090,000 | 70,645,000 | 61.9 |
| 1968 | 120,285,000 | 73,212,000 | 60.9 |
| 1972 | 140,777,000 | 77,719,000 | 55.5 |
| 1976 | 152,308,000 | 81,556,000 | 53.5 |
| 1980 | 164,595,000 | 86,515,000 | 52.6 |
| 1984 | 174,447,000 | 92,653,000 | 53.1 |
| 1988 | 182,600,000 | 91,602,291 | 50.2 |
| 1992 | 189,044,000 | 104,426,659 | 55.2 |

*Restrictions based on sex, age, race, religion, and property ownership prevented a significant portion of the adult population from voting in the nineteenth and early twentieth centuries. Of those who were eligible, however, the percentage casting ballots was often quite high, particularly during the last half of the nineteenth century.

Source: Population figures for 1824 to 1920 are based on estimates and early census figures that appear in Neal R. Pierce, *The People's President* (New York: Simon and Schuster, 1968), p. 206. Population figures from 1932 to 1984 are from the U.S. Department of Commerce, Bureau of the Census, *Statistical Abstract of the United States* (Washington, D.C., 1987), p. 250. Figures for 1988 and 1992 were compiled from official election returns supplied by the Federal Election Commission.

be more aware of the issues and more concerned about them than they were in some previous elections, particularly in 1984 and 1988. That concern, undoubtedly aroused by the recession, generated a higher than normal vote on election day. The candidates, primarily H. Ross Perot, may also have provided more incentive to vote. Perot's independent candidacy seemed to energize those who were most angry and frustrated with the major parties and their nominees and thus had less incentive to vote for them. Had Perot not run, some of the 19.7 million people who voted for him would probably have stayed at home.

Whether or not turnout continues to rise, however, may depend on longer-term trends such as citizen satisfaction with government and feelings of political efficacy as well as the standard motivations for voting: interest in the election, concern over the outcome, and feelings of civic responsibility. Naturally a person who feels more strongly about the election and its consequences is more likely to vote than one who does not care or cannot see what difference it would make who wins.

In addition to attitudinal factors, demographic characteristics that relate to turnout include education, income, and occupational status. As people become more educated, as they move up the socioeconomic ladder, as their jobs gain in status, they are more likely to vote. Education is the most important of these variables. It has the greatest bearing on whether people vote.[5]

Finally, state laws influence voting. In order to cast a ballot on election day, a citizen must be registered to vote. Within broad federal guidelines, the states prescribe the rules for registration. The failure to register accounts for a significant portion of nonvoting. Two political scientists, Raymond E. Wolfinger and Steven J. Rosenstone, estimated that simplifying registration could increase turnout by as much as 9 percent.[6] Their supposition is likely to be tested after 1995 when new federal legislation goes into effect that requires all states to permit registration by mail or at various state offices such as the bureau of motor vehicles. Approximately half the states already follow these procedures.

Turnout has partisan implications as well. The Republican party, composed of a larger proportion of well-educated, high-income, white-collar workers, usually gets a greater percentage of its adherents to vote than does the Democratic party. The higher Republican turnout has helped that party counter the Democrats' advantage in number of registered voters. In 1992, turnout among Republicans was marginally higher than among Democrats; however, the proportion of Republicans voting declined from 1988 while that of Democrats increased.[7]

Candidates and their advisers must take the voting behavior of the electorate into account when planning their campaign. They must also be conscious of the social basis of contemporary American politics—the racial, ethnic, religious, and even gender groupings that comprise each party's electoral coalition.

PARTISAN COALITIONS.    It was during the depression that the Democrats became the majority party. They built their coalition primarily along economic lines with the bulk of it coming from those in the lower socioeconomic strata. In addition, the party maintained the support of white southerners who had voted Democratic since the Civil War.

Today the Democrats still constitute the political party with which the largest proportion of the electorate identifies, but their proportionate advantage has declined. The Democrats' electoral coalition is much more fragile than it was in the period from the 1930s to the 1960s. White southern support has eroded within the last three decades while labor support has also declined, and the party has barely maintained the traditional backing it receives from Catholic voters (see Table 3-2). On the other hand, it has increased its support from African-Americans and Hispanics, retained its Jewish constituency, and cut into the Republican vote in the Northeast. In recent years the Democrats have also been the beneficiaries of a female vote, particularly from younger, working women. Democratic support is frequently concentrated in the cities in the large industrial states.

Table 3-2. Demography of Democrats and Republicans in the 1990s
(in percentages)

| | Republican | Democrat | Independent | No. of Interviews |
|---|---|---|---|---|
| **National** | 29 | 38 | 33 | 4,929 |
| **Sex** | | | | |
| Male | 30 | 36 | 34 | 2,476 |
| Female | 28 | 40 | 32 | 2,453 |
| **Age** | | | | |
| 18–29 years | 29 | 33 | 38 | 871 |
| 30–49 years | 29 | 37 | 34 | 2,014 |
| 50–64 years | 28 | 42 | 30 | 993 |
| 65 & older | 33 | 43 | 24 | 1,029 |
| Boomer (26–46) | 29 | 36 | 35 | 2,133 |
| **Region** | | | | |
| East | 24 | 41 | 35 | 1,197 |
| Midwest | 30 | 32 | 38 | 1,368 |
| South | 32 | 40 | 28 | 1,510 |
| West | 32 | 39 | 29 | 854 |
| **Race** | | | | |
| White | 32 | 34 | 34 | 4,319 |
| Nonwhite | 11 | 65 | 24 | 610 |
| Black | 9 | 71 | 20 | 457 |
| Hispanic | 23 | 52 | 25 | 367 |
| **Education** | | | | |
| College graduates | 36 | 32 | 32 | 1,185 |
| College incomplete/ technical | 33 | 34 | 33 | 1,295 |
| High school graduates | 28 | 38 | 34 | 1,575 |
| Less than high school graduates | 21 | 50 | 29 | 844 |
| **Income** | | | | |
| $40,000 & over | 35 | 32 | 33 | 1,474 |
| $25,000–$39,999 | 32 | 34 | 34 | 1,233 |
| $15,000–$24,999 | 26 | 41 | 33 | 902 |
| Under $15,000 | 23 | 51 | 26 | 1,013 |
| **Religion** | | | | |
| Protestant | 34 | 36 | 30 | 2,695 |
| Catholic | 26 | 42 | 32 | 1,428 |

Source: *The Gallup Poll Monthly,* July 1992, p. 49.

The Republicans were the majority party before the 1930s. During the depression the GOP lost the support of much of the working class and was unable to attract new groups to its coalition. Business and professional people, however, maintained their Republican affiliation, as did nonsouthern, white Protestants. Today, the Republican party receives much of its support from white-collar workers, professionals and managers, and those in the upper-middle and upper classes. The party has increased its popularity in the Sunbelt and the West, particularly in the more sparsely populated Rocky Mountain areas, but has lost popularity in the so-called Rust Belt of the Northeast and Midwest. Republicans have maintained their traditional support from Protestants, gaining adherents from Christian fundamentalist groups. Recently men have given GOP candidates at the national level more support than they have given their Democratic challengers.

What conclusions can we draw about the social basis of politics today? It is clear that the old party coalitions have changed and, in the Democrats' case, weakened. While class, religion, and geography are still related to party identification and voting behavior, they are not as strongly correlated as they were in the past. Voters are less influenced by group cues. They exercise a more independent judgment on election day, a judgment that is less predictable and more subject to be influenced by the campaign itself. These changes explain why the Republicans have been able to make inroads at the presidential level since 1968. Although they have not become a majority or even plurality of the electorate, they have reduced the Democrats' advantage.

### Financial Considerations

A third factor that affects the strategic environment of presidential campaigns is the funding provided by the federal government. In the past, candidates were dependent on the generosity of their backers and the support of their party. And considerable generosity was needed to finance these national efforts.

The spiraling costs of campaigning beginning in the 1960s, however, made candidates increasingly dependent on large donors. The number of individuals who contributed $10,000 or more grew dramatically during this period. The rapidly rising donations and expenditures created even greater inequalities than had existed in the past. In 1964, 1968, and 1972 the Republican nominees were able to spend more than twice as much as their Democratic counterparts. This became a bone of contention, since it was assumed that money contributed to electoral success.

A cursory look at total expenditures in presidential elections lends some support to this thesis. In general elections between 1860 and 1972 (the last election before public financing), the winner outspent the loser twenty-one out of twenty-nine times. Republican candidates have spent more than their Democrat opponents in twenty-five out of the twenty-nine elections during this period. The four times they did not, the Democrats won. These figures would suggest that the potential for winning is affected by and affects the capacity to raise money.

The high costs of campaigning, the dependence on large donors, and the inequities in the amounts candidates received and could spend prompted a Democratically controlled Congress in the 1970s to enact legislation for public funding of presidential elections.

The funding provision went into effect in 1976. At that time the federal contribution to the major party candidates was set at $20 million plus a cost-of-living adjustment. In 1992, when that adjustment was taken into account, each of the major candidates received $55.2 million.

The nominees of the major parties are automatically eligible for funds. Third-party and independent candidates do not qualify until they receive 5 percent of the presidential vote. Thereafter, they are eligible to get funds equal to their proportion of the popular vote until that vote drops below 5 percent. John Anderson, a third-party candidate in 1980, received $4.2 million for his 6.6 percent of the vote, enough to pay off his debts but not enough to have mounted a vigorous campaign. Moreover, he received it after the election. Billionaire H. Ross Perot chose not to accept federal funds in 1992. His 19 percent of the popular vote makes him eligible for federal funds in 1996 if he decides to run and to accept government support.

The law permits the national parties to spend two cents per citizen of voting age in support of their presidential nominees. In 1992 this amounted to $10.3 million. In addition a 1979 amendment to the Federal Election Campaign Act also allows state and local political parties to spend an unlimited amount of funds on voluntary efforts to turn out the vote. The printing and distribution of literature, the operation of phone banks, and the coordination of registration and get-out-the-vote drives are all included. This is referred to as "soft money." In 1992 the Republicans reported to the Federal Election Commission that they had spent $51.4 million in soft money compared to $36.3 million for the Democrats.[8]

The campaign finance legislation has had a profound effect on the conduct of presidential elections. It has equalized spending between the major party candidates. Theoretically, this should work to the Democrats' and to the incumbent's benefit. Equal spending denies the Republicans their traditional financial edge. It also makes it more difficult for a challenger, who lacks the news-making capacity of an incumbent, to get equal public attention.

In 1976 these advantages seemed to offset one another. In subsequent elections they did not. Superior Republican resources at the national, state, and local levels enabled the GOP to mount national media campaigns and selective grass-roots efforts for many of its candidates for national and state office including president and vice president. In contrast, the Democrats, who have suffered from a weaker financial and organizational position, could not benefit their tickets nearly as much, although they were more successful in 1992 than in previous years.

Independent efforts by nonparty groups such as political action committees (PACs), protected by the First Amendment to the Constitution, have also been important in presidential contests. In 1976, Democrat Carter was greatly aided by labor's efforts on his behalf as well as by members of the National Education Association in several key states. In the 1980s it was Republican candidates who were the principal benefactors of independent spending and election activities by individuals and groups. While these activities have continued, independent spending on behalf of presidential candidates has declined since 1984. In 1992 it was less than $5 million dollars.[9]

Finally, the law has affected and will continue to affect the major parties. Here, however, the law may be more harmful than beneficial because party candidates, not party organizations, receive the bulk of federal support. Moreover, the prohibition against private contributions has enlarged the role and impact of political action committees, although less at the presidential level than at the state and congressional level. On balance, the law has reduced the influence of the national parties over the campaigns of their candidates although they have regained some of their lost influence through their solicitation and distribution of soft money to their state and local affilitates. Limited funding has also prompted the candidates to utilize the mass media, not old-style party organizations, to reach the largest number of voters in the most cost-effective way.

### News Coverage

News coverage also affects the strategic environment. Today most people follow presidential campaigns on television. It is the prime source of news for approximately two-thirds of the population. Newspapers are a distant second, being the major source for only about 20 percent. Radio and magazines trail far behind.[10]

Since it is an action-oriented, visual medium, television reports the drama and excitement of the campaign. It does so by emphasizing the contest. Who is ahead? How are the candidates doing? Is the leader slipping? It is this horse-race aspect of the campaign that provides the principal focus during the nomination phase and, with a close contest, during the general election as well. This was certainly the case in 1992 when horse-race stories dominated the news during the early primary period and throughout the general election campaign.[11]

The need to stress the contest affects which issues are covered when issues are covered. Television in particular focuses on those that provide clear-cut differences between the candidates, those that provoke controversy, and those that can be presented in a simple, straightforward manner. These are not necessarily the issues that the candidates have stressed during their campaigns. In general, substantive, policy questions of what the government should do tend to receive little in-depth coverage. In 1992, next to the close race, it was stories about the candidates, their organizations, and their strategies and tactics that received the most emphasis.

Moreover, much of the coverage was negative. According to one analysis of the evening news on the three major television networks, good news was hard to find. Only 31 percent of Bush's coverage was positive compared to 37 percent for Clinton's and 46 percent for Perot's.[12] (See Figure 3-1.)

Although candidates may influence their news coverage, they cannot control it. Try as they may to counter an uncomplimentary evaluation and project a favorable image, it is very difficult to divert the media's focus or blunt their effect on the voters.

The time, money, and energy spent on image building suggests that it has a major impact on electoral behavior. Although there is little tangible evidence that the media campaign changes attitudes, it does generate interest, increase awareness, and affect perceptions of the candidates by the electorate. In this way, it influences voting.

Studies of presidential campaigning in the 1940s indicated that the principal impact of the print media was to activate predispositions and reinforce attitudes rather than to convert voters. Newspapers and magazines provided information but primarily to those who were most committed. The most committed, in turn, used the information to support their beliefs. Weeding out opposing views, they insulated themselves from unfavorable news and opinions that conflicted with their own.[13] With only a small percentage of the population citing newspapers as its primary source of data, the direct impact of print journalism on the political campaign is limited. However, the investigative reports of principal newspapers and magazines become part of the campaign debate and in this way help generate the issues and condition the candidates' agenda.

In contrast, television viewers are more captive of the picture than readers are of the printed page. Thus, television exposes the less com-

**Figure 3-1. Good Press: Positive Coverage on the Evening News for 1992**

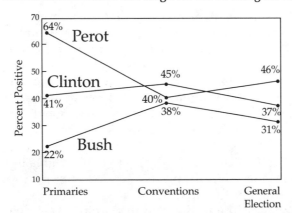

Source: "Clinton's the One: TV News Coverage of the 1992 General Election," *Media Monitor*, published by the Center of Media and Public Affairs, a non-partisan and non-profit research organization (November 1992), 5. Copyright © 1993 CMPA.

mitted to more information and the more committed to other points of view. Avoidance is more difficult.

Moreover, television news tends to be "more mediating, more political, more personal, more critical, [and] more thematic than old-style print."[14] Whereas newspapers describe events, indicating what candidates say and do, television presents the dramatic elements. It provides a visual slice of reality, not simply a compendium of people, places, and things.

But in presenting political news, television also compartmentalizes it, fitting a large number of stories into a thirty-minute broadcast (of which 22 minutes is news and the remainder is advertising). Of necessity, this restricts the time that can be devoted to any one item in the news. Campaign stories average one and a half minutes on the evening news, the equivalent of only a few paragraphs of a printed account. The portion of the story devoted to the candidate's words is much smaller. The average "sound bite" in 1992 was only 8.4 seconds; in 1988 it was 9.8 seconds.[15] Perhaps this explains why viewers do not retain much information from what candidates say and do.

Two political scientists, Thomas E. Patterson and Robert D. McClure, studied how television reported the news during the 1972 campaign and found:

1. Most election issues are mentioned so infrequently that viewers could not possibly learn about them.
2. Most issue references are so fleeting that they could not be expected to leave an impression on viewers.
3. The candidates' issue positions generally were reported in ways guaranteed to make them elusive.[16] "Television news adds little to the average voter's understanding of election issues," they wrote. "Network news may be fascinating. It may be highly entertaining. But it is simply not informative."[17]

From what sources, then, do people receive information? One of the most interesting findings of the Patterson and McClure study is that people actually get more information from the advertisements they see on television than from the networks' evening news programs. The reason seems to be that ads are more repetitive and more compact. When placed with other commercials in popular shows, they are difficult to avoid. In fact, television watchers pay about twice as much attention to political advertisements as they do to other kinds of commercials.

What effect does this have on the election? Who is influenced and how? Students of the electoral process suggest three principal effects for three different groups of voters.

*Strong Partisans:* The media tend to reinforce their feelings and loyalties. Acting as a catalyst, television, radio, and newspapers move members of this group in the direction of their inclinations. In other words, they make them more Democratic or more Republican and thus more likely to exercise their partisan judgment on election day.

*Weak Partisans* (including those who claim they are independent but lean in a partisan direction): The campaign is too short to change their beliefs or attitudes, but it is long enough to affect their perceptions of the candidates. By providing weak partisans with more information about the candidates and their stands, the media raise doubts or remove them. By so doing either they produce cross-pressures that lead to uncertainty and may ultimately cause partisan defections or nonvoting, or they may actually reduce pressure, thereby generating a partisan response.

*Independents* (those with no partisan affiliation and sometimes little interest in politics): The media bring these individuals into contact with the campaign, which in turn may excite interest, arouse concern, improve knowledge, and, in the end, affect judgment. In this way the media increase the likelihood of their voting and the influence of candidate evaluation on their voting decisions.

## THE PRESIDENTIAL CAMPAIGN

Campaigning by presidential candidates is a relatively recent phenomenon. For much of American history, personal solicitation by the party nominees was viewed as demeaning and unbecoming of the dignity and status of the presidency. It was not until 1860 that this tradition of nonparticipation by the candidates themselves was broken when Senator Stephen A. Douglas, Democratic nominee for president, spoke out on the slavery issue. Douglas did not set an immediate precedent. Presidential candidates remained on the sidelines for most of the nineteenth century. Party supporters made appeals on their behalf.

The second nominee who personally campaigned was William Jennings Bryan. Gaining the Democratic nomination following his famous "cross of gold" speech at his party's convention, Bryan pleaded his case for free silver to groups around the country. By his own account, he traveled more than eighteen thousand miles, made more than six hundred speeches, and, according to press estimates, spoke to almost five million people.[18] In contrast, Bryan's opponent of that year, William McKinley, campaigned from the front porch of his home.

Republican candidates did little more than front-porch oratory until the 1930s, but Democrats Woodrow Wilson and Al Smith took their campaigns to the public in 1912 and 1928, respectively. By 1932 active campaigning by the nominees became the rule rather than the exception. Franklin Roosevelt crisscrossed the country by railroad, making it possible for thousands of people to see him.[19] He employed radio to reach millions of others. Roosevelt's skillful use of this communication medium demonstrated the potential that a personal appeal can have for winning and leading.

Television accelerated this potential, making it easier for a candidate to reach millions of voters. But television also created new obstacles for the nominees and their parties. The physical appearance of the candidates became more important. Attention focused on the images they presented. New game plans had to be designed. These plans contained broad public appeals, appeals that were candidate oriented, appeals that were projected by sophisticated marketing techniques, appeals that were carefully targeted to specific groups within the electorate. Additionally, large, multitiered, functionally differentiated campaign organizations had to be developed.

## Running an Organization

A large, specialized political organization is essential to coordinate the myriad activities that must be performed in any presidential campaign. These include advance work, scheduling, press arrangements, issue and candidate research, speech writing, polling, advertising, grass-roots organizing, accounting, budgeting, legal activities, and liaison with state and local party committees and other "friendly" groups.

Organizations vary in structure and style. Some have been very centralized, with a few individuals making most of the major decisions; others have been more decentralized. Some have worked through or in conjunction with national and state party organizations; others seem to have disregarded these groups entirely and created their own field organizations. Some have operated from a comprehensive game plan; others have adopted a more incremental approach. The Goldwater organization in 1964, the Nixon operation in 1972, the Reagan and Bush efforts in 1984 and 1988, and the Clinton campaign of 1992 exemplified the tighter, hierarchical structure, in which a few individuals control decision making and access to the candidate. The Humphrey campaign in 1968, Mondale's effort in 1984, and, to some extent, the Bush campaign of 1992 had looser, more fluid structures with units within the organizations rivaling each other for influence and access to the candidate.

There are tensions in every campaign, tensions between the candidate's organization and the party's, between the national headquarters and the field staff, between the research and operational units, between government functions (for incumbents) and political activities, and between government and campaign staffs. Some of these tensions are the inevitable consequence of personnel operating under severe time constraints and pressures. Some are the result of the need to coordinate a large, decentralized party system for a national campaign. Some result from limited resources, large egos, and the struggle over who gets how much.

Some of these tensions were evident in the Dukakis campaign of 1988 and the Bush campaign of 1992. In 1988 Democratic leaders who had experience in other national presidential campaigns were not actively recruited or even encouraged to join the Dukakis effort. Not only did this produce ill will among Democrats, but it resulted in costly delays in addressing the critical strategic needs of the campaign. In 1992 it was a lack of coordination among the White House, the Republican National Committee, and the official Bush campaign that marred the president's reelection efforts. It was not until the final weeks of the campaign that the candidate's activities, speeches, and advertisements resonated a single, cohesive theme. In contrast, the Clinton organization was the model of efficiency. Its campaign left nothing to chance. Survey research and in-depth focus groups were used to design and test the candidate's messages. A rapid-fire response team enabled the campaign to answer Republican attacks within hours.

### Designing a Presidential Image

To become president it is necessary to act like one, to display the traits of an ideal president. Strength, boldness, and decisiveness are intrinsic to the public's image of the office. During times of crisis or periods of social anxiety these leadership characteristics are considered absolutely essential. The strength that Franklin Roosevelt was able to convey by virtue of his successful bout with polio and that Eisenhower imparted by his military command in World War II contrasted sharply with the perceptions of Stevenson in 1956, McGovern in 1972, and Carter in 1980 as weak, indecisive, and vacillating. Mondale in 1984 and Bush in 1988 and 1992 also suffered from the general perception that they lacked some of these leadership traits.

In addition to seeming strong enough to be president, it is also important to appear competent, to exhibit sufficient knowledge and skills for the job. Although Ross Perot's prowess as a successful business executive was commonly cited as a strength of his candidacy, particularly in the light of the country's economic woes, his lack of experience in government raised questions about his ability to be its top public official.

Honesty, integrity, and trustworthiness are also essential attributes for the presidency. Clinton's lack of candor about his personal life and his draft status and his tendency to equivocate on controversial issues became issues in the 1992 election.

When the public judges a candidate's qualities, it looks to past performance as a guide to future behavior. In most instances, this provides an advantage to the incumbent because it allows that candidate to claim those qualities deemed essential for the office. Being president produces recognition, esteem, and status. It also gives incumbents the ability to affect events or at least influence their timing, help certain individuals, groups, and areas of the country, and promote certain policies and programs that have political benefit. President George Bush used his discretionary authority to authorize emergency loans for victims of natural disasters, approve trade agreements, and continue defense programs that created or maintained jobs for thousands of workers.

While incumbency contributes to a perception of leadership, it does not guarantee it as George Bush found out in 1992. He was unable to demonstrate that he could be an agent for change or that he understood the country's economic problems and could deal with them as effectively as his Democratic opponent.

Challengers usually face a more difficult task than do incumbents. They must appear as presidential as possible. Carter in 1976, Reagan in 1980, Dukakis in 1988, and Clinton and Perot in 1992 had to provide the electorate with information about their leadership abilities. Walter Mondale had to demonstrate that he was an influential vice president, yet not responsible for the problems of the Carter years.

## Projecting an Appeal

Once a presidential image is established, it must be projected. This can be done in a variety of ways: in speeches and news conferences, in press releases and interviews, and in print, radio, and television advertising. Of all these methods, advertising, particularly on television, reaches the largest audience, has the most sustained impact, and is least subject to interference by media representatives. That is why recent presidential campaigns have allocated more than two-thirds of their budgets to this method of reaching the voters.

ADVERTISING.    To be effective, advertising must be presented in an interesting and believable way. It must maintain interest. For television, this frequently means action; the ad must move. For Reagan the need in 1980 was different. Fearful that a slick presentation would bring attention to the candidate's career as an actor, Reagan's media advisers presented him as a talking head with as few gimmicks and diversions as possible. In contrast, his 1984 advertising used the trappings of the presidency to demonstrate his leadership skills. Most incumbents take advantage of their status to use the White House and their presidential activities as a backdrop for their reelection campaign. Take Bush's commercial in 1992 that pictured scenes from the Persian Gulf War and then an empty Oval Office. "Who do you trust to be sitting in this chair?" an announcer asked, raising doubts about the steadiness of his two opponents.

Advertising tends to be targeted to different sections of the country and to different groups within the electorate. The objective of targeting is to bring the campaign home, to influence specific groups of voters who share many of the same concerns. This requires that issues and positions be relevant to the audience. The candidate's appearance, message, and language must mesh. Media buyers will normally code stations by their viewers and their program format so that the messages fit the audience both demographically and regionally.

Frequently, candidates work as hard to destroy their opponent's image as they do to build their own. This is known as confrontational advertising and has been used with regularity since 1964. That year perhaps the most famous (or infamous) negative ad was created for the Democrats. Called daisy girl, it was designed to reinforce the impression that Republican candidate Barry Goldwater was a trigger-happy zealot who would not hesitate to use nuclear weapons against a Communist foe.

The advertisement began with a little girl in a meadow plucking petals from a daisy. She counted to herself softly. When she reached eleven, her voice faded and a stern-sounding male voice counted down from nine. When he got to zero, there was an explosion, the little girl disappeared, and a mushroom-shaped cloud covered the screen. President Johnson was heard saying, "These are the stakes, to make a world in which all of God's children can live or go into the dark. The stakes are too high for you to stay at home." The ad ended with a plea to vote for Lyndon Johnson on election day.

The commercial was run only once. Goldwater supporters were outraged and protested vigorously. Their protest kept the issue alive. In fact, the ad itself became a news item, and parts of it were shown on television newscasts, thereby reinforcing the impression the Democrats wished to leave in the voters' minds.

The emphasis given confrontational, or negative, advertising has increased in recent years. In 1988 both candidates ran more ads that were critical of their opponents than ones that lauded their own accomplishments and qualifications for the office. One of Bush's hardest-hitting commercials featured a Massachusetts prison furlough program that Dukakis supported as governor. The ad pictured tough-looking inmates in prison garb walking through a revolving door. It suggested that Dukakis was soft on crime. An even more poignant and sensational spot, sponsored by a PAC that was supporting Bush, showed a picture of Willie Horton, a convicted murderer who stabbed a man and raped his female companion after escaping while on a furlough from a Massachusetts prison. Amid gruesome commentary about Horton's criminal acts, the ad contrasted the positions of Dukakis and Bush on crime, much to Dukakis's disadvantage. This ad was particularly controversial because it had racial overtones. Horton is African-American and his victims white.

Negative advertising by the Bush campaign and groups that supported his candidacy led Dukakis to run antinegative ads about Bush's negative advertising. In one, the governor was seen sitting in front of a television showing a Bush commercial that accused Dukakis of being against virtually every new weapons system for the military. An angry Dukakis turns off the set and says: "I'm fed up with it. Haven't seen anything like it in twenty-five years of public life, George Bush's negative TV ads: distorting my record, full of lies, and he knows it."

The amount of negative advertising, which became a campaign issue in 1988, had an impact on the 1992 election. It affected candidates' strategies, particularly those who were targets of such advertising. Dukakis had not responded quickly enough to Bush's negative advertising in 1988. He allowed impressions created by the ads to persist, thereby damaging his candidacy. By the end of the campaign 25 percent of the electorate knew who Willie Horton was, what he did, and who furloughed him; 49 percent thought Dukakis was soft on crime.[20]

Clinton did not make the same mistake in 1992. His campaign reacted skillfully and rapidly to Bush's attacks. In several instances, Clinton's media consultants even obtained copies of Bush's advertisements *before* they were aired, enabling them to craft responses that could be aired within hours of Bush's attacks. The Clinton people went so far as to prepare negative ads about their own candidate, show them to groups, and test their responses to these ads in order to be in a position to counter similar charges by Bush.[21]

A second impact of Bush's 1988 negative advertising campaign was that people were far more skeptical of the claims made in advertising during the 1992 campaign. A majority of the electorate did not believe Bush's ads and tuned them out over the course of the campaign. Although Clinton's and Perot's advertising was seen as more truthful by more voters, about a third of the electorate still questioned the candidates' veracity.[22]

The news media also exercise more scrutiny. In 1992 major news organizations such as the *New York Times* and the *Washington Post* printed television advertisements and assessed their accuracy, as illustrated in Box 3-1.

From the perspective of the candidates and their managers, political advertising works. It affects voter perceptions and reinforces attitudes and opinions. The environment can be predetermined, the words and pictures can be created and coordinated, and the candidate can be rehearsed to produce the desired effect.

In contrast, news is more difficult to influence. The candidate's message is mediated partially by the structure of the event and partially by how the media choose to cover it. Remarks may be edited for the sake of the story. A candidate can be interrupted, his comments interpreted, and his policies evaluated. The national press corps is particularly confrontational, and candidates in 1992 were encouraged to avoid tough interviews and press conferences with them in favor of softer, less hostile questions from average citizens in a town-meeting format or with talk-show hosts.

Another problem candidates often face is that their major statements can be overshadowed by minor events—if, for example, the candidate makes some goof or if hecklers are present. Antiabortion protesters dogged Geraldine Ferraro in 1984 and Michael Dukakis in 1988, making abortion an issue wherever they spoke. Under these circumstances, aspirants for the presidency and vice presidency exercise much less leverage. They are not powerless, however.

Campaign organizations work very hard to affect the coverage they receive. Speeches for presidential candidates are now scripted for their sound bites; events are staged with television in mind. Satellite broadcasting has made it possible for campaign press secretaries to give local newspaper reporters and television stations more direct access to the candidates. Interviews conducted by the local press are apt to be less hostile and more favorable than those conducted by the national reporters covering the campaign.

Although contemporary campaigns lack spontaneity, they are designed for maximum public impact. Symbols are used to convey images; themes are presented on a weekly or biweekly basis. Press releases, advertisements, and speeches are carefully synchronized to strengthen a candidate's appeal. Even seemingly off-the-cuff remarks are usually prepared and timed to contribute to the overall thematic effect.

The Clinton and Perot campaigns were fairly successful in maintaining their focus and themes. Clinton constantly talked about the economy and the need for change; Perot hammered away at inept economic and budgetary policy, privileged and inefficient government, and poor political leadership. Bush struggled to find a theme that resonated with the American people. He finally ended up by focusing on personal characteristics such as trust and experience, claiming that he was the most reliable of the three candidates.

DEBATES.    Debates are another good example of events that candidates go to great lengths to influence. More than any other single campaign activity, presidential debates have gained public attention. It is estimated that more than half of the adult population in the United States watched all of the 1960 Kennedy–Nixon debates, the first debate between presidential candidates, and almost 90 percent saw one of them.[23] Although less attention has been riveted on a single debate since then, millions still watch all or parts of them. Table 3-3 indicates the size of the viewing audience according to a Nielsen survey.

With so many people watching, meticulous planning goes into each debate. Representatives of the candidates study the locations, try to anticipate the questions, and brief and rehearse the candidates.[24] Mock studios are built and the debate environment simulated. In 1980 this elaborate preparation took a bizarre twist. Those who readied Ronald Reagan for his debate with President Carter obtained the briefing material that Carter's aides had prepared for him. Knowing the questions that Carter anticipated and the answers he was advised to give helped Reagan counter Carter's responses. The debate made him look good.

Candidates have viewed presidential debates as vehicles for improving their images and/or damaging their opponents. They seek to establish their leadership credentials and critique their opponent's. This worked to Bush's disadvantage in 1992 as both Clinton and Perot criticized his administration's policies.

Debates tend to help challengers more than incumbents. Since they are less well known, challengers have more questions raised about them, their competence, and their capacity to be president. The debates provide an opportunity to satisfy some of these doubts in a believable

## BOX 3-1.    ADVERTISING AND ANALYSIS IN 1992

### Bush: TV Spot Harshly Denounces Clinton's Record

The Bush campaign began broadcasting this 30-second commercial Wednesday in unidentified markets around the country.

**ON THE SCREEN** Opens with gloomy black and white images of a rainy day, a deserted road, weeds rustling in the wind. Key phrases from the narration, and sources for the statistics, are superimposed over similarly depressing images. Closes with a tree and a buzzard in the desert and these words, "America Can't Take That Risk."

**PRODUCER** The November Company.

**TELEVISION SCRIPT** Announcer: "In his 12 years as Governor, Bill Clinton has doubled his state's debt. Doubled government spending and signed the largest tax increase in his state's history. Yet his state remains the 45th worst in which to work. The 45th worst for children. It has the worst environmental policy.

"And the F.B.I. says Arkansas had America's biggest increase in rate of serious crime. And now Bill Clinton wants to do for America what he's done for Arkansas. America can't take that risk."

**ACCURACY** This ad is a case study in how accusations can be made and how facts can be used to bolster them or tear them down. The Bush campaign backs its accusations with statistics and cites its sources on the screen. The Clinton campaign refutes every accusation with its own statistics.

For example, while it is true that Arkansas doubled government spending, most of that growth came from inflation. The Clinton campaign has also cited figures from the National Governors' Association showing that all but six states have doubled general spending since Mr. Clinton took office.

**SCORECARD** This ad takes facts out of context to paint Mr. Clinton as a governor who brought only misery to Arkansas. In reality, Mr. Clinton has been considered a better than average governor of a small, poor state. It tries to scare viewers into thinking that a Clinton administration would bring only gloom and doom to the whole country. In 30 seconds, the ad tries to hit Mr. Clinton on the hot-button issues of the environment, children, crime and taxes—all issues that Mr. Bush has been attacked on.

Source: Richard L. Berke, "Bush: TV Spot Harshly Denounces Clinton's Record," *New York Times*, October 30, 1992, p. A19. Copyright © 1992 by The New York Times Company. Reprinted by permission.

(continued)

**BOX 3-1.**    *(continued)*

### Clinton: Issuing a Quick Response

Less than a day after the Bush campaign began broadcasting its commercial attacking Arkansas, the Clinton campaign produced this 30-second response, for broadcast in select markets beginning yesterday.

**ON THE SCREEN** Phrases appear that underscore the narration, like "Bush ads are misleading and wrong," and "Arkansas leads the nation in job growth." Beneath the words, in smaller type, appear sources for the phrases, like CBS, Bureau of Labor Statistics. Interspersed with the words are photographs of Gov. Bill Clinton at work in the Governor's office.

**PRODUCER** Clinton/Gore Creative Team.

**TELEVISION SCRIPT** Announcer: "CBS, CNN and newspapers across the country call George Bush's ads misleading and wrong. The fact is, under Bill Clinton's leadership Arkansas leads the nation in job growth, has the second-lowest tax burden and the lowest Government spending in the country.

"And he's balanced 12 budgets. They reduced infant mortality, and now have the highest graduation rate in the region. And in the past year, Arkansas's crime rate went down.

"No wonder *The Washington Post* says George Bush is lying about Bill Clinton's record, and why *The Oregonian* concluded, 'Frankly, we no longer trust George Bush.'"

**ACCURACY** While the Bush ad makers selectively used figures to attack Mr. Clinton's record, this ad selectively uses figures to build up his record and makes assertions out of context. The Clinton ad says Arkansas leads the nation in job growth, but the Bush campaign cites figures showing that has been true for only the last three months. While Mr. Clinton balanced 12 budgets, he was required to by state law.

The ad uses many citations to lend it credibility but sometimes goes overboard. It was not the institution of *The Washington Post* that said Mr. Bush was lying, but Judy Mann, a local columnist.

**SCORECARD** This ad inundates viewers with documentation to try to lessen the impact of one of the Bush campaign's harshest attacks. The ad also tries to portray Mr. Clinton as a successful Governor and the President as a man who cannot be trusted.

Source: Richard L. Berke, "Clinton: Issuing a Quick Response," *New York Times*, October 30, 1992, p. A19. Copyright © 1992 by The New York Times Company. Reprinted by permission.

setting and on a comparative basis. By appearing to be at least the equal of their incumbent opponents, challengers enhance their presidential image. There are fewer reasons for voting against them. In 1992 they worked to Clinton's and especially to Perot's benefit as indicated by Table 3-4. The impact of debates tends to be greater in a close election, where the perceptions of the candidates are more fluid.

In practice, debates tend to reinforce predispositions and attitudes. Those who are inclined toward a particular candidate tend to see that candidate in a more favorable light in the debate. Even a weak performance, such as Reagan's in his first debate with Walter Mondale in 1984, is not apt to change many voting decisions. Thus debates tend to be decisive only in very close elections in which influencing the perceptions of a relatively small proportion of voters could make a difference. In 1960 and again in 1976, the debates may have affected who won and who lost. In 1980 the one presidential debate probably contributed to Rea-

**Table 3-3. Television Viewership of Presidential and Vice-Presidential Debates, 1960–1992**

| Year | Candidates | Date | Audience Rating* (percent) | Persons (in millions) |
|------|-----------|------|---------------------------|----------------------|
| 1960 | Nixon–Kennedy | Sept. 26 | 59.5 | — |
| | | Oct. 7 | 59.1 | — |
| | | Oct. 13 | 61.0 | — |
| | | Oct. 21 | 57.8 | — |
| 1976 | Ford–Carter | Sept. 23 | 53.5 | 69.7 |
| | | Oct. 6 | 52.4 | 63.9 |
| | | Oct. 22 | 47.8 | 62.7 |
| | Dole–Mondale | Oct. 15 | 35.5 | 43.2 |
| 1980 | Carter–Reagan | Oct. 28 | 58.9 | 80.6 |
| 1984 | Reagan–Mondale | Oct. 7 | 45.3 | 65.1 |
| | | Oct. 21 | 46.0 | 67.3 |
| | Bush–Ferraro | Oct. 11 | 43.6 | 56.7 |
| 1988 | Bush–Dukakis | Sept. 25 | 36.8 | 65.1 |
| | | Oct. 13 | 35.9 | 67.3 |
| | Quayle–Bentsen | Oct. 5 | 33.6 | 46.9 |
| 1992 | Bush–Clinton–Perot | Oct. 11† | 38.3 | 62.4 |
| | | Oct. 15 | 46.3 | 69.9 |
| | | Oct. 19 | 45.2 | 66.9 |
| | Quayle–Gore–Stockdale | Oct. 13 | 35.9 | 51.2 |

*Note:* 1976–1988 debates include ABC, CBS, and NBC only; 1992 includes CNN. PBS data not included. Combined audience estimates are based on comparable durations.

*Percentage of television households viewing the debates during an average minute.
†Does not include CBS.

Source: *Nielsen Tunes in to Politics: Tracking the Presidential Election Years (1960–1992)* (New York: Nielsen Media Research, 1993), pp. 4–5, as reprinted in Harold W. Stanley and Richard Niemi, *Vital Statistics on American Politics* (Washington, D.C.: Congressional Quarterly, 1994), p. 76.

**Table 3-4. Who Won the 1992 Presidential Debates?**
*Question: Regardless of which candidate you happen to support, who do you think did the best job in the debate—George Bush, Bill Clinton, or Ross Perot?*

|  | Bush | Clinton | Perot | No One* | No Opinion | (No. of Interviews) |
|---|---|---|---|---|---|---|
| First debate (Oct. 11) | 16% | 30% | 47% | 5% | 2 | (452) |
| Second debate (Oct. 16–18) | 16 | 58 | 15 | 7 | 4 | (700) |
| Third debate (Oct. 19) | 28 | 28 | 37 | 7 | † | (423) |

*Volunteered response.
†Less than 0.5%.
Source: *Gallup Poll Monthly* (October 1992), p. 19.

gan's margin of victory. In 1992 they may have elevated Perot's vote, but in 1984 and 1988 the debates had a less discernible impact on the results.

### Building a Winning Coalition

Once appeals are designed and projected they must be targeted to potentially receptive voters. When doing this, candidates must consider their political bases of support as well as the geographic foundations of the Electoral College. The goal is to build a coalition that results in winning a majority of the electoral votes, not necessarily a huge popular victory.

For the Democrats this translates into two basic strategic objectives: Rekindle partisan loyalties and turn out a sizable vote. The two are related in that partisanship is a motivation for voting. In recent years the Democrats have faced higher defections of their party identifiers than have Republicans. To counter these defections, Clinton targeted moderate, middle-class Democrats, some of whom had voted for Reagan and Bush in the 1980s. He also appealed directly to independent voters. Claiming he was a new Democrat, Clinton discarded the party's liberal rhetoric and policy positions of the 1970s and 1980s in favor of more moderate language and a centrist position.

Prior to the 1980s, Republican candidates tended to make a more general, less partisan appeal, in part because of their party's minority status. As the gap between the Democrats and Republicans has narrowed, however, Republican presidential candidates have presented a more partisan message in their appeal to voters. As candidates of the more homogeneous of the two major parties, Republican presidential nominees have had less of a problem with partisan defections but they do need the votes of Democrats and especially independents to win.

Increasingly, contemporary presidential campaigns have been directed toward independents and weak party identifiers. In the 1980s the

Republicans were more successful in appealing to these groups, using symbols and slogans to reinforce their positions and stereotype their opponents. Bush's use of the Pledge of Allegiance in 1988 and attempted use of the family values issue in 1992 are illustrations. Here too the Democrats learned from their past mistakes. Anticipating that the Republicans would claim that their values and beliefs were more in tune with mainstream public opinion, the Democrats emphasized their commitment to these very same values and beliefs at their 1992 convention, thereby denying the Republicans an issue.

In addition to group appeals, campaigns also have a geographic thrust that must be consistent with the Electoral College. In such a thrust, the large states always receive attention as do the middle-sized, most competitive ones.

In the last three decades the Democrats have been forced to focus on certain Northeast and Midwest states because of their declining competitiveness in the South and Rocky Mountain areas. This gave the Republicans an advantage: They could concentrate their efforts and resources in a few of the key states that the Democrats needed to win since the GOP could count on winning the South and the West.

In 1976 and 1992, the Democrats found a way to overcome that Republican strategy. The key to their success was to be competitive in the South and strong in the largest states. In 1992 the Republicans were forced to spread their resources thinner than in previous elections. The Clinton camp targeted 32 states with 356 electoral votes and won in 31 of them, losing only North Carolina but picking up the untargeted states of Montana and Nevada. Even though Florida and Texas were not among their targeted states, they spent resources in them so that the Bush campaign could not take them for granted.

## THE MEANING OF THE ELECTION

### Polling the People

From the candidate's perspective, the name of the game is to win. From the voter's perspective, it is to decide who will govern for the next four years. Naturally, throughout the campaign there is considerable interest in what the probable results will be.

Prior to the election, pollsters take the pulse of the electorate. Those who work for the candidates do so to help the campaigns adjust and target appeals. Those who work for the media do so to provide news on the race and to forecast the results.

Since 1916 there have been nationwide surveys of public sentiment during the campaign. However, some of the early polls did not accurately forecast the results. The most notable gaffes occurred in 1936 and 1948, when major surveys predicted that Alfred M. Landon and Thomas E. Dewey, respectively, would win. The principal errors in these surveys were that they concluded their polling too early before election day and that their selection of people to be interviewed was not random. These problems, subsequently corrected, have resulted in preelection polls that have closely reflected the popular vote (see Table 3-5).

The final surveys are published before the election. They indicate the likely outcome, but they are not the final forecast. That comes on election night. The surveys result from a huge poll of voters as they leave the voting booths and are conducted for a consortium of the major news networks. This "exit poll" has two principal objectives: (1) to forecast the results as early as possible and before the actual ballots are completely counted and (2) to explain the reasons people voted as they did.

Here's how exit polls work. A large number of precincts across the country are randomly selected. Representatives of the media, often college students, interview voters as they leave the polls. The interview is intended to measure the beliefs and attitudes of the electorate. In the course of the interview, each voter is asked to complete a printed ballot and deposit it into a sealed box. Throughout the day, these ballots are collected and tabulated, and the results are telephoned to a central computer bank. After the election in a state has been completed, the findings of the poll are broadcast.

These early forecasts have engendered considerable controversy. Since the country is divided into separate time zones, projections of the results in the East and Midwest are known before voting is concluded in the Rocky Mountain and Pacific Coast states and in Alaska and Hawaii. At issue is whether these early projections affect that late voting. Although the evidence is not conclusive, it does suggest a slight decline in turnout but little vote switching as a consequence of these forecasts.[25]

The issue was raised in 1980 but with a slightly different twist. When the early returns and private polls indicated a Reagan landslide, President Carter appeared before his supporters at 8:30 P.M. Eastern Standard Time, while polls were still open in most parts of the country, and acknowledged defeat. His concession speech, carried live on each of the major networks, incurred extensive criticism, particularly from defeated West Coast Democrats. They alleged that the president's remarks discouraged many Democrats from voting, thereby contributing to their defeat as well. However, it is difficult to substantiate this claim. In general, turnout declined more in the East and Midwest than it did in the Far West in 1980. Even if there was a decline after Carter's concession, there is little evidence to suggest that Democrats behaved any differently from Republicans and independents. Hawaii, the last state to close its polls, voted for Carter. Similarly, in 1988, despite the forecasts aired on all the major networks that Bush had won, three of the last four states to close their polls voted for Dukakis. A similar problem did not exist in 1992. Clinton had a commanding lead, and Perot and Bush did not concede until most of the polls had closed in the continental United States.

Despite the criticism they have received, television networks are likely to continue to depend on exit polling because it provides them

**Table 3-5. Final Preelection Polls and Results, 1948–1992 (in percentages)**

| Year/Candidates | Gallup Poll | Roper (1948–1976) CBS/NYT Polls (1988 and 1992) | Harris Poll | Actual Results[*] |
|---|---|---|---|---|
| **1948** | | | | |
| Truman | 44.5 | 37.1 | | 49.6 |
| Dewey | 49.5 | 52.2 | | 45.1 |
| Others | 6.0 | 4.3 | | 5.3 |
| **1952** | | | | |
| Eisenhower | 51.0 | | | 55.1 |
| Stevenson | 49.0 | | | 44.4 |
| **1956** | | | | |
| Eisenhower | 59.5 | 60.0 | | 57.4 |
| Stevenson | 40.5 | 38.0 | | 42.0 |
| **1960** | | | | |
| Kennedy | 51 | 49 | | 49.7 |
| Nixon | 49 | 51 | | 49.5 |
| **1964** | | | | |
| Johnson | 64 | | 64 | 61.1 |
| Goldwater | 36 | | 36 | 38.5 |
| **1968** | | | | |
| Nixon | 43 | | 41 | 43.4 |
| Humphrey | 42 | | 45 | 42.7 |
| Wallace | 15 | | 14 | 13.4 |
| **1972** | | | | |
| Nixon | 62 | | 61 | 60.7 |
| McGovern | 38 | | 39 | 37.5 |
| **1976** | | | | |
| Carter | 48 | 51 | 46 | 50.1 |
| Ford | 49 | 47 | 45 | 48.0 |
| Others | 3 | 2 | 3 | 1.9 |
| Undecided | | | 6 | |
| **1980** | | | | |
| Reagan | 47 | | 46 | 50.7 |
| Carter | 44 | | 41 | 41.0 |
| Anderson | 8 | | 10 | 6.6 |
| Others | | | | 1.7 |
| Undecided | 1 | | 3 | |
| **1984** | | | | |
| Reagan | 59 | | 56 | 59.0 |
| Mondale | 41 | | 44 | 41.0 |
| Others/Undecided | | | 2 | |
| **1988** | | | | |
| Bush | 53 | 48 | 51 | 53.4 |
| Dukakis | 42 | 40 | 47 | 45.6 |
| Others/Undecided | 5 | 12 | 2 | 1.0 |

(*continued*)

Table 3-5. (continued)

| Year/Candidates | Gallup Poll | Roper (1948–1976) CBS/NYT Polls (1988 and 1992) | Harris Poll | Actual Results* |
|---|---|---|---|---|
| 1992 | | | | |
| Clinton | 44 | 44 | 44 | 43.0 |
| Bush | 37 | 35 | 38 | 37.5 |
| Perot | 14 | 15 | 17 | 18.9 |
| Others/Undecided | 5 | 6 | 1 | 1.6 |

*Prior to 1976 (with the exception of 1948) the percentage of undecided voters in polls and votes for minor candidates is not noted.

Source: Final Gallup poll, "Record of Gallup Poll Accuracy," *Gallup Opinion Index*, December 1992.

with a portrait of the electorate that usually contains a wealth of information about political and ideological preferences, positions on issues, and evaluations of the candidates. This information may be correlated with demographic data to discern voting patterns and to infer the reasons for the vote.

The problem with an analysis based on exit poll data, however, is that it is time-bound (election day) and limited to a portion of the electorate (those who vote before a certain hour in the key states). It does not permit inferences about the effect of the campaign on the electorate nor about the changing patterns of public opinion and preferences among different population groups. To make such inferences, it is necessary to interview and reinterview the same voters. Since 1948, researchers who have participated in the National Election Studies at the University of Michigan have been collecting and analyzing data gathered in this manner and making it available to scholars at colleges and universities across the country. These studies, which collect information on attitudes and opinions, have provided the most sophisticated understanding of voting behavior.

## Analyzing the Results

During the last three decades, partisan attitudes of the electorate have weakened. Candidate and issue orientations became more important influences on voting. In 1960, for example, the Democrats' large partisan advantage was the primary reason that John F. Kennedy beat Richard Nixon. However, the closeness of the election (Kennedy won by only 100,000 votes) can be explained by the impact of Kennedy's Catholic religion on voters, particularly in the heavily Protestant South. It is estimated that Kennedy lost approximately 1.5 million popular votes because he was a Catholic.[26] However, he might actually have gained electoral votes because of the concentration of Catholics in the large industrial states that have the most electoral votes.

In 1964, it was Goldwater's uncompromising ideology and positions on issues that helped provide Johnson with an overwhelming victory in all areas but the Deep South. Moderate Republicans and independents voted more Democratic than usual that year. Four years later, however, it was defections from the Democratic party that spurred the Wallace third-party candidacy and contributed to Nixon's triumph. In 1972, the Democrats were again divided. Over 40 percent of those who identified with the Democratic party voted for Nixon as did 66 percent of the independents and most of the Republicans. The perception of McGovern as incompetent as well as ideologically to the left of his party contributed to the larger than normal Republican vote.[27]

Short-range factors regarding issues and candidates were also evident in 1976, but they were not of sufficient magnitude to offset the longer-term partisan inclinations of the electorate. Carter won in 1976 primarily because he was the majority party nominee and secondarily because he was from the South, the first Democrat to win the South since 1960.[28] He was also perceived as having greater potential for strong and effective leadership than his Republican opponent, President Gerald Ford, who had pardoned his predecessor, Richard Nixon, for crimes he may have committed in office.

In 1980, however, Carter lost despite the fact that he was a Democrat and because he was no longer seen as having that leadership potential. Voters made a retrospective judgment on his record and found it wanting. Reagan, in contrast, won in 1980 primarily because he was seen as having the greater potential for leadership, not because of his ideology, his policy positions, or his personal appeal.[29]

Four years later the voters rewarded President Reagan for what they considered to be a job well done. With 59 percent of the popular vote and 525 (out of 538) electoral votes, Reagan won in a referendum on his performance in office. The electorate voted *for* him in 1984 just as they had voted *against* Carter in 1980. It was a retrospective vote. The American people approved of his leadership and wanted him to continue in office.

The 1988 election constituted still another referendum on the Reagan presidency, although obviously not on President Reagan. Vice President Bush benefited from the public's perception of good times and greater national security. Bush won an impressive victory, obtaining majorities in all areas of the country, a popular vote of 53 percent and 426 electoral votes.

Most of those who cast ballots for Reagan in 1984 continued to support Bush in 1988. He won overwhelmingly among Republicans and conservatives; among independents, Bush enjoyed a solid 12 percent lead. In contrast, Michael Dukakis, Bush's opponent in 1988, did well among Democrats and liberals. His problem, and that of any Democrat perceived as liberal, is that the Democratic proportion of the two-party vote has declined substantially and so has the percentage of the electorate that considers itself liberal.

In addition to ideology and party, the 1988 vote also evidenced clear class, race, and gender differences with the Republican doing better among voters who were wealthier, white, and male and the Democrat doing better among those in the lower socioeconomic groups, ethnic and racial minorities, and women. These trends continued in 1992.

Like the vote four years earlier, the electorate in 1992 made a retrospective judgment; in doing so, however, they rejected the incumbent. Bush's vote in 1992 fell among every population group. By comparison, Clinton's vote among various population groups was closer to Dukakis's in 1988 than was Bush's vote closer to his own in the previous election. The only demographic groups that continued to vote for the Republican candidate were the wealthy; white Protestants, especially born-again Christians; conservatives; and those who identified themselves as homemakers. Perot's numbers were fairly steady among the various population groups. He fared slightly better among Republicans than Democrats, men than women, and younger people than older voters.

The exit polling data for 1992 also indicates that Clinton held on to the traditional Democratic vote. A smaller percentage of Democrats than Republicans defected from their nominee. With fewer defections and more party identifiers, Clinton had an advantage over Bush, but one that could have been reversed had a sizable portion of independents voted for Bush. In the 1980s the independent vote had strongly favored the Republicans; in 1992, it did not. With Ross Perot doing substantially better among independents than party identifiers, and with Clinton holding his own among these voters, Bush received less than one-third of the independent vote.

In short, the voters made a retrospective judgment: George Bush did not deserve another four years in office. (See Table 3-6.) They supported the need for change although not necessarily all or even most of the particulars Clinton had proposed in the course of the campaign.

### Assessing the Mandate

Despite the many postelection analyses conducted by political scientists, journalists, and politicians, the meaning of the election results often remains unclear. The reasons that people vote for a candidate vary. Presidents are rarely given a clear mandate for governing even though they may try to claim one.

Unfortunately for most candidates, the promises they make during the campaign create expectations and goals that may be impossible to meet. Kennedy pledged to get the country moving again; Johnson to continue the momentum and create a Great Society; Nixon to bring a divided nation together; Carter to provide a more honest, open, responsive leadership; Reagan to assume a new, steadier course in economic

Table 3-6. Portrait of the American Electorate, 1984–1992 (in percentages)

| Percent of 1992 Total | 1984 | | 1988 | | 1992 | | |
|---|---|---|---|---|---|---|---|
| | Reagan | Mondale | Bush | Dukakis | Clinton | Bush | Perot |
| | 59 | 40 | 53 | 45 | 43 | 38 | 19 |
| 46 Men | 62 | 37 | 57 | 41 | 41 | 38 | 21 |
| 54 Women | 56 | 44 | 50 | 49 | 46 | 37 | 17 |
| 87 Whites | 64 | 35 | 59 | 40 | 39 | 41 | 20 |
| 8 Blacks | 9 | 90 | 12 | 86 | 82 | 11 | 7 |
| 3 Hispanics | 37 | 62 | 30 | 69 | 62 | 25 | 14 |
| 1 Asians | — | — | — | — | 29 | 55 | 16 |
| 65 Married | 62 | 38 | 57 | 42 | 40 | 40 | 20 |
| 35 Unmarried | 52 | 47 | 46 | 53 | 49 | 33 | 18 |
| 22 18–29 years old | 59 | 40 | 52 | 47 | 44 | 34 | 22 |
| 38 30–44 years old | 57 | 42 | 54 | 45 | 42 | 38 | 20 |
| 24 45–59 years old | 60 | 40 | 57 | 42 | 41 | 40 | 19 |
| 16 60 and older | 60 | 40 | 50 | 49 | 50 | 38 | 12 |
| 6 Not high school graduate | 50 | 50 | 43 | 56 | 55 | 28 | 17 |
| 25 High school graduate | 60 | 39 | 50 | 49 | 43 | 36 | 20 |
| 29 Some college education | 61 | 38 | 57 | 42 | 42 | 37 | 21 |
| 40 College graduate or more | 58 | 41 | 56 | 43 | 44 | 39 | 18 |
| 24 College graduate | — | — | 62 | 37 | 40 | 41 | 19 |
| 16 Postgraduate education | — | — | 50 | 48 | 49 | 36 | 15 |
| 49 White Protestant | 72 | 27 | 66 | 33 | 33 | 46 | 21 |
| 27 Catholic | 54 | 45 | 52 | 47 | 44 | 36 | 20 |
| 4 Jewish | 31 | 67 | 35 | 64 | 78 | 12 | 10 |
| 17 White born-again Christian | 78 | 22 | 81 | 18 | 23 | 61 | 15 |
| 19 Union household | 46 | 53 | 42 | 57 | 55 | 24 | 21 |
| 14 Family income under $15,000 | 45 | 55 | 37 | 62 | 59 | 23 | 18 |
| 24 $15,000–$29,999 | 57 | 42 | 49 | 50 | 45 | 35 | 20 |
| 30 $30,000–$49,999 | 59 | 40 | 56 | 44 | 41 | 38 | 21 |
| 20 $50,000–74,999 | 66 | 33 | 56 | 42 | 40 | 42 | 18 |
| 13 $75,000 and over | 69 | 30 | 62 | 37 | 36 | 48 | 16 |
| Family's financial situation is | | | | | | | |
| 25 Better today | 86 | 14 | — | — | 24 | 62 | 14 |
| 41 Same today | 50 | 50 | — | — | 41 | 41 | 18 |

*(continued)*

and foreign affairs; Bush to maintain peace and prosperity; and Clinton to change America by stimulating the economy, reducing the budget deficit, and providing affordable health care to all. Achieving these broad goals have proved difficult.

If these broad and comprehensive goals were not enough, presidential candidates also make specific promises to specific groups. Clinton promised to end discrimination against homosexuals in the military, to allow political refugees from Haiti and other countries into the United States, and to cut taxes for the middle class. Once in office he found it impossible to fulfill these promises and recanted, thereby alienating some of those to whom he had made the promises and also decreasing his credibility as president.

The gap between promises and performance is heightened by the emphasis that presidential candidates place on personal and institutional leadership during the campaign. By creating impressions of assertiveness, decisiveness, and potency, candidates may contribute to the de-

Table 3-6. (continued)

| Percent of 1992 Total | 1984 | | 1988 | | 1992 | | |
|---|---|---|---|---|---|---|---|
| | Reagan | Mondale | Bush | Dukakis | Clinton | Bush | Perot |
| 34 Worse today | 15 | 85 | — | — | 61 | 14 | 25 |
| 24 From the East | 53 | 47 | 50 | 49 | 47 | 35 | 18 |
| 27 From the Midwest | 58 | 41 | 52 | 47 | 42 | 37 | 21 |
| 30 From the South | 64 | 36 | 58 | 41 | 42 | 43 | 16 |
| 20 From the West | 61 | 38 | 52 | 46 | 44 | 34 | 22 |
| 35 Republicans | 92 | 7 | 91 | 8 | 10 | 73 | 17 |
| 27 Independents | 63 | 36 | 55 | 43 | 38 | 32 | 30 |
| 38 Democrats | 25 | 74 | 17 | 82 | 77 | 10 | 13 |
| 21 Liberals | 28 | 70 | 18 | 81 | 68 | 14 | 18 |
| 49 Moderates | 53 | 47 | 49 | 50 | 48 | 31 | 21 |
| 29 Conservatives | 82 | 17 | 80 | 19 | 18 | 65 | 17 |
| 68 Employed | 60 | 39 | 56 | 43 | 42 | 38 | 20 |
| 5 Full-time student | 52 | 47 | 44 | 54 | 50 | 35 | 15 |
| 6 Unemployed | 32 | 67 | 37 | 62 | 56 | 24 | 20 |
| 8 Homemaker | 62 | 38 | 58 | 41 | 36 | 45 | 19 |
| 13 Retired | 60 | 40 | 50 | 49 | 51 | 36 | 13 |
| 11 First-time voters | 61 | 38 | 51 | 47 | 48 | 30 | 22 |

Notes: 1992 data were collected by Voter Research and Surveys based on questionnaires completed by 15,490 voters leaving 300 polling places around the nation on election day. Data based on surveys of voters conducted by the *New York Times* and CBS News: 9,174 in 1984; and 11,645 in 1988. Those who gave no answer are not shown. Dashes indicate that a question was not asked or a category was not provided in a particular year. Family income categories in 1984: under $12,500, $12,500–$24,999, $25,000–$34,999, $35,000–$50,000, and over $50,000. In 1988: under $12,500, $12,500–$24,999, $25,000–$34,999, $35,000–$49,999, $50,000, and over. "Born-again Christian" was labelled "born-again Christian/fundamentalist" in 1992 and "fundamentalist and evangelical Christian" in 1988. Family financial situation is compared to four years ago in 1984 and 1988; 1984 numbers from NBC News.

Source: Voter Research and Surveys as printed in the *New York Times*, November 5, 1992, p. B9. Copyright © 1992 by the New York Times Company. Reprinted by permission.

cline of their own popularity once in office. In other words, expectations created during the campaign make governing more difficult once it is over and generate temptations for the president to engage in a continuous campaign.

## Converting the Electoral Coalition for Governance

Not only does the selection process inflate performance expectations and create a set of diverse policy goals, it also lessens the presidents' power to achieve them. Their political muscle has been weakened by the decline in the power of party leaders and the growth of autonomous state and congressional electoral systems.

Moreover, the electoral process has become highly personalized. Candidates create their own organizations and mount their own campaigns, but they pay a price for this independence. There are fewer political allies on whom they can count once in office.

The democratization of the selection process has also resulted in the separation of state, congressional, and presidential elections. In the aftermath of Watergate, Jimmy Carter made much of the fact that he did not owe his nomination to the power brokers within his party or his election to them or to members of Congress. But the same can be said for members of Congress and, for that matter, governors and state legislators. Presidents are not indebted to them nor are they indebted to presidents. The increasing independence of Congress decreases legislators' political incentives to follow the president's lead.

Bill Clinton found this out the hard way. He ran away from fellow Democrats in Congress during the 1992 election, not wanting to be tainted by the anti-incumbent, anti-Congress, anti-Washington attitude of voters. But he soon found that he needed the support of Democratic members of Congress to obtain his legislative objectives. Nor could he easily or effectively go over their heads to the voters. With only 43 percent of the vote, Clinton ran behind practically every Democrat who was elected or reelected to Congress in 1992 *in his or her own districts.*

Finally, personality politics has produced factions within the parties. It has created a fertile environment for the growth of interest group pressures. Without strong party leaders to act as brokers and referees, groups vie for the candidate's attention and favor during the campaign and for the president's after the election is over. This group struggle provides a natural source of opposition and support for almost any presidential action or proposal. It enlarges the arena of policy making and contributes to the multiplicity of forces that converge on most presidential decisions.

What can presidents do? How can they meet public expectations in light of the weakening of partisanship and the increased sharing of policy-making powers? How can they lead, achieve, and satisfy pluralistic interests at the same time?

Obviously, there is no set formula for success. Forces beyond the president's control may affect the course of events. Nonetheless, presidents must exercise as strong political leadership as possible. They must establish their own priorities and thereby shape public expectations of what they hope to do. These priorities need to be consistent with their election campaign and accord with the public mood. If that mood changes and/or if conditions change, presidents must recast their priorities as well. Bill Clinton was slow to do this in 1993. He was slow to realize that deficit reduction had replaced economic stimulus as the principal public concern. His refusal to withdraw or sufficiently compromise his stimulus package resulted in its defeat at the hands of a Republican filibuster in the Senate.

To be successful, presidents must take advantage of opportunities, particularly in the period following the election. They must construct their own policy alliances and thereby actualize potential supporters. Moreover, they must be careful not to alienate those whose support they will need to achieve their political objectives. Presidents who fail to focus their appeal and articulate it clearly and effectively to the general and specialized publics will have difficulty building the coalitions they need to govern.

With fewer natural allies, presidents face an almost inevitable decline in their popularity, which detracts from their ability to accomplish their goals. The growing influence of personality on people and events makes the president's job much tougher. As a consequence, during ordinary times presidents are forced to be facilitators even though they might prefer to be directors of change.

## CONCLUSION

The system of election designed by the framers of the Constitution has been substantially modified over the years. Theoretically, the Electoral College continues to select the president, but in practice the popular vote, aggregated by states, decides the outcome.

During much of America's electoral history political parties were the principal link between candidates and the voters. They chose the nominees, organized their campaigns, mobilized their support, and stood to gain if they were elected. Moreover, partisan attitudes conditioned the perceptions and voting behavior of much of the electorate.

Times have changed. Today there are more mediators and more mediums. Party professionals are less important than they were and campaign professionals more important. Pollsters, grass-roots organizers, and media experts now plan and run the general election campaigns. These handlers discern attitudes, design and project appeals, target voters, and mobilize what they hope will be a winning coalition. They utilize the techniques of market research and the vehicles of the modern electronic age. Radio and television (including satellite hookups and entertainment talk shows) plus direct mail and phone banks are the principal means used to reach voters. Party has a role, particularly in raising and distributing soft money, but it no longer exercises the dominant influence it once did over the presidential selection process.

The campaigns have become more candidate oriented. It is the candidates who now create their organizations, receive federal funds, and mount highly personalized appeals. Moreover, the electorate's personal evaluation of the candidates plays an increasingly important role in its voting decisions.

This personalization of the presidential selection process has serious implications for the exercise of presidential leadership. It tends to inflate public expectations yet reduces the capacity to achieve them. Presidents are more on their own. Their electoral coalition is not easily converted into a governing coalition, forcing them to devote more time, energy, and resources to mobilizing and maintaining outside support, to controlling the national news media's focus, and to worrying about reelection. All of this has made the president's leadership task more difficult.

## NOTES

1. The initial solution to this problem was to grant the president a long term of office but make him ineligible for reelection. This, however, created an additional dilemma. It provided little incentive for the president to perform well and denied the country the possibility of reelecting a person whose experience and success in office might make the incumbent better qualified than anyone else. Reflecting on these concerns, delegate Gouverneur Morris urged the removal of the ineligibility clause on the grounds that it "intended to destroy the great motive to good behavior, the hope of being rewarded by a re-appointment" (Gouverneur Morris, *Records of the Federal Convention*, ed. Max Farrand [New Haven, Conn.: Yale University Press, 1921], 2:33).

2. So great was the sectional rivalry, so parochial the country, so limited the number of people with national reputations that it was feared that electors would tend to vote primarily for those from their own states. To prevent the same states, particularly the largest ones, from exercising undue influence in the selection of both the president and vice president, this provision was included. It remains in effect today.

3. The most populous state at the time, New York, did not permit its electorate to participate in the selection of electors. Moreover, in three of the states in which Jackson won the electoral vote but lost in the House of Representatives, he had fewer popular votes than Adams. He captured the majority of electoral votes in two of these states because the electors were chosen on a district rather than on a statewide basis (William R. Keech, "Background Paper," in *Winner-Take-All: Report of the Twentieth Century Fund Task Force on Reform of the Presidential Election Process* [New York: Holmes and Meier, 1978], p. 50).

4. Much of this research has been conducted by The Center for Political Studies at the University of Michigan. Starting in 1952, the center began conducting national surveys, known as American National Election Studies, during presidential elections. The object of these surveys was to identify the major influences on voting behavior. A random sample of the electorate was interviewed before and after the election. Respondents were asked a series of questions designed to reveal their attitudes toward the parties, candidates, and issues. On the basis of these responses, researchers constructed an explanation of voting behavior in a very important book entitled *The American Voter*. See Angus Campbell et al., *The American Voter* (New York: Wiley, 1960).

5. Raymond E. Wolfinger and Steven J. Rosenstone, *Who Votes?* (New Haven, Conn.: Yale University Press, 1980), pp. 13, 226.

6. Ibid., p. 73.

7. Robert Pear, "The Turnout: 55% Voting Rate Reverses 30-Year Decline," *New York Times* (November 5, 1992), p. B4.

8. Federal Election Commission, "Record," 19 (May 1993), p. 6.

9. Federal Election Commission, "Record," 19 (July 1993), p. 5.

10. Only about 10 percent report that they pay much attention to magazine articles about the campaign. Those who listen to speeches or discussions on the radio also constitute a relatively small percentage. National Election Studies, Center for Political Studies, annual codebooks, 1952–1992.

11. "Clinton's the One: TV News Coverage of the 1992 General Election," *Media Monitor* (November 1992), p. 3.

12. Ibid.

13. Paul Lazarsfeld, Bernard Berelson, and Hazel Goudet, *The People's Choice* (New York: Columbia University Press, 1948); Bernard Berelson, Paul Lazarsfeld, and William McPhee, *Voting: A Study of Opinion Formation in a Presidential Campaign* (Chicago: University of Chicago Press, 1954).

14. Michael J. Robinson and Margaret A. Sheehan, *Over the Wire and on TV: CBS and UPI in Campaign '80.* (New York: Russell Sage Foundation, 1983), p. 9.

15. "Clinton's the One," *Media Monitor* (November 1992), p. 2.

16. Thomas E. Patterson and Robert D. McClure, *The Unseeing Eye* (New York: Putnam, 1976), p. 58.

17. Ibid., p. 54.

18. William J. Bryan, *The First Battle* (Port Washington, N.Y.: Kennikat Press, 1971), p. 618.

19. One reason that Roosevelt initiated the whistle-stop tour in 1932 was to overcome

the whispering campaign about his physical condition. Roosevelt had been crippled by polio. To demonstrate that he was not confined to a wheelchair, he appeared standing when he addressed groups from the rear platform of his train. However, Roosevelt could not get up or sit down without aid. So before the train arrived and after it left the station, Roosevelt's aides would assist him, out of public view.

20. Edwin Diamond and Adrian Marin "Spots," *American Behavioral Scientist* 32 (March/April 1989): 386.

21. F. Christopher Arterton, "Campaign '92: Strategies and Tactics of the Candidates," in Gerald M. Pomper, ed., *The Election of 1992* (Chatham, N.J.: Chatham House, 1993), p. 97.

22. Times-Mirror Center for the People and the Press, "The People, the Press, and Politics, Campaign '92: Air Wars," October 8, 1992, p. 2.

23. Elihu Katz and Jacob J. Feldman, "The Debates in the Light of Research: A Survey of Surveys," in Sidney Kraus, ed., *The Great Debates* (Bloomington, Ind.: Indiana University Press, 1962), p. 190.

24. If they do not, the results can be extremely harmful. Nixon did not look physically well for his first debate with Kennedy. Viewers rated his performance lower than those who listened on the radio. A more recent example occurred during the vice presidential debate in 1992. Admiral James Stockdale, Perot's running mate, seemed unprepared and unable to answer questions that were posed to him. His inability to do so seriously undermined his candidacy and the credibility of the Perot–Stockdale ticket.

25. In a 1964 survey of approximately 1,700 registered voters in California, Harold Mendelsohn found that few watched the early broadcasts and then voted. Most voted first. The impact of the early broadcasts on those who saw them and then cast ballots was about the same for supporters of Johnson and Goldwater (Harold Mendelsohn and Irving Crespi, *Polls, Television, and the New Politics* [Scranton, Pa.: Chandler, 1970], pp. 234–236). A similar study of the 1968 election conducted by other researchers arrived at a similar conclusion (Sam Tuchman and Thomas E. Coffin, "The Influence of Election Night Television Broadcasts in a Close Election," *Public Opinion Quarterly* 35 [1971]: 315–326. However, in the 1972 election, political scientists Raymond Wolfinger and Peter Linquiti concluded that there was a small decline in the West Coast vote after the Nixon victory had been predicted (Raymond Wolfinger and Peter Linquiti, "Tuning In and Tuning Out," *Public Opinion* 4 [1981]: 57–59).

26. Philip E. Converse et al., "Stability and Change in 1960: A Reinstating Election," in Angus Campbell et. al., *Elections and the Political Order* (New York: Wiley, 1966), p. 92.

27. Philip E. Converse, Aage R. Clausen, and Warren E. Miller, "Electoral Myth and Reality: The 1964 Election," *American Political Science Review* 59 (June 1965): 321–336; Arthur H. Miller et al., "A Majority Party in Disarray: Policy Polarization in the 1972 Election" (paper presented at the Annual Meeting of the American Political Science Association, New Orleans, Louisiana, September 4, 1973), p. 28.

28. Arthur H. Miller and Warren E. Miller, "Partisanship and Performance: Rational Choice in the 1976 Presidential Elections" (paper presented at the Annual Meeting of the American Political Science Association, Washington, D.C., September 1, 1977).

29. Arthur H. Miller and Martin P. Wattenberg, "Policy and Performance Voting in the 1980 Election" (paper delivered at the Annual Meeting of the American Political Science Association, New York, September 3, 1981), p. 15.

## SELECTED READINGS

Abramson, Paul R., John H. Aldrich, and David W. Rhode. *Change and Continuity in the 1988 Elections.* Washington, D.C.: Congressional Quarterly, 1990.

Campbell, Angus, Philip E. Converse, Warren E. Miller, and Donald E. Stokes. *The American Voter.* New York: Wiley, 1960.

Goldman, Peter. *The Quest for the Presidency, 1992.* Toronto: Bantam, 1993.

Jamieson, Kathleen Hall, and David S. Birdsell. *Presidential Debates.* New York: Oxford University Press, 1988.

Ladd, Everett Carll. "The 1992 Vote for President Clinton: Another Brittle

Mandate?" *Political Science Quarterly* 108 (1993): 1–28.

McCubbins, Mathew D., ed. *Under the Watchful Eye.* Washington, D.C.: Congressional Quarterly, 1992.

Nelson, Michael, ed. *The Elections of 1992.* Washington, D.C.: Congressional Quarterly, 1993.

Pomper, Gerald M., et al. *The Election of 1992: Reports and Interpretations.* Chatham, N.J.: Chatham House, 1993.

Troy, Gil. *See How They Ran: The Changing Role of the Presidential Candidate.* New York: Free Press, 1991.

Wayne, Stephen J. *The Road to the White House, 1992.* New York: St. Martin's Press, 1992.

Wolfinger, Raymond E., and Steven J. Rosenstone. *Who Votes?* New Haven, Conn.: Yale University Press, 1980.

# 4

# The President
# and the Public

"Public sentiment is everything. With public sentiment nothing can fail, without it nothing can succeed."[1] These words, spoken by Abraham Lincoln, pose what is perhaps the greatest challenge to any president: to obtain and maintain the public's support. As every student of the presidency quickly learns, presidents are rarely in a position to command others to comply with their wishes. Instead, they must rely on persuasion. A principal source of influence for presidents is public approval of their performance and their policies.

Presidents want both to please the public and to avoid irritating it. They also want to lead public opinion. Accomplishing these goals is premised to a large degree on knowing what the public is thinking. Gauging public opinion is a difficult task, however. Citizens' opinions on policy are often uncrystallized and lacking in coherence. Moreover, the tools available to measure public opinion, such as polls, the mail, and election results, are far from perfect and make it difficult to infer opinion on specific issues.

The president is in the limelight of American politics, and citizens come quite naturally to organize their political thinking and focus their hopes for the future around the White House. Although this attention provides the potential for presidential leadership of the public, it is purchased at a high cost. The public's expectations of the chief executive's policy performance, personal characteristics, and private behavior tend to be high. They are also often contradictory with regard to both policy and leadership style. It is quite clear that no leader can fully meet these expectations, yet they provide the context within which the president struggles to gain and maintain public support.

Probably the most visible political statistics in American life are the frequent measurements of the public's approval of the president. Political commentators duly note whether the president is doing better or worse than in the last poll (sort of a political batting average). But on what bases do people arrive at their evaluations of the president? Certain predispositions in the public, such as party affiliation and the positivity bias (a proclivity to evaluate people favorably), provide an important component of the explanation of presidential approval. Job-related personal characteristics and the president's handling of, and stands on, the issues are also important. On the other hand, the president's personality and the personal effects and short-run success of policies play a less important role.

Presidents are not passive followers of public opinion. In the words of Franklin Roosevelt, "All our great Presidents were *leaders* of thought at times when certain historic ideas in the life of the nation had to be clarified." His cousin, Theodore Roosevelt, had earlier observed: "People used to say of me that I . . . divined what the people were going to think. I did not 'divine.' I simply made up my mind what they ought to think, and then did my best to get them to think it."[2] Throughout most of Ronald Reagan's tenure in office, polls showed that the public wanted to lower the federal deficit and did not want to cut social programs. They were willing to decrease planned military spending to accomplish these goals. The president refused to go along.

Presidents offer several rationales for not following public opinion. President Nixon claimed he was not really acting contrary to public opinion at all but rather he represented the "silent majority" that did not express its opinion in activist politics. Similarly, presidents may argue that their actions are on behalf of underrepresented groups, such as the poor or an ethnic minority. The extreme case of this technique, of course, is for a president to say that he is representing a future (probably unborn) generation. This kind of rationale is used today on behalf of environmental and energy policies designed to save natural resources for the future population. Presidents have also wrapped themselves in the mantle of courageous statesmen following their principles and fighting the tides of public opinion.

Whatever the reasons given, presidents have generally not been content only to follow public opinion on issues or to let their approval ratings reach some "natural" level. Instead, they usually have engaged in substantial efforts to lead the public. Sometimes their goals have been to gain long-term support for themselves, while at other times they have been more interested in obtaining support for a specific program. Often both goals are present.

Moving the public provides one of the clearest tests of presidential leadership. Presidents who direct impose their priorities on the national agenda and create a constituency to follow their lead. Presidents who facilitate, on the other hand, reflect and perhaps intensify widely held views. Their challenge is to channel an already existing tide of public opinion to achieve their goals.

In this chapter we explore presidential attempts to understand public opinion and the public's expectations and evaluations of the chief executive. We are interested in both the nature of the attitudes the public has and, even more important, *why* it holds them. Such study will deepen our understanding not only of expectations and evaluations but of the obstacles the White House faces in measuring public opinion. We also examine presidential efforts to influence public opinion, including appealing directly to the public, controlling information, employing symbols, and engaging in public relations activities. We do not assume, of course, that presidents are always successful in influencing the public. Thus, we are equally concerned with the effectiveness of the various techniques of opinion leadership presidents use.

## UNDERSTANDING PUBLIC OPINION

Presidents need public support, and understanding public opinion can be a considerable advantage to them in gaining and maintaining it. At the very least, presidents want to avoid needlessly antagonizing the public. Thus, presidents need reliable estimates of public reactions to the actions they are contemplating. It is equally useful for presidents to know what actions and policies, either symbolic or substantive, the public wants. No politician wants to overlook opportunities to please constituents and, perhaps even more significant, to avoid frustrating them. By knowing what the public desires, presidents may use their discretion to gain its favor when they feel the relevant actions or policies are justified.

In addition, presidents often want to lead public opinion to support them and their policies. To do this they need to know the views of various segments of the public, whom they need to influence and on what issues, and how far people can be moved. Presidents usually do not want to use their limited resources on hopeless ventures. Nor do they want to be too far ahead of the public. If they are, they risk losing their followers and alienating segments of the population.

### Americans' Opinions

Before a president can understand what opinions the public holds, citizens must have opinions. Although Americans are usually willing to express opinions on a wide variety of issues, we generally cannot interpret their responses as reflecting crystallized and coherent views. Citizens' opinions are often rife with contradictions[3] because the public fails to give its views much thought and does not consider the implications of its policy stands for other issues. For example, national polls show consistently that the American people place a very high priority on balancing the budget. At the same time, majorities favor maintaining or increasing spending on virtually every component of domestic policy, but they also oppose increasing taxes enough to cover the costs of the policies.

Policy making is a very complex enterprise, and most voters do not have the time, expertise, or inclination to think extensively about most issues, especially those as distant from their everyday experiences as federal regulations, nuclear weapons, and bureaucratic organization. Even closer to home, after two decades of political controversy, nearly half of Americans do not realize that we must import oil.[4] The major domestic policy initiative of Ronald Reagan's second term was tax reform. Yet as the bill was nearing the end of its legislative path in the Senate, only 40 percent of the people had heard or read even "some" about it.[5]

On the other hand, *collective* public opinion has properties quite different from those of individual citizens, taken one at a time. There is evidence that the public holds real, stable, and sensible opinions about public policy and that these develop and change in a reasonable fashion in response to changing circumstances and new information. Changes that occur are usually at the margin and the result of different trade-offs among constant values.[6]

In short, as the White House attempts to understand American public opinion, it operates under the handicap that many people do not have opinions on issues of significance to the president, and many of the opinions that the public expresses are neither crystallized, coherent, nor informed. On the other hand, it is possible to grasp the essential contours of public opinion, especially where opinions are widely held, such as on issues that touch the public directly like economic conditions and civil rights. Moreover, the president may desire to know the distribution of whatever opinions that do exist. Under these circumstances, what means can the president rely upon to measure public opinion?

### Public Opinion Polls

One common tool for measuring public attitudes is public opinion polls. Whether they are commissioned on behalf of the White House or by various components of the mass media, they allow the president to learn how a cross section of the population feels about a specific policy, conditions in their lives, or his performance in office.

In an attempt to understand public opinion on matters of special concern to them, recent presidents have commissioned their own polls. Franklin D. Roosevelt was the first president to pay much attention to polls, which were just being developed scientifically during his tenure in office. All presidents since John F. Kennedy have retained private polling firms to provide them with soundings of American public opinion. In the last four administrations, pollsters have also played a large role as high-level political advisers.

Despite their widespread use in the modern White House, public opinion polls are not completely dependable instruments for measuring public opinion. An important limitation of polls is that questions usually do not attempt to measure the intensity with which opinions are held. People with intense views will probably be more likely to act on those views to reward or punish politicians than people who state a preference but for whom the issue is incidental and a matter of indifference.

A related problem with polls is that the questions asked of the public seldom mesh with the decisions that a president faces. He rarely considers issues in the "yes/no" terms presented by most polls. Evidence of widespread support for a program does not indicate how the public stands on most of the specific provisions under consideration. Yet such details do not lend themselves to mass polling because they require specialized knowledge that few Americans possess.

Another problem with polls is that responses may reflect the particular wording of the choices presented to citizens, especially for those people who lack crystallized opinions on issues. If questions are of the "agree/disagree" variety, there is a bias toward the "agree" alternative. If the "official" government position is indicated in a question, this often elicits a bias toward that position, especially on foreign policy issues. Public attitudes toward China softened considerably after President Nixon began making overtures toward establishing relations with the People's Republic.

On policies that are very controversial, it may be impossible to ascertain public attitudes without some "contamination" by the use of "loaded" symbols in the questions. When people were asked in a poll whether federal "welfare" programs should be turned over to state and local governments, 39 percent replied in the affirmative. In a survey the following month only 15 percent favored turning over federal programs for "aid to the needy" to state and local governments.[7]

A final limitation of polls from a presidential perspective is that, unless the president or his party pays for them, polls are not taken at his convenience. If opinion on an issue is measured at all, it is likely to be a one-time measurement, so the president will not be able to learn of changes in public sentiment. Thus, the president cannot rely on public polls to provide information on what the public is thinking on a given issue at a particular time.

Questions that inevitably arise when discussing presidents and polls include the following: How should presidents use public opinion data? Does use of these data constrain presidents rather than indicate where their persuasive efforts should be focused? Do presidents, in effect, substitute followship for leadership?

Presidents ritually deny that their decisions are influenced by polls. According to President Carter's chief media adviser, Gerald Rafshoon, "If we ever went into the president's office and said, 'We think you ought to do this or that to increase your standing in the polls,' he'd throw us out." Instead of using polls to determine his policies, Carter used them to measure how effective he was in getting his message across to the public and to determine the obstacles in his path.[8]

Other presidents have also claimed that they have not been captives of public opinion polls, but all recent presidents have used polls in their efforts to lead. The Nixon administration was often blatant in its use of polls to manipulate the public. According to Nixon aide Charles Colson, the White House used daily polls to tell how people were reacting to events, "and the next morning back off or intensify what you wanted to say."[10]

More than any other administration, the Reagan White House used polling in its decision-making process. Reagan's pollster, Richard Wirthlin, took polls every three or four weeks for the president (more often during a crisis) and met regularly with him and his top aides. Wirthlin's goal was to determine when the nation's mood was amenable to the president's proposals and what its reactions were to the president's actions. The White House wanted the timing of the president's proposals to be compatible with the political climate to maximize the probabilities of achieving the president's objectives; thus, polls were used to help set the presidential agenda.[11]

Presidents Bush and Clinton used their pollsters to perform similar functions, although Bush had a modest number of polls taken for him. Within a week of taking office, Clinton directed his aides to begin regularly polling on issues, and Clinton's pollster, Stan Greenberg, meets frequently with the president and sees one of his roles as making sure the president "gets a dose of the public's thinking, unfiltered."[12]

### Presidential Election Results

If presidents cannot always rely on polls to inform them about public opinion, theoretically they can gain valuable insights through interpretation of their own electoral support. In other words, perhaps they can learn what voters are thinking when they cast their ballots for president. Before such an approach can be useful for a president seeking to understand public opinion, the following conditions must be met:

1. Voters must have opinions of policies.
2. Voters must know candidates' stands on the issues.
3. The candidates that voters support must offer them the alternatives they desire.
4. There must be a large turnout.
5. Voters must vote on the basis of issues.
6. The president must be able to correlate voter support with voters' policy views.

As we saw in Chapter 3, these conditions rarely occur, making presidential election results a tenuous basis for interpreting public opinion.

### Mail from the Public

The mail is another potential means for the president to learn about public opinion. Although estimates vary and record keeping is inconsistent, there can be no doubt that the White House receives several million communications from the public each year, including several thousand letters, phone calls, and even electronic mail messages daily. The White

House staff screens the mail and keeps a log that summarizes opinion on critical issues. Correspondence that requires a response is forwarded to relevant agencies.

The president usually reads only a few items from a day's mail, and these are communications from personal friends, prominent and influential citizens, and interest group leaders. Although a few letters from ordinary citizens may be answered by the president, primarily as a public relations gesture, mail from important individuals and organizations is usually answered by top White House aides. At the beginning of his administration, President Clinton personally reviewed all substantive policy replies to members of Congress.

Even if the president could read more mail, it would not necessarily provide a useful guide to what the public is thinking about policy issues, since most of the mail does not focus on the issues with which the president must deal. In addition, those who communicate with the White House are not a cross section of the American people. They over-represent the middle and upper classes and people who agree with the president.

### Understanding Public Opinion in Perspective

Presidents find it difficult to understand public opinion. There is potential for slippage between what the public wants, what it is understood to want, and what it receives. There is also the possibility that the president will exceed the boundaries of what the public finds acceptable. There is no lack of examples of the White House being surprised by public reaction to events and presidential actions. These range from President Nixon's decision to invade Cambodia in 1970 and Ronald Reagan's efforts to halt increases in social security benefits in 1981[13] to President Clinton's nomination of Zoe Baird as attorney general and his proposal to lift the ban against gays in the military in 1993.

Even if presidents feel (or at least *say*) they understand public opinion on a particular issue, they do not necessarily follow it. For example, in a speech on the invasion of Cambodia in 1970, President Nixon stated: "I would rather be a one-term president and do what I believe is right than to be a two-term president at the cost of seeing America become a second-rate power and to see this nation accept the first defeat in its proud 190-year history."[14] Similarly, President Bush told his staff that if the United States had to fight Saddam Hussein to liberate Kuwait, "it's not going to matter to me if there isn't one congressman who supports this, or what happens to public opinion. If it's right, it's gotta be done."[15]

As we noted earlier, presidents often feel, with good reason, that they know more about policy than most members of the public and that they sometimes have to lead public opinion instead of merely follow it. Gerald Ford expressed this view:

I do not think a President should run the country on the basis of the polls. The public in so many cases does not have a full comprehension of a problem. A President ought to listen to the people, but he cannot make hard decisions just by reading the polls once a week. It just does not work, and what the President ought to do is make the hard decisions and then go out and educate the people on why a decision that was necessarily unpopular was made.[16]

## PUBLIC EXPECTATIONS OF THE PRESIDENT

When new presidents assume the responsibilities of their office, they enter into a set of relationships the contours of which are largely beyond their control. The nations with which they will negotiate, the Congress they must persuade, and the bureaucracy they are to manage, for example, have well-established routines and boundaries within which they function. These set the context of the president's relationships with them.

Public evaluations of the president also occur within an established environment: public expectations. The public has demanding expectations of what presidents should be, how they should act, and what their policies should accomplish. It is up to the chief executive to live up to these expectations. Although some presidents may succeed over time in educating the public to alter their expectations, the public's views change slowly and usually the changes that take place only create additional burdens for the president. In addition, the static nature of the president's personal characteristics and leadership style and the American political system's inherent constraints on executive power and capacity to choose the most effective policies limit his ability to meet the public's expectations. Frustration on the part of both the president and the public is inevitable in such a situation.

### High Expectations

The public's expectations of the president in the area of policy are substantial and include his ensuring peace, prosperity, and security. Table 4-1 shows the results of polls taken in December 1976 and 1980 following the elections of Presidents Carter and Reagan, respectively. Performance expectations of each president are quite high and cover a broad range of policy areas. We want the good life, and we look to the president to provide it.

In addition, there is a substantial gap between the expectations the public has of what presidents should accomplish (and for which it will hold them accountable) and the degree of success the public expects presidents to have in meeting its expectations. For example, at the time of Bill Clinton's election, most people expected him to be an "outstanding" or "above average" president and were optimistic about the next

Table 4-1. Early Expectations of Presidents Carter and Reagan

| Policy | Percent Who Feel They Can Expect | |
| --- | --- | --- |
| | Carter | Reagan |
| Reduced unemployment | 72 | 69 |
| Reduced inflation | * | 66 |
| Reduced cost of government | 59 | 70 |
| Increased government efficiency | 81 | 89 |
| Effective dealings with foreign policy | 79 | 77 |
| Strengthened national defense | 81 | 76 |

*Not available.

Source: "Early Expectations: Comparing Chief Executives," *Public Opinion*, February/March 1981, p. 39. Reprinted with the permission of The American Enterprise Institute for Public Policy Research, Washington, D.C.

four years with him in the White House (almost exactly the same results found in 1977, 1981, and 1989 for Carter, Reagan, and Bush, respectively).[17] At the same time, over 70 percent of the people did not expect him to keep his campaign promise not to raise taxes, and clear majorities did not expect him to reduce the deficit or control federal spending (see Table 4-2). The fact that the juxtaposition of these views might be unfair to the president does not seem to disturb many of his constituents.

Later in this book we will see that the president's influence on public policy and its consequences is quite limited most of the time. Nevertheless, the public holds the president responsible for them anyway. To quote President Carter: "When things go bad you [the president] get entirely too much blame. And I have to admit that when things go good, you get entirely too much credit."[18] Since conditions empha-

Table 4-2. Expectations of the Clinton Administration

*Do you think the Clinton administration will or will not be able to do the following?*

| | Will | Will Not |
| --- | --- | --- |
| Improve education | 69% | 25% |
| Help minorities and the poor | 68 | 27 |
| Improve health care | 64 | 30 |
| Improve the environment | 64 | 29 |
| Keep the nation out of war | 60 | 27 |
| Improve the economy | 59 | 35 |
| Reduce unemployment | 58 | 37 |
| Increase respect for the United States abroad | 50 | 40 |
| Control spending | 40 | 54 |
| Reduce the federal budget deficit | 38 | 54 |
| Avoid raising taxes | 20 | 74 |

Source: Gallup poll, November 10–11, 1992. Reprinted with permission of the Gallup Poll News Service.

sized in the press seem to be bad more than good, it is usually blame that presidents receive.

In addition to expecting successful policies from the White House, Americans expect their presidents to be extraordinary individuals. (This, of course, buttresses the public's policy expectations). The public desires the president to be honest, intelligent, cool in a crisis, caring, competent, and to possess a sense of humor. Substantial percentages also want the nation's leader to have imagination and charisma. Obviously, it is not easy to meet these expectations, and, as we have seen, presidents are watched very carefully to see whether they do.

The public not only has high expectations for presidents' official performance but also lofty expectations for their private behavior. Substantial percentages of the population strongly object if presidents engage in behavior that is very common in American society. For example, when the Watergate tapes revealed that President Nixon frequently used profane and obscene language in his private conversations, many Americans were outraged. The public demands that the president's public and private life be exemplary.

The tenacity with which Americans maintain high expectations of the president may be due in large part to the encouragement they receive from presidential candidates to do so. The lengthy process by which Americans select their presidents lends itself to political hyperbole. For one year out of every four, the public is enticed to expect more from the president than it is currently receiving. Evidently it takes this rhetoric to heart and holds presidents to ever higher standards, independent of the reasonableness of these expectations.

High expectations of presidents are also supported by political socialization; schoolchildren are often taught American history organized by presidential eras. Implicit in much of this teaching is the view that great presidents were largely responsible for the freedom and prosperity Americans enjoy. From such lessons it is a short step to presuming that contemporary presidents can be wise and effective leaders and, therefore, that the public should expect them to be so. Furthermore, commentators may compare contemporary presidents to an ideal president, compounded out of the strongest attributes of their predecessors.

Yet another factor encouraging high expectations of the White House is the prominence of the president. As the nation's spokesperson, the personification of the nation, the chief executive is the closest thing Americans have to a royal sovereign. On election presidents and their families, even their pets, dominate the news in America. Their great visibility naturally induces people to focus attention, and thus demands and expectations, upon them.

Related to the president's prominence is the tendency to personalize. Issues of public policy are often extremely complex. To simplify them, Americans tend to think of issues in terms of personalities, especially the president's. It is easier to blame a specific person for personal and societal problems than it is to analyze and comprehend the complicated mix of factors that really causes these problems. Similarly, it is easier to project frustrations onto a single individual than it is to deal with the contradictions and selfishness in people's own policy demands. At the midpoint of his term in office President Carter reflected: "I can see why it is difficult for a President to serve two terms. You are the personification of problems and when you address a problem even successfully you become identified with it."[19]

Part of the explanation for the public's high expectations of the president probably lies in its lack of understanding of the context in which the president functions. We shall see in later chapters that the president's basic power situation in the nation's constitutional system is one of weakness rather than strength. Yet this is widely misperceived by the public. Most people do not feel that the president has too little power.[20]

Do high expectations of our presidents affect the public's evaluations of their performance? Although we lack sufficient data to reach a definitive conclusion, there is reason to believe that they do. Sometimes the negative impact of high expectations in the public's support for the president is of the chief executive's own making. Jimmy Carter provides a good example of a president who was his own worst enemy in this regard. Both before and after taking office, he set very high standards for himself and his administration and assured the public that he would live up to them. Unfortunately, he was unable to keep many of his promises, such as balancing the budget and keeping his administration free from scandal.

Similarly, George Bush promised in dramatic fashion not to raise taxes and to create millions of jobs. When he agreed to a tax increase as part of a budget agreement with Congress and when the jobs failed to materialize, his opponents wasted no time in criticizing him. Bill Clinton began his administration on a sour note when he announced that he would not be able to provide a tax cut for the middle class or halve the deficit in four years as he had promised during the campaign.

We have, of course, no way to calculate precisely the influence of such unkept promises on the president's standing with the public, and many of them alone may be of little significance. Yet their collective impact undoubtedly depresses the president's approval ratings because they help to undermine the aura of statesmanship and competence that attracted support in the election campaign. According to Richard Wirthlin, President Reagan's pollster, expectations are the ultimate source of public frustration.[21] Perhaps presidents should lower expectations, especially at the beginning of their terms, so they will not mortgage their reputation and prestige to nuances of governing they have not yet learned.

### Contradictory Expectations

The contradictions in the public's expectations of the president present an additional obstacle to presidents in their efforts to gain public support. With contradictory expectations it is very difficult to escape criticism and loss of approval—no matter what they do.

Contradictory expectations of presidents deal with either the content of policy or their style of performance. Our expectations of policy are confused and seemingly unlimited. We want low taxes and efficient government, yet we do not want a decrease in public services. We desire plentiful gasoline, but not at a higher price. We wish inflation to be controlled, but not at the expense of higher unemployment or interest rates. We yearn for a clean environment, yet we are anxious to have industrial development.

It is true, of course, that the public is not entirely to blame for holding these contradictory expectations. Presidential candidates often enthusiastically encourage voters to believe that they will produce the proverbial situation in which the people can have their cake and eat it, too. In the 1980 presidential campaign Ronald Reagan promised, among other things, to slash government expenditures, substantially reduce taxes, increase military spending, balance the budget, and maintain government services. In 1992 Bill Clinton promised to halve the budget deficit and increase social services without raising taxes on most Americans.

Expectations of the president's leadership style are also crucial in the public's evaluation of the president. People want a president who embodies a variety of traits, some of which are contradictory.

1. We expect the president to be a *leader*, an independent figure who speaks out and takes stands on the issues even if the views expressed are unpopular. We also expect the president to preempt problems by anticipating them before they arise. Similarly, we count on the president to provide novel solutions to the country's problems. To meet these expectations the president must be ahead of public opinion, acting on problems that may be obscure to the general populace and contributing ideas that are different from those currently in vogue in discussions of policy.

   In sharp contrast to our expectations for presidential leadership are our expectations that chief executives be *responsive* to public opinion and that they be constrained by majority rule as represented in Congress. The public overwhelmingly desires Congress to have final authority in policy disagreements with the president, and it does not want the president to be able to act against majority opinion.[22]

   The contradictory expectations of leadership versus responsiveness place presidents in a no-win situation. If they attempt to lead, they may be criticized for losing contact with their constituents and being unrepresentative. Conversely, if they try to reflect the views of the populace, they may be reproached for failing to lead and for not solving the country's problems.

2. We expect our presidents to be open-minded politicians in the American tradition and thus exhibit *flexibility* and willingness to compromise on policy differences. At the same time we also expect the president to be *decisive* and to take firm and consistent stands on the issues. These expectations are also incompatible, and presidents can expect to be criticized for being rigid and inflexible when they are standing firm on an issue. Presidents will also be disparaged for being weak and indecisive when they do compromise.

3. A large majority of the public wants the president to be a *statesman*, to place the country's interests ahead of politics. Yet a majority of the same public also desires the president to be a skilled *politician*, and a substantial minority favors the president's exercising loyalty to his political party. A president who acts in a statesmanlike manner may be criticized for being too far above the political fray, for being an ineffective idealist and insufficiently solicitous of party supporters. Jimmy Carter began his term on such a note when he attempted to cut back on "pork barrel" water projects. A president who emphasizes a party program, however, may be criticized for being a crass politician, without concern for the broader national interest.

4. Americans like their presidents to run *open* administrations. They desire a free flow of ideas within the governing circles in Washington, and they want the workings of government to be visible to them and not sheltered behind closed doors. At the same time they want to feel that the president is *in control* of things and that the government is not sailing rudderless. If presidents allow internal dissent in White House decision making and do not try to hide or succeed in hiding this dissent from the public, they will inevitably be reproached for not being in control of their own aides. But if they should attempt either to stifle dissent or to conceal it from the public, they will be accused of being isolated, undemocratic, unable to accept criticism, and of attempting to muzzle opposition.

5. Finally, Americans want their presidents to be able to *relate* to the average person in order to inspire confidence in the White House and to have compassion and concern for the typical citizen. Yet, as we have shown throughout our discussion of expectations, the public also expects the president to possess characteristics far *different* from its own and to act in ways that are beyond the capabilities of most people. To confuse the matter further, the public also expects the president to act with a special dignity befitting the leader of this country and the free world and to live and entertain in splendor. In other words, presidents are not supposed to resemble the common man at all.

　　If presidents seem too common, they may be disparaged for

being just that—"common." One only has to think of the political cartoons of Harry Truman and Gerald Ford, implying that they were really not up to the job of president. On the other hand, if presidents seem too different, appear too cerebral, or engage in too much pomp, they will likely be denounced as snobbish and isolated from the people and as being too regal for Americans' tastes. Again, one has to think back only to the Nixon White House to recall such criticisms.

## PUBLIC APPROVAL OF THE PRESIDENT

The most visible and significant aspect of presidents' relations with the public is their level of approval. Presidents' efforts to understand and lead public opinion and their efforts to influence the media's portrayal of them are aimed at achieving public support. This support is related to their success in dealing with others, especially the Congress. The higher the public's level of approval of the president, the more support Congress gives administration programs.[23]

Whether they are based on perceptions encouraged by the White House, the media, or other political actors, or based on detached and careful study, opinions about the president and his policies are formed. People are also affected, sometimes quite directly, by the impact of foreign and domestic policies. In this section we examine issues, the president's personality and personal characteristics, and dramatic international events as possible explanations for presidential approval. In addition, there are certain less dynamic factors in the form of predispositions that citizens hold, such as political party identification and the positivity bias, that may strongly influence their evaluations of the president. Party in particular not only directly affects opinions of the president but also mediates the impact of other influences. Thus it is important that we examine predispositions as well as more specific opinions about the president and his policies.

### Party Identification

Evaluations of the president's performance reflect the underlying partisan loyalties of the public. Members of the president's party are predisposed to approve of his performance and members of the opposition party are predisposed to be less approving. Independents, those without explicit partisan attachments, fall between the Democrats and Republicans in their levels of approval of the president. The average difference in support between Democrats and Republicans over the past forty years has been nearly 40 percentage points, a very substantial figure. Independents fall in between, averaging a difference of about 20 percentage points from both Democrats and Republicans. The public was especially polarized along party lines during Ronald Reagan's tenure: The gap between Democrats and Republicans widened to 52 percentage points.

The impact of partisanship on evaluations of the president can also be seen by examining presidential approval at a cross section of time. In July 1974, shortly before he resigned, Richard Nixon registered overall support of 25 percent. Approval among Democrats had diminished to a meager 13 percent, and among Independents he received only a 23 percent approval rating. Yet even at the height of the Watergate crisis, 52 percent of Republicans gave the president their approval. Five years later, at the end of July 1979, Jimmy Carter, a Democratic president, saw his approval fall to an overall 29 percent. Republican approval stood at only 18 percent. Democrats, on the other hand, were more than twice as likely to support Carter, giving him 37 percent approval. Independents were in the middle at 27 percent.

### Positivity Bias

Another predisposing factor is the "positivity bias," which one authority defines as the tendency "to show evaluation of public figures and institutions in a generally positive direction."[24] Americans have a general disposition to prefer, to learn, and to expect positive relationships more than negative relationships and to perceive stimuli as positive rather than negative. They tend to have favorable opinions of people.

The causes of the positivity bias are not well known, but it seems to have the greatest potential for influence in ambiguous situations, such as the beginning of a president's term, when new occupants of the White House are unknown to the public as chief executives. There is a coming together after presidential campaigns. People want their new presidents to succeed and usually give them the benefit of the doubt.

Although the positivity bias should encourage presidential approval throughout a president's tenure, it is likely to be especially important at the beginning of a president's tenure, when no record exists. One way to see the impact of positivity bias is to compare the electoral percentage by which presidents first won election with their approval level in the first Gallup poll after inauguration. In Table 4-3 we find such a comparison (President Ford is excluded because he never won an election for the presidency).

The figures clearly show that, with the exception of Ronald Reagan and George Bush, a substantially larger percentage of the people are willing to give new presidents their approval at the beginning of their terms than were willing to vote for them two months earlier.

As presidents perform their duties, they become better known to citizens, who have more basis for judgments about them. Moreover, people may begin to perceive greater implications of presidential poli-

Table 4-3. Comparison of Electoral Percentages and Postinaugural Approval

| President | Popular Vote in First Election ($) | Approval in First Postinaugural Poll (%) |
|---|---|---|
| Eisenhower | 55 | 69 |
| Kennedy | 50 | 72 |
| Johnson | 61 | 71 |
| Nixon | 43 | 60 |
| Carter | 50 | 66 |
| Reagan | 51 | 51 |
| Bush | 53 | 51 |
| Clinton | 43 | 58 |

Source: Gallup poll.

cies for their own lives as time passes. If these are viewed unfavorably, the public may be more open to, and pay more attention to, negative information about the president.

A related factor may be at work in affecting presidents' approval by the public early in their terms. As people have little basis on which to evaluate the president, they may turn to others for cues. A new chief executive is generally treated favorably in the press. Moreover, there is excitement and symbolism inherent in the peaceful transfer of power, inaugural festivities, and "new beginnings." All of this creates a positive environment in which initial evaluations of elected presidents take place and buttresses any tendency toward the positivity bias.

Several studies have found evidence of what some authors term a *fait accompli*, or bandwagon effect. In other words, after an election people, especially those voting for the loser, tend to view the winner more favorably than they did before the election. The depolarization of politics following an election and the positivity bias itself probably help to create an environment conducive to attitude change.[25]

### The Persistence of Approval

We have seen that presidents typically begin their initial terms with the benefit of substantial support from the public. But how long does this honeymoon last? Conventional wisdom indicates not very long. The thrust of the argument is that soon presidents will have to begin making hard choices that will inevitably alienate segments of the population. Additional support for this view comes from a revealing response by President Carter in 1979 to a reporter's question concerning whether it was reasonable to expect the president to rate very highly with the American people. The president answered:

> In this present political environment, it is almost impossible. There are times of euphoria that sweep the Nation immediately after an election or after an inauguration day or maybe after a notable success, like the Camp

David Accords, when there is a surge of popularity for a President. But most of the decisions that have to be made by a President are inherently not popular ones. They are contentious.[26]

Despite the reasonableness of these expectations, presidential honeymoons are not always short-lived. Examining shifts in presidents' approval ratings reveals that although declines certainly do take place, they are neither inevitable nor swift. Eisenhower maintained his standing in the public very well for two complete terms. Kennedy and Nixon held their public support for two years, as did Ford, once he suffered his sharp initial decline. Johnson's and Carter's approval losses were steeper, although Johnson's initial ratings were inflated by the unique emotional climate at the time he assumed office. The same was true, of course, for Ford. Reagan's approval ratings were volatile, but he stood at 64 percent approval at the time of his second inauguration, 13 percentage points higher than when he began. George Bush maintained very high levels of public support until about the last year of his tenure.

Thus, honeymoons are not necessarily fleeting times during which new occupants of the White House receive a breathing period from the public. Instead, the president's constituents seem to be willing to give a new chief executive the benefit of the doubt for some time. It is up to each president to exploit this goodwill and build solid support for his administration in the public. This is why the first few months are often critical for setting the tone of the administration and shaping the reputation of the president.

### Long-Term Decline

In addition to examining approval levels within presidential terms, we also need to look for trends in public support across presidents. As we can see in Figure 4-1, from 1953 through 1965, with the single exception of 1958, at least 60 percent of the public approved the president on the average. Support from two out of three Americans was not unusual. Starting in 1966, approval levels changed dramatically. Since that time, presidents have obtained support from even a bare majority of the public only about half of the time.

What happened? We cannot provide a definitive answer to this question, but it is reasonable to argue that the war in Vietnam, a highly divisive policy following an era of peace, had a destructive effect on President Johnson's approval levels. Although Richard Nixon rebounded somewhat from his predecessor's low standing in the polls from 1966 to 1968, he did not rise back to pre-1966 levels, and Watergate sent his approval levels to new lows.

Just how much residual effect the factors of Vietnam and Watergate have had on the approval levels of subsequent presidents is impossible to determine with certainty. We do know that President Ford's pardon of Nixon tied Ford irrevocably to Watergate and that his public support

Figure 4-1. Average Yearly Presidential Approval, 1953–1993

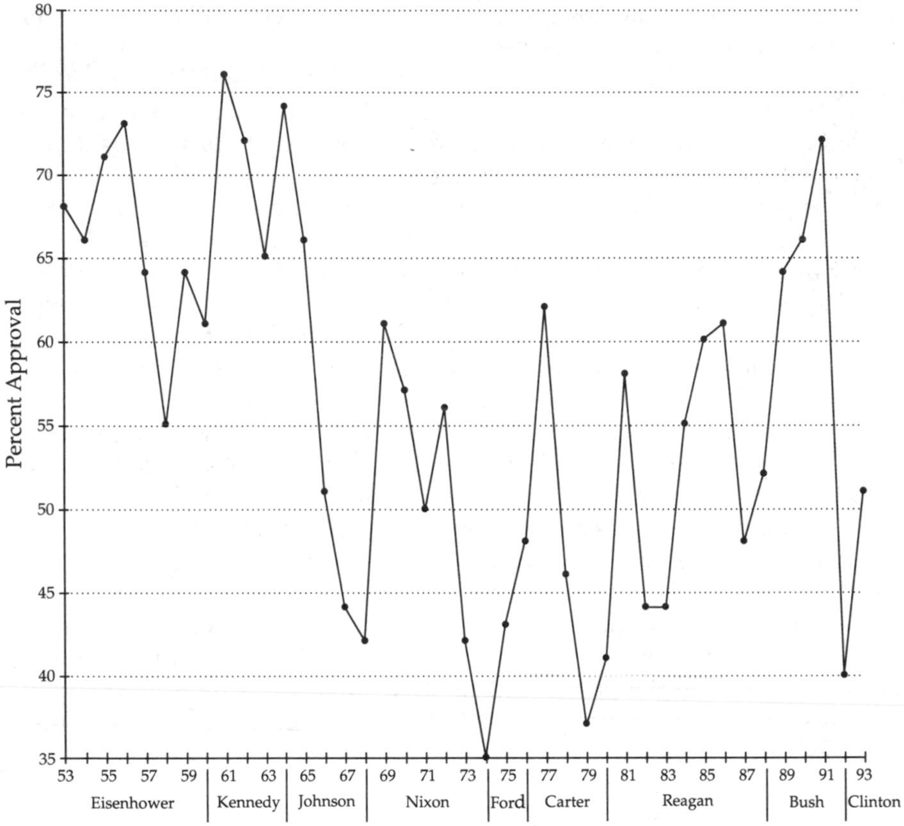

Source: Gallup Poll.

plunged immediately after announcing it. Moreover, there is survey evidence that Watergate had reduced the confidence of many people in the office of president.[27]

We also know that President Carter did not enjoy high levels of approval, and Ronald Reagan's approval varied considerably over the course of his presidency. Contrary to accounts in the popular media, Reagan sustained high levels of approval only for a two-year period beginning near the end of his first term. President Bush rose to great heights of public support, but fell to less than 40 percent approval during his last year in office and was defeated for reelection. Bill Clinton had the lowest approval ratings of any modern president in his first months in office—less than 40 percent in June 1993. Although the generally low level of support for some presidents may be purely a product of their individual actions and characteristics, it is difficult not to conclude that the events of the late 1960s and early 1970s have weakened the predispositions of many Americans to support the president. This conclusion is consistent with findings of a decline in the enthusiasm of voters for winning presidential candidates over the same period.[28]

AIR TEMP. 92°
WATER TEMP. 78°
WIND S.W. 6 M.P.H.
SUNBURN INDEX 8
OVERNIGHT
CHANGE
IN THE
PRESIDENT'S
APPROVAL
RATING -2%

Drawing by Ziegler; © 1989 The New Yorker Magazine, Inc.

## Personality or Policy?

One factor commonly associated with someone's approval is personality. In common usage the term "personality" refers to personal characteristics such as warmth, charm, and humor that may influence responses to an individual on a personal level. It is not unusual for observers to conclude that the public evaluates presidents more on style than substance, especially in an era in which the media and sophisticated public relations campaigns play such a prominent role in presidential politics. The fact that Americans pay relatively little detailed attention to politics and policy adds further support to the view that the president's personality plays a large role in the public's approval or disapproval. In other words, some argue that the public evaluates the president by how much it may like him as a person.

Dwight Eisenhower was unique among modern presidents in that his public standing preceded and was independent of his involvement in partisan politics. He was a likeable war hero who had recently been a principal leader in the highly consensual policy of defeating Germany in World War II. His image following the war was so apolitical that both parties approached him about running for president.

Nevertheless, Eisenhower was evaluated by the public as a partisan figure. Republicans were much more likely to approve his handling of

the presidency than were Democrats. Moreover, the differences between the approval levels of the two groups of party identifiers are
typical of those for other presidents. Thus, the personal component of
Eisenhower's public support may have kept his overall level of approval
high, but it did not protect him from evaluations as a partisan figure or
from fluctuations in approval related to other conditions and events in
the public's environment.

Personality may buttress presidential approval, but it is not a dynamic factor. In other words, it cannot explain shifts in the president's
standing with the public. Sharp changes in approval have occurred for
presidents whose public manners have remained unaltered. Although
impressions the public holds of the president's personality form early
and change slowly, what the public feels ought to be and the way people
evaluate what they see can change more rapidly. "Cleverness" can soon
be viewed as "deceit," "reaching down for details" as "a penchant for
the trivial," "evaluating all the alternatives" as "indecisiveness,"
"charm" as "commonness" or, even worse, "vulgarity," "staying above
politics" as "naivete." The contradictory expectations the people hold of
the president help to set the scene for these changing interpretations of
presidential behavior, allowing the public to switch emphasis in what it
looks for in a president and how it evaluates what it sees.

In addition, the public may "like" presidents but still disapprove of
the way they are handling their jobs. A poll near the middle of President
Carter's term found that almost twice as many people liked the president as approved of the manner in which he was handling the presidency.[29] Several years later a Gallup poll found that 74 percent of the public
approved of President Reagan as a person, but only 49 percent approved
of his performance as president.[30]

Thus, although we cannot specify the contribution of personality to
presidential approval, we do know that Americans appear to compart-
mentalize their attitudes toward the president. They have little difficulty
in separating the person from the performance. Changes in presidential
approval are in large part a response to what people see happening in
the world and not merely a reaction to a particular personality. Policy
matters play a large role in evaluations of presidents.

### Personal Characteristics

Much of the commentary on presidents in the press and in other
forums focuses on their personal characteristics, especially integrity, intelligence, and leadership abilities. When the public is asked about such
job-related characteristics, its responses are clearly related to its evaluations of the president. Assessments of characteristics such as the president's integrity, reliability, and leadership ability may change as new
problems arise, or in relation to the president's past performance. Certain characteristics may become more salient in response to changing

conditions. When the Iran–Contra affair became news, President Reagan's decision-making style became a prominent issue. Many people came to evaluate his focus on the "big picture" and detachment from the details of governing in a less positive light.

### Issues

Ultimately, we care about presidents because of issues of public policy. For an issue to have a significant influence on presidential evaluation, it must be salient to people, they must hold the president responsible for it, and people must make their evaluation in terms of the president's performance regarding the issue. Obviously, perceptions of reality mediate each of these components of assessing the president.

SALIENCE OF ISSUES.    For most of his tenure in office George Bush stood high in the polls despite the public's low rating of his performance on a wide variety of issues, ranging from abortion to the economy. How could the public approve of a president whom it considered was doing a poor job on so many issues? The answer is that the public evaluated the president primarily in terms of other issues, especially foreign policy, on which it approved of the president's performance.

Understanding presidential approval, then, requires identifying what is on the minds of Americans. People generally have only a few issues that are particularly important to them and to which they pay attention.[31] If a matter is not salient to people, it is unlikely that it will play a major role in their evaluations of the president. The importance of specific issues to the public also varies over time and is closely tied to objective conditions such as unemployment, inflation, international tensions, or racial conflict. In addition, different issues are likely to be salient to different groups in the population at any given time. Some may be concerned about inflation, others about unemployment, and yet others about an aspect of foreign policy.[32]

The relative weight of values and issues in evaluations of the president also varies over time. Valence or style issues are values such as patriotism, morality, or a strong national defense on which there is a broad consensus in the public and that are more basic than a position on a specific policy. The president's articulation of valence issues, directly and in the symbols he employs in his actions and speech, can affirm the values and beliefs that define citizens' political identities. As a result, valence issues may be powerful instruments for obtaining public support, for presidents often prefer to be judged on the basis of consensual criteria with which they can associate themselves.

The relative weight given to values and issues is not all that varies over time. So do the trade-offs among competing values and among individuals at any given time. Research has found that values are relatively constant over time, but that policy debates are rarely single-valued. Some values become more salient and some less so in making these trade-offs.[33] Antigovernment and antiwelfare attitudes give way to concerns for health and compassion if it is discovered that children are going hungry. In the debate over abortion, the salience of values represented by "life" and "choice" varies substantially among citizens.

Finally, within an issue area, bad news may outweigh the good in capturing the public's attention. Several scholars have found that people weigh negative information more heavily than positive, that is, it is more salient to them.[34] If the economy slumps, for example, this may be more salient to the public than if it continues to grow at a moderate rate. Thus, it is possible that presidents may be punished in the polls if the economy is not doing well, while they may not be rewarded for prosperity.[35] It may be that an issue only comes to the public's attention when it reaches a certain threshold level, which usually means that there is a problem.[36] This in turn may provide the basis for more vocal, and thus more salient, opposition to the president.

RESPONSIBILITY.     Even if a matter such as the economy is salient to the public, it is not likely to affect people's evaluations of the president unless they hold him responsible for it.[37] And the more the public attributes responsibility for an issue to the president, the more the issue is likely to affect evaluations of his performance.[38]

Despite the prominence of the chief executive, there are several reasons why people may not hold the president responsible for all the problems they face personally or for some problems that they perceive confront the country. Most people do not politicize their personal problems, and most of those concerned about personal economic problems do not believe the government should come to their assistance.[39] If people perceive that their economic problems are the result of their own failings or those of their immediate environment, then their personal economic circumstances should not necessarily lead to discontent with national political figures or institutions. A study asking who is "most responsible" for "economic problems" found that only 11 percent chose the president; 67 percent chose big business and big labor.[40]

There is also evidence of sophistication in the public's attributions of responsibility. For example, people do not necessarily exaggerate the importance of the president or ignore contextual and institutional factors beyond his control.[41] Some people may feel that those who preceded the president or who share power with him are to blame for important problems. In March 1991, 48 percent of the public placed much of the blame for the recession on the Reagan administration (which had left office three years before) compared with only 15 percent who placed the blame primarily on the Bush White House.[42]

PRESIDENTIAL PERFORMANCE ON AN ISSUE.     For an issue that is salient to the public and for which it holds the president accountable, the quality of the president's performance on that issue should become a factor in presidential approval. Many observers assume that, for example, if unemployment is rising, the president will be seen as doing a poor job. Perhaps this is true, but perceptions may not follow directly from objective indicators of the economy's performance.

The public may be less harsh in its evaluations of presidents who are struggling with difficult situations, even if they are not meeting with short-term success. Franklin D. Roosevelt may have enjoyed the public's tolerance in 1933 and 1934, not only because he could not be held responsible for the Great Depression but also because he was seen as doing the best that could be done under trying circumstances.

The unemployment level was virtually identical in the summer of 1984 as it was in the summer of 1992, but the public evaluated the economic performance of Presidents Reagan and Bush, respectively, quite differently. Reagan was rewarded for bringing it down while Bush suffered the consequences of economic stagnation.

In addition, a substantial and growing body of evidence supports the argument that the political attitudes of Americans are more influenced by what they see as important national issues than by their personal experience. Focusing on the most often discussed issue area, the economy, will clarify the point.

The conventional view is that people's evaluations of the president are affected strongly by their personal economic circumstances. That is, they are more likely to approve of the president if they are prospering personally than if they feel they are not. In recent years an impressive number of studies have found that personal economic circumstances are typically subordinated to other, broader considerations when people evaluate government performance or individual candidates.[43] More specifically, some scholars have argued that citizens evaluate the president on the basis of broader views of the economy than just their narrow self-interests. In other words, rather than asking what the president has done for them lately, citizens ask what the president has done for the *nation*.[44]

Furthermore, people typically differentiate their own circumstances from those of the country as a whole. For example, in a Gallup poll taken in 1992, only 21 percent were satisfied with the way things were going in the nation, but 79 percent were satisfied with the way things were going in their personal lives.[45]

This reasoning regarding the public's evaluation of the president also applies to factors other than the economy. The Vietnam War may have influenced citizens' evaluations of the president because of how they viewed it as a general policy rather than how it affected them personally. Jimmy Carter's standing in the public may have benefited for several months from favorable public perceptions of his handling of the Iranian hostage crisis, despite the fact the hostages were not freed during this period.

### Rally Events

To this point we have examined factors that may affect presidential approval systematically over time, but sometimes public opinion takes sudden jumps, as in the case of the 18 percentage point increase George Bush received in the polls after the Persian Gulf War began in January 1991. One popular explanation for these surges of support are "rally events." John Mueller, in his seminal definition of the concept, defined a rally event as one that is international, directly involves the United States and particularly the president, and is specific, dramatic, and sharply focused. Such events confront the nation as a whole, are salient to the public, and gain public attention and interest.[46]

The theory behind attributing significance to rally events is that the public will increase its support of presidents in times of crisis or during major international events, at least in the short run, because they are the symbol of the country and the primary focus of attention at such times. Moreover, people do not want to hurt the country's chances of success by opposing the president. The president meanwhile has an opportunity to look masterful and evoke patriotic reactions among the people. Conversely, there is also reason to expect the potential for the "rally around the flag" effect to be limited. Studies of American public opinion regarding national security have found little inherent deference to the president.[47]

The preponderance of evidence indicates that the rally phenomenon rarely appears and that the events that generate it are highly idiosyncratic and do not seem to differ significantly from other events that were not followed by surges in presidential approval. Moreover, the events that cause sudden increases in public support are not restricted to international affairs, and most international events that would seem to be potential rally events fail to generate much additional approval of the president.

### Summary

Public approval of the president is the product of many factors. At the base of evaluations is the predisposition of many people to support the president. Political party identification provides the basic underpinning of approval or disapproval and mediates the impact of other factors. The positivity bias and the bandwagon effect buttress approval levels, at least for a while.

Changes in approval levels appear to be due primarily to the public's evaluation of the importance of issues, the president's responsibility for them, and his performance in handling them. Citizens seem to focus on the president's efforts and his stands on issues rather than on his personality or how his policies affect them personally or even whether his policies are successful in the short run. Job-related personal characteristics of the president also play an important role in influencing the degree of presidential approval. Conversely, rally events may provide an occasional increment of support, but in general they do not seem to be very significant.

## LEADING THE PUBLIC

If public support can be a useful leadership resource for presidents, are they in a position to call upon it when needed? Commentators on the presidency often assume that the White House can persuade or even mobilize the public if the president is a skilled enough communicator. Before accepting this premise, however, a critical examination of the chief executive's efforts at leading the public is needed.

### Direct Opinion Leadership

The most visible and obvious technique employed by presidents to lead public opinion is to seek the public's support directly. Presidents frequently attempt to influence public opinion with speeches over television or radio or in person to large groups. Recent presidents have averaged one public appearance every day (George Bush and Bill Clinton have been especially active). Not all presidents are effective speakers, however, and not all look good under the glare of hot lights and the unflattering gaze of television cameras. Moreover, the public is not always receptive to the president's message.

All presidents since Truman have had media advice from experts on lighting, makeup, stage settings, camera angles, clothing, pacing of delivery, and other facets of speechmaking. Despite this aid and despite the experience that politicians inevitably have in public speaking, presidential speeches aimed at directly leading public opinion have typically not been very impressive. Only Kennedy, Reagan, and Clinton have mastered the art of speaking to the camera.

No matter how effective presidents might be as speakers, they still must contend with the predispositions of their audience. As we noted in our discussion of the campaign, members of the public screen the president's messages through their own views and values, posing a formidable challenge to persuasion. The president also cannot depend upon an attentive audience. Most people are not very interested in politics.

The relative importance the typical person attaches to a president's address is illustrated by the attention presidential staffs give to setting the date for the president's annual State of the Union message. They have to be careful to avoid preempting prime time on the night that offers the current season's most popular shows while at the same time trying to maximize their national viewing audience. In general, the size of the audience for televised presidential speeches has declined over time. For example, President Bush received only a 43 percent audience rating for his triumphal speech to a joint session of Congress following the success of the Gulf war.[48]

The public's general lack of interest in politics constrains the president's leadership of public opinion in the long run as well as on a given day. Although they have unparalleled access to the American people, presidents cannot make too much use of it. If they do, their speeches will become commonplace and lose their drama and interest. That is why presidents do not make appeals to the public, particularly on television, very often—four or five times a year on average.[49] Some presidents, such as Clinton, Reagan, and Nixon, have turned to radio and midday addresses in order to reserve prime-time televised addresses for more important issues.

Television is a medium in which visual interest, action, and conflict are most effective. Presidential speeches are unlikely to contain these characteristics. Although some addresses to the nation, such as President Johnson's televised demand for a voting rights act before a joint session of Congress in 1965, occur at moments of high drama, they do not typically do so.

Presidents not only have to contend with the medium but they also must concern themselves with their messages. The most effective speeches seem to be those whose goals are general support and image building rather than specific support. They focus on simple themes rather than complex details. Calvin Coolidge used this method successfully in his radio speeches, as did Franklin Roosevelt in his famous "fireside chats." The limitation of such an approach, of course, is that general

**President Clinton delivers a speech during Memorial Day ceremonies at the Vietnam Veteran Memorial in Washington on Monday, May 31st, 1993.**
AP/WideWorld Photos.

support cannot always be translated into public backing for specific policies.

SUCCESS OF APPEALS.     We should not be surprised, then, that direct appeals to the public often fail. Ronald Reagan was certainly interested in policy change and went to unprecedented lengths to influence public opinion. Nevertheless, numerous national surveys of public opinion found that Americans did not move their general ideological preference to the right, and support for regulatory programs and spending on health care, welfare, urban problems, education, environmental protection, and aid to minorities increased rather than decreased during Reagan's tenure. On the other hand, support for increased defense expenditures was decidedly lower at the end of his administration than when he took office. In the realm of foreign policy, whether the issue was military spending, arms control, military aid and arms sales, or cooperation with the Soviet Union, public opinion by the early 1980s had turned to the left—*ahead* of Reagan. He was especially frustrated in his goal of obtaining public support for aid to the Contras in Nicaragua.[50]

Regarding the latter issue, Reagan voiced his disappointment in his memoirs:

> For eight years the press called me the "Great Communicator." Well, one of my greatest frustrations during those eight years was my inability to communicate to the American people and to Congress the seriousness of the threat we faced in Central America.[51]

Despite the limitations of their abilities to exercise direct opinion leadership over the public, presidents are aided by the willingness of Americans to *follow* their lead, especially on foreign policy. Foreign policy is more distant from the lives of most Americans than is domestic policy and is therefore seen as more complex and based on specialized knowledge. Thus people tend to defer more to the president on foreign issues than on domestic ones that they can relate more easily and directly to their own experience. Studies have shown public opinion undergoing changes in line with presidents' policies on the liberation of Kuwait, the invasion of Grenada, testing nuclear weapons, relations with the People's Republic of China, isolationism, and both the escalation and deescalation of the war in Vietnam.[52]

One scholar ascertained public opinion on six potential responses to the 1979–1980 hostage crisis in Iran. Then he asked those who opposed each option if they would change their view "if President Carter considered this action necessary." The policy options and the public's responses to them are shown in Table 4-4.[53] In each case a substantial percentage of the public changed its opinion in deference to the supposed opinion of the president. Similarly, a poll of Utah residents found that two-thirds of them opposed basing the deployment of MX missiles in Utah and Nevada. But an equal number said they would definitely or

Table 4-4. Reconsidering Iran Hostage Crisis Policy Opinions in Response to
the President

| Policy | Original Approval (%) | Approval after Reconsideration (%) | Change Due to President (%) |
|---|---|---|---|
| Wait and see | 58 | 83 | 25 |
| Return Shah to Iran | 21 | 53 | 32 |
| Send Shah elsewhere | 74 | 87 | 13 |
| Naval blockade | 62 | 85 | 23 |
| Threaten to send troops | 43 | 73 | 30 |
| Send troops | 29 | 62 | 33 |

Source: Lee Sigelman, "Gauging the Public Response to Presidential Leadership," *Presidential Studies Quarterly* 10 (Summer 1980): 431. Permission granted by the Center for the Study of the Presidency, publisher of *Presidential Studies Quarterly*.

probably support President Reagan if he decided to go ahead and base the missiles in those states.[54]

Not all results are so positive, however. In one study different sample groups were asked whether they supported a domestic policy proposal dealing with welfare and a proposal dealing with foreign aid. One of the groups was told President Carter supported the proposals. The authors found that attaching the president's name to either proposal not only failed to increase support for them but actually had a negative effect because those who disapproved of Carter reacted very strongly against proposals they thought were his.[55]

As we learned earlier, the public generally does not have crystallized opinions on issues and is therefore often easy to sway in the short run. But this volatility also means that any opinion change is subject to slippage. As issues fade into the background or as positions on issues confront the realities of daily life, opinions that were altered in response to presidential leadership may quickly be forgotten. This is especially likely to occur where the president's influence on public opinion seems to be greatest: foreign policy.

A balanced view of the president's ability to lead public opinion directly must take into consideration both the potential for and the obstacles to leadership. The limited evidence available indicates that presidents are much more likely to be successful in influencing public opinion when they have high approval ratings themselves.[56] As in so many other presidential relationships, the direct leadership of public opinion provides opportunities, especially in foreign policy, but no guarantees of success. It is for this reason that presidents often rely on more subtle methods of opinion leadership.

### Information Control

A technique for influencing public opinion that is less direct than appeals to the public is information control. This comes in many forms, ranging from withholding information from the public to lying. If the public is unaware of a situation or has a distorted view of it, then presidents may have more flexibility in achieving what they desire. Often they desire public passivity as much as they want public support.

WITHHOLDING INFORMATION.    The classification of information under the rubric of "national security" is a frequently used means of withholding information. Most people support secrecy in handling national security affairs, especially in such matters as defense plans and strategy, weapons technology, troop movements, the details of current diplomatic negotiations, the methods and sources of covert intelligence gathering, and similar information about the defense, negotiations, and intelligence gathering of other nations. However, there has been controversy over the amount of information classified and whether classification is used by the president and other high officials to influence public opinion. When officials withhold information that might aid the public in evaluating their performance in office and in answering general questions of public policy but that might embarrass them if made public, they may provide a distorted view of reality and increase or maintain support for themselves.

There are other means of withholding information. Many critics felt that George Bush's Christmas Eve pardons of former Secretary of Defense Casper Weinberger and five other officials were motivated by his desire to preempt testimony regarding the Iran–Contra scandal.

DEEMPHASIS OF INFORMATION.    Presidents can also employ more subtle methods of manipulating information in an effort to influence public opinion. They can, for example, order that information collected by the government be deemphasized. When the economy was not doing well in 1971, the White House ordered the Bureau of Labor Statistics to discontinue its monthly briefing of the press on prices and unemployment. Similarly, during the Vietnam War the Defense Department gave much more attention in its public announcements to deserters from enemy forces than to deserters from the armed forces of our South Vietnamese allies. In each case the government possessed information that might negatively influence public perceptions of the president and his administration. It chose not to emphasize this "bad news."

COLLECTION OF INFORMATION.    Going a step further, presidents can simply order that information on a policy not be collected. This, of course, prevents the public from fully evaluating their performance. President Johnson had invested a great deal in his Great Society domestic programs and did not want to cut back on them when large amounts of funds were needed for the Vietnam War. Although warned by the Council of Economic Advisers at the end of 1965 of the need for a tax increase to avoid the inflation that would result from having both "guns and butter," he refused to request one. Instead Johnson kept the precise expenditures on the war from Congress and the public.[57] No serious effort was ever made to determine the true costs of U.S. involvement in the war, and Americans felt the ravages of inflation for years to come.

TIMING OF THE RELEASE OF INFORMATION.    Sometimes information is provided, but the timing of its release is used to try to influence public opinion. On November 2, 1970, the White House announced the most recent casualty figures from Vietnam. They were at a five-year low and their announcement was made on Monday instead of Thursday as usual, presumably because the 1970 congressional elections were being held the next day. The Carter administration revealed that the Pentagon had developed a new technology that made aircraft virtually invisible to enemy detection devices. This disclosure coincided with an administration effort during the 1980 presidential election campaign to show that it was working to strengthen national defense. Taking the opposite tack, the Ford administration announced that the country was in a recession one week after the 1974 congressional elections. The Reagan administration knew that its economic forecasts had been too optimistic, but it did not change them until after the crucial vote on the president's tax cut proposal in 1981.

OBFUSCATION OF INFORMATION.    Presidents and their aides may also attempt to obscure or distort the truth in order to confuse or mislead the public. President Eisenhower regularly gave purposefully ambiguous answers at his press conferences.[58] A classic example of this technique is an answer Nixon's press secretary Ron Ziegler gave to a reporter's questions about the Watergate tapes.

> I would feel that most of the conversations that took place in those areas of the White House that did have the recording system would, in almost their entirety, be in existence, but the special prosecutor, the court, and I think, the American people are sufficiently familiar with the recording system to know where the recording devices existed and to know the situation in terms of the recording process, but I feel, although the process has not been undertaken yet in preparation of the material to abide by the court decision, really, what the answer to that question is.[59]

When George Bush agreed to accept "tax revenue increases" as part of the 1990 budget agreement with Congress, his announcement was so confusing that it took officials in Washington several days to determine whether he meant increases resulting from increased economic growth, from a cut in capital gains taxes, or from an increase in tax rates—and his press secretary refused to define the president's terms.

DISTORTION.    Distortion comes in many forms. One of the most common is to provide impressive statistics without going into the details of how they were compiled. Reagan's budget director, David Stockman, admitted "rigging the [budget] numbers to the point that even we couldn't understand them."[60] In 1982 President Reagan told the American people that more than half the stores investigated by the government were selling items that were prohibited for purchase with food stamps. He omitted the fact that the stores that were investigated were ones already suspected of abuse.

In March 1993 Secretary of Labor Robert Reich called a special news conference to argue that the figures his department was releasing— showing that February 1993 had experienced a large gain in jobs—were misleading because 90 percent of the jobs were just part-time. He wanted to show that the Clinton administration's economic stimulus program was still necessary, but he arrived at his figures through spurious inferences that were later widely criticized in the economics community.

Presidents have also used tricks to make budgets appear smaller. In his last year in office President Johnson introduced the "unified budget," which included trust funds previously excluded from the budget, such as those for social security, unemployment benefits, highway construction, and retirement pensions of railroad workers. The fact that the trust funds were running a surplus allowed him to cut the size of the projected federal deficit—at least on paper—because these surplus trust funds could not be used to cover the deficit in the regular budget. President Nixon introduced the "full employment" budget in fiscal 1972. His ruse was to calculate the federal revenues not at what was expected but at what they would be if there were full employment (which there was not). This subterfuge allowed him to show a smaller overall deficit. In more recent times presidents (and Congress) have used what are termed "off-budget" expenditures to reduce the size of the budget—on paper.[61] In 1993 Bill Clinton proposed to increase the percentage of taxable income of certain social security recipients. This would increase the taxes paid by these people, but his administration listed the proposal as a spending cut![62]

It is not only what goes into compiling a "fact" that is important for the public's evaluation of it, but also the context of events in which the "fact" occurs. In 1964 Lyndon Johnson went before Congress to ask for a resolution supporting retaliation against North Vietnam for two attacks on U.S. ships in the Gulf of Tonkin. The Gulf of Tonkin Resolution was subsequently passed with only two dissenting votes and marked a watershed in the nation's military actions in Vietnam. As the president desired, it was passed in the context of strong public support for retaliating against "unprovoked" attacks against Americans.

The public might have been less enthusiastic in its backing of military reprisals, however, if it had known what the president knew about the context in which the North Vietnamese actions took place. First, the United States had secretly been gathering intelligence and supporting covert South Vietnamese operations against North Vietnam for several years before the incidents in the Gulf of Tonkin. Some of these activities were going on in the vicinity at the time of the attacks on U.S. ships, and the North Vietnamese might have thought our ships were involved. The second piece of crucial contextual information that was withheld from the American people was that there was considerable reason to doubt that the second attack ever occurred! As President Johnson later said (in private, of course), "For all I know, our Navy was shooting whales out there."[63] Although it is possible that at the time the president had honestly concluded that the attack had in fact occurred, there is little doubt that the public's approval of retaliatory actions would have been more restrained if it had had this information.

Attempts to distort information are not always successful. By 1967 two-thirds of the American people felt the Johnson administration was not telling them all it should know about the Vietnam War. In 1971 a similar percentage felt the same way about the Nixon administration.[64] Out of such attitudes emerged a credibility gap and low levels of popular standing for these presidents.

PREVARICATION.    The most extreme form of information control is lying. Do presidents lie? The answer is yes. The range of subjects of lies is great and includes the topics of the country's military situation in Vietnam; its role in the 1954 coup in Guatemala; the U-2 incident; the nation's role in the Bay of Pigs invasion; the presence of missiles in Cuba in 1962; the U.S. role in the overthrow of President Diem of South Vietnam; the attempted bribery by the United States of the prime minister of Singapore; the motivations behind the American invasion of the Dominican Republic in 1965; the reasons that the USS Liberty was sunk by our Israeli allies in the 1967 Six-Day War; the nation's attempts to prevent the election of Marxist Salvador Allende as president of Chile; the Watergate cover-up; the invasion of Grenada; trading hostages with terrorists; presidential plans for appointments, travel, and policies; whether President Bush was pushing for a meeting with the president of the Soviet Union; and even the president's review of requests to use the White House tennis courts.[65]

In his press conference on September 28, 1982, President Reagan responded to questions on the economy with descriptions of the growth of the gross national product, the rate of increase in the unemployment rate under his predecessor, the proportion of the population in the work force, and the increase in the purchasing power of the average family. All of these were assertions about the economy's performance, and all of them were motivated by a desire to put it in the best possible light. Unfortunately, all of these statements were also untrue![66] Whether the president's responses were carefully planned or the result of his misunderstanding of the statistics is unclear.

One thing is clear. The American people resent being lied to. A poll near the end of 1986 found that 72 percent of the sample did not agree that it was acceptable for the government to lie—even to achieve foreign policy goals.[67] At the same time, the Reagan administration was losing credibility on a wide range of issues: Substantial majorities of the public, for example, did not believe its claims concerning the secret sale of arms to Iran, its denial of a trade of a captured Soviet spy for the release of an American newsman detained in Moscow, and its denial that an American pilot shot down over Nicaragua was a CIA agent.[68] It was also criticized for releasing false reports that Libya was planning new terrorist attacks.

INFORMATION CONTROL IN PERSPECTIVE.    What can we conclude from our discussion of information control? Perhaps the most obvious pattern that we have found is that it is most common in the national security area. The reason is simple: It is difficult for the public to challenge official statements about events in other countries, especially military activities, which often are shrouded in secrecy. It is much easier to be skeptical about domestic activities that American reporters can scrutinize and to which they can provide alternative views. In addition, people can relate many domestic policies to their own experiences more easily than they can relate most foreign and military policies. When officials' statements do not correspond to people's experiences, they have a built-in basis for skepticism.

Information control is employed to deny information not only to a foreign adversary but also to the American public. In virtually all of the examples involving national security policy, from the U-2 flight over the Soviet Union to the secret bombing of Cambodia, the "enemy" knew the truth. Only the American public was left in the dark.

Information control is an unfortunate and, regrettably, common technique used by presidents. Their goal is to influence public opinion by controlling the information upon which the public bases its evaluations of chief executives and their policies and upon which it determines if there is cause for concern. Although we have no way to measure the impact of these efforts, it is probably safe to say that some are successful and some lead to embarrassment and a loss of credibility for the president and his administration.

## The Use of Symbols

The language used in political discourse may have an influence on public opinion independent of the subject under discussion. One important aspect of political language is the use of symbols, things that are simple or familiar that stand for things complex or unfamiliar. Symbols are frequently used to describe politicians, events, issues, or some other aspect of the political world. Naturally, symbols are not synonyms for what they describe. The choice of symbols inevitably highlights certain aspects of an issue or event and conceals others. Thus, if presidents can persuade a substantial segment of the public to adopt symbols favorable to them, they will be in a position to influence public opinion.

Because of the potential power of symbols in shaping public opinion, presidents have encouraged the public to adopt certain symbols as representative of their administrations. Franklin Roosevelt dubbed his administration the "New Deal," and Harry Truman termed his the "Fair Deal." Each symbol was an oversimplification for new and extremely complex policies, but each served to reassure many Americans that these policies were for their good. Similarly, John Kennedy's "New Frontier" and Lyndon Johnson's "Great Society" served as attractive symbols of their administrations.

Symbols are also used to describe specific policies. President Johnson declared a "War on Poverty" despite the fact that many saw the "war" as more of a skirmish. President Nixon went to considerable efforts to have the public view the January 1973 peace agreement ending the involvement of American troops in Vietnam as "peace with honor," clearly a controversial conclusion. He also claimed his administration represented "law and order," a claim that is especially ironic in light of the Watergate debacle.

Perhaps the most important and effective televised address President Reagan made to the nation in 1981 was his July 27 speech seeking the public's support for his tax-cut bill. In it he went to great lengths to present his plan as "bipartisan." It was crucial that he convince the public that this controversial legislation was supported by members of both parties and was therefore, by implication, fair. Despite the fact that House Democrats voted overwhelmingly against the president's proposal two days later, he described it as "bipartisan" eleven times in the span of a few minutes! No one could miss the point.

As these examples indicate, symbols can be manipulated in attempts not only to lead public opinion but also deliberately to mislead it. During the Watergate controversy Richard Nixon repeatedly referred to his unwillingness to cooperate fully with Congress and the special prosecutor as necessary to protect the office of the presidency (a powerful symbol), not himself as a particular president. This is an argument frequently used by presidents when they oppose legislation that would limit their power.

The White House tries to label opponents as well as policies. President Nixon's chief of staff, H. R. Haldeman, accused critics of Nixon's Vietnam peace plan of being traitors, and the president made no disclaimer. Vice President Agnew classified administration critics as "radical-liberals" and "effete snobs."

The presidency uniquely lends itself to symbolic manipulation. As chief of state the president personifies the government and our nation's heritage. Presidents use this opportunity to enhance their public standing. They are frequently seen on television welcoming heads of state or other dignitaries to the White House, dedicating federal projects, speaking before national groups, or performing ceremonial functions, such as laying a wreath at the Tomb of the Unknown Soldier in Arlington National Cemetery.

Foreign travels provide even greater opportunities for the president to be viewed as the representative of America and as a statesman above partisan politics. Dealing with the leaders of other nations on matters of international importance and being greeted by cheering crowds of Egyptians, Poles, or Italians, the president is a source of pride as the representative of our country, the embodiment of our goals, and the bearer of our goodwill. As we shall see, presidents are aware of this and may schedule activities so they will be covered on prime-time television.

The president also participates in many ceremonial roles dealing with domestic matters. These include having pictures taken with the winner of the national spelling bee, the teacher of the year, or the March of Dimes poster child; lighting the national Christmas tree; and issuing proclamations celebrating national holidays such as Thanksgiving and Veterans Day and lesser-known celebrations such as National Pickle Week.

All of this activity as chief of state, the president hopes, will help foster the view that he is a fitting head of state and competent to run the country and make important and difficult decisions. Presidents want to try to relieve some of the fears and anxieties of the public and provide hope for and confidence in the future. If they are successful in projecting an image of dignity and ability, which may or may not be accurate, they will make it easier for the public to vest its allegiance in them as visible, human sources of authority and to accept decisions it might otherwise oppose.

While engaging in these and other functions, presidents often make appeals to patriotism, traditions, and our history (and its greatness) to move the public to support them, reminding people of their common interests. They also frequently invoke the names of revered leaders of the past, such as Lincoln or Truman, who made difficult decisions on the basis of high principles, and relate themselves or their decisions to these paragons.

Presidents also make gestures to show that they are really "one of the people." President Carter made considerable use of this technique, desiring to be seen as a people's president. At his inauguration he walked (instead of rode) down Pennsylvania Avenue from the Capitol to the White House after taking the oath of office. He conducted a "fireside chat" over national television, seated before a blazing fire and dressed casually in a sweater instead of a suit. He also staged a press conference in which private individuals could call in from around the country and directly ask him questions, and he held many town meetings where he could be questioned directly by local citizens.

Bill Clinton has followed in the same vein, holding a variety of televised town meetings and devoting two hours each week to meeting with average citizens. He undercut his image of a people's president, however, when he held up air traffic at Los Angeles International Airport while he waited for a Hollywood hairstylist to come to Air Force One and give him a $200 haircut.

Despite the considerable efforts presidents make to manipulate symbols, they are not always successful. The Nixon administration tried to find a slogan that captured its essence, including the "New Federalism," the "New American Revolution," the "Generation of Peace," and the "Open Door," but none of these metaphors caught on with the press or the public. Gerald Ford wore a WIN (for "Whip Inflation Now") button to represent his economic priorities during a televised address before a joint session of Congress, but it only became an object of derision.[69]

Many observers feel that a president's failure to lead the public to adopt broad symbols for his administration can cause severe problems in relations with the public. Presidents Carter and Bush both faced substantial criticism for lacking unifying themes and cohesion in their programs and for failing to inspire the public with a sense of purpose, an idea to follow. Instead of providing the country with a sense of their vision and priorities, they emphasized discrete problem solving. President Clinton began his presidency in the same pattern.

On the other hand, Ronald Reagan understood instinctually that his popular support was linked to his ability to embody the values of mythic America. He projected a simple, coherent vision for his presidency that served him well in attracting adherents and in countering criticism when the inevitable contradictions in policy arose. He continually invoked symbols of his vision of America and of its past, an optimistic view that did not thrive on close encounters with reality—but that did sustain public support. For example, he maintained his identification with balanced budgets although he never submitted a budget that was even close to being balanced, and his administration was responsible for more deficit spending than all previous administrations combined.

According to Pat Buchanan, who served as the White House director of communications, "For Ronald Reagan the world of legend and myth is a real world. He visits it regularly and he's a happy man there."[70] In his 1965 autobiography, Reagan described his feelings about leaving the military at the end of World War II: "All I wanted to do . . . was to rest up awhile, make love to my wife, and come up refreshed to a better job in an ideal world."[71] The reader would never know that Reagan never left Hollywood during the war! But perceptions are as important as reality in politics, and many people responded positively to the president's vision of history and his place in it.

### Public Relations

In its efforts to mold public opinion, the White House employs public relations techniques modeled after those of commercial advertising firms. One indicator of the importance of public relations to contemporary presidents is the presence of advertising specialists in the White House. Michael Deaver, one of the three aides forming the "troika" at the top of the White House hierarchy in Ronald Reagan's first term, was a public relations specialist. His role was that of a general adviser with special responsibilities for developing and coordinating public relations.

These responsibilities included orchestrating the president's public appearances and scheduling and coordinating public appearances by other administration officials to help ensure that they publicized the president's policies and had maximum impact and that their public postures were consistent and not distracting.

The use of public relations specialists has become customary. One of President Johnson's closest aides, Jack Valenti, came to the White House from the advertising business and went into the motion picture industry when he left. Richard Nixon carried the hiring of public relations experts even further. His chief of staff, H. R. Haldeman, his press secretary and later close adviser, Ron Ziegler, and several other aides came to the White House from advertising firms. President Carter put Gerald Rafshoon, the advertising director for his 1976 campaign, on the White House staff. Soon after Bill Clinton's election, the Democratic National Committee negotiated contracts with the political and communication consultants who ran the president's campaign, hiring them to sell his legislative program.

Aside from serving as an indicator of the importance presidents place on public relations, the presence of these aides may influence the substance and especially the timing of policy. Being human, all presidents are subject to the temptation to do the most popular thing. For example, an analysis of President Johnson's public statements on Vietnam shows that he varied their content—that is, their "hawkishness"—with the audience he was addressing.[72] The potential for subordinating substance to style is clearly present. This is especially true when presidents hire public relations aides like Michael Deaver, who freely admitted that he had little interest in matters of public policy and argued that "image is sometimes as useful as substance."[73]

There is also the potential for running the White House like an advertising agency. A close observer of the Reagan administration found that one matter permeated staff meetings of top White House officials: how the topic under discussion would play in the media.[74] In addition, since an advertising specialist's orientation is to stress a uniform image, the power of such persons can be a centralizing force in an administration. Emphasis on "team play" inevitably leads to the discouragement of dissent and irregularity because they blunt the impact of the president's image. The parallels between this description and the Nixon White House are especially striking.

SPREADING THE WORD.    The primary goal of White House public relations efforts is to build support for the president and his policies. Part of this job is "getting the word out" about the president, his views, and his accomplishments. Bill Clinton appeared on MTV within six weeks of taking office. Lyndon Johnson constantly sought more publicity and even arranged to have favorable articles placed in the *Congressional Record* with prefatory remarks provided by the White House.

Richard Nixon took a special interest in public relations. His office of communications tried to stimulate books on Nixon, suggested ideas for feature articles about the president and his family, wrote speeches for leading administration officials, attempted to exercise more control over the public relations of the executive branch, held regional press briefings to publicize younger members of the administration, stacked a televised press conference with Nixon supporters, and pressured the Bureau of Labor Statistics to issue announcements of the number of new jobs created in the economy (as the unemployment rate failed to fall). The office also placed representatives of the administration on television shows and lecture platforms and dispersed information to editors, commentators, and reporters and to ethnic, religious, geographic, professional, and other types of groups interested in particular policies.

Reaching the enormous television audience of about 50 million viewers of the evening news is especially important to the White House, and the president's staff builds his schedule around efforts to do so. As President Ford's deputy press secretary put it: "Whenever possible, everything was done to take into account the need for coverage. After all, most of the events are done for coverage. Why else are you doing them?"[75]

Public relations efforts may focus on certain presidential characteristics. Photographs portraying the president as family oriented or a pet owner are common. Reagan White House aides ghost-wrote, under the president's name, a story on keeping physically fit and had it published in a popular Sunday newspaper magazine supplement. The idea was to subtly make the point that Ronald Reagan was not too old for the job. In January 1976 President Ford held a special budget briefing so he could display that he was "competent," a subject over which there had been considerable debate in the press.[76]

Many aspects of public relations were employed in the early days of the Reagan administration. The president focused on his priority item: the economy. Publicity was carefully planned at the time of his first speech urging budgetary reductions. Press briefings were held, and administration officials appeared on all three Sunday interview shows— "Issues and Answers," "Meet the Press," and "Face the Nation"— "Nightline," the "MacNeil-Lehrer Report," and one of the morning news shows. Throughout, the White House paid close attention to the image of the president as well, trying to portray him as busy and engaged in important decision making, not remote and passive.

Presidents and their aides tailor messages they wish to transmit to the public to the needs of the press. According to one former speechwriter for President Reagan,

> You can take a Reagan speech . . . and I can point out to you the four or five sound bites we built in the speech. We wrote them that way. . . . trying to give the lead to the media. . . .[77]

President Carter emphasized short two- or three-minute statements to the White House press over longer addresses because he knew that is all that would be shown on the evening news broadcasts. Similarly, announcements are timed so that reporters can meet their papers' deadlines. Those made too late in the evening will not appear in the next morning's newspapers and those made too late in the afternoon will miss publication in the evening papers.

If the White House wants to decrease the coverage of an event, it can wait until after the evening news programs to announce it. Then it might be buried among the next day's occurrences. It can also pass the word to administration officials to avoid appearing on interview programs or holding press conferences.

The White House tries to avoid associating the president with bad news. Better to let a subordinate serve as the lightning rod. When the United States pulled the marines out of Lebanon, it was announced after President Reagan flew to his California ranch for a vacation and was not available for questions.[78] Other lightning rods for Reagan included James Watt on the environment, David Stockman for budget cuts, and Drew Lewis regarding the strike by air traffic controllers. The highest-priority domestic policy legislation in the president's second term was reform of the federal income tax. It was originally presented as Donald Regan's plan rather than the president's, diverting criticism to the treasury secretary.

President Eisenhower used two of his top officials, White House Chief of Staff Sherman Adams and Secretary of State John Foster Dulles, to deflect criticism that would otherwise be aimed at him. He let his subordinates promulgate and take responsibility for actions that were likely to be unpopular while he accepted the credit for more popular decisions.[79]

Presidents may also try to avoid being caught up in controversies. Presidents Reagan and Bush addressed the annual Washington anti-abortion rally by phone, even though it was held only a short distance from the White House. They wanted to avoid being seen with the leaders of the movement on the evening news. Similarly, President Clinton left a recorded message for those participating in a 1993 gay rights rally in the capital.

Conversely, the White House loves good news, so it tries to distribute it over time so each incident receives full coverage. What the president does *not* want is for bad news to drive out the good. Yet it happens. The first major piece of legislation that President Clinton signed was the popular Family Leave Act. Coverage of the signing ceremony was diluted, however, by media attention focused on Zoe Baird's withdrawal from consideration as attorney general.

MEDIA EVENTS.    In addition to general efforts to publicize the president, the White House often stages "media events" in hope of obtaining additional public support. When President Bush unveiled his proposal for a constitutional amendment to prohibit burning the American flag, he chose to do it at the Iwo Jima Memorial in Arlington National Cemetery. Similarly, he announced his support for renewal of the Clean Air Act in Jackson Hole, Wyoming, with the Grand Tetons as the backdrop.

President Nixon's trip to China in 1972 was a great media event. The White House obtained agreement from the Chinese to allow live television coverage, and the networks sent three large cargo planes of equipment and more than one hundred technicians, producers, and executives to do the job. Of course, the White House was not passive in obtaining media coverage. The president's plane arrived in Peking and returned to Washington during prime time. The latter was accomplished only by sitting on the ground in Anchorage, Alaska, for nine hours! The president was very much aware of the huge viewing audience. In his opening remarks at the first banquet in Peking, he referred to the fact that "more people are seeing and hearing what we say than on any other occasion in the whole history of the world."

President Carter engaged in most of the public relations activities of his predecessors and added a few innovations of his own. In addition to staging a call-in and several town meetings, Carter traveled to New York City to sign the bill authorizing federal aid to the city. The White House signing of the Camp David Accords between Egypt and Israel on prime-time television was a spectacular media event.

No administration was more attentive to the potential of media events than Ronald Reagan's. As Michael Deaver put it, "You get only forty to eighty seconds on a given night on the network news, and unless you can find a visual that explains your message you can't make it stick."[80] Deaver carefully scripted every second of the president's public appearances, right down to placing tape on the floor telling Reagan where to stand for the best camera angles.[81]

Some of the staged events in the Reagan administration were quite spectacular. In the election year of 1984, for example, the president followed Nixon's precedent and toured China. Later that spring, not coincidentally when the Democratic primaries were reaching their climax, Reagan attended an economic summit meeting in Europe. His aides felt the subject matter of the summit was too dry to attract much attention in the public, so they had him engage in a folksy visit to Ireland (the town of Ballyporeen was selected for the presidential visit only after it was checked for visual charm), some stately hobnobbing with Queen Elizabeth (filled with colorful pageantry), and the delivery of an emotional speech at an American cemetery in Normandy commemorating the fortieth anniversary of D-Day. The visuals were superb, and they later appeared in campaign commercials.

At times media events can be used quite cynically. When Reagan was under fire for not supporting civil rights, he paid a visit to a black family that had had a cross burned in its front yard. The White House did not mention that the cross burning had occurred five years earlier. When the president's pollster found that the public overwhelmingly disapproved of the administration's reductions in aid to education, Michael Deaver arranged for Reagan to make a series of speeches emphasizing quality education. As Deaver later gloated, public approval of the president regarding education "flip-flopped" without any change in policy at all.[82]

Sometimes, media events backfire on the White House. George Bush's first nationally televised address featured him displaying a bag of crack cocaine purchased across the street from the White House. The president was embarrassed, however, when the press learned that the administration had lured a drug dealer to Lafayette Park, not known for heavy drug trafficking, in order to buy drugs "across from the White House."

Some of the emphasis on media events is the White House's response to the nature of the media, which we examine in the next chapter. According to Larry Speakes, the White House press spokesman during most of Ronald Reagan's tenure in the White House,

> We knew that television had to have pictures to present its story. . . . So when Reagan was pushing education, the visual was of him sitting at a little desk and talking to a group of students, or with the football team and some cheerleaders, or in a science lab. Then we would have an educators' forum where the president would make a noteworthy statement. We learned very quickly that the rule was no picture, no television piece, no matter how important our news was.[83]

Thus, when housing starts began to increase during the depths of the 1982 recession, Reagan went to Dallas where he visited a subdivision under construction. Pictures of the president talking with carpenters made the story, which was covered much more extensively than if the White House had simply released a statement on improving economic conditions.[84]

## CONCLUSION

Presidents' relations with the public are complex. They need its support in order to play an effective leadership role, yet they have a difficult time obtaining it. Expectations are high and contradictory, and the public's desires are hard to ascertain. Although the public appears to award or withhold its support of the chief executive largely on job-performance grounds, its perceptions of issues and the president's actions may be hazy. Just how the public reaches its conclusions about the president's performance is not well understood. In theory, however, there is ample opportunity for the president, directly and through the press, to influence public perceptions.

Given this environment, presidents are not content to follow public opinion. In their search for public support they invest substantial amounts of time, energy, ingenuity, and personnel in techniques that include direct appeals to the public, use of symbols, information control, and public relations. Some of this activity is quite legitimate, and some is not. Some of it follows Richard Nixon's view that "It's not *what* Presidents do but how they do it that matters."[85]

There is no guarantee of success in these efforts, however, and they often fail to achieve their desired effects. The president, even a "great communicator," is not able to move the public much on his own. The chief executive is not a director who leads the public where it otherwise would not go, reshaping the contours of the political landscape. Instead, presidents are facilitators who reflect and perhaps intensify widely held views and endow their constituencies' views with structure and purpose through their interpretations of them. As President Carter's press secretary, Jody Powell, put it:

> [With] Communications and the management of them, the impact is marginal. The substance of what you do and what happens to you over the long haul is more important, particularly on the big things like the economy. . . . Poor communications comes up after a problem is already there, if an economic program doesn't work, if it is ill-conceived, or if circumstances change... . . . The ability to turn a sow's ear into silk purses is limited. You can make it into a silkier sow's ear, that's all.[86]

Nevertheless, presidents continue to employ these tactics, adding their own wrinkles to those of their predecessors as they seek public support.

## NOTES

1. First debate with Stephen A. Douglas, August 21, 1858, in Roy P. Asler, ed., *The Collected Works of Abraham Lincoln* (New Brunswick, N.J.: Rutgers University Press, 1953), p. 27.

2. Franklin Roosevelt and Theodore Roosevelt, quoted in Emmett John Hughes, "Presidency vs. Jimmy Carter," *Fortune*, December 4, 1978, pp. 62, 64; our italics.

3. See Stanley Feldman and John Zaller, "The Political Culture of Ambivalence: Ideological Responses to the Welfare State," *American Journal of Political Science* 36 (February 1992): 268–307.

4. "U.S. Dependence on Foreign Oil," *Gallup Poll Monthly*, February 1991, p. 35.

5. CBS News/*The New York Times* Poll, June 24, 1986, table 9.

6. Benjamin I. Page and Robert Y. Shapiro, *The Rational Public* (Chicago: University of Chicago Press, 1992); and James A. Stimson, *Public Opinion in America: Moods, Cycles, and Swings* (Boulder, Colo.: Westview, 1991).

7. Advisory Commission on Intergovernmental Relations, *Changing Public Attitudes on Governments and Taxes* (Washington, D.C.: Advisory Commission on Intergovernmental Relations, 1981), pp. 1–4.

8. See Dom Bonafede, "Carter and the Polls—If You Live by Them, You May Die by Them," *National Journal*, August 19, 1978, pp. 1312–13.

9. See, for example, Lawrence R. Jacobs, "The Recoil Effect: Public Opinion and Policymaking in the U.S. and Britain," *Comparative Politics* 24 (January 1992): 199–217.

10. Quoted in John Anthony Maltese, *Spin Control* (Chapel Hill, N.C.: University of North Carolina Press, 1992), p. 3.

11. Interview with Richard Wirthlin, West Point, N.Y., April 19, 1988; Maltese, *Spin Control*, p. 185.

12. Quoted in James A. Barnes, "The Endless Campaign," *National Journal*, February 20, 1993, p. 461.

13. See, for example, Saul Pett, "Interview Draws Rare Portrait of Carter," *New Orleans Times-Picayune*, October 23, 1977, sec. 1, p. 13; Richard M. Nixon, *RN: The Memoirs of Richard Nixon* (New York: Grosset and Dunlap, 1978), pp. 935, 945; and Herbert G. Klein, *Making It Perfectly Clear* (Garden City, N.Y.: Doubleday, 1980), p. 341.

14. Richard M. Nixon, "Addresses to the Nation on the Situation in Southeast Asia," *Public Papers of the President of the United States: Richard Nixon, 1970* (Washington, D.C.: U.S. Government Printing Office, 1971), p. 410.

15. Quoted in Tom Matthews, "The Road to War," *Newsweek*, January 28, 1991, p. 65.

16. Gerald R. Ford, "Imperiled, Not Imperial," *Time*, November 10, 1980, p. 31.

17. See *The Polling Report* 5 (January 30, 1989): 2–4.

18. President Carter, quoted in Godfrey Hodgson, *All Things to All Men: The False Promise of the Modern American Presidency* (New York: Simon and Schuster, 1980), p. 25.

19. "Carter Interview," *Congressional Quarterly Weekly Report*, November 25, 1978, p. 3354.

20. See, for example, Gallup poll, *Attitudes toward the Presidency*, January 1980, p. 21.

21. Interview with Richard Wirthlin, West Point, N.Y., April 19, 1988.

22. George Gallup, Jr. and Frank Newport, "Wary Americans Favor Wait and See Posture in Persian Gulf," *The Gallup Monthly Report*, November 1990, p. 14; Jack Dennis, "Dimensions of Public Support for the Presidency" (paper presented at the Annual Meeting of the Midwest Political Science Association, Chicago, April 1975), tables 4, 8; Hazel Erskine, "The Polls: Presidential Power," *Public Opinion Quarterly* 37 (Fall 1973): 492, 495.

23. George C. Edwards III, *At the Margins* (New Haven, Conn.: Yale University Press, 1989), chap. 6.

24. David O. Sears, "Political Socialization," in Fred I. Greenstein and Nelson Polsby, eds., *Micropolitical Theory*, vol. 2 of *Handbook of Political Science* (Reading, Mass.: Addison-Wesley, 1975), p. 177.

25. See George C. Edwards III, *The Public Presidency* (New York: St. Martin's, 1983), p. 261, n. 13.

26. "Remarks of the President at a Meeting with Non-Washington Editors and Broadcasters," White House Transcript, pp. 11–12.

27. "Institutions: Confidence Even in Difficult Times," *Public Opinion*, June/July 1981, p. 33.

28. Martin P. Wattenberg, "The Reagan Polarization and the Continual Downward Slide in Presidential Candidate Popularity," *American Politics Quarterly* 14 (July 1986): 219–45.

29. *Gallup Opinion Index*, November 1978, pp. 8–9.

30. "Reagan: A Likeable Guy," *Public Opinion*, December/January 1981, p. 24.

31. Philip E. Converse, "The Nature of Belief Systems in Mass Publics," in David Apter, ed., *Ideology and Discontent* (New York: Free Press, 1964), pp. 206–61.

32. Charles W. Ostrom, Jr. and Dennis M. Simon, "The President's Public," *American Journal of Political Science* 32 (November 1988): 1096–1119.

33. Stimson, *Public Opinion in America*, pp. 24–25.

34. David J. Lanoue, *From Camelot to the Teflon President* (New York: Greenwood Press, 1988); Howard S. Bloom and H. Douglas Price, "Voter Response to Short-Run Economic Conditions: The Asymmetric Effect of Prosperity and Recession," *American Political Science Review* 69 (December 1975): 1240–54; Samuel Kernell, "Presidential Popularity and Negative Voting: An Alternative Explanation of the Midterm Congressional Decline of the President's Party," *American Political Science Review* 71 (March 1977): 44–66; Richard R. Lau, "Two Explanations for Negativity Effect in Political Behavior," *American Journal of Political Science* 29 (February 1985): 119–38; Clyde Wilcox and Dee Allsop, "Economic and Foreign Policy as Sources of Reagan Support," *Western Political Quarterly* 44 (December 1991): 941–58. But see Morris P. Fiorina and Kenneth A. Shepsle, "Is Negative Voting an Artifact?" *American Journal of Political Science* 33 (May 1989): 423–39.

35. Lanoue, *From Camelot to the Teflon President*; George C. Edwards III, "Comparing Chief Executives," *Public Opinion*, June/July 1985, p. 54. But see Michael S. Lewis-Beck, *Economics and Elections* (Ann Arbor, Mich.: University of Michigan Press, 1988).

36. Ostrom and Simon, "The President's Public."

37. See, for example, Jon Hurwitz and Mark Peffley, "The Means and Ends of Foreign Policy as Determinants of Presidential Support," *American Journal of Political Science* 31 (May 1987): 236–58.

38. Shanto Iyengar, *Is Anyone Responsible?* (Chicago: University of Chicago Press, 1992), chap. 8; Shanto Iyengar, "Television News and Citizens' Explanations of National Affairs," *American Political Science Review* 81 (September 1987): 815–31.

39. Richard A. Brody and Paul Sniderman, "From Life Space to Polling Place," *British Journal of Political Science* 7 (July 1977): 337–60; Paul Sniderman and Richard A. Brody, "Coping: The Ethic of Self-Reliance," *American Journal of Political Science* 21 (August 1977):

501–22. See also Stanley Feldman, "Economic Self-Interest and Political Behavior," *American Journal of Political Science* 26 (August 1982): 449–52; Kay L. Schlozman and Sidney Verba, *Injury to Insult: Unemployment, Class and Political Response* (Cambridge, Mass.: Harvard University Press, 1979).

40. K. Jill Kiecolt, "Group Consciousness and the Attribution of Blame for National Economic Problems," *American Politics Quarterly* 15 (April 1987): 203–22.

41. Iyengar, *Is Anyone Responsible?* p. 80.

42. Robin Toner, "Poll Finds Postwar Glow Dimmed by the Economy," *New York Times*, p. A11. The poll is a CBS News/*New York Times* poll of March 2–4, 1991.

43. See Edwards, *The Public Presidency*, chap. 6; George C. Edwards III, *Presidential Approval* (Baltimore: Johns Hopkins University Press, 1990); Lee Sigelman and Yung-mei Tsai, "Personal Finances and Voting Behavior: A Reanalysis," *American Politics Quarterly* 9 (October 1981): 371–400; Pamela Johnston Conover, Stanley Feldman, and Kathleen Knight, "Judging Inflation and Unemployment: The Origins of Retrospective Evaluations," *Journal of Politics* 48 (August 1986): 565–88; Pamela Johnston Conover, "The Impact of Group Economic Interests on Political Evaluations," *American Politics Quarterly* 13 (April 1985): 139–66; Stanley Feldman, "Economic Self-Interest and the Vote: Evidence and Meaning," *Political Behavior* 6 (No. 3, 1984): 229–52; M. Stephen Weatherford, "Evaluating Economic Policy: A Contextual Model of the Opinion Formation Process," *Journal of Politics* 45 (November 1983): 866–88; D. Roderick Kiewiet, *Macroeconomics and Micropolitics: The Electoral Effects of Economic Issues* (Berkeley, Calif.: University of California Press, 1983); William Schneider, "Opinion Outlook: A National Referendum on Reaganomics?" *National Journal*, October 9, 1982, p. 1732; M. Stephen Weatherford, "Economic Voting and the 'Symbolic Politics' Argument: A Reinterpretation and Synthesis," *American Political Science Review* 77 (March 1983): 158–74; Jeffrey W. Wides, "Perceived Economic Competency and the Ford/Carter Election," *Public Opinion Quarterly* 43 (Winter 1979): 535–43; Gregory B. Markus, "The Impact of Personal and National Economic Conditions on the Presidential Vote: A Pooled Cross-Sectional Analysis," *American Journal of Political Science* 32 (February 1988): 137–54; John R. Owens, "Economic Influences on Elections to the U.S. Congress," *Legislative Studies Quarterly* 9 (February 1984): 123–50; Lewis-Beck, *Economics and Elections*; Donald R. Kinder, Gordon S. Adams, and Paul W. Gronke, "Economics and Politics in the 1984 American Presidential Election," *American Journal of Political Science* 33 (May 1989): 491–515; Donald R. Kinder and Walter R. Mebane, Jr., "Politics and Economics in Everyday Life," in Kristen Monroe, ed., *The Political Process and Economic Change* (New York: Agathon, 1983), pp. 141–80.

44. See, for example, Michael B. MacKuen, Robert S. Erikson, and James A. Stimson, "Peasants or Bankers? The American Electorate and the U.S. Economy," *American Political Science Review* 86 (September 1992): 597–611; Donald R. Kinder, "Presidents, Prosperity, and Public Opinion," *Public Opinion Quarterly* 45 (Spring 1981): 1–21; Richard Lau and David O. Sears, "Cognitive Links between Economic Grievances and Political Responses," *Political Behavior* 3 (No. 4, 1981): 279–302; Diana C. Mutz, "Mass Media and Depoliticization of Personal Experience," *American Journal of Political Science* 36 (May 1992): 495–96.

45. *Gallup Report*, March 1992, pp. 47–50.

46. John E. Mueller, *War, Presidents, and Public Opinion* (New York: Wiley, 1970), pp. 208–13.

47. See, for example, Market Opinion Research, *Americans Talk Security*, No. 12, January 1989, pp. 31–32, 106.

48. Samuel Kernell, *Going Public*, 2nd ed. (Washington, D.C.: CQ Press, 1992), p. 113.

49. Paul Brace and Barbara Hinckley, "Presidential Activities from Truman through Reagan: Timing and Impact," *Journal of Politics* 55 (May 1993): 387.

50. See Edwards, *At the Margins*, chap. 7, fns. 48–51; Benjamin I. Page and Robert Y. Shapiro, *The Rational Public* (Chicago: University of Chicago Press, 1992); Stimson, *Public Opinion in America*; and William G. Mayer, *The Changing American Mind* (Ann Arbor, Mich.: University of Michigan Press, 1992).

51. Ronald Reagan, *An American Life* (New York: Simon and Schuster, 1990), p. 471. See also p. 479.

52. Eugene J. Rossi, "Mass and Attentive Opinion on Nuclear Weapons Test and Fallout, 1954–1963," *Public Opinion Quarterly* 29 (Summer 1965): 280–97; Robert S. Erikson, Norman R. Luttbeg, and Kent L. Tedin, *American Public Opinion: Its Origins, Content, and Impact*, 2nd ed. (New York: Wiley, 1980), p. 144; Mueller, *War, Presidents, and Public Opinion*, pp. 69–74; CBS News/*The New York Times* Poll, October 28, 1983, p. 2; Page and Shapiro, *The Rational Public*, p. 182; and Barry Sussman, "Reagan's Talk Gains Support for Policies,"

*Washington Post*, October 30, 1983, sec. A, pp. 1, 18. But see Page and Shapiro, *The Rational Public*, pp. 242, 250.

53. Lee Sigelman, "Gauging the Public Response to Presidential Leadership," *Presidential Studies Quarterly* 10 (Summer 1980): 427–33. See also Pamela Johnston Conover and Lee Sigelman, "Presidential Influence and Public Opinion: The Case of the Iranian Hostage Crisis," *Social Science Quarterly* 63 (June 1982): 249–64.

54. "Most Utah Residents Say 'No' to MX Missile Deployment," *Bryan-College Station Eagle*, September 15, 1981, p. 5A.

55. Lee Sigelman and Carol K. Sigelman, "Presidential Leadership of Public Opinion: From 'Benevolent Leader' to Kiss of Death?" *Experimental Study of Politics* 7 (No. 3, 1981): 1–22.

56. Benjamin I. Page and Robert Y. Shapiro, "Presidential Leadership through Public Opinion," in George C. Edwards III et al., eds., *The Presidency and Public Policy Making* (Pittsburgh: University of Pittsburgh Press, 1985), pp. 22–36.

57. See, for example, Joseph A. Califano, Jr., *The Triumph and Tragedy of Lyndon Johnson* (New York: Simon and Schuster, 1991), pp. 173, 340.

58. Fred I. Greenstein, "Eisenhower as an Activist President: A Look at New Evidence," *Political Science Quarterly* 94 (Winter 1979–1980): 588–90.

59. Israel Shenker, "Obfuscation Foes against Ziegler and an Air Attache," *New York Times*, November 28, 1974, sec. 1, p. 35.

60. David Stockman, *The Triumph of Politics* (New York: Harper and Row, 1986), p. 173. See also pp. 132, 353.

61. These expenditures are primarily federal loans to the public for specified investment and assistance projects, federal guarantees of loans made by private issuers, and lending activities of federally sponsored enterprises, such as the Farm Credit Administration, Federal Home Loan Bank system, Student Marketing Association, and the Federal National Mortgage Association. Although they involve billions of dollars of outlays, these funds are not included in the regular budget.

62. For other budgetary distortions, see Tim Muris, "Budget Manipulations," *The American Enterprise* (May/June 1993): 24–28.

63. Joseph C. Goulden, *Truth Is the First Casualty* (Chicago: Rand McNally, 1969), p. 160.

64. Mueller, *War, Presidents, and Public Opinion*, pp. 112–13.

65. For a more complete discussion see Edwards, *The Public Presidency*, pp. 60–64. See also Larry Speakes, *Speaking Out* (New York: Scribner's, 1988), pp. 141, 160–62, 172.

66. Dick Kirschten, "Reagan and Reality," *National Journal*, October 16, 1982, p. 1765.

67. See, for example, CBS News/*The New York Times* Poll, October 30, 1986, table 29.

68. William Schneider, "Opinion Outlook," *National Journal*, November 29, 1986, pp. 2908–09.

69. Mark J. Rozell, *The Press and the Ford Presidency* (Ann Arbor, Mich.: University of Michigan Press, 1992), pp. 10, 65.

70. Steven V. Roberts, "Return to the Land of the Gipper," *The New York Times*, March 9, 1988, p. A28.

71. Ronald Reagan, *Where's the Rest of Me? The Autobiography of Ronald Reagan* (New York: Karz, 1965), p. 138.

72. Lawrence C. Miller and Lee Sigelman, "Is the Audience the Message? A Note on LBJ's Vietnam Statements," *Public Opinion Quarterly* 42 (Spring 1978): 71–80. See also Malcolm Goggin, "The Ideological Content of Presidential Communications," *American Politics Quarterly* 12 (July 1984): 361–84.

73. Michael K. Deaver, *Behind the Scenes* (New York: William Morrow, 1987), p. 73. See also pp. 126–27, 135.

74. Laurence I. Barrett, *Gambling with History* (New York: Penguin, 1983), p. 442.

75. Michael Baruch Grossman and Martha Joynt Kumar, *Portraying the President: The White House and the News Media* (Baltimore: Johns Hopkins University Press, 1981), p. 29.

76. Ibid., p. 234; Rozell, *The Press and the Ford Presidency*, p. 190.

77. Quoted in "Press Secretaries Explore White House News Strategies," *Political Communication Report* 2 (March 1991), p. 4.

78. Lou Cannon, *President Reagan: The Role of a Lifetime* (New York: Simon and Schuster, 1991), p. 453.

79. Fred I Greenstein, *The Hidden-Hand Presidency: Eisenhower as Leader* (New York: Basic Books, 1982), pp. 90–92.

80. Deaver, *Behind the Scenes*, p. 141.
81. See Donald T. Regan, *For the Record* (San Diego: Harcourt Brace Jovanovich, 1988), pp. 247–49.
82. Rich Jaroslovsky, "Manipulating the Media Is a Specialty for the White House's Michael Deaver," *The Wall Street Journal*, January 5, 1984, p. 44.
83. Speakes, *Speaking Out*, p. 220.
84. Quoted in "Press Secretaries Explore White House News Strategies," *APIP Report* 1 (January 1991), pp. 2–3.
85. John Ehrlichman, *Witness to Power: The Nixon Years* (New York: Simon and Schuster, 1982), p. 267.
86. Jody Powell, quoted in Michael Baruch Grossman and Martha Joynt Kumar, "Carter, Reagan, and the Media: Have the Rules Changed or the Poles of the Spectrum of Success?" (paper presented at the Annual Meeting of the American Political Science Association, New York, September 3–6, 1981), p. 18. See also p. 26.

## SELECTED READINGS

Brody, Richard A. *Assessing the President: The Media, Elite Opinion, and Public Support*. Palo Alto, Calif.: Stanford University Press, 1991.

Cronin, Thomas E. "The Presidency and Its Paradoxes." In Thomas E. Cronin and Rexford G. Tugwell, eds., *The Presidency Reappraised*, 2nd ed. New York: Praeger, 1977.

———. "The Presidency Public Relations Script." In Rexford G. Tugwell and Thomas E. Cronin, eds., *The Presidency Reappraised*. New York: Praeger, 1974.

Edwards, George C., III. *Presidential Approval*. Baltimore: Johns Hopkins University Press, 1990.

———. *The Public Presidency*. New York: St. Martin's, 1983.

Graber, Doris, ed. *The President and the Public*. Philadelphia: Institute for the Study of Human Issues, 1982.

Kernell, Samuel. *Going Public*, 2nd ed. Washington, D.C.: Congressional Quarterly, 1992.

Kinder, Donald R. "Presidents, Prosperity, and Public Opinion." *Public Opinion Quarterly* 45 (Spring 1981): 1–21.

Krosnick, Jon A., and Donald R. Kinder, "Altering the Foundations of Support for the President through Priming." *American Political Science Review* 84 (June 1990): 497–512.

Lau, Richard, and David O. Sears. "Cognitive Links between Economic Grievances and Political Responses." *Political Behavior* 3, no. 4 (1981): 279–302.

Miller, Lawrence C., and Lee Sigelman. "Is the Audience the Message? A Note on LBJ's Vietnam Statements." *Public Opinion Quarterly* 42 (Spring 1978): 71–80.

Miroff, Bruce. "The Presidency and the Public: Leadership as Spectacle." In Michael Nelson, ed., *The Presidency and the Political System*. Washington, D.C.: Congressional Quarterly, 1988.

Sigelman, Lee. "Gauging the Public Response to Presidential Leadership." *Presidential Studies Quarterly* 10 (Summer 1980): 427–33.

Sigelman, Lee, and Carol K. Sigelman. "Presidential Leadership of Public Opinion: From 'Benevolent Leader' to Kiss of Death?" *Experimental Study of Politics* 7, no. 3 (1981): 1–22.

Tulis, Jeffrey K. *The Rhetorical Presidency*. Princeton, N.J.: Princeton University Press, 1987.

Wayne, Stephen J. "Great Expectations: What People Want from Presidents." In Thomas E. Cronin, ed., *Rethinking the Presidency*. Boston: Little, Brown, 1982.

# 5

# The President
# and the Media

Despite all their efforts to lead public opinion, presidents do not directly reach the American people on a day-to-day basis. It is the media that provide people with most of what they know about chief executives, their policies, and the consequences of their policies. The media also interpret and analyze presidential activities, even the president's direct appeals to the public.

The media, or press, is the principal intermediary between the president and the public, and relations with the press are an important aspect of the president's efforts to lead public opinion. Presidents who are portrayed in a favorable light will face fewer obstacles in obtaining public support than presidents who are treated harshly by the media.

Because of the importance of the press to the president, the White House goes to great lengths to encourage the media to project a positive image of the president and his policies. These efforts include coordinating the news, holding press conferences, and providing a range of services such as formal briefings, interviews, photo opportunities, background sessions, travel accommodations, and daily handouts.

In addition to the chief executive's efforts to influence the media, there is another side of this relationship we must examine: the content of the news. Ultimately, it is the written and spoken word that concerns the president. Leaks of confidential information and what is seen in the White House as superficial and biased reporting exacerbate the tensions inherent in relations between the president and the press. Presidents commonly view the press as a major obstacle to their obtaining and maintaining public support. Criticism of media coverage as being trivial and distorted and as violating confidences is a standard feature of most administrations. The White House feels that this type of reporting hinders its efforts to develop public appreciation for the president and his policies.

In this chapter we examine the nature and structure of presidential relationships with the press, emphasizing both the context of these relationships and the White House's attempts to obtain favorable coverage through holding press conferences and providing services for the press. We also focus on the substance of the media's coverage of the president, discussing the controversial issues of leaks to the press and superficiality and bias in the news. Finally, we consider the evidence regarding the important but generally overlooked question of the effects of press coverage of the White House on public opinion.

If the president fits the model we have termed director, he will receive favorable press coverage of his administration and reliably use the press to advance his interests. In contrast, a facilitator president will experience a more adversarial relationship, one characterized by more neutral coverage and a constant struggle by the White House to obtain both space and sympathetic treatment in the media.

## THE EVOLUTION OF MEDIA COVERAGE

Today we are accustomed to turning to our newspapers or television sets to learn conveniently about what the president has said or done. Things have not always been this way. Before the Civil War, newspapers were generally small, heavily partisan, and limited in circulation. Between 1860 and 1920 a number of changes occurred that permanently altered the relationship between the president and the press.

Several technological innovations, including the electric printing press, the telegraph, the typewriter, the telephone, Linotype, and woodpulp paper, made it both possible and economical to produce mass-circulation newspapers carrying recent national news. Aside from the sales efforts of the newspapers themselves, the increasing literacy of the population helped to create a market for these papers.

The growing interest in national affairs as a result of the new importance of the national government also helped newspapers. The government began to regulate the economy with the Interstate Commerce Commission and its antitrust efforts. It expanded its role in world affairs during the Spanish-American War and World War I. Both of these events kindled support for and great interest in the activities of the government in Washington. The increased interest in national affairs was also caused by the renewed prominence of the presidency following an era of congressional ascendancy. Theodore Roosevelt took an activist view of the presidency and exploited the new opportunities to reach the public provided by the mass-circulation press. He used the White House as a "bully pulpit" to dramatize himself and the issues in which he was interested. He sought and gained extensive access to the press in order to forge a more personal relationship with the American people.

Ever since the first Roosevelt occupied the White House, news about the president has played an increasingly prominent role in the printed press, both in absolute terms and relative to coverage of Congress or the national government as a whole. Research on the contemporary presidency has found that almost three-fourths of national government news focuses on the president.[1]

Presidents have found that they need the press because it is their primary link to the people. The press, in turn, finds coverage of the president indispensable in satisfying its audience and in reporting on the most significant political events. The advent of radio and television has only heightened these mutual needs.

The history of relations between the president and the press has not involved unlimited goodwill. President George Washington complained that the "calumnies" against his administration were "outrages of common decency" motivated by the desire to destroy confidence in the new government.[2] John Adams was so upset at criticism in the press that he supported the Sedition Act and jailed some opposition journalists under its authority.

Thomas Jefferson, certainly one of our greatest defenders of freedom, became so exasperated with the press as president that he argued that "even the least informed of the people have learned that nothing in a newspaper is to be believed." He also felt that "newspapers, for the most part, present only the caricature of disaffected minds. Indeed, the abuses of freedom of the press have been carried to a length never before known or borne by any civilized nation." These observations, it should be noted, come from the man who earlier had written that "were it left to me to decide whether we should have a government without newspapers or newspapers without a government, I should not hesitate to prefer the latter."[3]

Almost two centuries later things have not changed very much. Although all presidents have supported the abstract right of the press to criticize them freely, most have not found this criticism very comfortable while in office. They have viewed some of the press as misrepresenting (perhaps maliciously) their views and actions, failing to perceive the correctness of their policies, and dedicated to impeding their goals. As the Iran–Contra scandal unfolded, Ronald Reagan complained of the press circling the White House like "sharks."

No matter who is in the White House or who does the reporting, presidents and the press tend to be in conflict. Presidents are inherently policy advocates and want to be able to define a situation and receive favorable coverage. They will naturally assess the press in terms of its aiding or hindering their goals. The press, on the other hand, has the responsibility for presenting reality. While the press may fail in its efforts, it will assess itself on that criterion. Presidents want to control the amount and timing of information about their administrations, while the press wants all the information that exists without delay. As long as their goals are different, presidents and the press are likely to be adversaries.

## RELATIONS BETWEEN THE PRESIDENT AND THE PRESS

### The White House Press Corps

Who are the reporters that regularly cover the White House? The regulars represent diverse media constituencies. These include daily newspapers like the *Washington Post* and *The New York Times*; weekly newsmagazines like *Time* and *Newsweek*; the wire services like the Associated Press (AP) and United Press International (UPI); newspaper chains like Hearst, Scripps-Howard, Newhouse, and Knight-Ridder; the television and radio networks; the foreign press; and "opinion" magazines like the *New Republic* and the *National Review*.

In addition, photographers, columnists, television commentators, and magazine writers are regularly involved in White House–press interactions. More than seventeen hundred persons have White House press credentials. Fortunately, not everyone shows up at once. Fewer than seventy reporters and fifteen photographers regularly cover the White House, and the total of both increases to more than one hundred when an important announcement is expected. Attendance at a presidential press conference may number about three hundred.

The great majority of daily newspapers in America have no Washington correspondents, much less someone assigned to cover the White House. The same can be said for almost all of the country's individual television and radio stations. These papers and stations rely heavily upon the AP and UPI wire services, each of which covers the White House continuously and in detail with several full-time reporters.

### The Presidential Press Operation

The White House's relations with the media occupy a substantial portion of the time of a large number of aides. About one-third of the high-level White House staff is directly involved in media relations and policy of one type or another, and most staff members are involved at some time in influencing the media's portrayal of the president.

The person in the White House who most often deals directly with the press is the president's press secretary. Probably the central function of press secretaries is to serve as conduits of information from the White House to the press. They must be sure that clear statements of administration policies have been prepared on important policy matters. The press secretaries usually conduct the daily press briefings, giving prepared announcements and answering questions. In forming their answers they often do not have specific orders on what to say or not to say. They must be able to think on their feet to ensure that they accurately reflect the president's views. Sometimes these views may be unclear, however, or the president may not wish to articulate his views. Therefore, press secretaries may seem to be evasive or unimaginative in public settings. They also hold private meetings with individual reporters, where the information provided can be more candid and speculative.

To be effective in the conduit role the press secretary must maintain credibility with reporters. Credibility rests on at least two important pillars: (1) truth and (2) access to and respect of the president and senior White House officials. Press secretaries viewed as not telling the truth or (like President Clinton's press secretary, Dee Dee Myers, at the beginning of the administration) as not being close to top decision makers (and therefore not well informed) will not be effective presidential spokespersons because the press will give little credence to what they say. Credibility problems have arisen for several press secretaries as a result of these perceived deficiencies.

Press secretaries also serve as conduits from the press to the president. They must sometimes explain the needs of the press to the president. For example, all of Lyndon Johnson's press secretaries tried to persuade the president to issue advance information on his travel plans to the press. When he refused, they provided it anyway and then had it expunged from the briefing transcript so the president would not see it. Press secretaries also try to inform the White House staff of the press's needs and the rules of the game, and they help reporters gain access to staff members.

Press secretaries typically are not involved in substantive decisions, but they do give the president advice, usually on what information should be released, by whom, in what form, and to what audience. They also advise the president on rehearsals for press conferences and on how to project the proper image and use it to political advantage.

Since the time of William Loeb, Theodore Roosevelt's press secretary, the White House has attempted to coordinate executive branch news. Presidents have assigned aides to clear the appointments of departmental public affairs officials, to keep in touch with the officials to learn what news is forthcoming from the departments, and to meet with them to explain the president's policy views and try to prevent conflicting statements from emanating from the White House and other units of the executive branch. Specialists have had responsibility for coordinating national security news.

Of course, such tactics do not always work. President Ford wanted to announce the results of the *Mayaguez* operation from the White House, but he found to his disappointment that the Pentagon had already done so, making any presidential announcement anticlimactic. At the beginning of his second year in office, President Reagan issued an order that required advance White House approval of television appearances by cabinet members and other top officials, but it soon lapsed.

Coordinating the news from the White House itself has also been a presidential goal. Presidents have sometimes monitored and attempted to limit the press contacts of White House aides, who have annoyed their bosses by using the media for their own purposes. President Reagan, for example, instituted a policy midway through his administration that required his assistant for communications to approve any interview with any White House official requested by a member of the media. All requests were monitored and entered on a computer so the White House could keep tabs on whom reporters wanted to see. Since even the White House press cannot wander through the East or West wings on their own, the only way to speak to aides without administration approval was to call them at home, a practice discouraged by presidential assistants and generally avoided by the media. Such efforts to limit press access are exceptional, however, and have proved to be largely fruitless.

Recent administrations have also made an effort to coordinate publicity functions within the White House, attempting to present the news in the most favorable light, such as preventing two major stories from breaking on the same day, smothering bad news with more positive news, and timing announcements for maximum effect.

All recent presidents, including Eisenhower, who had a reputation to the contrary, have read several newspapers each day, especially *The New York Times* and the *Washington Post*. Kennedy, Johnson, and Reagan were also very attentive to television news programs. Johnson had a television cabinet with three screens so he could watch all three commercial networks at once. But even this was not enough to satisfy his thirst for news. He also had Teletypes that carried the latest reports from the AP and UPI wire services installed in the Oval Office, and he monitored them regularly.

President Nixon rarely watched television news and did not peruse large numbers of newspapers or magazines, but he was extremely interested in press coverage of his administration. He had his staff prepare a daily news summary of newspapers, magazines, television news, and the AP and UPI news wires. Often this summary triggered ideas for the president, who gave orders to aides to follow up on something he read. The news summary also went to White House assistants. Subsequent presidents have continued the news summary, altering it to meet their individual needs, and have circulated it to top officials in their administrations. The Carter White House instituted a separate magazine survey and even a weekly summary of Jewish publications when it became concerned about a possible backlash within the American Jewish community against the administration's Middle East policy.

### Presidential Press Conferences

The best-known direct interaction between the president and the press is the presidential press conference. Presidents Truman through Reagan generally employed a large room (such as the State Department auditorium or the East Room in the White House) for press conferences, usually relying on public address systems. The large number of reporters covering press conferences and the setting in which they take place have inevitably made them more formal than in the days when Franklin D. Roosevelt held forth from his desk in the Oval Office. Transcripts of the press conferences were first made during Eisenhower's tenure, and the conferences were televised live beginning in the Kennedy administration.

Presidents took other steps that contributed to the formalization of press conferences. Beginning with Truman, they underwent formal briefings and "dry runs" in preparation for questions that might be asked. Presidents asked their aides and the departments and agencies to submit possible questions and suggested answers, and sometimes they called for further information. In 1982 President Reagan began holding full-scale mock news conferences.

Guessing at questions is not too difficult. There are obvious areas of concern, and questions raised at White House and departmental briefings and other meetings with reporters provide useful cues. The president can also anticipate the interests of individual reporters and can exercise discretion over whom to recognize. In Reagan's news conferences, reporters were assigned seats, and the president, using a seating chart, called them by name. In one case Reagan called on a reporter only to discover that he was not even attending the conference. The reporter, watching the news conference in his living room at home, asked a question anyway but only his family heard it. The next day the newspapers had a field day reporting the incident.

Presidents since Truman frequently have begun their press conferences with carefully prepared opening statements. Examples include President Kennedy's 1962 blast at the steel companies for raising their prices (eventually leading to the increases being rescinded) and President Carter's five-minute monologue on his administration's accomplishments in a televised press conference during the 1980 presidential election. Lyndon Johnson was especially likely to deliver an opening statement. These statements have given presidents an opportunity to reach the public on their own terms. Opening statements may also reduce the opportunities for questions while at the same time they may focus questions on issues of the president's choosing (contained in the statement).

From the press's perspective, the change in the nature of presidential press conferences from semiprivate to public events diminished their utility in transmitting information from the president to the press. Since every word they say is transmitted verbatim to millions of people, presidents cannot speak as candidly as, say, Franklin D. Roosevelt could. Nor can they speculate freely about their potential actions or evaluations of persons, events, or circumstances. Instead, they must choose their words carefully, and their responses to questions are often not very enlightening. In addition, more reporters have meant more persons with different concerns and thus less likelihood of follow-up questions to cover a subject in depth. Spontaneity in questions and answers has been largely lost.

The White House has seen things differently, however. As President Kennedy's press secretary, Pierre Salinger, put it: "The idea of going to television . . . was to jump over the press and go directly to the people."[4] Thus, the White House has tried to use the press as a prop to speak to the public. In response, the networks have become more reluctant to cover presidential news conferences. Only one network covered President Clinton's first prime-time press conference, and then only for thirty minutes.

Presidents are firmly in control of their press conferences, and they can state that they will not entertain questions on certain topics. They may also evade questions with clever rhetoric or simply answer with a "no comment." Or they can use a question as a vehicle to say something they planned ahead of time. If necessary they can reverse the attack and focus on the questioner, or conversely, they can call on a friendly reporter for a "soft" question. Eisenhower used a skilled evasiveness and impenetrable syntax to avoid direct answers to embarrassing or politically sensitive questions, something not unusual among presidents.

Presidents and their staffs have sometimes found it convenient to plant questions with the press, letting it be known that certain questions will receive interesting answers. In other words, presidents end up asking themselves questions. This practice started at least as early as Franklin Roosevelt, and Eisenhower and Johnson often made use of it.

The frequency of press conferences has varied. Franklin Roosevelt held about seven a month; Truman cut this figure in half. Eisenhower further reduced their frequency, holding about two press conferences each month, a rate maintained by Kennedy and Johnson. Carter and Ford averaged closer to one press conference per month, while Nixon and Reagan held only about one press conference every two months. Naturally, the more time that has elapsed between press conferences, the more events and governmental actions that will have transpired since the last press conference. The more that has transpired, the more wide-ranging the questions are likely to be. And the more wide-ranging the questions, the more superficial the coverage of any one topic is likely to be.

Figures on the frequency of press conferences should not be accepted at face value, however. What presidents count as press conferences varies considerably, and the figures for average frequency of press conferences may conceal wide fluctuations in the time between conferences. The trend is clearly in the direction of fewer formal press conferences, however, especially for chief executives who do not perform well in unstructured settings.

In a break with precedent, President Bush virtually abandoned formal, prime-time press conferences, preferring frequent brief, informal morning sessions with reporters, often called on short notice. It was difficult for the commercial networks to provide live broadcasts without costly interruptions of scheduled programs, and many reporters were absent. Oddly, in an age of television, Bush's format was aimed at newspapers.

Bush made little connection between his public relations and his policy initiatives. He held more press conferences in a year than Ronald Reagan did in eight years and met frequently with reporters in informal ways as well. Yet he used these sessions to respond to journalists' inquiries rather than as part of an effort to advance his own policies. He talked to the press, not over it.

Bill Clinton took office with an antagonistic attitude toward the national media and planned to bypass it rather than use it as part of his political strategy. He waited two months before holding his first formal news conference and five months before he held one in prime-time viewing hours. After a rocky start in his press relations, the president hired David Gergen, who had been a communications adviser in Republican administrations, as a top aide and made himself somewhat more accessible to the national press.

No matter what the format, many of the questions asked of the president involve trivial topics. One reason for this is deference to the president. Reporters meet the president on his territory, not theirs, and dutifully rise when he enters the room. An adversarial relationship may exist outside the press conference, but it is rarely reflected during the sessions themselves. The author of a study of press conferences found only two occasions in fifteen years when the number of hostile questions asked by reporters at any press conference exceeded three.[5]

The artificial nature of press conferences, especially on television, may lead to distortions. On the one hand, a truly spontaneous answer to a question may be candid, but it also may be foolish or expose the president's ignorance of an area. Generalizations based on such a reply may be inaccurate because the president may actually be well informed but require more than a few seconds to think about a complex problem. On the other hand, some presidents may be glib, charming, and attractive, and therefore perform well in a spontaneous press conference but really not be very competent. The advent of television has further increased the potential for distortion, since a president's physical attractiveness, delivery, and flair for the dramatic may leave more of an impression on the public mind than the substance of his answers.

### Services for the Press

In order to get their messages across to the American people and to influence the tone and content of press presentation of those messages, presidents have provided services for the press. One of the most important is the backgrounder. The president's comments to reporters may be "on the record" (remarks may be attributed to the speaker); "on background" (a specific source cannot be identified but the source's position and status can, such as a "White House source"); "deep background" (no attribution); or "off the record" (the information reporters receive may not be used in a story). For purposes of convenience we shall term all sessions between White House officials (including the president) and the press that are not "on the record" as "backgrounders." All recent presidents, especially Johnson and Ford, have engaged in background discussion with reporters, although President Nixon's involvement was rare. Some presidents, especially Eisenhower and Nixon, have relied heavily upon their principal foreign policy advisers to brief reporters on foreign affairs.

The most common type of presidential discussion with reporters on a background basis is a briefing. In these sessions the president typically explains a policy's development and what it is expected to accomplish. Interestingly, the president does not appear to stress the substance of policy and seldom makes "hard" news statements in background briefings because this would irritate absent members of the press. The reporters watch the president perform, and since the president controls the conditions of these briefings, the chances of making a favorable impression are good.

Reporters tend to view middle-level aides as the best information sources. They have in-depth knowledge about the substance of programs, and they are generally free from the constraints of high visibility, so they are in a good position to provide useful backgrounders. Backgrounders are particularly important for these officials because presidents are generally intolerant of staff members who seek publicity for themselves, and most interviews with White House staff are on this basis. Sometimes aides say more than their superiors would like in order to prod the president in a particular policy direction.

Backgrounders have a number of advantages for the White House. Avoiding direct quotation allows officials to speak on sensitive foreign policy and domestic policy matters candidly and in depth, something domestic politics and international diplomacy would not tolerate if speakers were held directly accountable for their words. The White House hopes such discussions will help it communicate its point of view more clearly and serve to educate journalists, perhaps preparing them for future policies, and make them more sympathetic to the president's position in their reporting. An impressive performance in a background session can show the White House to be competent and perhaps elicit the benefit of the doubt in future stories. Moreover, background sessions can be used to scotch rumors and limit undesirable speculation about presidential plans and internal White House affairs.

On the other hand, backgrounders may be aimed at the public (in the form of trial balloons that the White House can disclaim if they meet with disapproval) or at policymakers in Washington. They may also be directed at other countries. To discourage the Soviet Union's support of India in its war with Pakistan, Henry Kissinger told reporters in a backgrounder that the Soviet policy might lead to the cancellation of President Nixon's trip to Moscow. Since the statement was not officially attributed to Kissinger, it constituted less of a public threat to the Soviet Union, while at the same time it communicated the president's message.[6]

Reporters have generally been happy to go along with protecting the identities of "spokespersons" and "sources" (although an experienced observer can identify most of them) because the system provides them more information than they would have without it. This increase of information available to reporters adds to the information available to the public, and it probably helps advance journalistic careers as well.

Backgrounders, of course, have also provided the White House opportunities to disseminate misleading or self-serving propaganda anonymously. Sometimes such propaganda concerns intramural warfare, an especially common theme in the Ford administration but also appearing in the Nixon and other administrations.

In addition to the more informal sessions, briefings are held each weekday for the White House press. In the daily briefings reporters are provided with information about appointments and resignations, decisions of the president to sign or not to sign routine bills and explanations for these actions, and the president's schedule (appointments, meetings, future travel plans, and availability to the press). More significantly from the standpoint of the press, the briefing provides presidential reactions to events, the White House "line" on issues and whether it has changed, and a reading of the president's moods and ideas. This information is obtained through prepared statements or answers to reporters' queries. Responses to the latter are often prepared ahead of time by the White House staff. The daily briefings, of course, also provide the press with an opportunity to have the president's views placed on the public record, which eases the burdens of reporting.

Usually the president's press secretary or his or her deputy presides over these briefings, although sometimes the president participates. White House staff members and executive branch officials with substantial expertise in specific policy areas such as the budget or foreign affairs sometimes brief the press and answer questions at the daily briefing or at special briefings, especially when the White House is launching a major publicity campaign.

Interviews with the president and top White House staff members are a valuable commodity to the press, and sometimes the White House uses them for its purposes. President Nixon traded an exclusive interview to Hugh Sidey of *Time* for a cover story on him. In order to obtain an interview with President Ford, even the venerable Walter Cronkite agreed to use only questions the president could handle easily. At other times the White House may give exclusives to a paper like *The New York Times* in return for getting a story in which it is interested a prominent place in the paper.[7]

Providing the press exclusive information may be as ingratiating as an exclusive interview and may be used to distract reporters from more embarrassing stories. At other times the White House may trade advance notice of a story for information reporters possess about developments elsewhere in the government that are not clear to the president and his staff.

Recent presidents, with the exception of Richard Nixon, have regularly cultivated elite reporters and columnists, the editors and publishers of leading newspapers, and network news producers and executives with small favors, social flattery, and small background dinners at the White House. (Nixon turned these chores over to top aides.) President Clinton had the television network anchors to lunch at the White House before delivering his first prime-time address to the nation. The first call ABC anchorperson Peter Jennings received after winning his job was from Ronald Reagan.[8] Since the 1960s the White House has had first a designated person and then an office for media liaison to deal directly with the representatives of news organizations, such as editors, publishers, and producers, in addition to the press office that deals with reporters' routine needs.

There are many additional services that the White House provides for the press. It gives reporters transcripts of briefings and presidential speeches and daily handouts announcing myriad information about the president and his policies, including advance notice of travel plans and upcoming stories. Major announcements are timed to accommodate the deadlines of newspapers, magazines, and television networks.

Photographers covering the president are highly dependent on the White House press office, which provides facilities for photographers on presidential trips and arranges photo opportunities, making sure they will produce the most flattering shots of the president (such as Johnson's left profile). President Reagan even prohibited impromptu questions from reporters at photographing sessions. Moreover, the official White House photographers provide many of the photographs of the president that the media use. Naturally, these are screened so that the president is presented favorably.

When the president goes on trips, at home or abroad, extensive preparations are made for the press. These preparations include arranging transportation and lodging for the press, installing equipment for radio and television broadcasting, obtaining telephones for reporters, erecting platforms for photographers, preparing a detailed account of where and with whom the president will be at particular times, providing elaborate information about the countries the president is visiting, forming pools of press members to cover the president closely (as in a motorcade), and scheduling the press plane to arrive early so the press can cover the president's arrival.

As many of these services suggest, the press is especially dependent upon the White House staff in covering presidential trips, particularly foreign trips. The number of sources of information is generally reduced, as is the access of the press to the principal figures it wishes to cover. Thus the president's aides are in a good position to manipulate press coverage to their advantage. Coverage of foreign trips is generally favorable, although less so than in the past now that reporters with expertise in foreign affairs accompany the president, and the press points out the relationship of the trip and its goals and accomplishments to the president's domestic political problems. (It is interesting that foreign travel does not seem to increase the president's approval ratings.)[9]

Even in Washington, however, reporters are very much in a controlled environment. Reagan aides went so far as to have the motor of the president's helicopter revved so he could not hear questions shouted by the press as he left for a weekend at Camp David. Similarly, the president held no press conferences at all during the 1984 presidential campaign.

Reporters may not freely roam the halls of the White House, interviewing whomever they please. In one of its first acts, the Clinton White House even barred reporters from the area behind the press room, where the offices of the press secretary and communications director are located (this policy was changed after a few months). Reporters are highly dependent upon the press officer for access to officials, and about half their interviews are with the press secretary and his or her staff. Much of their time is spent waiting for something to happen or watching the president at formal or ceremonial events. Since most news stories about such occurrences show the president in a favorable light, the press office does everything possible to help reporters record these activities. Similarly, the White House is happy to provide photographs featuring the president's "warm," "human," or "family" side. These please editors and the public alike.

Briefings, press releases, and the like can be used to divert the media's attention from embarrassing matters. The Reagan White House adopted a strategy of blitzing the media with information to divert its attention after the press raised questions about the president's sleeping through Libyan attacks on United States forces off the coast of Africa.[10] To avoid publicity about illegal transfers of arms to Nicaragua, the Reagan White House spearheaded a drive for an "Economic Bill of Rights."[11]

More frequently, the White House, by adopting an active approach to the press, gains an opportunity to shape the media's agenda for the day. Through announcements and press releases it attempts to focus attention on what will reflect positively on the president. Such information frequently generates questions from reporters and subsequent news stories. Representatives of the smaller papers, who have few resources, are more heavily dependent upon White House-provided news than are the larger news bureaus, including the major networks. They are the most likely to follow the White House's agenda. Moreover, since White House reporters, especially the wire services, are under pressure to file daily "hard news" reports, the White House is in a strong position to help by providing information, much of it trivial and all of it designed to reflect positively on the president. As a Ford official put it: "You can predict what the press is going to do with a story. It is almost by formula. Because of this they are usable."[12]

Many observers, including journalists, feel that the press tends to parrot the White House line, so conveniently provided at a briefing or in a press release, especially early in a president's term. The pressure among journalists to be first with a story increases the potential for White House manipulation inherent in this deferential approach, as concerns for accuracy give way to career interests.

Presidents have undoubtedly hoped that the handouts, briefings, and other services they and their staffs provide for reporters will gain them some goodwill. They may also hope that these services will keep the White House press from digging too deeply into presidential affairs. In addition, they want to keep reporters interested in the president's agenda because bored journalists are more negative in their reporting and may base their stories on trivial incidents like the president's stumbling on a plane.

In addition, the White House controls a commodity of considerable value to the press: information on the president's personal life. Most reporters are under pressure to provide stories on the minutiae of the president's life, no matter what he does. Some White House aides have found that the provision of such information can co-opt journalists or sidetrack them from producing critical stories. Some reporters will exploit the opportunity to please their editors instead of digging into more significant subjects; others reciprocate their favorable treatment by the White House with positive stories about the president.

Seeing yet another opportunity to influence the press, the White House has provided services for the local as well as the national and Washington-based media. Relations with the local media took a significant step forward in the Nixon administration. In an effort to bypass the more liberal national press and to develop goodwill, President Nixon held briefings for local news executives or had senior administration officials give them. He also sent administration briefing teams around the country to discuss his legislative proposals with local media representatives. The local press, they found, was very responsive to this attention, often giving the president substantial publicity and using the White House story ideas and sometimes even the background materials it provided. Special mailings of news releases and documents to newspapers, television and radio stations, journal writers, citizens groups, and private individuals were also made.

Subsequent presidents learned that dealing directly with the nonnational press was very useful in obtaining coverage of the president's message in the local and specialty media. Once the Washington press reports an issue, it tends to drop it and move on to the next one, yet repetition is necessary to convey the president's views to the generally inattentive public. Moreover, the Washington press tends to place more emphasis on the support of or opposition to a program than on its substance, although the White House wants to communicate the latter.

The Nixon administration's efforts at dealing with the local press were continued and expanded. Gerald Ford invited local news announcers to the White House for taped personal interviews to be used exclusively in their home stations. He also held press conferences for reporters from the local press. Every other week President Carter had local newspapers and broadcast journalists come to Washington to meet him and be briefed by administration officials. The information provided in these meetings was not released to the general press for twenty-four hours so that the out-of-town journalists could file their exclusive stories. At the end of 1978 the White House began to provide thirty- and forty-second taped radio spots free of charge to radio stations that called a toll-free White House number. All White House press releases and texts are now available by computer to anyone subscribing to the service. President Clinton meets frequently with journalists representing local media.

Recent presidents have arranged to be interviewed from the White House by television and radio stations through satellite hookups. This allows the White House to tailor unedited messages for specific groups and reach directly into the constituencies of members of Congress.

Presidents who engage in servicing (and lobbying) the local media undoubtedly hope that they will receive a sympathetic hearing from journalists grateful to be invited to the White House and perhaps susceptible to presidential charm. They also hope that by providing information directly to the local media they can evade the closer scrutiny of the Washington- and New York-based national media, with its greater resources to challenge White House versions of events and policies and to investigate areas of government not covered by briefings or press releases. Naturally, they hope they can create some goodwill that will be reflected in news stories on the local level.

## PRESS COVERAGE OF THE PRESIDENT

### Leaks

In early 1982 President Reagan read the riot act to his cabinet, denouncing the release of confidential information to the press by anonymous sources as one of the major problems facing his administration. He was particularly concerned about leaks regarding his upcoming budget proposals for defense spending, a number of foreign policy matters, and the urban enterprise zones proposal that he wanted to save for his State of the Union message.[13] The president's frustration is evident in the quip with which he opened a press conference held at about the same time: "I was going to have an opening statement, but I decided that what I was going to say I wanted to get a lot of attention so I'm going to wait and leak it."

Ronald Reagan was hardly the first president to be upset by leaks. Sometimes they can be potentially quite serious, as when the U.S. negotiating strategy of the first SALT talks was disclosed during the Nixon administration. When the Pentagon Papers were leaked to the public, President Nixon felt that there was a danger that other countries would lose confidence in our ability to keep secrets and that information on the delicate negotiations then in progress with China might also be leaked, endangering the possibility of rapprochement.[14] At other times they are just embarrassing, as when internal dissent in the administration is revealed to the public. President Johnson feared leaks would signal what he was thinking, and he would lose his freedom of action as a result.

Who leaks information? The best answer is "everybody." Presidents themselves do so, sometimes inadvertently. As Lyndon Johnson once put it: "I have enough trouble with myself. I ought not to have to put up with everybody else too."[15] Top presidential aides may also reveal more than they intend. When a leak regarding President Reagan's willingness to compromise on his 1981 tax bill appeared in *The New York Times*, White House aides tracked down the source of the story and found it was budget director David Stockman.[16] A year earlier a leak revealing secret CIA arms shipments to Afghan rebels was attributed to the office of the president's chief national security adviser.[17] Lt. Col. Oliver North charged that members of Congress had leaked the fact that the United States had intercepted Libyan radio messages, which in turn enabled it to capture the hijackers of the *Achille Lauro* cruise liner. But *Newsweek* magazine reported that the source of the leak was none other than Oliver North himself.

Most leaks, however, are deliberately planted. As one close presidential aide put it, "99 percent of all significant secrets are spilled by the principals or at their direction."[18] Presidents are included in those who purposefully leak. *Newsweek* used to hold space open for the items John Kennedy would phone to his friend Benjamin Bradlee right before the magazine's deadline.[19]

There are many reasons for leaks. They may be used as trial balloons to test public or congressional reaction to ideas and proposals or to stimulate public concern about an issue. Both the Ford and Carter White House used this technique to test reaction to a tax surcharge on gasoline. When the reaction to these proposals turned out to be negative, they denied ever contemplating such a policy. President Clinton's task force on health care reform engaged in a series of leaks regarding a wide range of health policy options. At other times information is leaked to reporters who will use it to write favorable articles on a policy.

Diplomacy is an area in which delicate communications play an important role. Leaks are often used to send signals to other nations of our friendship, anger, or willingness to compromise. For example, during negotiations with the Japanese regarding restricting imports, the Reagan administration leaked a story that the talks were going badly to pressure Japan into moderating its position. At the same time leaks provide the president with the opportunity to disavow publicly or to reinterpret what some might view as, for example, an overly "tough" stance or an unexpected change in policy.

Leaks may also be used to influence personnel matters. The release of information letting a stubborn official know that the official's superiors wish him or her to leave may force a resignation and thus save the problem of firing the official, or, conversely, make the official's position a public issue, increasing the costs of such a firing. Similarly, the release of information on an appointment before it is made places presidents in an awkward position and can help ensure that they follow through on it or prematurely deny they have such plans.

Some leaks are designed to force the president's hand on policy decisions. During the Indian–Pakistani War, President Nixon maintained a publicly neutral stance but was really favoring Pakistan. When this was leaked there was inevitably pressure to be neutral in action as well as in rhetoric. Conversely, in the case of Lyndon Johnson, a leak that he was thinking about a decision could ensure that he would take no such action.

Leaks may serve a number of other functions for individuals. They may make one feel important or help one gain favor with reporters. Leaks may also be used to criticize and intimidate personal or political adversaries in the White House itself or protect and enhance reputations. In the Ford administration, White House counsel Robert Hartmann and the chief of staff Richard Cheney often attacked each other anonymously in the press. Several members of the White House staff attacked Press Secretary Ron Nessen in an effort to persuade the president to replace him. When negotiations with North Vietnam broke down in late 1972, White House aides employed leaks to dissociate the president from his national security adviser.

Presidents sometimes leak information for their own political purposes. Lyndon Johnson leaked information on nuclear weapons to answer Barry Goldwater in the 1964 presidential election. A Nixon aide leaked a false story to *The Wall Street Journal* that the president was considering seeking legislation to reduce the independence of the Federal Reserve Board and that the board's chairman, Arthur Burns, was a hypocrite because he sought a personal salary increase while he was

" I HAD TO SWITCH YOUR LIE DETECTOR TEST THIS AFTERNOON FROM 3 TO 1 BECAUSE YOU'RE SCHEDULED TO LEAK SOME INFORMATION AT 2 ! "

Cartoon by Wayne Stayskal (1983). From *Chicago Tribune*. Reprinted by permission: Tribune Media Services.

asking the rest of the country to dampen its demands. The UPI received a somewhat similar story. These leaks were attempts to make Burns more responsive to White House demands. The Nixon White House often employed leaks as a political tactic.

The Reagan White House was able to influence the first reports on the study done on the deaths of 241 marines in Beirut in 1983. By leaking the findings about lax security measures, presidential aides were able to focus press attention on security lapses rather than the criticism of the ill-defined nature of the marines' mission in Lebanon.[20]

In all of these cases government officials were using the press for their purposes and not vice versa. Although reporters may well be aware of being used, the competitive pressure of the news business makes it difficult for them to pass up an exclusive story. Nevertheless, most good reporting, even investigative reporting, does not rely heavily upon leaks. Instead, reporters put together stories by bits and pieces.

It is generally fruitless to try to discover the source of a leak. The Reagan administration tried everything from lie detector tests to logging every journalist's interview on a computer, but nothing stopped the leaks. According to White House Chief of Staff Donald Regan, "In the Reagan Administration the leak was raised to the status of an art form. Everything, or nearly everything, the President and his close associates did or knew appeared in the newspapers and on the networks with the least possible delay."[21]

## Superficiality

Early in this century Woodrow Wilson complained that most reporters were "interested in the personal and trivial rather than in principles of policies."[22] Things have not changed much in the ensuing generations. In a background briefing in 1979 President Carter complained to reporters: "I would really like for you all as people who relay Washington events to the world to take a look at the substantive questions I have to face as a president and quit dealing almost exclusively with personalities."[23] In this section we examine the question of the superficiality of the coverage of the presidency and the reasons for it.

Today media coverage of national news is characterized by brevity and simplicity. Editors do not want to bore or confuse their viewers, listeners, or readers. They often resort to the use of themes ("another example of rivalries within the White House"), symbols (a supermarket checkout line may represent inflation), and personification (an unemployed mother of five) to simplify issues. Moreover, most reporting is about events, actions taken or words spoken by public figures, especially if the events are dramatic and colorful, such as ceremonies and parades. Conflicts between clearly identifiable antagonists (the president versus the Speaker of the House) is highly prized, particularly if there is something tangible at stake, such as the passage of a bill.

The amount of information transmitted under such conditions is limited. This type of news coverage is ill-equipped to deal with the ambiguities and uncertainties of most complex events and issues. Moreover, it provides little in the way of the background and contextual information that is essential for understanding political events. Although the electronic media, especially television, are the most typical source of news for Americans, they do the poorest job of providing information to the public. According to CBS anchorman Dan Rather, "You simply cannot be a well-informed citizen by just watching the news on television."[24]

Human interest stories, especially those about presidents and their families, are novel and easier for the public to relate to than are complex matters of public policy. They are always in high demand. Nancy Reagan's new White House china received more attention in the press than most issues. Socks, the Clinton's cat, became an overnight celebrity following the 1992 presidential elections. Scandals involving public persons of all kinds receive high-priority coverage. Disasters and incidents of violence make for excellent film presentations, are novel, contain ample action, and are portrayed in easily understood terms. The intricacies of a presidential tax proposal are not so fortunate.

Studies show that coverage of presidential election campaigns is often superficial, especially on television. Coverage of issues is spotty. The stands candidates take on issues are usually old news to reporters, who must suffer through hearing the same speech, with slight varia-

**Even the president's cat becomes the object of media attention.**
Copyright © 1992 Agence France-Presse Photo. Reproduced with permission.

tions added for local audience appeal, again and again. The candidates' stands are not viewed as news. In general, substantive issues are reported in terms of their impact on politics rather than in terms of their merits.[25]

Clear-cut differences on issues between candidates have the potential for confrontation, even if the drama results from skillful tape editing, and these differences are emphasized within the space allotted to coverage. Such issues are not typical, however. Media coverage does not reflect the blend of issues advocated by the candidates. Moreover, the press generally ignores issues that the candidates neglect, even though they may be significant to the typical citizen. What does receive extensive coverage, as we saw in Chapter 3, is the "horse race"—the campaign as opposed to what the campaign is ostensibly about. Stories feature conflict, make brief points, are easily understood (often in either/or terms), and, especially on television, have film value.

Superficial news coverage is not limited to elections. Most of the White House press activity comes under the heading of the "body watch." In other words, reporters focus on the most visible layer of the president's personal and official activities and provide the public with a step-by-step account. They are interested in what the president is going to do, how his actions will affect others, how he views policies and individuals, how he presents himself, and whose stars are rising and falling, rather than in the substance of policies or the fundamental processes operating in the executive branch.

Editors expect this type of coverage, and reporters do not want to risk missing a story. As the Washington bureau chief of *Newsweek* said: "The worst thing in the world that could happen to you is for the President of the United States to choke on a piece of meat, and for you not to be there."[26] When President Bush vomited at a state dinner in Japan, television networks had a field day, running the tape of the president's illness again and again.

Journalists are not allowed at Camp David with one exception. About twenty minutes before the president's helicopter lands, two reporters are allowed to sit in something akin to a duck blind about 150 yards from where the helicopter lands and observe the landing. They leave immediately after, without ever speaking to the president. Why do they bother? They are there for the "death watch"—to be on hand in case the president's helicopter crashes.

The emphasis of news coverage is on short-run, "instant history." Perspective on the events of the day is secondary. Thus, embarrassing items such as blunders and contradictions made by presidents and their staff are widely reported, especially if the president is low in the polls (providing a consistent theme). Similarly, major presidential addresses are often reported in terms of how the president looked and spoke, as well as the number of times the speech was interrupted by applause as much as in terms of what was said.

Presidential slips of the tongue or behavior are often blown out of all proportion. In the second debate between Gerald Ford and Jimmy Carter during the 1976 presidential campaign, Ford made a slip and said that Eastern Europe was "free from Soviet domination." Everyone, including the president, knew that he had misspoken. Unfortunately for Ford, he refused to admit his error for several days while the press had a field day speculating about his basic understanding of world politics. Similarly, when Richard Nixon described the persons "blowing up the campuses" as "bums," the press extended the adjective to all students, something the president had not meant. The uproar following this "news" can well be imagined.

In its constant search for "news," the press, especially the electronic media, is reluctant to devote repeated attention to an issue, although this might be necessary to explain it adequately to the public. As a deputy press secretary in the Carter administration said: "We have to keep sending out our message if we expect people to understand. The Washington Press corps will explain a policy once and then it will feature the politics of the issue."[27] This is one incentive for the president to meet with the non-Washington press.

One of the causes of superficial press coverage of the presidency is the demands of news organizations for information that is new and different, personal and intimate, revealing and unexpected. According to the White House correspondent for a major newspaper chain: "It's a lot easier for me to get [my stories] into several newspapers in the chain with a story about Amy [President Carter's daughter] than with a story about an important policy decision."[28] ABC White House correspondent Sam Donaldson commented, in much the same vein, "A clip of a convalescent Reagan waving from his window at some circus elephants is going to push an analytical piece about tax cuts off the air every time."[29]

Given the emphasis on the short run and the demand for details of the president's activities, reporters face continual deadlines. There is little time for reflection, analysis, or comprehensive coverage.

A related factor contributing to the trivialization of the news is the great deal of money and personnel needed to cover presidents, including following them around the globe on official business and on vacations. Because of this investment and because of the public's interest in the president, reporters must come up with something every day. Newsworthy happenings do not necessarily occur every day, however, so reporters either emphasize the trivial or blow events out of proportion. While covering a meeting of Western leaders on the island of Guadeloupe, Sam Donaldson faced the prospect of having nothing to report on a slow news day. Undaunted, he reported on the roasting of the pig the leaders would be eating that evening, including "an exclusive look at the oven in which the pig would be roasted."[30] Similarly, the White House press often focuses on the exact wording of an announcement in an effort to detect a change in policy. Frequently it finds significance where none really exists.

There are more than organizational imperatives at work in influencing coverage of the president, however. Reporters' backgrounds and personal interests also underlie the trivialization of the news. They are often ill at ease with abstractions, and when they talk to each other about politics, they emphasize the superficial aspects—who will be elected, what bills will pass, what personalities the principal actors have, who has power.

The typical White House reporter lacks special background on the presidency. Moreover, the White House press frequently lacks policy expertise relevant to understanding the issues with which the president deals. Thus, its focus on politics and personalities rather than on issues is not surprising.

To delve more deeply into the presidency and policy requires not only substantial expertise but also certain technical skills. Washington reporters in general and White House reporters in particular do little documentary research. They are trained to do interviews and transmit handouts from press secretaries and public information officials rather than to conduct research. Moreover, in-depth research requires a slower pace and advance planning, and journalists tend to be comfortable with neither.

Sometimes several factors influence coverage of the presidency at the same time. Despite the glamour attached to investigative reporting following the Watergate scandal, not much of it takes place. Most reporters are unwilling or unable to take the time necessary for investigative work and the coordination required with other reporters and news bureau staff to cover all leads successfully. The ethic of journalism is to go it alone, and the incentives are generally to get news out fast. Similarly, the slowness of the process of using the Freedom of Information Act to force the release of documents inhibits its use. A final hindrance to investigative reporting is the reluctance of many editors to publish analyses sharply divergent from the president's position without some confirmation from what they consider to be an authoritative source who would be willing to go on the record in opposition to the president.

Not only does the press provide superficial coverage of the stories it reports, but many important stories about the presidency are missed altogether because of the emphasis of the media. Implementation of policy, the predominant activity of the executive branch, is very poorly covered because it is not fast-breaking news; it takes place mostly in the field, away from the reporters' natural territory, and it requires documentary analysis and interaction with civil servants who are neither famous nor experts at public relations. Similarly, the White House press misses most of the flow of information and options to the president from the rest of the executive branch.

### Bias

Bias is the most politically charged issue in press relations with the president. Bias is also an elusive concept with many dimensions. Although we typically envision bias as news coverage favoring identifiable persons, parties, or points of view, there are more subtle and more pervasive forms of bias that are not motivated by the goal of furthering careers or policies.

Many studies covering topics such as presidential election campaigns, the Vietnam War, and local news conclude that the news media are not biased *systematically* toward a particular person, party, or ideology, as measured in the amount or favorability of coverage. The bias found in such studies is inconsistent; the news is typically characterized by neutrality.[31] After six years as President Reagan's press secretary, Larry Speakes concluded that the news media had generally given the administration "a fair shake" and that "they probably gave us a longer honeymoon than we deserved."[32]

Some people may equate objectivity with passivity and feel that the press should do no more than report what others present to it. This simple passing on of news is what occurs much of the time, and it is a fundamental reason for the superficiality of news coverage. Sometimes, however, reporters may feel the necessity of setting the story in a meaningful context. The construction of such a context may entail reporting what was *not* said as well as what was said; what had occurred before; and what political implications may be involved in a statement, policy, or event. If the press is passive, it can be more easily manipulated, even representing fiction as fact.

This discussion of the general neutrality of news coverage in the mass media pertains most directly to television, newspaper, and radio reporting. Columnists, commentators, and editorial writers usually cannot even pretend to be neutral. Newspaper endorsements for presidential candidates typically overwhelmingly favor Republicans (1992 was an exception).[33] Newsmagazines are sometimes less neutral than newspapers or television. In the 1940s, 1950s, and 1960s Henry Luce used *Time* to criticize Harry Truman, to campaign for his view of a China policy, to help elect Dwight Eisenhower as president, and to support the Vietnam War, and the magazine has continued to favor Republican presidents. Unfair but picturesque adjectives are often used in newsmagazines to liven up stories. So are cartoons and drawings, which are generally unflattering to the president.

A number of factors help to explain why most mass-media news coverage is not biased systematically toward a particular person, party, or ideology. Reporters tend not to be partisan or strong ideologues; nor are they politically aligned or holders of strong political beliefs. Journalists are typically not intellectuals or deeply concerned with public policy. Moreover, they share journalism's professional norm of objectivity. The organizational processes of story selection and editing also provide opportunities for softening judgments of reporters. The rotation of assignments and rewards for objective news gathering are further protections against bias. Local television station owners and newspaper publishers are in a position to apply pressure regarding the presentation of the news, and, although they rarely do so, their potential to act may restrain reporters.

Self-interest also plays a role in constraining bias. Individual reporters may earn a poor reputation if others view them as biased. The television networks, newspapers, newsmagazines, and the wire services, which provide most of the Washington news for newspapers, have a direct financial stake in attracting viewers and subscribers and do not want to lose their audience by appearing biased, especially when multiple versions of the same story are available to major news outlets. Slander and libel laws and the "political attack" rule, providing those personally criticized on the electronic media with an opportunity to respond, are formal limitations on bias.

To conclude that the news contains little explicit partisan or ideological bias is not to argue that the news does not distort reality in its coverage. It does! Even under the best of conditions, some distortion is inevitable due to simple error or such factors as lack of careful checking of facts, the efforts of the news source to deceive, and short deadlines.

In a very important sense, values are pervasive in the news, and it is difficult to imagine how it could be otherwise. As members of our society, journalists are imbued with such values as democracy, capitalism, and individualism, and these unconsciously receive positive treatment in the media. Similarly, journalists have concepts of what is "new," "abnormal," and "wrong" and notions of how the world works (e.g., how power is distributed) and how to draw inferences that guide them in their efforts to gather and present the news.

Journalism also contains a structural bias. Selecting, presenting, editing, and interpreting the news inevitably require judgments about what stories to cover and what to report about them because there is simply not enough space for everything. Thus the news can never mirror reality. In addition, the particular ways in which the news is gathered and presented have consequences for distortion in news coverage.

We have already seen that the news is fundamentally superficial and oversimplified and is often overblown, all of which provides the public a distorted view of, among other things, presidential activities, statements, policies, and options. The emphasis on action and the deviant (and therefore "newsworthy" items) rather than on patterns of behavior and the implication that most stories represent more general themes of national significance contribute further to this distortion. Personalizing the news downplays structural and other impersonal factors that may be far more important in understanding the economy, for example, than individual political actors.

We have also seen that the press prefers to frame the news in themes, which both simplify complex issues and events and provide continuity of persons, institutions, and issues. Once these themes are established, the press tends to maintain them in subsequent stories. Of necessity, themes emphasize some information at the expense of other data, often determining what information is most relevant to news coverage and the context in which it is presented.

Once a stereotype of President Ford as a "bumbler" was established, every stumble was magnified as the press emphasized behavior that fit its mold. He was repeatedly forced to defend his intelligence, and many of his acts and statements were reported as efforts to "act" presidential. Once Ford was typecast, his image was repeatedly reinforced and was very difficult to overcome.[34] The same thing happened to Vice President Dan Quayle.

Sometimes themes are established by the press to attract an audience for coverage of an event. A study of television coverage of the 1972 Democratic National Convention found that, although the networks were neutral as to partisanship, they portrayed the convention as more disorderly and conflictual than it actually was. Television's requirements for themes and conflict encouraged reporters to focus on differences between delegates, and the technique of switching from camera to camera gave the impression of rapidly shifting action.[35]

Reporters often fail to alert readers and viewers about the tentativeness of much of what the press reports. Although sources may be unreliable, motives obscure, facts disputed or confused, and meanings unclear, the news is presented in a straightforward manner that communicates little notion of uncertainty. Similarly, reporters often do not make it clear that they have made inferences in their reporting. Such presentations enhance the credibility of journalists who deliver the news, but they provide the potential for distortion in the process.

Some observers feel that the press is biased against whomever holds office at the moment and that reporters want to expose them in the media. Reporters, they argue, hold disparaging views of most politicians and public officials, finding them self-serving, lacking in integrity and competence, hypocritical, and preoccupied with reelection. Thus it is not surprising that journalists see a need to expose and debunk them through general derogation. This orientation may be characterized as neither liberal nor conservative, but reformist.[36]

White House reporters are always looking to expose conflicts of interest and other shady behavior of public officials. Moreover, many of their inquiries revolve around the question, "Is he up to the job?" Reporters who are confined in the White House all day may attempt to make up for their lack of investigative reporting with sarcastic and accusatory questioning. Moreover, the desire to keep the public interested and the need for continuous coverage may create a subconscious bias in the press against the presidency that leads to critical stories.

News coverage of the presidency often tends to emphasize the negative (although the negative stories are typically presented in a seemingly neutral manner).[37] In the 1980 election campaign the press portrayed President Carter as mean and Ronald Reagan as imprecise rather than Carter as precise and Reagan as nice. The emphasis, in other words, was on the candidates' negative qualities. As the following excerpt from Jimmy Carter's diary regarding a visit to Panama in 1978 illustrates, "objective" reporting can be misleading:

> I told the Army troops that I was in the Navy for 11 years, and they booed. I told them that we depended on the Army to keep the Canal open, and they cheered. Later, the news reports said that there were boos and cheers during my speech. I reckon that was an accurate report![38]

On the other hand, one could argue that the press is biased *toward* the White House. Reporters' general respect for the presidency is often transferred to individual presidents. Framed at a respectful distance by the television camera, the president is typically portrayed with an aura of dignity working in a context of rationality and coherence on activities benefitting the public. Word selection often reflects this orientation as well. In addition, at least until recently, journalists followed conventions that protected politicians and public officials from revelations of private misconduct.

The White House enjoys a consistent pattern of favorable coverage in newspapers, magazines, and network news. The most favorable coverage comes in the first year of a president's term, before there is a record to criticize or critics for reporters to interview. Coverage focuses on human interest stories of the president and his appointees and their personalities, goals, and plans. The president is pictured in a positive light as a policymaker dealing with problems. Controversies over solutions arise later. Newspaper headlines also favor the president, and news of foreign affairs provides basic support for the policies and personalities of the administration.[39]

Ultimately, the issue of bias may hang on questions of nuance. As Bill Moyers, public affairs analyst and former presidential press secretary, put it, "Depending on who is looking and writing, the White House is brisk or brusque, assured or arrogant, casual or sloppy, frank or brutal, warm or corny, cautious or timid, compassionate or condescending, reserved or callous."[40] Given the limitations of language and the lack of agreement on the exact nature of reality, it is almost impossible for the media to please everyone.

## MEDIA EFFECTS

The most significant question about the substance of media coverage, of course, is about the impact it has, if any, on public opinion. Most studies on media effects have focused on attitude changes, especially in voting for presidential candidates, and have typically found little or no evidence of influence. Reinforcement of existing attitudes and opinions has been the strongest effect of the media.[41] In the words of one expert,

Most media stories are promptly forgotten. Stories that become part of an individual's fund of knowledge tend to reinforce existing beliefs and feelings. Acquisition of new knowledge or changes in attitude are the exception rather than the rule.[42]

There are other ways to look for media effects, however.

The media are more likely to influence perceptions than attitudes. The press can influence the perceptions of what public figures stand for and what their personalities are like, what issues are important, and what is at stake. If the media raise certain issues or personal characteristics to prominence, the significance of attitudes that people already hold may change and thus alter their evaluations of, say, presidential performance, without their attitudes themselves changing. In other words, the media can influence the criteria by which the president is judged.

The public's familiarity with political matters is closely related to the amount and duration of attention they receive in the mass media.[43] The media also have a strong influence on the issues the public views as important.[44] "Many people readily adopt the media's agenda of importance, often without being aware of it."[45] Moreover, when the media cover events, politicians comment on them and take action, reinforcing the perceived importance of these events and ensuring more public attention.

In addition, media coverage of issues increases their importance in the public's evaluation of political figures. In the words of a leading authority on the impact of television news on public opinion, "The themes and issues that are repeated in television news coverage become the priorities of viewers. Issues and events highlighted by television news become especially influential as criteria for evaluating public officials."[46]

There is growing evidence that network news helps to provide a frame of reference for issues, and this affects evaluations of presidents. When the news began covering the Iran–Contra affair, Ronald Reagan's public approval took an immediate and severe dip as the public applied new criteria of evaluation.[47] Experiments found that President Carter's overall reputation and, to a lesser extent, his apparent competency were affected by network news. The standards people used in evaluating presidents, what they felt was important in their job performance, seemed to be influenced by the news they watched on television.[48]

The public's information on and criteria for evaluating candidates parallel what are presented in the media: campaign performance, personality traits, mannerisms, and personal background rather than positions on issues, ability to govern, and relevant experience. Moreover, what the press emphasizes about elections (the horse race) is what the people say is important about them, what they discuss about them in private conversations, and what they remember about them.[49]

Although it cannot be conclusively proven that media coverage contributes to the public's deemphasis of the professional capacities and policy plans of candidates, it is reasonable to speculate that press emphasis on the horse race and personality traits encourages the public to view campaigns in these terms. Thus, although the press may not directly influence voters to support a particular candidate, it probably amplifies the public's predispositions to view public affairs through personalities rather than more complex factors.

Earlier we saw that the press gave substantial coverage to President Ford's misstatement about Soviet domination of Eastern Europe. This coverage had an impact on the public. Polls show that most people did not realize the president made an error until they were told so by the press. After that, pro-Ford evaluations of the debate declined noticeably as voters' concerns for competence in foreign policy making became salient.[50] A somewhat similar switch occurred after the first debate between Walter Mondale and Ronald Reagan in 1984.[51]

The press probably has the greatest effect on public perceptions of individuals and issues between election campaigns, when people are less likely to activate their partisan defenses. The prominent coverage of Gerald Ford's alleged physical clumsiness was naturally translated into suggestions of mental ineptitude. In the president's own words:

> Every time I stumbled or bumped my head or fell in the snow, reporters zeroed in on that to the exclusion of almost everything else. The news coverage was harmful, but even more damaging was the fact that Johnny Carson and Chevy Chase used my "missteps" for their jokes. Their antics— and I'll admit that I laughed at them myself—helped create the public perception of me as a stumbler. And that wasn't funny.[52]

Once such an image is established in the mass media, it is very difficult to change, as reporters continue to emphasize behavior that is consistent with their previously established themes.

During the Iranian hostage crisis ABC originated a nightly program entitled "America Held Hostage," Walter Cronkite provided a "countdown" of the number of days of the crisis at the end of each evening's news on CBS, many feature stories on the hostages and their families were reported in all the media, and the press gave complete coverage to "demonstrations" in front of the U.S. embassy in Tehran. The latter were often artificially created for consumption by Americans. This crisis gave President Carter's approval rating a tremendous boost, at least for a while. Conversely, when the American ship *Pueblo* was captured by North Korea, there were many more American captives, but there were also no television cameras and few reporters to cover the situation. Thus the incident played a much smaller role in American politics.

Those with only marginal concern for politics may be especially susceptible to the impact of the media because they have few alternative sources of information and less-developed political allegiances. Thus, they have fewer strongly held attitudes to overcome. Similarly, coverage of new issues that are removed from the experiences of people and their political convictions is more likely to influence public opinion than coverage of continuing issues.

Almost all citizens are basically ignorant of such areas of the world as Central America, Afghanistan, and Sudan. The press plays a pivotal role in shaping perceptions of the personalities and issues involved in conflicts abroad (generally only conflicts receive coverage) and the nation's stake in the outcomes of the disputes. In such situations we have seen that there is substantial potential for distortion. The public is heavily dependent on the media for information and has little basis for challenging what it reads and sees in the news. The illustrations of the conflict—scenes of combat or demonstrations, for example—may become the essence of the issue in the public's mind. The underlying problems, which the president must confront, may be largely ignored.

Presidents need public understanding of the difficulty of their job and the nature of the problems they face. The role of the press here can be critical. Watching television news seems to do little to inform viewers about public affairs; reading the printed media is more useful. This may be because reading requires more active cognitive processing of information than watching television, and there is more information presented in newspapers.

We have seen that press coverage of the president is superficial, oversimplified, and often overblown, providing the public a distorted picture of White House activities. This trivialization of the news drowns out coverage of more important matters, often leaving the public ill-informed about matters with which the president must deal, ranging from the renegotiation of the Panama Canal Treaty to funding social security benefits. The preoccupation of the press with personality and the results of policies does little to help the public appreciate the complexity of presidential decision making, the trade-offs involved in policy choices, and the broad trends outside the president's control.

In the previous chapter we saw that the president's access to the media is at least a potential advantage in influencing public opinion. Press focus on the president has disadvantages as well. It inevitably leaves the impression that the president *is* the federal government and crucial to our prosperity and happiness. This naturally encourages the public to focus its expectations on the White House. So does the national frame of reference provided by a truly mass media and the media's penchant for linking coverage of even small matters with responses from the president or presidential spokespersons.

Moreover, the extraordinary attention the press devotes to presidents magnifies their flaws. Even completely unsubstantiated charges against them may make the news because of their prominence. Familiarity may not breed contempt, but it certainly may diminish the aura of grandeur around the chief executive.

Similarly, commentary following presidential speeches and press conferences may influence what viewers remember and may affect their opinions.[53] Although the impact of commentary on presidential addresses and press conferences is unclear, it is probably safe to argue that it is a constraint on the president's ability to lead public opinion. In the words of two observers:

> Critical instant analysis undermines presidential authority by transforming him from presentor to protagonist. . . . Credible, familiar, apparently disinterested newsmen and -women, experts too, usually agreeing with each other, comment on the self-interested performance of a politician. Usually the president's rhetoric is deflated, the mood he has striven to create dissipated.[54]

While reviewing evidence of the impact of the media on public opinion concerning the president, it is important to keep in mind the significant limitations on this influence. Characteristics of readers and viewers—including short attention spans, lack of reading ability, selective perception (especially for those who have well-developed political views), general lack of interest in politics, lack of attentiveness to the media when exposed to it, and forgetfulness—limit the impact of the media. So does the ability of people to reject or ignore evaluations (implicit or explicit) in stories.[55]

The nature of the news message also affects the impact of the media. The great volume of information available in the news; the limited time available in which to absorb it (especially for television viewers); the superficial coverage of people, events, and policies; the presentation of the news on television and in most newspapers in disconnected snippets; and the lack of guidance through the complexities of politics all constrain the influence of the media on public opinion. As a result, people often do not understand the news and actually learn little in the way of specifics from it. The lack of credibility of news sources among some readers and viewers further limits the impact of the media.

Visuals may also distract from verbal messages. Leslie Stahl of CBS News did a long report on Ronald Reagan during the 1984 presidential campaign, criticizing him for deceiving the American people with public relations tactics. Instead of the complaints she expected from the White House, however, she received thanks. Reagan's press aides appreciated the pictures of the president campaigning and were not concerned with the journalist's scathing remarks.[56]

## CONCLUSION

The mass media play a prominent role in the public presidency, providing the public with most of its information about the White House and mediating the president's communications with constituents. Presidents need the press in order to reach the public, and relations with the press are an important complement to the chief executive's efforts at leading public opinion. Through attempting to coordinate news, holding press conferences, and providing a wide range of services for the press, the White House tries to influence its portrayal in the news.

The president's press relations pose many obstacles to efforts to obtain and maintain public support. Although it is probably not true that press coverage of the White House is biased along partisan or ideological lines or toward or against a particular president, it frequently presents a distorted picture to the public and fails to impart an appropriate perspective from which to view complex events. Moreover, presidents are continuously harassed by leaks to the press and are faced with superficial, oversimplified coverage that devotes little attention to substantive discussion of policies and often focuses on trivial matters. This type of reporting undoubtedly affects public perceptions of the president, usually in a negative way. It is no wonder that chief executives generally see the press as a hindrance to their efforts to develop appreciation for their performance and policies in the public.

It is clear that the president is a facilitator rather than a director in relation to the press. He is in a constant struggle with the press and cannot depend on it to stress what he feels is most important about his administration or to provide favorable coverage in the stories it produces. Presidents vary in their success in using the media to promote their goals, but they all are limited in doing so by the nature and independence of the "fourth branch" of government.

Before leaving this chapter, we feel it is important to put the subject in perspective. Americans benefit greatly from a free press. This should not be forgotten as we examine the media's flaws. The same press that provides superficial coverage of the presidency also alerts people to abuses of authority and to attempts to mislead public opinion. It is also much less biased than the heavily partisan newspapers that were typical early in the nation's history. The press is an essential pillar in the structure of a free society.

Moreover, perhaps the fundamental reason that press coverage is much less than its critics would like it to be is that it must appeal to the general public. When the public, or a sizable segment of it, demands more of the mass media, it undoubtedly will receive it. In short, although mass-media coverage of the presidency is often poor, it could be much worse and it is probably about what the public desires. The media reflect as well as influence American society.

## NOTES

1. Doris A. Graber, *Mass Media and American Politics*, 4th ed. (Washington, D.C.: Congressional Quarterly Press, 1993), pp. 289–91; Elmer E. Cornwell, Jr., "Presidential News: The Expanding Public Image," *Journalism Quarterly* 36 (Summer 1959): 275–83; and Alan P. Balutis, "The Presidency and the Press: The Expanding Presidential Image," *Presidential Studies Quarterly* 7 (Fall 1977): 244–51.

2. Richard Harris, "The Presidency and the Press," *New Yorker*, October 1, 1973, p. 122; Dom Bonafede, "Powell and the Press: A New Mood in the White House," *National Journal*, June 25, 1977, p. 981.

3. Quoted in Harris, "The Presidency and the Press," p. 122; and Peter Forbath and

Carey Winfrey, *The Adversaries: The President and the Press* (Cleveland: Regal Books, 1974), p. 5.

4. Quoted in "Press Secretaries Explore White House News Strategies," *APIP Report* 1 (January 1991), p. 2.

5. Jarol B. Manheim, "The Honeymoon's Over: The News Conference and the Development of Presidential Style," *Journal of Politics* 41 (February 1979): 60–61.

6. Graber, *Mass Media and American Politics*, p. 308.

7. Michael Baruch Grossman and Martha Joynt Kumar, *Portraying the President: The White House and the News Media* (Baltimore: Johns Hopkins University Press, 1981), pp. 59–60, 63–64, 280–81.

8. Interview with Peter Jennings, New York, N. Y., October 18, 1987.

9. Paul Brace and Barbara Hinckley, *Follow the Leader: Opinion Polls and the Modern Presidents* (New York: Basic Books, 1992), chap. 3.

10. Dom Bonafede, "The Washington Press: It Magnifies the President's Flaws and Blemishes," *National Journal*, May 1, 1982, pp. 267–71.

11. Graber, *Mass Media and American Politics*, p. 301.

12. David L. Paletz and Robert M. Entman, *Media–Power–Politics* (New York: Free Press, 1981), pp. 55–56.

13. "Reagan Outburst on Leaks," *Newsweek*, January 18, 1982, p. 23; and Walter S. Mossberg, "Reagan Prepares Curbs on U.S. Officials to Restrict News Leaks on Foreign Policy," *The Wall Street Journal*, January 13, 1982, p. 7.

14. William Safire, *Before the Fall: An Inside View of the Pre-Watergate White House* (New York: Doubleday, 1975), p. 373; and Henry Kissinger, *Years of Upheaval* (Boston: Little, Brown, 1981), p. 116.

15. Lyndon Johnson, quoted in George Christian, *The President Steps Down: A Personal Memoir of the Transfer of Power* (New York: Macmillan, 1970), p. 203.

16. "The U.S. vs. William Colby," *Newsweek*, September 28, 1981, p. 30.

17. "The Tattletale White House," *Newsweek*, February 25, 1980, p. 21.

18. Robert T. Hartmann, *Palace Politics: An Inside Account of the Ford Years* (New York: McGraw-Hill, 1980), p. 38.

19. William J. Lanouette, "The Washington Press Corps: Is It All That Powerful?" *National Journal*, June 2, 1979, p. 898.

20. Lou Cannon, *President Reagan: The Role of a Lifetime* (New York: Simon and Schuster, 1991), p. 452.

21. Donald T. Regan, *For the Record: From Wall Street to Washington* (San Diego, Calif.: Harcourt Brace Jovanovich, 1988), p. xiv.

22. Woodrow Wilson, quoted in William Small, *To Kill a Messenger: Television News and the Real World* (New York: Hastings, 1970), p. 221.

23. President Carter, quoted in Michael Baruch Grossman and Martha Joynt Kumar, "Carter, Reagan, and the Media: Have the Rules Really Changed or the Poles of the Spectrum of Success?" (paper presented at the Annual Meeting of the American Political Science Association, New York, September 3–6, 1981), p. 8.

24. Dan Rather, quoted in Hoyt Purvis, ed., *The Presidency and the Press* (Austin, Tex.: Lyndon B. Johnson School of Public Affairs, 1976), p. 56.

25. See George C. Edwards III, *The Public Presidency* (New York: St. Martin's, 1983), p. 149, and sources cited therein. See also Bruce Buchanan, *Electing a President* (Austin: University of Texas Press, 1991), chap. 4; Graber, *Mass Media and American Politics*, pp. 226, 269; and Thomas E. Patterson, "The Press and Its Missed Assignment," in *Elections of 1988*, ed. Michael Nelson (Washington, D.C.: CQ Press, 1989).

26. Quoted in Grossman and Kumar, *Portraying the President*, p. 43.

27. Quoted in ibid., p. 26.

28. Quoted in ibid., p. 231.

29. Sam Donaldson, quoted in "Washington Press Corps," *Newsweek*, May 25, 1981, p. 90.

30. Sam Donaldson, *Hold On, Mr. President* (New York: Random House, 1987), pp. 196–97.

31. See Edwards, *The Public Presidency*, p. 156, and sources cited therein.

32. Larry Speakes, quoted in Eleanor Randolph, "Speakes Aims Final Salvos at White House Practices," *Washington Post*, January 31, 1987, p. A3.

33. John P. Robinson, "The Press as King-Maker: What Surveys from Last Five Campaigns Show," *Journalism Quarterly* 51 (Winter 1974): 587–94, 606.

34. See Mark J. Rozell, *The Press and the Ford Presidency* (Ann Arbor, Mich.: University of Michigan Press, 1992).

35. David L. Paletz and Martha Elson, "Television Coverage of Presidential Conventions: Now You See It, Now You Don't," *Political Science Quarterly* 91 (Spring 1976): 109–31.

36. See Edward Jay Epstein, *News from Nowhere: Television and the News* (New York: Vintage, 1973), pp. 215–20; Herbert J. Gans, *Deciding What's News* (New York: Vintage, 1979), pp. 68–69, 187; and Stephen Hess, *The Washington Reporters* (Washington, D.C.: Brookings Institution, 1981), p. 88.

37. Graber, *Mass Media and American Politics*, p. 227. On the 1992 presidential campaign, see "Clinton's the One," *Media Monitor* 6 (November 1992): 3–5.

38. Jimmy Carter, *Keeping Faith: Memoirs of a President* (New York: Bantam, 1982), pp. 179–80.

39. On this topic, see Edwards, *The Public Presidency*, p. 162, and sources cited therein.

40. Bill D. Moyers, "The Press and Government: Who's Telling the Truth?" in Warren K. Agee, ed., *Mass Media in a Free Society* (Lawrence, Kans.: University Press of Kansas, 1969), p. 19.

41. For an overview, see Cliff Zukin, "Mass Communication and Public Opinion," in Dan D. Nimmo and Keith R. Sanders, eds., *Handbook of Political Communication* (Beverly Hills, Calif.: Sage, 1981), pp. 359–90.

42. Graber, *Mass Media and American Politics*, p. 208, see also pp. 222–29.

43. Benjamin I. Page and Robert Y. Shapiro, *The Rational Public* (Chicago: University of Chicago Press, 1992), pp. 12–13.

44. Shanto Iyengar, Mark D. Peters, and Donald R. Kinder, "Experimental Demonstrations of the 'Not-So-Minimal' Consequences of Television News Programs," *American Political Science Review* 76 (December 1982): 848–58; James P. Winter and Chaim H. Eyal, "Agenda-Setting for the Civil Rights Issue," *Public Opinion Quarterly* 45 (Fall 1981): 376–83; Michael Bruce MacKuen and Steven Lane Coombs, *More than News* (Beverly Hills, Calif.: Sage, 1981), chaps. 3–4; Fay Lomax Cook, Tom R. Tyler, and Edward G. Goetz, "Media and Agenda-Setting: Effects on the Public, Interest Group Leaders, Policy Makers, and Policy," *Public Opinion Quarterly* 47 (Spring 1983): 16–35; David L. Portess and Maxwell McCombs, eds., *Agenda Setting: Readings on Media, Public Opinion, and Policymaking* (Hillsdale, N.J.: Lawrence Erlbaum Associates, 1991); Doris A. Graber, "Agenda-Setting: Are There Women's Perspectives?" in *Women and the News*, ed. Laurily Epstein (New York: Hastings House, 1978), 15–37.

45. Graber, *Mass Media and American Politics*, p. 216.

46. Shanto Iyengar, *Is Anyone Responsible?* (Chicago: University of Chicago Press, 1992).

47. Jon A. Krosnick and Donald R. Kinder, "Altering the Foundations of Support for the President Through Priming," *American Political Science Review* 84 (June 1990): 497–512; and Iyengar, *Is Anyone Responsible?* chap. 8.

48. Iyengar, Peters, and Kinder, "Experimental Demonstrations of the 'Not-So-Minimal' Consequences of Television News Programs."

49. Thomas E. Patterson, *The Mass Media Election: How Americans Choose Their President* (New York: Praeger, 1980), pp. 84–86, 98–100, 105, and chap. 12; Doris A. Graber, "Personal Qualities in Presidential Images: The Contribution of the Press," *Midwest Journal of Political Science* 16 (February 1972): 295; and Graber, *Mass Media and American Politics*, pp. 275–78.

50. Frederick T. Steeper, "Public Response to Gerald Ford's Statements on Eastern Europe in the Second Debate," in George F. Bishop, Robert G. Meadow, and Marilyn Jackson-Beeck, eds., *The Presidential Debates: Media, Electoral, and Public Perspectives* (New York: Praeger, 1978), pp. 81–101.

51. Michael J. Robinson, "News Media Myths and Realities," in Kay Lehman Schlozman, ed., *Elections in America* (Boston: Allen and Unwin, 1987), p. 149.

52. Gerald R. Ford, *A Time to Heal: The Autobiography of Gerald R. Ford* (New York: Harper and Row, 1979), p. 289; see also pp. 343–44.

53. Dwight F. Davis, Lynda Lee Kaid, and Donald L. Singleton, "Information Effects of Political Commentary," *Experimental Study of Politics* 6 (June 1977): 45–68; Lynda Lee Kaid, Donald L. Singleton, and Dwight F. Davis, "Instant Analysis of Televised Political Addresses: The Speaker versus the Commentator," in Brent D. Ruben, ed., *Communication Yearbook* I (New Brunswick, N.J.: Transaction Books, 1977), pp. 453–64; and John Havick, "The Impact of a Televised State of the Union Message and the Instant Analysis: An Experiment" (unpublished paper, Georgia Institute of Technology, 1980, typescript).

54. Paletz and Entman, *Media–Power–Politics*, p. 70.
55. Doris A. Graber, *Processing the News*, 2nd ed. (New York: Longman), pp. 90–93.
56. Interview with Leslie Stahl, West Point, N.Y., 1986.

## SELECTED READINGS

Braestrup, Peter. *Big Story*. Garden City, N.Y.: Anchor, 1978.

Edwards, George C., III. *The Public Presidency*. New York: St. Martin's, 1983.

Epstein, Edward Jay. *News from Nowhere: Television and the News*. New York: Vintage, 1973.

Gans, Herbert J. *Deciding What's News*. New York: Vintage, 1979.

Grossman, Michael Baruch, and Martha Joynt Kumar. *Portraying the President: The White House and the News Media*. Baltimore: Johns Hopkins University Press, 1981.

Hallin, Daniel C. "The Media, the War in Vietnam, and Political Support," *Journal of Politics* 46 (February 1984): 2–24.

Hess, Stephen. *The Washington Reporters*. Washington, D.C.: Brookings Institution, 1981.

Iyengar, Shanto. *Is Anyone Responsible?* Chicago: University of Chicago Press, 1992.

Iyengar, Shanto, and Donald R. Kinder. *News That Matters*. Chicago: University of Chicago Press, 1987.

Kaid, Lynda Lee, Donald L. Singleton, and Dwight Davis. "Instant Analysis of Televised Political Addresses: The Speaker versus the Commentator." In Brent D. Ruben, ed., *Communication Yearbook I*. New Brunswick, N.J.: Transaction Books, 1977.

Paletz, David L., and Robert M. Entman. *Media–Power–Politics*. New York: Free Press, 1981.

Patterson, Thomas E. *The Mass Media Election: How Americans Choose Their President*. New York: Praeger, 1980.

Robinson, Michael Jay. "The Impact of Instant Analysis." *Journal of Communication* 27 (Spring 1977): 17–23.

Robinson, Michael Jay, and Margaret A. Sheehan. *Over the Wire and On TV: CBS and UPI in Campaign '80*. New York: Russell Sage Foundation, 1983.

Steeper, Frederick T. "Public Response to Gerald Ford's Statements on Eastern Europe in the Second Debate." In George F. Bishop, Robert G. Meadow, and Marilyn Jackson-Beeck, eds., *The Presidential Debates: Media, Electoral, and Public Perspectives*. New York: Praeger, 1978.

# 6

# The President's Office

A president's tasks are many and varied. The job is too big for any one person to perform. Presidents need help. They need help in making, promoting, and implementing their decisions. They need help in attending to the symbolic and ceremonial functions of the office. They need help in articulating their beliefs, communicating their policy, and responding to public moods, opinions, and expectations.

The executive departments and agencies were obviously intended to provide such help, but they alone have not been sufficient. Their interests, needs, and ongoing responsibilities have not been synonymous with the president's all the time or even most of the time. Besides, they serve a number of masters. In addition to the chief executive, they must look to Congress for their programs and budgets and to their clientele for policy requests and political support. With an increasing number of issues overlapping departmental jurisdictions and an increasing number of matters requiring presidential attention, presidents need their own advisory bodies and institutional structures for assistance.

They need them for three principal reasons: to obtain information on people and policies; to maintain linkage to the constituencies within and outside the government with whom they must interact; and to ensure that their priorities are clear, their decisions are implemented, and their interests are protected. Only if these needs are satisfied can presidents exercise effective leadership.

Although presidents cannot lead alone, their dependence on others creates potential problems for them. The information they receive on people or policy can be incorrect, biased, or simply too narrow. Their link to the community can be severed or overloaded by too much or too little activity. Overzealous behavior by their staff can result in a loss of perspective, a failure to consider all options or consult with a range of people, and unwise or even illegal behavior. None of this serves the president's interests. In short, presidents need good staff support. But good staff support, in turn, requires telling presidents what they may not want to hear, being sensitive to diverse and often critical political forces, and operating according to recognized and accepted rules and procedures.

In this chapter we will examine the institutional components of presidential leadership and their operation within the governmental system: the cabinet, the Executive Office, and the president's personal office, the White House. Beginning with the oldest of these advisory bodies, the cabinet, we briefly describe its creation, evolution, and its demise. We then explore the institutionalization of advisory responsibilities in the Executive Office. Here the emphasis is on the growth of this bureaucracy within a bureaucracy and its impact on the president and the performance of presidential responsibilities. After a historical sketch of the evolution of the White House, we examine patterns of staffing and their relationship to the style and objectives of the president. In the final section we assess the increasing importance of the vice presidential office and also the president's spouse.

## ORGANIZING EXECUTIVE ADVICE

### The Evolution of the Cabinet

The Constitution did not create a separate advisory council for the president. The framers had discussed the idea but rejected it largely out of the fear that presidents might try to sidestep responsibility for their own actions by using their council as a foil. In order to avoid the fiction, popular in England at the time, that the king could do no wrong, that any harmful action he committed was always the result of poor or even pernicious advice from his counselors, the Constitution designated that presidents could demand written opinions of their subordinates. Having these in writing, it was hoped, would pinpoint responsibility.

Although presidents had been expected to use their department secretaries in both administrative and advisory capacities, there was no expectation that the secretaries would function as the principal body of advisers. However, in 1791, when George Washington prepared to leave the capital city, he authorized his vice president, secretaries of state, treasury, and war, and the chief justice to consult with each other on governmental matters during his absence. The following year, the president began to meet more frequently with the heads of the executive departments but without the vice president and the chief justice. During the undeclared naval war with France, these meetings became more frequent. It was James Madison who referred to this group as the president's cabinet. The name stuck. Jefferson's resignation as secretary of state in 1794 in protest over the administration's policies fixed the partisan nature of the group. Members were expected to provide counsel as well as support.

For the next 140 years, the cabinet functioned as the president's principal advisory body for both foreign and domestic affairs. Administrative positions on controversial proposals were often thrashed out at cabinet meetings. Presidents also turned to their cabinets for help in supporting them on Capitol Hill. The personal relationships between the individual secretaries and members of Congress frequently put the cabinet officials in a better position than the president to obtain this support. Strong cabinets and weak presidents characterized executive advisory relationships during most of the nineteenth century.

The president's position began to change as his capacity for exerting personal influence improved. The ability to shape public opinion and mobilize partisan support, evident during the administrations of Theodore Roosevelt and Woodrow Wilson, strengthened the president's hand in dealing with Congress and with his own department heads. Beginning in 1921, the power to affect department and agency decision making through the budget process also contributed to a stronger presidency.

As a consequence of these changes, cabinet meetings became more of a forum for discussion than a mechanism for making decisions. Franklin Roosevelt even trivialized the forum. His practice was to go around the table asking each participant what was on his or her mind. Frequently after the session, several secretaries remained to discuss their important business with him without other secretaries in attendance.

Although Truman emphasized the importance of the cabinet upon taking office (as have most of his successors), he did not meet with it regularly. Rather than utilizing the department secretaries as an advisory body, Truman turned to them individually as Roosevelt had done and relied on a few senior staff aides in the White House for help in formulating policy.

The cabinet enjoyed a resurgence under Eisenhower, meeting some 230 times during his eight years in office. The president personally presided over most of these meetings and used his presence to achieve consensus on policy. The sessions themselves often featured elaborate presentations of proposals by individual department heads and their staffs. These presentations, replete with visual aides and supporting materials, were the prelude to final decisions on the administration's legislative program prior to its presentation to Congress.

Johnson also met with his cabinet frequently, more so as his administration progressed. According to Professor James E. Anderson, Johnson used it as a management tool: to exchange information and ideas, to develop a sense of group-mindedness, a team approach; and to promote internal coordination and oversight of key presidential initiatives.[1] The president dominated the sessions, sometimes employing them as a sounding board for new proposals and sometimes as a vehicle for issuing directives to his department heads.[2] Unlike Eisenhower and Johnson, other contemporary presidents have not turned to the cabinet as a collectivity for advice or administration.

Kennedy rarely met with his cabinet, and Nixon, despite his announced intention to revert to a cabinet system, held few meetings and relegated department heads to positions of lesser importance in his administration. Ford and Carter held cabinet meetings at the beginning of their administrations and then slowly discontinued them. Carter, for example, met with the cabinet every week during his first year in office, every other week during his second year, once a month during his third year, and sporadically during his final year. Neither used their cabinets as key advisory bodies.

Although Reagan met less frequently with the full cabinet as his presidency progressed, he employed a cabinet model of decision making. Known as a cabinet council system, it was organized on the basis of broad policy areas. The councils, composed of various departmental secretaries, performed some of the same advisory functions that the cabinet as a group did during and before the Eisenhower administration. They deliberated policy recommendations, developed administration positions, and helped coordinate the implementation of key presidential decisions. Staff support was provided by the White House. Nominally chaired by the president, the councils were run in his absence by one of the department heads who had been designated as chairman *pro tempore*. In Reagan's first term there were seven cabinet councils; in the second there were three. The frequency with which the councils met to discuss administration policy was also reduced in the second term as the number of new policy initiatives declined.

Bush continued to use the cabinet counsel system as it had evolved in Reagan's second term. However, he turned to it with less regularity over the course of his administration, preferring instead to consult with informal groups of policy advisers, particularly on economic and national security issues. It was his secretary of the treasury, director of the Office of Management and Budget, chairman of the Council of Economic Advisers, and White House chief of staff, not the formal Cabinet Council on Economic Affairs, to whom he turned for advice during the recession that plagued the last years of his administration.

Clinton has also adopted a variation of the cabinet council system. Senior White House aides in domestic, economic, and national security affairs coordinate advisory and policy implementation responsibilities with cabinet heads and other White House staffers. Clinton's system has encouraged the president to get deeply involved in issues as they are being developed. It has also facilitated interagency cooperation, reducing the influence that any single cabinet member exercises over making policy or serving as an administration spokesperson.

### The Cabinet's Demise

While the cabinet council system of the last three presidents has not been an unqualified success (see Chapter 12), it has addressed and partially overcome some of the principal weaknesses of the contemporary cabinet, notably its size and its diversity. Table 6-1 lists the departmental components of the contemporary cabinet. In addition to the secretaries, the vice president, senior White House aides, and other executive officials of cabinet rank may attend its sessions. The increasingly technical nature of policy making and the need for highly specialized information

**Table 6-1. The Cabinet,* 1994**

| Department | Year Created | President | Rankings Budget Outlays (1992) | Rankings Number of Civilian Personnel (1993) |
|---|---|---|---|---|
| State | 1789 | Washington | 13 | 10 |
| Treasury | 1789 | Washington | 3 | 3 |
| Interior | 1849 | Polk | 12 | 7 |
| Agriculture | 1862 | Lincoln | 4 | 5 |
| Justice | 1870 | Grant | 11 | 6 |
| Commerce (formerly part of Department of Commerce and Labor, 1903) | 1913 | Wilson | 14 | 9 |
| Labor (formerly part of Department of Commerce and Labor, 1903) | 1913 | Wilson | 5 | 12 |
| Defense (consolidated Department of War, 1789, and Department of Navy, 1798) | 1947 | Truman | 2 | 1 |
| Housing and Urban Development | 1965 | Johnson | 9 | 13 |
| Transportation | 1966 | Johnson | 7 | 8 |
| Energy | 1977 | Carter | 10 | 11 |
| Health and Human Services (formerly part of Department of Health, Education, and Welfare, 1953) | 1980 | Carter | 1+ | 4 |
| Education (formerly part of Department of Health, Education, and Welfare, 1953) | 1980 | Carter | 8 | 14 |
| Veteran Affairs | 1988 | Reagan | 6 | 2 |

*President Clinton has proposed to Congress that the Environmental Protection Agency be elevated to cabinet status.
+Includes social security.

also made it difficult for secretaries to be sufficiently versed in the intricacies of issues outside of their own areas to carry on an intelligent discussion. At best this limited participation at cabinet meetings to the few who were informed and competent; at worst it reduced the level of the discussion and extended the time of debate.

There are other reasons for the cabinet's decline. Increasing pressure from outside groups forced secretaries to assume more of an advocacy role for their respective departments (referred to as "going native"), particularly in meetings in which they had to go on the record or even in closed sessions which could be leaked to the press. The tendency to advocate department interests increased over the course of an administration. The cabinet meetings thus became more confrontational and less useful as a device for reaching a consensus or building one after policy decisions had been made. The cabinet council system has helped to avoid this "going native" problem by keeping the focus on the president's agenda and by effectively integrating the policy-making operations of the White House and the executive departments.

Moreover, the need and desire to extend personal influence discouraged department secretaries from discussing their concerns in a group setting. Cabinet members usually prefer the president's ear alone, and contemporary presidents have tended to encourage one-on-one situations to maximize their own flexibility, increase their own bargaining power, and conserve their own time. Reagan and Eisenhower have been the exceptions.

These factors help explain why presidents tend to meet with their cabinets less over time, particularly in the last years of their administrations.[3] They also suggest why presidents have increasingly differentiated among their secretaries in seeking advice. The heads of certain departments have tended to exercise closer and more collaborative relationships with the president. These tend to be the most influential secretaries, those who comprise the so-called inner cabinet: State, Treasury, Justice, and Defense.[4]

In contrast, the other secretaries, who are considered members of the outer cabinet, tend to have a more distant relationship with the president because of the nature of their departments and clientele. According to political scientist Thomas E. Cronin, "These departments experience heavy and often conflicting pressures from clientele groups, from congressional interests, and from state and local governments, pressures that often run counter to presidential priorities."[5] Advocating departmental interests and exercising administrative responsibilities make it more difficult for secretaries to perceive problems from the president's perspective and recommend solutions that accord with the president's needs rather than theirs. This has given presidents little choice but to develop their own institutional and personal staffs.

### The Executive Office

The Executive Office of the President (EOP) was established by executive order in 1939. Its title, however, is a misnomer. Its functions are not primarily executive, nor is it a single office. The people in the EOP do work for a single client, the president.

The principal objective of the EOP has always been to help presidents perform central, nondelegable tasks, including those involved in their expanded policy-making roles. For the most part, administrative responsibilities have been avoided. The various offices in the EOP have not taken over the ongoing responsibilities of the departments and agencies, although they have helped coordinate some interagency projects.

Nor is the Executive Office a monolithic agency. It has always consisted of a number of specialized staffs. The first EOP was composed of five separate units, including the Bureau of the Budget and the White House. Over the years many different boards, offices, and councils have been placed within its purview. Today the EOP consists of twelve offices, two executive residences, a staff of approximately sixteen hundred, and a budget of over $180 million.[6] Figure 6-1 lists its current units, authorized personnel, and budget allocations.

While the EOP has evolved in size and function, it has not done so in a systematic, carefully planned way. Rather, its development has been a product of historical accident, the needs of different administrations, and the goals of different presidents. Most chief executives have changed the Executive Office in some way, adding or deleting some of it.

**Figure 6-1. Executive Office of the President—At Its Inception and Today**

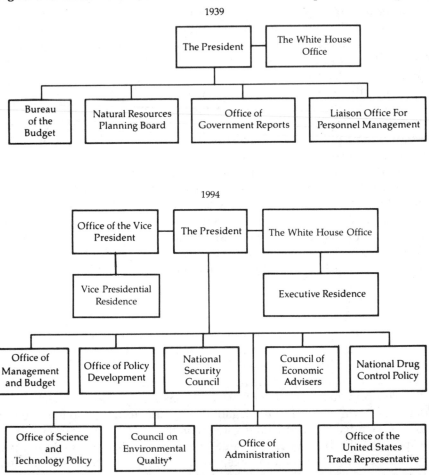

*The Clinton administration proposed the elimination of the Council on Environmental Quality but Congress refused to do so and appropriated funds for it.

Some have attempted to overhaul it entirely. The most extensive reorganization occurred during the first term of the Nixon presidency.

Unhappy with the piecemeal expansion of the executive branch that had occurred prior to 1968, President Nixon appointed a council at the beginning of his administration to review the entire branch structure including the organization and operation of the EOP. Meeting over a fourteen-month period, this advisory council proposed recommendations to centralize and streamline the executive branch, thereby making it more responsive to the president's political needs. Included were recommendations to create a separate domestic policy-making staff and to reorganize and retitle the Bureau of the Budget.

The changes not only affected the composition of the Executive Office but decision making within it. More political positions, filled by presidential nominees, were created. This had the effect of decreasing the role and influence of civil servants. It also shifted power from the departments and agencies to the presidency. Political appointees in the upper echelon of the White House and the Office of Management and Budget (OMB) dominated activities, ran the processes, advised the president, and made sure that his wishes were carried out.

Criticism of the hierarchical structure of the Nixon presidency, the heavy-handed tactics of his principal aides, and the inaccessibility of the president to others in the executive branch and Congress led to a moderating effect and less-centralized control during the Ford and Carter presidencies. Ford was more accessible to department and agency heads and more receptive to their input than was his predecessor. He did not use the EOP to impose a perspective on them as the Nixon administration attempted to do. Carter, too, gave his department secretaries considerable latitude in articulating and promoting their positions and in administering their own departments.

Carter also reorganized the EOP, decreasing the number of offices and reducing its personnel. The smaller office, however, did not increase the president's capacity to manage the government. Unable to impose discipline on the various departments and agencies, Carter was eventually forced to fire two cabinet secretaries who consistently undercut his position on Capitol Hill and in their own departments. Presidents Reagan and Bush did not make major structural changes in their Executive Office.

President Clinton did. At the beginning of his administration, he announced with much fanfare that he intended to reduce the size of the president's office by 25 percent. The reduction, a symbolic belt tightening in the light of the president's deficit reduction plan, proposed the elimination of several small EOP offices, consolidated others, and greatly reduced the size of one of the largest, the office of National Drug Control Policy.[7] Considerable controversy, however, surrounded the administration's claim of an actual 25 percent reduction in White House staff. The figure included personnel on an advisory space council that met infrequently, reductions in two EOP offices, Administration and

National Drug Control Policy, normally not considered part of the White House, the proposed elimination of the Council on Environmental Quality with which Congress refused to go along, and an increase in part-time employment and private contracted services.[8]

### Consequences of Structural Change

The transformations that have occurred in the EOP have made the structure of that office more consistent with the personal styles of individual presidents. This has resulted in short-term advantages for the president, but long-term disadvantages for the presidency. Together, they have produced instability in organization, irregularity in operations, and turnover in personnel. Relations between the president and executive branch agencies have been subject to continuing uncertainty with each new administration. Transitions between administrations have been made more arduous with the slow process of appointments contributing to the problem. The wheel has to be reinvented constantly.

Despite the initial objective of the office to help the president oversee the operational responsibilities and policy-making efforts of the executive departments and agencies, not to substitute for them, separate policy-making units have been established, moving closer and closer to the Oval Office. Despite the initial desire to staff the EOP with civil servants, political appointees have increased in number and in influence. Despite the initial goal to keep the Executive Office small in size and general in capabilities, it has become a larger, more highly specialized presidential bureaucracy.

This growth, differentiation, and politicization have worked at cross-purposes. On one hand, they have increased the political sensitivity of the president and the ability of the White House to exercise centralized control over the rest of the executive branch; on the other, they may have decreased the president's capacity to obtain neutral policy advice. Discontinuities in policy between and even within administrations have resulted.

There is another problem. Politicization has caused the presidency's institutional memory to fade. Turnover within the EOP has increased, often placing the president's people at a competitive disadvantage when dealing substantively with officials from the departments and agencies.[9]

Although the establishment of a presidential bureaucracy has increased the presidency's discretion and influence, it has also generated internal rivalry and competition. Senior presidential aides enjoy status by virtue of their access to and interaction with the president. They also exercise considerable authority within their functional areas. This status and that authority have contributed to tension between department and agency heads and the White House which, in turn, has accentuated problems of maintaining loyalty and mobilizing support within an administration. Information leaks are now a perennial problem for every president.

While the establishment of an institutional mechanism within the presidency has increased the president's ability to meet the multiple demands of the office, it has also helped perpetuate those demands. Bureaucracies have a self-perpetuating character. By performing functions and meeting expectations, these structures encourage those expectations to persist. Subsequent presidents who do not meet them are criticized.

Finally, the development of the presidency has enhanced the institution's power, but it has probably decreased the president's personal influence on that institution. Chief executives are either forced to immerse themselves in the details of administration, consuming valuable time and energy in the process, or to delegate that responsibility to others. If they choose to delegate, as most presidents have done, then they face the danger of having key operational and policy decisions shaped by others acting on their behalf. When presidents fail to delegate, on the other hand, their perspectives can become clouded by small details and decisions. Moreover, they are also more prone to be blamed for problems that may emerge. Ronald Reagan fell victim to the dangers of overdelegation, and Jimmy Carter to those of underdelegation.

## PROVIDING A PRESIDENTIAL STAFFING SYSTEM

In addition to the support the institution requires, presidents need assistants to help them perform their personal duties and responsibilities. Until the creation of an official White House staff in 1939, that help was mainly clerical and frequently in short supply.

### The Early Years

For the first seventy years, Congress did not even provide the president with secretarial support. Early presidents were expected to write their own speeches and answer their own correspondence. Most employed a few aides and paid them out of their own salary. These assistants tended to be young and undistinguished. Frequently, they were related to the president. They were paid low wages and generally performed menial tasks.

In 1857 Congress enacted a separate appropriation for a personal secretary, but the position did not assume great importance or even much potential at the time. If anything, the quality of the secretaries actually employed by presidents declined. Andrew Johnson's aide, his son Robert, was an alcoholic; Grant's secretary, General Orville E. Babcock, was indicted for fraud; Hayes's assistant, William Rogers, was generally regarded as incompetent.[10]

The secretary's role and influence began to expand with the administration of Chester Arthur. Daniel G. Rollings, who had assisted Arthur as vice president, helped him draft speeches and legislative messages.[11]

Grover Cleveland's chief aide, Dan Lamont, performed a variety of political and personal tasks. His influence was attested by the press corps' labeling him "assistant president"; he was the first presidential assistant to receive such an appellation.

In the twentieth century, the secretary's functions were gradually increased. Theodore Roosevelt's principal aide, William Loeb, Jr., began to deal with the press on a regular basis. Wilson's secretary, Joseph Tumulty, controlled access to the Oval Office and functioned as an appointments secretary, political adviser, administrative manager, and public relations aide.

The number of presidential assistants also began to increase during this period. Whereas Benjamin Harrison could house his entire staff on the second floor of the White House near his own living quarters, in McKinley's administration, a separate group of offices had to be constructed outside the mansion for the president's staff. When the West Wing was completed in 1909, the president's aides occupied an even larger space near the president's office.

Hoover doubled the number of his administrative aides from two to four and was also helped by more than forty others: clerks, typists, messengers, and so on. Franklin Roosevelt expanded presidential support still further. In addition to a small administrative staff, he had key aides, budgeted to the executive departments but available for White House work. The creation of a separate White House unit as part of the Executive Office enabled Roosevelt to move several of these individuals to the official White House staff, but it did not end the practice of using detailees for presidential tasks.

### The Personalized White House, 1939 to the Mid-1960s

In establishing the first White House office, Roosevelt designed a highly personal staff system. Six key administrative aides performed action-forcing assignments for the president, ones that were dictated by Roosevelt's immediate needs and activities. The president ran the staff operation himself, making assignments, receiving reports, and generally coordinating activities. Presidential assistants were expected to be anonymous. They were given general responsibilities. No one exercised exclusive jurisdiction over "their" function or program. On the contrary, lines of authority were purposely blurred and assignments overlapped. Roosevelt even encouraged competition among his aides to maximize his information and extend his influence. According to Professor Richard E. Neustadt, he enjoyed "bruised egos."[12]

The organization of Roosevelt's White House was a prescription for personal control. It satisfied Roosevelt's needs. It was not, however, a model his successors could easily follow because it conformed to Roosevelt's style, not theirs. The increasing responsibilities of the presidency dictated a larger, more specialized staff structure.

The White Houses of Truman and Eisenhower were more hierarchial in form and more carefully differentiated in function than Roosevelt's, although senior aides in both administrations continued to operate with a great deal of informality with one another and enjoyed easy access to the president. Of the two staffs, Eisenhower's was the larger and more formal. Areas of responsibility were more clearly designated.

Eisenhower had a penchant for organization and adopted a system along the lines of the one he experienced in the military. A chief of staff oversaw the operation and regulated the flow of visitors and memoranda to the Oval Office. Unlike Roosevelt and Truman, who desired to maximize their information and involvement, Eisenhower preferred a system that relieved him of numerous detailed decisions. He desired to set general policy and then work behind the scenes to build political support for it. To some extent he used his staff as a shield to enhance his own flexibility.

While the Roosevelt, Truman, and Eisenhower operations differed somewhat in size, structure, and style, they had much in common. By contemporary standards they were relatively small and operated more as a personal extension of the president than as an institutional extension of the presidency. With the exception of Eisenhower's chief of staff, Sherman Adams, presidential aides did not possess the status and clout of department secretaries. Their influence stemmed from their mediating role, their ability to obtain information, and their proximity to the president. When the White House called, the president's personal interests were usually the reason.

### The Institutionalized White House, Mid 1960s–Present

Changes began to occur in the 1960s. They had a profound effect not only on the way the White House was structured and worked but on the operation of the entire executive branch itself. Presidential aides became better known, exercised more power, and tended to monopolize the president's attention and his time. The White House grew in size, specialization, and responsibilities. Today it has approximately 400 people on its budget plus another 100 to 150 detailed to it for specific assignments and a budget of almost $39 million for the fiscal year 1994.

The most notable change during the Kennedy–Johnson period was the institutionalization of policy-making functions by and in the White House. Senior presidential aides became the principal policy advisers. They supervised their own staffs, which were based in the Executive Office. These staffs competed with the departments and agencies for influence. The institutionalization of policy making in the White House had three major effects. First, it gave the president more discretion and allowed him to take more personal credit for policy developed by his administration. Second, it gave the presidency a capacity to formulate policy distinct from and independent of the departments and agencies. Third, it accelerated the shift of power from the departments and agencies to the White House. Cabinet secretaries were no longer the president's only advisers within their respective spheres. In some cases they were not even primary advisers. Their status declined accordingly while that of the president's assistants increased.

The growth of the White House naturally affected the relationship between presidents and their aides, particularly at the middle and lower levels of the White House. Informality was replaced by a more formal arrangement. Personal interaction with the president became more difficult and less frequent for more members of the staff. Perquisites, such as office location, mess privileges, and portal to portal limousine service, began to differentiate aides and their status in the White House hierarchy. The president's time became an even more precious and closely guarded commodity.

How presidents related to their senior aides was still a matter of personal style. Kennedy consciously attempted to emulate Franklin Roosevelt's model but without the internal competition that Roosevelt generated. Senior Kennedy staffers, many of whom had worked together on the 1960 election campaign, were a close-knit group. They operated in an ad hoc, collegial manner. Many of the recommendations for major presidential decisions and actions were the product of group decisions.

Lyndon Johnson inherited Kennedy's staff structure and did little to change it initially beyond the addition of several of his long-time aides. Over the course of his administration, however, the jurisdiction of those who worked in the White House became more clearly defined. Policy advisers, in particular, exercised considerable influence within their respective spheres in developing recommendations and options for the president.

Nixon gave his senior policy aides even greater power and enlarged their functions accordingly. His White House was structured like a pyramid and managed by a chief of staff and two principal policy aides. Ironically, Nixon had begun his presidency by announcing a return to a cabinet form of government in which the heads of the principal executive departments would be the prime initiators and implementors of administration policy. He contemplated a small White House staff composed of a handful of senior advisers. Nixon's personal style, however, clashed with this type of staffing system.

After a relatively short time, Nixon instituted changes that resulted in a larger, more specialized White House staff that numbered in excess of five hundred people, with sizable policy staffs in the national security and domestic areas supporting presidential activities.

The Nixon White House had clear lines of authority and vertical patterns of decision making. From a managerial perspective it operated smoothly. From a political perspective there were problems that impeded the president's ability to make and implement policy. The system insulated Nixon from the departments and agencies, members of Congress, and even from many of his own staff. Access to him was limited to a few top aides. The difficulty of communicating with the president produced dissatisfaction with White House decision-making procedures, although in the short run it also enhanced the clout of the White House aides who coordinated the processes and saw the president on a regular basis.

After his reelection in 1972, Nixon sought to expand his personal and political influence by transferring trusted White House officials to important positions in the departments and agencies. The events of Watergate aborted the plan, immobilized the White House, and raised doubts about the wisdom of having a large personal staff whose blind loyalty to the president impaired their judgment and his.

Ford and Carter both reacted to the Nixon experience in slightly different ways. Ford improved access to the president; Carter cut down on the size and status of the White House and the perquisites of those working there.

At first, both presidents also tried to organize their White House like the spokes of a wheel with themselves at the hub. Theoretically, top aides, operating autonomously within their own offices but collegially as a staff, were to have direct and easy access to the president. There was to be no chief of staff.

In practice, the system did not work well. Turf battles quickly erupted within the White House and between it and other executive agencies. These internal disputes plagued both administrations for most of their time in office.

Presidential advising was also adversely affected. The presentation of a wide range of options to the president was not assured. Each administration had difficulty establishing and articulating priorities. Presidential interests were not always protected or promoted.

Eventually, a more efficient operating structure emerged in each administration. Coordination between the White House and the departments improved. A chief of staff was appointed, and each president began to use his own time more wisely. Lines of authority were more clearly designated.

The lessons of the Ford and Carter experiences were not lost on subsequent presidents. What were these lessons? First, the White House had grown too large and too specialized during the 1970s to operate effectively without a tight administrative structure and efficient operating procedures. Second, while considerable autonomy was necessary for those engaged in policy making and consensus building, the individual offices in the White House that dealt with these activities had to be coordinated if the administration was to speak with a single voice and act in a unified manner. Third, although White House involvement in a host of presidential activities could not be easily reduced, the activities and initiatives of the president could be more carefully marshalled.

Ronald Reagan's approach when he began his presidency was to maintain a large, structurally differentiated White House, even expanding the staff to include more outreach efforts. A more centralized management orientation was imposed with the cabinet council system used to coordinate the input of departments into the policy-making process.

The system worked well in Reagan's first term and at the end of his second largely because of the personal interaction of the senior aides who oversaw the operation of the White House and linked its staff to the president. Reagan delegated considerable responsibility to his chief of staff and, during his first term, to the individuals responsible for public relations and policy development. Together this triumvirate, consisting of James Baker, chief of staff; Michael Deaver, deputy chief of staff; and Edwin Meese, counselor to the president, orchestrated the staff's activity, monitored the operation of the different White House units, briefed the president on a daily basis, and acted on his behalf.

Personnel changes at the beginning of Reagan's second term, however, produced a very different environment for White House decision making. Instead of a small group coordinating policy and public relationships, a single chief of staff dominated all aspects of White House activity. Instead of adjusting policy objectives to the political realities of the times, a more consistent ideological perspective was imposed. Instead of having the president speak out on a variety of issues, an administration spokesperson took over more of the burden. The result was a White House operation that eased the president's load as it shielded him from external opinions and limited his contact with the outside world. The machinations of several members of the national security staff that culminated in the Iran–Contra affair as well as the president's unprepared and disengaged reaction to the affair illustrate the dangers for presidents of delegating too much power and providing too little supervision of the White House. In its final two years, the Reagan White House returned to a more collaborative, coordinated, politically sensitive operation.

The early Bush White House followed the pattern established during the final Reagan years. A chief of staff, John Sununu, oversaw White House operations as well as closely monitored the flow of people and papers to the president. Senior staff aides for the most part reported through Sununu to the president. Sununu's abrasive manner and controlling personality, his strong ideological perspective, and his penchant for publicity got him into trouble, decreased his usefulness to the president, and eventually forced him to resign from office. Charged with ethical violations that included the personal use of White House air and ground transportation, Sununu soon found himself the object of ridicule, fueled by negative criticism from those in the Congress and the executive branch whom he had offended.

Not only did Sununu's predicament embarrass the administration, but it created the appearance of an administration that lacked internal discipline and strong presidential control. Sununu's replacement, Department of Transportation Secretary Samuel Skinner, was not able to impose order on the policy-making and mobilizing activities of the administration. Although Bush's third chief of staff, James Baker, former Reagan chief and Bush secretary of state, exercised greater discipline over White House–executive branch operations and relations, he was not able to exert control over the president's reelection campaign.

The Clinton White House was also beset by internal, start-up problems that persisted into the fifth month of the presidency. Lines of authority were unclear; senior staff meetings were large, long, and discursive; there were frequent leaks of pending or proposed decisions; access to the president was not sufficiently limited nor was effective use made of his time. Poor staff work resulted in a slow and sloppy appointment process, inadequate communication and consultation with members of Congress, mixed messages to the public, and embarrassing presidential activities such as a $200 haircut on Air Force I when it was sitting on a runway at Los Angeles airport.[13]

These blunders, which contributed to low public approval ratings for Clinton, indicated that the president was not being well served by his staff. After only five months in office, Clinton initiated structural and personnel changes in the White House. He appointed David Gergan, former aide to Republican presidents Nixon, Ford, and Reagan, as counselor. Gergan directed the external activities of the administration, clarifying, simplifying, and focusing the president's message as well as improving relations with the media that would transmit it to the public. He also had an interest in keeping Clinton on the moderate policy course articulated during his 1992 presidential campaign. George Stephanopolus, former communications director, moved to a new position of senior adviser. His charge was to look at the implications of decisions and actions Clinton contemplated, identifying the "you-can't-do-it-issues" that the president should avoid. Thomas "Mac" McLarty, White House chief of staff, was relieved of overseeing its day-to-day operations, thereby allowing him to represent the president with the Washington community, particularly with members of Congress. Roy Neel, McLarty's new deputy and formerly head of Vice President Gore's staff, took over functional control of the White House. (See Figure 6-2 for the contemporary White House structure.)

### Trends in White House Staffing

Since its creation, the White House has undergone significant growth. It has become more specialized. Greater presidential needs and responsibilities have resulted in a larger and more functionally differentiated office. Most recent presidents have added to the structure. Eisenhower established a congressional liaison office; Kennedy created a national security adviser and staff; Johnson instituted a domestic counterpart; Nixon expanded both policy staffs as well as the press and communications offices; Ford added an economic assistant and a modest public liaison operation; Carter vastly enlarged the public liaison function as well as created an office for intergovernmental affairs; Reagan added a political affairs office and a secretariat for cabinet administration

Figure 6-2. The Contemporary White House

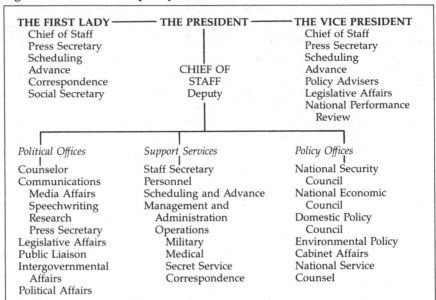

| THE FIRST LADY —— THE PRESIDENT —— THE VICE PRESIDENT |
| Chief of Staff | | Chief of Staff |
| Press Secretary | | Press Secretary |
| Scheduling | | Scheduling |
| Advance | CHIEF OF | Advance |
| Correspondence | STAFF | Policy Advisers |
| Social Secretary | Deputy | Legislative Affairs |
| | | National Performance |
| | | Review |

| *Political Offices* | *Support Services* | *Policy Offices* |
| Counselor | Staff Secretary | National Security |
| Communications | Personnel | Council |
| Media Affairs | Scheduling and Advance | National Economic |
| Speechwriting | Management and | Council |
| Research | Administration | Domestic Policy |
| Press Secretary | Operations | Council |
| Legislative Affairs | Military | Environmental Policy |
| Public Liaison | Medical | Cabinet Affairs |
| Intergovernmental | Secret Service | National Service |
| Affairs | Correspondence | Counsel |
| Political Affairs | | |

in addition to a short-lived office of planning and evaluation. Clinton created a national economic council to coordinate economic policy making and an enlarged communications office to mount public relations campaigns for his major initiatives. Although the number of full-time staff budgeted to the White House has been reduced, largely for reasons of politics and public relations, the functions and capabilities of the office are as large as ever.

The institutional components reflect these functions. There is little presidents can do to alter them as long as the expectations and obligations they inherit remain large. They may tinker with the structure, but they cannot radically change it.

Over time, the White House becomes more important to presidents. Over time, their need for a more centrally managed and efficiently run staff becomes obvious in large part because presidents find that they depend more and more on their assistants for information, advice, and liaison activities in addition to the servicing of their own needs.

White House staffs tend to expand over the course of an administration, and presidents come to rely increasingly on their staffs as leaks and loyalty problems surface and as press and public criticism mounts. Ironically, the larger and more powerful the staff becomes, the more resistant it is to the president's personal control. Like any large organization, it develops a structure and a routine of its own.

Moreover, the staff operation tends to exhibit self-perpetuating tendencies. These tendencies may even be reinforced as personnel leave and subordinates are promoted to replace them. Turfs are established and protected. Standard operating procedures evolve. The White House achieves greater autonomy over priority decision making. It begins to engulf the president particularly when the president depends increasingly on it.

Presidents exert the most influence on their staff at the top among their senior aides. Their personal style affects staff interaction, priorities, and, to a lesser extent, the operation of individual White House offices. Whether presidents choose to overlap their aides' jurisdiction or carefully delineate their authority, to have them compete or operate in a collegial manner, to delegate decision making or get involved in the details themselves is their prerogative, although there are consequences for each of these ways of doing business.

### Evaluating the Staffing System

There have been three basic models that presidents have employed to organize their White Houses: the *collegial* model that Kennedy used, and with which Carter and Clinton began; the *competitive* system that Franklin Roosevelt engineered; and the *formal, centrally managed* model that characterized the Nixon presidency, and, to a lesser extent, the Eisenhower and Reagan White Houses. Each of these staffing arrangements has its pros and cons.

The collegial system is characterized by a relatively small group of senior aides who work informally together to advise the president and plan and coordinate administration positions and responses. The key ingredient is their working together. The system is predicated on the ability of the president's top assistants to adopt a team approach and generate loyalty and to do so without centralized direction and control.

Most collegial staffs come directly from the presidential campaign. One danger with recruiting campaign staff is that they often lack executive experience. Running a campaign and operating a White House are not the same nor do they involve the same skills. Moreover, campaign aides are apt to be "true believers" who mistrust those who do not share these beliefs and did not participate in the presidential campaign. They may also be less willing to compromise to achieve their campaign policy objectives. Staffing problems, resulting from the appointment of inexperienced campaign aides, surfaced during the first years of the Carter and Clinton administrations.

Another danger of the collegial system is that the team may be too cohesive, their perceptions too uniform, and their advice too complementary. The psychologist Irving Janis refers to this problem as "groupthink" and suggests that it is most apt to occur in crisis situations. What happens, according to Janis, is that the crisis generates a desire for unity among policy advisers. Critical opinions are suspended and a consensus is produced.[14]

A number of high-level administration decisions may have been influenced by this groupthink effect. The ill-fated decision by almost all of Kennedy's advisers to support an invasion of the Bay of Pigs in Cuba in 1961 is an illustration that Janis uses to support his thesis. Other examples include the reaction to the Japanese attack on Pearl Harbor, the response to North Korean aggression, the escalation of the Vietnam War, and the White House response to the Iraqi invasion of Kuwait.

Presidents have sought to avoid the danger of groupthink. When the Bay of Pigs attack failed, Kennedy consciously would absent himself from the staff deliberations so that discussion could be more candid. Ford would request opposing points of view in meetings he attended. Carter and Bush insisted on being presented with a wide range of options.

To coordinate advisers and relieve the president from being overburdened with detailed decisions, a formalistic, centrally managed system with clear lines of authority has been used. In such a system senior aides are given authority within their functional areas but report through a hierarchy that organizes and coordinates the entire operation. The chief of staff presides over the structure.

The chief's job is to ensure that the White House is run efficiently and effectively, to provide the president with a range of information and options, and to make certain that decisions are implemented in accordance with the president's wishes. The chief may also be an advocate, but not at the expense of these other responsibilities. Finally, the chief of staff must be a lightning rod for criticism, deflecting it from the president.

The problem with an hierarchial system controlled by a single individual is that it can be too efficient. Important decisions can get made before they reach the Oval Office. At the top, a presidential assistant can become an assistant president. This occurred during the Reagan administration when Chief of Staff Donald Regan unduly restricted the flow of people and paper into the Oval Office, thereby isolating President Reagan.

In general, a centrally managed system aggravates the proclivity toward isolation that White Houses usually evidence over time. It can work to insulate presidents and those around them from public as well as private criticism. The risk, similar to the groupthink effect, is that sufficient weight will not be given to countervailing views. Bad policy decisions and poor political judgments can result.

What should presidents do? Which structural model in whole or part would best facilitate the achievement of their policy objectives and political goals and do so at the least cost? The answer depends on the kinds of decisions that need to be made and the president's personal style of decision making. We explore both of these variables in the chapters that follow.[15]

In general, those presidents who wish to maximize their involvement, their discretion, and their influence benefit more from a fluid advisory relationship. On the other hand, those who prefer to make the final decision themselves, leaving the burden of soliciting and coordinating advice to others, are better served by a more formal arrangement. Kennedy, Johnson, Carter, and Clinton fall into the first category; Nixon and Reagan into the second, although in each case too much fluidity or too much structure can be dangerous. Ford and Bush fall somewhere in between the two groups.

Presidents who wish to depart from existing policy, particularly that which is based on strong outside interests, would tend to gain most from the flexible advisory arrangement. The less formal the structure, the more quickly it can respond to changing conditions and the more easily it can produce innovative policy. Kennedy is an example of a president who had these objectives, who desired new and creative policy. Johnson is another. Nixon and Carter, in contrast, were less interested in innovation and more interested in obtaining the careful analysis that a well-staffed White House policy operation could produce.

To use the leadership dichotomy we have presented, if the president wishes to exert leadership as a facilitator, then the office can tolerate more open discussion, produce more options, and provide more interactive patterns than if the president wishes to be a director of change. The director comes with a vision, usually developed and articulated during the campaign, and uses the White House to refine and promote it. Clinton tried to do this with his economic stimulus, deficit reduction, and health care plans, but found that he could not get his policy adopted unless he incorporated the views of others whose support he needed. He thus was forced to move from a relatively closed policy-making system to one that openly solicited the opinions of the larger political community in which any president must operate.

There is no one formula for good presidential staffing, but good presidential staffing is a critical component of the formula for effective presidential leadership. Although presidents may be more dependent on others than they were in the past, they can still affect the staffing they receive. They can and do influence the personnel, organization, and operation of their own office. That is why, if they are victimized by their own staff, they usually have themselves at least partially to blame.

## INVOLVING THE VICE PRESIDENT

Presidential support has been supplemented in recent years by the activities of the vice president and his staff. These activities range from providing policy advice and making political appeals to performing a variety of ceremonial functions. It was not always this way.

For years the vice presidency was regarded as a position of little importance. It was the brunt of jokes and laments. The nation's first vice president, John Adams, complained, "My country has in its wisdom contrived for me the most insignificant office that ever the invention of man contrived or his imagination conceived."[16] Thomas Jefferson, the second person to hold the office, was not quite as critical. Describing his job as "honorable and easy," he added, "I am unable to decide whether I would rather have it or not have it."[17]

Throughout most of the nineteenth century, the vice president performed very limited functions. Other than succeeding to the presidency, the holder of this position had only one designated constitutional responsibility—presiding over the Senate and voting in case of a tie. Nor did presidents enlarge these responsibilities very much. Vice presidents played only a peripheral role within their respective administrations, so much so that when Professor Woodrow Wilson wrote his treatise on American government in the 1880s, he devoted only one paragraph to the vice president. "The chief embarrassment in . . . explaining how little there is to be said about it," Wilson concluded, is that "one has evidently said all there is to say."[18] John Nance Garner, Franklin Roosevelt's first vice president, offered perhaps the most earthy refrain in his much-quoted comment that the office was "hardly worth a pitcher of spit."

Were Adams, Jefferson, and Garner alive today, they would have to reevaluate their assessments. The position has increased enormously in importance. Roosevelt's sudden death, Eisenhower's illness, and Kennedy's assassination cast attention on the vice president and generated support for clarifying succession during presidential disability and for filling the vice presidency should it become vacant. These events also contributed to the enhancement of the office by encouraging presidents to do more to prepare their vice president for the number one job.

Eisenhower was the first of the modern presidents to upgrade the vice president's role. He invited Richard Nixon, his vice president, to attend cabinet, National Security Council, and legislative strategy meetings. During his illness, Nixon presided over these sessions. According to Bradley H. Patterson, Jr.:

> Nixon was present at over 171 Cabinet meetings and chaired at least 20 of them in Ike's absence. He attended more than 217 NSC meetings and presided at some 26 of those, joined 173 legislative leaders' meetings, chairing two of them. The Cabinet and the National Security Council papers were sent to Nixon; his policy assistant attended both the post-Cabinet debriefings at the White House and the meetings of the NSC Planning Board. Eisenhower's privileged daily Staff Notes information memoranda were also taken to the vice president.[19]

In addition, as vice president, Nixon was sent on a number of well-publicized trips for the administration.

Lyndon Johnson was also involved in a variety of activities. As John Kennedy's vice president, he helped coordinate administration efforts to eliminate racial discrimination and promote exploration of outer space. He participated in legislative lobbying efforts, joining Kennedy at the White House breakfasts for congressional leaders. He also traveled abroad on behalf of the administration. Nonetheless, Johnson was not enamored with the job. To biographer Doris Kearns he stated: "Every time I came into John Kennedy's presence, I felt like a goddamn raven hovering over his shoulder. Away from the Oval Office, it was even worse. The Vice Presidency is filled with trips around the world, chauffeurs, men saluting, people clapping, chairmanships of councils, but in the end, it is nothing. I detested every minute of it."[20]

Despite their own experiences, neither Johnson nor Nixon added new responsibilities to the office, although both continued to have their vice presidents perform a variety of ceremonial, diplomatic, and political roles, such as chairing committees, making speeches, and representing the administration at international and national events. Hubert Humphrey, Johnson's vice president, and Spiro Agnew, Nixon's vice president, were not influential presidential advisers. Humphrey was not invited to the Tuesday lunch group strategy sessions for the Vietnam War, and Agnew found his access to the president more and more limited as the administration progressed. Neither exercised major influence on the formulation of important policy initiatives within their administrations.

Nelson Rockefeller, Gerald Ford's vice president, had the opportunity to do so. He was given good personal access to the president and an important policy-making role—to oversee the development of domestic programs. Quickly, however, his priorities clashed with those of others within the administration. Coming under increasing criticism from conservative Republicans, he announced his intention not to seek the vice presidency in the 1976 election and subsequently removed himself from an active policy-making and advisory role.

Whereas Rockefeller did not realize the vice president's potential as a presidential adviser, Walter Mondale did. He was the first vice president to have an office in the West Wing of the White House. Moreover, his staff was integrated with the president's.

Mondale saw Carter on a regular basis. While he had no ongoing administrative responsibilities, he was given *carte blanche* to be included in any conference, see any paper, and participate in any study that he desired. Carter writes in his memoirs that Mondale " . . . received the same security briefings I got, was automatically invited to participate in all my official meetings, and helped to plan strategy for domestic programs, diplomacy, and defense."[21] Carter also provided opportunities for Mondale to shape policy, and he did. He was also instrumental in improving congressional relations for the administration, heading a priority-setting mechanism, facilitating administration lobbying on key bills, helping to establish a public liaison operation in the White House, and using his own political connections to groups outside the government to improve coalition building for the president.

When President Reagan wished to demonstrate his concern with crisis management, drug enforcement, and government relations, he appointed Vice President Bush to head committees studying these issues. Bush also served as a personal envoy of the president in visits to North Atlantic Treaty Organization (NATO) countries, on a fact-finding trip to Lebanon, and by attending the funerals of several foreign policy leaders. When he was in Washington he attended key White House meetings with the president, had a one- on-one lunch with Reagan on a weekly basis, and was in the loop on major administrative policy decisions.[22] His aides represented him at the senior staff meetings.

Dan Quayle played a role in the Bush administration similar to the one that Bush played in the Reagan administration, but Quayle attracted more public attention. As vice president, Quayle was sent on a number of fact-finding and morale-boosting trips to Latin America, Europe, and the Persian Gulf. He nominally chaired the committee overseeing space exploration as Lyndon Johnson had done during the Kennedy administration. He also served as a liaison to conservative groups and members of Congress.

Quayle's most important policy-making role was as head of a business-oriented group known as the Council of Competitiveness. The objective of this council was to prevent the government from imposing regulations that had the effect of making American businesses less competitive. In this capacity, Quayle engineered the delay, reduction, or elimination of regulations that threatened to have an adverse effect on business. Although he was an active participant in internal discussions within the administration, he was not perceived to be an influential policy adviser.

Vice President Al Gore has had considerable policy and personal influence within the Clinton administration, particularly within his areas of expertise—the environment and advanced technology. He has participated in the selection of the cabinet and some subcabinet appointments, reviewed the drafts of presidential speeches, and headed a committee to "reinvent government." The committee proposed organizational and management reforms to make government more efficient and less costly. Overseeing the implementation of these reforms also falls within the vice president's responsibilities.

Gore has also been a key lobbyist for the administrations's major legislative initiatives and has played a role in overseeing regulatory policy. Like other vice presidents, he has also attended party functions, engaged in personal and presidential diplomacy, and participated in public outreach efforts for the administration.

One reason for the influence of contemporary vice presidents has been their willingness to exercise power behind the scenes. Another has been to let the president take the credit. According to Paul C. Light, these experiences suggest four cardinal rules for vice presidents:

1. *Never complain to the press.* One of Rockefeller's continuing problems in the Ford administration was his high profile in the press. Leaks were easily traced to the vice president's office.
2. *Never take credit from the president.* The vice president must remember who is president and who is not.
3. *Fall in line.* No matter how much the vice president opposes a

presidential decision, he or she must support the final policy. The vice president does not have to become a vocal supporter or lobbyist, but must fall in line like any other staffer.

4. *Share the dirty work.* Though the vice president may not like endless travel (and nights in Holiday Inns, as Mondale once complained), it is all part of being a team player. Mondale, for example, was on the road 600 days during his term.[23]

The growth of the vice presidency has not only benefited the vice president, but it has also worked to the president's advantage. It has provided him with additional resources for the performance of his ceremonial and symbolic functions, and additional policy advice from an official who shares his national and political perspective.

Each of these advantages, however, can become a disadvantage if the vice president rivals the president for political influence, policy direction, or personal power. Presidents want strong and loyal support, but they do not relish internal opposition, particularly from those who are a heartbeat or an election away from replacing them. That is why the vice president's influence is still dependent to a much larger extent on the president's personal needs than on the institutional responsibilities of the office.

## THE PRESIDENT'S SPOUSE

The president's spouse has the potential to become an important component of the contemporary presidency. Hillary Rodham Clinton's role as chief architect and lobbyist for the Clinton administration's health care proposal has enlarged the role that a spouse can play. Mrs. Clinton, however, was not the first wife to perform nonsocial and ceremonial functions in the White House. Edith Wilson, Eleanor Roosevelt, and Rosalyn Carter also engaged in activities with political consequences and policy implications.

After Woodrow Wilson was felled by a severe stroke, Mrs. Wilson, along with presidential adviser Colonel House, helped him assume or appear to assume his responsibilities in his last year in office. Eleanor Roosevelt also helped her husband overcome a medical disability. Because the president was crippled by polio and unable to get around, Mrs. Roosevelt became in effect another pair of eyes and ears for him. She traveled across the country on the president's behalf, collecting information, releasing trial balloons, and acting as his personal liaison to individuals and groups.

Of the more contemporary first ladies, Rosalyn Carter and her predecessor Betty Ford had broad interests in mental health issues that they pursued in the White House. Mrs. Carter was the first presidential spouse to attend cabinet meetings and also had a weekly business lunch with the president.

Other presidential wives, including Betty Ford and Nancy Reagan, also spoke out on health-related issues. Mrs. Reagan's "just say no" campaign was used to highlight the administration's educational efforts to combat illegal drugs. Although she was not involved in policy making, Mrs. Reagan influenced the president's scheduling, particularly his travels. She also was instrumental in ousting those whom she believed were not serving the president well. Her efforts played a major role in the departure of Chief of Staff Donald Regan and Attorney General Edwin Meese.

Hillary Rodham Clinton's participation in the policy and personnel decisions of the Clinton administration has been more extensive than any of her predecessors. Designated to coordinate the administration's health care initiatives, Mrs. Clinton has met with members of Congress, industry representatives, and policy experts.[24] She has also held town meetings in which many individuals and groups were invited to speak and held numerous interviews with the media after the plan was unveiled.

Her role has been controversial. Critics have complained that her unique relationship to the president makes her less vulnerable to the usual constraints on presidential advisers, placing her in a position to impose her own views on the president and those around him and to intercede and prevent others from reaching the president. By law, no member of the president's immediate family may hold an appointive position within the federal government. The law, however, does not prevent Mrs. Clinton or any other spouse from performing presidentially directed tasks for free. Much like the vice president's responsibilities, most aspects of the job of the president's spouse are conditioned by evolving precedent, but must ultimately be approved by the president.


## CONCLUSION

Today the tasks of contemporary presidents are far too numerous, require too much knowledge, and may be fraught with too many obstacles for presidents to undertake them alone. They need the information and advice of others; they need to build and maintain political alliances; and they need to increase the credit and reduce the blame for their actions. All of these needs are serviced by their presidential office.

The founders undoubtedly would have been surprised and probably dismayed by the growth and institutionalization of that office. They conceived of the president in narrower terms, as a chief executive with subsidiary responsibilities. They also envisioned his need for subordinates and advisers. Still, nothing in their deliberations suggests an institution as large, complex, and influential as the presidential office has become.

Most of this growth has occurred in the twentieth century, much of it since World War II. The office has become larger, more specialized, and increasingly politicized. It has developed an independent capacity to advise and inform the president, to formulate and prioritize policy, to orchestrate and oversee department and agency input, and to build public and congressional support.

As a result of this growth, senior presidential aides have become more important, more prestigious, and more visible. They occupy more of the president's time. In contrast, department secretaries have lost some of their status, their access to the president, and their exclusive influence over policy within their departments' primary spheres.

Not only has the creation and maintenance of a presidential office occurred at the expense of the departments and agencies, but it may also have occurred at some cost to the president. While the influence of the presidency and its capacity to affect policy have undoubtedly been enhanced, the president's personal ability to oversee his staff on an ongoing basis has not. In fact, it has been made more difficult by the large size of the office and the number of functional responsibilities it performs.

This has placed contemporary presidents in a dilemma. They need a large, functionally differentiated staff to exercise leadership, yet their leadership is frequently at the mercy of that staff. Thus, the expansion of the presidential office has been a mixed blessing. Created to meet increased expectations, it has generated new ones. Designed to coordinate and facilitate executive branch decision making, it has produced serious tensions between the White House and the departments. Tailored to systematize advice to the president, it has proliferated that advice and sometimes has worked to isolate presidents from their advisers.

Yet, its expansion has obviously been necessary. It has been both a cause and effect of the growth of government, of the executive branch, and of the president's leadership responsibilities.

## NOTES

1. James Anderson, "A Revised View of the Johnson Cabinet," *Journal of Politics* 48 (1986): 531.

2. Ibid.: 534–35.

3. The need to develop a team approach and produce new policy is most acute at the beginning of an administration when cabinet input is desired. Toward the end, the implementation of that policy, often the prerogative of a single department, consumes more time. The increasing constraints on a president's time resulting from periods of extended foreign travel or the quest for reelection also make it difficult for presidents to continue to meet with their cabinet on a regular basis.

4. President-elect Clinton acknowledged the importance of these particular secretaries when he announced his intention to name a woman to one of these top four positions. After nominating and then withdrawing the name of Zoe Baird for attorney general, Clinton nominated and the Senate confirmed Janet Reno as attorney general, the first woman to hold this office.

5. Thomas E. Cronin, *The State of the Presidency* (Boston: Little, Brown, 1980), p. 283.

6. The White House budget is supplemented by other executive departments that provide services for the president and his staff. These include units of the Department of Defense—the White House Communications Agency (secure communications), the Air Force (air transportation), the Army (explosive detection and ground transportation), and

the Navy (helicopter transportation, Marine guards, food, and medical facilities)—the General Service Administration (buildings and grounds), National Park Service (visitors and the fine arts collection), National Archives (custody of official documents), Secret Service (protection of the president, vice president, and their families as well as those of former presidents), and the State Department (official visits and receptions for foreign dignitaries).

7. Thomas McLarty, "White House Press Briefing," February 9, 1993, p. 2.

8. Ann Devroy, "Adding Up Clinton's Cuts," *Washington Post*, September 30, 1993, pp. A1, 7.

9. For the case for centralization and politicization, see Terry M. Moe, "The Politicized Presidency," in John E. Chubb and Paul E. Peterson, eds., *The New Direction in American Politics* (Washington, D.C.: Brookings Institution, 1985), pp. 235–71.

10. William C. Spragens, "White House Staffs, 1789–1974," in Bradley D. Nash et al., eds., *Organizing and Staffing the Presidency* (New York: Center for the Study of the Presidency, 1980), pp. 20–21.

11. Ibid.

12. Richard E. Neustadt, "Approaches to Staffing the Presidency," *American Political Science Review* 54 (December 1963): 857.

13. Clinton's haircut not only damaged his popular image as a person who experienced poverty and shared the values of the common people, but also inconvenienced thousands of travelers whose planes could not land at the airport because of the security concerns posed by Air Force I's location on a runway.

14. Irving Janis, *Groupthink* (Boston: Houghton Mifflin, 1982).

15. For an excellent article that examines the fit between organizational structure and personal style, see Bruce Buchanan, "Constrained Diversity: The Organizational Demands of the Presidency," *Presidential Studies Quarterly* (1990): 791–822.

16. John Adams, *The Works of John Adams*, ed. C. F. Adams (Boston: Little, Brown, 1850), vol. 1, p. 289.

17. Thomas Jefferson, *The Writings of Thomas Jefferson*, ed. P. L. Ford (New York: Putnam, 1896), vol. 1, pp. 98–99.

18. Woodrow Wilson, *Congressional Government* (New York: Meridian Books, 1956; originally printed in 1885), p. 162.

19. Bradley H. Patterson, Jr., *The Ring of Power* (New York: Basic Books, 1988), p. 287.

20. Lyndon Johnson, quoted in Doris Kearns, *Lyndon Johnson and the American Dream* (New York: Harper & Row, 1976), p. 164.

21. Jimmy Carter, *Keeping Faith* (New York: Bantam Books, 1982), p. 39.

22. His attendance at these meetings got him into trouble when the Iran–Contra affair became public. Accused of knowing of the plan and being part of the group that approved it, Bush denied his involvement, claiming that he could not even remember the discussion of it at key White House meetings. One week before the 1992 election, however, the special prosecutor, who was investigating the planning and execution of the operation, indicated that he believed that Bush attended the critical meetings in which the plan was discussed and thus knew about it. This charge severely damaged Bush's credibility and undercut the trust issue that he had raised during the campaign.

23. Paul C. Light, "Second Counts: Filling the New Vice Presidency" (paper presented at the Brookings Institution, Washington, D.C., 1984), pp. 20–21.

24. A report in the *Washington Post* indicated that Mrs. Clinton consulted with members of Congress over 100 times during the first 200 days of the Clinton presidency (Donnie Radcliffe, "The Capitol Climb of the First Lady," *Washington Post*, September 21, 1993, pp. D1, 2).

## SELECTED READINGS

Anderson, James E. "A Revised View of the Johnson Cabinet." *Journal of Politics* 48 (1986): 529–37.

Buchanan, Bruce. "Constrained Diversity: The Organizational Demands of the Presidency." *Presidential Studies Quarterly* (1990): 791–822.

Campbell, Colin. *Managing the Presidency*. Pittsburgh: University of Pittsburgh Press, 1986.

Cohen, Jeffrey E. *The Politics of the U.S. Cabinet: Representation in the Executive Branch, 1789–1984.* Pittsburgh: University of Pittsburgh Press, 1988.

Hart, John. *The Presidential Branch.* New York: Pergamon, 1987.

Janis, Irving. *Groupthink.* Boston: Houghton Mifflin, 1982.

Kernell, Samuel, and Samuel L. Popkin, eds. *Chief of Staff: Twenty-Five Years of Managing the Presidency.* Berkeley, Calif.: University of California Press, 1986.

Kessel, John H. "The Structures of the Carter White House." *American Journal of Political Science* 27 (1983): 431–63.

———. "The Structures of the Reagan White House." *American Journal of Political Science* 28 (1984): 231–58.

Light, Paul C. *Vice Presidential Power.* Baltimore: Johns Hopkins University Press, 1984.

Moe, Terry M. "The Politicized Presidency." In John E. Chubb and Paul E. Petersen, eds. *The New Direction in American Politics.* Washington D.C.: Brookings Institution, 1985, pp. 235–71.

Patterson, Bradley H., Jr. *The Ring of Power.* New York: Basic Books, 1988.

Pfiffner, James P., ed. *The Managerial Presidency.* Belmont, Calif.: Brooks-Cole, 1990.

Pfiffner, James P., and R. Gordon Hoxie, eds. *The Presidency in Transition.* New York: Center for the Study of the Presidency, 1989.

Reedy, George. *The Twilight of the Presidency.* New York: New American Library, 1987.

Rockman, Bert A. "The Style and Organization of the Reagan Presidency." In Charles O. Jones, ed. *The Reagan Legacy.* Chatham, N.J.: Chatham House, 1988, pp. 3–29.

Walcott, Charles, and Karen M. Hult. "Organizing the White House: Structure, Environment, and Organizational Governance." *American Journal of Political Science* 31 (1987): 109–125.

# 7

# Presidential Decision Making

The essence of the president's job is making decisions—about foreign affairs, economic policy, and literally hundreds of other important matters. The task is a difficult one, and many obstacles to rational decision making are present. Leadership in the area of decision making is of a different nature than in the other arenas of presidential activity we examine in this book. Presidents need to ensure that they have before them a full range of options and the appropriate information necessary for evaluating them.

The president's leadership in decision making requires the establishment of a working relationship with subordinates and an organization in the White House that serves presidential decision-making needs. Often the president will have to persuade his own appointees in the White House and the bureaucracy to provide him with the options and information that he requires. As we will see, they have many incentives not to do so.

There are other obstacles as well. Lack of time to consider decisions and previous commitments of the government may constrain a president's decision making. So may the president's own personal experiences and personality.

Director presidents will have a full range of options and information at their disposal, and they will be relatively unencumbered by environmental constraints on their range of choices. More subject to the influence of contextual factors, facilitator presidents will be more dependent on their environment for options and information and more constrained in their decision making.

Figure 7-1 is a graphical representation of the influences on presidential decision making. In the outer circles are the broad contexts in which decisions take place; in the inner circles are the more immediate influences. In this chapter we examine the influence the factors represented in the outer five rings have on presidential decision making. In the following chapter we consider the impact of the president's personal characteristics.

Figure 7-1. Influences on Presidential Decision Making

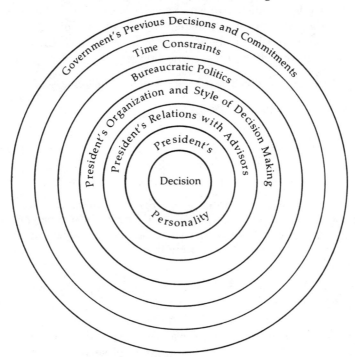

## PREVIOUS COMMITMENTS

The first step in understanding presidential decision making is to recognize that presidents operate under severe constraints in their decision making, no matter what their approaches to making decisions. As Kennedy aide Theodore Sorensen has observed:

> We assume that the President makes decisions. . . . Presidents rarely, if ever make decisions . . . in the sense of writing their conclusions largely on a clean slate. They make choices. They select options. They exercise judgments. But the basic decisions, which confine their choices, have all too often been previously made by past events or circumstances, by other nations, by pressures or predecessors or even subordinates.[1]

Thus, the president's decisions usually fall within parameters set by prior commitments of the government that obligate it to spend money, defend allies, maintain services, or protect rights.[2]

For example, when Bill Clinton took office in January 1993, the American people were in general agreement that the federal deficit was the most important matter for the new president to tackle. Clinton was not able to start from scratch and consider how best to allocate federal expenditures, however. As we discuss in Chapter 13, almost the entire federal budget was already committed before Clinton took the oath of office. A president could propose to save money by, say, eliminating the navy or ending the provision of health care for the indigent, but such solutions would receive little support. Clinton's decision making was restricted to marginal changes in the budget.

## TIME CONSTRAINTS

The diverse obligations of the president and his top aides impose severe constraints on the amount of time they can devote to generating and evaluating options and information. According to a Carter aide:

> When the President asks to see all the potential alternatives, it is an impossible request. Not only do we have to limit the range to the few that just might work but we have to cut back to save on time. The staff already has too much to do without attempting that kind of analysis—it involves too much time.[3]

Overloaded advisers may rely on others, equally overloaded, to bring crucial information to the attention of the president. Several of President Truman's advisers believed there was a serious danger of Chinese intervention in the Korean War if the president attempted to reunite all of Korea under a non-Communist government. However, no one went to him to argue that he should reverse his decision allowing General MacArthur to invade Communist North Korea. Each person thought that someone else would do it.[4]

The president and his advisers rarely have the luxury of anticipating new issues. According to Zbigniew Brzezinski, President Carter's national security assistant, at the time the fateful revolution in Iran began,

> our decision making circuits were heavily overloaded. The fall of 1978 was the time of the Camp David process and its aftermath. This was also the time of the stepped-up SALT negotiations, and during the critical December days we would literally rush from one meeting, in which the most complex positions on telemetry encryption or cruise missile definition would be hammered out, to another meeting on the fate of Iran. The fall . . . was also the period of the critical phase in the secret U.S.-Chinese negotiations. . . . In addition, the crisis in Nicaragua was beginning to preoccupy and absorb us. Finally, [Secretary of State] Cy Vance was heavily involved in key negotiations abroad, notably in the Middle East, while for [Secretary of Defense] Harold Brown this was the period of most difficult battles with the President over the defense budget. . . . It was unfortunately not a time in which undivided attention could be focused easily and early on what became a fatal strategic and political turning point.[5]

Sometimes deadlines make it necessary for the president and his aides to cease the consideration of information and options and make a decision. In the words of President Reagan's budget director, David Stockman:

I just wish that there were more hours in the day or that we didn't have to do this so fast. I have these stacks of briefing books and I've got to make decisions about specific options. . . . I don't have time, trying to put this whole package together in three weeks, so you just start making snap judgments.[6]

Because of such time limits, the less controversial parts of elaborate policies often receive too little attention and contain too much logrolling.

If a study about an issue is not available when policymakers must make a decision, the report will go unread. If the report is required by a certain date and more than one person has been engaged to produce it, there is an incentive for the participants to "soften" their views in order to reach a consensus. This, in turn, can mask problems inherent in the policies they recommend. Moreover, the pressure of hammering together a report under a strict deadline may make it quite incoherent.

# ORGANIZATION AND STYLE OF DECISION MAKING

Each president is unique and has broad discretion in structuring his decision making in the White House. There are many ways to do this, and each has consequences for the effectiveness of the advisory system. In this section we explore the ways in which the organization and style of the presidential advisory process can affect the president's consideration of options and information.

## White House Organization

Many commentators on the presidency stress the formal aspects of White House organization, but they may be overemphasized, at least as they relate to presidential decision making. As Kennedy aide Theodore Sorensen has commented, "To be preoccupied with form and structure— to ascribe to . . . form and structure a capacity to end bad decisions— is too often to overlook the more dynamic and fluid forces on which presidential decisions are based."[7]

There is virtual unanimity among observers of the presidency that one cannot develop an ideal organization for the White House that is appropriate for every president. The organization of the White House will inevitably reflect the personality and work habits of the incumbent. Moreover, the chief executive's personal style will dominate any organizational scheme. If presidents have a penchant for acting without adequate study, they will defeat any advisory system that they have established in the White House. According to an experienced presidential aide, "The nature of the *man* is absolutely crucial and decisive, altogether overriding the issue of organization."[8]

As discussed in Chapter 6, White House structure may also reflect the goals of presidents. Those like Franklin Roosevelt, John Kennedy,

Lyndon Johnson, and Bill Clinton who were concerned with producing innovative policies have displayed a tendency toward flexible staff arrangements.

Presidents may simultaneously use several approaches to organizing their decision making, depending on their level of interest in a policy area, their policy priorities, and the strengths and limitations of their principal advisers in each policy area. For example, President Ford employed a hierarchical model of centralized management for foreign policy in which he concentrated responsibility in Henry Kissinger's hands. In economic policy, he employed a managed multiple advocacy system in which collegial discussions among a wider range of advisers occurred. In the area of domestic policy, where he did not want to undertake policy initiatives, he delegated responsibility to Vice President Rockefeller and dealt with issues on an ad hoc basis.[9] George Bush employed much the same structure in each of these policy areas.

Organizational charts may be misleading. When asked by a fellow White House assistant about drawing up an organization chart of the Johnson White House, Bill Moyers replied:

> Such an exercise is a gross misuse of a good man's time; nothing useful can come from it since the White House staff reflects the personal needs of the President rather than a structural design. . . . There is no pattern to it that can be fitted to a chart.[10]

Henry Kissinger adds that the influence of a presidential assistant "derives almost exclusively from the confidence of the President, not from administrative arrangements."[11]

We should not be surprised, then, that top Carter aides sometimes "walked" their memos into the president's office when he was gone, circumventing the prescribed system for the circulation of memoranda to the president (to ensure that all relevant views were gathered), and then made sure that their memos were on top of the president's pile. President Eisenhower's decision-making process was really much more fluid than the rigid hierarchy that would appear on an organization chart. Nixon adviser John Connally regularly bypassed the White House chain of command.

Sometimes what appears to be crucial presidential consultation with advisers is actually much less. One of the crucial moments in America's involvement in Vietnam came in July 1965 when President Johnson committed the United States to large-scale combat operations. In his memoirs Johnson goes to considerable lengths to show that he considered very carefully all the alternatives available at the time. The detailed account by one of his aides of the dialogue between Johnson and some of his advisers shows the president probing deeply for answers, challenging the premises and factual bases of options, and playing the devil's advocate. Yet a presidency scholar has argued persuasively that this "debate" was really a charade, staged by the president to lend legitimacy to the decision he already had made.[12] Richard Nixon has been accused of similar behavior.

After analyzing sources of decisional problems in foreign policy, political scientist Alexander George concluded

> There appears to be no single structural formula by which the chief executive and his staff can convert the functional expertise and diversity of viewpoints of the many offices concerned with international affairs into consistently effective policies and decisions.[13]

We may confidently add that this is also true for domestic policy decisions.

On the other hand, organization does make a difference. As we saw in the previous chapter, the two most common White House organizational schemes are the hierarchical and the "spokes of the wheel." Recent presidents have found that they require a chief of staff to coordinate the flow of White House business and to give them time to focus on priorities and reflect on questions of basic strategy.

Both Gerald Ford and Jimmy Carter began their tenures trying to employ the spokes-of-the-wheel approach, but both had to alter their organizational scheme to establish more of a hierarchical system headed by a chief of staff. The following comments by President Ford explain why this was necessary and also indicate the significance of organization:

> Initially, when I became President, I did not want to have a powerful chief of staff. . . . I was aware of the trouble . . . top assistants had caused my predecessors. I was determined to be my own chief of staff. . . . I would have five or six senior assistants with different areas of responsibility . . . and they would be able to see me at regular intervals during the day. . . . But as I was to discover soon enough, it simply didn't work. Because power in Washington is measured by how much access a person has to the President, almost everyone wanted more access than I had access to give. I wanted to have an "open" door, but it was very difficult; my working days grew longer and longer, and the demands on my time were hindering my effectiveness. Someone . . . had to be responsible for scheduling appointments, coordinating the paper flow, following up on decisions I had made and giving me status reports on projects and policy development. I didn't like the idea of calling this person chief of staff, but that in fact was the role he would fill.[14]

Hierarchical staff organizations save the president's time and promote thorough evaluation of options. Yet many observers of the presidency are concerned with such arrangements because the hierarchy that screens information may also distort it. This does not occur because presidential aides "capture" the president, however. Even in the Nixon administration, with its famed "palace guard" around the president, whatever isolation occurred in the Oval Office was with the full concurrence and encouragement of the president. The president used his staff to serve his own needs and to keep out those whom he did not want to see. As long-time presidential adviser Clark Clifford put it, "In the end, every President gets the advice—and the advisers—that, in his heart, he really wants."[15] Moreover, we lack systematic evidence that Nixon's chiefs of staff provided Nixon with a distorted view of the issues with which he desired to deal.

The president's staff also needs to screen issues so that only those requiring direct involvement by the chief executive will be presented. If attempts are made to solve all the problems that come to the White House, the president will spread his and his advisers' attention too thinly, wasting time and scarce resources. In addition, the more the president does, the more problems for which others will hold him accountable. Presidents Ford, Carter, and Clinton had tendencies toward becoming involved in relatively minor matters and were criticized, in some cases, even by their own aides, for lacking the appropriate breadth of vision and understanding necessary to shape and guide the government.

Presidents—Eisenhower, Nixon, Ford, and Reagan are examples—often want their advisers to reach a consensus on an issue and make a recommendation to them before it receives much consideration in the Oval Office. This does not mean that they will accept the recommendation, however. Gerald Ford's description of his approach is typical:

> I myself liked to have consensus developed before a problem came to my desk for decision, but then I reserved the right to go behind that consensus to find out what the differing views were in the process. In that way I got a feel as to whether it was just a weak compromise or whether it was a legitimate one that provided the best answer.[16]

### The Form of Advice

Different presidents prefer to receive advice in different forms. Presidents Nixon and Carter preferred to reach their decisions on the basis of written memoranda on the pros and cons of various options. President Clinton also relies heavily on detailed memoranda. In contrast, Presidents Eisenhower, Kennedy, Johnson, Ford, and Bush used memos to focus discussion but frequently discussed issues with advisers in relatively open settings. President Reagan had a more detached style, reading less than other recent presidents while talking directly to a small number of aides.

There are advantages and disadvantages of both the verbal and paper approaches. The latter requires that options that go to the president be thoroughly "staffed out," that is, that relevant officials comment upon them after careful analysis. As Henry Kissinger explains, if this does not occur,

> the danger is real that plausibility is confused with truth and verbal fluency overwhelms cool analysis . . . . [I]n the absence of staff work, decisions

may be made which the facts do not support, where individuals talk to impress and not to elucidate at a time when precision is crucial. The temptation . . . is . . . to allow a fleeting and superficial consensus to ratify unexamined assumptions. There are the simultaneous risks of paralysis and recklessness. Principals cannot really know the consequences of their recommendations unless those recommendations have been translated into specific operational terms.[17]

Reviewing advice on paper also saves the president time and protects the confidentiality of communications. It may also provide an outlet for those who find it difficult to express themselves directly to the president in order to articulate their views. The most vociferous critic out of the president's presence can become the meekest lamb when meeting the president personally. This inhibition in speech is not unusual. Most presidents find that people's oral skills often desert them when they are in the Oval Office.

On the other hand, the requirement that communications to the president be written and thoroughly researched may deny the chief executive access to some useful information and ideas. Some aides simply resist writing memos, as did Jody Powell, one of President Carter's closest advisers. Face-to-face discussions with advisers may also provide the president with information that is not reflected in the written word. Direct confrontation between advocates of diverse positions allows the participants to pinpoint their critiques of each other's positions and raise relevant follow-up points. Oral discussions also provide opportunities for advisers to highlight the most important points and crucial nuances in arguments and for presidents to learn the intensity of officials' views and the confidence with which they hold them. This may alert the chief executive to the level of support he may expect from officials who oppose his ultimate decision. In addition, some ideas, especially those that are highly sensitive, can be best or perhaps only advanced personally and informally in the give-and-take of conversation, and some may not be ready for memoranda but deserve mention so the president will be aware of the fullest range of options.

In order for face-to-face discussions among advisers and the chief executive to be useful, the president must be able to accommodate the interpersonal tensions inherent in an advisory system of close give-and-take. Yet not all presidents possess this tolerance. Ronald Reagan hated conflict. So did Richard Nixon, whose personality was not amenable to dealing with oral confrontations. He dreaded meeting new people, especially if they were in a position to rebuff or contradict him. To avoid tension, he spoke elliptically and had a tendency to agree with whomever he was speaking (only to disavow it later). Thus, the president conducted as much business as possible by memos, in which he was more likely to express his true views and less likely to meet with opposition. To avoid confrontations he sometimes called carefully constructed meetings that included one dissenter and began by agreeing with that person and then allowed himself to be talked out of that position, leaving the holdout isolated and more likely to join in a consensus view.

Nixon's aversion to open disagreement both affected the quality of his decision-making process and led him to alter policy decisions to achieve consensus. According to national security adviser Henry Kissinger:

> So much time, effort, and ingenuity were spent in trying to organize a consensus of the senior advisers that there was too little left to consider the weaknesses in the plan or to impose discipline on the rest of the government. There was no role for a devil's advocate. At every meeting, to gain the acquiescence of the potential recalcitrant, Nixon would offer so many modifications that the complex plan he was seeking to promote was eventually consumed. . . . Each of these steps may have been minor; the cumulative impact was considerable.[18]

The oral approach also carries the danger that the president will make a decision based on the last person talked to instead of on the basis of careful consideration of alternatives. President Ford sometimes did this, as when he agreed to support Secretary of Labor John Dunlap on a labor relations bill, only to face the opposition of the rest of his cabinet and top advisers when the bill passed. The president vetoed the bill amid embarrassing publicity on his policy reversal, angering labor interests, which felt betrayed, and undercutting his secretary of labor, who resigned over the matter.

Another requirement for the oral approach to be effective is that the president must not dominate the discussion. If he does, he may not devote sufficient attention to the advice he receives and may influence that advice by his comments. According to Hamilton Jordan, Jimmy Carter's White House chief of staff:

> I had learned when Jimmy Carter was Governor that if I wanted to change his mind or challenge him on something that was important or complicated, it was best to do it in writing. If I went into his office to argue with him, armed with five reasons to do something, I would rarely get beyond point one before he was aggressively countering it. I seldom got to the second or third point.[19]

Similarly, another Carter aide found that the president was formidable in face-to-face encounters and often persuaded him to his view, even though upon reflection he concluded the president was actually wrong on the matter. When personally confronted, the president may be on the defense; written differences of opinion may be easier to accept.

### Multiple Advocacy

Closely related to the form in which presidents receive advice is the range of options they receive and the effectiveness with which those options are presented. The president should not be dependent upon a single channel of information, as occurred, for example, when the president and other high officials, including the Joint Chiefs of Staff, relied upon the CIA's estimates of the success of the 1961 invasion of Cuba at the Bay of Pigs. It occurred again in 1965 when the president relied on the American embassy in the Dominican Republic for the information that led to the U.S. invasion of the island. Moreover, the key assumptions of alternatives should be evaluated by officials who did not develop them and thus have no personal stake in them. Only the CIA evaluated the Bay of Pigs plan, with disastrous consequences.

Quality decision making requires more than that the president be presented with a diversity of views. It is also necessary that each point of view be represented by an effective advocate. This is not always the case, however, because differences exist among advisers in persuasive skills, intellectual ability, policy expertise, power, status, standing with the president, and analytical staff support. These disparities may distort the decision-making process by giving some viewpoints an undue advantage. As Kennedy aide Theodore Sorensen has observed, "The most formidable debater is not necessarily the most informed, and the most reticent may sometimes be the wisest."[20]

Multiple advocacy also forces a larger number of issues to the top, that is, to the president; debate and give-and-take on them require a substantial commitment of time on the part of both the president and his staff, and time is a scarce commodity in the White House. According to a Ford assistant, "Multiple advocacy is very nice on paper. It just can't work in the White House. We don't have time to make sure all the advisors have access to the President. This is not day-care; it is survival of the fittest."[21] In addition, the president may not be interested in all his advisers have to offer on a policy about which he cares little.

Multiple advocacy also runs a considerable risk of increasing staff conflict. Presidents must engage in the delicate balancing act of being in firm control of the process of decision making while encouraging free and open discussion. This is difficult enough to accomplish while they are considering options. It is even more of a challenge after they decide on a course of action because it is not uncommon for both winners and losers among presidential advisers to be less than gracious and turn to backstabbing and leaks to the press.

George Bush was well-informed, knowledgeable, experienced, and involved in decision making. He wanted to hear a wide range of options, and he worked at maintaining civility and openness in discussion. Negotiations within his administration and with Congress over the Clean Air Act, for example, represented effective multiple advocacy. However, there may be a cost to sustaining such a system. One author has argued that at times positions and alternatives regarding the Persian Gulf War were not sufficiently focused and decisions were not always clear.[22]

Some political scientists have suggested that the president needs a process manager to balance the resources of his advisers and strengthen the weaker advocates, ensure that all options are articulated and have effective advocates, set up additional channels of information, arrange for independent evaluations of decisional premises and options when

necessary, and generally monitor the decision-making process and identify and correct any malfunctions. This delicate role can easily be undermined if the custodian is also a policy adviser, presidential spokesperson, enforcer of decisions, administrative operator, or watchdog for the
president's power stakes. He or she must remain an "honest broker"
concerned with the process of advising the president. This adviser must
also keep his or her own staff small so that it will not become specialized
and circumvent established channels of advice.

In some decision-making situations an adviser may adopt the role of
"devil's advocate" in order to provide a challenge to the dominant point
of view. The devil's advocate may relieve some of the stress of decision
making because officials feel they have considered all sides of an issue,
and there may be some public relations benefits for publicizing that the
president considered a full range of views. Decision makers may also
benefit from listening to and rebutting challenges to their course of
action, and those least enthusiastic about a decision may be more willing
to join in a consensus view if there has been debate before it is reached.

Nevertheless, the devil's advocate does not necessarily improve the
quality of White House decision making. Since the devil's advocate is
playing a role and is not a true dissenter, he or she is unlikely to persist
in opposition or try to form coalitions or employ all resources to persuade others. Such an advocate is not really engaged in a truly competitive struggle. Moreover, officials may discount ahead of time the comments of one who persistently plays the devil's advocate role. Yet if
devil's advocacy is not routinized, there is no assurance it will be operating when it is needed to provide balance to an argument.

Even if a president chooses to consider a range of viewpoints, he
may not benefit fully from them. For example, Gerald Ford has been
criticized for falling back on his experience as a legislator and reaching
decisions by weighing the views of others and then leaning in the direction of the consensus opinion. Presidential authority is diluted when the
chief executive bases decisions on the number of advisers on a side
rather than on his own informed judgment.

### Presidential Involvement

In his classic study of presidential power, Richard Neustadt alerted
future presidents that they would need information, including tangible
details, to construct a necessary frame of reference for decision making.[23] As we have seen, presidents cannot assume that any person or
advisory system will provide them with the options and information
they require. Thus, presidents must reach out widely for them.

If a president fails to do so, to actively oversee the decision-making
system, the consequences may be profound. Bill Clinton was blindsided
by the negative congressional and public response to his proposal to lift
the ban on gays in the military. He saw the issue as one of discrimination, but many others saw it in other terms—as an issue of morality or of

military readiness or both. By not seeking other perspectives, he subjected himself to a firestorm of criticism and had to backtrack on his policy.

Other presidents have faced similar problems. On January 17, 1986, President Ronald Reagan signed a document, technically called a "finding," that paved the way for the United States to sell arms secretly to Iran in hopes of obtaining the release of American hostages held in the Middle East. The finding also created the opportunity to generate profits on the arms sales that could be, and were, diverted covertly to the Contras fighting the Nicaraguan government.

The finding was presented to the president by his national security adviser, Vice Admiral John Poindexter. It had a cover memo, prepared by Lt. Col. Oliver North, but the president did not read the memo. Although the memo pointed out that the plan was opposed by the secretaries of state and defense, the memo presented neither their views nor justifications for the assertions of success the memo made. Yet the president did not insist that better staff work be done. Eleven days earlier, before the National Security Council meeting he called to discuss it took place, the president had signed a similar finding that also had not been fully staffed, not realizing that the paper was only a proposal for discussion. As he put it in his memoirs, "Because I was so concerned about getting the hostages home, I may not have asked enough questions about how the Iranian initiative was being conducted."[24]

The arms sale policy was a failure and undermined the nation's strongly asserted position of not trading arms, or anything else, for hostages. When details of this policy decision began to emerge later in the year, there was a loud public outcry. The president's standing fell substantially in the polls, and his political clout was diminished. Things got even worse when the diversion of funds to the Contras came to light. At this point the president fired North, accepted the resignation of Poindexter, and had to endure a year of congressional hearings and a critical investigation by a special commission he appointed to examine his handling of the matter.

A spate of books written by top officials in the Reagan administration (detractors term them "kiss and tell") revealed that Ronald Reagan was a peculiarly detached decision maker. As we noted in Chapter 6, he had strong views on the basic goals of public policy but left it to others to implement his broad vision. Aides prepared detailed scripts on index cards for his use in meetings. His detachment and lack of mastery of the details of policy hindered his evaluation of policy options.

## PRESIDENTIAL RELATIONSHIPS WITH ADVISERS

The president requires the services of personal aides to carry out his duties. Since he must rely so heavily upon his aides and work so closely with them, he naturally chooses persons of similar attitudes and compatible personalities. Moreover, strong personalities, which typically characterize presidents, create environments to their liking and weed out irritations.

Many, perhaps most, people find it difficult to stand up to the president and disagree with him. Several of President Reagan's top aides had doubts about his economic policies even in 1981 but did not relay them to the president until after the program was enacted. At times advisers are strong advocates of a position before a meeting with the president and then completely switch their arguments during the meeting after they learn the president has accepted the opposite view. It was because of this phenomenon that President Kennedy often absented himself from meetings of his advisers during the Cuban missile crisis. He wanted everyone to feel free to speak his or her mind.

Sometimes advisers find it difficult to disagree with the president because of the latter's strong, dynamic, or magnetic personality. These traits are certainly not unusual in successful politicians, especially presidents. Former White House assistant Chester Cooper has written that President Johnson often polled his foreign policy advisers one at a time to hear their views on the Vietnam War. Each would respond "I agree,"

"All those in favor say 'Aye.'"
"Aye."        "Aye."        "Aye."
        "Aye."        "Aye."

Drawing by H. Martin; © 1979 The New Yorker Magazine, Inc.

although Cooper, and undoubtedly others, did *not* agree. Cooper even dreamed of answering no, but he never did.[25] Other Johnson administration officials report of a similar tendency of those around the president to tell him what they thought he wanted to hear about the war rather than what they really thought.

One reason for the reluctance of presidential aides to challenge the president is that they are completely dependent upon him for their jobs, their advancement, and the gratification of their egos. Cabinet members are nearly as dependent, although they may have support in Congress or from interest groups. Because aides usually desire to perpetuate their positions, they may refrain from giving the president "unpleasant" information or from fighting losing battles on behalf of their principles. Even Nixon's White House chief of staff, H. R. Haldeman, felt that he had to survive in his own job and therefore failed to fight sufficiently the dark side of the president's character.

Thus, the president often finds it difficult to evoke critical responses from staff members. Gerald Ford observed:

> Few people, with the possible exception of his wife, will ever tell a President that he is a fool. There's a majesty to the office that inhibits even your closest friends from saying what is really on their minds. They won't tell you that you just made a lousy speech or bungled a chance to get your point across. . . . You can tell them you want the blunt truth; you can leave instructions on every bulletin board, but the guarded response you get never varies.
>
> And yet the President—any President—needs to hear straight talk. He needs to be needled once in a while, if only to be brought down from the false pedestal that the office provides. He needs to be told that he is, after all, only another human being with the same virtues and weaknesses as anyone else. And he needs to be reminded of this constantly if he's going to keep his perspective.[26]

All of these tendencies may be reenforced by a president who "punishes" aides who present options and information he does not like. Lyndon Johnson was such a person. He forced top aides and officials who dissented on Vietnam to leave his administration, and he went so far as to reduce contact with such key people as Secretaries of Defense Robert McNamara and Clark Clifford and Vice President Hubert Humphrey.

Johnson's press secretary George Reedy observed that the White House had an inner political life of its own. Thus, the staff carefully studied the president's psyche to gain and maintain access to him. They wanted to be around when there was good news to report and discreetly absent when the news was bad, hoping someone else would receive the blame. Naturally, this gamesmanship helped to distort Johnson's view of reality.

Richard Nixon had little interest in critiques of his weak points, and those who attempted to criticize him did not maintain their influence very long. Even as secure and personable a president as Franklin Roosevelt is reported to have allowed only those who did not challenge him to remain around.

The dampening effect that behavior like Johnson's or Nixon's can have on discussions even outside the Oval Office can be substantial. Office of Congressional Relations chief Lawrence O'Brien and Vice President Hubert Humphrey were in constant contact for months before they became aware of each other's views on Vietnam. Because President Johnson equated criticism with disloyalty, even the highest officials in the White House kept their dissent to themselves.

Strong presidents may also, in effect, tell their advisers what advice to offer them. Richard Nixon turned to John Connally for "tough" advice, such as when he wanted someone to urge him to mine the harbor at Haiphong, North Vietnam. A Nixon aide once observed the president and Connally cruising down the Potomac on the presidential yacht, the *Sequoia*, as Nixon was trying to talk his adviser into recommending that he institute wage and price controls on the economy.

Presidents with heightened fears of security leaks may place loyalty above competence, independence, or openness as a criterion for evaluating and relying upon advisers. They may also control the information flow tightly and keep even insiders in the dark. One of the reasons President Johnson relied so heavily on a group of five or six high officials (called the Tuesday lunch group) to advise him on the Vietnam War was that he felt the larger National Security Council leaked too much information. According to Secretary of State Dean Rusk, "The Tuesday luncheons were where the really important issues regarding Vietnam were discussed in great detail. This was where the real decisions were made. And everyone there knew how to keep his mouth shut."[27]

Ironically, one inhibition on freedom of dissension in the White House and in the upper levels of the bureaucracy is public opinion. If the president allows open discussion of policy views, then there will inevitably be disagreement. This disagreement is often then presented in the press as evidence that the president is not in control and that the White House lacks a sense of direction. Thus, by being open the president may lose some public support but by being closed to options and information he may make poor decisions.

Feuding and infighting for power and access to the president among ambitious aides are also obstacles to rational decision making. This rivalry takes several forms. One of the most common techniques is to attack rivals through leaks to the press that they are out of favor with the president or not competent to carry out their duties. Sometimes the leaks place competitors for power in a favorable context but one that will displease the president, who may value credit and publicity for himself rather than his aides.

In recent years the Nixon, Ford, and Reagan administrations stand out for the extent of their internal feuding and infighting. One high-level Reagan aide disclosed how he and other White House officials tried to undercut Secretary of State Alexander Haig. "In a classic case of Washington infighting, we threw virtually every booby trap in his way that we could, planted every story, egged the press on to get down on him."[28]

All of this feuding encourages self-interested behavior by presidential advisers that may distort their vision and cause them to overextend their arguments and present unbalanced discussions of options and their consequences to the president. There is also a tendency for competing advisers to seek to aggrandize influence and monopolize the counsel on which presidential decisions are based, providing insufficient information, analysis, and deliberation for decisions. Staff rivalry also detracts from the efficiency of White House operations as it wastes time and lowers staff morale. Moreover, publicity on feuding in the White House can embarrass the president when it is covered in the press, which it inevitably is.

High officials in Washington know that their ability to function effectively with the bureaucracy depends on being known for their effectiveness with the president. Dean Rusk, former secretary of state, argues that "the real organization of government at higher echelons is . . . how confidence flows down from the President."[29] To maintain their reputations for effectiveness with the president, officials may not strongly advocate positions that they consider sound if they feel the president is unlikely to adopt their proposals. An official does not usually want to be known as one whose advice the president rejected.

An additional potential hindrance to sound advice for the president is the loss of perspective by White House aides. Because working in the White House is a unique experience, a narrowing of viewpoint may easily occur. Especially for top aides, the environment is luxurious, secure, and heady, and the exercise of power is an everyday experience. The potential for isolation is real, and the chief executive must fight these insulating tendencies. President Johnson was very sensitive about his aides losing perspective, and thus he closely controlled the use of White House perks and stripped his staff of pretensions with a "merciless persistency."[30]

Advisers' conceptions of their jobs influence their delivery of information and options. President Eisenhower's secretaries of defense, Charles Wilson and Neil McElroy, considered themselves managers of the department and did not become heavily involved in disputes over foreign policy or strategic doctrine. By contrast, Secretary of Defense Robert McNamara adopted an aggressive stance as an adviser. But McNamara's colleague, Secretary of State Dean Rusk, did not consider it his job to participate in policy disputes with his colleagues or the president. In fact, many observers thought he did not effectively present State Department views on important foreign policy issues.

## BOX 7-1.    WHAT DIFFERENCE DOES IT MAKE?

It is much easier to describe how presidents make decisions than it is to show what difference it makes. However, one recent study examined how presidents Eisenhower and Johnson appraised the choices before them on a similar issue, American intervention in Vietnam (in 1954 and 1964–65, respectively). Eisenhower chose not to intervene, while Johnson eventually sent more than half a million American troops.

Eisenhower, who had headed organizations of enormous size and complexity as a military commander, was sensitive about the impact of the structure of advisory systems on the process of analyzing policies and making decisions. His system produced spirited, open debate before him, with aides challenging him, often tenaciously, even though he openly expressed his own opinions. He was exposed to diverse views (not "loaded" presentations of options), sharply focused alternatives, and advice separated from parochial interests. In addition, he supplemented his formal advisory system with an informal, fluid process of consultation that interacted with and reinforced the formal system.

Contrary to the conventional wisdom of the time, Ike was clearly in charge and kept his options open. He reasoned explicitly about the means and ends, the trade-offs, and the consequences of options, and he thought strategically, viewing issues as parts of more comprehensive patterns. In all this he set the tone for decision making in his administration.

Johnson, in contrast, was insensitive to the impact of advisory structures. His advisory system was an organizational shambles, marked by an absence of regular meetings and routinized procedures, shifts in the membership of advisory and decision-making groups, a reliance on out-of-channel advocacy, weak staff work, and other impediments to rigorous policy analysis.

A heavy reliance on informal advising by a few people and a lack of systematized staff work left many policy disagreements unresolved and unexamined. Frequently options were neither coherently assembled nor carefully considered, and there was a lack of broad strategic debate in which the underlying assumptions of policy were questioned. Policy differences at all levels were typically not sharply stated and directly analyzed, and there was a lack of forums for contradictory views to be clarified, studied, and debated. The views of most dissenters were not rejected after discussion; instead, they were simply not discussed. The lack of systematic policy analysis and the reliance on a few advisors left the upper and lower levels of the foreign policy community separated, and the impact of advice was more a function of skill and resources in bureaucratic politics than the logic of the argument.

In many ways the president was his own worst enemy. He immersed himself in detail rather than focusing on broad policy questions, and he was insulated from confrontation of advisors' views. LBJ did not press for additional alternatives or question incisively the options pre-

BOX 7-1.    *(continued)*

sented to him. Continuing the pattern of his years in the Senate, he was preoccupied with searching for consensus within, probing for areas of agreement rather than disagreement. His personal interactions with his advisors encouraged a narrowing, not a broadening of options, and his intolerance of disagreement had a chilling effect on the range of advice he received.

In sum, Eisenhower was a planner and conceptualizer, LBJ an individualistic political operator. Eisenhower was preoccupied with analyzing policy and Johnson with the politics of making it. Each constructed an advisory system to meet his needs. At least in the case of Vietnam, these advisory systems, as well as the people who composed them and the presidents themselves, made a difference in the options the president chose.

Source: John P. Burke and Fred I. Greenstein, *How Presidents Test Reality: Decisions on Vietnam, 1954 and 1965* (New York: Russell Sage Foundation, 1989).

## BUREAUCRATIC POLITICS AND DECISION MAKING

A primary source of options and information for the president is the bureaucracy. Yet it is not a neutral instrument. Individuals and the agencies they represent have interests of their own to advance and protect and do not necessarily view issues from the president's perspective. Moreover, the structure of the flow of information and the development of options may also hinder decision making in the White House.

### Organizational Parochialism

Government agencies have a tendency toward inbreeding. The selective recruitment of new staff helps to develop homogeneous attitudes. Those attracted to work for government agencies are likely to support the policies carried out by those agencies, whether they be in the fields of social welfare, agriculture, or national defense. Naturally, agencies prefer hiring like-minded persons. Within each agency the distribution of rewards creates further pressure to view things from the perspective of the status quo. Personnel who do not support established organizational goals and approaches to meeting them are unlikely to be promoted to important positions. Moreover, all but a few high-level policymakers spend their careers within one agency or department. Since people want to believe in what they do for a living, this long association strongly influences the attitudes of bureaucrats.

Related to long-time service in an agency is the relatively narrow range of each agency's responsibilities. Officials in the Department of

Education, for example, do not deal with the budget for the entire national government but only with the part that pertains to their programs. It is up to others to recommend to the president what is best for national defense, health, or housing. With each bureaucratic unit focusing on its own programs, there are few people to view these programs from a wider, national perspective.

Influences from outside an agency also encourage parochial views among bureaucrats. When interest groups and congressional committees support an agency, they expect continued bureaucratic support in return. Since these outsiders generally favor the policies the bureaucracy has been carrying out all along (which the outsiders probably helped initiate), what they really want is "more of the same."

All of these factors result in a relatively uniform environment in which policy making takes place. Intraorganizational communications pass mainly among persons who share similar frames of reference and who reinforce bureaucratic parochialism by their continued association.

The influence of parochialism is strong enough that even some presidential appointees, who are in office for only short periods of time, are "captured" and adopt the narrow views of their bureaucratic units. The dependence of such officials on their subordinates for information and advice, the need to maintain organizational morale by supporting established viewpoints, and pressures from their agencies' clienteles combine to discourage high-ranking officials from maintaining broad views of the public interest.

President Nixon observed that "it is inevitable when an individual has been in a Cabinet position or, for that matter, holds any position in Government, [that] after a certain length of time he becomes an advocate of the status quo; rather than running the bureaucracy, the bureaucracy runs him."[31] Thus, parochialism can lead officials to see different faces on the same issue.

When President Carter considered asking Congress for an authorization for a 20 percent cutback in wheat acreage and the placing of several million tons of food and feed grains in reserve, there was an intense internal debate in which the Department of Agriculture, reacting to the demands of farmers, wanted an even bigger cutback; the Treasury Department and the Council of Economic Advisers opposed any cutback out of concern for future consumer prices and the export potential of the United States should food shortages develop; and the State Department was concerned about the proposal's effect on international negotiations regarding an international grain reserve. In other words, policymakers in different bureaucratic units with different responsibilities saw the same policy in a different light and reacted differently to it.

A president can benefit from the diversity of views across organizational units, but the White House must recognize that each view is likely to be articulated from a "biased" perspective. It was to combat this parochialism that President Reagan went to considerable lengths to insulate his new cabinet appointees from the traditional agency arguments in defense of programs the White House had slated for cuts. They received their initial briefings from the president, the director of the Office of Management and Budget, and citizens groups rather than from the bureaucracy; were often assigned deputies with close personal and ideological ties to the White House; and were given little time to react to the president's proposals.

### Maintaining the Organization

As a result of parochialism in the bureaucracy, career officials come to believe that the health of their organization and its programs is vital to the national interest. In their eyes, this well-being depends in turn on the organization's fulfilling its missions, securing the necessary resources (personnel, money, authority), and maintaining its influence. Organizational personnel can pursue their personal quests for power and prestige, the goals of their organization, and the national interest all at the same time without perceiving any role conflicts. Moreover, policymakers in different organizational units are prone to see different faces on the same issues because of their different organizational needs.

The single-mindedness of policymakers attached to various agencies causes them to raise options and gather information that support the interests of their organization and avoid or oppose options and information that challenge those interests. In this way, the goals of maintaining an organization may *displace* the goals of solving the problems for which the organization was created. As one former high White House official has written, "For many cabinet officers, the important question was whether their department would have the principal responsibility for the new program—not the hard choices that lay hidden within it."[32]

Within most organizations there is a dominant view of the *essence* of the organization's mission and the attitudes, skills, and experience employees should have to carry out that mission. Organizations usually propose options they believe will build upon and reinforce the essential aspects of their organizations. Although its bombing campaigns had not had unqualified success in previous wars, the air force lobbied for strategic bombing and deep interdiction in the Vietnam War. One way to do this was to argue for bombing as a central feature of U.S. policy in order to show its utility. The lack of success only reinforced the air force's efforts to step up bombing even further; the air force never admitted it was not accomplishing its objectives. An organization will also vigorously resist efforts of others to take away, decrease, or share its essence and the resources deemed necessary to realize that essence.

In their struggles over roles and missions, bureaucrats may distort the information and options provided to senior officials. In Vietnam the air force and navy were each concerned that the other might encroach on its bombing missions; the navy was also concerned about justifying the high cost of its aircraft carriers. Thus, they competed in their efforts at air warfare. The aspect of this interservice competition that was most damaging to the accuracy of the perceptions high-level decision makers had of American success in the war was the battle over the relative effectiveness of each service's air warfare. Each was concerned for future budgets and missions and could not let the other get the upper hand. Thus, each exaggerated its own performance, expecting the other to do likewise.

Budgets are another vital component of strategies to maintain an organization. This is true for grant-awarding agencies, as well as for agencies with large operational capabilities like the military services and the Department of Agriculture. Because staff within governmental organizations generally believe their work is vital to the national interest, and because conventional wisdom stipulates that a larger budget enables an organization to perform its functions more effectively, units normally request an increase in funding and fight decreases. The size of a group's budget not only determines the resources available for its services but also serves as a sign of the importance others attach to the organization's functions.

Agency personnel also examine any substantive proposal to ascertain its impact on the budget. They rarely suggest adding a new function to their responsibilities if it must be financed from monies already allocated for ongoing activities. Moreover, components of large organizations, like units in the military or the Department of Health and Human Services, are concerned about maintaining or increasing their percentage of the larger unit's budget.

An organization's staff members are likely to raise and support options that give them autonomy. In their view they know best how to perform their essential mission. They resist options that would place control in the hands of higher officials or require close coordination with other organizations. This desire for autonomy helps explain why several agencies independently gather and evaluate national security intelligence from their own perspective. As Richard Nixon complained when he was disappointed in the intelligence reports he received, "Those guys spend all their time fighting each other."[33]

Because organizations seek to create and maintain autonomous jurisdictions, they rarely oppose each other's projects. This self-imposed restraint reduces the conflict between organizations and correspondingly reduces the options and information available to the president. In dealing with their superiors, the leaders of an organization often guard their autonomy by presenting only one option for a new program. The rationale is that if higher officials cannot choose among options, they cannot interfere with the organization's preference. Once an agency of government has responsibility for a program, it has a tendency to evaluate it positively. Thus,

> After the American presence in Vietnam was increased and the programs enlarged . . . each bureaucratic organization then had its own stakes. The

military had to prove that American arms and advice could succeed. The Foreign Service had to prove that it could bring about political stability in Saigon and build a nation. The CIA had to prove, especially after the Bay of Pigs fiasco, that it could handle covert action and covert paramilitary operations lest it chance having its operational missions in general questioned. The Agency for International Development (AID), like the State Department and the military, had to prove that pacification could work and that advice and millions of dollars in assistance could bring political returns. . . . [B]y 1965 almost all career professionals became holier than the Pope on the subject of U.S. interests in Vietnam.[34]

## Organizational and Personal Influence

To achieve the policies they desire, organizations and individuals seek influence. In pursuing power, officials often further distort the processes of generating options and gathering information for the president. One way for organizations to increase their influence is to defer to one another's expertise. The operations of all large-scale organizations, including governments, require a considerable degree of specialization and expertise. Those who possess this expertise, whether within executive agencies or congressional committees, naturally believe they know best about a subject in their field, and they therefore desire primary influence over the resolution of issues in their subject area. Because each set of experts has a stake in deference to expertise (they each receive benefits from it), reciprocal deference to expertise becomes an important theme in policy making. One result of this reciprocity is that fewer challenges to expert views are aired than might otherwise be the case.

For several decades there has been an implicit agreement between the Departments of State and Defense that each would stay out of the other's affairs. During the Vietnam War the State Department often took no part in shaping war policies and refrained from airing its views on many of them. Contributing to this restraint was Secretary of Defense McNamara's adamant belief that the State Department should not challenge the military's appraisal of the actual progress of the war. Once when the director of the State Department's Bureau of Intelligence and Research attempted to do so, McNamara forcefully elicited a promise from Secretary of State Dean Rusk that such a challenge would not recur. He thus deliberately blocked the flow of information on the war. This meant that policymakers had to defer to Defense Department assessments that were often inaccurate and biased toward military rather than political solutions.

Although deference to expertise is not always a satisfactory way of resolving conflicts in policy making, it is often the only possible course of action. Governmental agencies are the sole source of data and analysis on many issues. As their work becomes more and more specialized, it becomes more and more difficult to check their information and evaluations. This problem is exacerbated by a need for secrecy on most national security policies, which makes it necessary to limit even further the number of participants in the policy-making process.

To take full advantage of deference to expertise and to increase their influence further, organizations seek to prevent their own experts from disseminating conflicting information and options. Contrary information and evaluations undercut the credibility of a unit's position. Moreover, by presenting several real options, a unit increases the range of possible policy decisions and commensurately decreases the probability that the option favored by the unit's leaders will be selected. Thus, the Joint Chiefs of Staff rarely disagree in their recommendations. The relevant departments never really presented President Carter options on welfare reform, in part because they were afraid he would select an alternative they opposed. No one would insist to the president that reform would be costly because they feared he would then reject reform efforts.[35]

If there are disagreements among the experts in an organizational unit, efforts to produce an appearance of unanimity can reduce the experts' recommendations to broad generalizations. A record of agreement on the least disputed common denominators usually fails to mention many controversial points that may be crucial to the ultimate success of the policy at issue. When compromise positions reach the president in a form that suggests a unified consensual judgment, they can give him a false sense of security because he may lack an awareness of the potential problems buried within the recommendations.

For bureaucrats interested in their own careers, the prospect of a deferred promotion or even dismissal makes them reluctant to report information that undercuts the official stands of their organizations. The example of the Foreign Service officers who frankly (and accurately) reported on the strength of the Communists in China during the late 1940s was not quickly forgotten in the bureaucracy. They were driven from the Foreign Service for allegedly pro-Communist sympathies. Over forty years later, in 1992, CIA Director Robert Gates announced that many within the CIA felt that intelligence reports were tailored to please superiors.

Some officials anticipate sanctions even in the absence of their being exercised. One of the most embarrassing incidents of Jimmy Carter's early presidency was the scandal surrounding Bert Lance, his close friend and the director of the Office of Management and Budget. Lance eventually resigned under pressure after details of his business and personal financial dealings were made public. For our purposes the question is, why did the president not know of these problems?

At least a large part of the answer seems to be that officials responsible for reviewing Lance's background soft-pedaled the reports in an effort to cultivate the goodwill of the new administration. The deputy comptroller general (who was acting comptroller) later testified that he knew of Lance's problems but downplayed them to avoid losing his job. Indeed, he hoped to be appointed comptroller general. It also appears that the relevant United States attorney closed his investigation of Lance early, over the objections of several of his subordinates, hoping not to irritate the new president so that he could keep his job and qualify for a federal pension.

Experts can create an illusion of competition when they agree to compare their preferred action to unfeasible alternatives. Lyndon Johnson's advisers have been criticized for juxtapositioning in 1964 their favored option of bombing North Vietnam against two phony options: In effect, blow up the world or scuttle and run.

## Bureaucratic Structure

The structure of administrative organizations is one of the factors that impedes the flow of options and information to higher-level decision makers. Most bureaucracies have a hierarchical structure, and the information on which decisions are based usually passes from bottom to top. At each step in this ladder of communication, personnel screen the information from the previous stage. Such screening is necessary because the people at the top—presidents—cannot absorb all the detailed information that exists on an issue and must have subordinates summarize and synthesize information as it proceeds upward. The longer the communication chain, the greater the chance that judgments will replace facts; nuances or caveats will be excluded; subordinates will paint a positive face on a situation to improve their own image or that of their organization; human error will distort the overall picture; and the speculations of "experts" will be reported as fact.

Screening, summarizing, and human error are not the only pitfalls in the transmission of information. When subordinates are asked to transmit information that can be used to evaluate their performance, they have a tendency to distort information in order to put themselves in the most favorable light. For example, many of the military's assessments of damage done to Iraqi forces and weaponry in the Gulf war turned out to be erroneous, inflated substantially by soldiers in the field.

Subordinates sometimes distort facts by not reporting those that indicate danger. President Kennedy was not apprised of the following problems with the contingency plan for the Bay of Pigs: The men participating in the invasion had not been told to go to the mountains if the invasion failed; between the beach and the mountains which supposedly offered refuge was a large swamp; and only one-third of the men had received guerrilla training. Instead, he was simply informed that if the invasion failed, the men would go to the mountains and carry out guerrilla warfare. At other times subordinates may exaggerate the evidence in support of their favored alternative in order to increase the probability of its being chosen.

Even in the hierarchical executive branch, the president cannot depend on information being centralized. There was a great deal of information pointing to the Japanese attack on Pearl Harbor, for example, but it was never fully organized. No one brings forward all the political, economic, social, military, and diplomatic considerations of a policy in a recognizable manner for the president's deliberation because the bureaucracy relevant to any policy is too decentralized and too large and produces too much paper to coordinate information effectively.

The president may attempt to compensate for the problems of hierarchy by sending personal aides or outsiders to assess a situation directly and propose options. However, the person assigned to the task may determine the nature of the report more than the situation itself. Moreover, the president cannot bypass senior officials very often without lowering their morale and undercutting their operational authority.

President Kennedy's chief White House national security adviser, McGeorge Bundy, ordered that cables to the State Department, the Central Intelligence Agency (CIA), and the Pentagon be sent directly to the White House and not just to the Washington headquarters of those departments where they could be summarized and analyzed for transmittal to the president. But this practice could not correct the distortion that may have gone into the cables in the first place, and someone had to summarize and synthesize the tremendous volume of information before it reached the president. President Bush discovered the same problems when he asked for direct information channels from the field.

Organizations use routines or standard operating procedures (SOPs) to gather and process information in a methodical fashion. However, the character of the SOPs may delay the recognition of critical information, distort the quality of information, and limit the options presented to policymakers.

In the case of the Cuban missile crisis, several weeks before the president was aware of the missiles there was a good deal of information in the U.S. intelligence system pointing to their presence. But the time required by SOPs to sort out raw information and double check it delayed recognition of the new situation. Organizational routines also masked signs forecasting the 1974 leftist coup in Portugal. Officials from the intelligence services of the CIA, the Defense Department, and the State Department testified after the event that their routines did not focus much attention on Portugal, and they could not shift personnel rapidly to a new area of concern.

SOPs affect not only *if* and *when* information is collected but also the substance of the information. In Vietnam the military's concentration on the technical aspects of bombing caused it to substitute a set of short-run physical objectives for the ultimate political goals of the war. Military reports emphasized physical destruction per se rather than the political impact of such destruction. The enemy's capacity to recruit more men or rebuild a structure never seemed to enter into the calculations.

Standard operating procedures give disproportionate weight to information entering the system from regular channels. For example, the United States was highly dependent on the Shah of Iran and Savak, the Shah's secret police organization, for information about Iran. Until a few months before the Shah was deposed, they reported to the CIA and President Carter that there was no likelihood of revolution. The White House rejected more pessimistic reports from journalists and others outside the regular flow of information.

SOPs structure the process of decision making by preselecting those who will be asked for advice and predetermining when they will be asked. There are routine ways of invading foreign countries and of determining agency budgets. Some persons will be involved at earlier stages than others, and some will be viewed as having more legitimate and expert voices in policy discussions. When Lyndon Johnson limited his circle of personal advisers on the Vietnam War to a half-dozen top officials, those at a lower rung in the foreign policy hierarchy found it harder to have their dissents heard. In addition, there was little opportunity for others in the cabinet to challenge the war policy because they were not in the right decision-making channels.

Purely analytic units often have problems in being heard. According to Henry Kissinger:

> I can think of no exception to the rule that advisers without a clear-cut area of responsibility eventually are pushed to the periphery by day-to-day operators. The other White House aides resent interference in their spheres. The schedulers become increasingly hesitant in finding time on the President's calendar.[36]

Thus, information is most likely to influence policy making if the position of those who have it ensures they must be consulted before a decision is made.

Standard operating procedures also affect the nature of the alternatives proposed by bureaucratic units. Bureaucracies typically propose their standard ways of doing things rather than innovative solutions to problems. These standard policies may not be appropriate for the problem at hand.

As a result of problems with established routines, presidents often create special task forces of "outside" experts to develop new programs. Such bodies, brought together for a new purpose, are less likely than established agencies to be blinded by SOPs.

Because only decision makers directly responsible for a policy are normally consulted on "secret" matters, fewer advisers contribute to secret deliberations than to debate on more open issues. This reduces the range of options that are considered in a secret decision and limits the analysis of the few options that are considered. The secrecy of President Johnson's Tuesday lunch group, which made the important decisions on the Vietnam War, prevented an advance agenda. Thus, decisions were made without a full review of the options beforehand. Secrecy also makes it easier for those directly involved to dismiss (intentionally or unintentionally) the dissenting or offbeat ideas of outsiders as the products of ignorance, which is unfortunate because secret information is often inaccurate or misleading. President Kennedy wished he had not been successful in persuading *The New York Times* not to publish the plans for the Bay of Pigs invasion; he afterward felt that publicity might have elicited some useful critiques.

## CONCLUSION

Presidents face an enormously difficult and complex task in making decisions on a wide range of issues. They must work within the parameters of the national government's prior commitments and are further constrained by the limited time they can devote to considering options and information on any one policy. In addition, they face a number of other potential hazards in reaching decisions. The struggling facilitator, not the dominating director, is the description that matches the process of presidential decision making most of the time.

There are a variety of ways for presidents to organize the White House and acquire advice. Not all of them are equally useful in ensuring that presidents are presented with a full range of options, each supported with effective advocacy. Moreover, presidents may experience problems with their aides' reluctance to present candid advice, which may be aggravated by presidents themselves, and by their efforts to increase their influence.

Bureaucratic politics also plays a role in determining the options and information presidents receive and the forms in which they are presented. Agencies and their personnel inevitably have narrower perspectives than the White House and desire to maintain and expand their programs, status, and influence. Those ambitions often bias the options and information presented to the White House. The ways in which bureaucratic units collect, process, and transmit options and information and the secrecy that sometimes accompanies them may add further distortion to what the president sees.

It is important that presidents be sensitive to the many obstacles to effective decision making and attempt to avoid or compensate for them as best they can, realizing that perfectly rational decision making is unattainable.

## NOTES

1. Theodore Sorensen, quoted in John C. Donovan, *The Politics of Poverty*, 2nd ed. (Indianapolis: Pegasus, 1973), p. 111.

2. On continuity in foreign policy despite changes in the occupant of the presidency, see William J. Dixon and Stephen M. Gardner, "Presidential Succession and the Cold War: An Analysis of Soviet–American Relations, 1948–1988," *Journal of Politics* 54 (February 1992): 156–75.

3. Quoted in Paul C. Light, *The President's Agenda: Domestic Policy Choice from Kennedy to Carter* (Baltimore: Johns Hopkins University Press, 1982), p. 179.

4. Richard E. Neustadt, *Presidential Power and the Modern Presidents* (New York: Free Press, 1990), pp. 121–22.

5. Zbigniew Brzezinski, *Power and Principle: Memoirs of a National Security Adviser, 1977–1981* (New York: Farrar, Straus, and Giroux, 1983), p. 358; see also p. 396.

6. David Stockman, quoted in William Greider, "The Education of David Stockman," *Atlantic*, December 1981, p. 34.

7. Theodore C. Sorensen, *Decision-Making in the White House: The Olive Branch or the Arrows* (New York: Columbia University Press, 1963), p. 3.

8. Bryce Harlow, quoted in Emmet John Hughes, *The Living Presidency: The Resources and Dilemmas of the American Presidential Office* (Baltimore: Penguin, 1973), p. 345.

9. Roger B. Porter, "Gerald Ford: A Healing Presidency," in Fred I. Greenstein, ed., *Leadership in the Modern Presidency* (Cambridge, Mass.: Harvard University Press, 1988).

10. Bill Moyers, quoted in Larry Berman, "Political Scientists in Presidential Libraries: How Not to Be a Stranger in a Strange Land" (paper presented at the Annual Meeting of the American Political Science Association, Washington, D.C., September 1979), n. 52.

11. Henry Kissinger, *White House Years* (Boston: Little, Brown, 1979), p. 47; see also p. 1455.

12. Larry Berman, *Planning a Tragedy: The Americanization of the War in Vietnam* (New York: Norton, 1982).

13. Alexander L. George, "The Case for Multiple Advocacy in Making Foreign Policy," *American Political Science Review* 66 (September 1972): 766.

14. Gerald R. Ford, *A Time to Heal: The Autobiography of Gerald R. Ford* (New York: Harper and Row, 1979), p. 147; see also p. 186.

15. Clark Clifford, *Counsel to the President* (New York: Random House, 1991), p. 636.

16. Gerald R. Ford, "Imperiled, Not Imperial," *Time*, November 10, 1980, p. 31.

17. Kissinger, *White House Years*, p. 602; see also p. 40.

18. Ibid., p. 996.

19. Hamilton Jordan, *Crisis: The Last Year of the Carter Presidency* (New York: Putnam, 1982), p. 42.

20. Sorensen, *Decision-Making in the White House*, p. 62.

21. Quoted in Light, *The President's Agenda*, p. 200.

22. Bob Woodward, *The Commanders* (New York: Simon and Schuster, 1991), pp. 41–42, 299–302.

23. Neustadt, *Presidential Power*, chaps. 6 and 7.

24. Ronald Reagan, *An American Life* (New York: Simon and Schuster, 1990), pp. 540–41.

25. Chester L. Cooper, *The Lost Crusade: America in Vietnam* (New York: Dodd, Mead, 1970), p. 223.

26. Ford, *A Time to Heal*, pp. 187–88; see also Reagan, *An American Life*, p. 536.

27. Dean Rusk, quoted in Leon V. Sigal, *Reporters and Officials: The Organization and Politics of Newsmaking* (Lexington, Mass.: Heath, 1973), p. 147.

28. Larry Speakes, *Speaking Out* (New York: Scribner's, 1988), p. 244–45.

29. "Mr. Secretary: On the Eve of Emeritus," *Life*, January 17, 1969, p. 62B.

30. Jack Valenti, *A Very Human President* (New York: Norton, 1975), pp. 115–16.

31. Richard M. Nixon, *Public Papers of the Presidents: Richard Nixon, 1972* (Washington, D.C.: U.S. Government Printing Office, 1974), p. 1150.

32. Harry McPherson, *A Political Education* (Boston: Little, Brown, 1972), p. 298.

33. H. R. Haldeman, *The Ends of Power* (New York: Times Books, 1978), p. 107.

34. Leslie H. Gelb with Richard K. Betts, *The Irony of Vietnam: The System Worked* (Washington, D.C.: Brookings Institution, 1979), p. 239.

35. Laurence E. Lynn, Jr., and David deF. Whitman, *The President as Policymaker: Jimmy Carter and Welfare Reform* (Philadelphia: Temple University Press, 1981), pp. 116, 269.

36. Henry Kissinger, *Years of Upheaval* (Boston: Little, Brown, 1982), p. 74.

## SELECTED READINGS

Allison, Graham. *Essence of Decision: Explaining the Cuban Missile Crisis.* Boston: Little, Brown, 1971.

Anderson, Paul A. "Decision Making by Objection and the Cuban Missile Crisis," *Administrative Science Quarterly* 28 (June 1983): 201–22.

Barilleaux, Ryan J. *The President and Foreign Affairs*. New York: Praeger, 1985.

Bendor, Jonathan, and Thomas H. Hammond. "Rethinking Allison's Models," *American Political Science Review* 86 (June 1992): 301–22.

Berman, Larry. *Planning a Tragedy: The Americanization of the War in Vietnam*. New York: Norton, 1982.

Best, James J. "Who Talked to the President When?" *Political Science Quarterly* 103 (Fall 1988): 531–45.

Burke, John P. *The Institutional Presidency*. Baltimore: Johns Hopkins University Press, 1992.

Burke, John P., and Fred I. Greenstein. *How Presidents Test Reality: Decisions on Vietnam, 1954 and 1965*. New York: Russell Sage Foundation, 1989.

Downs, Anthony. *Inside Bureaucracy*. Boston: Little, Brown, 1967.

Gelb, Leslie H., with Richard K. Betts. *The Irony of Vietnam: The System Worked*. Washington, D.C.: Brookings Institution, 1979.

George, Alexander L. *Presidential Decisionmaking in Foreign Policy: The Effective Use of Information and Advice*. Boulder, Colo.: Westview Press, 1980.

Halperin, Morton H. *Bureaucratic Politics and Foreign Policy*. Washington, D.C.: Brookings Institution, 1974.

Hult, Karen. "Advising the President." In George C. Edwards III, John H. Kessel, and Bert A. Rockman, eds., *Researching the Presidency*. Pittsburgh: University of Pittsburgh Press, 1993.

Kessel, John H. "The Structures of the Reagan White House." *American Journal of Political Science* 28 (May 1984): 231–58.

March, James G., and Herbert A. Simon. *Organizations*. New York: Wiley, 1958.

Neustadt, Richard E. *Presidential Power and the Modern Presidents*. New York: Free Press, 1990.

Porter, Roger. "Gerald R. Ford: A Healing Presidency." In Fred I. Greenstein, ed., *Leadership in the Modern Presidency*. Cambridge, Mass.: Harvard University Press, 1988, pp. 199–227.

Simon, Herbert A. *Administrative Behavior: A Study of Decision-Making Processes in Administrative Organization*. 3rd ed. New York: Free Press, 1976.

Wayne, Stephen J. "President Bush Goes To War: A Psychological Analysis from a Distance." In Stanley A. Renshon, ed., *The Political Psychology of the Gulf War: Leaders, Publics, and the Process of Conflict*. Pittsburgh: University of Pittsburgh Press, 1993.

# 8

# The Personalized Presidency

In Chapter 6 we discussed the office of the presidency. The size of that office, its structures and modes of operation, and its patterns of communication, coordination, and decision making all affect what presidents do and how effectively they do it. Presidential decisions and actions are also influenced by the environment in which they occur. We focused on that environment in Chapter 7 and listed a variety of factors that impinge on decision making either directly or indirectly. These included advisory patterns, organizational structures, bureaucratic politics, and standard operating procedures as well as longer-term external forces and events such as the political climate, economic and social conditions, and public attitudes and opinions.

But presidents are not robots. Nor do we believe that all their decisions are fated. They have choice and exercise it. It matters how skilled they are, how smart they are, and how quickly they absorb information and make decisions. Their attitudes and values, their view of their roles and tasks, and their long- and short-term goals can all affect their decisions and conduct in office. Moreover, how they feel on a particular day, whether they are sick or healthy, tired or rested, sad or happy, frustrated or contented, may also have an impact. Beneath these feelings, their personality, cognitive skills, and interactive behavior will affect either directly or indirectly their perceptions, evaluations, and ultimately their judgments and actions as president.

The type of leadership role presidents desire and the one they usually pursue, whether they try to direct or facilitate change, follow in large part from their personal needs and abilities. Theodore Roosevelt needed to maintain a strong, public presence as president; Calvin Coolidge preferred to operate in a low-key manner outside of public view; Lyndon Johnson had to dominate personal relations; both he and Richard Nixon wanted to exercise strategic control; Ronald Reagan was more laid back and willing to delegate; Bill Clinton needs to be involved.

Whether presidents are successful in the role they choose to pursue depends in large part on the fit between their personality and the public mood, on their capacity to influence people and shape events, and on their ability to make the right choices and avoid problems and decisions that can be dealt with by others. This chapter will discuss these person-alized aspects of the presidency. After treating the purely formal, consti-tutional requirements for office, it will examine factors that affect presi-dents' preferences and, ultimately, their ability to lead: their social and political background, their physical attributes and general health, their psychological character and style of doing business, and their cognitive skills and perceptions. Additionally, patterns of interaction within the White House that directly or indirectly impinge on presidential priorities and their implementation will also be discussed. In this manner the chapter will address the critical question that the American electorate faces and must answer every four years: What difference does it make *who* is elected president?

## QUALIFICATIONS FOR OFFICE

The framers of the Constitution were naturally aware that personal factors could and would affect presidential performance. Although they hoped that presidents would have altruistic motives and set exemplary standards in their public and private behavior, they could not predicate the powers and responsibilities of the office on this assumption. Rather they had to take precautions against the potential abuse of power by the executive, abuses they believed they had experienced during the coloni-al period under the reign of George III.

Thus, they devised a constitutional structure to constrain the presi-dent and other federal officials from exceeding their authority and pro-vided a mechanism for removing them if they did. Reeligibility was seen as a motive for good behavior. Moreover, they envisioned the indirect selection process in the Electoral College as more likely to achieve an informed, intelligent, rational judgment than a direct election by the general public. Presumably the electors could spot dangerous character problems more readily than the average voters, or so the framers be-lieved.

Conceiving that character was more a product of personality than position, the delegates at the Philadelphia Convention did not impose a long list of qualifications for the office. On the contrary, they listed only three constitutional requirements. The president must be a natural-born citizen who has been a resident in the United States for fourteen years and is at least thirty-five years old. The citizenship and residence quali-fications were designed to prevent those with allegiances to other coun-tries, by virtue of their birth or residential preference, from becoming president and thereby being in a position to subvert the national inter-ests of the United States. The age requirement was imposed because the delegates at the Philadelphia Convention believed that the presidency demanded a higher level of maturity than any other position in the United States government. Minimum age for the House of Representa-tives was set at twenty-five and for the Senate at thirty.

With the possible exception of age, those formal requirements have precluded few who might otherwise be considered qualified from seeking the presidency. However, a set of informal requirements, as noted in Chapter 2, has in practice restricted eligibility to a much smaller subset of the population. Despite the notion, so appealing in democratic theory, that the nation's highest position should be one to which any citizen can aspire and achieve, the fact is that presidents as a group have not represented a microcosm of American society.

## SOCIAL AND POLITICAL BACKGROUND

To put it simply, American presidents have not been typical Americans. They have been advantaged by virtue of their wealth, the professional positions they have held, and the personal contacts they have made. Born into families of high social status and considerable economic means, they have benefited from greater educational and professional opportunities than their peers have enjoyed.

Despite the log cabin myth, perpetuated by Abraham Lincoln's rise to political prominence, most presidents have not had humble origins. In fact, Lincoln did not either.[1] The early presidents in particular were men of high social class. Eight of our presidents were the product of only four families: John Adams and John Quincy Adams (father and son), William Henry Harrison and Benjamin Harrison (grandfather and grandson), Theodore Roosevelt and Franklin Roosevelt (cousins), and James Madison and Zachary Taylor (common grandparents). At least half of those who have served in the White House during the twentieth century had backgrounds of social or political prominence. Only Calvin Coolidge, Richard Nixon, and Ronald Reagan might be said to have suffered from poverty in their youth. Bill Clinton's family was not wealthy, but by Arkansas standards they were probably middle class. Said one of his neighbors, Rose Crane, who knew Clinton since the third grade:

> Compared to the kids he ran into at Georgetown and Oxford and Yale, he was poor as a church mouse. . . . But they were not poor, not in the sense of Arkansas poor. I was terribly envious of Bill, in a childhood sort of way, for three things he had that I thought would probably make the entire world okay, if I had them: One was that they had a big red Coca-Cola box in the garage, and the Coke truck came and filled it up. Two, they had a convertible. And three, Virginia [Bill's mother] always had all of the bones and all of the skin out of chicken and dumplings, and there were little tiny pieces of white meat in the chicken and dumplings. And if your mother would do that, and you had a convertible and a Coca-Cola box, it was a perfect world.[2]

The advantages that higher income and social status can provide can be seen in the educational levels and professional activities that presidents as a group have attained. Most have been well educated. Of those who held office in the twentieth century, only Harry S Truman did not attend a university. Most, in fact, have undergraduate and graduate degrees (see Table 8-1).[3]

Education has been used as a springboard for professional careers that have culminated in public service. Most presidents held elective office prior to being president. Eisenhower was the last not to have done so, although he did run and defeat Senator Robert A. Taft in the Republican presidential primaries. The increasing public dimensions of the office have also put a premium on communication skills, which contributed to actor Ronald Reagan's rise to political prominence and success in office.

Whereas social and political position have given certain individuals an advantage in winning the presidency, they may have also contributed to their success in governing, or at least that is what two sociologists have concluded. E. Digby Baltzell and Howard G. Schneiderman correlated the social class origins of presidents with recent evaluations by historians and political scientists of those who have served as president. They found that presidents from higher social classes tended to be more favorably evaluated than those from lower social classes.[4]

Coming from an upper-class background did not help George Bush. In fact, it contributed to the perception, especially during the economic recession, that he just did not understand the problems of the average American family. In contrast, Bill Clinton made much of his humble background during the 1992 presidential campaign, asserting that it enabled him to empathize with the plight of those in the lower and middle classes.

## PHYSICAL ATTRIBUTES AND GENERAL HEALTH

Although background and upbringing may be only indirectly related to presidential performance, other factors such as physical and mental health and personal attributes have a more direct effect. Take feelings, for example. Few would deny that people's feelings affect their job performance. For presidents these feelings could increase or decrease their willingness to listen to options, their capacity to weigh alternatives and make the best decision, and their ability to persuade others to support their choice. They could also affect their energy level, their capacity to withstand the rigors of the office, their concentration, even their tolerance.

Despite the importance of health, information about the medical pathologies of presidents has been extremely limited. Even today, the medical diagnoses and treatments of presidents are presented in a sketchy way, particularly at the onset of a health problem. The principal reason that health problems are understated is that presidents and their advisers want to prevent precipitous public reactions to an illness or injury to the president and desire to maintain continuity of policy both

**Table 8-1. Social and Political Background of Twentieth-Century Presidents**

| Presidents | Years Served | Father's Occupation | Own Occupation | Undergraduate College |
|---|---|---|---|---|
| William McKinley | 1897–1901 | Businessman | Lawyer | Allegheny College |
| Theodore Roosevelt | 1901–1909 | Businessman | Lawyer | Harvard |
| William H. Taft | 1909–1913 | Lawyer | Lawyer | Yale |
| Woodrow Wilson | 1913–1921 | Minister | Educator | Princeton |
| Warren G. Harding | 1921–1923 | Physician | Journalist | Ohio Central |
| Calvin Coolidge | 1923–1929 | Storekeeper | Lawyer | Amherst |
| Herbert Hoover | 1929–1933 | Blacksmith | Engineer | Stanford |
| Franklin D. Roosevelt | 1933–1945 | Businessman | Lawyer | Harvard |
| Harry S Truman | 1945–1953 | Farmer | Businessman | None |
| Dwight D. Eisenhower | 1953–1961 | Mechanic | Military | U.S. Military Academy |
| John F. Kennedy | 1961–1963 | Businessman | Journalist | Harvard |
| Lyndon B. Johnson | 1963–1969 | Farmer | Educator | Southwest Texas Teachers College |
| Richard Nixon | 1969–1974 | Streetcar motorman | Lawyer | Whittier College |
| Gerald Ford | 1974–1977 | Businessman | Lawyer | University of Michigan |
| Jimmy Carter | 1977–1981 | Farmer | Farmer, businessman | U.S. Naval Academy |
| Ronald Reagan | 1981–1989 | Shoe salesman | Actor | Eureka College |
| George Bush | 1989–1993 | Businessman, politician | Businessman, politician | Yale |
| William Clinton | 1993– | Salesman | Politician | Georgetown |

within the government and between it and other governments. Thus, it was not revealed until weeks after Ronald Reagan left the hospital following the attempt on his life how close he had actually come to death. Similarly, Grover Cleveland's two cancer operations, Woodrow Wilson's incapacity after a stroke, Franklin Roosevelt's worsening health, and John F. Kennedy's affliction with Addison's disease were not made known to the public during their presidencies.

Additionally, presidents may not even tell their own physicians exactly how they feel.[5] Nor does the president's doctor thoroughly examine him every day. Ross T. McIntire, Franklin Roosevelt's personal physician, described his typical morning examination of the president:

> In accordance with the routine decided on, I parked my car before the White House every morning around 8:30 and went to the President's bedroom for a look-see. Neither the thermometer nor stethoscope was produced, there was no request for a look at the tongue or a feel of the pulse, and only rarely was a direct question ever asked. Finding myself a comfortable chair, I sat a bit while breakfast was being eaten or the morning papers looked over.
>
> A close but seemingly casual watch told all I wanted to know. The things that interested me the most were the President's color, the tone of his voice, the tilt of his chin, and the way he tackled his orange juice, cereal, and eggs. . . . [6]

McIntire observed the president in a similar manner at the end of the day.[7]

Presidents seem to have had more than their share of illnesses and poor health while in office. George Washington had pneumonia, rheumatism, and a persistent back problem; Andrew Jackson was sick during much of his eight years as president; William Henry Harrison died in office after a bout with viral pneumonia, which he contracted on Inauguration Day; Zachary Taylor also died in office, succumbing to gastroenteritis early in his presidency; Lincoln suffered from headaches and depression, which may have been an indication that he suffered from Marfan syndrome, a genetic disease that affects joints and connective tissues; Wilson had a debilitating stroke; Harding had heart disease, a weak stomach, and died from a misdiagnosed seizure; Garfield and McKinley were shot and probably lost their lives from improper and inept medical treatment.

In the modern era, Franklin Roosevelt's health deteriorated as president, and he died in office from a coronary. Eisenhower had three major illnesses: coronary thrombosis in 1955, acute ileitis in 1956, and a minor stroke in 1957. In addition to Addison's disease, Kennedy aggravated a back problem he had since college and treated it throughout his presidency with special braces, exercises, and a chair designed to alleviate pressure. He also took a cortisone-based medicine to relieve his back pain. Lyndon Johnson had both a gall bladder and hernia operation while in office and caught pneumonia on at least one occasion. The burdens of Vietnam and Watergate put both Johnson and Richard Nixon under severe mental strain, although in general Richard Nixon, Gerald Ford, and Jimmy Carter enjoyed relatively good health as president. Ronald Reagan had operations for the removal of malignant growths in his colon and on his face, as well as suffering serious injury during the assassination attempt in 1981. George Bush had Graves disease, a thyroid-related illness, that often results in hyperactivity and severe mood swings. Bill Clinton has a chronic allergy problem that makes him congested and hoarse much of the time. His condition is treated by injections and throat sprays.

The effects of these medical problems on presidential performance, of course, vary. In general, the more serious the illness or injury is, the longer the recovery period, the more removed the president becomes from the day-to-day functioning of the office, and the more likely that critical decisions are delayed or delegated to others. What is more difficult to discern is how decision making is affected when presidents are not up to speed, when their judgment is affected by medication or pain.

Health issues are related to the aging process. Presidents are older than most Americans. Their mean age upon assuming office has been fifty-four. Reagan was the oldest, first elected at sixty-nine, while Theodore Roosevelt and Kennedy have been the youngest, inaugurated at forty-three. Bill Clinton was forty-six. The reason that the framers set a minimum age was their assumption that maturity, wisdom, and experience were products of age, but so is infirmity.

Older people may be less able to engage in vigorous activities and at a certain point tend to become slower mentally, have shorter attention spans and reduced memory, and, sometimes, are less able to handle stress.[8] The nation's oldest president, Ronald Reagan, joked about his dozing off at cabinet meetings; he frequently forgot names, dates, and other pertinent details and carried index cards to remind him of information he needed to know. His memory deteriorated in his second term.

Obviously, the electoral success of presidents, particularly in the contemporary period in which much personal campaigning is frequently required, testifies to some extent to their physical stamina and may auger well for their fitness as president. On the other hand, every campaign takes its toll. Moreover, skillful media consultants and campaign organizers can create an impression of activity and vigor when the reality may be much less compelling. In 1944 Franklin Roosevelt's aides staged a series of public appearances for the president to refute rumors that his health was declining. In 1984 Ronald Reagan's campaign manager projected the impression of much election activity by getting the president on the evening news every night in another campaign-related event. During much of the campaign, however, the evening news event was his *only* one of the day. Rumors about George Bush's health became so rampant during his 1992 reelection campaign that his doctor released a detailed report that indicated that the president was in excellent health.

In addition to their lower energy levels, older people are also more prone to sickness and disability than are those in their younger and middle years.[9] The onerous duties and awesome responsibilities of the office have aggravated these manifestations of the aging process. Typically, before and after pictures of the president reveal the physical signs of aging: thinning, receding, and graying hair; facial wrinkles and blemishes; double chins; and the like. Take Lyndon Johnson, for example. Historian Eric Goldman, who worked in the Johnson White House, commented on the changes in Johnson's appearance during the five years that he was president:

> On March 31, 1968, I and the millions of others sat at our television sets for a speech of President Johnson's that he had labeled as especially important. I had not seen LBJ on television for quite a while and I was shocked. My mind went back over the changes in his appearance and manner during his five years in the White House. There were the days immediately after the assassination—the rangy, rugged figure, every antenna alert, trailed by edgy aides, looking around him with those hard, piercing eyes, always as if he were sniffing out a friend and foe, always as if he were remembering that a smile or a handshake might be needed here or there. . . .
>
> Now, in March 1968 an old, weary, battered man was on the television screen. The face was deeply lined and aging; the drawl occasionally cracked and wavered. His manner gave no intimation of FDR, and little of the LBJ of 1964. Rather it suggested a lecturish, querulous schoolmaster.[10]

Although the Johnson experience may not be typical, it is suggestive of the physical toll that the presidency can exact.

Statistics on the longevity of those who have served in the nation's highest office tend to support the "killing" nature of the job. As a group, presidents have had shorter life spans than their contemporaries.[11] Excluding the four presidents who were assassinated at a relatively young age, the longevity of the thirty-one others who have died is shorter than that of their peers, particularly if other demographic variables such as race, gender, sex, educational level, and professional background are taken into account. Presidents also live shorter lives than the average member of Congress or Supreme Court justice.[12]

Although the numbers are small and generalizations hazardous, these statistics lend support to the conventional wisdom that the presidency is a very arduous and stressful position. In their conversations and writings, presidents have referred to the constant pressures they were under. In the words of President Johnson:

> The work of the President is demanding and unrelenting. It is always there to be done. Of all the 1886 nights I was President, there were not many when I got to sleep before 1 or 2 A.M., and there were few mornings when I didn't wake up by 6 or 6:30. It became a question of how much the physical constitution could take. I frankly did not believe in 1968 that I could survive another four years of the long hours and unrelenting tensions I had just gone through.[13]

One of the difficulties of being president is that there is no escape. Presidents cannot go on vacation and forget about their work. They are always on duty, always the center of attention. In his memoirs, *Mandate for Change*, President Eisenhower wrote:

> A President is President no matter what his location. For example, during eight weeks in Denver 1954 my staff and I worked every day other than Sundays, including six that I spent in the mountains at Fraser, Colorado. During those weeks I saw 225 visitors, not including my own immediate staff, made four official trips out of Denver, delivered six speeches, made three television appearances, attended five official luncheons or dinners, considered 513 bills from Congress, signing 488 into law and vetoing 25. Finally, I signed 420 other official papers or documents—all of the business of direct concern to the running of the Executive Branch.[14]

George Bush was on vacation at his home in Maine when Iraq invaded Kuwait. Not wanting to be perceived as captive to events as Carter was after U.S. diplomats were taken hostage in Iran, Bush recreated with a vengeance. As described by *Newsweek* reporter Tom Mathews, there was "nonstop golf and horseshoes, iron-man jogs, marathon sets of tennis, relentless trolls for bluefish aboard his speedboat, Fidelity."[15]

It is difficult to know how much of this frenzied activity was abnormal for Bush given the activity level he usually displayed at work or play. Some of it may also have been the result of his overactive thyroid. However, the frustration of being blind-sided by Saddam Hussein and not being able to reverse the Iraqi invasion of Kuwait undoubtedly contributed to his near manic behavior during this period.

Medical studies link long hours, persistent pressures, and a stressful environment to a variety of physical and mental illnesses: high blood pressure, cardiovascular disease, stroke, and, generally, lower resistance to communicable diseases. Perhaps this explains why presidents who have served more than four years in office have had more serious health problems and shorter life spans than those who completed one term or less. Similarly, presidents judged less successful and who, as a consequence, may have encountered more frustration and difficulty have lived shorter lives than those who were evaluated as more successful.

## PSYCHOLOGICAL ORIENTATION

Common sense suggests that personality affects behavior, but scientifically, it is difficult to prove. Personality is not directly observable. It must be inferred from observable behavior. That inference, in and of itself, is likely to be based on unverifiable assumptions such as those postulated by Sigmund Freud, Carl Jung, Alfred Adler, or more contemporary psychological theorists.

Although discerning the precise effect of personality on behavior and thereby distinguishing its impact from other variables may be beyond the scope of contemporary social science, it is still important to focus on personality and examine it within the context of the contemporary presidency. The increasing emphasis given to personal character by the media, by candidates, and by those in office demands that it receive scholarly attention as a critical component of political leadership.

Two basic types of studies focus on the relationship between personality and performance. One, known as psychobiography, seeks to explain a single president's behavior on the basis of a comprehensive psychological analysis of his life. Frequently beginning with his youth, adolescence, and early political experiences, the study progresses through his career as a public official. Examples of presidential psychobiographies that have been frequently cited include Alexander George and Juliette L. George, *Woodrow Wilson and Colonel House*; Fawn Brodie, *Thomas Jefferson*; Doris Kearns, *Lyndon Johnson and the American Dream*; Bruce Mazlish, *In Search of Nixon*; and Betty Glad, *Jimmy Carter: In Search of the Great White House*.[16]

The other type of analysis, more comparative in scope, seeks to generalize about presidential behavior on the basis of certain psychological dimensions. It seeks to discern the ways in which personality may affect seeking the presidency and then exercising power within it—how personality shapes, motivates, conditions responses, and influences judgments. One of the most stimulating and influential studies that addresses these questions is James David Barber's, *The Presidential Character*.[17]

### Presidential Character

Originally published in 1972, Barber's book seeks to explain and, under certain conditions, predict generalized reactions on the bases of several dimensions of personality. His objective is to create a framework that can be used to categorize a president's psychological tendencies and then use that categorization as an explanatory and predictive tool. Since psychological orientation per se is not discernible to the naked eye, it must be inferred from behavior that is. Three manifestations of that behavior are words, work, and personal interaction. Together, they provide clues to aspects of an individual's personality.

Which aspects are most relevant? From the standpoint of presidential performance, Barber suggests three: character, style, and world view.

Character is the least discernible but most basic of these components. In Barber's words, it "is the way the President orients himself toward life"—how he views himself.[18] Self-esteem underlies character. Naturally, the better a president feels about himself, the more easily he will be able to accept criticism, think rationally, and learn on the job.

If character is the inner core, style is the outer garb. It constitutes the way a "President goes about doing what the office requires him to do—to speak, directly or through media, to large audiences; to deal face to face with other politicians, individually and in small, relatively private groups; and to read, write, and calculate by himself in order to manage the endless flow of details that stream onto his desk. No President can escape doing at least some of each."[19] Style varies with the president and with the times. It is important because it is a predictable coping mechanism, a way of handling people, tasks, and communication.

The third component is world view. Barber defines it as "how he [the president] sees the world and his lasting opinions about what he sees."[20] It consists of "his primary, politically relevant beliefs, particularly his conceptions of social causality, human nature, and the central moral conflicts of the time."[21]

According to Barber, these three psychological components form a pattern of motives, habits, and beliefs that result in behaviors that are evident throughout life. Moreover, these behaviors and the psychological foundation on which they rest are not easily changed. Once developed, they tend to persist. Thus, while politicians shift and may even reverse their stands on policy, usually to resonate better with changes in public opinion, their personality and its manifestations remain more stable; as a consequence, they are better predictors of how politicians will perform in public office. This makes the study of personality important not only to those who wish to understand the "whys" of presidential behavior but also to those who must decide which candidates have the temperament, style, and vision that is most likely to succeed in office. Helping the American electorate in its voting decisions is an important objective of Barber's work.

To provide some analytic tools that the average citizen can use to make this evaluation, Barber develops a typology based on two observable personality dimensions: activity and affect. Activity is the level of energy that is devoted to the job—whether a person is basically active or passive. Affect concerns the level of satisfaction that is obtained from the work—whether a person's political life is a positive or negative experience. In Barber's words, "The activity baseline refers to what one does, the affect baseline to how one feels about what he does."[22] There are four possible combinations, which are summarized in Table 8-2.

Of these four character types, the active-positive is clearly the one Barber believes is best suited for the presidency. Such a person brings to the office the level of activity needed to sustain the multiplicity of roles the president must assume. Moreover, the positive attitude toward work generates its own psychological and physical benefits. It contributes to energy level; it eases the inevitable interpersonal conflicts that result from competing perspectives, interests, policy goals, and ambitions; and it increases tolerance. Presidents who enjoy their work tend to be more eager to take on new and difficult challenges. Each of the other personality types has built-in weaknesses that could impede them in the performance of their presidential duties—perhaps affecting their vision, impairing their judgment, or causing decisions or actions that may not be in their best interests.

Barber's model assumes that typecasting can provide a valuable clue to the potential difficulties that might develop in the presidency. Although Barber cannot predict these difficulties with certainty, or antici-

Table 8-2. Presidential Character Types

| *Active-Positive* | *Active-Negative* |
|---|---|
| This presidential type is characteristic of an energetic president who enjoys his work and who tends to be productive and capable of adjusting to new situations. Such a person generally feels confident and good about himself. | This type describes a president who works hard but does not gain much pleasure from it, and who tends to be intense, compulsive, and aggressive. He may pursue his public actions in a self-interested manner. Such a person generally feels insecure and uses his position to overcome these feelings of inadequacy and even impotency. |
| *Passive-Positive* | *Passive-Negative* |
| This type describes a relatively receptive laid-back individual who wants to gain agreement and mute dissent at all costs. Such a person is apt to feel pessimistic and unloved on a deep psychological level. As president, the passive-positive individual attempts to compensate for these feelings by being overly optimistic and by continually trying to elicit agreement and support from others. | This presidential type can be said to abhor politics and withdraw from interpersonal relationships. Such an individual is ill-suited for political office, much less the nation's highest one. He or she suffers from low self-esteem and a sense of uselessness and is apt to take refuge in generalized principles and standard procedures. |

Source: Adapted from James David Barber, *The Presidential Character,* 4th ed. (Englewood Cliffs, N.J.: Prentice-Hall, 1992), pp. 9–10.

pate particular reactions to particular events, he can indicate general tendencies and reactions to which certain personality types are prone. One problem, however, with making electoral judgments on the basis of this type of analysis is that those presidents who have been characterized as most psychologically qualified have not always turned out to be the most effective. Table 8-3 lists Barber's categorization of twentieth-century presidents, beginning with William Howard Taft.

Franklin Roosevelt is an example of an active-positive type who is generally regarded as a great president, while Woodrow Wilson, who is also well regarded by historians, is active-negative. Two recent extremely popular presidents, Dwight Eisenhower and Ronald Reagan, are not even active (and in Eisenhower's case not positive either, according to Barber), while Gerald Ford and Jimmy Carter, who were much less popular (and many would argue much less successful), are both active and positive. So is George Bush, whose public approval fluctuated greatly during his presidency. Among the nineteenth-century presidents, Abraham Lincoln, generally considered one of America's greatest

**Table 8-3. The Personality Types of Contemporary Presidents**

| Active-Positive | Active-Negative |
|---|---|
| Franklin D. Roosevelt | Woodrow Wilson |
| Harry S Truman | Herbert Hoover |
| John F. Kennedy | Lyndon B. Johnson |
| Gerald Ford | Richard M. Nixon |
| Jimmy Carter | |
| George Bush | |
| | |
| Passive-Positive | Passive-Negative |
| William Howard Taft | Calvin Coolidge |
| Warren G. Harding | Dwight D. Eisenhower |
| Ronald Reagan | |

Source: James David Barber, *The Presidential Character*, 4th ed. (Englewood Cliffs, N.J.: Prentice-Hall, 1992).

presidents, has been categorized as active-negative by political scientist Jeffrey Tulis.[23]

What is the problem? Has Barber made a major methodological error or has he merely miscategorized some presidents? Much controversy has surrounded these and other questions. Barber's critics have alleged that his categories are too broad and ambiguous, that his activity and affect dimensions are too crude because they are dichotomous, and that psychological tendencies themselves do not neatly fit into one and only one box, an allegation that Barber admits although he believes that it is possible to identify a dominant tendency.

There is another difficulty with Barber's analysis. In addition to being reductionist—reducing the causes of very complex behavior to a single psychological explanation—Barber's argument also tends to be tautological. Categories are defined first rather than being derived from empirical evidence, and the definitions are then used to explain empirical phenomena. This generates self-fulfilling prophesies, according to political scientist Alexander George.[24] If they turn out to be correct, as they did in the case of Nixon, then Barber can claim that the psychological explanation is a valid one; if the predictions do not occur, then he could assert that the environment was not ripe for the psychological tendencies to produce their expected reaction. None of these criticisms invalidates the model, but they do question its scope, application, and general utility as an explanatory and predictive tool.

In addition to the methodological problems, there may be another reason that psychological types and presidential success do not always mesh. Barber himself alludes to this reason when he discusses the interaction of personality, the power situation in which presidents find themselves, and the national climate of expectations. Presidents must make decisions and take actions within a potent political environment over which they have limited influence. Thus, although their character, style, and world view are relatively constant, the power mix and public moods are not. An environment that allows one president to achieve policy objectives may prevent another from doing so. Active-positive presidents in particular are prone to circumvent existing structures and processes—often at their own peril—in attempting to achieve results.[25] Franklin Roosevelt's failed attempt to pack the Supreme Court is a case in point.[26] Bill Clinton's refusal to consider partisan opposition to some of his early legislative policy proposals, such as his economic stimulus plan, may be another.

Moreover, the environment that may have contributed to the election or success in office of one personality type may change. This happened to George Bush. Elected to continue the policies of the Reagan administration, Bush was unable to alter his basic approach to the economy in the light of the recession that occurred in the final years of his presidency. His unwillingness to initially acknowledge the economic problem, to develop a plan to combat it, and to devise a strategy for getting Congress and the public to support him made Bush appear ill-suited for a job for which he seemed so well suited earlier in his presidency.

### Mood Cycles

In a sequel to his analysis of personality, Barber examines mood in a book entitled *The Pulse of Politics*.[27] In it, he proposes a typology of electoral periods based on three basic dominant moods: *conflict*, a clash of competing interests; *conscience*, an appeal to principle and honesty; and *conciliation*, a desire for tranquility, goodwill, and compromise.[28] Barber sees these periods as cyclical, each reoccurring every twelve years. The most successful presidents are likely to be those whose personalities best fit the mood of the period and can adapt to changes in that mood over the course of their presidencies.

A variety of reasons may explain why some personality types do not fit the times. The public may make a poor judgment on election day; voters may not have had viable options; partisan or other factors may affect the outcome. However, the more the public knows about the personalities of the nominees, the more likely it will make a wise voting decision.

The dynamics of the public pulse combined with the stability of personality provide a potential down-the-road problem for presidents. Selected in part because their personality may have coincided with the public mood at the time of the election, presidents may have difficulty adjusting when that mood changes. As a consequence, they may be more apt, particularly under stress, to react impulsively on the basis of their own psychological needs rather than in a manner that more rationally calculates public costs and benefits. That is why the active-positive type has an advantage, but, as the George Bush example illustrates, it does not guarantee success. External factors beyond the president's control may affect the outcome far more than character can.

The influence of a variety of factors on behavior point to the difficulties of using a psychological model to explain and anticipate presidential performance. Nonetheless, character is an important component of that behavior, and Barber's contribution is that he has focused attention on it. His model, despite its substantial limitations, continues to frame much of the debate on how the president's character affects performance in office.

## COGNITIVE DIMENSIONS

There is a link between personality dimensions and political perspectives. Beliefs people have are shaped by how they view themselves and others within their environment. Personal character and needs condition the processing of information, the consideration of options, and the making of decisions.

### Impact of World Views

Presidents and their aides bring to office sets of beliefs about politics, policy, human nature, and social causality—or, in other words, beliefs about how the world works and why it does so. These beliefs serve decision makers by providing a frame of reference for raising and evaluating policy options, filtering information and giving it meaning, establishing potential boundaries of action, and supplying an approach to decision making itself. Beliefs also help busy officials cope with complex decisions to which they can devote limited time, and they predispose them to act in certain directions.

Although sets of beliefs are inevitable and help to simplify the world, they can be dysfunctional as well. First, they may distort the identification of a problem that requires attention. This is perhaps most dramatically illustrated in the case of surprise attacks by one country on another. In these situations beliefs often interfere with effective analysis when they filter information and give it meaning because "the primary problem in major strategic surprise is not intelligence [information] but political disbelief."[36] The Bush White House was surprised when Iraq invaded Kuwait in 1990, even though it had substantial evidence of a massive military build-up on the Kuwaiti border.

Belief systems also influence the determination of the objectives of public policies. Decisions about U.S. participation in the Vietnam War were molded by the views of top officials. The premises they shared included the contentions that a non-Communist Vietnam was important to the security and credibility of the United States; the war-torn country was a critical testing ground of the ability of this country to counter Communist support for wars of national liberation; communism was a

## BOX 8-1.    BILL CLINTON: RUNNING, PERSEVERING, AND PLEASING

Bill Clinton's biological father died in an automobile accident before he was born. His mother remarried after several years. Bill's stepfather, Roger Clinton, was reputed to be a kind and generous man, but he was also an alcoholic. Under the influence of liquor, he tended to be abusive and violent toward his family. On occasions when he was a teenager, Bill had to call for outside help to settle family disputes that threatened to become violent. In one incident when he was fourteen years old, young Clinton actually confronted his stepfather, warning him never to hit his mother or stepbrother again. "If you want them, you'll have to go through me," he said.[29]

Virginia (Bill's mother) and Roger Clinton eventually got divorced, but after Roger was dying of cancer, they remarried. While a student at Georgetown University, Bill recalls driving from Washington to Duke University Hospital to visit his stepfather. One particular trip, which occurred over Easter weekend, left an indelible mark on Clinton's memory. He recalled that he and his stepfather went to a religious service at Duke's chapel:

> It was, God, beautiful. I think he knew that I was coming down there just because I loved him. There was nothing else to fight over, nothing else to run from. It was a wonderful time in my life, and I think in his.[30]

These events, which candidate Clinton vividly recalled during his presidential campaign, cast a major imprint on his personality and helped forge a character that shaped his political life. Three personality features—his limitless ambition, his perseverance in the face of adversity, and his desire to please and heal—have reappeared throughout his career, including his presidency.

Bill Clinton is goal oriented. The goals represent steps on a political ladder that led in his own mind toward the presidency ever since he shook hands with John F. Kennedy at the White House in 1963: band major in high school, president of his freshman and sophomore classes at college, Rhodes scholar, Yale Law School, Arkansas attorney general at 30, and governor at 32, the youngest in the country since Harold Stassen of Minnesota. Defeated once, Clinton was reelected five times and achieved national prominence as leader of the National Governors' Association and head of the Democratic Leadership Conference.

Clinton explains his nonstop political career as a kind of reaction to his biological father's death and to the precariousness of life as he saw it:

> For a long time I thought I would have to live for both of us in some ways. . . . I think that's one reason I was in such a hurry when I was younger. I used to be criticized by people who said, "Well, he's too ambitious," but to me, because I grew up sort of subconsciously on his

**BOX 8-1.**    *(continued)*

timetable, I never knew how much time I would have. . . . It gave me an urgent sense to do everything I could in life as quickly as I could.[31]

Clinton's frantic pursuit has not been without its setbacks. Elected two years in a row as class president at Georgetown, he was defeated in an attempt to be head of the school council; elected as the youngest governor in Arkansas history, he was defeated in his quest for reelection; asked to give the nominating speech for Michael Dukakis at the 1988 Democratic Convention, he bored delegates with a long-winded, passionless address, arousing their attention and applause only when he said, "In conclusion . . ."; acknowledged as the leading Democrat for his party's nomination in 1992, his campaign was rocked by charges of marital infidelity, draft dodging, and conflicts of interest while he was governor of Arkansas. In each case he survived these hurtles that threatened to capsize his political career.

The ability to persevere, to hang in there and survive adversity, may also be traceable to the events of his youth. After his biological father's death, Bill's mother also persevered under difficult circumstances. She sent her two-year-old son to live with her parents while she went to complete her nursing education. Her remarriage to Roger Clinton improved the family's financial situation but also brought the alcohol-related problems of an abusive stepfather into the household. This was the environment in which Bill Clinton developed his instinct to survive.

One way to survive in this type of environment was for Clinton to adopt an interpersonal strategy as a "healer," a compromiser, a peacemaker. For his whole life, getting along for Bill Clinton has meant trying to please as many diverse interests as possible. Journalist Peter Applebome defines this as a "compulsive need to please, to bring people together at some hazily defined, accommodating center—as if he [Clinton] were still re-enacting in politics the role he played at home."[32]

Both supporters and opponents have noted Clinton's passion to please. According to John Brummett, the editor of *Arkansas Times Magazine,* "He tries not to say no to anyone. He has an obsession to please. For years, I've seen legislators from different sides of the same question come out of his office, all thinking he's on their side."[33] Supporters see this as a desirable trait, responsible for his political successes. Says Betsey Wright, his chief of staff for six years when Clinton was governor of Arkansas, "Part of what attracted me to Bill is he's always been secure enough as a person to be able to listen, to be able to negotiate, to hear other points of view."[34] Critics, however, see another side: that of one who is trying to please others to further his own interests. The appellation "Slick Willie," coined by Arkansas newspaper columnist Paul Greenberg, was intended to describe this aspect of Clinton's personality: "a tendency to tell people whatever it is they wanted to hear."[35]

Clinton does overpromise in public, and this tendency has gotten

**BOX 8-1.**    *(continued)*

him into trouble. It has made him look weak and vacillating, reenforcing the "Slick Willie" image. Once in office, he finds that he cannot obtain his policy goals unless he modifies them. But backing off, he is accused of being unprincipled, of not standing for anything. The tendency to please has also led to another charge: that Clinton compromises too easily, that he can be had. Both of these character-related problems surfaced during his early months in the White House.

The political difficulties Clinton encountered during his first term as governor and his early months as president can be traced in part to his haste, to his desire to do too much too quickly, and to his failure to consider the political realities of his environment. After rejection by the voters of Arkansas in 1981 and a precipitous decline in public approval during his first five months as president, Clinton changed; he did what he needed to do to survive. He got some new advisers, including a few older, experienced hands; consulted with his opponents; redefined his priorities; refocused his attention; articulated a simpler, clearer message; and moderated his programs, moving closer to the political center where his skills as an energetic, intelligent compromiser would be most effective.

Ambition, perseverance, and a desire to heal are three character tendencies that have had a profound impact on Bill Clinton's entire political career. These aspects of his character undoubtedly will continue to affect his presidency. They may not dictate specific words and actions, but within the environment in which Clinton finds himself, they are bound to affect what he does, how he does it, and, to some extent, how he is perceived. In this way, character will continue to affect his performance in office.

world conspiracy; South Vietnam would fall to the North without American aid; and if South Vietnam fell to communism, other countries would shortly follow. When these views were coupled with President Johnson's more general premises that all problems were solvable and that the United States could do anything, this country's intervention was a foregone conclusion.

The doctrinal consensus on Vietnam made it difficult to challenge U.S. policy. Defining doctrine in terms of necessity foreclosed policy options. As a result, "no comprehensive and systematic examination of Vietnam's importance to the United States was ever undertaken within the executive branch. Debates revolved around how to do things better and whether they could be done, not whether they were worth doing."[37]

Similarly, Robert McFarlane, President Reagan's former national security adviser, testified before the special congressional committee investigating the Iran–Contra affair that no government-wide analysis of American interests in Nicaragua was ever made. Answers to the most important questions were simply assumed.

Finally, the world views of top decision makers affect the options they raise to deal with issues and the choices they make among these options. Decision making regarding the Cuban missile crisis is often cited as an example of deliberate, comprehensive consideration of alternatives, but President Kennedy precluded diplomatic and nonmilitary responses to the situation at the outset and actually considered a fairly narrow range of military options. He believed that the presence of Soviet missiles in Cuba greatly increased the threat to the national security of the United States and that the Soviet Union would remove the missiles only if forced to so by the threat of American military sanctions. His decisions followed directly from those premises.

A president's view of a problem and proposed response to it is especially likely to foreclose consideration of alternatives in a crisis when there is a premium on rapid and decisive action. In the period directly preceding the actual fighting in the Gulf war, General Colin Powell, chairman of the Joint Chiefs of Staff, wanted to consider the option of the continuation of economic sanctions against Iraq. President Bush, however, told him there was not time to try such a strategy.[38]

### Managing Inconsistency

The environment in which the president operates is complex and uncertain. Yet the human mind is not comfortable with these characteristics. It has certain cognitive needs and prefers stable views to a continuous consideration of options. About a month before the commencement of hostilities in the Gulf war, George Bush told an interviewer: "I've got it boiled down very clearly to good and evil. And it helps if you can be that clear in your own mind."[39]

It does not follow that the president should not continue to consider options and information once a policy decision has been made. The decision may have been a poor one. Yet busy aides are typically reluctant to risk irritating an even busier president by attempting to reopen a question he thought was settled. In the words of two close observers of decision making:

> Once a president sets policy, it becomes a herculean task for senior officials and bureaucrats to argue against it. Presidents have to make clear up and down the line that they want to hear criticisms and alternatives from their subordinates before they read them in the press, and that dissenters will be rewarded as well as team players. They should press for agreement on coherent policies but also leave the door open to revising judgment.[40]

It is especially difficult to review decisions regarding national security while fighting is taking place. Speaking from experience, Vice President Hubert Humphrey wrote: "Once a wartime decision has been made and men's lives have been lost, once resources are committed—and most dangerously, once a nation's honor has been committed—what you are doing becomes almost Holy Writ. Any division, dissension, or diversion is suspect."[41]

Decision makers often experience stress as they try to cope with the complexity of decisions, especially in times of crisis. In a revealing incident President Warren G. Harding explained to a friend:

> John, I can't make a damn thing out of this tax problem. I listen to one side and they seem right, and then God! I talk to the other side and they seem just as right, and there I am where I started. I know somewhere there is a book that would give me the truth, but hell, I couldn't read the book. I know somewhere there is an economist who knows the truth, but I don't know where to find him and haven't the sense to know him and trust him when I did find him. God, what a job![42]

Fortunately, most of those occupying the Oval Office have had greater confidence in their intellectual capacity than Harding.

The mind often simplifies reality to deal with the world's complexities and resolves uncertainty by ignoring or deemphasizing information that contradicts existing beliefs. These inference mechanisms operate unconsciously, and they may have as great an influence on a person's beliefs as objective evidence. Consequently, most policymakers remain unreceptive to a major revision of their beliefs in response to new information, especially if they have had success in the past with applying their general beliefs to specific decisions or if they have held their beliefs for a long time. Moreover, they are unlikely to search for information that challenges their views or for options contrary to those they advocate. Instead, they tend to incorporate new information in ways that render it comprehensible within their existing frames of reference. In other words, they rationalize it to support their previously held beliefs.

One relatively simple technique for managing inconsistency consists in attaching very negative consequences to alternatives, as top policymakers did to the option of "scuttle and run" from Vietnam. By concluding that the role of the United States in international relations would be seriously diminished by such action, decision makers dismissed an alternative that was widely advocated outside the government.

Officials may also employ selective information to make inferences that a particular situation could not possibly occur. If policymakers accept this inference of impossibility, there is no need for them to consider information pointing to the "impossible" situation, alternatives to prevent or respond to it, or what effect it would have on the alternatives that *are* being considered. Most officials believed that the Japanese could not attack Pearl Harbor. Because they were not expecting an attack, American officials did not notice the signs pointing toward it. Instead, they paid attention to signals supporting their current expectations of enemy behavior.

Another means of reducing inconsistency and thereby decreasing the pressure to consider alternatives is similar to what we commonly term "wishful thinking." Information inconsistent with ongoing policy may be deemphasized by believing that undesirable conditions are only temporary and will ameliorate in response to current policy. Officials used this type of reasoning to garner support for the continued escalation of the Vietnam War. All that was needed to force the enemy to succumb, they argued, was to keep up the pressure. More generally, in the face of contradictory or ambiguous indicators of the progress of the war, they listened most carefully to the optimistic rather than the pessimistic reports or the caveats to positive assessments and hoped for the best.

Yet another means of resolving uncertainty and simplifying decision making is reasoning by analogy. The conclusions supported by this type of reasoning seem to have strength independent of the available evidence, probably because the analogies simplify and provide a coherent framework for ambiguous and inconsistent information.

Metaphors and similes simplify a complex and ambiguous reality by relating it to a relatively simple and well-understood concept. If one is then used as the basis of an analogy, the possibilities for error are considerable. Part of the theoretical underpinning for the Vietnam War was often characterized as the "domino theory" of international relations, which holds that the United States must prevent countries from falling to the Communists because once one country falls, the one next to it will fall, and then the next—just like falling dominoes. The simplistic nature of the metaphor indicates how much room exists for differences between it and reality.

Discrediting the source of information and options is another means of reducing the complexity and resolving the contradictions with which policymakers have to deal. At first, President Johnson handled the critics of his Vietnam War policy quite well, inviting them to his office and talking to them for hours. But as opposition increased and polls indicated a dip in his popularity, he responded to criticism by discrediting its source. He maintained that Senator William Fulbright (the chairman of the Senate Foreign Relations Committee) was upset at not being named secretary of state; the liberals in Congress were angry at him because he hadn't gone to Harvard, because the Great Society was more successful than the New Frontier, and because he had blocked Robert Kennedy from the presidency; the columnists opposed him to make a bigger splash and to follow James Reston and Walter Lippman; and the young were hostile because they were ignorant.

At other times presidents may simply avoid information they fear will force them to face disagreeable decisions that complicate their lives and produce additional stress. Richard Nixon is a classic example. In his memoirs he writes of putting off confronting his own attorney general, John Mitchell, because of his hypersensitivity and desire not to know the truth about Mitchell's involvement in Watergate in case it was unpleasant. He just could not bring himself to talk to Mitchell personally. Similarly, the president found it too painful to discuss Watergate with experienced officials he had brought back to the White House to help restore confidence in his administration. It was easier to rely solely on those personally close to him in dealing with the scandal. Referring to Nixon's ability to engage in self-delusion and avoid unpleasant facts, White House Chief of Staff H. R. Haldeman argues that the "failure to face the irrefutable facts, even when it was absolutely clear that they were irrefutable, was one of our fatal flaws in handling Watergate at every step."[43]

Each of the cognitive processes that reduce uncertainty and complexity can be a reasonable response to a situation. The point is that people have a tendency to rely on them not only by conscious choice but because of their need for certainty and simplicity. In each of the examples cited above, the president and his advisers made use of an inference mechanism that diverted their attention from vital information and led them to ignore appropriate options. Potential actions that were considered disastrous would have been far less so than those that were taken, situations thought to be impossible actually occurred, hoped-for results from policies never materialized, inferences were based upon inappropriate analogies, and worthwhile criticism was rejected. Thus, the inference mechanisms that top decision makers employ to manage inconsistency may jeopardize rational decision making.

At the same time, it is important to recognize the interplay between motivation and cognition. Many people can tolerate at least some inconsistency, and there are other motives aside from consistency that drive behavior, including accuracy, fairness, efficiency, accountability, ideological biases, and time pressure. So presidents and their advisers have a variety of cognitive strategies available to them and may choose to "face the facts" rather than simplify if they have sufficient motivation. Understanding which motivations are operative in a given situation remains one of the most intriguing questions of presidential politics.

## PRESIDENTIAL STYLE

Presidents set the tone for their White Houses. How they approach their job and interact with their aides, what they demand from their subordinates, and how much supervision they exercise over them have a lot to do with how the White House functions and how well presidents are served.

Stylistic differences are a product of personal needs and experience. Some presidents work constantly. Carter, Bush, and Clinton put in twelve- to fourteen-hour days on a regular basis (see Box 8-2). Eisenhower and Reagan had a more leisurely schedule. Reagan worked from 9 A.M. to 5 P.M., Monday through Thursday; he would usually leave early Friday afternoon for the presidential retreat at Camp David in Maryland.

BOX 8-2.    CLINTON'S DAYBOOK, MARCH 17, 1993

| | |
|---|---|
| T.B.A. | Jog |
| 9:00–9:15 A.M. | Intelligence Briefing, Oval Office |
| 9:15–9:30 | National Security Briefing, Oval Office |
| 9:30 | Staff Briefing, Oval Office |
| 10:15 | Remarks to Electronics Industry Association, Old Executive Office Building |
| 10:40–10:55 | Drop by, National Council of Senior Citizens |
| 11:00–11:15 | Staff Briefing, Oval Office |
| 11:15–11:30 | Meeting with Prime Minister Albert Reynolds of Ireland |
| 11:30 | St. Patrick's Day Shamrock Presentation, Roosevelt Room |
| 12:00–1:30 P.M. | St. Patrick's Day Lunch, Capitol Hill |
| 2:00–2:30 | Office Time |
| 2:45–2:50 | Phone call to William J. Clinton of Seattle (a ten-year-old with a birth defect) |
| 3:00–3:15 | Meeting with Stan Greenberg, the President's polltaker, Oval Office |
| 3:15–4:00 | Office Time |
| 4:00–4:30 | Meeting with Ted Turner, Oval Office |
| 5:00–7:00 | Health Care Reform Meeting, Roosevelt Room |
| 7:30–8:15 | Office Time |
| BC and HRC RON, White House* | |

*Bill Clinton and Hillary Rodham Clinton, rest of night at White House

Source: *New York Times*, March 21, 1993, p. 24.

Some presidents have to dominate relationships with their subordinates. Lyndon Johnson was one of these people. He monopolized discussions and was unable to accept criticism. Others, such as Kennedy and Ford, treated their senior staff almost as equals.

Some presidents need to operate in a very protective environment. Nixon saw only a few trusted aides and wanted all recommendations and advice written and presented as option papers. Carter and Clinton, although much more open than Nixon, also operated primarily off paper. Eisenhower and Reagan preferred oral briefings to written memoranda. Ford is said to have maintained a revolving door into and out of the Oval Office as did Clinton at the very beginning of his administration.

Some presidents need to be involved in almost everything. Johnson, Carter, Bush, and Clinton maintained a hands-on approach to decision making. Others such as Eisenhower and Reagan waited for decisions to reach them. Nixon and Ford were more active but Nixon was not involved in a lot of detailed, middle-level decisions. He left much of the budget decision making to his budget director.

Presidents create the mood and condition the way their White House operates. In general, the more personable, accessible, and tolerant they are, the happier the staff. Efficiency, however, is not always promoted by the chief executive's being a nice person.

Each White House has its particular style. During the Nixon years, that style was described as *macho*. Aides had to prove how tough they were, how long they worked, and how many sacrifices they were making for the job. In contrast, Presidents Ford and Carter permitted a looser operation. They were more tolerant, more open, and less imposing.[44]

The early Clinton White House is another good example of a fluid staff system, described by *New York Times* reporter Richard L. Berke as "controlled pandemonium."[45] Senior aides got involved in a variety of overlapping issues; meetings were frequent and attendance open to all interested staff; there was little discipline; media leaks on proposed personnel selections and policy alternatives were rampant. The president contributed to this seemingly chaotic environment by involving himself in details usually reserved for staff—subcabinet appointments, early policy development, speech drafting, even scheduling and travel. It was not until several well-publicized and embarrassing incidents, which included the attempted firing of the entire White House travel office, that changes were instituted in the personnel and operation of the Clinton White House.

## WHITE HOUSE STAFF RELATIONSHIPS

Character, world views, and style are not limited to the president. Aides also have orientations and feelings that affect their work. Moreover, the environment in which they work conditions the decisions and actions that are made. For example, the long hours presidential assistants must work, the unrelenting pressures they are under, the complex issues with which they must deal, and the significant and often long-term implications of their decisions cannot help but affect how they interact and communicate with one another and how they perform their jobs.

The work is arduous. The hours are extensive. Aides usually arrive before the president and leave after he departs. For most, a sixty- to eighty-hour week is standard. Arriving early in the morning and staying into the evening five days a week, senior and middle-level aides usually work a full day on Saturday and frequently a half day on Sunday either in the office or at home.

Group pressures also serve to reinforce the White House work ethic. Members of the presidential staff tend to be conscious of the hours that others work. "There's always a customary desire to be around when the phone rings" was the way one Carter aide put it.[46] A Clinton staffer likened the White House to "a campus full of overachievers—everybody wants to be the last one to turn out the lights."[47]

The long hours generate fatigue and lower tolerance. They make touching all bases a more burdensome chore. There is a tendency to circumvent those who might place obstacles in the way of decisions or actions. Thus in the Reagan administration, the secretaries of defense and state were not included in many Iran–Contra meetings when it became clear they opposed selling arms to the Iranian government. Clinton aides avoided consulting and even communicating with Republican members of Congress who opposed the president's economic and budget proposals.

In addition to the workload, the pressures of deadlines, crises, and decisions that can have a major impact on the president's reputation are enormous. Combined with time constraints and high performance expectations, they contribute to a very stressful environment that affects behavior on and off the job. William Clark, one of Reagan's national security advisers, had to leave his job after suffering from migraine headaches and nightmares.[48] For years the White House has had a reputation as a "divorce mill." Stories of aides adopting unhealthy coping mechanisms, such as philandering and alcohol abuse, abound. One particularly tragic illustration of these pressures was the suicide of Vincent Foster, deputy counsel in the Clinton administration, who apparently took his own life after he and several others were named in a *Wall Street Journal* article criticizing the counsel's operation.

Not only is sufficient time often lacking to perform quality work, but the constant need to deal with a highly complex and politically divided governmental system—and often achieve a consensus—further complicates the task. One official in the Ford White House contrasted his expectations as a state official with the reality of working in the White House.

> When I worked for the state of Illinois, I used to scream about the damn Feds. Why can't they do that; why can't they make a decision and get this whole thing straightened out? You're sure there is a button to push to get something done, but when you get here you find that it's not there. Rather, there's a flow chart telling you how many steps in the process you have to go through. It can be very frustrating.[49]

Richard Cheney, Ford's chief of staff and Bush's defense secretary, echoed a similar refrain:

> There is a tendency before you get to the White House or when you're just observing it from the outside to say, "Gee, that's a powerful position that person has." The fact of the matter is that while you're here trying to do

things, you are far more aware of the constraints than you are of the power. You spend most of your time trying to overcome obstacles getting what the president wants done.[50]

Internal competition also tends to be heightened by these job-related pressures. The greater the work demands on staff, both in terms of quantity and quality, and the more severe the sanctions for shoddy or tardy performance, the more likely the environment will promote self-interested, competitive behavior.

Internal rivalries are not generated solely by the White House environment, however. The kinds of people who are attracted to jobs as presidential aides are also a proximate cause of their behavior. The White House tends to draw very ambitious people. Landon Butler, deputy assistant to President Carter, observed the intermix between ambition and service in a diary he prepared during the Carter transition:

> Our personal destinies get all mixed in with our work. The uncertainty of who gets invited into the government is bringing out the worst in people. They are overreaching. I'm getting angry. It's affecting my judgment. Will the White House be like this?[51]

Staff competition, of course, does not always adversely affect the running of the White House, although it does tend to make working there less pleasant. The Franklin Roosevelt White House, where a competitive staff structure reaped benefits for a president interested in maximizing his information, options, and influence, illustrates that some internal competition can be advantageous. On the other hand, infighting usually detracts from the efficiency of operations and lowers the morale of staff. When carried into the public arena, it can cause political embarrassment for the president.

A competitive environment also encourages self-interested behavior that can warp vision, overextend arguments, and lead to inaccurate or unbalanced presentations of issues, options, and their consequences for the president. All of this contributes to the dangers George Reedy saw and described in his book, *The Twilight of the Presidency*.[52]

Reedy was concerned with the isolation of presidents, with their making of decisions and taking of actions in an environment that did not accord with reality. He saw the deference paid to presidents by their aides, a propensity for telling them what they wanted to hear, and an obsession with satisfying their every whim as contributing to this potential danger. To make good decisions, Reedy contended, the president needs accurate information, not pleasantries; wise recommendations, not self-motivated advocacy; and intelligent support, not blind loyalty.

All of the pressures and deadlines, the internal competition, and the tendencies toward isolation cannot help but have an impact on the presidency. Presidents have no choice. They have to delegate since their tasks exceed their time, energy, and, often, their expertise. How their aides interact with them, with each other, and with their executive and congressional counterparts affects presidential performance in a direct and often immediate way. Presidents themselves can influence this pattern of interaction but they cannot control it. To some extent, all presidents are at the mercy of the organizational, operational, and personal proclivities of their staff. But this is particularly true for presidents who wish to direct change and thus tend to concentrate their advisory and decision-making structures in their White House staffs.

## CONCLUSION

When all is said and done, *who* the president is matters. Social background, physical well-being, presidential character, cognitive views, and personal style and staff interaction all condition performance in office. How they affect that performance is difficult to measure with precision, but their impact must be considered when trying to explain presidential actions or predict presidential responses.

A case can also be made that some of these characteristics are better than others; that is, they are more desirable because they are more likely to lead to the president's achievement of his policy and political goals. James David Barber and others have argued that voters should take the character of the candidates into account when making their decisions on election day. They do, although most people do not have the kind and amount of information that may be necessary to render an informed, intelligent, psychologically oriented judgment.

Nonetheless, if socialization, physical condition, and psychological orientation—which includes character, world views, and style—affect behavior, then they must have an impact on the president's capacity to lead. One would expect that those people who have demonstrated the most outstanding leadership skills in our democratic society will have a wide range of personal experience, particularly on the issues with which they must deal as president; will be physically and mentally healthy; will be stable, independent, and self-assured; will have a sophisticated understanding of domestic and international policy problems; and will relate easily and effectively to those around them. Some presidents have obviously demonstrated many of these tendencies and characteristics, but a surprising number of those presidents who have been highly evaluated did not.

As a group, the presidents who have been viewed as most successful have tended to come from the country's social and economic elite. Some of them have experienced serious health problems in office. Some have manifested psychological needs that seem to have influenced their desire for the nation's highest office as well as their conduct in it, energizing them or immobilizing them in different kinds of situations. The perspectives of some of the most accomplished presidents have also been limited or skewed. In contrast, some of the less accomplished presidents have had more humble origins, enjoyed better health, and have not been weighed down with heavy psychological baggage that made it difficult for them to separate their personal needs from their public policy decisions. Does this suggest that the norm is not the ideal for outstanding American presidents? It may, but it also points to the very complex environment in which presidents function—an environment that not only affects presidential decisions and actions but also influences personal tendencies and characteristics that, themselves, affect those decisions and actions.

Our conclusion is that leadership is not only a consequence of who the leader is but of how that leader interacts with others in the changing social, economic, and political milieu in which he must operate. Those who are better able to perceive change and adjust to it are apt to be more successful than those who do not and cannot. Moreover, not only does a great leader require the capacity to exercise significant leadership skills, but that leader also needs an environment in which those skills can be effectively exercised.

Returning to our distinction between two leadership types, we conclude that bad times, crises, or some cataclysmic event is probably necessary for leadership of the director of change variety, while good times in a politics-as-usual environment contributes to a president performing a facilitator role.

## NOTES

1. Digby Baltzell and Howard G. Schneiderman, "Social Class in the Oval Office," *Society* 25 (September/October 1988): 45.

2. Rose Crane, quoted in James Morgan, "An Arkansas State of Mind," *The Washington Post Magazine*, July 12, 1992, p. 17.

3. Bill Clinton is the first Rhodes scholar to be elected president.

4. Baltzell and Schneiderman, "Social Class in the Oval Office," p. 44.

5. Thomas C. Wiegele suggests that presidents may suppress pain because of their penchant for struggle, for overcoming political adversity, particularly the rigors of the campaign and then of governance (Thomas C. Wiegele, "Presidential Physicians and Presidential Health Care: Some Theoretical and Operational Considerations Related to Political Decision Making," *Presidential Studies Quarterly* 20 [Winter 1990]: 83–84).

6. R. T. McIntire, *White House Physician* (New York: G.P. Putnam's Sons, 1946), pp. 63–64.

7. Ibid.

8. Jame E. Birren and K. Warner Schaie, Handbook of *The Psychology of Aging*, 2d ed. (New York: Van Nostrand, 1985); James F. Fries and Lawrence M. Crapo, *Vitality and Aging* (San Francisco: Freeman, 1981); James N. Schubert, "Age and Active-Passive Leadership Style," *American Political Science Review* 82 (1988): 763–72.

9. Robert E. Gilbert, "Personality, Stress and Achievement: Keys to Presidential Longevity," *Presidential Studies Quarterly* 15 (Winter 1985): 33–50.

10. Eric Goldman, *The Tragedy of Lyndon Johnson* (New York: Knopf, 1969), pp. 511–12.

11. Gilbert, "Personality, Stress, and Achievement": 35–36, 43–44.

12. Ibid.: 44.

13. Lyndon Johnson, *The Vantage Point* (New York: Holt, Rinehart and Winston, 1971), p. 425.

14. Dwight D. Eisenhower, *Mandate for Change* (New York: Doubleday, 1963), p. 267.

15. Tom Mathews, "The Road to War," *Newsweek*, January 28, 1991, p. 60.

16. Alexander George and Juliette L. George, *Woodrow Wilson and Colonel House* (New York: John Day, 1956); Fawn Brodie, *Thomas Jefferson* (New York: W. W. Norton, 1974); Doris Kearns, *Lyndon Johnson and the American Dream* (New York: Harper & Row, 1976); Bruce Mazlish, *In Search of Nixon* (New York: Basic Books, 1972); and Betty Glad, *Jimmy Carter: In Search of the Great White House* (New York: W. W. Norton, 1980).

17. James David Barber, *The Presidential Character*, 4th ed. (Englewood Cliffs, N.J.: Prentice Hall, 1992).

18. Ibid., p. 5.

19. Ibid.

20. Ibid.

21. Ibid.

22. Ibid., p. 9.

23. Jeffrey Tulis, "On Presidential Character," in Joseph M. Bessette and Jeffrey Tulis, eds., *The Presidency in the Constitutional Order* (Baton Rouge, La.: Louisiana State University Press, 1981), pp. 292–301.

24. Alexander George, "Assessing Presidential Character," in Aaron Wildavsky, ed., *Perspectives on the Presidency* (Boston: Little, Brown, 1975), pp. 110–11.

25. Barber, *The Presidential Character*, p. 426.

26. Ibid., pp. 243–46.

27. James David Barber, *The Pulse of Politics* (New York: W. W. Norton, 1980).

28. Ibid., pp. 3–4.

29. William J. Clinton, as quoted in Peter Applebome, "Bill Clinton's Uncertain Journey," *New York Times Magazine*, March 8, 1992, p. 60.

30. Ibid.

31. William J. Clinton, as quoted in David Maraniss, "Clinton's Life Shaped by Early Turmoil," *Washington Post*, January 26, 1992, pp. A1, 17.

32. William J. Clinton, quoted in Applebome, "Clinton's Uncertain Journey," p. 60.

33. John Brummett, quoted in "As Governor, Clinton Remade Arkansas in His Own Image," *New York Times*, March 31, 1992, p. A16.

34. Betsey Wright, quoted in Bill McAllister and David Maraniss, "Clinton: An Instinctive Dealmaker," *Washington Post*, March 28, 1992, p. A12.

35. Paul Greenberg, as quoted in Joel Brinkley, "Clinton Remade Home State in Own Image," *New York Times*, March 31, 1992, p. A16.

36. Richard K. Betts, *Surprise Attack: Lessons for Defense Planning* (Washington, D.C.: Brookings Institution, 1982).

37. Leslie H. Gelb with Richard K. Betts, *The Irony of Vietnam: The System Worked* (Washington, D.C.: Brookings Institution, 1979), p. 190; see also pp. 353–54, 365–67.

38. Bob Woodward, *The Commanders* (New York: Simon and Schuster, 1991), pp. 41–42, 299–302.

39. Quoted in Kenneth T. Walsh, "Commander in Chief," *U.S. News and World Report*, December 31, 1990–January 7, 1991, p. 24.

40. Leslie H. Gelb with Richard K. Betts, *The Irony of Vietnam: The System Worked* (Washington, D.C.: Brookings Institution, 1979), p. 365.

41. Hubert Humphrey quoted in Hamilton Jordan, *Crisis: The Last Year of the Carter Presidency* (New York: Putnam, 1982), p. 250.

42. Warren G. Harding, as quoted in William Allen White, *Masks in a Pageant* (New York: Macmillan, 1928), pp. 422–23.

43. H. R. Haldeman, *The Ends of Power* (New York: Times Books, 1978), p. 34.

44. Stephen J. Wayne, "Working in the White House: Psychological Dimensions of the Job" (paper presented at the Annual Meeting of the Southern Political Science Association, New Orleans, La., November 1977).

45. Richard L. Berke, "Inside White House: Long Days, Late Nights," *New York Times*, March 21, 1993, p. 1.

46. Wayne, "Working in the White House," pp. 9, 34.

47. Burt Solomon, "When the Potomac Becomes. . . A Turbulent River of No Return," *National Journal*, July 31, 1993, 1936.

48. Ibid.

49. Wayne, "Working in the White House," p. 35.

50. Ibid.

51. Landon Butler, "Transition Diary," *Newsweek*, January 24, 1977, p. 29.

52. George Reedy, *The Twilight Of the Presidency* (New York: New American Library, 1987).

## SELECTED READINGS

Baltzell, E. Digby, and Howard G. Schneiderman. "Social Class in the Oval Office." *Society* 25 (September/October 1988): 42–49.

Barber, James David. *The Presidential Character*, 4th ed. Englewood Cliffs, N.J.: Prentice-Hall, 1992.

Betts, Richard K. *Surprise Attack: Lessons for Defense Planning*. Washington, D.C.: Brookings Institution, 1982.

Buchanan, Bruce. *The Citizen's Presidency: Standards of Choice and Judgment.* Washington, D.C.: Congressional Quarterly, 1987.

——. *The Presidential Experience: What the Office Does to the Man*. Englewood Cliffs, N.J.: Prentice-Hall, 1978.

Burke, John R., and Fred I. Greenstein. "Presidential Personality and National Security Leadership: A Comparative Analysis of Vietnam Decisionmaking." *International Political Science Review* 10 (1989): 73–92.

Fiske, Susan T. "Cognition and Motivation." In George C. Edwards III, John H. Kessel, and Bert A. Rockman, eds., *Researching the Presidency*. Pittsburgh: University of Pittsburgh Press, 1993, pp. 233–65.

George, Alexander. "Assessing Presidential Character." In Aaron Wildavsky, ed., *Perspectives on the Presidency*. Boston: Little Brown, 1975, pp. 91–134.

——. *Presidential Decisionmaking in Foreign Policy: The Effective Use of Information and Advice*. Boulder, Colo.: Westview Press, 1980.

Gilbert, Robert E. "Personality, Stress and Achievement: Keys to Presidential Longevity." *Presidential Studies Quarterly* 15 (Winter 1985): 33–50.

Hargrove, Erwin C. "Presidential Personality and Leadership Style." In Edwards et al., *Researching the Presidency* pp. 69–109.

Janis, Irving L. *Groupthink*. Boston: Houghton Mifflin, 1982.

Reedy, George E. *The Twilight of the Presidency.* Rev. ed. New York: New American Library, 1987.

# 9

# The President and
# the Executive Branch

Public policies are rarely self-executing. They require a staff of experts, people who have an understanding of the substantive issues, institutional processes, and political implications involved in turning statutes, executive orders, and the like into services and benefits for the nation. These are the people who work in the executive branch. Some are civil servants, others are political appointees. Both are charged with the implementation of public policy.

The president sits atop the executive branch, the organization of which is pictured in Figure 9-1. As the title of chief executive implies, the president has responsibility for executing or implementing government policies. Implementation includes issuing and enforcing directives; disbursing funds; making loans; awarding grants; signing contracts; collecting data; disseminating information; analyzing problems; assigning and hiring personnel; creating organizational units; proposing alternatives; planning for the future; and negotiating with private citizens, businesses, interest groups, legislative committees, bureaucratic units, and even other countries.

In this chapter we examine presidents' efforts, in conjunction with their subordinates in the executive branch, to implement public policies. Presidents who are directors will be able to dominate this process and ensure that policies are executed as they wish; presidents who are facilitators will face just as great a challenge in leading the executive branch as in leading those who are not directly in their chain of command. We will find that, despite the unquestioned importance of implementation, it receives relatively low priority in the White House. We shall also find that presidents face an uphill fight in implementing the policies for which they are responsible. Thus, we focus on the obstacles to effective policy implementation, including communication, resources, implementors' dispositions, bureaucratic structure, and executive follow-up, to understand better the difficulties the president faces.

Before we move on, we should clarify an important point. The president's role in implementation is not always as direct as in giving a speech, negotiating with Congress, or making decisions. Moreover, implementation typically occurs over an extended period of time and far

**Figure 9-1. Organization of the Executive Branch**

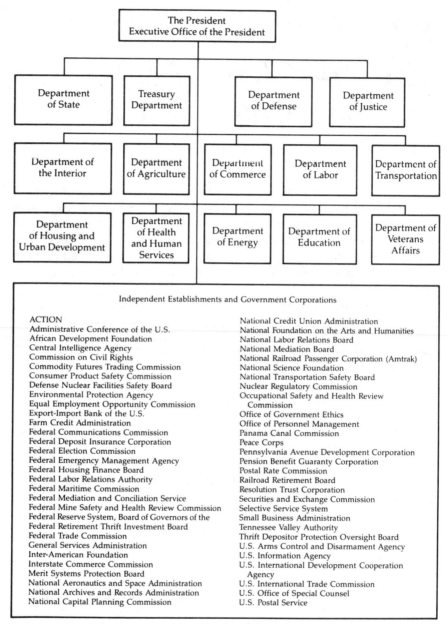

Source: Office of the Federal Register, *The United States Government Manual, 1992–1993* (Washington, D.C.: U.S. Government Printing Office, 1992), p. 21.

from the confines of the White House. In addition, the implementation of federal policy usually requires the efforts of many people, often thousands, at the federal, state, and local levels and in the private sector. As a result, many observers of the presidency mistakenly restrict their discussions of the president as chief executive to actions he personally takes. To avoid this error we cast our view more broadly in order to understand the problems with which presidents must contend as they seek to carry out their responsibilities for implementing policies, including those they initiate, those established in previous administrations, and those passed over their objections.

## IMPLEMENTATION PROBLEMS

Since policy implementation is so complex, we should not expect it to be accomplished in a routine fashion. Even presidents cannot assume that their decisions and orders will be carried out. Indeed, their experiences in recent years would turn even the most optimistic observers into cynics. Once again we see the validity of Richard Neustadt's warning that presidents are rarely in a position to simply issue commands and have them obeyed.

In 1962 President John Kennedy ordered U.S. Army troops located in Memphis to the campus of the University of Mississippi at Oxford to control rioting that resulted from the attempts of a black, James Meredith, to enroll. As the hours passed after giving the order, the commander in chief saw no progress toward Oxford. Frustrated, he demanded of Secretary of the Army Cyrus Vance, "Where are the troops?" No one seemed to know. When he talked on the phone to the general who supposedly was leading the troops, the general indicated he was awaiting orders from the Pentagon.[1] This was hardly Kennedy's only frustration in policy implementation. Kennedy once told an aide not to abandon the minor project of remodeling Lafayette Park across the street from the White House. "Hell," the president exclaimed, "this may be the only thing I'll ever get done."[2]

President Ronald Reagan also had implementation troubles. For example, a potentially severe gap in our national defenses was created when several plants involved in producing the material for nuclear weapons had to be shut down when flaws in their design and operations endangered the public's health. Equally damaging, some White House aides took foreign policy into their own hands and funneled funds illegally from the sale of arms to Iran to the Contras in Nicaragua.

Given the frustration that presidents experience, we should not be surprised when President Carter complained, "Before I became president, I realized and I was warned that dealing with the federal bureaucracy would be one of the worst problems I would have to face. It has been even worse than I had anticipated."[3]

## LACK OF ATTENTION TO IMPLEMENTATION

Policy implementation has had a low priority in most administrations. Presidents have many obligations, of which implementing policy is only one. Policies must be developed, decisions made, legislation passed, controversies defused or contained, and the public courted, to name only the most obvious. Moreover, presidents often lack experience in administration and find other tasks more compatible with their skills and interests.

Foreign affairs are always a top priority of presidents because of their importance, the unique constitutional responsibilities of the president for them, and the strong interest in international relations many presidents bring to office. Besides, presidents often feel they can accomplish more in the international arena than at home wrestling over domestic issues with an unresponsive Congress or a recalcitrant executive branch. Ceremonial functions performed in the role of chief of state are traditions maintained by the president to broaden public support. For example, within six weeks of George Bush's assuming office, he had traveled to Canada, Japan, China, and Korea and had trips planned to Europe and other parts of the world. All of these activities typically have priority over implementation.

In addition, the incentives to invest time in implementation are few. Presidents have only a short time in office and in their first terms must constantly think about reelection. This encourages a short-run view in the White House, and presidents are more likely to try to provide the public with immediate gratification through the passage of legislation or the giving of speeches than with efforts to manage the implementation of policies. As one Office of Management and Budget official put it:

> The people in the White House are there for such a short time. The pressure is on making some impact and getting some programs passed. There is not enough time or reward in thinking carefully about effectiveness and implementation. The emphasis is really on quantity, not quality. The President could never be reelected on the effectiveness theme. "We didn't do much, but it is all working very well." Do you think a President could win with that?[4]

Presidents know they will receive little credit if policies are managed well because it is very difficult to attribute effective implementation to them personally. Moreover, to most people the functioning of government often is not very visible. Both citizens and the press, when they pay attention to government at all, are most interested in controversial scandals, the passage of new policies, or ceremonial functions. Policies such as inflation or civil rights, which have an immediate and direct effect on their lives, attract their attention. Yet even here the press and public are mainly concerned with the impact of policies, not the process of their implementation. Although implementation directly influences the final results, this does not seem to be enough to entice the mass public and the press that caters to it to turn their attention to policy implementation.

As a result of these incentives, presidents devote a comparatively small amount of their time to policy implementation. Similarly, too little consideration is given to problems of implementation in the formulation of policies. Again, the proper incentives are missing. According to a Carter aide: "We all believe there should be more planning. The President has stressed the need for more caution. But when we fall behind, the President will impose a deadline. It is still a political system; and political systems are interested in results, not implementation."[5]

Thus, despite the president's clear responsibility for policy implementation, it typically receives relatively little attention from the White House. Although this may seem inevitable, it is not without its costs. As an aide to President Reagan commented: "It's unfortunately true that the management of the bureaucracy becomes one of the lowest priorities of almost every administration that comes to this city. Every administration pays a heavy price for it before it's over."[6]

## COMMUNICATION OF PRESIDENTIAL DECISIONS

The first requirement for effective implementation of presidential decisions or policies for which the president is responsible is that those who are to implement a decision must know what they are supposed to do. Policy decisions and implementation orders must be transmitted to the appropriate personnel before they can be followed. Naturally, these communications need to be accurate, and they must be accurately perceived by implementors. Implementation directives must also be clear. If they are not, implementors may be confused about what they should do, and they will have discretion to impose their own views on the implementation of policies, views that may be different from those of the president. Consistency in the communication directives is also crucial. Contradictory decisions confuse and frustrate administrative staff and constrain their ability to implement policies effectively.

### Transmission

Before subordinates can implement a presidential decision, they must be aware that the decision has been made and an order to implement it issued. This is not always as straightforward a process as it may seem. Ignorance or misunderstanding of decisions frequently occurs. Although the executive branch has highly developed lines of communication throughout the bureaucracy, this does not guarantee that communications will be transmitted successfully. The Bay of Pigs fiasco illustrates this point. On April 17, 1961, a force of 1,200 Cuban refugees, recruited, trained, and supplied by the Central Intelligence Agency (CIA), landed ninety miles south of Havana with the announced goal of overthrowing the Communist-oriented regime of Fidel Castro. Within three days the "invasion" had been crushed, inflicting a disastrous blow to American prestige, not to mention that of the new president, John F. Kennedy. The CIA never told the leader of the brigade sent to invade Cuba until it was too late that the president had ordered the soldiers to go to the mountains and fight a guerilla war if the invasion failed. The CIA disregarded the president's order, which it thought might weaken the brigade's resolve to fight or encourage the brigade to go to the mountains too quickly.

Sometimes aides and other officials ignore presidential directives with which they disagree primarily to avoid embarrassment for their chief. Such orders are generally given in anger and without proper consultation. President Nixon especially liked to let off steam by issuing outrageous orders. At one time he instructed Secretary of State William Rogers to "fire everybody in Laos," and he often told aides to "go after" reporters. These and similar outbursts were ignored by H. R. Haldeman and the aides close to Nixon. They knew the president would view things differently when he calmed down.[7] In situations such as these, close associates of presidents have provided them safe outlets for their frustrations and protected them from their worst instincts.

In most instances, implementors have considerable discretion in interpreting their superiors' decisions and orders. Orders from the White House are rarely specific. Personnel at each rung in the bureaucratic ladder must use their judgment to expand and develop them. Obviously this process invites distortion of communications, and the further down in the bureaucracy presidential implementation directives go, the greater the potential for distortion. Moreover, as we shall see, subordinates do not always interpret the communications of superiors in a way that advances the goals of the president. Bureaucrats often use their discretion to further their personal interests and those of their agencies. Interest groups also take advantage of the discretion granted bureaucrats by pushing for their own demands at intermediate and low decision-making levels. It is for these reasons that observers of the federal bureaucracy often recommend that presidents and other high officials make every attempt to commit their directives to writing (in detail where possible), use personalized communications where appropriate, and show persistence in attempting to convey accurately their orders to those who actually implement policies.

In general, the more decentralized the implementation of a public policy, the less likely that it will be transmitted to its ultimate implementors accurately. Decentralization usually means that a decision must be communicated through several levels of authority before it reaches those who will carry it out. The more steps a communication must traverse from its original source, the weaker the signal that is ultimately received will be. A president can tell a secretary of state to go to another country and deliver a policy pronouncement to its prime minister, with little concern that the message will not be accurately transmitted. But he cannot have the same confidence about messages aimed at caseworkers in a social security office or soldiers in the field. The distance between the White House and the implementors is too great.

At times, executives and their staffs prefer *not* to transmit policy directives personally; they would rather get others to communicate for them. President Johnson wanted Secretary of the Treasury Henry Fowler to apply "jawboning," or powerful persuasion, to try to lower interest rates. Because Fowler opposed such efforts, Johnson decided not to communicate his wishes to the secretary directly. Instead he called House Banking Committee Chairman Wright Patman, a supporter of "jawboning," and asked him to pressure Fowler. Any time a step is added to the chain of communication, the potential for distortion is increased. Those who speak for others will have their own styles, their own views, and their own motivations. Not even presidents can depend upon other people to transmit directives exactly as they would desire.

Some presidents do not have personalities that are well suited to direct communication. This seems to have been particularly true of Richard Nixon. Fearing rejection and confrontation, he adopted an indirect administrative style to avoid possible unpleasantness. He spoke elliptically to those who disagreed with him to avoid being rebuffed and typically failed to issue unambiguous orders directly to his subordinates. He did not like to say no personally or to discipline recalcitrant officials. When he found opposition within his administration, either he tried to accomplish his objectives without his adversaries being aware of it or he had intermediaries take them written or verbal orders. The president shunned personal efforts at persuading or inspiring subordinates.[8]

Nixon's unwillingness to communicate directly with his subordinates fostered an environment in which discipline and cohesion were often low. It also revealed disunity in his administration that outsiders could exploit, further eroding cohesion. Officials in positions of power, such as Secretary of State Williams Rogers, could increase their discretion by implementing orders with which they disagreed only if they were transmitted personally to them by the president, which they rarely were.[9]

The press also may serve as a means of presidential communicating in more straightforward ways. Those in the White House often believe that since most high-level bureaucrats read the *New York Times* and the *Washington Post*, they can communicate with these officials about policy matters more rapidly through news stories than through normal channels. The White House also uses other media outlets such as television, newsmagazines, and specialized publications to send messages to government officials. Such messages may indicate a policy decision or position, or they may signal that an official White House statement was merely to appease special interests and should not be taken literally. On the other hand, the information provided in a story or as a response to a reporter's question is unlikely to be sufficient for guiding the implementation of a complex policy. Indeed, it may be in error. Yet it is to the nuances contained in such communications that ears in Washington are often most attuned.

## Clarity

If policies are to be administered as presidents desire, their implementation directives must not only be received, but they also must be clear. Often the instructions transmitted to implementors are vague and do not specify when or how a program is to be carried out, however. Lack of clarity provides implementors with leeway to give new meaning to policies, meaning that sometimes inhibits intended change or brings about unintended change.

The lack of clarity in many implementation orders can be attributed to several factors. Perhaps the most important is the sheer complexity of policy making. When they establish policy, neither presidents nor members of Congress have the time or expertise to develop and apply all the requisite details for how it will be carried out. They have to leave most (and sometimes all) of the details to subordinates, usually in the executive branch. Thus, although it is the president's responsibility to implement policies of the national government, no matter who initiates them, much of this responsibility must be delegated to others.

The difficulty in reaching consensus on the goals of policies also inhibits clarity in implementation directives. In the United States we share wide agreement on the goals of avoidance of war, equal opportunity, and efficiency in government, but this consensus often dissolves when specific policy alternatives are under consideration. Lyndon Johnson once said, "If the full implications of any bill were known before its enactment, it would never get passed."[10] Clearly, imprecise decisions make it easier for presidents to develop and maintain winning coalitions. Different people or groups can support the same policy for different reasons. Each may hold its own conception of the goal or goals the program is designed to achieve. Ambiguous goals also may make it less threatening for groups to be on the losing side of a policy conflict, and this may reduce the intensity of their opposition.

The problems of starting up a new program may also produce confusion in implementation instructions. Often the passage of a new policy is followed by a period of administrative uncertainty in which there is a considerable time lag before any information on the program is disseminated. This period is followed by a second one in which rules are made but are then changed quickly as high-level officials attempt to deal with the unforeseen problems of implementing the policy and of their own earlier directives.

A cynical yet realistic explanation for lack of clarity in federal statutes is that Congress does not want them to be detailed. Congress would rather let executive branch agencies provide the specifics, not because of the latter's expertise, but in order to let the agencies take the blame for the rules that turn out to be unworkable or unpopular. Title IX of the Education Act Amendments of 1972 stated that "no person in the United States shall, on the basis of sex, be excluded from participation in, or be denied the benefits of, or be subject to discrimination under an education program or activity receiving Federal financial assistance." Such broad language allowed Congress to sidestep many touchy questions and leave their resolution to the president and his appointees. Moreover, individual members of Congress can gain credit with their constituents by intervening on their behalf regarding the application of regulations. In addition, if goals are not precise, Congress cannot be held accountable for the failure of its policies to achieve them. All of this only adds to the president's burden in guiding the bureaucracy.

Sometimes efforts are made to restrict the discretion of implementors. The Voting Rights Act of 1965 reduced the discretion of local voting registrars by limiting the use of literacy tests or similar voter qualification devices. In some cases the administration of voting registration was physically taken over by federal officials so that local officials could not inhibit voter registration. Another example of limiting implementors' discretion occurred in early 1973 when the Nixon administration issued new rules that restricted the way funds could be expended to aid the poor through social services. Funds could be used only for persons with specifically defined conditions of need and then only under a system of detailed accounting of the services provided. This was an attempt by the Nixon administration to restrict the options available to social workers.

It is generally easier for the president to reduce the discretion of officials with orders to stop doing something than to start doing something. For example, an absolute ban on providing funds for abortions for poor women is more likely to be unambiguous and more likely to be noticed if it is violated than an order to begin implementing a new policy. The implementation of most policies, however, requires positive actions, not prohibitions. Moreover, usually a series of positive actions extending over a long period of time and involving the technical expertise of numerous persons throughout a bureaucratic hierarchy is necessary to implement a policy. The complexity of such policy making makes it very difficult for a president to communicate and enforce rules that effectively reduce the discretion available to most policy implementors.

Vague policy decisions often hinder effective implementation, but directives that are too specific may also adversely affect implementation. Implementors sometimes need the freedom to adapt policies to suit the situation at hand. Myriad specific regulations can overwhelm and confuse personnel in the field and may make them reluctant to act for fear of breaking the rules, which seems to be what occurred in the Federal Emergency Management Agency as it tried to help the victims of Hurricane Andrew in 1992. President Clinton gave the agency clearer direction and a shorter time frame in which to provide emergency assistance to Midwest flood victims during the spring and summer of 1993, and the agency responded with greater dispatch and efficiency.

Strict guidelines may also induce a type of goal displacement in which lower-level officials become more concerned with meeting specific requirements than with achieving the basic goals of the program. By rigidly adhering to the letter of a regulation, they may become so bogged down in red tape that the purpose of the rule is forgotten or defeated. Conversely, implementors sometimes simply ignore rigid regulations.

### Consistency

Inconsistency as well as vagueness in guidance from the president may provide operating agencies with substantial discretion in the interpretation and implementation of policy, discretion that may not be exercised to carry out a policy's goals. Environmental policy during the Nixon administration is an example. The president made a rhetorical commitment to supporting the National Environmental Policy Act (NEPA), but in practice his policy priorities were not significantly tied to environmental matters. Similarly, the Office of Management and Budget, the president's principal tool for controlling the federal bureaucracy, did not treat environmental policy goals as a major consideration in the evaluation of the activities of all federal agencies as NEPA intended. Federal officials received inconsistent signals from the White House concerning the importance of environmental policy and were left to resolve the question largely on their own.

Many of the factors that produce unclear communications are also responsible for inconsistent directives. The complexity of public policies, the difficulties in starting up new programs, and the multiple objectives of many policies all contribute to inconsistency in policy communications. Another reason that decisions are often inconsistent is that the president and top officials are constantly attempting to satisfy a diverse set of interests that may represent views on both sides of an issue. Policies that are not of high priority to the president may simply be left to flounder in a sea of competing demands.

## RESOURCES

Implementation orders may be accurately transmitted, clear, and consistent, but if the president lacks the resources necessary to carry out policies, established at his discretion or by Congress, implementation is likely to be ineffective. Important resources include money, staff of sufficient size and with the proper skills to carry out its assignments, and the information, authority, and facilities necessary to translate proposals on paper into functioning public services.

### Money

Sometimes the problem the president faces in implementing policy and delivering services is simply a lack of money. President Clinton's efforts to provide increased access to education and training for Americans are severely constrained by the lack of funds. Elliot Richardson, when he was secretary of the Department of Health, Education and Welfare, discovered that the funds Congress appropriated for programs permitted his department to reach only very small percentages of those eligible for the benefits. When his staff estimated the cost of having the department's service-delivery programs reach each eligible person, it turned out to exceed the entire federal budget for that year!

## Staff

Certainly an essential resource in implementing policy is staff. In an era in which "big government" is under attack from all directions, it may seem surprising to learn that a principal source of implementation failure is inadequate staff. Although nearly 5 million military and civilian personnel work for the federal executive branch (see Table 9-1), and therefore the president, there are still too few people with the requisite skills to do an effective job implementing many policies. We must evaluate the bureaucracy not only in terms of absolute numbers, but also in terms of its capabilities to perform desired tasks.

The federal government provides a wide range of services through its own personnel, such as national defense, immigration control, and maintenance of recreational facilities. Each of these and others like them are labor-intensive areas, and thus the services provided are directly related to the size and quality of the staff available to the relevant agencies over which the president presides. Yet there is substantial evidence that agencies and departments are woefully understaffed. For example, a shortage of staff at the Federal Drug Administration (FDA) has been responsible for delays in the testing of new drugs to combat AIDS, millions of illegal aliens elude our understaffed border guards every year, and some observers fear that the lack of maintenance of national parks will lead to permanent deterioration of such treasured American vacation spots as Yosemite and Yellowstone.

Although staff size can be critical for almost every policy, it is more so for some than others. Insufficient staff is especially critical to implementation when the policy involved is one that imposes unwelcome constraints on people, whether these be the requirements of grant policies, regulatory policies, or criminal law. Since such policies generally involve highly decentralized activities, a large staff is necessary if this behavior is to be monitored. It is much easier for the chief executive to implement a policy such as social security that distributes benefits recipients desire. More personnel are required to enforce limitations on people than to write checks to them.

Yet the lack of staff makes compliance data difficult to obtain. Thus, the president and his subordinates often have to rely upon information about compliance from those who are doing the complying. This occurs in a wide range of policies, including school desegregation, hospital care, and environmental protection. Quite naturally, this system of information raises questions about effective implementation. It should

**Table 9-1. Federal Employment in the Executive Branch**
(Civilian employment as measured by full-time equivalents, in thousands)

| Agency | 1992 Actual | 1993 Base | 1993 Estimate | 1994 Estimate | 1995 Estimate | Change: 1993 Base to 1995 |
|---|---|---|---|---|---|---|
| Cabinet agencies: | | | | | | |
| Agriculture | 113.4 | 113.3 | 112.1 | 110.8 | 108.9 | −4.3 |
| Commerce | 35.2 | 36.4 | 36.0 | 35.5 | 34.9 | −1.5 |
| Defense (civilian) | 972.9 | 927.2 | 927.2 | 895.2 | 865.2 | −62.0 |
| Defense (military) | 1808.1 | — | 1728.3 | 1620.6 | — | — |
| Education | 4.9 | 5.0 | 4.9 | 4.8 | 4.8 | −0.2 |
| Energy | 19.7 | 20.6 | 20.4 | 20.0 | 19.7 | −0.9 |
| Health and Human Services | 128.8 | 130.0 | 128.7 | 126.7 | 124.8 | −5.2 |
| Housing and Urban Development | 14.1 | 13.6 | 13.5 | 13.3 | 13.1 | −0.5 |
| Interior | 75.3 | 77.9 | 77.2 | 76.0 | 74.8 | −3.1 |
| Justice | 91.7 | 98.4 | 97.4 | 95.9 | 94.4 | −3.9 |
| Labor | 19.7 | 19.8 | 19.6 | 19.3 | 19.0 | −0.8 |
| State | 25.5 | 26.0 | 25.8 | 25.4 | 25.0 | −1.0 |
| Transportation | 69.9 | 71.1 | 70.0 | 69.3 | 68.3 | −2.8 |
| Treasury (civilian) | 162.8 | 165.2 | 163.6 | 163.1 | 161.6 | −3.6 |
| Treasury (Coast Guard) | 38.2 | — | 38.1 | 37.8 | — | — |
| Veteran Affairs | 229.0 | 232.4 | 232.1 | 234.2 | 225.7 | −6.7 |

Other agencies (excluding Postal Service):

| | | | | | |
|---|---|---|---|---|---|
| Agency for International Development | 4.4 | 4.4 | 4.3 | 4.3 | 4.2 | −0.2 |
| Corps of Engineers | 27.4 | 27.4 | 27.2 | 26.8 | 26.3 | −1.1 |
| Environmental Protection Agency | 17.4 | 18.3 | 18.1 | 17.8 | 17.6 | −0.7 |
| Equal Employment Opportunity Commission | 2.8 | 2.8 | 2.9 | 3.0 | 3.0 | 0.1 |
| Federal Emergency Management Agency | 2.6 | 2.7 | 2.7 | 2.7 | 2.6 | −0.1 |
| Federal Deposit Insurance Corporation and Resolution Trust Corporation† | 21.8 | 21.3 | 21.3 | 22.8 | 22.8 | 1.6 |
| General Services Administration | 22.8 | 22.7 | 22.5 | 22.1 | 21.8 | −0.9 |
| National Aeronautics and Space Administration | 24.5 | 24.9 | 24.2 | 23.8 | 23.9 | −1.0 |
| National Archives and Records Administration | 2.6 | 2.8 | 2.7 | 2.7 | 2.6 | −0.1 |
| National Labor Relations Board | 2.1 | 2.1 | 2.1 | 2.1 | 2.1 | |
| Nuclear Regulatory Commission | 3.4 | 3.4 | 3.3 | 3.3 | 3.2 | −0.2 |
| Office of Personnel Management | 5.9 | 6.1 | 6.0 | 5.9 | 5.9 | −0.2 |
| Panama Canal Commission | 8.6 | 8.7 | 8.7 | 8.8 | 9.0 | 0.3 |
| Securities and Exchange Commission | 2.5 | 2.7 | 2.7 | 2.6 | 2.6 | −0.1 |
| Small Business Administration | 4.0 | 4.0 | 4.0 | 3.9 | 3.9 | −0.2 |
| Smithsonian Institution | 4.4 | 4.9 | 4.8 | 4.8 | 4.7 | −0.2 |
| Tennessee Valley Authority | 20.0 | 19.1 | 18.9 | 18.5 | 18.4 | −0.8 |
| United States Information Agency | 8.3 | 8.7 | 8.6 | 8.5 | 8.4 | −0.3 |
| All other small agencies | 21.0 | 22.0 | 21.6 | 21.2 | 21.0 | −1.0 |
| U.S. Postal Service | 792.0 | — | — | — | — | — |

Source: Budget of the United States Government, Fiscal Year 1994, pp. 38–39, A-441, A-859.

come as no surprise to us, then, when faulty welds are discovered in the trans-Alaskan pipeline, federal grants to state and local governments are misspent, or hazardous wastes are found to be polluting water supplies.

The president's executive branch agencies do not even come close to meeting these needs. The fear of creating a totalitarian bureaucratic monster and the pressures to allocate personnel to more direct services, such as the provision of agricultural expertise to farmers, keep staffs that monitor implementation small. In addition, the scarcity of payroll funds coupled with the irresistible urges of policymakers to provide public services (at least in form) ensure that staffs will generally be inadequate to implement programs.

Because of lack of staff and because of traditional federal government deference to the states, federal programs rely heavily upon state agencies for their implementation. This, however, does not solve the president's problem of lack of staff at the federal level; it merely transfers the problem to the states. Since this shortage of personnel exists at every level of government, delegating the implementation of a policy to a lower level of government rarely alleviates the problem.

Sometimes presidents turn limited staff to their advantage. The Reagan administration actually decreased staff in areas such as antitrust, civil rights, and environmental protection in an effort to reduce enforcement activities to which it was opposed.[11]

In addition to numbers, skill is an important characteristic of staff for implementation. One problem the president faces is the shortage of people with management skills among career executives. Personnel with substantive skills are also often in short supply in the executive branch. This is especially true when a government agency is carrying out or regulating highly technical activities. Inadequately trained inspectors for the Environmental Protection Agency were found to be missing more than half of the serious violations in their inspections of facilities handling and storing hazardous waste.

Sometimes the necessary personnel are very difficult to hire because of the higher incomes and greater flexibility they can enjoy by working in the private sector. The military's problems in attracting physicians is a prime example. At other times, the needed staff may simply not exist even in the private sector, and a government agency must invest in developing expertise. The federal government's efforts to regulate energy prices and allocations in the 1970s illustrate both problems. No one really knew how to accomplish these tasks, and few people outside the energy companies had the background to understand the industry. Thus, employees of the Federal Energy Office relied upon "on the job training."

Staff skills are especially critical for new policies or those involving technical questions. Routine functions, such as dispersing funds, building roads, training troops, hiring typists, or purchasing goods, are relatively straightforward in their operation, and a wealth of information exists on how to carry them out. But the implementors of policies such as controlling hospital costs or developing a jet fighter do not share these advantages. They are being asked to meet goals no one has ever met. Thus, it is one thing for Congress or the White House to mandate a change in policy, but it is something quite different for the executive branch officials who work for the president to figure out how to do it.

As a result, some responsibilities will simply not be met, or they will not be met on time. Inefficiency is also likely to characterize the implementation of such policies. Some efforts will prove to be mistakes, and implementors will have to try again. Moreover, regulations may be inappropriate, causing other government units or organizations in the private sector to purchase equipment, fill out forms, or stop certain activities unnecessarily. Ideally, for example, before an agency acts to implement a law by ordering costly changes in an industry or its products (such as automobiles), the agency should be able to predict the effects of the change on the economic health of the industry in question. Such information, however, is frequently lacking, and the president may be severely criticized as a result.

### Authority

Authority is often a critical resource in policy implementation. The president actually has relatively little direct authority. Congress vests most authority in subordinate executive officials. Sometimes agency officials simply lack authority, even on paper, to implement a policy properly. For example, the policy being implemented may provide no sanctions against those violating the law, or the agency may lack authority to initiate administrative or judicial actions.

Many observers feel that the Federal Drug Administration (FDA) lacks adequate powers to protect the public from drugs and devices that may be potentially dangerous to some, such as silicon breast implants, the sleeping pill Halcion, and the sedative Versed. The FDA does no testing of its own and must rely entirely on the test results submitted by manufacturers. Yet it lacks the subpoena power to obtain drug company documents when its suspicions are aroused regarding the withholding of data about adverse drug reactions or fraudulent representation of test results. It often even lacks access to potentially damaging company documents that reveal a manufacturer's involvement in product liability cases. When formal authority does exist, it is frequently mistaken by observers for effective authority. But authority on paper is one thing; authority effectively exercised is quite another.

Executive branch officials may be reluctant to exercise authority for a number of reasons. One of the potentially most effective sanctions is the withdrawal of funds from a program. Cutting off funds is a drastic action. It may be embarrassing to all those involved and antagonize the implementors of a program whose active support is necessary for effective implementation. Cutting off federal funds from projects also alienates the members of Congress from the areas losing the money. Requiring states or cities to repay misspent funds can also have severe political consequences. In addition, terminating a project or withdrawing federal funds may hurt most those whom the policy is designed to aid. Schoolchildren, the elderly, or the poor are often the real victims of cutbacks. If a company loses federal contracts because of racial or sexual discrimination, it may be forced to lay off workers. Those with the least seniority may be the minorities the policy is trying to help. Similarly, cutting off federal funds for the educationally disadvantaged because of misallocation is most likely to hurt students from poor families. In general, the White House does not even try to exercise this authority.

The desire for self-preservation keeps many of the president's agencies from withdrawing funds. Agencies like the Federal Highway Administration and the Department of Education are primarily involved in channeling grants to other levels of government. To survive they must give away money. If they fail to do so, they may look bad to Congress and superior executive officials. This may hurt them in their future quests for budgets and authority, resources of great significance for most bureaucrats. Thus, they may sacrifice the social objectives of a program to the "maintenance" objectives of the bureaucratic unit.

Although executive officials often lack effective authority over other public officials, this lack of control is small compared with their lack of authority over private individuals, groups, and businesses, upon whom the successful implementation of policies often depends. Therefore, they must make their policies attractive to the private sector. As a result of these efforts, the enforcement of policies such as those dealing with safety in the workplace rarely results in serious penalties for noncompliance. Environmental pollution, however, is another matter, one in which large settlements between alleged polluters and the Environmental Protection Agency have been negotiated.

### Facilities

Physical facilities may also be critical resources in implementation. Without the necessary buildings, equipment, supplies, and even green space, implementation won't succeed. National parks are overcrowded; military equipment, ranging from rifles to spare parts for airplanes, has often been in short supply; those patrolling our borders lack the appropriate ships and planes to prevent the smuggling of illegal drugs; and we lack adequate storage facilities for our national oil reserves.

There is also often a shortage of sophisticated equipment. Computers are essential to the implementation of modern defense policy; they issue paychecks, assign personnel, navigate ships, and track missiles. Nevertheless, studies of the military's computers have found that the Defense Department has been saddled with thousands of obsolete machines that leave the military services ill prepared for a modern war. Similar problems have beset other agencies, such as the Internal Revenue Service, the Immigration and Naturalization Service, and the Social Security Administration.

Although the president can request funds for new or additional facilities, both the White House and Congress may hesitate to raise taxes to pay for them. Moreover, as was the case for staff, Congress often prefers to spread resources over many policies rather than to fund fewer programs adequately. Internal government procurement rules ("red tape") may add additional burdens to those trying to purchase expensive equipment such as computers.

## DISPOSITIONS

If implementors are well disposed toward a particular policy, they are more likely to carry it out as the president intended. But when implementors' attitudes or perspectives differ from the president's, the process of implementing a policy becomes infinitely more complicated. Many policies fall within a "zone of indifference." These policies will probably be implemented faithfully because implementors do not have strong feelings about them. Other policies, however, will be in direct conflict with the policy views or personal or organizational interests of implementors. When people are asked to execute orders with which they do not agree, inevitable slippage occurs between policy decisions and performance. In such cases implementors may exercise their discretion, sometimes in subtle ways, to hinder implementation. As President Ford said:

> There are bureaucratic fiefdoms out in the states or in various regions, and the people who occupy those pockets of power want to do things in their own way. They are pros at it. They have been disregarding Presidents for years, both Democratic and Republican.[12]

Implementors may oppose a policy, and their opposition can prevent a policy option from even being tried. For some time there had been a policy debate over whether there should be a work requirement for those receiving welfare payments and able to work. During the Nixon administration, however, many top officials concluded that welfare administrators would not enforce a work requirement provision, even in the face of presidential exhortations and congressional demands. Thus, they had to turn to other alternatives, such as tax incentives, to encourage welfare recipients to work. On another occasion, Nixon ordered Secretary of Defense Melvin Laird to bomb a hideaway of Palestine Liberation Organization guerrillas, a move that Laird opposed. According to the secretary, "We had bad weather for forty-eight hours. The Secretary of Defense can always find a reason not to do something."[13] Thus, the president's order was stalled for days and was eventually rescinded. President Reagan's national security adviser explained that the United States could not employ a strategy of selective use of force in order to support diplomatic efforts to keep peace in Lebanon because of the lack of cooperation between the Departments of State and Defense.

The opposition of presidential subordinates to a policy may also defeat some of its immediate goals after it becomes law. President Carter ordered federal agencies to discourage the development of low-lying areas in danger of damage by flooding. Twenty-five months later only fifteen of the seventy-five agencies that had received the directive had issued regulations specifying how they were going to comply with the president's wishes. Forty-six of the agencies had not even taken the first step toward adopting regulations. The primary reason for this lack of action was not bureaucratic indolence. Instead, it was the opposition of agencies to the substance of the president's order.

Similarly, Ronald Reagan's efforts to build up special commando units for unconventional warfare and counterterrorist operations were hampered by the failure of the air force to provide adequate aircraft to deliver the forces and of the army to provide the units with the proper equipment.

Differences in organizational viewpoints may also impede the cooperation between agencies that is so often necessary in policy implementation. The army requires aircraft, all of which belong to the air force (at its insistence), to transport troops. Yet transporting troops is a low priority for the air force, which is more interested in strategic bombers and fighter planes. Thus, it typically does not fight for resources for troop transport planes or choose to allocate its scarce resources to that function, thereby undermining the ability of the army to carry out *its* function.

There may also be differences in viewpoints within an agency between presidential subordinates with different program responsibilities. There was intra-agency conflict over the implementation of the National Environmental Policy Act. Secretaries of transportation, for example, had a difficult time getting development-oriented agencies in the department, such as the Federal Highway Administration, to consider seriously the environmental consequences of their projects.

Bureaucratic units also resist vigorously the efforts of others to take away or share the resources deemed necessary to accomplish their missions. Turf fights over jurisdiction are not unusual in the executive branch. According to Richard Nixon, when J. Edgar Hoover directed the FBI, he "totally distrusted the other intelligence agencies—and, whenever possible, resisted attempts to work in concert with them."[14] At one point the director cut off all liaison activities with the other intelligence agencies, such as the Central Intelligence Agency, the Defense Intelligence Agency, and the National Security Agency. This hindered President Nixon's efforts to control dissension at home.

### Staffing the Bureaucracy

Implementors' dispositions may pose obstacles to policy implementation. But if existing personnel do not implement policies the way top officials desire, why are they not replaced with people more responsive to leaders?

APPOINTMENTS.    The president has authority to appoint directly about 625 top officials in the executive branch. This total includes the White House staff, between one and four dozen individuals in each of the cabinet-level departments, about ten persons in each of the major independent agencies (such as the National Aeronautical and Space Administration), the heads of some lesser agencies, and the commissioners of the independent regulatory agencies (as their terms expire). Of the nearly 5 million employees in the executive branch, far less than 1 percent are appointed by the president and his designees. This is an obvious constraint on the ability of any administration to alter personnel.

After being elected, a president has less than three months to search for a new team to take over the government. Moreover, this must be done by the president-elect and aides who are exhausted from the long, arduous election campaign and have many other demands on their time, such as preparing a budget and a legislative program. Members of the cabinet and other appointees usually have little advance notice of their selection and are busy wrapping up their other responsibilities and doing their homework on the issues relevant to their new positions prior to their confirmation hearings. Thus, they, too, often resort to haphazard recruiting techniques when they make their appointments.

Presidents are also constrained politically in their appointments. Usually they feel these appointments must show a balance of geography, ideology, ethnicity, sex, and other demographic characteristics salient at the time. Thousands of persons are urged upon an administration by themselves, members of Congress, or people in the president's party. Few of these persons are qualified for available jobs, but due to political necessity, more than a few are appointed. Political favors may please political supporters, but they do not necessarily provide the basis for sound administration. Moreover, such appointments may result in incompatibilities with the president that lead to politically costly dismissals.

The interest groups that appointments are designed to please keep a watchful eye throughout a president's tenure in office on who is appointed to what position. Not only is "balance" important at the beginning of a new administration, but it remains a constraint on recruiting personnel. Thus, in the middle of a term White House aides may be ordered to find a Mexican-American woman to serve as United States treasurer. A president also might desire to reward new groups. After the 1972 presidential election, Richard Nixon wanted his cabinet and sub-cabinet to represent more accurately his broadened electoral coalition. This led to a renewed emphasis on the demographic characteristics of appointees, delays in filling positions, and, most significantly, compromises in the quality of some appointees, such as many of those placed in top positions in the Labor Department to please the president's new "hard hat" constituency. It also led to a humorous incident in which Claude Brinegar was selected as secretary of transportation partly on the basis of his Irish Catholic background. The White House was in error, however; Brinegar was really a German Protestant.

A different type of "political" constraint may arise if a strong member of an administration opposes a person the president desires to appoint. Usually the president can overcome this opposition within the ranks, but sometimes the price may be too high. In his second term President Nixon wanted to appoint John Connally secretary of state but did not do so because of the opposition of his chief adviser on national security matters, Henry Kissinger. Instead, Kissinger was named secretary of state.

A surprising but nonetheless real limitation on personnel selection is that presidents often do not know individuals who are qualified for the positions they have to fill. Following his election in 1960, John F. Kennedy told an aide: "For the last four years I spent so much time getting to know people who could help me get elected President that I didn't have time to get to know people who could help me, after I was elected, to be a good President."[15] Thus, presidents often appoint persons they do not know to the highest positions in the federal government.

Early in their terms many presidents have not imposed their preferences for subcabinet-level officials upon those whom they appoint to head departments and agencies. The reason has partially been the lack of organization in the personnel system. In addition, however, there has been a concern that since top officials will be held accountable for agencies' performances, they should be able to appoint subordinates whom they like and who will complement their own abilities and help them accomplish their jobs. Naturally, top officials generally request this freedom. High officials also fight to name their subordinates because if they lose to the White House on personnel matters, their standing within their departments will drop.

The Reagan administration, on the other hand, insisted on White House clearance of all subcabinet appointments. Although there is disagreement about the quality of the personnel appointed to high-level executive branch positions during this period, there is consensus on the view that Reagan's appointees were unusually loyal to the president and committed to his conservative ideology.

The Bush administration reverted to the more common practice of giving department and agency heads discretion in making political appointments. It was more concerned with the competence and personal loyalty to the president of its political appointees than with their ideology.

The Clinton White House clears subcabinet appointments and has put a high priority on recruiting minorities and women to high office. This process slowed his initial appointments, so a large percentage of top departmental positions were unfilled six months into his tenure, as indicated in Table 9-2.

As presidential terms extend from weeks into months and years,

Table 9-2. Presidential Appointments: The Early Clinton Experience*

| | Political Positions | Clinton Nominees | Senate Confirmed | Vacancies† |
|---|---|---|---|---|
| Agriculture | 17 | 9 | 9 | 7 |
| Commerce‡ | 30 | 12 | 9 | 20 |
| Defense | 52 | 22 | 18 | 26 |
| Education‡ | 20 | 11 | 11 | 7 |
| Energy | 23 | 10 | 8 | 14 |
| HHS | 20 | 13 | 10 | 9 |
| HUD | 15 | 13 | 13 | 2 |
| Interior | 17 | 11 | 10 | 7 |
| Justice‡ | 30 | 10 | 9 | 16 |
| Labor | 19 | 11 | 9 | 9 |
| State | 41 | 28 | 28 | 6 |
| Transportation | 18 | 11 | 9 | 7 |
| Treasury | 31 | 16 | 15 | 9 |
| Veterans | 14 | 7 | 7 | 4 |
| Totals | 347 | 184 | 165 | 143 |

*January 21, 1993–August 6, 1993.
†The number of vacancies has been reduced to reflect the 39 political appointees held over from the Bush administration. Included are those serving terms that did not expire when Clinton took office, such as the six members of the Joint Chiefs of Staff, and officials chosen by Clinton to stay on, such as the inspectors general of the departments of Commerce, Education, Energy, Transportation and Veterans Affairs.
‡Nominees in each agency were withdrawn. These five are not included in the nominee column.

Source: Congressional Research Service as published in *Congressional Quarterly,* September 4, 1993, p. 2310.

every White House experiences frustrating problems in policy implementation and tends to take a direct interest in personnel matters below the levels of department and agency heads. For example, in mid-1978 the Carter administration began a review of subcabinet officials with the object of weeding out those who were incompetent or disloyal (something that cannot be taken for granted, as you can see in Box 9-1). Tim Kraft was promoted to the position of assistant for political affairs *and* personnel (indicating an appreciation for the linkage between the two). Kraft and his staff began taking more interest in appointees: "We have told the personnel people in the departments that we want to be consulted on all appointments, whether they are presidential appointments or appointments to high GS [civil service] positions."[16]

Despite its frequent use, political clearance is often a crude process. Many policy views fit under a party label. Democrats range from very liberal to very conservative, and the range for Republicans is nearly as great. Moreover, political appointees may be motivated by materialistic or selfish aims and not necessarily be responsive to the president. A person may want an ambassadorship, or a young lawyer may seek experience in the Justice Department or a regulatory agency in hope of cash-

## BOX 9-1.    THE POWER OF APPOINTMENT?

*The following memorandum was written by White House aide James Rowe to Attorney General Francis Biddle on April 1, 1943.*

### CONFIDENTIAL—NOT FOR THE FILES

#### Memorandum for the
#### Attorney General

I have your note to speak to you about May Ward, whom Earl Harrison wants to get rid of. I cannot speak to you about May Ward because the very name leaves me speechless. It was inevitable that sooner or later Harrison, being a new Commissioner, would find out that May Ward was doing nothing, never had done anything, and never would do anything—and, inevitably, he would decide she should be fired. Everyone sooner or later gets the bright idea that May Ward should be fired—and everyone sooner or later finds out that idea was not so bright after all.

May Ward was once a Democratic politician with some weight in Massachusetts. Being one of the faithful she was properly rewarded as Commissioner of Immigration, in the days when they had District Commissioners. She got along all right because she had nothing to do and people liked her. When the reorganization plans came along, the President quite logically abolished these useless jobs. He soon heard from May on the subject, and since he takes his orders from her just like the rest of us, she was soon back on the pay roll where she has resided happily ever since, with the exception of sporadic efforts by the Department of Justice to get rid of her.

We almost got her once. Schofield fired her, Matt McGuire backed him up and when she got to the White House I backed Matt up. It was a terrifying experience and I still wonder how I had the courage to go through it. You would not understand unless you had been face to face with May. I understand Bob Jackson left town when he heard she was coming. That is merely another indication of his wisdom.

Soon a terrific bombardment descended upon the President, channeled mostly through Mrs. Roosevelt who performed the unpleasant task of attempting to act as a buffer state for the President against May. This was much like Latvia being a buffer against Russia.

May had all six Democratic Congressmen from Massachusetts working at top-speed for her. She really does not have any political influence because I have carefully checked it. But I can well understand their predicament. It was much easier to push Presidents and Attorneys General around than explain to May that really she shouldn't be on the pay roll if she wouldn't do any work. I recall having the impression that May drove the six Congressmen down Pennsylvania Avenue in tandem, much like a dog team with May cracking the whip.

I have forgotten who was running the Democratic Committee at the

**BOX 9-1.** *(continued)*

time but I do recall they formed a baying Greek chorus for May. She had rehearsed them thoroughly. Such minor matters as national policies were forgotten as May laid siege to Washington. She made Jubal Early look like an amateur.

To be brief and succinct, the President signed a truce of unconditional surrender, May went back on the pay roll and there she stays. If I may respectfully suggest, Sir, for all of me she can stay there.

If, however, you are outraged by the thought that May is battening upon the taxpayers and contributing nothing, I suggest you fire her. Before you do it, I suggest you have the signature of the President, of the esteemed Democratic Chairman, and of your honorable self all on one piece of paper, in the form of a ukase.

One personal boon I crave of you. If you do decide to fire her, please give me advance warning—so I can get out of town.

James Rowe, Jr.

Addendum: My memory has just been jogged by Kitty Gilligan. I have gone back to my own file on May and have extracted the attached, very confidential memorandum, anent May. I hope you now see what you are up against.

Why not fire Earl? It would be easier.

*Rowe enclosed a note from the president dated July 25, 1941, in which he wrote, "If you love me you will get this woman a job. If you don't have something for her by Tuesday, I will either have to shoot you or commit suicide. FDR."*

Source: James Rowe papers, FDR Library.

ing in on it later for a high-paying job in the private sector. Political appointees may also remain loyal to their home-state political organizations, interest group associations, or sponsors in Congress—rather than to the White House.

Conversely, if political appointees are viewed as too close to the White House, they may be "shut out" in their departments and from their departments' client groups and thus be of limited usefulness to the president. No matter how loyal to the president appointees are, they need to know what to do and how to do it once they obtain their positions. People with these capabilities, as we have seen, are not easy to find. Moreover, too many political lieutenants in a department may separate the top executive from the bureaucracy and its services. They may also decrease the executive's opportunities to build personal support within the bureaucracy through communication, consultation, and access.

CIVIL SERVICE    Most executive branch employees rank below appointed officials in the federal hierarchy. Almost all civilian employees are covered by the protection of personnel systems designed to fill positions on the basis of merit and protect employees against removal for partisan political reasons. The military has a separate personnel system designed to accomplish the same goals.

Political appointees often bring to office a distrust of the permanent bureaucracy, a suspicion fueled by presidential election campaigns such as those of Jimmy Carter and Ronald Reagan in which the winning candidate runs as a Washington outsider and engages in "bureaucrat bashing." (George Bush and Bill Clinton, however, abstained from the temptation to criticize the bureaucracy in their campaigns.) Regardless of the attitudes they bring with them to government, most political appointees before they leave office come to regard members of the civil service as both competent and responsive to their leadership.[17]

If the president or a presidential appointee finds that a civil servant is obstructing implementation of the president's policies, he or she has some potential remedies. Those at the top of the civil service, those in the Senior Executive Service (SES), may be transferred and may be demoted more easily than in the past. Although members of the SES compose only a small percentage of the civil service (there are about 8,000 members of the SES), they are among the most powerful members of the career bureaucracy and the most crucial to implementing the president's policies.

Those below the SES are more difficult to move. It is possible for an incompetent or recalcitrant civil service employee to be dismissed, but this rarely happens. It takes more time, expertise, and political capital to fire a civil servant than most officials have or are willing to invest in such an effort. Transferring unwanted personnel to less troublesome positions is one of the most common means of quieting obstructive bureaucrats. In President Carter's words, it is "easier to promote and transfer incompetent employees than to get rid of them."[18] Transferring unwanted personnel is much easier when the civil servants in question opt not to use the technicalities and protections of the civil service system or their allies in Congress and interest groups. Ironically, these are the type of persons most likely to be dedicated to the notion of a civil service and therefore the ones an executive would probably least desire to replace. In addition, transferring personnel is not a panacea for the problems of implementors' dispositions because it does not solve problems; it just relocates them.

As the size and scope of the federal government have grown since the 1960s, so has distrust, especially among Republican presidents. Over this period there has been a trend toward politicizing the bureaucracy, emphasizing the White House's operational control of the executive bureaucracy rather than traditional patronage. The number of political appointees at the top of the executive bureaucracy has increased substantially, as has the number of political appointees at lower ranks.

Employing a related technique (developed by his predecessors), President Reagan made efforts to place political appointees in career positions just before leaving office.

Politicizing the bureaucracy has drawbacks, however. It is difficult to recruit high-quality political appointees to some of the lower sub-cabinet positions. In addition, layering political appointees at the top of bureaucratic units undermines the motivation of the career service and closes off career options to them. Finally, the short tenure in the same job of typical political appointees (about two years) diminishes their ability to implement policy effectively.

The Nixon and Ford administrations were able to place many persons who had favorable attitudes toward the Republican administrations' domestic policies in top career and politically appointed managerial positions. Yet, the number of vacancies the Nixon and Ford administrations were able to fill was limited. After eight years of Republicans in the White House, nearly 70 percent of the existing top career and political executives had assumed their positions before the Nixon administration. (The figure for career executives alone was 85 percent.) Thus, filling vacancies is unlikely to be a sufficient strategy to alter the attitudes in the bureaucracy. The president must also influence those already holding their jobs.[19]

### Incentives

Changing the personnel in government bureaucracies is difficult, and it does not ensure that the implementation process will proceed

*"I'm leaving, sir, to become a disgruntled former Administration official."*

Drawing by Dana Fradon; © 1983 The New Yorker Magazine, Inc.

smoothly. Another potential technique the president can use is to alter the dispositions of existing implementors through the manipulation of incentives. Since people generally act in their own interest, the manipulation of incentives by high-level policymakers may influence their actions. Increasing the benefits or costs of a particular behavior may make implementors more or less likely to choose it as a means of advancing their personal, organizational, or substantive policy interests.

As we have seen, the ability of top officials to exercise sanctions is severely limited. Rewards are the other side of the incentive coin, but they are even more difficult for executives to administer than penalties. Individual performance is difficult to reward with pay increases. President Carter once complained that "more than 99 percent of all federal employees got a so-called 'merit' rating."[20] Raises are almost always given across-the-board, with everyone in the same category of employment receiving a similar percentage increase in salary regardless of differences in performance. The Civil Service Reform Act of 1978 created the potential for awarding merit pay increases or bonuses for many managers, supervisors, and top executives in the federal civil service, but Congress has appropriated little money for these raises and few civil servants have received them. Usually personal performance can be rewarded only by promotions, and they are necessarily infrequent. In addition, presidential subordinates who oppose or who are indifferent to a policy are unlikely to employ incentives to further its implementation.

## THE BUREAUCRATIC STRUCTURE

Policy implementors may know what to do and have sufficient desire and resources to do it, but they may still be hampered in implementation by the structures of the organizations in which they serve. Two prominent characteristics of bureaucracies are standard operating procedures (SOPs) and fragmentation. Both may hinder presidential policy implementation.

### Standard Operating Procedures

Standard operating procedures (SOPs) are routines that enable public officials to make numerous everyday decisions. They have many benefits for the chief executive. They save time, and time is valuable. If a social security caseworker had to invent a new rule for every potential client and have it cleared at higher levels, few people would be helped. So detailed manuals are written to cover as many particular situations as officials can anticipate. SOPs also bring uniformity to complex organizations, and justice is better served if rules are applied uniformly. This is true for the implementation of welfare policies that distribute benefits to the needy, as well as for criminal law policies that distribute sanctions.

Uniformity also makes personnel interchangeable. A soldier can be transferred to any spot in the world and still know how to carry out a function by referring to the proper manual, a substantial advantage for the commander in chief.

Although designed to make implementing policies easier, at least in theory, SOPs may be inappropriate in some cases and function as obstacles to action. Presidents have had many a plan thwarted by standard government practices. They certainly frustrated President Franklin D. Roosevelt:

> The Treasury is so large and far-flung and ingrained in its practices that I find it is almost impossible to get the action and results I want. . . . But the Treasury is not to be compared with the State Department. You should go through the experience of trying to get any changes in the thinking, policy, and action of the career diplomats and then you'd know what a real problem was. But the Treasury and the State Department put together are nothing as compared with the Na-a-vy. . . . To change anything in the N-a-a-vy is like punching a feather bed. You punch it with your right and you punch it with your left until you are finally exhausted, and then you find the damn bed just as it was before you started punching.[21]

Standard operating procedures may hinder policy implementation by inhibiting change. Designed for typical situations, SOPs can be ineffective in new circumstances. In 1962 the United States discovered the presence of Soviet missiles in Cuba and reacted by blockading the island. President John F. Kennedy was very concerned about the initial interception of Soviet ships, and he sent Secretary of Defense Robert McNamara to check with Chief of Naval Operations George Anderson on the procedures being followed. McNamara stressed to Anderson that the president did *not* want to follow the normal SOP whereby a ship risked being sunk if it refused to submit to being boarded and searched. Kennedy did not want to goad the Soviet Union into retaliation. But Admiral Anderson was not cooperative. At one point in the discussion, he waved the *Manual of Naval Regulations* in the secretary's face and shouted, "It's all in here." To this McNamara replied, "I don't give a damn what John Paul Jones would have done. I want to know what you are going to do now."[22] The conversation ended when the admiral asked the secretary of defense to leave and let the navy run the blockade according to established procedures.

Sometimes SOPs cause organizations to take actions superior officials do not desire, as the Cuban missile crisis dramatically illustrates. Despite President Kennedy's explicit order that the initial encounter with a Soviet ship not involve a Soviet submarine, the United States Navy, according to established procedure, used its "Hunter-Killer" antisubmarine warfare program to locate and float above Soviet submarines within six hundred miles of the continental United States. Also following standard "Hunter-Killer" procedures, the navy forced several Soviet submarines to surface. This drastic action was not ordered by the president or the secretary of defense. It "just happened" because it was the programmed response to such a situation. The highest officials, who ostensibly had authority over the navy, never imagined standard procedures would supplant their directives. SOPs become deeply embedded in an organization and are difficult to control, even in times of crisis.

New policies are the most likely to require a change in organizational behavior and are therefore the most likely to have their implementation hindered by SOPs. In October 1983, 241 United States Marines were killed while they slept in a terrorist attack on their barracks outside Beirut, Lebanon. A presidential commission appointed to examine the causes of the tragedy concluded that, among other factors contributing to the disaster, the marines in the peacekeeping force were "not trained, organized, staffed or supported to deal effectively with the terrorist threat."[23] In other words, they had not altered their SOPs regarding security, basic to any military unit, to meet the unique challenges of a terrorist attack.

### Fragmentation

A second aspect of bureaucratic structure that may impede implementation is fragmentation. Fragmentation is the dispersion of responsibility for a policy area among several organizational units.

The extent of governmental fragmentation is widespread. In the field of welfare, for example, more than one hundred federal human services programs are administered by ten different departments and agencies. The Department of Health and Human Services has responsibility for the Aid to Families with Dependent Children program; the Department of Housing and Urban Development provides housing assistance for the poor; the Department of Agriculture runs the food stamp program; and the Department of Labor administers training programs and provides assistance in obtaining employment. President Carter declared, "There are too many agencies doing too many things, overlapping too often, coordinating too rarely, wasting too much money—and doing too little to solve real problems."[24] The more actors and agencies involved with a particular policy and the more interdependent their decisions, the less the probability of successful implementation.

Over the years Congress has created many separate agencies and has favored categorical grants that assign specific authority and funds to particular agencies in order to oversee more closely and intervene more easily in the administration of policies. Dispersing responsibility for a policy area also disperses "turf" to congressional committees. In water resource policy, three committees in the House and three committees in the Senate have authority over the Army Corps of Engineers, the Soil Conservation Service, and the Bureau of Reclamation, respectively. None of these committees wants to relinquish its hold over these agencies. Thus, the agencies and programs that deal with a common problem remain divided among three departments.

Like congressional committees, agencies are possessive about their jurisdictions. Usually department or agency heads vigorously oppose executive branch reorganizations that encroach upon their sphere of influence. President Carter requested that funds for state drug abuse programs be divided into single, consolidated grants for mental health, drug, and alcohol abuse services. Congress refused to consent to this proposal, however. Professionals in the alcohol and drug abuse programs feared that their programs would be downgraded if they lost their separate legislative identities and were combined with mental health programs. They blocked the president's attempt to reduce program fragmentation. President Clinton proposed to merge the FBI with the Drug Enforcement Agency (DEA), both units *within* the Justice Department. DEA officials, fearful of losing their agency identity and perhaps their jobs, mobilized sympathetic members of Congress to oppose the move.

Interest groups are a third force supporting fragmentation. When Lyndon Johnson tried to move the Maritime Administration from the Department of Commerce to the Department of Transportation, he was successfully opposed by the AFL-CIO. Although it made sense administratively to house the Maritime Administration with other transportation-related agencies, labor leaders feared a bureaucratic reorganization would jeopardize their close relationship with the Maritime Administration. Groups also develop close working relationships with congressional committees and do not want to lose their special access in a reorganization of committee jurisdictions that might follow an executive branch reorganization.

Often a combination of interest groups and legislative committees oppose reorganization. The Department of Education, proposed by President Carter, is composed almost exclusively of education programs from the old Department of Health, Education and Welfare. Head Start, Indian education, the school lunch program, GI bill benefits, job training, and some vocational and rehabilitation education programs remained where they were because of opposition to their being moved. For example, the Senate Agriculture Committee opposed change out of fear of losing oversight responsibility for child nutrition programs, and the American Food Service Association opposed change because it feared nutrition would not be a high priority with educators.

The nature of public policy also is a factor in producing fragmentation. Broad policies, such as those dealing with environmental protection, are multidimensional and overlap with dimensions of other policies, such as agriculture, transportation, recreation, and energy. Thus, presidents cannot easily organize government agencies around just one policy area.

Fragmentation implies diffusion of responsibility, and this makes coordination of policies difficult. The resources and authority necessary for the president to attack a problem comprehensively are often distributed among many bureaucratic units. For example, President Bush found that his high-priority efforts to interdict illegal drugs at the country's borders required coordination among the Treasury Department's Customs Service; the Department of Justice's Drug Enforcement Agency, the Federal Bureau of Investigation, and Border Patrol; and the Transportation Department's Coast Guard. During the invasion of Grenada, President Reagan learned that an army officer on the island had to use his credit card to place a call to North Carolina in order to speak to a ship just offshore! The army and navy had not coordinated their communications systems.

Duplication in the provision of public services is another result of bureaucratic fragmentation. President Carter complained, "There are . . . at least 75 agencies and 164,000 Federal employees in police or investigative work. Many of them duplicate or overlap state and local law enforcement efforts unnecessarily."[25]

Fragmentation may result in two or more agencies working at cross-purposes. According to Richard Nixon:

> One department's watershed project, for instance, threatens to slow the flow of water to another department's reclamation project downstream. One agency wants to develop an electric power project on a certain river while other agencies are working to keep the same area wild. Different departments follow different policies for timber production and conservation, for grazing, for fire prevention and for recreational activities on the federal lands they control, though the lands are often contiguous.[26]

Not only do such conflicts defeat the purposes of the programs involved, but they also force the president's highest-level aides and departmental executives to spend great amounts of time and energy negotiating with one another. This is wasteful, and it may result in compromises representing the lowest common denominators of officials' original positions. Unfortunately, bold and original ideas may be sacrificed for intragovernmental harmony.

Sometimes responsibility for a policy area is so fragmented that certain functions fall between the cracks. Some tasks do not fit neatly within an agency's formal authority. A former intelligence official writes of serving in a Scandinavian embassy and hiring someone to read the local Communist literature. From this a useful chart showing the hierarchy of the Communist party was developed. The project was cut from the budget, however, because coverage of the Communist movement was considered to be a CIA function, yet the CIA could not carry out this function because it was "overt," and the CIA was a clandestine organization.[27] Thus, the project fell between the divisions of organizational responsibility, and useful information was not available to the White House or others in government.

## FOLLOW-UP

Because of all the hindrances to effective policy implementation, it seems reasonable to suggest that implementation would be improved if presidents followed up on their decisions and orders to see that they have been properly implemented. The following example illustrates the importance of follow-up.

President Nixon ordered the CIA to destroy its stockpile of biological weapons. CIA Director Richard Helms relayed the president's order to the deputy director for plans (the head of the covert action division), and he in turn relayed it to a subordinate. Five years later two lethal toxins were discovered in a secret cache. A middle-level official had disobeyed the president's order, later retired, and his successor had assumed that the storage of the toxins had official approval. When called before Congress, Helms testified that he had undertaken no follow-up check on his own order, and when asked who told him the toxins were destroyed, he replied, "I read it in the newspapers." Indeed, if the official who discovered the toxins had not received a directive from the new CIA director, William Colby, to be on the constant lookout for illegal action, he might not have checked on the legality of the toxins, and they would still be sitting there.[28]

The importance of follow-up was made apparent to Nixon at many other points in his administration. Once he ordered the demolition of two old Department of Defense buildings on the Mall near the White House, but it took more than a year to get them down. White House aide William Safire explains:

> Because the President of the United States took a continuing interest, because at least two of his aides were made to feel that its success was a crucial test of their ability and because the President kept prodding, issuing orders, refusing to be "reasonable," a few miserable buildings were finally knocked down and their occupants reassigned.

After the demolition the president called together his aides. With "pride, relief, and wonderment," he told them, "We have finally gotten something done."[29]

Thus a president must constantly check up on his orders. Nevertheless, most recent presidents, including Nixon himself, have not followed this advice. Follow-up on the whole has been haphazard. Presidents and their staffs have been too busy with crisis management, electoral politics, or getting legislation passed to delve into the details involved in monitoring policy implementation. Moreover, presidents lack systematic information about the performance of agencies. And some presidents are philosophically opposed to engaging in much follow-up. Ronald Reagan believed that the chief executive should set broad policy goals and general ground rules and then appoint good people to accomplish the goals. He did not believe presidents should constantly monitor their subordinates.[30]

One technique presidents could use to increase their capacity to follow up on their decisions is to enlarge the size of their personal staffs. This strategy can create additional burdens for the White House, however. Because chief executives can personally deal effectively with only a few people, they are forced to relay implementation orders and receive feedback through additional layers of their own staffs. This, in turn, increases both the possibility of communication distortion and the burden of administration, which the staff is supposed to lighten. The more authority is delegated to persons at the top of a hierarchy, the more possibilities there are for inadequate coordination, interoffice rivalries, communication gaps, and other typical administrative problems. Moreover, a large number of aides with limited access to a top official such as the president increases the chance of their carrying out orders given in anger. Those with limited access will be less likely to know the executive well enough or have enough confidence to hold back on implementing their supervisor's instructions.

A large staff for a president has another drawback. Only a few people can credibly speak for the president. If too many people begin giving orders in the president's name, for example, they will undermine the credibility of all those claiming to speak for him. This credibility is important for aides trying to help the president implement policies. As one Carter aide explained: "If you are perceived by people in a given agency as being close to the president because you have an office in the West Wing, your phone calls will be returned more rapidly and your requests for information or action will be taken more seriously."[31]

Presidential assistants carry the contingent authority of the president, authority that is essential to accomplish anything at all since under the law presidential assistants have no authority of their own. But presidential authority is undermined if numerous people attempt to exercise it.

Excessively vigorous staff involvement in implementation decisions may cause other problems. For example, some observers of recent presidential administrations have concluded that as larger numbers of bright, ambitious, energetic assistants probe into the activities of departments and agencies, they will bring more issues for decision to the president, issues that were formerly decided at lower levels in the bureaucracy. Bureaucrats will begin to pass the buck upward, and more and more decisions must then be made by the White House. This can easily make the Executive Office of the President top-heavy and slow. Involvement in the minutiae of government also may divert resources (including time) from the central objectives and major problems of a president's administration. In addition, if White House aides become intimately involved in the management of government programs, they may lose the objectivity necessary to evaluate new ideas regarding "their" programs.

Overcentralization of decision making at the highest levels may have other negative consequences. It may discourage capable people from serving in government posts where their authority is frequently undercut. It may lower morale and engender resentment and hostility in the bureaucracy. This may impede future cooperation; decrease respect for lower officials among their subordinates; reduce the time bureaucratic officials have for internal management because they must fight to maintain access to and support of the chief executive; and weaken the capability of agencies to streamline or revitalize their management. Similarly, too much monitoring of subordinates' behavior may elicit hostility or excessive caution and lack of imagination in administering policy.

Another factor inhibiting follow-up is secrecy. Secretly executed policies, such as those implemented by the CIA, require few reports to Congress or to superiors in the executive branch. Consequently, officials' actions are not routinely monitored. Since members of Congress risk criticism for violating national security if they make public any secret information, they are reluctant to do so and have incentives to forgo their responsibility for oversight and follow-up of certain secret policies. When President Johnson's fear of leaks regarding decisions on the Vietnam War led him to restrict his direct communications to a few top officials (the Tuesday lunch group), he did without a prearranged agenda or minutes of the meetings that would have recorded decisions and made possible follow-up on them.

An organization's personnel may be aware of implementation problems but fail to report them to the president or other administration officials. There are several reasons for this. An obvious one, which we noted earlier, is that subordinates may fear that reporting implementation failures will reflect poorly on their own performance and also possibly anger their superiors. Employees may also have a natural loyalty to their organization or to others in the organization who might be hurt by their negative reports. Further, the informal norms against reporting negative information may be very strong. Thus, employees may withhold information from their superiors to escape social ostracism in their peer groups. Finally, some bureaucrats may feel the president is simply too busy to bother with matters of policy implementation.

Even when information indicating poor policy implementation is available to the president and other top executive officials, they may fail to use it. Information coming from the field is often fragmentary, circumstantial, inconsistent, ambiguous, and unrepresentative—in sum, unreliable. In addition, we noted in the previous chapter that such information may be lost in the huge volume of information circulating in the executive branch. It is very difficult for the president to have a clear idea of how a complex policy is actually implemented.

Organizations may fail to report problems in policy implementation for political reasons, such as the fear of losing public or legislative support for their programs. Also, within some organizations rivalries between headquarters and field personnel make the latter reluctant to expose themselves to negative reactions to their implementation efforts.

Although there are limitations on performing follow-up properly, this does not mean follow-up cannot work. And we have seen substantial evidence that it needs to be done. One study found that the Nixon administration's efforts to monitor and evaluate the actions of welfare caseworkers, especially to review them for errors that allowed ineligible persons to receive funds under the Aid to Families with Dependent Children program, had a significant influence on reducing the number of persons receiving welfare. (Unfortunately, it appears that this approach also resulted in many eligible persons not receiving welfare payments.)[32]

The Reagan administration made headway in monitoring agency regulations when it required the Office of Management and Budget (OMB) to review all regulations proposed by executive agencies. This procedure allows the president to influence or block individual regulations more effectively than before. An additional requirement is that agencies inform OMB of upcoming regulations, which aids the White House in preempting the proposal of regulations it opposes or influencing them before they are proposed (when the political costs of opposition are less). Finally, the White House requires agencies to provide cost–benefit analyses of their proposed regulations. Since this type of analysis is often as much art as it is science, ideological preferences may determine the conclusions, which in turn may be used to resist regulations to which the administration is opposed.[33]

## CONCLUSION

The president faces many obstacles in implementing public policies. Although he is the "chief executive," he typically is not in a position to command his own branch's bureaucracy. Moreover, he operates in an environment of scarce resources and few incentives to devote time and energy to implementation. The president emerges from this process as a facilitator rather than a director.

Improving implementation will be very difficult. The roots of most implementation problems are embedded deeply in the fabric of American government and politics. Moreover, as long as presidents remain more concerned with shaping legislation to pass in the Congress than with the implementation of the law after it is passed, as long as they persist in emphasizing public relations rather than policy, and as long as "crisis" situations continue to dominate their time, little progress is likely to be made in improving policy implementation. Moreover, until there are more political incentives for officials to devote more attention to policy implementation and to develop better administrative skills, these priorities probably will not change. Given both the low visibility of many policy implementation activities and the lack of interest in them, the prospects for a change in incentives are not very favorable.

### NOTES

1. Lawrence F. O'Brien, *No Final Victories* (New York: Ballantine Books, 1974), p. 142.

2. John Kennedy, quoted in John Herbers, "Nixon's Presidency: Centralized Control," *New York Times*, March 6, 1973, p. 20.

3. President Carter, quoted in G. Calvin Mackenzie, "Personnel Appointment Strategies in Post-War Presidential Administrations" (paper delivered at the Annual Meeting of the Midwest Political Science Association, Chicago, April 1980), introductory page.

4. Quoted in Paul C. Light, *The President's Agenda: Domestic Policy Choice from Kennedy to Carter* (Baltimore: Johns Hopkins University Press, 1982), p. 145.

5. Quoted in Ibid., p. 152.

6. David Gergen, quoted in "How Much Can Any Administration Do?" *Public Opinion* (December/January 1982): 56.

7. See, for example, William Safire, *Before the Fall: An Inside View of the Pre-Watergate White House* (New York: Doubleday, 1975), pp. 112–13, 285–87, 353, and 566–67; and H. R. Haldeman, *The Ends of Power* (New York: Times Books, 1978), pp. 58–59, 111–12, and 185–87.

8. See, for example, Henry Kissinger, *White House Years* (Boston: Little, Brown, 1979), pp. 26, 28–29, 45–46, 48, 141–42, 158–59, 264, 482, 729, 806, 879, 887, 900, 909, 917, and 994.

9. Ibid., pp. 28–29, 264, and 900.

10. Lyndon Johnson, quoted in Doris Kearns, *Lyndon Johnson and the American Dream* (New York: Harper and Row, 1976), p. 137.

11. See, for example, Dan B. Wood and James E. Anderson, "The Politics of U.S. Antitrust Regulation," *American Journal of Political Science* 37 (February 1993): 1–39; Richard Waterman and Dan B. Wood, "The Dynamics of Political Control of the Bureaucracy," *American Political Science Review* 85 (September 1991): 801–28; Dan B. Wood, "Principals, Bureaucrats, and Responsiveness in Clean Air Enforcement," *American Political Science Review* 82 (March 1988): 213–34.

12. Gerald R. Ford, "Imperiled, Not Imperial," *Time*, November 10, 1980, p. 30.

13. Melvin Laird, quoted in Seymour M. Hersh, *The Price of Power: Kissinger in the Nixon White House* (New York: Summit, 1983), pp. 235–36.

14. Richard M. Nixon, *RN: The Memoirs of Richard Nixon* (New York: Grosset and Dunlap, 1978), pp. 472–73, 513.

15. John F. Kennedy, quoted in Kenneth P. O'Donnell and David F. Powers, *Johnny, We Hardly Knew Ye: Memories of John Fitzgerald Kennedy* (New York: Pocket Books, 1972), p. 270.

16. Tim Kraft, quoted in Dom Bonafede, "Carter Sounds Retreat from 'Cabinet Government,'" *National Journal*, November 18, 1978, pp. 1852–57; see also "Rafshoon and Co.," *Newsweek*, January 29, 1979, p. 23.

17. James P. Pfiffner, *The Strategic Presidency* (Chicago: Dorsey, 1988), p. 98.

18. Jimmy Carter, quoted in "Civil Service Reform," *Congressional Quarterly Weekly Report*, March 11, 1978, p. 660.

19. Richard L. Cole and David A. Caputo, "Presidential Control of the Senior Civil Service: Assessing the Strategies of the Nixon Years," *American Political Science Review* 73 (June 1979): 399–413.

20. Jimmy Carter, quoted in "Press Conference Text," *Congressional Quarterly Weekly Report*, March 11, 1978, p. 655.

21. Franklin D. Roosevelt, quoted in M. S. Eccles, *Beckoning Frontiers* (New York: Knopf, 1951), p. 336.

22. Quoted in Graham T. Allison, *Essence of Decision: Explaining the Cuban Missile Crisis* (Boston: Little, Brown, 1971), pp. 131–32.

23. *Report of the DOD Commission on Beirut International Airport Terrorist Act, October 23, 1983*, December 20, 1983, p. 133.

24. Jimmy Carter, quoted in "Carter Criticizes Federal Bureaucracy," *Congressional Quarterly Weekly Report*, June 3, 1978, p. 1421.

25. Ibid.

26. Richard Nixon, "Government Reorganization—Message from the President," in Stanley Bach and George T. Sulzner, eds., *Perspectives on the Presidency: A Collection* (Lexington, Mass.: Heath, 1974), p. 257.

27. William Colby, *Honorable Men: My Life in the CIA* (New York: Norton, 1975), pp. 101–2.

28. Ibid., pp. 440–41; and "Intelligence Failures, CIA Misdeeds Studied," *Congressional Quarterly Weekly Report*, September 20, 1975, p. 2025.

29. Safire, *Before the Fall*, pp. 250–60.

30. Ronald Reagan, *An American Life* (New York: Simon and Schuster, 1990), p. 161.

31. Quoted in Wayne, "Working in the White House: Psychological Dimensions of the Job" (paper delivered at the annual meeting of the Southern Political Science Association, New Orleans, La., November 1977), pp. 16–17.

32. Ronald Randall, "Presidential Power versus Bureaucratic Intransigence: The Influence of the Nixon Administration on Welfare Policy," *American Political Science Review* 73 (September 1979): 795–810.

## SELECTED READINGS

Aberbach, Joel D., and Bert A. Rockman. "Clashing Beliefs within the Executive Branch: The Nixon Administration Bureaucracy." *American Political Science Review* 70 (June 1976): 456–68.

Allison, Graham. *Essence of Decision: Explaining the Cuban Missile Crisis.* Boston: Little, Brown, 1971.

Chambers, Raymond L. "The Executive Power: A Preliminary Study of the Concept and Efficacy of Presidential Directives." *Presidential Studies Quarterly* 7 (Winter 1977): 21–36.

Cole, Richard L., and David A. Caputo. "Presidential Control of the Senior Civil Service: Assessing the Strategies of the Nixon Years." *American Political Science Review* 73 (June 1979): 399–413.

Cooper, Joseph, and William W. West. "Presidential Power and Republican Government: The Theory and Practice of OMB Review of Agency Rules." *Journal of Politics* 50 (November 1988): 864–95.

Derthick, Martha. *Agency Under Stress.* Washington, D.C.: Brookings Institution, 1990.

Edwards, George C., III. *Implementing Public Policy.* Washington, D.C.: Congressional Quarterly, 1980.

Heclo, Hugh. *A Government of Strangers: Executive Politics in Washington.* Washington, D.C.: Brookings Institution, 1977.

Kaufman, Herbert. *Administrative Feedback.* Washington, D.C.: Brookings Institution, 1973.

Mackenzie, G. Calvin. *The In-and-Outers.* Baltimore: Johns Hopkins University Press, 1987.

Malek, Frederic V. *Washington's Hidden Tragedy: The Failure to Make Government Work.* New York: Free Press, 1978.

Moe, Terry M. "The Politicized Presidency." In John E. Chubb and Paul E. Peterson, eds., *The New Directions in American Politics.* Washington, D.C.: Brookings Institution, 1985.

Nathan, Richard P. *The Administrative Presidency.* New York: Wiley, 1983.

Peterson, Paul E., Barry G. Rabe, and Kenneth K. Wong. *When Federalism Works.* Washington, D.C.: Brookings Institution, 1986.

Radin, Beryl A., and Willis D. Hawley. *The Politics of Federal Reorganization.* New York: Pergamon Press, 1988.

Sapolsky, Harvey M. *The Polaris System Development: Bureaucratic and Programmatic Success in Government.* Cambridge, Mass.: Harvard University Press, 1972.

Wood, Dan B. "Principals, Bureaucrats, and Responsiveness in Clean Air Enforcement." *American Political Science Review* 82 (March 1988): 213–34.

Waterman, Richard W. *Presidential Influence and the Administrative State.* Knoxville, Tenn.: University of Tennessee Press, 1989.

Waterman, Richard W., and Dan B. Wood. "The Dynamics of Political Control of the Bureaucracy." *American Political Science Review* 85 (September 1991): 801–28.

# 10

# The President and Congress

If one were to write a job description of the presidency, near the top of the list of presidential responsibilities would be that of working with Congress. According to Lyndon Johnson, "There is only one way for a President to deal with Congress, and that is continuously, incessantly, and without interruption."[1] Since our system of separation of powers is really one of shared powers, presidents can rarely operate independently of Congress. Although they require the cooperation of Congress, they cannot depend on it. Thus, one of the president's most difficult and frustrating tasks is trying to persuade Congress to support his policies.

The differences in our contrasting views of presidential leadership are perhaps most clear in the area of executive–legislative relations. Director presidents will dominate Congress, reliably obtaining its support for their policies and precluding legislative initiatives to which they are opposed. Facilitators, on the other hand, will find the going much tougher. They will often fail to achieve their legislative goals and almost always have to struggle to win at all. Congress may pass major legislation over their opposition. Frustration and stalemate will characterize such a presidency.

In this chapter we examine the president's leadership of Congress. Because it is important to understand the context of presidential–congressional interaction, we begin with a discussion of the president's formal legislative powers and the inevitable sources of conflict between the two branches. We then move to an examination of the potential sources of presidential influence in Congress, including party leadership, public support, and legislative skills. In our discussion we emphasize both how presidents attempt to persuade members of Congress and the utility of each source of influence.

## FORMAL LEGISLATIVE POWERS

Presidents today have a central role in the legislative process. They are expected to formulate and promote policies. They are expected to coordinate them within the executive branch, to introduce them to Congress, and to mobilize support for them on Capitol Hill and, increasingly, with the general public.

These expectations suggest a broad scope of legislative authority for the president. In actuality, however, the constitutional basis for this authority is quite limited. Only four duties and responsibilities were designated by Article 2: (1) to inform Congress from time to time on the state of the union; (2) to recommend necessary and expedient legislation; (3) to summon Congress into special session and adjourn it if the two houses cannot agree on adjournment; and (4) to exercise a qualified veto.

With the exception of the veto, these responsibilities stem primarily from the president's unique position within the political system: the only official other than the vice president who was to have continuous tenure, a national perspective, and the ability to respond quickly and decisively to emergencies. As the framers of the Constitution saw it, these job-related qualifications placed the president in a unique position to inform Congress, to recommend legislation, and to summon it into session if necessary.

The rationale for the veto was different. Justified within the Constitutional Convention as a defensive weapon, the veto was proposed as a device by which the president could prevent executive powers from being usurped by the legislature. The founders feared that the institutional balance would become undone and that the Congress would be the likely perpetrator. The extent to which their fears were justified and the use of the veto as a political and constitutional weapon are examined later in this chapter.

Over the years presidents have used their legislative responsibilities to enlarge their congressional influence. The State of the Union message is a good example. In the nineteenth century it was a routine message dealing primarily with the actions of the executive departments and agencies for the previous year. Beginning with Jefferson and continuing through Theodore Roosevelt, the address was sent to the Congress to be read by the clerk of the House and then distributed to the members. Woodrow Wilson revived the practice of the first two presidents and delivered the speech himself. Subsequently, presidents have timed the address to maximize its public exposure. Today it is an important vehicle by which presidents can articulate the legislative goals of their administrations, recite their accomplishments, present their agendas, and try to mobilize support for their programs.

Similarly, presidents have transformed their responsibility to recommend necessary and expedient legislation into an annual agenda-setting function. Although nineteenth-century presidents formulated some legislative proposals and even drafted bills in the White House, it was not until the twentieth century that the practice of presidential programming developed on a regular basis. Wilson and Franklin Roosevelt submitted comprehensive legislative proposals to Congress. Truman packaged them in the State of the Union address. With the exception of Eisenhower in his first year in office, every subsequent president has followed the Truman tradition.

To some extent the Congress has found the president's legislative initiatives advantageous. In some cases it has insisted upon them. For example, the 1921 Budget and Accounting Act, the 1946 Employment Act, and the 1974 Budget Act require the president to provide Congress with annual reports and an annual executive budget.

The calling of special sessions by the president has fallen into disuse. The length of the current legislative year combined with changes in the calendar have made this function largely obsolete. The last special session occurred in 1948. In the past, however, presidents frequently would call special sessions after their inauguration to gain support for their objectives and to initiate "their" Congress. Until the passage of the Twentieth Amendment in 1933, Congress began its session on or about December 1. This made every other session of Congress "a lame duck" and forced a newly elected president to wait nine months for the newly elected Congress. Between the Lincoln and Franklin Roosevelt administrations there were nineteen special sessions.

## SOURCES OF CONFLICT BETWEEN THE EXECUTIVE AND LEGISLATIVE BRANCHES

Presidents must influence Congress because they generally cannot act without its consent. Under our constitutional system of separation of powers, Congress must pass legislation and can override vetoes. The Senate must ratify treaties and confirm presidential appointments to the cabinet, the federal courts, regulatory commissions, and other high offices. Yet these overlapping powers do not explain the president's need to influence Congress. Theoretically, the two branches *could* be in agreement. In fact, the president and some members of Congress will always disagree because of their personalities or past histories. Yet these differences are not the source of systematic conflict. The source lies in the structure and processes of American politics.

In "The Federalist, No. 46," James Madison focused on the greatest source of conflict between the president and Congress: their different constituencies.

> The members of the federal legislature will likely attach themselves too much to local objects. . . . Measures will too often be decided according to their probable effect, not on the national prosperity and happiness, but on the prejudices, interests, and pursuits of the governments and the people of the individual states.[2]

Only presidents (and their vice presidential running mates) are chosen in a national election. Each member of Congress is elected by only a fraction of the populace. Inevitably, presidents must form a broader electoral coalition in order to win their office than any member of Congress. Moreover, two-thirds of the senators are not elected at the same time as the president, and the remaining senators and all the House members seem to be increasingly insulated from the causes of presidential victories. In addition, the Senate overrepresents rural states because each state has two senators regardless of its population. Thus, the whole that the president represents is different from the sum of the parts that each legislator represents. Each member of Congress will give special access to the interests that he or she represents, but Congress as a body has more difficulty representing the nation as a whole.

The internal structures of the executive and legislative branches also cause differences between the president and Congress. The executive branch is hierarchically organized, facilitating the president's examining a broad range of viewpoints on an issue and then weighing and balancing various interests. This structure also helps the president to view the trade-offs among various policies. The president must take a comprehensive view of those policies, supporting all the major policies emanating from the executive branch.

On the other hand, each house of Congress is highly decentralized. The party structure is not a unifying force within the United States legislature, as we shall see later. Committee memberships are frequently unrepresentative of each chamber, and members of each committee may defer to members of the other committees. Thus, members representing special interests have a disproportionate say over policy regarding those interests.

One of the functions of decentralizing power and responsibility in Congress is to allow for specialization in various policy areas. However, because of specialization, legislators tend to rely upon the cues of party leaders, state party delegations, relevant committee leaders of their party, and other colleagues to decide how to vote. These cue givers, however, are chosen because they represent constituencies or ideologies that are similar to those of the member who is consulting them. They do not represent a cross section of viewpoints.[3]

Members of Congress are not generally in a position to make trade-offs between policies. Because of its decentralization, Congress usually considers policies serially, that is, without reference to other policies. Without an integrating mechanism, members have few means by which to set and enforce priorities and to emphasize the policies with which the president is most concerned, particularly when Congress is controlled by the opposition party. In addition, Congress has little capability, except within the context of the budget, to examine two policies, like education and health care, in relation to each other. Not knowing that giving up something on one policy will result in a greater return on another policy, members have little incentive to engage in trade-offs. Congress is also poorly organized to deal comprehensively with major policy domains. It distributes its workload among committees with jurisdictions that often do not cover entire policy areas such as welfare, national security, or economic stability.

Thus, although the structure of Congress ensures that a diversity of views will be heard and that many interests will have access to the legislative process, it does not follow that *each* member will hear all the views and see the proponents of each interest. Indeed, the decentralization of Congress almost guarantees that the information available to it as a whole is not a synthesis of the information available to each legislator. The Congress as a whole does not ask questions; individual members do. Thus, not all members receive the answers.

The hierarchical structure of the executive branch, with the president at the pinnacle, forces the president to take responsibility for the entire executive branch. Moreover, when the president exercises power, it is clear who is acting and who should be held accountable. Congress, on the other hand, is not responsible for implementing policies, and each member is relatively obscure compared with the president. Since Congress is so decentralized, any member can disclaim responsibility for policies or their consequences. Members of Congress, therefore, can and do make irresponsible or self-serving decisions and then let the president take the blame.

All of this can be very frustrating to the president. As Gerald Ford, who spent most of his adult life in Congress, wrote after leaving the White House:

> When I was in the Congress myself, I thought it fulfilled its constitutional obligations in a very responsible way, but after I became President, my perspective changed. It seemed to me that Congress was beginning to disintegrate as an organized legislative body. It wasn't answering the nation's challenges domestically because it was too fragmented. It responded too often to single-issue special interest groups and it therefore wound up dealing with minutiae instead of attacking serious problems in a coherent way.[4]

Another source of conflict between the president and Congress is the difference in information and expertise available to them. There has been a substantial increase in congressional staff in recent years, including the expansion or addition of analytic units such as the General Accounting Office, the Congressional Research Service in the Library of Congress, the Office of Technology Assessment, and the Congressional Budget Office. Nevertheless, members of Congress usually do not have access to the same quantity and quality of expertise as that available to the president.

Aside from the fact that the executive branch includes five million civilian and military employees plus hundreds of advisory committees while Congress employs only about 25,000 persons (about one-third of whom work in supporting agencies, including the Library of Congress), the expertise of the two branches differs. Members of Congress tend to hire generalists, even on committee staffs. Some individuals develop great expertise in a particular field, but others may only be amateurs compared with their counterparts in the executive branch. Many are selected to serve legislators' needs and desires, which have little to do with policy analysis, and neither house has a merit system, a tenured career service, or a central facility for recruiting the best available talent.

Because the president and Congress have different information and expertise available to them, they may well see issues from different perspectives. The president's views will generally be buttressed with more data and handled more expertly, inevitably giving the chief executive different views and more confidence in those views.

We have seen that the structure of American government exerts strong pressure on the two branches to represent different sets of interests and to view policies differently. This, in turn, sets the stage for conflict and virtually compels a president to try to influence Congress.

## PARTY LEADERSHIP

"What the Constitution separates our political parties do not combine."[5] Richard Neustadt wrote these words three decades ago to help explain why presidents could not simply assume support from the members of their party in Congress. The challenge of presidential party leadership in Congress remains just as great and is just as important today as it was when Neustadt wrote his famous treatise on presidential power.

### Party Support of the President

Representatives and senators of the president's party are almost always the nucleus of coalitions supporting the president's programs. As one White House aide put it: "You turn to your party members first. If we couldn't move our own people, we felt the opportunities were pretty slim."[6] No matter what other resources a president may have, without seats in Congress held by his party, he will usually find it very difficult to move his legislative program through Congress. Thus, leading his party in Congress is the president's principal task as he seeks to counter the tendencies of the executive and legislative branches toward conflict inherent in the system of checks and balances.

Tables 10-1 and 10-2 show the support given presidents by members of each party on roll-call votes on which the presidents took a stand. Clearly, there is a substantial difference between the levels of support presidents receive from members of the two parties, with the gap generally exceeding 25 percentage points. Although the presidents of each party varied considerably in their policies, personalities, and political environments, their fellow partisans in Congress gave them considerably more support than they gave presidents of the opposition party.

With a president of their own in the White House, party members in Congress may alter their voting tendencies.[7] For example, Republi-

Table 10-1. Presidential Support by Party, 1953–1990 (in percentages)*

| Year | President's Party | House Democrats | House Republicans | Senate Democrats | Senate Republicans |
|------|-------------------|-----------------|-------------------|------------------|--------------------|
| 1953 | R | 45% | 70% | 42% | 66% |
| 1954 | R | 34 | 74 | 36 | 74 |
| 1955 | R | 42 | 52 | 37 | 70 |
| 1956 | R | 38 | 72 | 35 | 69 |
| 1957 | R | 48 | 52 | 44 | 69 |
| 1958 | R | 52 | 55 | 37 | 66 |
| 1959 | R | 34 | 72 | 28 | 73 |
| 1960 | R | 46 | 64 | 41 | 66 |
| 1961 | D | 73 | 26 | 68 | 31 |
| 1962 | D | 72 | 30 | 64 | 31 |
| 1963 | D | 75 | 21 | 63 | 37 |
| 1964 | D | 78 | 26 | 63 | 56 |
| 1965 | D | 75 | 24 | 64 | 44 |
| 1966 | D | 67 | 20 | 53 | 35 |
| 1967 | D | 70 | 28 | 56 | 42 |
| 1968 | D | 63 | 36 | 46 | 41 |
| 1969 | R | 48 | 57 | 42 | 65 |
| 1970 | R | 41 | 60 | 35 | 63 |
| 1971 | R | 41 | 71 | 33 | 65 |
| 1972 | R | 46 | 68 | 34 | 66 |
| 1973 | R | 31 | 65 | 24 | 64 |
| 1974 | R | 38 | 59 | 31 | 53 |
| 1975 | R | 37 | 68 | 36 | 67 |
| 1976 | R | 32 | 67 | 29 | 62 |
| 1977 | D | 61 | 32 | 62 | 39 |
| 1978 | D | 65 | 34 | 64 | 36 |
| 1979 | D | 64 | 26 | 67 | 39 |
| 1980 | D | 63 | 31 | 60 | 38 |
| 1981 | R | 39 | 72 | 33 | 81 |
| 1982 | R | 30 | 61 | 35 | 72 |
| 1983 | R | 28 | 71 | 39 | 73 |
| 1984 | R | 32 | 66 | 31 | 74 |
| 1985 | R | 28 | 68 | 27 | 76 |
| 1986 | R | 23 | 72 | 26 | 80 |
| 1987 | R | 26 | 75 | 27 | 70 |
| 1988 | R | 24 | 70 | 29 | 68 |
| 1989 | R | 34 | 71 | 36 | 77 |
| 1990 | R | 25 | 72 | 31 | 69 |

*On roll-call votes on which the winning side was supported by fewer than 80 percent of those voting.
R = Republican
D = Democrat

Source: George C. Edwards III, *At the Margins: Presidential Leadership of Congress* (New Haven, Conn.: Yale University Press, 1989), Table 3.1; updated by author.

Table 10-2. Partisan Support for Presidents, 1953–1990 (in percentages)*

|  | Presidents | | |
|  | Democratic | Republican | Difference |
|---|---|---|---|
| *House* | | | |
| Democrats | 69% | 36% | 33† |
| Republicans | 38 | 66 | 28 |
| *Senate* | | | |
| Democrats | 61 | 34 | 27 |
| Republicans | 35 | 69 | 34 |

*On roll-call votes on which the winning side was supported by fewer than 80 percent of those voting.
†Differences expressed as percentage points.
Source: George C. Edwards III, *At the Margins: Presidential Leadership of Congress* (New Haven, Conn.: Yale University Press, 1989), Table 3.3; updated by author.

cans have a tendency to be more supportive of internationalist foreign policies and are more likely to accept governmental economic activity when a Republican is president. Democrats, on the other hand, have a tendency to move in the opposite direction when there is a Republican in the White House. In 1981, with a conservative Republican as president, many Republicans in Congress shifted to supporting foreign aid and increasing the national debt ceiling even though they had opposed these policies under the previous Democratic administration of Jimmy Carter. Similarly, many members of the president's party who voted for a bill when it was originally passed switch and vote against the same legislation if their party leader vetoes it.

Although the president receives more support from members of his party than from the opposition, this is not necessarily the result of their shared party affiliation. It is difficult to tell whether a member of the president's party votes for the president's policies because of shared party affiliation, basic agreement with those policies, or some other factor. Undoubtedly, members of the same party share many policy preferences and have similar electoral coalitions supporting them. In 1981 President Reagan won several crucial votes in Congress on his taxing and spending proposals. He was immediately credited with extraordinary party leadership because nearly 100 percent of the Republicans in Congress supported his programs. If we examine voting on budget resolutions under Democrat Jimmy Carter, however, we find nearly the same degree of Republican party unity in the House. Thus, we should not necessarily ascribe Reagan's success to party loyalty. Republican members of the House had been voting a conservative line well before Ronald Reagan came to Washington.

Despite the proclivity of members of Congress to support presidents of their party, the White House also experiences substantial slippage in party cohesion in Congress. Table 10-2 shows that presidents can count on their own party members for support no more than two-thirds of the time (even on key votes). This forces them to adopt an activist orientation toward party leadership and to devote as much effort to converting party members to support them as to mobilizing members of their party who already agree with them.

### Leading the Party

That members of the president's own party are more open to presidential influence is clear. Members of the president's party typically have personal loyalties or emotional commitments to their party and their party leader, which the president can often translate into votes when necessary. Thus, members of the president's party vote with him when they can, giving him the benefit of the doubt, especially if their own opinion on an issue is weak. Moreover, this proclivity for supporting the president increases the effectiveness of other sources of party influence.

One of these sources is the desire of members of the presidential party not to embarrass "their" administration. This attitude stems from two motivations. The first is related to the sentiments discussed above, but the second is more utilitarian. Members of the president's party have an incentive to make the president look good because his standing in the public may influence their own chances for reelection. They also want a record of legislative success to take to the voters. In 1993 the need to end gridlock between the president and Congress was a unifying force among Democrats in both the House and the Senate, motivating them to support President Clinton.

Presidents may also find it easier to obtain party unity behind their programs if their party regains control of one or both houses of Congress at the time of their election. Many new members may feel a sense of gratification for the president's coattails. Moreover, the prospect of exercising the power to govern may provide a catalyst for party loyalty while the loss of power may temporarily demoralize the opposition party. All of the motivations to support the president are, of course, buttressed by basic distrust of the opposition party.

WORKING WITH CONGRESSIONAL LEADERS.    Each party has a set of floor and committee leaders in the House and Senate, and in theory they should be a valuable resource for their party's leader in the White House. The president needs both their advice and their resources for making head counts and other administrative chores. Because of their role perceptions, because their reputations for passing legislation give them a clear stake in the president's success, and because they are susceptible to the same sentiments and pressures toward party loyalty as are other members of Congress, floor leaders of the president's party in Congress are usually very supportive of the White House. In the month before Ronald Reagan's inauguration, the new Senate majority leader, Howard Baker, declared, "I intend to try to help Ronald Reagan [carry out] the commitments he made during the campaign."[8]

Committee leaders of the president's party usually have a similar orientation. Representative Daniel Rostenkowski, chair of the House Ways and Means Committee, told President Clinton, "You send the proposals, and I'll be the quarterback." Senator Daniel Patrick Moynihan, the chair of the Senate Finance Committee, declared, "The most important thing for me coming to the job . . . is that I want to get the president's agenda through."[9]

Yet party floor leaders are not always dependable supporters. They certainly are not simply extensions of the White House. House Majority Leader Richard Gephardt and House Majority Whip David Bonior broke with President Clinton over the North American Free Trade Agreement and led the opposition to it. There is little the White House can do in such a situation. Presidents do not lobby for candidates for congressional party leadership positions and virtually always remain neutral during the selection process. They have no desire to alienate important members of Congress whose support they will need.

Similarly, committee chairpersons and ranking minority members are usually determined by seniority. Furthermore, the chairpersons always come from the majority party in the chamber, which often is not the president's. For all practical purposes, the president plays no role at all in determining the holders of these important positions. Moreover, the norm of supporting a president of one's party is weaker for committee leaders than for floor leaders.

Presidents and their staff typically work closely with their party's legislative leaders, meeting regularly for breakfast when Congress is in session. Sometimes these meetings include the leaders of the opposition party as well. These gatherings provide opportunities for an exchange of views and for the president to keep communication channels open and maintain morale. The significance of these efforts has varied, however. On one extreme, Nixon's meetings were often pro forma, serving more as a symbolic ritual than a mechanism for leadership. On the other, Johnson used them as strategy sessions, integrating congressional leaders into the White House legislative liaison operation.

Equally as important as the congressional party leaders' relations with the president are their relations with their party colleagues in Congress. Major changes have occurred in the past generation that have weakened the ability of party leaders to produce votes for the president. According to Gerald Ford:

> Today a President really does not have the kind of clout with the Congress that he had 30 years ago, even in matters that affect national security. There is not the kind of teamwork that existed in the '50s, even if the President and a majority of the Congress belong to the same party. The main reason for this change is the erosion of the leadership in the Congress. Party leaders have lost the power to tell their troops that something is really

significant and to get them to respond accordingly. The days of Sam Rayburn, Lyndon Johnson and Everett Dirksen are gone. That has adversely affected the Congress's ability to do things even in very difficult circumstances involving the national interest.[10]

One reason that party leaders have lost much of their power over their "followers" is the increased dispersion of power in Congress. The face of Congress has changed over the past two decades. Seniority is no longer an automatic path to committee or subcommittee chairs, and chairpersons must be more responsive to the desires of committee members. There are also more subcommittees and more subcommittee chairpersons now, and these subcommittees have a more important role in handling legislation. While the power of subcommittees has increased, that of the southern oligarchies has declined. Members of both parties have larger personal, committee, and subcommittee staffs at their disposal as well as new service adjuncts such as the Congressional Budget Office. This new freedom and these additional resources, combined with more opportunities to amend legislation, make it easier for members of Congress to challenge the White House and the congressional leadership and to provide alternatives to the president's policies.

The president's program is also now subject to more cross-cutting demands within Congress as a result of split and joint committee referrals for some legislation. This further complicates the task of influencing members of Congress because it is difficult to lobby several committees at once with the limited resources available to the president. Similarly, more than a quarter of the members of Congress sit on committees that raise, budget, or appropriate funds. No wonder presidents have trouble getting their budgets passed.

Yet other reforms have increased the burden of leaders. The increased number of roll-call votes and thus the increased visibility of representatives' voting behavior have generated more pressure on House members to abandon party loyalty, making it more difficult for the president to gain passage of legislation. Reforms that have opened committee and subcommittee hearings to the public have had the same effect. There has also been a heavy turnover in the personnel of Congress in recent years, and new members have brought with them new approaches to legislating. They are less likely to adopt the norms of apprenticeship and specialization than were their predecessors in their first terms. Instead, they have eagerly taken an active role in all legislation. They place a heavy emphasis on individualism and much less on party regularity.

Thus, congressional party leaders now have more decision makers to influence. They can no longer rely on dealing with the congressional aristocracy and expect the rest of the members to follow. According to one Johnson assistant:

In 1965, there were maybe ten or twelve people who you needed to corral in the House and Senate. Without those people, you were in for a tough time.

Now, I'd put that figure upwards of one hundred. Believe it, there are so many people who have a shot at derailing a bill that the President has to double his effort for even routine decisions.[11]

Although the party leadership at least in theory possesses sanctions that it can exercise to enforce party discipline, including exercising discretion on committee assignments, patronage, campaign funds, trips abroad, and aid with members' pet bills, in reality this discretion exists primarily on paper. Most rewards are considered a matter of right, and it is the leadership's job to see that they are distributed equitably. Party leaders do not dare to withhold benefits because they fear being overturned by the rank and file. Senate Majority Leader Robert Dole sometimes termed his position that of "majority pleader." Threats of sanctions in such a situation are unconvincing and thus rarely occur.

OBSTACLES TO PARTY UNITY.    The primary obstacle to party cohesion in support of the president is the absence of a consensus among members of the president's party on policies, especially if the president happens to be a Democrat. This diversity of views often reflects the diversity of constituencies represented by party members. The frequent defection from support of Democratic presidents by the conservative southern Democrats, or "boll weevils," is one of the most prominent features of American politics. Under Presidents Kennedy, Johnson, and Carter there was approximately a 25 percentage point difference between northern and southern Democrats in support of the president. When constituency opinion and the president's proposals conflict, members of Congress are more likely to vote with their constituencies, to whom they must return for reelection.

Republican presidents often lack stable coalitions as well. As we noted earlier, Ronald Reagan received nearly unanimous support from his party on his 1981 proposals to reduce taxes and expenditures. The next year, when he proposed legislation to increase taxes, to restrict abortions and forced busing for integration, and to allow school prayer, things were different. Republicans were in the forefront of the opposition to these policies.

A shift in the status of party members may present another obstacle to party unity. Just as regaining power may encourage party unity, having to share it may strain intraparty relations. When a party that has had a majority in Congress regains the White House, committee and floor leaders of that party will typically be less influential because they will be expected to take their lead on major issues from the president. This may cause tensions within the party and make party discipline more difficult.

Yet other obstacles may confront a president trying to mobilize his party in Congress. If the president's party has just regained the presidency but remains a minority in Congress, its members need to adjust from their past stance as the opposition minority to one of a "governing" minority. This is not always easily done, however, as Richard Nixon found when he sought Republican votes for budget deficits.

Further difficulties may stem from the fact that the winning presidential candidate may not be the natural leader of the party. Indeed, as in the case of Jimmy Carter, and to a lesser extent Bill Clinton, they campaigned against the party establishment and were not identified with the Democratic party program that existed at the time. Naturally when a new president arrives in Washington under these conditions, intraparty harmony is not likely to materialize overnight, and appeals for party loyalty may fall on less than receptive ears.

MIDTERM ELECTION CAMPAIGNING.    Members of Congress who are of the president's party are more likely to support the president than are members of the opposition party; presidents do their best to exploit this potential of partisan support. Nevertheless, such actions are inevitably at the margins of coalition building because they take place within the confines of the partisan balance of the Congress. To exploit fully the benefits of party leadership, presidents need as many of their fellow partisans in Congress as possible. Once members of Congress are elected, however, they almost never change their party affiliation, and the rare instances when they do have not resulted from presidential persuasion. Thus, if presidents are to alter the party composition of Congress, they must help to elect additional members of their party. One way to try to accomplish this goal is to campaign for candidates in midterm congressional elections.

Sometimes presidents are so unpopular that the candidates of their party do not want their support. President Johnson adopted a low profile during the 1966 campaign because of his lack of public support (below 50 percent in the Gallup Poll). In 1974, before he resigned, President Nixon wanted invitations to campaign for Republicans to prove that he was not political poison, but he had few offers as the Watergate crisis reached a head.

Nevertheless, modern presidents have often taken an active role in midterm congressional elections. In 1970, President Nixon was heavily involved in the congressional elections. He chose Vice President Spiro Agnew to carry the main burden of making speeches and offered him the services of several White House aides and speech writers. Behind the scenes Nixon was running the show, however, making strategic decisions such as selecting issues to raise and to avoid, labeling particular Democratic candidates as "radicals," encouraging people (mostly representatives) to run for the Senate, and deciding whom to support. He also made numerous campaign speeches.

President Carter also was an active campaigner in 1978, speaking on behalf of Democratic candidates all across the country. Ronald Reagan did the same in 1982, although some candidates asked him to stay away because of the recession, with which many voters identified him. In 1986 he stumped the country in an unsuccessful effort to preserve the Republican majority in the Senate. George Bush made numerous speeches for Republican candidates in 1990.

Table 10-3. Changes in Congressional Representation of the President's Party
           in Midterm Elections

| Year | President | House | Senate |
|------|-----------|-------|--------|
| 1954 | Eisenhower | −18 | −1 |
| 1958 | Eisenhower | −47 | −13 |
| 1962 | Kennedy | −4 | +3 |
| 1966 | Johnson | −47 | −4 |
| 1970 | Nixon | −12 | +2 |
| 1974 | Ford | −47 | −5 |
| 1978 | Carter | −15 | −3 |
| 1982 | Reagan | −26 | 0 |
| 1986 | Reagan | −5 | −8 |
| 1990 | Bush | −9 | −1 |

Presidential efforts in midterm elections have had quite limited success.[12] As Table 10-3 shows, a recurring feature of American politics is the decrease in representation of the president's party in Congress in midterm congressional elections. We can also see this as far back as Woodrow Wilson's efforts in 1918, which were rewarded by the loss of both houses of Congress (even George Washington's Federalists lost seats in the House in the first midterm election in 1790).

PRESIDENTIAL COATTAILS.    Another way in which presidents may influence the partisan composition of Congress is through their coattails. Presidential coattails are part of the lore of American politics. Politicians project them in their calculations, journalists attribute them in their reporting, historians recount them, and political scientists analyze them. Yet we have limited understanding of how they affect the outcomes in congressional elections. A coattail victory is a victory for a representative of the president's party in which presidential coattail votes provide the increment of the vote necessary to win the seat.

Coattail victories, whether they bring in new members or preserve the seats of incumbents, can have significant payoffs for the president in terms of support for the administration's programs. Those members of the president's party who won close elections may provide an extra increment of support out of a sense of gratitude for the votes they perceive they received due to presidential coattails or out of a sense of responsiveness to their constituents' support for the president.

Yet research has found that the outcomes of very few congressional races are determined by presidential coattails.[13] In 1988 George Bush won election while his party actually lost seats in both houses of Congress. The Democrats lost ten seats in the House and gained none in the Senate when Bill Clinton won election in 1992 (he ran behind all but a handful of members of Congress in their states or districts). This is nothing new. In 1792 George Washington easily won reelection, but the opposition Democrat-Republicans captured the House of Representatives. The results of elections over the past forty years are shown in Table 10-4. Most House seats are too safe for a party, and especially for an incumbent, to have the election outcome affected by the presidential election. Senate elections are more affected by the president's standing with the public,[14] but the president's party typically gains no seats at all in a presidential election year.

Thus, presidents cannot expect personally to carry like-minded running mates into office to provide additional support for their programs. On the contrary, rather than being amenable to voting for the president's policies due to shared convictions, representatives are free to focus on parochial matters and to respond to narrow constituency interests. Similarly, although we cannot know the extent to which representatives have felt gratitude to presidents for their coattails and thus have given them additional legislative support in the past, we do know that any such gratitude is rarely warranted. The more representatives are aware of the independence of their elections from the president's, the less likely they are to feel that they must "thank" the president with an additional increment of support.

BIPARTISANSHIP.   On July 27, 1981, President Reagan delivered an exceptionally important and effective televised address to the nation seeking the public's support for his tax-cut bill. In it he went to great lengths to present his plan as "bipartisan." It was crucial that he convince the public that this controversial legislation was supported by members of both parties and was therefore, by implication, fair. Thus, he described it as "bipartisan" *eleven* times in the span of a few minutes! No one was to miss the point. The president required the votes of Democrats in the House to pass his bill, and he wanted their constituents to apply pressure to them to support it.

Despite the advantage that presidents have in dealing with members of their party in Congress, they are often forced to solicit bipartisan support. There are several reasons for this. First, the opposition party

Table 10-4. **Changes in Congressional Representation of the President's Party in Presidential Election Years**

| Year | President | House | Senate |
|------|-----------|-------|--------|
| 1952 | Eisenhower | +22 | +1 |
| 1956 | Eisenhower | −2 | −1 |
| 1960 | Kennedy | −22 | −2 |
| 1964 | Johnson | +37 | +1 |
| 1968 | Nixon | +5 | +6 |
| 1972 | Nixon | +12 | −2 |
| 1976 | Carter | +1 | 0 |
| 1980 | Reagan | +34 | +12 |
| 1984 | Reagan | +14 | −2 |
| 1988 | Bush | −3 | −1 |
| 1992 | Clinton | −10 | 0 |

may control one or both houses of Congress. Thus even if all members of the president's party supported the administration on its key initiatives, that would not be sufficient. Between 1953 and 1992 Republican presidents faced a Democratic House of Representatives for twenty-six years and a Democratic Senate for twenty years.

A second reason for bipartisanship is that presidents cannot depend on all the members of their party to support them on all issues. Tables 10-1 and 10-2 show clearly that members of the president's own party frequently oppose the president. As Jimmy Carter wrote, "I learned the hard way that there was no party loyalty or discipline when a complicated or controversial issue was at stake—none."[15] Southern Democrats support Democratic presidents less consistently than do northern Democrats.

Not only do partisan strategies often fail, but they also may provoke the other party into a more unified posture of opposition. Where there is confrontation, there can be no consensus, and consensus is often required to legislate changes on important issues. Presidents are also inhibited in their partisanship by pressures to be "president of all the people" rather than a highly partisan figure. This role expectation of being somewhat above the political fray undoubtedly constrains presidents in their role as party leaders.

Despite the frequent necessity of a bipartisan strategy, it is not without costs. Bipartisanship often creates a strain with the extremes within the president's party as a Republican president tries to appeal to the left for Democratic votes and a Democratic president to the right for Republican votes. Although it is true that the Republican right wing and Democratic left wing may find it difficult to forge a coalition in favor of alternatives to their own president's policies, it is not true that they must therefore support their president. Instead, they may complicate a president's strategy by joining those who oppose administration policies.

The ultimate limitation on a bipartisan strategy is that, as Tables 10-1 and 10-2 demonstrate, the opposition party is generally not a fertile ground for obtaining policy support. Democratic presidents have often been frustrated in their efforts to deal with Republicans. President Clinton faced virtually unanimous Republican opposition to his economic and deficit-reduction programs in 1993. Republican presidents also face obstacles to obtaining bipartisan support. Only twenty-three House Democrats supported Ronald Reagan on both the important budget and tax votes in 1981, despite the president's persuasive efforts, the perception that the president had a mandate, and the pull of ideology. Nevertheless, presidents cannot ignore the opposition party and even a few votes may be enough to bring them a majority.

## PUBLIC SUPPORT

Although congressional seats held by members of the president's party may be a necessary condition for presidential success in Congress, they are not a sufficient one. The president needs public support as well.

In the words of Eisenhower aide and presidential authority Emmet John Hughes, "Beyond all tricks of history and all quirks of Presidents, there would appear to be one unchallengeable truth: the dependence of Presidential authority on popular support."[16]

### Public Approval

In his memoirs, President Johnson wrote, "Presidential popularity is a major source of strength in gaining cooperation from Congress."[17] Thus, following his landslide electoral victory, he assembled the congressional liaison officials from the various departments and told them that his victory at the polls "might be more of a loophole than a mandate" and that since his popularity could decrease rapidly, they would have to use it to their advantage while it lasted.[18]

President Carter's aides were quite explicit about the importance of public approval in their efforts to influence Congress. One stated that the "only way to keep those guys [Congress] honest is to keep our popularity high."[19] The president's legislative liaison officials generally agreed that their effectiveness with Congress ultimately depended upon the president's ability to influence public opinion. As one of them said, "When you go up to the Hill and the latest polls show Carter isn't doing well, there isn't much reason for a member to go along with him. There's little we can do if the member isn't persuaded on the issue."[20] The Reagan administration was especially sensitive to the president's public approval levels. According to one top aide, "Everything here is built on the idea that the president's success depends on grassroots support."[21]

Why is presidential approval or popularity such an important source of influence in Congress? According to a senior aide to President Carter:

> When the President is low in public opinion polls, the Members of Congress see little hazard in bucking him. . . . After all, very few Congressmen examine an issue solely on its merits; they are politicians and they think politically. I'm not saying they make only politically expedient choices. But they read the polls and from that they feel secure in turning their backs on the President with political impunity. Unquestionably, the success of the President's policies bears a tremendous relationship to his popularity in the polls.[22]

The public's evaluations of the president may be taken as indicators of broader opinions on politics and policy. Moreover, members of Congress must anticipate the public's reactions to their support for or opposition to the president and his policies. They may choose to be close to or independent from the president, depending upon his public standing, to increase their chances of reelection. Polls find that a significant percentage of voters see their votes for candidates for Congress as support for or opposition to the president.[23] Members of Congress may also use the president's standing in the polls as an indicator of his ability to mobilize public opinion against his opponents.

Public approval operates mostly in the background and sets the limits of what Congress will do for or to the president. Widespread support gives a president leeway and weakens resistance to the administration's policies. It provides a cover for members of Congress to cast votes to which their constituents might otherwise object. They can defend their votes as support for the president rather than on substantive policy grounds alone.

Lack of public support strengthens the resolve of those inclined to oppose the president and narrows the range in which he receives the benefit of the doubt, as Bill Clinton discovered when his approval ratings dipped into the 35 percent range in mid-1993. In addition, low ratings in the polls may create incentives to attack the president, further eroding an already weakened position. For example, after the arms sales to Iran and the diversion of funds to the Contras became a *cause célèbre* in late 1986, it became more acceptable in Congress and in the press to raise questions about Ronald Reagan's capacities as president. Disillusionment is a dangerous phenomenon for the White House.

The impact of presidential approval on presidential support occurs at the margins of coalition building, within the confines of other influences. No matter how low a president's standing in public polls or how close it is to the next election, the president still receives support from a substantial number of senators and representatives. Similarly, no matter how high approval levels climb or how large a president's winning percentage of the vote, a significant portion of the Congress may still oppose his policies. Members of Congress are unlikely to vote against the clear interests of their constituents or the firm tenets of their ideology out of deference to a widely supported chief executive. Approval gives a president leverage, not control.

Thus, public approval is a necessary but not a sufficient source of influence in Congress. It is most useful in combination with party supporters in each house of Congress. If either approval or seats are lacking, the president's legislative program will be in for rough sledding. The consequences of the absence of each source of influence are described by two presidential assistants, the first to Nixon and the second to Carter:

> Nineteen seventy-two did not help us. It was similar to Eisenhower in 1956. We had tremendous public and electoral support. But that and a dime couldn't buy a cup of coffee. It was still a question of what we didn't have: what we didn't have was enough Republican congressmen.

> The 292 Democrats in Congress were potential supporters—that was only three fewer than LBJ had. But with the close election and the drop in approval, they remained that way: potential. We couldn't force them to be active supporters.[24]

As the most volatile leadership resource, public approval is the factor most likely to determine whether or not an opportunity for policy change exists. Public approval makes other resources more efficacious. The president's party is more likely to be responsive if the chief executive is high in public esteem, the public is more easily moved, and legislative skills become more effective. Thus, public approval is the resource that has the most potential to turn a typical situation into one favorable for change.

The fact that presidential approval is an important potential source of influence in Congress provides a strong incentive for the president to try to gain popular support. But, as we learned earlier, presidential approval is an effective source of presidential influence, but not one that can be easily manipulated.

### Mandates

Another indicator of the public's opinion of the president is the results of the presidential election. Electoral mandates can be powerful symbols in American politics. They accord added legitimacy and credibility to the newly elected president's proposals. Moreover, concerns for both representation and political survival encourage members of Congress to support the president if they feel the people have spoken.

More important, mandates change the premises of decisions. Following the 1932 election, the essential question became how government should act to fight the depression rather than whether it should act. Similarly, following the 1964 election, the dominant question in Congress was not whether to pass new social programs, but rather how many to pass and how much to increase spending. In 1981 the tables were turned. Ronald Reagan's victory placed a stigma on big government and exalted the unregulated marketplace and large defense efforts. Reagan had won a major victory even before the first congressional vote.

Although presidential elections can structure choices for Congress, merely winning an election does not give a president a mandate. Every election produces a winner, but mandates are much less common. Even large electoral victories such as Richard Nixon's in 1972 and Ronald Reagan's in 1984 carry no guarantee that Congress will interpret the results as mandates from the people to support the president's programs, especially if the voters also elect majorities in Congress from the other party.

The winners in presidential elections usually claim to have been accorded a mandate, of course, but in the absence of certain conditions few observers accept these assertions at face value. Conditions that promote the perception of a mandate include a large margin of victory, the impression of long coattails, hyperbole in the press analyses of the election results exaggerating the one-sidedness of the victory, a surprisingly large victory accompanying a change in parties in the White House, a campaign oriented around a major change in public policy, and the consistency of the new president's program with the prevailing tides of opinion in both the country and his party.

Since it is unusual for these conditions to be met (Bill Clinton's 1992 election was accompanied only by the last two), perceptions of mandates are rarely strong. Presidents can do little about these perceptions. Some are simply elected under more favorable conditions for legislative leadership than others. When mandates do occur or are effectively claimed, the issue becomes one of exploiting the special opportunities they provide.

## PRESIDENTIAL LEGISLATIVE SKILLS

In this section of our discussion of presidential influence in Congress we examine other White House efforts to persuade members of Congress to support the president's legislative proposals. Some of these activities are aimed at building goodwill in the long run and others at obtaining votes from individual members of Congress on specific issues. Whatever the immediate goal, the nature of the legislative process in America demands that presidents apply their legislative skills in a wide range of situations. In the words of one presidential aide:

> Senator A might come with us if Senator B, an admired friend, could be persuaded to talk to him. Senator C wanted a major project out of Chairman D's committee; maybe D, a supporter of our bill, would release it in exchange for C's commitment. Senator E might be reached through people in his home state. If Senator F could not vote with us on final passage, could he vote with us on key amendments? Could G take a trip? Would the President call Senator H?[25]

### Congressional Liaison

Although the Constitution establishes separate institutions, the operation of the government requires those institutions to work together. Presidents are expected to propose legislation and to get it enacted into law. As our previous discussion suggests, they need all the help they can get. To assist them in these efforts as well as with their other ongoing legislative responsibilities, a congressional liaison staff, based in the White House, has operated since 1953. The size of this staff and the duties it performs have expanded significantly in recent years.

The growth of the president's liaison mechanism has occurred in three stages. In its initial phase during the Eisenhower administration, the congressional relations office was small in size, adopted a low profile, and utilized a bipartisan approach in dealing with Congress. Wary of infringing on the legislature's prerogatives or of operating on its turf, the president's agents worked by telephone from the White House rather than in the halls of Congress, communicated mainly with and through the legislative leadership, and used gentle persuasion rather than arm twisting to achieve their goals. Eisenhower himself was not heavily involved in the details of legislation, although he did have contact with members of Congress, especially with the Republican leaders.

The congressional relations office assumed a more aggressive posture in its second phase, which occurred during the Kennedy–Johnson years. With a larger and more comprehensive legislative agenda to advocate, the staff expanded its size and its functions. In addition to pushing major White House policy initiatives, the president's liaison team began funneling legislative views into the executive decision-making process. The increasing development of policy by the White House made this input desirable from a congressional perspective.

Presidential assistants involved in legislation became more numerous, more visible, and more partisan. Attempts were made to organize executive department and agency liaison staffs more effectively behind the president's major priorities. Pressures were exerted on committee chairs, informal legislative groups, and, in general, on more members on more issues. Rewards were also more generously bestowed. "The White House certainly remembers who its friends are," Lawrence F. O'Brien, head of the office, both warned and promised legislators early in the Kennedy administration.[26]

In an effort to improve the atmosphere for the administration on Capitol Hill and to meet an increasing need of Congress, the White House began providing casework services for members and their staffs. This care and feeding operation soon became a congressional expectation, one that subsequent White Houses could not shirk. Social lobbying increased as well.

By the end of the 1960s certain functions had come to be regarded as traditional liaison activities. In addition to catering to the constituency needs of members of Congress, these included gathering intelligence, tracking legislation, coordinating department and agency efforts, and working with the leadership on priority programs. These functions continue to be performed today, but the level of White House involvement and the scope of its activities have expanded even further. The principal reason for that expansion is the difficulty that contemporary presidents have had in mobilizing majority coalitions in support of their policy proposals.

Phase three in the evolution of the presidency's liaison mechanism began in the Carter administration. Frustrated by its inability to get Congress to enact its policy recommendations in the first year and a half of the administration, the Carter White House began to broaden its interaction with Congress and utilize outside forces to help build legislative support. The president increased the size of his congressional relations office despite his highly publicized reduction of White House personnel. Internal task forces on key initiatives were formed to coordinate the administration's congressional activities. A mechanism for setting priorities for highly visible issues was established. More sophisticated information retrieval systems and computerized mail logs were developed to process congressional mail and assess voting patterns. Even the president, a private person by nature, began to interact more regularly with members of Congress, particularly the leadership.

In conjunction with these changes, other presidential offices got more involved with Congress and the legislative process. Although it did not solicit congressional views, the president's domestic policy staff became more receptive to them. Members of Congress and their staffs were given opportunities to affect the development of proposed legislation *before* it was sent to Congress. A public liaison office was established to organize outside groups[27] and community leaders into coalitions behind the administration's proposals. Once established, these coalitions, orchestrated by the White House, mounted grass-roots efforts and directed them toward Congress. They identified the positions of members on key issues, targeted those who were wavering, had them contacted by group representatives from their own constituencies, and supplemented these activities by organizing mass letter-writing and telephoning campaigns. These constituency-based pressures were designed to make it easier for members of Congress to vote with the president regardless of their party affiliation.

During the Reagan presidency, especially the first term, a legislative strategy group, consisting of senior presidential aides, operated out of the chief of staff's office to coordinate these "outreach" efforts and tie them to administrative lobbying on Capitol Hill. Other White House offices, in addition to congressional relations and public liaison, also got involved in congressional affairs. A newly constituted political office handled patronage and other party-related matters while an intergovernmental affairs office orchestrated state and local officials behind other administration initiatives.

The Bush administration did not orchestrate its congressional liaison operation as precisely or as effectively as did the Reagan administration. There was no legislative strategy group. Rather, key White House staff were given responsibility for negotiating and lobbying major legislative initiatives: Richard Darman, the OMB director, took the lead on budget matters; Roger Porter, assistant to the president for domestic and economic policy, handled the Clean Air Act and other domestic legislation; James Baker, secretary of state, oversaw most legislation that affected U.S. foreign policy and was heavily involved in the lobbying preceding the vote to authorize the use of force in the Persian Gulf; John Sununu, chief of staff, was involved on all major issues. The legislative affairs office dealt with more routine matters, including congressional correspondence, social invitations, and vote counts. Fred McClure, head of the office, provided the president with information on potential congressional reactions to his decisions, especially vetoes.

Bill Clinton appointed an experienced Washington lobbyist, Howard Paster, as head of his legislative affairs office. Despite a liaison staff recruited from Congress, Democratic control of both houses, and a president who indicated that he wanted to work closely with legislators to end government gridlock, the Clinton liaison effort ran into trouble initially. It failed to alert the president to Republican opposition to his economic stimulus plan and to the problems that some of his nominees encountered in their Senate confirmation hearings. In addition to misreading some of Congress' intentions, the office irritated Republican and junior Democratic members of Congress with its strategy of dealing primarily with the Democratic leadership on major presidential initiatives. Paster was accused of being too detail-oriented, too willing to compromise, and too liberal. These accusations, combined with the difficulty Clinton encountered with recalcitrant members of Congress, forced senior White House aides, particularly chief of staff Thomas "Mac" McLarty, and some department heads to play an increasing liaison role with Congress. The president also became an active lobbyist on behalf of his major legislative initiatives as did his wife on health care. He met with and called numerous legislators prior to key votes. As a result, Congress eventually passed many of Clinton's first year proposals, but often only after a difficult battle.

In summary, congressional liaison has developed and expanded because it serves the needs of *both* executive and legislative branches. For the Congress, it helps integrate legislative views into executive policy making, services constituency needs, forces presidents to indicate their legislative priorities, provides channels for reaching compromises, and helps the leadership to form majority coalitions. For presidents, it enables them to gain a congressional perspective, to communicate their views to Congress, to mobilize support for their programs, and to reach accommodations with the legislature. Such efforts to bridge the constitutional separation have helped to overcome some of the hurdles in the formulation of public policy.

We now turn to the particular legislative techniques that presidents and their liaison aides must utilize in their efforts to win support for the administration's proposals on Capitol Hill.

### Personal Appeals

A special aspect of presidential involvement in the legislative process is the personal appeal for votes. According to presidential scholar Richard Neustadt, "When the chips are down, there is no substitute for the President's own footwork, his personal negotiation, his direct appeal, his voice and no other's on the telephone."[28] Members of Congress are as subject to flattery as other people and are impressed when the president calls.

Calls from the president must be relatively rare to maintain their usefulness. They will have less impact if they are made too often. Moreover, members might begin to expect calls, for which the president has limited time, or they may resent too much high-level pressure being applied to them. On the other hand, they may exploit a call and say that they are uncertain about an issue in order to extract a favor from the president.

Presidents become intensely involved only after the long process of lining up votes is almost done and their calls are needed to win on an important issue, a situation that arises only a few times a year. A good example occurred on the House vote on the budget reconciliation bill in 1993. President Clinton focused on key members of Congress, whose votes served as cues for other members, and members who were un-committed or weakly committed in either direction. These members were identified by studying the head counts prepared by the White House congressional liaison office and the congressional party whips. The president was able to garner a few votes and eked out a narrow victory.

Despite the prestige of their office, their invocations of national interest, and their persuasiveness, presidents often fail in their personal appeals. President Eisenhower liked to depend heavily on charm and reason. In 1953 he tried to persuade Republican chairman Daniel Reed of the House Ways and Means Committee to support the continuance of the excess profits tax and to oppose a tax cut. "I used every possible reason, argument, and device, and every kind of personal and indirect contact," he wrote, "to bring Chairman Reed to my way of thinking." But he failed.[29] Lyndon Johnson was renowned for his persuasiveness but nevertheless failed on many issues, ranging from civil rights and education to Medicare and the Panama uprising. "No matter how many times I told Congress to do something," he wrote, "I could never force it to act."[30] If Eisenhower and Johnson often failed in their efforts at persuasion, we should not be surprised that other presidents did also.

### Bargaining

It is part of the conventional wisdom that the White House regularly "buys" votes through bargains struck with members of Congress. There can be no question that many bargains occur and that they take a variety of forms. Reagan's budget director, David Stockman, recalled that "the last 10 or 20 percent of the votes needed for a majority of both houses [on the 1981 tax cut] had to be bought, period." The concessions for members of Congress included special breaks for oil-lease holders, real estate tax shelters, and generous tax loopholes for corporations. "The hogs were really feeding," he declared. "The greed level, the level of opportunism, just got out of control."[31] Nevertheless, bargaining, in the form of trading support on two or more policies or providing specific benefits for representatives and senators, occurs less often and plays a less critical role in the creation of presidential coalitions in Congress than one might think. For obvious reasons, the White House does not want to encourage the type of bargaining Stockman described.

The president cannot bargain with Congress as a whole because it is too large and decentralized for one bargain to satisfy everyone. Also, the president's time is limited, as are the administration's resources—only so many appointive jobs are available and the federal budget is limited. Moreover, funding for public works projects is in the hands of Congress. Thus, most of the bargains that are reached are implicit. The lack of respectability surrounding bargaining also encourages implicitness.

In addition, if many direct bargains are struck, word will rapidly spread, everyone will want to trade, and persuasive efforts will fail. A good example occurred in 1993 when President Clinton proposed to increase user fees for grazing and mineral rights on federal land. After protests from Western senators, whose votes he needed for his budget, the president told them he would remove the fees from his budget and deal with them separately in a bill later in the session. His decision opened a Pandora's box because it signaled to every interest group in Washington that he would cave in to pressure. He was quickly inundated with requests to change his budget in other ways, particularly his proposed energy tax. The word was out that the president could be "rolled."

Fortunately for the president, bargaining with everyone in Congress is not necessary. Except on vetoes and treaties, only a simple majority of those voting is needed. A large part of Congress can be "written off" on any given vote. Moreover, as we have seen, presidents generally start with a substantial core of party support and then add to this number those of the other party who agree with their views on ideological or policy grounds. Others may provide support on the basis of goodwill that a president has generated through White House services, constituency interest, or because of high levels of public support. Thus, the president needs to bargain only if all these groups do not provide a majority for crucial votes, and bargaining is needed only with enough people to provide that majority.

Since resources are scarce, presidents will usually try to use them for bargaining with powerful members of Congress, such as committee chairs or those whose votes are the most important. There is no guarantee that a tendered bargain will be accepted, however. The members may not desire what the president offers, or they may be able to obtain what they want on their own. This is, of course, particularly true of the most powerful members, whose support the president needs most. Sometimes members of Congress do not want to trade at all because of constituency opinion or personal views. At other times the president is unwilling to bargain.

Most of the pressure for bargaining actually comes from the Hill. When the White House calls and asks for support, representatives and senators frequently raise a question regarding some request that they have made. In the words of a presidential aide, "Every time we make a special appeal to a Congressman to change his position, he eventually comes back with a request for a favor ranging in importance from one of the President's packages of matches to a judgeship or cabinet appointment for a 'worthy constituent'."[32]

More general bargains also take place. In the words of Nixon's chief congressional aide, William Timmons: "I think they [members of Congress] knew that we would try our best to help them on all kinds of requests if they supported the President, and we did. It kind of goes without saying." His successor in the Ford administration, Max Friedersdorf, added his assurance that people who want things want to be in the position of supporting the president. This implicit trading on "accounts" is more common than explicit bargaining.[33]

For the White House, a member of Congress indebted to the president is easier to approach and ask for a vote. For the member, previous support increases the chances of a request being honored. Thus, office holders at both ends of Pennsylvania Avenue want to be in the other's favor. The degree of debt determines the strategy used in presidential requests for support. Although services and favors increase the president's chances of obtaining support, they are not usually exchanged for votes directly. They are strategic and not tactical weapons.

### Services and Amenities

Since a member of Congress who is indebted to the president is easier to approach and ask for a vote, the White House provides many services and amenities for representatives and senators. Although these favors may be bestowed on any member of Congress, they actually go disproportionately to members of the president's party. Personal amenities used to create goodwill include social contact with the president, flattery, rides on Air Force One, visits to Camp David, birthday greetings, theater tickets for the presidential box at the Kennedy Center, invitations to bill-signing ceremonies, pictures with the president, briefings, and a plethora of others, the number and variety of which are limited only by the imagination of the president and his staff.

Also, the White House often helps members of Congress with their constituents. A wide range of services is offered, including greetings to elderly and other "worthy" constituents, signed presidential photographs, presidential tie clasps and other White House memorabilia, reprints of speeches, information about government programs, White House pressure on agencies in favor of constituents, passing the nominations of constituents on to agencies, influence on local editorial writers, ceremonial appointments to commissions, meetings with the president, and arguments to be used to explain votes to constituents. The president may also help members of Congress please constituents through patronage, pork-barrel projects and government contracts, and aid with legislation of special interest to particular constituencies.

Campaign aid is yet another service the White House can provide party members, and the president may dangle it before them to entice support. This aid may come in various forms, including campaign speeches by the president and executive officials for congressional candidates, funds and advice from the party national committees, presidential endorsements, pictures with the president, and letters of appreciation from the president. Some aid is more ingenious, as when Lawrence O'Brien, then postmaster general, held a stamp dedication ceremony, complete with parade and associated festivities, in Representative Stan Greigg's hometown in 1966.

All administrations are not equally active in providing services and amenities for members of Congress. The Johnson and Reagan White Houses fall on the "active" end of this spectrum while the Nixon and Carter presidencies fall on the other end. Yet the important point is that any such differences are relatively small in comparison to the efforts made by every recent administration to develop goodwill among its party members in Congress. Although this activity is to presidents' advantage and may earn them a fair hearing and the benefit of the doubt in some instances, party members consider it their right to receive benefits from the White House and are unlikely to be especially responsive to the president as a result.

## Pressure

In 1982 one of President Reagan's aides told of how he persuaded two Republican members of the House to vote for the president's budget cuts. The representatives feared the political repercussions in their constituencies of supporting the president, so the aide promised them the maximum campaign aid the law allows a party to give a candidate and won their votes. When asked what would have happened if the congressmen had not given in, the aide replied, "I would have nailed them to the wall."[34]

Thus, just as presidents can offer the carrot, they can also wield the stick. Moreover, the increased resources available to the White House in recent years provide increased opportunities to levy sanctions in the form of the withholding of favors. As the deputy chairman of the Republican National Committee said, there is more money than ever "to play hardball with. We're loaded for bear."[35] The threats of such actions are effective primarily with members of the president's party, of course, because members of the opposition party do not expect to receive many favors from the president.

Although sanctions or threats of sanctions are far from an everyday occurrence, they do happen. These may take the form of excluding a member from White House social events, denying routine requests for White House tour tickets, and shutting off access to the president. Each of these personal slights sends a signal of presidential displeasure. More dramatically, after Democratic Senator Richard Shelby complained about President Clinton's budget package, the White House announced that it was moving the management team for a space shuttle contract from Alabama to Texas, a loss of jobs for the senator's state. To add insult to injury, Senator Shelby was given only one ticket to the White House ceremony honoring the University of Alabama football team; Senator Howell Heflin, Alabama's other senator, was given eleven.

Heavy-handed arm twisting is unusual, however. More typical is the orchestration of pressure by others. The Reagan White House was especially effective in this regard. Operating through party channels, its Political Affairs Office, and its Office of Public Liaison, the administration was able to generate pressure from party members' constituents, campaign contributors, political activists, business leaders, state officials, interest groups, party officials, and, of course, cabinet members. The Clinton administration has tried the same strategy, but with much less success in the early months of the administration.

Despite the resources available to presidents, if members of Congress wish to oppose them, there is little the White House can do to stop them. This is true for those in the president's party as well as those in the opposition. The primary reason is that the parties are highly decentralized; national party leaders do not control those aspects of politics that are of vital concern to members of Congress: nominations and elections. Members of Congress are largely self-recruited, gain their party's nominations by their own efforts and not the party's, and provide most of the money and organizational support needed for their elections. Presidents can do little to influence the results of these activities, and usually they don't even try. As President Kennedy said in 1962, "Party loyalty or responsibility means damn little. They've got to take care of themselves first. They [House members] all have to run this year—I don't and I couldn't hurt most of them if I wanted to."[36]

### Consultation

Consulting with members of Congress on legislation can be advantageous for the White House. Members of Congress appreciate advance warning of presidential proposals, especially those that affect their constituencies directly. No official, especially an elected one, wants to be blindsided. Politicians quite naturally want to be prepared to take credit or avoid blame. Moreover, when a policy fails, members of Congress are unlikely to support the president in the perilous landing of the policy if they are not involved in the take-off.

Consultation before announcing a bill may also be useful in anticipating congressional objections. It may, in fact, be possible to preempt some of the opposition with strategic compromises and to garner some advance commitments. At the very least, members of Congress will feel that they have had an opportunity to be heard. They take pride in their work and may be offended if they feel the White House has not taken them seriously.

Despite these advantages, presidential consultation with Congress has often played a modest role in presidential–congressional relations.[37] It is not easy to do. Arriving at a common position within the executive branch may tax the resources and patience of the White House, particularly at a time when other exigencies press on the president and senior staff. Extending the negotiations to the legislature (and thus the public) and broadening the conflict may render the process of policy formulation unmanageable and increase its costs significantly. White House officials often are also concerned with the nature of Congress, which they often view as parochial, sieve-like, and prone to transforming important matters of state into pork-barrel issues.

An additional challenge is determining with whom the White House should consult. The decentralization of power within Congress presents a substantial burden to executive branch officials wishing to consult with all the relevant members of Congress, especially on jurisdictionally complex matters. In some cases even identifying the appropriate senators and representatives is difficult.

Time is an ever-present factor in White House operations, and it influences consultation with Congress as well. If severe deadlines are imposed on the production of a presidential initiative, such as the 1977 energy proposal, consultation may be difficult. At least fifty congressional staff members, recommended by key members of Congress, participated in President Clinton's task force on health care, which was unveiled eight months after taking office. In contrast, few members were consulted on the president's earlier economic stimulus package or his original budget proposal. In addition, a president with an extensive legislative agenda may send a large number of bills to Congress, restricting the time officials can devote to consulting on any one of them.

A president with firm ideas on policy is unlikely to relish consulting with Congress in order to make compromises to satisfy congressional desires. In addition, some presidential proposals are designed by the White House to assuage constituency groups or fulfill campaign promises, which significantly constrains the possibilities of modification of these bills in response to congressional consultation.

Some observers propose that the White House involve relevant members of Congress in the process of developing the president's legislative program, the rationale being that those who have been involved in formulating a bill are more likely to support it once it is sent to the Hill. This process is not typical, however, because chief executives have found it too cumbersome to include members of Congress, especially those of the opposition party, in writing legislation, and most members of Congress prefer to protect their status as members of an independent branch.

### Setting Priorities

An important aspect of a president's legislative strategy can be establishing priorities among legislative proposals. The goal of this effort is to set the congressional agenda. If the president is not able to focus the attention of Congress on his priority programs, these bills may become lost in the complex and overloaded legislative process. Congress needs time to digest what the president sends, time to come up with independent analysis, time to schedule hearings and markups of bills. Unless the president gives some indication of what is most important, Congress will simply put the proposals in a queue and they will compete with each other for attention, often with disastrous results for the president.

This is especially likely to be a problem if much of the president's program must go through a single committee, as was the case for Jimmy Carter and the House Ways and Means Committee in 1977. Thus, it is wise to spread legislative proposals among several committees so they can be working on different parts of the president's agenda at the same time.

Setting priorities is also important because presidents and their staff can lobby effectively for only a few bills at once. Moreover, the president's political capital is inevitably limited, and it is sensible to focus it on the issues the administration cares about most. In 1977 Jimmy Carter spent his political capital on ending pork-barrel water projects, not one of his priority items. In 1993 Bill Clinton risked losing focus on his economic and health care programs by proposing a host of controversial policies on abortion, gays in the military, campaign reform, and environmental protection, among others. Many of these policies were in response to pressures from segments of his party for action after twelve years of Republican presidents.

It is particularly important that priorities be clearly established in the first year in office when presidential influence in Congress is likely to be greatest. After the transition period more items are likely to be on the agenda. In 1981 Ronald Reagan focused attention on his priority programs and obtained passage of a large tax cut, a substantial increase in defense expenditures, and sizable decreases in the rate of spending increases for domestic policies. By 1982, however, the "honeymoon" was over and the legislative agenda was crowded.

The White House can put off dealing with the full spectrum of national issues for a period of months at the beginning of the term of a new president, but it cannot do so indefinitely. Eventually it must make decisions about them. By the second year the agenda is full and more policies are in the pipeline as the administration attempts to satisfy its constituencies and responds to unanticipated or simply overlooked problems. Presidents like Bill Clinton with large legislative agendas and more diverse political constituencies find it more difficult to set priorities than those, like Ronald Reagan, with only a small number of proposals and relatively homogeneous supporters.

Moreover, presidents themselves may distract from their own legislative priorities. They have so many demands to speak and decide on issues that it is impossible for White House schedulers to organize their schedules to focus the attention of Congress and the public for an extended period of times on their major goals. As Clinton White House Communications Director George Stephanopolous put it,

> On the campaign trail, you can just change the subject. But you can't just change the subject as President. You can't wish Bosnia away. You can't wish David Koresh away. You can't just ignore them and change the subject.[38]

Congress is also quite capable of setting its own agenda, providing competition for the president's proposals. Of the thirteen major legislative actions (as defined by *Congressional Quarterly*) of the Ninety-ninth Congress (1985–1986), the White House took the lead on only one of them. In 1987 President Reagan found Congress already working on the two primary domestic policy initiatives for his last two years in office, catastrophic health insurance and welfare reform.

### Moving Fast

As noted, the president should move quickly to exploit the honeymoon atmosphere that typically characterizes the early months of a new administration. First-year proposals have a better chance of passing Congress than do those sent to the Hill later in an administration. Lyndon Johnson explained, "You've got to give it all you can in that first year. . . . You've got just one year when they treat you right."[39]

The danger, of course, is proposing a policy without thorough analysis in order to exploit the favorable political climate of the honeymoon. This appears to have occurred with the budget cuts Reagan proposed in early 1981. The departments, including cabinet members, and their expertise were kept at a distance in the executive decision-making process. Although taking time to draft proposals does not guarantee that they will be well conceived, it is by no means clear that rapid drafting of legislation is in the best interests of the nation.

It is easier for a president who has a small agenda and one that is essentially negative in character, such as Ronald Reagan's agenda of cutting taxes or spending, to exploit the honeymoon. It is much more difficult to draft complex legislation rapidly, a problem Jimmy Carter faced in his first year when he tried to deal with issues such as energy, welfare reform, and the containment of health costs. Bill Clinton faced similar problems with his health care reform program. Kennedy and Johnson had the advantage of a party program that had been building up during the 1950s when the Democrats were not in the White House.

### Structuring Choice

Framing issues in ways that favor the president's programs may set the terms of the debate and thus the premises on which members of Congress cast their votes. The key vote on Ronald Reagan's budget cuts in 1981 was on the rule determining whether there would be a single vote of yea or nay in the House. Once the rule was adopted, the White House could frame the issue as a vote for or against the popular president, and the broad nature of the reconciliation bill shifted the debate from the losses of individual programs to the benefits of the package as a whole. Although Reagan could not win an important individual vote on cutting a social welfare program, by structuring the choice facing Congress, he needed only to win one vote and could avoid much of the potential criticism for specific reductions in spending.

Portraying policies in terms of criteria on which there is a consensus and playing down divisive issues are often at the core of efforts to structure choices for Congress. Federal aid to education had been a divisive issue for years before President Johnson proposed the Elementary and Secondary Education Act in 1965. To blunt opposition, he successfully changed the focus of debate from teachers' salaries and classroom shortages to fighting poverty and from the separation of church and state to aiding children. This change in the premises of congressional decision making eased the path for the bill.

Although the structuring of choices can be a useful tool for the president, there is no guarantee that it will succeed, and opponents of the president's policies are unlikely to defer to an administration's attempts to structure choices on the issues. Democrats framed the debate over President Bush's proposal to cut taxes on capital gains as being for or against giving benefits to the wealthy, while Republicans were able to frame the debate over President Clinton's 1993 jobs stimulus bill as being for or against high taxes and pork-barrel spending.

### The Context of Influence

In our discussion of the president's legislative skills, it is important that we keep in mind the general context in which a president is forced to operate today, a period characterized by congressional assertiveness. The diminished deference to the president by individual members of Congress and by the institution as a whole naturally makes presidential influence more problematical.

Current presidents also have the misfortune to preside during a period of substantial economic scarcity, whereas the Kennedy–Johnson years were characterized by stable prices, sustained economic growth, and general prosperity. The prosperity of the 1960s provided the federal government with the funds for new policies, with little risk. Taxes did not have to be raised and sacrifices did not have to be made in order to help the underprivileged. Since the late 1970s, resources have been more limited, helping to make the passage of new welfare or health programs, for example, more difficult. When resources are scarce, presidents are faced with internal competition for them and the breakdown of supporting coalitions. They must choose between policies rather than building coalitions for several policies through logrolling.

In light of the above discussion, it is not surprising that the relations of recent presidents with Congress have been characterized often by stalemate. The environment for presidential influence has been deteriorating.

### Impact of Legislative Skills

In general, presidential legislative skills must compete, as does public support, with other, more stable factors that affect voting in Congress, including party, ideology, personal views and commitments on specific policies, and constituency interests. By the time a president tries to exercise influence on a vote, most members of Congress have made up their minds on the basis of these other factors.

Systematic studies have found that, once we control for the status of their party in Congress and their standing with the public, presidents renowned for their legislative skills, such as Lyndon Johnson, are no more successful in winning votes, even close ones, or obtaining congressional support than those, such as Jimmy Carter, who are considered to have been less adept in dealing with Congress.[40] Even skilled presidents cannot change the contours of the political landscape and create opportunities for change very much. Yet they can recognize favorable configurations of political forces, such as existed in 1933, 1965, and 1981, and effectively exploit them to embark on major shifts in public policy.

## THE VETO

Sometimes presidents not only fail to win passage of their proposals but Congress passes legislation to which they are strongly opposed. Since all bills and joint resolutions except those proposing constitutional amendments must be presented to the president for approval, the president has another opportunity to influence legislation: the veto.

When Congress passes an item that must be submitted to the president, the president has several options. Within ten days (Sundays excepted) of its presentation the president may (1) sign the measure, in which case it becomes the law of the land; (2) withhold his signature and return the measure to the house in which it originated with a message stating the reasons for withholding approval; or (3) do nothing.

A bill or joint resolution that the president returns to Congress has been *vetoed*. It can then become law only if each house of Congress repasses it by a two-thirds majority of those present. Congress may override the presidential veto at any time before it adjourns *sine die* (that is, before the end of that particular Congress).

Early presidents exercised their veto power sparingly and ostensibly for the purpose of voiding legislation they deemed to be unconstitutional in its content or sloppy and improper in design. The first six presidents vetoed a total of eight bills; the seventh president, Andrew Jackson, vetoed twelve. Jackson used his negative to prevent legislation he opposed from becoming law. His example was followed by others.

The president can veto only an entire bill. Unlike most state governors, presidents do not have an item veto, which allows just specific provisions of a bill to be vetoed. As a result of this constraint, members of Congress use a number of strategies to avoid a possible veto of a particular proposal. For example, Congress may add increased appropriations or riders (i.e., nongermane provisions) that the White House might not want to bills that it otherwise desires, forcing the president to decide whether to accept these unattractive provisions in order to gain the legislation. In most such cases, presidents do not use their vetoes. For example, after President Carter vetoed a bill providing for increased salaries for Public Health Service physicians, Congress added the pay raise to mental health services legislation, a pet project of First Lady Rosalyn Carter. The president signed the bill.

In 1987 Congress passed the entire discretionary budget of the federal government in one omnibus bill. The president had to accept the whole package or lose appropriations for the entire government. President Reagan frequently called for a constitutional amendment giving the president an item veto, and Presidents Bush and Clinton have followed his example. They have argued that an item veto would allow the president to stop unnecessary spending within massive appropriations bills and thus help to bring the budget under control. Yet Congress is reluctant to give the president additional power, and there is reason to expect that the legislature could easily devise methods of protecting appropriations in danger of being vetoed.

If the president does nothing after receiving a measure from Congress, it becomes law after ten days (Sundays excepted) if Congress remains in session. If it has adjourned during the ten-day period, thus preventing the president from returning the bill to the house of its origination, the bill is *pocket vetoed*. A pocket veto kills a piece of legislation just as a regular veto does. Historically somewhat fewer than half of all vetoes have been pocket vetoes. Table 10-5 presents data on the vetoes by recent presidents.

Presidents have sometimes attempted to use the pocket veto by taking no action on measures sent to them just before Congress went into a temporary recess, claiming that the recess prevented them from returning their veto for congressional consideration. (In 1964 President Johnson pocket vetoed a bill during a congressional recess and then recalled and signed it.) However, in 1976 after the Nixon and Ford White Houses had lost litigation on the issue, the Ford administration promised that the president would not use the pocket veto during congressional recesses as long as an official of Congress was designated to be on hand to receive his vetoes. Since Congress is in session nearly all year, most people thought only an adjournment *sine die* would provide the opportunity for a pocket veto. Ronald Reagan used the pocket veto during a recess at the end of the 1981 session without apparent problems, but thirty-three House Democrats filed suit in federal court to challenge his pocket veto during the congressional recess at the end of 1983 of a bill making aid to El Salvador dependent on human rights

Table 10-5. Regular and Pocket Vetoes

| President | Regular Vetoes | Pocket Vetoes | Total Vetoes |
|---|---|---|---|
| Eisenhower | 73 | 108 | 181 |
| Kennedy | 12 | 9 | 21 |
| Johnson | 16 | 14 | 30 |
| Nixon | 26 | 17 | 43 |
| Ford | 48 | 18 | 66 |
| Carter | 13 | 18 | 31 |
| Reagan | 39 | 39 | 78 |
| Bush | 31 | 15 | 46 |

progress. In 1984 a federal appeals court ruled against the president. President Bush also claimed to have pocket vetoed some bills during congressional recesses, but Congress treated them like regular vetoes.

The last column in Table 10-5 indicates that vetoes are infrequently used. Not only are the absolute numbers low, but fewer than 1 percent of the bills passed by Congress (which number several hundred per session) are vetoed. The table also shows that presidents who faced Congresses controlled by the opposition party (Eisenhower, Nixon, Ford, Reagan, and Bush) used more vetoes, as we would expect. They were more likely to be presented with legislation that they opposed. Bill Clinton vetoed no bills in his first year in office.

Table 10-6 illustrates another important fact about vetoes. Regular vetoes are generally sustained, but overriding does occur, especially when the president's party is in the minority in Congress. Some very important legislation has been passed over the president's veto. In the post–World War II era such legislation includes the Taft–Hartley Labor Relations Act (1947), the McCarran–Walter Immigration Act (1952), the McCarran–Wood Internal Security Act (1950), and the War Powers Resolution (1973).

Sometimes presidents choose not to veto a bill either because, as mentioned earlier, they feel the good in the legislation outweighs the

Table 10-6. Vetoes Overridden

| President | Regular Vetoes | Vetoes Overridden | Percentage of Vetoes Overridden |
|---|---|---|---|
| Eisenhower | 73 | 2 | 3 |
| Kennedy | 12 | 0 | 0 |
| Johnson | 16 | 0 | 0 |
| Nixon | 26 | 7 | 27 |
| Ford | 48 | 12 | 25 |
| Carter | 13 | 2 | 15 |
| Reagan | 39 | 9 | 23 |
| Bush | 31 | 1 | 3 |

bad or because they do not want their veto to be overridden. Thus, President Ford did not veto the 1975 food stamp legislation, which he opposed, because only forty-six members of the House and Senate had supported his own proposal.

When a bill is introduced in either house of Congress, the chamber's parliamentarian classifies it as public or private. Generally, public bills relate to public matters and deal with individuals by classifications or categories, such as college students or the elderly. A private bill, on the other hand, names a particular individual or entity who is to receive relief, such as payment of a pension or a claim against the government or the granting of citizenship. Up until 1969 presidents usually vetoed more private than public bills. Recent presidents have vetoed very few private bills, however.

The veto is an inherently negative element in the president's arsenal, but sometimes it may be used to shape legislation. Presidents frequently veto or threaten to veto bills unless certain provisions are removed or altered. President Bush, a Republican facing large Democratic majorities in Congress, repeatedly made strategic use of the veto to move Congress in his direction. In a typical example, he vetoed a substantial increase in the federal minimum wage in 1989. This encouraged Congress to pass a more modest increase, one acceptable to the president. In a more unusual situation, President Reagan threatened to veto the omnibus appropriations bill in 1987, which contained the money necessary for running the government for the following year, if Congress did not include certain provisions that he favored. Fearing a shutdown of the government, Congress acquiesced.

Once exercised, the veto's usefulness as a threat ends and the chances of the president's obtaining positive action from Congress are substantially diminished. In 1988 Reagan vetoed the defense authorization bill because he objected to some funding provisions and restrictions on his discretion in procurement and arms control. Angered because it felt the president had violated an agreement on the bill and was grandstanding to aid George Bush's presidential campaign, Congress repassed the bill with essentially cosmetic changes. Moreover, the veto threat must be exercised with caution lest it be used too often and be too easily overcome. Thus, although a president's vetoes are normally successful in stopping legislation, they are less effective when used as inducements to pass legislation that the White House desires, and they are utilized in this way only in exceptional cases.

## CONCLUSION

Presidents face an uphill battle in dealing with Congress. Their formal powers of recommending legislation to Congress and vetoing bills help set the legislature's agenda and prevent some of what they oppose from passing. Yet these prerogatives are of only marginal help.

Conflict between the executive and legislative branches is inherent in the U.S. system of government. The overlapping powers of the two branches, their representation of different constituencies, the contrast of the hierarchical, expert nature of the executive and the decentralized, generalist Congress, and different time frames within which they operate guarantee that, except in extraordinary circumstances, conflict between them will remain a central feature of American politics.

The chief executive's assets in dealing with Congress are unimpressive. Party leadership is a potential source of influence in Congress, and presidents receive considerably more support from members of their party than from the opposition. Much, or even most, of this support is the result of members of the same party sharing similar policy views rather than the influence of the president's party leadership. Nevertheless, presidents work closely with their party and its leaders in Congress and gain some increment of support as a result of party loyalty. Party support is undependable, however, as constituency interests, a lack of policy consensus, and other factors intervene and diminish the importance of the party label. Congressional party leaders are typically in weak positions to move their troops in the president's direction. Ideally, presidents could influence the election of members of their party to Congress, but presidential coattails are very short and midterm campaigning seems to have limited payoffs. Thus, presidents generally have to seek support from opposition party members, but their efforts at bipartisanship, although necessary, may strain relations with the less moderate wing of their own party.

Presidents are more likely to receive support in Congress when they have the public's approval than when they sit low in the polls. Unfortunately, as we have seen in Chapter 4, they cannot depend on the public's support, nor can they be sure of being able to mobilize new support. Moreover, public approval is usually a necessary but not a sufficient source of influence. Even when presidents are high in the polls, they will find it difficult to pass their programs if their party lacks a substantial number of congressional seats.

The White House engages in a large-scale legislative liaison effort to create goodwill and influence votes on a more personal level. Bargains are consummated, services and amenities are provided, arms are twisted, presidential phone calls are made, and advance consultation is done. Yet there are severe limits on a president's time and resources. Presidents can also increase the chances of their success by moving programs early in their tenure and not letting those programs clog the legislative process. However, many presidents find it difficult or impossible to control the congressional agenda so neatly. Although presidential legislative skills are crucial in winning some votes, their importance is often exaggerated. Thus, presidents must constantly struggle to succeed in having their policies enacted into law.

Presidential leadership of Congress is at the margins most of the time. In general, successful presidential leadership of Congress has not been the result of the dominant chief executive of political folklore, who reshapes the contours of the political landscape to pave the way for change. Rather than creating the conditions for important shifts in public policy, the effective president is the less heroic figure of the facilitator, who works at the margins building coalitions to recognize and exploit opportunities presented by a favorable configuration of political forces.

The president remains an important influence on Congress but rarely dominates it. Ronald Reagan was considered a strong chief executive and began with a string of victories in Congress. But after the Democrats won control of the Senate in the 1986 elections and his approval ratings plummeted in the wake of the Iran–Contra scandal, he was successful only 44 percent of the time in 1987 and 47 percent in 1988 in getting measures passed. Budgeting was one of his principal tools for affecting public policy, yet the budgets he proposed to Congress were typically pronounced "DOA"—dead on arrival. George Bush reached record levels of public approval in the wake of the Gulf war in 1991, but his legislative program remained stalled. Members of Congress truly compose an independent branch and in recent years have more often taken the lead in initiating major changes in public policy than the president.

## NOTES

1. Lyndon Johnson, quoted in Doris Kearns, *Lyndon Johnson and the American Dream* (New York: Harper and Row, 1976), p. 226.

2. James Madison, "The Federalist No. 46," in *The Federalist* (New York: Modern Library, 1937), p. 307.

3. See, for example, John W. Kingdon, *Congressmen's Voting Decisions*, 3rd ed. (Ann Arbor, Mich.: University of Michigan Press, 1989); Donald R. Matthews and James A. Stimson, *Yeas and Nays* (New York: Wiley, 1975).

4. Gerald R. Ford, *A Time to Heal: The Autobiography of Gerald R. Ford* (New York: Harper and Row, 1979), p. 150.

5. Richard E. Neustadt, *Presidential Power and the Modern Presidents* (New York: Free Press, 1990), p. 29.

6. Quoted in Paul C. Light, *The President's Agenda: Domestic Policy Choice from Kennedy to Carter* (Baltimore: Johns Hopkins University Press, 1982), p. 135.

7. See Terry Sullivan, "Bargaining with the President: A Simple Game and New Evidence," *American Political Science Review* 84 (December 1990): 1167–96, on party members switching to support the president when he needs their support.

8. Howard Baker, quoted in James L. Sundquist, *The Decline and Resurgence of Congress* (Washington, D.C.: Brookings Institution, 1981), p. 402.

9. Quoted in "Recasting Senate Finance: Moynihan to Take Helm," *Congressional Quarterly Weekly Report*, December 12, 1992, p. 3796.

10. Gerald R. Ford, "Imperiled, Not Imperial," *Time*, November 10, 1980, p. 30.

11. Quoted in Light, *The President's Agenda*, p. 211.

12. See Jeffrey E. Cohen, Michael A. Krassa, and John A. Hamman, "The Impact of Presidential Campaigning on Midterm U.S. Senate Elections," *American Political Science Review* 85 (March 1991): 165–80.

13. George C. Edwards III, *The Public Presidency* (New York: St. Martin's, 1983), pp. 83–93.

14. James E. Campbell and Joe A. Sumners, "Presidential Coattails in Senate Elections," *American Political Science Review* 84 (June 1990): 513–24; Alan I. Abramowitz and Jeffrey A. Segal, *Senate Elections* (Ann Arbor, Mich.: University of Michigan Press, 1992), pp. 121, 233, 238.

15. Jimmy Carter, *Keeping Faith: Memoirs of a President* (New York: Bantam, 1982), p. 80.

16. Emmet John Hughes, *The Living Presidency* (Baltimore: Penguin, 1974), p. 68.

17. Lyndon B. Johnson, *The Vantage Point: Perspectives of the Presidency, 1963–1969* (New York: Popular Library, 1971), p. 443.

18. Ibid., p. 323.

19. Quoted in "Run, Run, Run," *Newsweek*, May 2, 1977, p. 38.

20. Quoted in "Carter Seeks More Effective Use of Departmental Lobbyists' Skills," *Congressional Quarterly Weekly Report*, March 4, 1978, p. 585.

21. Quoted in Sidney Blumenthal, "Marketing the President," *The New York Times Magazine*, September 13, 1981, p. 110.

22. Dom Bonafede, "The Strained Relationship," *National Journal*, May 19, 1979, p. 830.

23. See, for example, CBS News/*The New York Times* Poll, October 30, 1986, tables 21, 27.

24. Quoted in Light, *The President's Agenda*, pp. 29, 31; see, more generally, pp. 28–31.

25. Harry McPherson, *A Political Education* (Boston: Little, Brown, 1972), p. 192.

26. Lawrence F. O'Brien, quoted in Neil McNeil, *Forge of Democracy* (New York: McKay, 1963), p. 260.

27. On this, see Mark A. Peterson, "The Presidency and Organized Interests: White House Patterns of Interest Group Liaison," *American Political Science Review* 86 (September 1992): 612–25.

28. Richard E. Neustadt, "Presidency and Legislation: Planning the President's Program," in Aaron Wildavsky, ed., *The Presidency* (Boston: Little, Brown, 1969), p. 596.

29. Dwight D. Eisenhower, *Mandate for Change, 1953–1956* (New York: Signet, 1963), pp. 254–55.

30. Johnson, *The Vantage Point*, p. 40.

31. David Stockman, *The Triumph of Politics* (New York: Harper and Row, 1986), pp. 251, 253, 260–61, 264–65; see also William Greider, "The Education of David Stockman," *Atlantic Monthly*, December 1981, p. 51.

32. Gary W. Reichard, *The Reaffirmation of Republicanism: Eisenhower and the Eighty-Third Congress* (Knoxville, Tenn.: University of Tennessee Press, 1975), p. 173.

33. William Timmons and Max Friedersdorf, quoted in "Turning Screws: Winning Votes in Congress," *Congressional Quarterly Weekly Report*, April 24, 1976, pp. 952–53.

34. Quoted in "Playing Hardball," *The Wall Street Journal*, August 18, 1982, p. 1.

35. Quoted in ibid.

36. John Kennedy, quoted in Theodore Sorensen, *Kennedy* (New York: Bantam, 1966), p. 387.

37. See Mark A. Peterson, *Legislating Together* (Cambridge, Mass.: Harvard University Press, 1990).

38. Quoted in Thomas L. Friedman and Maureen Dowd, "Amid Setbacks, Clinton Team Seeks to Shake Off the Blues," *New York Times*, April 25, 1993, Sec 1., p. 12.

39. Lyndon Johnson, quoted in McPherson, *A Political Education*, p. 268.

40. George C. Edwards III, *At the Margins: Presidential Leadership of Congress* (New Haven, Conn.: Yale University Press, 1989), chap. 9. See also Jon R. Bond and Richard Fleisher, *The President in the Legislative Agenda* (Chicago: University of Chicago Press, 1990), chap. 8.

## SELECTED READINGS

Edwards, George C., III. *At the Margins: Presidential Leadership of Congress.* New Haven, Conn.: Yale University Press, 1989.

———. *Presidential Influence in Congress.* San Francisco: W. H. Freeman, 1980.

———. *The Public Presidency.* New York: St. Martin's, 1983.

Fisher, Louis. *Constitutional Conflicts between Congress and the President*, 3rd ed. Lawrence, Kans.: University Press of Kansas, 1991.

Jones, Charles O. *The Trusteeship Presidency: Jimmy Carter and the United States Congress*. Baton Rouge, La.: Louisiana State University Press, 1988.

Light, Paul C. *The President's Agenda: Domestic Policy Choice from Kennedy to Carter*. Baltimore: Johns Hopkins University Press, 1982.

Neustadt, Richard E. *Presidential Power and the Modern Presidents*. New York: Free Press, 1990.

Peterson, Mark A. *Legislating Together*. Cambridge, Mass.: Harvard University Press, 1990.

Ragsdale, Lyn. "The Fiction of Congressional Elections as Presidential Events." *American Politics Quarterly* 8 (October 1980): 375–98.

Spitzer, Robert J. *The Presidential Veto*. Albany, N.Y.: State University of New York Press, 1988.

Wayne, Stephen J. *The Legislative Presidency*. New York: Harper and Row, 1978.

West, Darrell M. "Activists and Economic Policymaking in Congress." *American Journal of Political Science* 32 (August 1988): 662–80.

# 11

# The President and the Judiciary

The president's interactions with the Congress and the bureaucracy are constant and receive considerable attention. Relations with the third branch of government, the judiciary, however, are in many ways more intermittent and less visible. Nevertheless, chief executives have important relationships with the courts, with opportunities to influence public policy for years to come through their nominations to the bench. The executive branch, operating through the solicitor general's office, is also a frequent litigant in the federal courts, especially at the Supreme Court level. Such litigation provides another opportunity for the president to influence judicial decisions.

In addition, presidents may end up with responsibility for enforcing court decisions, even though they were not directly involved in them. Sometimes enforcing the law actually means complying with decisions directed at the White House. Although such instances are not common, they may provide moments of high political drama and have important consequences for our political system. Finally, the Constitution gives the president the right to exercise some judicial powers directly through the granting of pardons, amnesty, and clemency for those accused or convicted of federal crimes.

The distinction between the director and facilitator presidential types is less clear in relationships with the judiciary than with Congress. Both the director and facilitator will take advantage of the opportunity to nominate compatible judges to the federal bench, but the director will be able to mold the courts more, moving them to reach decisions of which he approves and to overturn previous decisions that he opposes. The facilitator will be more constrained in placing his first choices on the bench and will not dominate their judicial decision making. His victories will result from the views of the judges he nominates to the bench rather than from his influence over them once they don their judicial robes.

## JUDICIAL SELECTION

The president's primary means of exercising leadership of the judicial branch is the nomination of federal judges. In this section we examine the process of judicial selection for the federal courts and the types of persons who become federal judges.

### Selection of Lower-Court Judges

We begin with the federal district courts and the courts of appeals, which include most federal judges and which handle most federal cases. The president nominates persons to fill these slots for lifetime service. The Senate must confirm each nomination by a majority vote. Because of the Senate's role, the president's discretion ends up being much less than it appears.

Senatorial courtesy is the customary manner in which the Senate disposes of state-level federal nominations for such positions as judgeships and U.S. attorneys. Under this unwritten tradition, nominations for these positions are not confirmed when opposed by a senator from the state in which the nominee is to serve (all states have at least one federal district court) or, in the case of courts of appeals judges, the state of the nominee's residence if the senator is of the same party as the president. To invoke the right of senatorial courtesy, the relevant senator usually simply states a general reason for opposing a nomination. Other senators then honor their colleague's views and oppose the nomination, regardless of their personal views or the candidate's merits.

The first instance of senatorial courtesy occurred in 1789, when President George Washington failed to have Benjamin Fishbourn confirmed as naval officer of the port of Savannah because of the opposition of Georgia's two senators. Since that time senatorial courtesy has become more and more established. By 1840, senators were virtually naming federal district court judges. In addition, at times senatorial courtesy has been successfully invoked by a senator not of the president's party.

A related practice began in the mid-1950s when the Senate Judiciary Committee initiated the practice of circulating a "blue slip" to the senators from the state in which a prospective judge was to serve, asking for permission to hold a hearing. Even those not from the president's party could object to a nominee by not returning the slip to the committee. Senators have not exercised this prerogative very often to defeat a nomination, however, and in 1979 the chairman of the Judiciary Committee, Edward Kennedy, announced that the committee would reserve the right to review independently and overrule a senator's failure to return a slip. Since then the issue has not been pressed by a senator or the White House.

When a president fails to heed the tradition of senatorial courtesy, the results can be embarrassing. On April 1, 1976, President Ford nominated William B. Poff to a federal judgeship in Virginia. Virginia's Republican senator, William Scott, had previously given notice of his opposition to Poff and of his support for another candidate, Glenn Williams. It is important to note that Scott himself agreed that Poff was qualified for the position. He just felt Williams's philosophy was closer to his own. Thus, on April 15 Scott formally announced his opposition to Poff's nomination in a letter to the Senate Judiciary Committee, simply terming Poff "unacceptable." On May 5 the committee chairman, Senator James Eastland, moved to table the nomination, and it was tabled without objection.

Presidents are not without assets in such a situation, but they rarely will find it worthwhile to fight a senator over a district court judgeship. These judges seldom interfere with their policies. If they desire to do so, presidents can refuse to appoint anyone to the position in an attempt to pressure a senator into supporting their nominee in order to avoid a backlog of federal cases in the state. Or they may make an appointment during a congressional recess at the end of a session. Although the nominee must still be confirmed in the next session of Congress, he or she may have had an opportunity to demonstrate such exemplary capabilities on the bench by then that the Senate will look more favorably on the appointment.

Because of the strength of these informal practices, presidents usually check carefully with the relevant senator or senators ahead of time to avoid making a nomination that will fail to be confirmed. In many instances this is tantamount to giving the power of nomination to these senators. Typically, when there is a vacancy for a federal judgeship, the senator (or senators) of the president's party from the state where the judge will serve suggest one or more names to the attorney general and the president. If neither senator is of the president's party, the state's representatives of the president's party or other state party leaders may make suggestions. Then the Department of Justice and the Federal Bureau of Investigation conduct competency and background checks on these persons, and the president usually selects a nominee from those who survive the screening process. It is very difficult for the president to reject the recommendation of a senator of his party in favor of someone else if the person recommended clears the hurdles of professional standing and integrity. Thus, the Constitution is turned on its head and the Senate ends up making nominations, which the president then approves.

The attorney general typically asks the Standing Committee on the Federal Judiciary of the American Bar Association (ABA) for its evaluation of potential nominees. Others have input in judicial selection as well. The ABA committee or the Department of Justice may ask sitting judges, usually federal judges, to evaluate prospective nominees. Sitting judges may also initiate recommendations to advance or retard someone's chances of being nominated. In addition, candidates for the nomination are often active on their own behalf. They have to alert the relevant parties that they desire the position and orchestrate a campaign of support on their behalf. As one appellate judge observed, "People don't get judgeships without seeking them. Anybody who thinks judicial office seeks the man is mistaken. There's not a man on the court who didn't do what he thought needed to be done."[1]

Presidents usually have more influence in the selection of judges to the federal courts of appeals than to federal district courts. Since the decisions of appellate courts are generally more significant than those of lower courts, the president naturally takes a greater interest in appointments to these courts. At the same time, individual senators are in a weaker position to determine who the nominee will be because the jurisdiction of an appeals court encompasses several states. Although custom and pragmatic politics require that these judgeships be apportioned among the states, the president has discretion in how this is done and therefore has a greater role in recruiting appellate judges than district court judges. Even here, however, senators from the state in which the candidate resides may be able to veto a nomination.

Jimmy Carter attempted to alter the role of senators in the judicial selection process. Shortly after his election as president, Carter struck a deal with Senator James Eastland, chairman of the Senate Judiciary Committee, that the president would have a free hand in nominations to the federal courts of appeal but would continue to defer to senators in nominations to the federal district courts. The president then established the United States Circuit Judge Nominating Commission and appointed members to its thirteen panels. Each panel was composed of laypeople as well as lawyers and included women and minorities. When a vacancy occurred, the relevant panel interviewed potential nominees and recommended three to five persons to the president to fill the position, basing their evaluations on broad merit criteria. President Carter made his selection from this list of names.

In 1978 Congress added wording to an act creating new federal judgeships that asked the president to establish standards for selecting federal district court judges and emphasized the importance of merit selection and greater representation for women and minorities. President Carter subsequently requested senators to make special efforts to identify qualified women and minority candidates (although he had no authority to force them to comply). In response, senators from most states adopted the use of nominating commissions to recommend candidates for federal district courts. The selection of members and the composition and operation of the commissions varied widely, as did the use of the names they produced. Nevertheless, states with these commissions produced judges with higher ratings by the ABA and a greater percentage of women and African Americans than states without commissions, although there were notable exceptions on both sides.

Things changed once again following Ronald Reagan's election as president. He abolished the Circuit Judge Nominating Commission and invited the Republican senator(s) from the relevant state (or Republican House members if there was no senator) to identify prospective candidates for federal judgeships. Senators were encouraged to apply screening devices to ensure that their recommendations were based on merit, but he specified no particular type of mechanism. George Bush asked senators to submit three names for each district court appointment and ordered those handling judicial nominations in his administration to open the process to a wide range of qualified people.

### Backgrounds of Lower-Court Judges

What kind of people are selected as judges as a result of this process? The data in Tables 11-1 and 11-2 show that federal judges are not a representative sample of the American people. They are all lawyers (although this is not a constitutional requirement), and they are overwhelmingly white males. Only George Bush and Jimmy Carter have appointed a substantial number of women to the federal bench, and Carter is the only president to have appointed a significant percentage of minority group members. Bill Clinton is likely to exceed Carter's efforts.

Federal judges have also typically held office as a judge or prosecutor, and often they have been involved in partisan politics. This involvement is generally what brings them to the attention of senators and the Department of Justice when they seek nominees for judgeships. As former United States attorney general and circuit court judge Griffin Bell once remarked:

> For me, becoming a federal judge wasn't very difficult. I managed John F. Kennedy's presidential campaign in Georgia. Two of my oldest and closest friends were two senators from Georgia. And I was campaign manager and special, unpaid counsel for the governor.[2]

Perhaps the most striking finding in Tables 11-1 and 11-2 is the fact that presidents rarely appoint someone to a judgeship who does not share their party affiliation. Merit considerations obviously occur after partisan screening. Judgeships are patronage plums that may serve as rewards for political service to either the president or senators of his party, as consolation prizes for unsuccessful candidates, or even to "kick upstairs" an official in order to remove him or her from an executive branch post. When the president nominates someone of the other party for a judgeship, it is usually because of ideological congruity with the nominee or to obtain support in a state where his party is weak.

Partisanship also plays a role in the creation of judgeships. Because of their keen interest in them, members of Congress are reluctant to create judicial positions to be filled by a president of the minority party in Congress.[3] For example, Democrats in Congress rejected President Eisenhower's efforts to create new judgeships in every year of his second term, 1957–1960, even though he offered to name Democrats to half the new positions. In 1962, however, a similar bill easily passed

Table 11-1. Backgrounds of Recent U.S. District Court Appointees

|  | Bush | Reagan | Carter | Ford | Nixon | Johnson |
|---|---|---|---|---|---|---|
| Total number of appointees | 148 | 290 | 202 | 52 | 179 | 122 |
| Occupation (%) |  |  |  |  |  |  |
| Politics/gov't | 11 | 13 | 4 | 21 | 11 | 21 |
| Judiciary | 42 | 37 | 40 | 35 | 29 | 31 |
| Large law firm | 26 | 18 | 14 | 10 | 11 | 2 |
| Moderate size firm | 15 | 19 | 20 | 25 | 28 | 19 |
| Solo or small firm | 5 | 10 | 14 | 10 | 19 | 23 |
| Professor of law | 1 | 2 | 3 | — | 3 | 3 |
| Other | 1 | 1 | 1 | — | — | — |
| Experience (%) |  |  |  |  |  |  |
| Judicial | 47 | 47 | 55 | 42 | 35 | 34 |
| Prosecutorial | 39 | 44 | 39 | 50 | 42 | 46 |
| Neither one | 32 | 28 | 28 | 31 | 36 | 34 |
| Party (%) |  |  |  |  |  |  |
| Democrat | 5 | 5 | 93 | 21 | 7 | 94 |
| Republican | 89 | 93 | 4 | 79 | 93 | 6 |
| Independent | 6 | 2 | 3 | — | — | — |
| Past party activism (%) | 61 | 59 | 61 | 50 | 49 | 49 |
| Religious origin or affiliation (%) |  |  |  |  |  |  |
| Protestant | 64 | 60 | 60 | 73 | 73 | 58 |
| Catholic | 26 | 30 | 28 | 17 | 18 | 31 |
| Jewish | 7 | 9 | 12 | 10 | 8 | 11 |
| Ethnicity or race (%) |  |  |  |  |  |  |
| White | 90 | 92 | 79 | 89 | 96 | 93 |
| Black | 7 | 2 | 14 | 6 | 3 | 4 |
| Hispanic | 4 | 5 | 7 | 2 | 1 | 3 |
| Asian | — | 1 | 1 | 4 | — | — |
| Sex (%) |  |  |  |  |  |  |
| Male | 80 | 92 | 86 | 98 | 99 | 98 |
| Female | 20 | 8 | 14 | 2 | 1 | 2 |
| Average age | 48 | 49 | 50 | 49 | 49 | 51 |

Source: Sheldon Goldman, "Bush's Judicial Legacy: The Final Imprint," *Judicature* 76 (April/May 1993): 287. Reprinted with permission of *Judicature*, the journal of the American Judicature Society.

Congress with Democrat John Kennedy in the White House. This partisan behavior was nothing new. In 1801 the newly elected Jeffersonians repealed a law creating separate judges for the circuit courts of appeal that had been passed by the outgoing Federalists a few months earlier.

There is no doubt that various women's, racial, ethnic, and religious groups desire to have as many of their members as possible appointed to the federal bench. At the very least judgeships have symbolic importance for them. Thus, presidents face many of the same pressures for

Table 11-2. Backgrounds of Recent U.S. Appeals Court Appointees

| | Bush | Reagan | Carter | Ford | Nixon | Johnson |
|---|---|---|---|---|---|---|
| Total number of appointees | 37 | 78 | 56 | 12 | 45 | 40 |
| Occupation (%) | | | | | | |
|   Politics/gov't | 11 | 6 | 5 | 8 | 4 | 10 |
|   Judiciary | 60 | 55 | 47 | 75 | 53 | 58 |
|   Large law firm | 16 | 13 | 11 | 8 | 4 | 5 |
|   Moderate size firm | 11 | 10 | 16 | 8 | 22 | 18 |
|   Solo or small firm | — | 1 | 5 | — | 7 | 10 |
|   Professor of law | 3 | 13 | 14 | — | 2 | 3 |
|   Other | — | 1 | 2 | — | 7 | — |
| Experience (%) | | | | | | |
|   Judicial | 62 | 60 | 54 | 75 | 58 | 65 |
|   Prosecutorial | 30 | 28 | 32 | 25 | 47 | 48 |
|   Neither one | 32 | 35 | 38 | 25 | 18 | 20 |
| Party (%) | | | | | | |
|   Democrat | 5 | — | 82 | 8 | 7 | 95 |
|   Republican | 89 | 97 | 7 | 92 | 93 | 5 |
|   Independent | 5 | 1 | 11 | — | — | — |
| Past party activism (%) | 70 | 69 | 73 | 58 | 60 | 58 |
| Religious origin or affiliation (%) | | | | | | |
|   Protestant | 59 | 55 | 61 | 58 | 76 | 60 |
|   Catholic | 24 | 31 | 23 | 33 | 16 | 25 |
|   Jewish | 16 | 14 | 16 | 8 | 9 | 15 |
| Ethnicity or race (%) | | | | | | |
|   White | 89 | 97 | 79 | 100 | 98 | 95 |
|   Black | 5 | 1 | 16 | — | — | 5 |
|   Hispanic | 5 | 1 | 4 | — | — | — |
|   Asian | — | — | 2 | — | 2 | — |
| Sex (%) | | | | | | |
|   Male | 81 | 95 | 80 | 100 | 100 | 98 |
|   Female | 19 | 5 | 20 | — | — | 3 |
| Average age | 49 | 50 | 52 | 52 | 54 | 52 |

Source: Goldman, "Bush's Judicial Legacy": 293. Reprinted with permission of *Judicature*, the journal of the American Judicature Society.

representativeness in selecting judges that they experience in naming their cabinet.

What is less clear is what policy differences result from presidents' appointing persons with different backgrounds to judgeships. The number of female and minority group judges has been too few and their service too recent to serve as a basis for generalizations about their decisions. There have been many members of each party appointed to the federal bench, however. It appears that, in general, Republican judges are somewhat more conservative than Democratic judges.[4]

### Selection of Supreme Court Justices

Like lower-court judges, justices of the Supreme Court must be approved by a majority of those voting in the Senate. There have been no recess appointments to the Court since the Senate voiced its disapproval of the practice in 1960. When the chief justice's position is vacant, the president may nominate either someone already on the Court or someone from outside it to fill the position. Usually presidents choose the latter course to widen their range of options, but if they decide to elevate a sitting associate justice, as President Reagan did with William Rehnquist in 1986, he or she must go through a new confirmation by the Senate.

The president operates under many constraints in selecting persons to serve on the lower federal courts, especially the district courts. Although many of the same actors are present in the case of Supreme Court nominations, their influence is typically quite different. The president is vitally interested in the Court because of the importance of its work and will generally be intimately involved in the recruitment process.

Unlike the case of federal judges, presidents have been personally acquainted with many of the people they have nominated to the Court, reflecting their involvement in the selection process, and it is not unusual for an administration official to receive a nomination. Presidents also often rely on the attorney general and the Justice Department to identify and screen candidates for the Court.

There are few matters as important to justices on the Supreme Court as the ideology, competence, and compatibility of their colleagues, and thus it is not surprising that they, especially chief justices, often try to influence nominations to the Court. Chief Justice William Howard Taft, a former president, was especially active during his tenure in the 1920s, and Warren Burger played a prominent role in the Nixon administration. Nevertheless, although presidents will listen to recommendations from justices, they feel no obligations to follow them.

Senators play a much less prominent role in the recruitment of Supreme Court justices than in the selection of lower-court judges, especially for the district courts. No senator can claim that the jurisdiction of the Supreme Court falls within the realm of his or her special expertise, interest, or sphere of influence. Thus, presidents typically consult with senators from the state of residence of a nominee after they have decided whom to select. At this point senators are unlikely to oppose a nomination because they like having their state receive the honor and are well aware that the president can simply select someone from another state if he chooses to do so.

Candidates for nomination are also much less likely to play a significant role in the recruitment process. Although there have been exceptions, most notably William Howard Taft, people do not usually campaign for a position on the Court. Little can be accomplished through such activity, and, because of the Court's standing, it might offend those who do play important roles in selecting nominees.

The American Bar Association's Standing Committee on the Federal Judiciary has played a varied but typically more modest role at the Supreme Court level than for nominations to lower courts. Usually the committee is asked to evaluate candidates for the Supreme Court only after the president has nominated them. The committee prefers to screen potential nominees before they are nominated, however, so it will not be in the position of opposing the president's choice. Indeed, it has never found a nominee unqualified to serve on the Court.

Through 1993, 107 persons have served on the Supreme Court. Of the 146 nominees, 3 were nominated and confirmed twice, 8 were confirmed but never served, and 28 failed to secure Senate confirmation. The president, then, has failed 20 percent of the time to appoint the person of his choice to the Court, a percentage much higher than for any other federal position. Thus, although home-state senators do not play prominent roles in the selection process for the Court, the Senate as a whole does.

Six nominees have failed to receive Senate confirmation in this century (see Table 11-3). Their difficulties are instructive. Liberal and civil rights groups opposed John J. Parker, Clement Haynsworth, and G. Harrold Carswell, and organized labor was in active opposition against the first two as well. Abe Fortas (who was already on the Court and who had been nominated as chief justice) was opposed by conservative interests and was charged with ethical violations, as was Haynsworth. Carswell was the only one of this group whose competence was seriously questioned. Haynsworth's and Carswell's troubles were compounded because they were Republican appointees facing a Democrat-controlled Senate, while Fortas was nominated at the end of President Johnson's term, and Senate Republicans refused to confirm him in the hope that a Republican president would be elected and have the opportunity to nominate a new chief justice.

On June 26, 1987, Justice Lewis Powell announced his retirement

**Table 11-3. Senate Rejections of Supreme Court Nominees in the Twentieth Century**

| Nominee | Year | President |
|---|---|---|
| John J. Parker | 1930 | Hoover |
| Abe Fortas* | 1968 | Johnson |
| Clement F. Haynsworth, Jr. | 1969 | Nixon |
| G. Harrold Carswell | 1970 | Nixon |
| Robert H. Bork | 1987 | Reagan |
| Douglas H. Ginsburg* | 1987 | Reagan |

*Nominations withdrawn. Fortas was serving on the Court as an associate justice and was nominated to be chief justice.

from the Supreme Court. President Reagan had already been able to elevate Justice William Rehnquist to be chief justice and also had appointed Sandra Day O'Connor and Antonin Scalia. With yet another appointee, he would have a solid bloc of conservative votes on the Court for years to come.

He nominated Judge Robert H. Bork to fill the vacancy. Everyone agreed that Bork was an intelligent and serious legal scholar. Bork had also served in the Justice Department. (He was the one who had fired special prosecutor Archibald Cox in the famous Saturday Night Massacre of Watergate fame.) At this point agreement on his qualifications ended, however.

Bork testified before the Senate Judiciary Committee for twenty-three hours. At the end, his supporters portrayed him as a distinguished scholar who would practice "judicial restraint," deferring to Congress and state legislatures and adhering to the precedents of the Supreme Court. Conversely, his opponents saw him as an extreme judicial activist who would use the Supreme Court to achieve conservative political ends, reversing decades of court decisions. A wide range of interest groups entered the fray, mostly in opposition to the nominee, and in the end, following a bitter floor debate, the Senate rejected the president's nomination by a vote of 58 to 42.

Six days after the Senate vote on Bork, the president nominated Douglas H. Ginsburg to the high court. Just nine days later, however, Ginsburg withdrew his nomination after disclosures that he had smoked marijuana at parties while a law professor at Harvard. Not until the spring of 1988 did Reagan finally succeed in filling the vacancy with Anthony Kennedy.

In June 1991, at the end of the Supreme Court's term, Associate Justice Thurgood Marshall announced his retirement from the Court. Shortly thereafter, President Bush announced his nomination of another African-American, federal appeals judge Clarence Thomas, to replace Marshall on the Court. Since Thomas was a conservative, this decision was consistent with the Bush administration's emphasis on placing conservative judges on the federal bench.

The president claimed that he was not employing quotas when he chose Thomas to replace the only African-American ever to sit on the Supreme Court. Not everyone believed him, but liberals were placed in a dilemma. On the one hand, they favored a minority group member serving on the nation's highest court. On the other hand, Thomas was unlikely to vote the same way as Thurgood Marshall. Instead, he presented the prospect of strengthening the conservative trend in the Court's decisions. In the end, this ambivalence inhibited spirited opposition to Thomas, who was circumspect about his judicial philosophy in his appearances before the Senate Judiciary Committee. The committee sent his nomination to the Senate floor on a split vote.

Just as the Senate was about to vote on the nomination, however, charges of sexual harassment leveled against Thomas by University of

**President Clinton with Supreme Court justice nominee Judge Ruth Bader Ginsburg.**
AP/WideWorld Photos.

Oklahoma law professor Anita Hill were made public. Hearings were reopened on the charges in response to criticism that the Senate was sexist for not seriously considering them in the first place. For several days citizens sat transfixed before their television sets as Professor Hill calmly and graphically described her recollections of Thomas's behavior. Thomas then emphatically denied any such behavior and charged the Senate with racism for raising the issue. Ultimately, public opinion polls showed that most people believed Thomas. He was confirmed by a vote of 52 to 48, the closest vote on a Supreme Court nomination in more than a century.

To avoid problems such as those that confronted the recent nominees who were not confirmed, the Clinton administration undertook detailed background checks of potential nominees and floated several names to test public reaction prior to the president's announcement of his choice, Judge Ruth Bader Ginsburg. In this way Clinton avoided a potentially contentious nomination battle that might embarrass his administration. However, he left himself open to the charge that he was indecisive and uncertain about whom he wanted to nominate.

The examples of recent failed nominations indicate that presidents are most likely to run into trouble under certain conditions: when their party is in the minority in the Senate or when they make a nomination at the end of their term. Both of these conditions increase the probability of substantial opposition and defeat. Equally important, opponents of a nomination are typically motivated by ideological concerns but usually must be able to question a nominee's competence, temperament, or ethics in order to defeat a nomination. Such questions provide a rationale for opposition that can attract moderates and make ideological protests seem less partisan.[5]

### Characteristics of Justices

Competence and ethical behavior are important to presidents for reasons beyond merely obtaining Senate confirmation of their nominees to the Court. Skilled and honorable justices reflect well on the president and will likely do so for many years. Moreover, they are more effective advocates and thus can better serve the president's interests. In addition, presidents usually have enough respect for the Court and its work that they do not want to saddle it with a mediocre justice. Although the criteria of competence and character screen out some possible candidates, they still leave a wide field from which the president may choose. Other characteristics then play prominent roles.

Like their colleagues on the lower federal courts, Supreme Court justices share many characteristics that are quite unlike those of the typical American. All have been lawyers and all but four (Thurgood Marshall, nominated in 1967, Sandra Day O'Connor, nominated in 1981, Clarence Thomas, nominated in 1991, and Ruth Bader Ginsburg, nominated in 1993) have been white males. Most have been in their fifties and sixties when they took office, from the upper-middle to upper class, and Protestants.[6]

Race and gender have become more salient criteria in recent years. In the 1980 presidential campaign Ronald Reagan promised to appoint a woman to the first vacancy on the Court if he were elected. Geography once was a prominent criterion for selection to the Court, but it is no longer very important. Presidents do like to spread the slots around, however, as when Richard Nixon decided that he wanted to nominate a Southerner. At various times there have been what some have termed a "Jewish seat" and a "Catholic seat" on the Court, but these are not binding on the president. For example, after a half century of having a Jewish justice, there was none between 1969 and 1993, until President Clinton nominated Ruth Bader Ginsburg to the Court.

Although presidents often have selected Supreme Court justices at least in part for their symbolic appeal to geographic, gender, racial, and religious interests, such appointees may not actually be providing these groups much policy representation. There is evidence that most symbolic appointees do not vote for their own group's policy attitudes any more than other members of the Court.[7]

Partisanship remains an important influence on the selection of justices; only 13 of 107 members were nominated by presidents of a different party. Moreover, many of the 13 exceptions were actually close to the president in ideology, as was the case in Richard Nixon's appointment of

Lewis Powell. Herbert Hoover's nomination of Benjamin Cardozo seems to be one of the few cases where partisanship was completely dominated by merit as a criterion for selection. Usually over 90 percent of a president's judicial nominations are of members of his own party.

The role of partisanship is not really surprising, even at the level of our highest court. Most presidents' acquaintances are in their party, and there is usually a certain congruity between party and political views. The president may also use Supreme Court nominations as a reward, as when President Eisenhower nominated Earl Warren as chief justice. As leader of the California delegation to the 1952 Republican convention, Warren had played a crucial role in Eisenhower's obtaining the Republican nomination for president. Many justices have at one time been active partisans, which gave them visibility and helped them obtain the positions from which they moved to the Court.

Typically justices have held high administrative or judicial positions before moving to the Supreme Court. Most have had some experience as a judge, often at the appellate level, and many have worked for the Department of Justice. Some have held high elected office, and a few have had no government service but have been distinguished attorneys. The fact that not all justices, including many of the most distinguished ones, have had previous judicial experience may seem surprising, but the unique work and environment of the Court renders this background much less important than it might be for other appellate courts.

## PRESIDENT–SUPREME COURT RELATIONS

At the top of two complex branches of government stand the president and the Supreme Court. Each has significant powers. In a system of shared powers such as ours, it is not surprising that the president is interested in influencing the Court. In this section we examine efforts of the White House to mold the Court through filling vacancies, setting its agenda, and influencing and enforcing its decisions. We also look at interbranch relations involving advising and other services.

### Molding the Court

As we have noted, one of the most significant powers of the president is molding the Supreme Court through nominations. Since justices serve for life, the impact of a president's selections will generally be felt long after that president has left office. Because of this, the policy preferences of candidates for the Supreme Court are important to most presidents, and they typically make substantial efforts to ascertain them. When they succeed, they can slow or alter trends in the Court's decisions. Franklin Roosevelt's nominees substantially liberalized the Court, while Richard Nixon's turned it in a basically conservative direction.

Presidents and their aides survey candidates' decisions (if they served on a lower court), speeches, political stands, writings, and other expressions of opinion. They also turn for information to people who know the candidates well. The most direct means of learning candidates' views on policy would be simply to ask them, but this must be done in a delicate manner. Most officials feel it is improper to question judicial candidates about upcoming judicial decisions, so conversations must be limited to broader discussions of issues. The Reagan administration was especially concerned about ideology and had each potential nominee (for all judicial vacancies) fill out a lengthy questionnaire and be interviewed by officials in the Department of Justice.[8] The Bush administration, also attentive to nominating conservative judges, continued this practice.[9]

As a result of all this effort, presidents are generally satisfied with the actions of their nominees, especially those who have prior judicial experience to examine.[10] Nevertheless, it is not always easy to identify the policy inclinations of candidates, and presidents have been disappointed in their selections about a fourth of the time. President Eisenhower, for example, was displeased with the liberal decisions of both Earl Warren and William Brennan. Once when asked whether he had made any mistakes as president, he replied, "Yes, two, and they are both sitting on the Supreme Court."[11] Earlier, Woodrow Wilson was shocked by the very conservative positions of one of his nominees, James McReynolds. On a more limited scale, Richard Nixon was certainly disappointed when his nominee for chief justice, Warren Burger, authored the Court's decision calling for immediate desegregation of the nation's schools shortly after his confirmation. This did little for the president's "southern strategy."

Presidents make what in their views are errors in nominations to the Court for several possible reasons. They and their aides may have done a poor job of probing the views of candidates. Moreover, once on the Court, justices may change their attitudes and values over time because of new insights gained in their position, the normal process of aging, or the influence of other members of the Court. (Virtually all justices between 1801 and 1835 were strongly affected by Chief Justice John Marshall.) Justices are also often constrained by their obligation to follow precedents (when they are clear).

Some presidents have been relatively unconcerned with ideology in their nominations. In periods of relative political and social calm or when there is a solid majority on the Court that shares their views and that is likely to persist for several years, presidents might give less weight to policy preferences than to other criteria in choosing justices.

Presidents cannot have much impact on the Court unless they have vacancies to fill, of course. Although on the average there has been an opening on the Supreme Court every two years, there is a substantial variance around this mean. Franklin D. Roosevelt had to wait five years before he could nominate a justice. All the while he was faced with a Court that found much of his New Deal legislation unconstitutional. In more recent years Jimmy Carter was never able to nominate a justice. Indeed, between 1972 and 1984 there were only two vacancies on the Court. On the other hand, Richard Nixon was able to nominate four justices in his first three years in office.

Sometimes unusual steps are taken to enhance or limit a president's ability to fill vacancies. The size of the Supreme Court was altered many times between 1801 and 1869. In 1866 Congress reduced the size of the Court from ten to eight members so that Andrew Johnson could not nominate any new justices. When President Grant took office, Congress increased the number to nine, since it had confidence he would nominate members to its liking. This number has remained unchanged since then, and it now seems inviolate. Franklin D. Roosevelt attempted to "pack" the court in 1937, when he proposed to add a justice to the Court for every justice currently serving who was over seventy and had served ten years. This proposal was an obvious attempt to change the direction of Court decisions on his economic policies, and after a prolonged political battle Congress refused to approve it. The refusal, however, was given only after the Court made a strategic reversal and began approving liberal legislation. Thus, Roosevelt lost the battle but won the war.

The president's role in Supreme Court judicial selection is not limited to the nomination of justices. It extends to the creation of positions as well. Justices are typically not prone to retirement, but presidents sometimes are frustrated enough at Court decisions to attempt to accelerate the creation of vacancies. Thomas Jefferson and his supporters tried to use impeachment to remove justices and thus gain control of the judiciary that was largely Federalist (and thus anti-Jefferson). This strate-

*"Do you ever have one of those days when every-thing seems un-Constitutional?"*

Drawing by Joe Mirachi; © 1974 The New Yorker Magazine, Inc.

gy was abandoned, however, when the Senate in 1805 failed to convict Justice Samuel Chase, who had made himself vulnerable with his partisan activities off the bench and injudicious remarks on it.

More often, presidents have relied on indirect pressure. Theodore Roosevelt resorted to leaks in the press in an unsuccessful effort to induce two justices to resign. More recently, the Nixon administration orchestrated a campaign to force liberal justice Abe Fortas to resign after he was accused of financial improprieties.

Justices are not helpless pawns in the game of politics, of course, and may try to time their retirements so a president with compatible views will choose their successor. This is one reason that justices remain on the Court for so long, even when they are clearly infirm. William Brennan and Thurgood Marshall, the most senior justices on the Court in the 1980s, stayed through the Reagan years because their liberal views contrasted sharply with those of the president. William Howard Taft, a rigid conservative, even feared a successor being named by conservative Republican Herbert Hoover!

Such tactics do not always succeed. In 1968 Chief Justice Earl Warren submitted his resignation to President Johnson, whom he felt would select an acceptable successor. When Johnson's choice of Abe Fortas failed to win confirmation, however, the opportunity to nominate the new chief justice passed to Warren's old California political rival, the newly elected president, Richard Nixon.

### Arguments in the Courts

The president may influence what cases the courts hear as well as who hears them. The solicitor general is a presidential appointee who must be confirmed by the Senate and serves in the Department of Justice. It is he or she (not the attorney general) who supervises the litigation of the federal executive branch. In this position the solicitor general plays a major role in determining the agenda of federal appellate courts. Although able to exercise wide discretion, he or she is subject to the direction of the attorney general and the president, the latter playing a role in major cases.

The solicitor general decides which of the cases lost by the federal government in the federal district courts or the courts of appeals will be appealed to the next higher court. The courts of appeal must hear properly appealed cases, but the Supreme Court, for all practical purposes, has complete control over its own docket. Thus, it is significant that the Court is far more likely to accept cases the solicitor general wants to be heard than those from any other party.[12] Moreover, the amount of litigation involved is quite large. In recent years, the federal government has been a party to about half the cases heard in federal courts of appeal and the Supreme Court.

The executive branch also participates in cases to which it is not directly a party. The solicitor general files *amicus curiae* (friend of the court) briefs supporting or opposing the efforts of other parties before the Court. These cases range from school busing for racial integration to abortion rights to equal pay for women. Once again, the Court usually grants the government's request to participate in this way.

When a case reaches the Supreme Court, the solicitor general supervises the preparation of the government's arguments in support of its position, whether it is a direct party or an *amicus*. These arguments are often reflected in Court decisions and thus become the law of the land. Since the government has participated in almost every major controversy decided by the courts in the past fifty years, the potential influence of the executive branch on public policy through the courts is substantial. Moreover, both as a direct party or as an *amicus*, the federal government wins a clear majority of the time.[13]

The government's success is due to several factors. The solicitor general builds credibility with the Court by not making frivolous appeals and in a few instances even by telling the Court the government should not have won cases in lower courts. Equally important, the solicitor general and his or her staff (again, not the attorney general) develop more expertise in dealing with the Court than anyone else, since they appear before it more frequently, and they provide the Court with high-quality briefs.

On a very rare occasion the president may directly attempt to influence a Court decision. In a very unusual move in 1969, Department of Justice officials visited Justice Brennan and Chief Justice Warren to alert them that the administration was worried about the outcomes of some wiretapping cases that were on the Court's agenda. The administration was concerned that the Court's decisions would force the discontinuance of its surveillance of embassies or its prosecutions based on the information obtained from them. According to Warren, this visit had no influence on the Court's decision making.[14]

### Enforcing Court Decisions

Another important relationship between the judicial and executive branches involves the enforcement of court decisions. Although the executive branch provides the federal courts with United States marshals, they are too few and lack sufficient authority to be of systematic aid, especially if a court order is directed against a coordinate branch of government. Thus, the courts often must rely on the president to enforce their decisions, especially their more controversial ones.

The Constitution is, not surprisingly, ambiguous as to the president's responsibility for aiding the judicial branch. Although it never explicitly discusses the point, the Constitution does assign the president the responsibility to "take care that the laws be faithfully executed." Typically, presidents have responded to support the courts, or at least the rule of law. On several occasions, such as during the efforts of Presidents Eisenhower and Kennedy to integrate educational institutions, presidents have gone so far as to employ federal troops to ensure compliance with court orders.

Presidents may use the carrot as well as the stick to encourage others to comply with Court decisions. One of the most significant and controversial Supreme Court decisions of this century has been that of *Brown* v. *Board of Education* (347 U.S. 483, 1954), calling for an end to segregation in the public schools. Compliance with this decision was a long and tortuous process, but it was aided by the passage of laws that provide federal aid only for school districts that do not segregate and that provide schools with extra funds to help ease the process of desegregation.

There have been exceptions to presidential cooperation, however. In *Worcester* v. *Georgia* (6 Peters 515, 1832), the Court found that Georgia had no authority over Cherokee Indian lands and that missionaries arrested there by the state should be released. The Court also implied that it was the president's responsibility to enforce its decision. Georgia refused to comply with the decision, however, and President Andrew Jackson took no actions to enforce it. He is reputed to have stated, "Well, [Chief Justice] John Marshall has made his decision, now let him enforce it."

### Other Relationships

In the earliest years of our nation the line of separation between the executive and judicial branches was vague and often crossed. President George Washington consulted with the chief justice on a range of matters and received written advisory opinions on matters of law. Washington even used the first two chief justices as diplomats to negotiate with other countries. The chief justice was also placed on a commission to manage the fund for paying off the national debt.

This interbranch cooperation did not last long, however. The diplomatic efforts of justices were criticized by many, the Court decided against providing further advisory opinions, and informal consultation between the White House and justices declined. The Court also refused to examine pension claims for the secretary of the treasury. The years of Jefferson's presidency were marked by hostility between the president and the judiciary, which was populated primarily by his Federalist political enemies.

The most notable formal exceptions in recent years to a strict separation between the two branches have been Justice Robert Jackson's service as chief American prosecutor at the Nuremberg trials of Nazi leaders following World War II and Chief Justice Earl Warren's chairmanship of the commission investigating the assassination of President Kennedy. Abe Fortas received a great deal of criticism for his activities as an informal adviser to President Johnson on a wide range of issues. In the words of one biographer, while on the Court, "Fortas served as political advisor, speechwriter, crisis manager, administration headhunter, legal expert, war counselor, or just plain cheerleader."[15]

This type of relationship has occurred from time to time, however, principally between justices and the presidents who appointed them, continuing a pattern established before the justice reached the Court. Felix Frankfurter continued to advise Franklin D. Roosevelt after he took his seat on the court, as did Louis Brandeis for Wilson,[16] Chief Justice Fred Vinson for Truman,[17] and a number of others throughout our history.

More striking perhaps is the fact that Chief Justice Warren Burger appears to have discussed issues pending before the Court with, and reported internal activities of the Court to, President Nixon and other top administration officials.[18] This would seem like a breach of the separation of powers. Burger also appears to have asked Nixon to use his influence with congressional Republicans to discourage them from proceeding with their attempt to impeach Justice William O. Douglas.

## COMPLYING WITH THE COURT

It is one thing for the White House to enforce a court decision against someone else, and something quite different for it to comply with an order directed at the president when he has lost a case in the Supreme Court. At that point interesting constitutional questions arise that have the potential for substantial interbranch conflict. As we will see, however, presidents typically do comply with court orders, a task made easier by the general deference of the courts to the chief executive.

### Presidential Compliance

The Constitution is ambiguous as to which branch shall have the final say in interpreting it. Jefferson, for example, argued that each branch has the authority to interpret the Constitution regarding its own actions. Thus, the president would be the final judge of his own conduct. Others disagreed and felt the Supreme Court should be the ultimate judge of the constitutionality of the executive's activities.

The Court made some progress in resolving this question in *Marbury* v. *Madison* (1 Cranch 137, 1803). The case involved the requests of Marbury and others to have the Supreme Court order Secretary of State James Madison to deliver their commissions as justices of the peace in the District of Columbia. Congress had created these positions at the end of President John Adams's term, and he had appointed Federalists to serve in them but had not gotten their commissions to them by the time he left office. The new president, Thomas Jefferson, wanted to appoint fellow party members to the positions and therefore refused to deliver the commissions after he took office.

The Court held that although Marbury and his co-plaintiffs were entitled to receive their commissions, the law that gave the Supreme Court original jurisdiction over the case was unconstitutional. Thus, the Court could not order the president or his secretary of state to act. It thereby avoided a confrontation with Jefferson. At the same time, the Court proclaimed the administration's actions to be unlawful and, more significantly, asserted its right to make the final judgment on the constitutionality of actions of the other branches of government.

*Marbury* did not really settle the question of the president's obligation to accept and follow the Court's interpretation of the Constitution because the president could argue that the law the Court voided pertained directly to the judicial branch. It was not until *Dred Scott* v. *Sanford* (19 Howard 393, 1857) that the Court again declared an act of Congress unconstitutional, and this time the law was not directly related to the judiciary. In the meantime the question of the final arbiter of the Constitution remained open.

Several presidents, including Jefferson, Lincoln, and Franklin D. Roosevelt, have threatened privately to disobey Court decisions that went against them, but in each case defiance was unnecessary because the Court supported them. The most blatant instance of a president's threatening to disobey a Court order occurred in a case in which the Court was asked to enjoin President Andrew Johnson from administering military governments in southern states following the Civil War. In oral argument before the Court, the president, speaking through his attorney general, let it be known that he would not comply with a decision enjoining him from implementing the laws. The Court, in turn, found in *Mississippi* v. *Johnson* (4 Wallace 475, 1867) that it lacked jurisdiction to stop the president from performing official duties that required executive discretion. We should also note that Johnson had vetoed these bills when Congress passed them, but he faced impeachment if he failed to execute them.

Presidents typically have obeyed Court decisions, even if it were costly to do so. There are two prominent examples of this in recent years that we will briefly examine. Near the end of President Truman's tenure and during the Korean War, the United Steelworkers of America gave notice of an industrywide strike. Concerned about steel production during wartime, the president ordered the secretary of commerce to seize and operate the steel mills. The steel companies then asked the courts to find the president's actions unconstitutional, and in *Youngstown Sheet and Tube Co.* v. *Sawyer* (343 U.S. 579, 1952), the Supreme Court did so. It found that the president lacked inherent power under the Constitution to seize the steel mills and that Congress had chosen not to give him statutory power to do so. Thus, in a rare occurrence, the president was ordered to reverse his actions, and Truman immediately complied.

The Watergate scandal produced another important case involving presidential prerogatives. The special prosecutor, Leon Jaworski, subpoenaed tapes and documents relating to sixty-four conversations President Nixon had with his aides and advisers. Jaworski needed the material for prosecution of Nixon administration officials. The president claimed that executive privilege protected his private conversations with his assistants and refused to produce the subpoenaed material. The case worked its way quickly to the Supreme Court.

In *United States* v. *Nixon* (418 U.S. 683, 1974), the Court unanimously ordered the president to turn the subpoenaed material over to the special prosecutor. Although Nixon had threatened not to comply with anything less than a "definitive" decision, he obeyed the Court. The Court held that a claim of executive privilege unrelated to military, diplomatic, or national security matters cannot be absolute and in this case must give way to considerations of due process of law in criminal proceedings. Moreover, the justices reaffirmed that it was they and not the president who must be the final judge in such matters. Nixon resigned the presidency about two weeks later.

Presidents have not always been responsive to court orders, however. For example, in *United States* v. *Burr* (25 Fed. Cas. 187, No. 14,964, 1807), President Jefferson was subpoenaed to appear at the treason trial of Aaron Burr and produce a letter. Jefferson refused to appear at the trial, but he did provide the document, stressing that he did so voluntarily and not because of judicial writ. Similarly, President James Monroe was subpoenaed as a witness in a trial, but he sent a written response instead.

The Civil War raised many difficult constitutional questions for the Court and the president. One set of cases found President Abraham Lincoln simply ignoring court orders. The president had suspended the writ of habeas corpus, which requires the government to explain why a person has been detained, and in the most famous of these cases, a citizen held prisoner by the military sued for his freedom. Chief Justice Roger Taney ordered his release, but Lincoln refused to give him up to the United States marshal sent to bring him into court. The chief justice (on circuit court duty) then held in *Ex parte Merryman* (17 Fed. Cas. 144, No. 9,487, 1861) that the president had exceeded his constitutional authority (the Constitution gives only Congress the power to suspend habeas corpus), but Lincoln simply ignored the decision and Merryman remained under arrest. Lincoln argued that he had not violated the Constitution but that in any case it would be better for the president to violate a single provision to a limited extent than to have anarchy because of failure to suppress the rebellion in the South.

Another aspect of presidential compliance with Court decisions is the administration of laws that the Court has approved and that the president opposes. This issue has arisen most directly with the claims of some presidents to the right to decide not to execute laws they view as unconstitutional, even if they had received court approval. Jefferson's opposition to the Alien and Sedition acts, passed under his predecessor John Adams and upheld by the courts, led him to stop all prosecutions and pardon all those convicted under these laws when he took office.

Andrew Jackson dismantled the Bank of the United States although the Court had approved it as constitutional.

This issue has never been really resolved, and presidents have often been lax in administering laws that they oppose. In modern times the Nixon administration was ordered by federal courts to enforce more strictly laws to eliminate segregation and sex discrimination in public educational institutions. Such court orders are rare, however.

If presidents are dissatisfied with Supreme Court decisions, their first thought is usually directed toward appointing new members with views similar to theirs. There are some other options, however. They might join in congressional efforts to remove certain types of cases from the Court's appellate jurisdiction. Congress has succeeded in such an action only once, however—on jurisdiction to hear appeals on certain writ of habeas corpus cases following the Civil War—and in this case the president supported the Court.

The president might support efforts to pass a constitutional amendment to overturn a Court interpretation of the Constitution, as George Bush did when the Court held that burning the American flag was protected speech. President Reagan supported amendments to allow prayer in public schools and to prohibit abortions. Such efforts rarely succeed, however, and Reagan's and Bush's did not. On the other hand, when the Court has made a statutory interpretation, it can be reversed by simply changing the law to clarify the intentions of those supporting the policy. In a notable example, in 1953 President Eisenhower supported legislation that deeded federal mineral rights on offshore lands to the states after the Court had held in 1951 that the federal government owned the rights.

### Deference to the President

A principal reason that complying with judicial decisions has rarely posed a problem for the president is the small number of instances in which the courts have held presidential actions to be in violation of the Constitution. Rarely have even these decisions interfered significantly with the president's policies, the *Youngstown* case being a major exception. More typically these cases have dealt with matters such as presidential instructions to customs officials or the suspension of the writ of habeas corpus.

Most presidential actions are not based upon the president's prerogatives under the Constitution and therefore do not lend themselves to constitutional adjudication. Effective opposition to most presidential policies must focus on the broader political arena. Moreover, it is especially difficult to prevent the president from acting. Most challenges occur only after the fact. On some occasions it is possible to oppose the president through challenging the constitutionality of laws he supported and Congress passed. Such efforts are rarely successful, but they were important during the early years of the New Deal, as we have seen. In the end, however, President Roosevelt prevailed.

In the area of foreign and defense policy, the Court has interpreted the Constitution and statutes to give the president broad discretion to act. In general the history of litigation regarding challenges to the president's actions in the field of national security policy has been one of avoidance, postponement of action, or deference to the chief executive. The judiciary has been content to find that discretionary actions of the executive branch were beyond its competence to adjudicate.[19]

Since the Civil War, presidents have been allowed especially broad powers in wartime. In that conflict the Supreme Court approved President Lincoln's deployment of troops during hostilities in the absence of a declaration of war and gave the chief executive discretion to determine the extent of force the crisis demanded and when an emergency existed. Similarly, it upheld the president's blockade of the South, expansion of the army and navy beyond statutory limits, calling out the militia, and most of his suspensions of habeas corpus.

In World War I, Congress delegated President Woodrow Wilson broad authority to regulate commissions, transportation, and the economy; to draft soldiers; and even to censor criticism, all with the approval of the Court. Franklin D. Roosevelt exercised even broader economic powers during World War II: he relocated Japanese-Americans from the West Coast to relocation centers and confiscated their property, and he bypassed the courts to establish special military commissions to try Nazi saboteurs, again with the Court's okay.

During the period of U.S. military involvement in Vietnam, there was never a declaration or other formal congressional authorization for the war. Many people, including many legal authorities, felt that this country's participation in the war without a formal declaration by Congress was unconstitutional, and several dozen cases were brought in federal court by opponents of the war to challenge various aspects of its legality. Yet the Supreme Court simply refused to hear all but one of these cases and never issued a written opinion regarding the war. A combination of deference to the president and pragmatic politics (what would happen if the war were declared unconstitutional while troops were engaged in combat?) rendered the Court irrelevant to the issue.[20]

It is interesting that in times in which presidents are most likely to stretch their power (that is, in wartime), the courts are the least likely to intervene. When they do, the war may be over. For example, following both the Civil War and World War II, the Supreme Court held that civilians could not be tried by military tribunals when the civilian courts were open. In each case, however, the president at which the decision was directed was no longer living.

Outside of war, the courts have found that presidents also have substantial discretion to act in the areas of foreign affairs and defense. They have broad prerogatives to act in negotiating and executing international agreements, withholding state secrets from the public, allocating international airline routes, terminating treaties, making executive agreements, recognizing foreign governments, protecting American interests abroad with military activities, punishing foreign adversaries, and acquiring and divesting foreign territory.

In the domestic sphere the president's prerogatives are closely linked to maintaining order. Thus, presidents have discretion to declare and terminate national emergencies and even martial law. They may also call out the militia or the regular armed forces to control internal friction and keep the peace.

Of course, a president does not always receive supportive decisions from the courts. President Nixon, for example, was told he could not impound funds appropriated by Congress, engage in electronic surveillance without a search warrant, or prevent the publication of the Pentagon Papers. He also was forced to turn over the Watergate tapes. Yet Nixon's presidency was atypical. Most presidents operate under few constraints from the courts.

It is not unusual for actions of executive branch officials to be found in violation of statutes passed by Congress, usually for exceeding the discretionary limits in the law. In these situations the judiciary is finding that the law, not the Constitution, must be changed, or perhaps just clarified, before the president's agents can take certain actions. Depending on the prevailing view in Congress, this may pose little problem for the president. At any rate, rarely are the issues involved central to his program.

## JUDICIAL POWERS

In addition to enforcing court orders, presidents have some judicial instruments of their own. They can issue pardons, grant clemency, and proclaim amnesty. These powers are exclusively theirs and theirs alone.

Over the years the exercise of this judicial authority by presidents has sparked controversy. Gerald Ford's unconditional pardon of his predecessor, Richard Nixon, in 1974 became a major political issue that adversely affected his electability two years later. Issued prior to a conviction or even an indictment of the former president, the pardon "for all offenses against the United States which Richard Nixon has committed or may have committed or taken part in during the period from January 20, 1969, through August 9, 1974," precluded any criminal prosecution. Although Ford was accused of subverting the legal process, his power to issue the pardon was not disputed.[21] Whether Nixon's acceptance of it amounted to an admission of guilt is also unclear.

In addition to the issuance of unconditional pardons, presidents can grant conditional ones. In 1954 the Supreme Court upheld President Eisenhower's commutation of a death sentence provided that the individual never be paroled. In 1972 President Nixon granted executive clemency to former labor leader James Hoffa on the condition that he refrain from further union activities.

Presidents may also issue general amnesty to those who have impeded war efforts. President Lincoln exercised this authority in 1863 in an effort to persuade southern deserters to return to the Union. His successor, Andrew Johnson, granted a universal amnesty in 1868 to all those who participated in the insurrection in order to heal the wounds of the Civil War. Twentieth-century presidents have used this power to pardon those convicted of crimes who subsequently served in the military and to prevent the imposition of wartime penalties (still on the books) on those who failed to register for the draft during peacetime.

The most sweeping and controversial amnesty proclamation in recent times occurred in 1977. Implementing one of his campaign promises, President Carter pardoned all Vietnam draft resisters and asked the Defense Department to consider the cases of military deserters during that war on an individual basis. Congress attempted to undercut Carter's general pardon by prohibiting the use of funds to execute his order. It was unsuccessful, however, because the president's directive to the Justice Department did not require a separate appropriation.

## CONCLUSION

Presidents are involved in vital relationships with the judicial branch, especially the Supreme Court. They attempt to influence its decisions through the process of selecting judges and justices and the arguments of their subordinates before the courts. There are strong congressional constraints on them in the selection of judges, however, and presidents sometimes err in their choice of nominees. Although the executive branch has skilled litigators before the federal appellate courts and has a clear record of success, the chief executive is ultimately dependent upon the judgment of members of a branch of government much more independent of him than the legislature. The president is once again a facilitator, not a director, of change.

A judicial decision does not end the president's relationship with the courts on an issue. In their capacity as chief executives, presidents may be obliged to enforce decisions, a responsibility that sometimes conflicts with their policy goals. Moreover, although the judiciary is generally deferential to presidents, the courts may order them to comply with a holding against an action of theirs. Such decisions do not touch most of what presidents do, but in some instances they do hamper their actions. Thus, the president's relations with the courts are characterized both by conflict and by harmony, and influencing judicial decisions remains an important, but at times frustrating, priority for the White House.

## NOTES

1. Quoted in J. Woodford Howard, Jr., *Courts of Appeals in the Federal Judicial System: A Study of the Second, Fifth, and District of Columbia Circuits* (Princeton, N.J.: Princeton University Press, 1981), p. 101.

2. Griffin Bell, quoted in Nina Totenberg, "Will Judges Be Chosen Rationally?" *Judicature* 60 (August/September 1976): 93.

3. See Jon R. Bond, "The Politics of Court Structure: The Addition of New Federal Judges, 1949–1978," *Law and Policy Quarterly* 2 (April 1980): 181–88.

4. C. K. Rowland, Robert A. Carp, and Ronald Stidham, "Judges' Policy Choices and the Value Basis of Judicial Appointments," *Journal of Politics* 46 (August 1984): 886–902; C. K. Rowland and Bridget Jeffery Todd, "Where You Stand Depends on Who Sits: Platform Promises and Judicial Gatekeeping in the Federal District Courts," *Journal of Politics* 53 (February 1991): 175–85; Ronald Stidham, Robert A. Carp, and C. K. Rowland, "Patterns of Presidential Influence on the Federal District Courts: An Analysis of the Appointment Process," *Presidential Studies Quarterly* 14 (Fall 1984): 548–60; C. K. Rowland, Donald R. Songer, and Robert A. Carp, "Presidential Effects on Criminal Justice in the Lower Federal Courts: The Reagan Judges," *Law and Society Review* 22 (No. 1, 1988): 191–200; John Gottschall, "Reagan Appointments to the United States Court of Appeals: The Continuation of a Judicial Revolution," *Judicature* (June/July 1986): 48–54; Timothy B. Tomasi and Jess A. Velona, "All the President's Men? A Study of Ronald Reagan's Appointments to the U.S. Courts of Appeals," *Columbia Law Review* 87 (May 1987): 766–93; and Robert A. Carp, Donald Songer, C. K. Rowland, Ronald Stidham, and Lisa Richey-Tracy, "The Voting Behavior of Judges Appointed by President Bush," *Judicature* 76 (April-May 1993): 298–302. On the impact of female and minority judges, see Thomas G. Walker and Deborah J. Barrow, "The Diversification of the Federal Bench: Policy and Process Ramifications," *Journal of Politics* 47 (May 1985): 596–617.

5. See John Massaro, *Supremely Political* (Albany: SUNY Press, 1992); Charles M. Cameron, Albert D. Cover, and Jeffrey A. Segal, "Senate Voting on Supreme Court Nominees: A Neoinstitutional Model," *American Political Science Review* 84 (June 1990): 525–34; Jeffrey Segal, "Senate Confirmation of Supreme Court Justices: Partisan and Institutional Politics," *Journal of Politics* 49 (November 1987): 998–1015.

6. On the background of justices, see John R. Schmidhauser, *Judges and Justices: The Federal Appellate Judiciary* (Boston: Little, Brown, 1979).

7. Thomas R. Marshall, "Symbolic versus Policy Representation on the U.S. Supreme Court," *Journal of Politics* 55 (February 1993): 140–50.

8. David M. O'Brien, "The Reagan Judges: His Most Enduring Legacy?" in Charles O. Jones, ed., *The Reagan Legacy* (Chatham, N.J.: Chatham House, 1988), pp. 60–101.

9. Sheldon Goldman, "The Bush Imprint on the Judiciary: Carrying on a Tradition," *Judicature* 74 (April–May, 1991): 294–306.

10. Robert Scigliano, *The Supreme Court and the Presidency* (New York: Free Press, 1971).

11. Dwight Eisenhower, quoted in Henry J. Abraham, *Justices and Presidents: A Political History of Appointments to the Supreme Court*, 3rd ed. (New York: Oxford University Press, 1992), p. 266.

12. On the Court's accepting cases, see Doris Marie Provine, *Case Selection in the United States Supreme Court* (Chicago: University of Chicago Press, 1980); and Stuart H. Teger and Douglas Kosinski, "The Cue Theory of Supreme Court Certiorari Jurisdiction: A Reconsideration," *Journal of Politics* 42 (August 1980): 834–46.

13. On the solicitor general's success, see Jeffrey A. Segal, "Courts, Executives, and Legislatures," in John B. Gates and Charles A. Johnson, eds., *The American Courts* (Washington, D.C.: CQ Press, 1991), pp. 376–82.

14. Earl Warren, *The Memoirs of Chief Justice Earl Warren* (Garden City, N.Y.: Doubleday, 1971), pp. 337–42.

15. Bruce Allen Murphy, *Fortas* (New York: William Morrow, 1988), p. 235. Murphy chronicles the Johnson–Fortas relationship in great detail. See also Joseph A. Califano, Jr., *The Triumph and Tragedy of Lyndon Johnson* (New York: Simon and Schuster, 1991), pp. 95–96, 118, 120, 153–54, 161–63, 189, 191, 205, 213–18, 298, 306, 312–15.

16. Bruce Allen Murphy, *The Brandeis/Frankfurter Connection: The Secret Political Activities of Two Supreme Court Justices* (New York: Oxford University Press, 1982).

17. See Clark Clifford, *Counsel to the President* (New York: Random House, 1991), p. 215; and David McCullough, *Truman* (New York: Simon and Schuster, 1992), p. 897.

18. John Ehrlichman, *Witness to Power: The Nixon Years* (New York: Simon and Schuster, 1982), p. 133.

19. See, for example, Craig R. Ducat and Robert L. Dudley, "Federal District Judges and Presidential Power During the Postwar Era," *Journal of Politics* 51 (February 1989): 98–118.

20. Anthony A. D'Amato and Robert M. O'Neil, *The Judiciary and Vietnam* (New York: St. Martin's, 1972).

21. There were many allegations of a deal between the two men. Some observers accused Ford of having agreed to the pardon in exchange for his nomination as vice president by Nixon. Ford vehemently denied that such an agreement had been made in sworn testimony before the House Judiciary Committee in 1974.


## SELECTED READINGS

Abraham, Henry J. *Justices and Presidents: A Political History of Appointments to the Supreme Court*, 3rd ed. New York: Oxford University Press, 1992.

Bond, Jon R. "The Politics of Court Structure: The Addition of New Federal Judges, 1949–1978." *Law and Policy Quarterly* 2 (April 1980): 181–88.

Caplan, Lincoln. *The Tenth Justice: The Solicitor General and the Rule of Law*. New York: Random House, 1987.

Danelski, David J. *A Supreme Court Justice Is Appointed*. New York: Random House, 1964.

Ducat, Craig R., and Robert L. Dudley. "Federal District Judges and Presidential Power During the Postwar Era." *Journal of Politics* 51 (February 1989): 98–118.

Murphy, Bruce Allen. *Fortas*. New York: William Morrow, 1988.

O'Brien, David M. "The Reagan Judges: His Most Enduring Legacy?" In Charles O. Jones, ed., *The Reagan Legacy*. Chatham, N.J.: Chatham House, 1988, pp. 60–101.

Rowland, C. K., Robert A. Carp, and Ronald Stidham. "Judges' Policy Choices and the Value Basis of Judicial Appointments." *Journal of Politics* 46 (August 1984): 886–902.

Rowland, C. K., and Bridget Jeffery Todd. "Where You Stand Depends on Who Sits: Platform Promises and Judicial Gatekeeping in the Federal District Courts." *Journal of Politics* 53 (February 1991): 175–85.

Schmidhauser, John R. *Judges and Justices: The Federal Appellate Judiciary*. Boston: Little, Brown, 1979.

Scigliano, Robert. *The Supreme Court and the Presidency*. New York: Free Press, 1971.

Stidham, Ronald, Robert A. Carp, and C. K. Rowland. "Patterns of Presidential Influence on the Federal District Courts: An Analysis of the Appointment Process." *Presidential Studies Quarterly* 14 (Fall 1984): 548–60.

Walker, Thomas G., and Deborah J. Barrow. "The Diversification of the Federal Bench: Policy and Process Ramifications." *Journal of Politics* 47 (May 1985): 596–617.

# 12

# Domestic Policy Making

The framers of the Constitution gave the president a policy role, but they did not expect him to dominate that policy. Yet that is precisely what has occurred. Seizing on the initiative that the Constitution provides—and which their central perspective, institutional structure, and political support facilitate—presidents have become chief policy-makers. Today, the public expects presidents to establish and achieve national goals. They are expected to redeem campaign promises, to respond to policy emergencies, and to propose solutions to the country's social, economic, and political ills on a regular basis. Failure to address critical issues and rectify national problems will likely result in public criticism and perhaps even electoral defeat if unsatisfactory conditions persist.

The problem that presidents face in performing their leadership role is that public expectations often exceed their ability to meet them. They have at their disposal significant policy expertise, but the experts are not always in agreement on what to do or how to do it. They have consider-able institutional resources in the presidential office and the executive branch, but they cannot control the behavior of those in other branches of government, much less those outside the government who affect that behavior. They have difficulty even overseeing the actions of those who are presumably subordinate to them. Finally, they have political clout but it varies with time and circumstances, and they cannot always exercise it effectively. Thus, the president's policy role is not an easy one, but it is a critical one for success in office. This chapter will focus on the problems inherent in presidential leadership of public policy.

The president's domestic policy role did not evolve gradually. It developed in response to policy problems during the twentieth century. To begin the chapter, we describe those responses, chronicling the growth of the president's role. Next we discuss the mechanism and processes that have been established to help meet these enlarged responsibilities. Initially we focus on the work of the Office of Management and Budget (known as the Bureau of the Budget prior to 1970) in the clearance and coordination of policy initiatives and regulations emanating from the executive departments and agencies. We then turn to the White House and to the development of a domestic policy office. In this section we also examine the impact of differing organizational models, policy goals, and personal styles on presidential policy making. Finally, we look at policy-making strategies: How can external forces be accommodated and how can internal agendas be constructed and accomplished? We place particular emphasis on the politics of agenda building—the content, packaging, and timing of domestic policy proposals.

## THE DEVELOPMENT OF A POLICY ROLE

The framers of the Constitution did not envision the president as chief domestic policymaker. They did, however, anticipate that the institution would have a policy-making role. Within the framework of the separation of powers, the president was given the duty to recommend necessary and expedient legislation and latitude in the execution of the law. Taken together, this duty and that discretion provided the constitutional basis upon which a substantial policy-making role could be built.

For the first one hundred years, presidents recommended measures, took positions, and occasionally even drafted bills, but they did not formulate domestic policy on a regular basis. Beginning with Theodore Roosevelt and continuing with Woodrow Wilson, presidential participation in the policy-making process expanded. Theodore Roosevelt developed a close relationship with Speaker of the House Joseph Cannon. The two consulted frequently on major policy initiatives. Cannon's power as Speaker and party leader enabled him to gain support for proposals Roosevelt initiated or favored.

Woodrow Wilson expanded the president's role even further. Seeing his responsibilities as analogous to the British prime minister's—to propose an integrated set of measures that addressed social and economic problems and then to utilize personal and political influence to get them enacted—Wilson personally supervised the development of policy in his administration. He chose priorities, helped formulate legislation, and exhorted his cabinet and members of Congress to support it. Wilson himself went to Congress on several occasions and was the first president since John Adams to use the State of the Union address to articulate his goals directly to Congress.

Wilson's program, known as the New Freedom, included labor measures, tariff reform, and consumer protection. He introduced legislation that led to the creation of the Federal Reserve system. Working primarily with the leaders of his party on Capitol Hill, he secured the passage of many of his domestic proposals, including the Adamson Act (which provided an eight-hour day for railroad workers), the Clayton Antitrust Act, and the act that established the Federal Trade Commission. He led the country into World War I but was unable to obtain Senate approval for the Treaty of Versailles, the agreement ending hostilities.

Wilson's Republican successors (Harding, Coolidge, and Hoover) did not expand the presidency's policy-making responsibilities. Their conservative philosophy undoubtedly influenced their conception of a limited role. This philosophy, combined with the dispersal of power in Congress, did not encourage extensive legislative activity or an aggressive presidential posture. From the perspective of the 1920s, the Republican interlude was a return to "normalcy," as Warren Harding termed it. From today's perspective it was a brief respite in the evolution of the president's domestic role.

### Institutionalizing Presidential Initiatives

Franklin Roosevelt, more than any other president, enlarged the domestic role and shaped contemporary expectations of the presidency. Coming into office in the throes of a depression, Roosevelt believed it absolutely essential for the president to take the policy initiative. In his first inaugural address, he stated:

> I am prepared under my constitutional duty to recommend the measures that a stricken Nation in the midst of a stricken world may require. These measures or such other measures as Congress may build out of its experience and wisdom, I shall seek within my constitutional authority to bring to speedy adoption.[1]

Having a sizable Democratic majority that was inclined to support his initiatives and being the kind of person who was not averse to using his personal influence to get them adopted, Roosevelt quickly and dramatically became deeply involved in the policy process.

During the first one hundred days of the New Deal, Roosevelt and his aides formulated a series of measures to address the nation's most pressing economic problems. Designed to regulate and stimulate financial, agricultural, and business sectors, these proposals, which Congress enacted into law, also created new executive and regulatory agencies. These agencies expanded the bureaucracy, but they did not necessarily improve the president's ability to oversee the implementation of "his" laws.

In the period from 1934 to 1936 another series of programs, fashioned by the president and his aides, was subsequently passed by Congress. Known as the second phase of the New Deal, these proposals included labor reform, social security, soil conservation, and various public works projects. New administrative structures were also established to administer these programs.

By the end of the Roosevelt era, the president's role as domestic policymaker was firmly established. In fact, when Harry S Truman, Roosevelt's successor, asked Congress for legislation to combat inflation, he was criticized by the Republican majority for not presenting a draft bill. When Eisenhower failed to propose a legislative program during his first year as president, he was criticized from both sides of the aisle. "Don't expect us to start from scratch on what you people want," an irate member of the House Foreign Affairs Committee told an Eisenhower official. "That's not the way we do things here. You draft the bills and we work them over."[2]

Whereas Roosevelt extended presidential initiatives primarily into the economic sphere, Presidents Kennedy and Johnson expanded them to include social welfare and civil rights measures.[3] Medical aid to the elderly, public housing, community health, minimum wages, and conservation and education programs plus a variety of civil rights policies were crafted during their administrations. By the end of the 1960s the domestic policy initiative was firmly focused in the White House.

Presidents were expected to set their policy agendas and determine the contours of legislative debate; they were expected to draft legislation and to work for its enactment. As time went on, they were also expected to mobilize public coalitions in support of their legislative proposals. And when Congress was slow in acting or obstructionist in its response, presidents were expected to find other ways of fulfilling their policy promises. Executive orders and other administrative actions became vehicles by which they could accomplish some of their policy goals. Republican presidents in particular, when confronted by Democratic Congresses, resorted to their executive powers to achieve their policy goals.

## Changing Policy Environment

That the decade of the 1960s was a period of unbridled prosperity, replete with low inflation and high employment, permitted the expansion of government services. Most elements of the society benefited. Presidents reaped political advantage from their policy-making role. As chief providers, they were charged with finding solutions to the country's domestic ills. These solutions took the form of federal programs to the disadvantaged. However, the weakening of the economy in the 1970s and early 1980s, combined with the persistence of social problems that the 1960's legislation was intended to ameliorate, cast doubt about the efficacy of these programmatic solutions. It also placed increasing burdens on presidents in the performance of their policy-making role.

Higher inflation, greater unemployment, declining productivity, increasing foreign competition, and decreasing natural resources limited the capacity of the federal government to respond to economic and social ills. Beginning with the Nixon administration and continuing through the Bush years, presidents attempted to slow the federal government's involvement in the domestic sector. President Nixon initiated a program of New Federalism in which the national government's revenues were to be shared with the states in exchange for a larger state and local role in providing social services. President Reagan carried this initiative one step further. In an attempt to shrink the public sector and reduce the responsibility of the federal government, he proposed a swap in which the states would take over the welfare and food stamp programs while the federal government would run the Medicare program. Nixon's revenue-sharing policy was enacted; the Reagan program was not. However, during the Reagan administration, the revenue-sharing program was ended and the national government's share of domestic programs declined.

In addition to the devolution of federal responsibilities to the states, Presidents Carter, Reagan, and Bush proposed reductions or elimination of other domestic programs. Entitlement programs, such as social security, medicare, and veterans' benefits, were not cut for the most part.

These three presidents also reduced the government's regulatory activity. The Carter administration successfully pushed the deregulation of the airline, railroad, and trucking industries. The Reagan administration relaxed the enforcement of many regulations, particularly in the areas of consumer protection, worker safety, and the environment. Bush appointed Vice President Quayle to head a Council on Competitiveness to ensure that American businesses were not adversely affected by regulations issued by the government.

The persistence of large budget deficits combined with Congressional opposition to increased federal spending also constrained the Clinton administration. The president's program to have government provide innoculations for all children, increased funding for the Head Start program for preschoolers, and direct loans to college students in exchange for national service were all scaled back to meet contemporary fiscal realities and the public perception, prevalent since the mid-1970s, that the federal government is neither an effective nor economical provider of social services.

Reducing government programs, expenditures, and regulations has not been easy. While the general public favors cutting government spending, specialized publics in the form of interest groups oppose reductions to "their" programs. The increasing ability of many of these groups to mobilize their constituencies behind their specific policy interests has created powerful forces toward the maintenance of the status quo. Moreover, presidents have found it necessary to pursue policies for which large constituencies have been lacking, such as raising taxes or capping benefits for entitlement programs.

Contemporary presidents are in a bind. How can they address pressing national problems without involving the federal government in some way in the solution? How can they meet public needs with existing economic resources and large budget deficits? How can they build political support for programs that lack organized national constituencies? How can they maintain their electoral and governing coalitions without being captive of those within these coalitions? These problems have led one astute observer, Paul C. Light, to conclude that domestic policy making places the president in a no-win situation: "The cost of presidential policy has grown, while the President's ability to influence outcomes has declined."[4]

How can presidents overcome this dilemma? How can they meet contemporary expectations of their policy-making role? In the next part of this chapter, we will explore this question by examining the mechanisms and processes that have been developed to aid the president in this increasingly difficult task.

## THE OFFICE OF MANAGEMENT AND BUDGET AND THE EXECUTIVE BRANCH

Presidents cannot make policy alone. They need others to provide them with information and expertise, to coordinate and implement their decisions and actions, to articulate their positions publicly and privately, and to build coalitions in support of them on Capitol Hill and within the executive branch. Initially many of these functions were performed by the Bureau of the Budget, working in conjunction with a small White House staff.

### Exercising Central Clearance

The Bureau of the Budget was originally established in 1921 to help the president prepare an annual budget and submit it to Congress. In performing this function the budget agency annually reviewed the requests for funds of the executive departments and agencies. Beginning in the 1930s, this centralized clearance process was extended to include all executive branch requests for legislation, regardless of whether or not money would be expended. In each case, the budget officials had to decide whether the proposal was in accord with the president's program, consistent with the president's objectives, or at the very least, not opposed by the president. Any proposal that the Bureau of the Budget believed conflicted with presidential policy could not be advanced by the departments and agencies.

In making their judgments, the analysts in the Budget Bureau used presidential campaign statements, major addresses and reports, and special messages to Congress. If there was a major issue about which the Budget Bureau was uncertain how the president's program applied or what the program actually was, the White House would be consulted. This situation was rare, however. As a consequence, the Budget Bureau's decision was usually final. Although an appeal could be made to the White House by the departments and agencies, the practice was not encouraged and was rarely successful. Presidents wanted the clearance procedure to work, and it did. In fact they extended it to include the positions that departments and agencies take on legislation and the testimony their officials present to Congress.

The Congress also found the process useful. Beginning in 1947, standing committees of both houses requested that the Bureau of the Budget indicate the president's position on legislation that did not originate in the executive departments and agencies.

From the president's perspective, the central clearance process offered a number of benefits: (1) it provided a mechanism for imprinting a presidential seal of approval on those proposals that the administration supported and withholding it from those it opposed; (2) it made the departments and agencies more aware of each other's views; (3) it helped resolve interagency disputes and promote interagency coordination. One of its most important functions was the resolution of conflict. Rather than kill a proposal, the Budget Bureau tried to have the objectionable parts removed and mediate the differences between the agencies.

From the department's perspective, however, the clearance requirement was seen as a constraint and the Bureau of the Budget as the policing agency. The civil servants who worked in the budget agency were regarded as the people who said no.

The central clearance process continues to operate today in much the same manner as it did in the past. However, it has become more politicized in the sense that civil servants play a less important role and political appointees a more important one in making key clearance decisions.

It is a behind-the-scenes operation, but occasionally it engenders public controversy. A case in point occurred in May 1989 when the Office of Management and Budget, the successor to the Bureau of the Budget, altered the congressional testimony of Dr. James E. Hansen, director of NASA's Goddard Institute for Space Studies, weakening his conclusion that man-made gases were primarily responsible for the so-called "greenhouse effect," the warming of the earth's atmosphere by depleting the ozone layer. When congressional leaders found out about the change after it was reported in the *New York Times*, they criticized the administration for trying to repress scientific evidence that conflicted with its policy.

The controversy points to the increasing political role of the Office of Management and Budget (OMB). It is the political appointees in the OMB and in the White House who make the critical decisions on what does or does not accord with the program of the president. In the greenhouse controversy, it was White House and cabinet officials, in addition to those in the OMB, who participated in the decision.

### Coordinating Executive Advice

In addition to applying the president's position on the policy proposals and the stands of the executive agencies, the Office of Management and Budget performs another coordinating function. It solicits and summarizes recommendations on enrolled bills, legislation that has passed both houses of Congress and is awaiting presidential action.

After Congress has enacted the legislation, the Office of Management and Budget circulates copies of it to all executive branch units that have been involved in its development, would be involved in its implementation, or have a substantive interest in the program itself. The departments and agencies have forty-eight hours in which to make a recommendation to the president. Their recommendations, accompanied by supporting arguments and frequently by drafts of signing and veto statements, are then summarized by the OMB, which adds a recommendation of its own and sends the entire file to the White House within the first five days of the ten-day period the president has to approve or disapprove the legislation. A similar process, designed to solicit the views of key White House aides, was also begun in 1965. A diagram of the central clearances and enrolled bill processes is shown in Figure 12-1.

Today, when presidents are ready to make decisions on pending

**Figure 12-1. The Enrolled Bill Process**

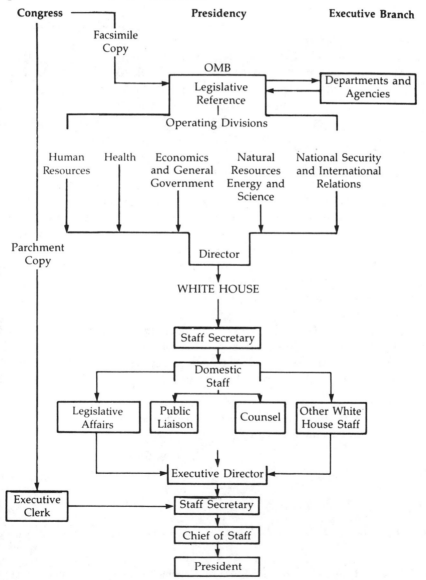

legislation, they have the benefit of the advice of a large number of executive officials. And because they have limited time and expertise of their own, they usually follow it.

Of all the executive participants in the process, presidents seem to be most influenced by the OMB and secondarily by the principal agency into whose jurisdiction the legislation falls. An OMB recommendation to approve the bill is almost always accepted. As the agency that says no most often, its advice to the president to sign the legislation seems to be regarded as an all-clear signal by the White House. Rarely does a president disregard this opportunity to approve legislation. On the other hand, the OMB's advice to veto might be ignored if there is significant political pressure in favor of the legislation.

A study of executive recommendations and presidential actions on enrolled bills from the beginning of the Johnson administration in 1963 to 1982 by Richard L. Cole and Stephen J. Wayne found that the OMB's recommendation to veto was followed only a little more than half the time, as indicated in Table 12-1.[5] When other executive agencies also urged the president to disapprove the legislation, the chances of a veto increased to 64 percent. In general, the more unified the advice given to the president, the more likely that advice will be taken.

### Reviewing Agency Regulations

The role of the OMB as policy overseer was extended at the end of the 1970s by the enactment of the Paperwork Reduction Act. A new unit was established in the OMB, the Office of Information and Regulatory Affairs, to administer the legislation. Initially, its principal task was to ensure that excessive reporting requirements were not imposed by agencies of the federal government. Within one month of assuming office, President Reagan enlarged the charter of this office to include a review of all pending executive regulations to implement new or existing legislation to make sure that they were necessary and, if issued, would be cost effective. In 1985 he further extended its scope—to include all pre–rule-making activities of the executive departments and agencies—and its charge—to decide whether the pending rules unduly interfered

Table 12-1. OMB Recommendations and Presidential Actions, 1963–1982*
         (in percentages)

| | OMB Recommendation | |
| --- | --- | --- |
| Presidential Action | Approve | Disapprove |
| Approve | 95 | 44 |
| Disapprove | 5 | 56 |

*Includes all bills on which there was at least one executive branch recommendation to veto.
$N = 536$.

Source: Richard L. Cole and Stephen J. Wayne, unpublished research.

with the private sector, families, or state and local government responsibilities.

In order to conform to the new guidelines and protect their own
autonomy, executive branch agencies decreased the volume of the new
rules they promulgated during the Reagan administration. This decline
was consistent with the administration's philosophy to reduce the role
of the national government within the domestic arena and its campaign
promise to try to eliminate governmental burdens on the private sector.

During the Bush administration, however, the number of regulations began to increase. To counter conservative criticism that the government was becoming more intrusive, Bush placed a moratorium on
the issuance of new regulations in the fall of 1991 as he readied his
reelection campaign.

The Clinton administration has continued to use this OMB office to
monitor agency regulations. However, the procedures for reviewing
agency regulations were modified by an executive order issued by the
president on September 30, 1993. Intended to open up the regulatory
review process, the order requires federal officials to disclose their contacts with interest group representatives and requires the groups to
submit their opinion in writing on pending regulations. A timely schedule for the review process has also been established. To discourage
needless and costly regulations, federal agencies are now obligated to
analyze the costs, benefits, and cumulative impact of all significant regulations, defined as those whose annual effect is $100 million or more on
the economy. The administration has charged Vice President Gore with
coordinating its regulatory priorities and agendas.

As a consequence of this regulatory oversight, the presidency
through its surrogate, the OMB, has extended influence over executive
branch activities. Not only have departments and agencies been discouraged from issuing new regulations, but those that have been issued are
now subject to clearance and, if necessary, to modification.

Moreover, the OMB's stature with outside groups has also been
enhanced. Business and professional organizations can now appeal directly to the budget agency to remove or modify regulations if they are
thwarted by the issuing department or agency. This appeals process also
works to increase the OMB's influence at the expense of the departments and agencies and also at the expense of Congress. It circumvents
the "iron triangle" relationship that has traditionally existed among the
executive branch agencies, the congressional committees that oversee
them, and outside interest groups, putting the OMB in a position to
negate the political compromises that may have been made among these
parties.

### Presenting an Annual Program

Since 1948, presidents have developed an annual legislative program and presented it to Congress in the form of special and required

messages and addresses. This programming process developed out of the president's need to articulate policy goals and to generate a record on which to appeal to voters. It also satisfied the need of Congress for an agenda on which to focus its activities.

During the Truman and Eisenhower administrations, the Bureau of the Budget coordinated the process that produced this program for the president. It did so initially as part of its annual budget review. When departments and agencies were asked to submit their budgets for the next fiscal year, they were also asked to submit ideas for new proposals that would require funding. The Budget Bureau collected these ideas and forwarded them to the White House, which decided which of them to include in the president's program. The State of the Union address became the vehicle for presenting these policy proposals to Congress.

From the president's perspective, tapping a wide range of executive ideas and goals proved useful. It increased administration options. In the words of Clark Clifford, who as special counsel to Harry Truman initially directed the White House's programming operations:

> The purpose of obtaining this information was to have the background of the needs and also the opinions of the departments and agencies of government so that we would be able to extract from that voluminous source of information a legislative program. While much of it was self-serving, at least we felt that we had tapped knowledgeable and experienced people in government. Sometimes in that general request a real pearl would appear. It is like a diver swimming around and all of a sudden there would appear a pearl as large as a hen's egg. In my opinion, that alone would justify the effort.[6]

This departmental orientation to policy making ended in the 1960s. The desire of Presidents Kennedy and Johnson to generate new initiatives, combined with their view of the bureaucracy as a pretty conservative place where innovative ideas were not likely to originate, resulted in a shift of focus from inside the executive branch to outside the government. In the words of President Johnson:

> I had watched this programming process for years, and I was convinced that it did not encourage enough fresh or creative ideas. The bureaucracy of the government is too preoccupied with day to day operations, and there is strong bureaucratic inertia dedicated to preserving the status quo. As a result, only the most powerful ideas can survive. Moreover, the cumbersome organization of government is simply not equipped to solve complex problems that cut across departmental jurisdictions.[7]

To generate new ideas, both Kennedy and Johnson set up task forces composed of campaign supporters, academicians, business and labor leaders, but not bureaucrats. Their job was to investigate a problem and present the president with a solution without regard to political considerations or costs. These factors were taken into account by the president and his aides when deciding which of the proposals to pursue.

Under Johnson the number of task forces increased, but their composition and their recommendations were secret. The purpose of the secrecy was to enable the president to take credit for ideas he liked but at the same time not be burdened by those he did not. The secrecy also permitted the president to ascertain the opinions of influential members of Congress without embarrassment to him or them. The Johnson aide who communicated with those in Congress would normally preface his remarks with the question, "The president hasn't decided to do this, but if he did, how would you respond?"

The high priority on new domestic policy proposals in both the Kennedy and Johnson administrations and the desire of both presidents to be personally involved in their development put an even greater burden for their initiation, coordination, and synthesis on White House aides. Moreover, the size of this effort and the number of task forces that were involved forced an expansion in the personnel who regularly dealt with domestic policy matters. By the mid-1960s, a separate White House staff was created to systematize the programming operation. This staff, although small and fairly general by contemporary standards, was the forerunner of the larger, more differentiated structure that has functioned as an operating arm of the presidency thereafter.

As a consequence of the growing White House role in policy making, the status and influence of the departments and agencies and the people who ran them declined. A two-track programming system eventually emerged with the departments and agencies on the second track. While they continued to submit proposals with their annual budget estimates, these submissions had less of an impact on the president's major domestic objectives. As power shifted to the White House, the Budget Bureau's influence in determining major presidential priorities also declined.

## THE DOMESTIC POLICY OFFICE AND THE WHITE HOUSE

The first domestic policy office was organized by the White House in 1965 to coordinate Lyndon Johnson's Great Society program. Charged with staffing Johnson's outside task forces and then reviewing their recommendations, the office developed policy initiatives for the president and then converted them into a legislative format, an executive order, or a departmental regulation.

President Nixon enlarged and institutionalized this White House policy-making operation. In 1970 he created a Domestic Council composed of his domestic cabinet secretaries and a supporting staff. Organized as a separate unit in the Executive Office of the President and directed by a senior White House aide, the staff quickly assumed dominance over the process. The council met infrequently. In fact, cabinet secretaries had difficulty even communicating with the president on an individual basis, much less as a group.

Since Nixon preferred a memorandum or option paper, the policy debate had to be in written form. Moreover, since he preferred a formal, hierarchical mode of operation, proposals, memos, and option papers had to be sent through official channels. John Ehrlichman, Nixon's chief domestic adviser and executive director of the council, supervised staff operations. All domestic policy documents to and from the president passed through his office.

The council's work was done primarily by committees organized on the basis of projects or missions. Composed of subcabinet departmental officials but organized and run by Ehrlichman's staff, the committees operated as internal task forces. Their functions were similar to the Johnson external task forces—to examine issues, conduct studies, and prepare recommendations for the president. Once a course of action was chosen by the president, the committees reconvened for the purpose of implementing his decision.

The Domestic Council staff member who presided over the group had to make certain that recommendations to President Nixon were in conformity with his basic goals and that the options he selected were properly converted into legislative proposals or executive actions. In this way a White House orientation was imposed on the policy-making process.

The Nixon council system was subsequently modified in 1972. Its staff was reduced in size. Senior personnel were reassigned to other departments and agencies. Some have contended that this was a thinly veiled attempt by the president to rein in the executive bureaucracy.[8]

As part of the policy reorganization, three cabinet secretaries were given additional responsibilities for coordinating domestic policy within three broad areas: human resources, natural resources, and community development. The events of Watergate, culminating first in Ehrlichman's resignation and eventually in Nixon's, ended this "super cabinet" experiment but did not deter future presidents from trying to exercise as tight control as possible over the domestic policy-making activities of their departments and agencies.

A domestic policy office has continued to function in each subsequent administration. Although its title has changed and its influence has varied, its principal functions have remained essentially the same— the development and coordination of major policy initiatives for the president. During its heyday in the Nixon administration, the Domestic Council was the primary domestic policy unit. It ran the process by which major administration initiatives were developed, and its executive director was the president's main domestic adviser. During the Ford period, the council played a much less important role. It was resuscitated by Carter. Stuart Eizenstat, the head of the office and assistant to the president for domestic affairs, was an influential adviser who also helped in negotiations with Congress.

Ronald Reagan's penchant for turning to his department secretaries for advice, his cabinet council system, and his opposition to new and costly domestic programs reduced the role of the White House's domestic policy staff to largely administrative tasks. It provided institutional support for the cabinet councils and helped the president by handling more perfunctory policy matters such as messages to Congress, liaison with interest groups, and policy-oriented speeches.

Under Bush the office and its director, Dr. Roger Porter, maintained a low profile. Porter, a distinguished political scientist who has written extensively about presidential decision making, sought to fashion an operation that coordinated department input rather than inhibited it. His model was multiple advocacy, a system that allows cabinet secretaries to be policy advocates for their departmental interests but also encourages them to reach a consensus on policy issues through negotiation. The formulation of a clean air policy that culminated in the clean air legislation of 1990 is a good example of how this process can work effectively.

A multiple advocacy approach to policy making, however, takes time. Also, it tends toward incrementalism rather than innovation. Thus, when faced with policy emergencies or the need for something different, it is apt to be less effective.

The absence of a well-defined policy agenda by the Bush administration and, specifically, its failure to deal adequately with the economic problems of the 1991–1992 recession subjected the president and his domestic policy advisers to increasing public criticism. Although a policy counselor was added toward the end of Bush's third year in office and an economic czar promised if he were reelected, the president was unable to convince the American people that his administration had the personnel, motivation, or intellectual capacity to address the nation's pressing economic and social issues.

The Clinton administration did not face this problem. Having promised to address these concerns with new policy solutions during his campaign, having immersed himself in domestic issues as governor of Arkansas and chairman of the Democratic Leadership Conference, having surrounded himself with a large number of policy advisers, Clinton's initial need was to prioritize all the policies he had proposed and his advisers had designed. A secondary issue was the extent to which input into those policies would be permitted from people outside the campaign and the White House.

Even before his inauguration, Clinton had decided to differentiate economic and domestic policy-making processes and advisers. He established a National Economic Council, headed by senior aide Robert Rubin, to design a unified economic program and then oversee the development of each of its principal components—the economic stimulus package, the deficit reduction plan, and proposals to make American businesses more competitive.

A chief domestic adviser, Carol Rasco, was also appointed to coordinate domestic policy making, oversee the Office of Program Development, and coordinate the Domestic Policy Council.[9] In addition the president assigned specific domestic initiatives to others within his administration. Hillary Rodham Clinton was given prime responsibility for the administration's health care reforms, assisted by another senior adviser, Irv Magaziner. Another assistant worked on the national service program. Other domestic initiatives in education, housing, and welfare emanated from the departments. The flexibility of this arrangement facilitated the development of new policies, but it also produced overlapping authority, coordination problems, some turf fights, and long and frequent meetings among the president's principal advisers and their staff aides.

In summary, domestic policy staffs have functioned since the Johnson administration to design and coordinate policy. The size of these staffs has varied from a high of approximately eighty at the end of Nixon's first term to about thirty to forty in other administrations. A senior presidential assistant has headed the office.

In the course of its operation, the White House policy staff has worked closely with the OMB. In general, priority policy making has been the prerogative of the president's domestic advisers while the clearance, coordination, and review of less important policy matters remain the job of the OMB. Conflict and cooperation have alternately characterized the relationship between these two presidential staffs. From time to time turf battles have also erupted between those responsible for economic advice and those charged with domestic policy making.

### Structural Orientation

The relationship between the domestic policy staff and the executive departments and agencies has been critical to the success of the president's policy efforts. While most presidents-elect ritually promise to institute a cabinet government upon taking office, they often find this undesirable and do not follow through on this promise.

In general, contemporary presidents have adopted one of two approaches to policy making. They have either assumed a White House orientation in which their senior aides dominate the process or they have adopted a cabinet-orientation system in which department secretaries exercise greater influence. The Nixon, Clinton, and, to a lesser extent, Carter presidencies illustrate the first approach, and the Reagan and Bush presidencies exemplify the latter.

In the White House approach, strong, influential domestic advisers funnel recommendations to the president. They filter and broker ideas. Their influence stems primarily from their control over the information flow to and from the president and the analytic network upon which that information rests.

The senior advisers tend to be advocates as well as mediators. Presidents rely on them for advice. This enhances their status and provides them with greater influence, not only with the president but also with others who wish to affect the president's policy judgments.

In contrast, the cabinet approach is less centralized. Cabinet secretaries, individually and collectively, have a greater impact. The White House policy office functions as a liaison and secretariat rather than as a policy initiator. It coordinates executive branch activity rather than dominates it. The senior adviser is more of a broker than an advocate.

Presidents Reagan and Bush utilized this approach in their cabinet council system. The councils, organized on the basis of substantive issue areas, provided a forum for the discussion of policy issues that crossed departmental lines. The system, patterned on a model Ronald Reagan used as governor of California, involved the president when final policy decisions were to be made. It provided a setting in which he could hear the issues debated, have points clarified, and then retire to make a decision.[10] Ralph Bledsoe, executive secretary to the Domestic Affairs Council during most of Reagan's second term, described how the councils worked in the Reagan administration:

> Interagency working groups are still the primary means by which policy issues are identified and scoped. Working groups and task forces are responsible for preparation of the issues and options papers to be discussed by the councils. As with the cabinet councils, issues are usually discussed in one or more council meetings without the President in attendance. When an issue is ready to be forwarded to the President for discussion and/or a decision, the council directs that a paper be prepared reflecting the council's views. If the President is being asked for a policy decision, the paper is in decision memorandum format, usually including a statement of the issue, background information, a discussion of decision options with advantages and disadvantages of each, and a recommendation, if appropriate. Following a meeting with the President, at which council members present their advice and views, the President will usually make a decision that is then communicated to the appropriate departments and agencies for implementation.[11]

Reagan wanted the councils to generate broad discussion, help develop consensus, and provide a mechanism for implementing administration decisions in accordance with his wishes. To work, end-runs had to be avoided, an administrative structure tied to the White House had to be established, and decisions had to be made that were consistent with the general ideological perspective of the administration. Secretaries could not simply be departmental advocates.

These conditions were more prevalent during the first term of the Reagan administration than during the second. Cabinet secretaries in key policy areas, particularly economic affairs and administration and management, tended to work through the council structure and not around it. However, in other areas the influence of the OMB and the group that met regularly to plan the administration's legislative strategy reduced the role of the cabinet councils on key administration priorities.

Any policy-making apparatus has its limitations. A council system is no exception. It requires many hours of meetings and group discussions. It is prone to leaks and may also be subject to a "groupthink" mentality, the emergence of a consensus that discourages careful and candid consideration. In Reagan's second term and during Bush's presidency, these structural limitations, changes in personnel, and the absence of clear and urgent policy objectives effectively reduced the influence of the cabinet councils. Bush also was more of a hands-on decision maker than Reagan and was less willing to rely solely on council discussion for his decisions.

## Stylistic Differences

In addition to the structural orientations presidents have adopted, their policy goals and personal styles have also affected White House policy making. The desire for innovative policy, particularly evident during the Kennedy, Johnson, and Clinton presidencies, spurred the development of new sources for ideas and programs. All three presidents turned to outside task forces to supplement the input they received from those inside their administrations. In contrast, the goals of retrenchment and consolidation, particularly evident during the Reagan administration, turned the focus back to executive officials appointed by the president who shared the president's ideological and policy perspectives.

While Kennedy and Johnson did not believe the bureaucracy could develop innovative policy, they were confident that civil servants would be able and willing to implement that policy once it had been initiated. Reagan lacked that confidence. He did not think that career bureaucrats could be trusted to execute the demise of their own programs. Clinton's position at the beginning of his administration was unclear.

All recent presidents have tried to keep tabs on their principal policy objectives by using their staff to promote and protect their interests. How the staff worked and how much power it wielded related in part to the president's style and penchant for exercising central authority. Those presidents who wished to involve themselves in the details of decision making seemed to have more flexible staff structures. Johnson, Carter, and Clinton had domestic policy offices that facilitated their reaching down the policy-making chain to make decisions. These presidents also had difficulty delegating authority to others. In contrast, Ford and Reagan were delegators who relied on their advisers for recommendations on what decisions to make and when to make them. Their policy operations were designed to relieve them of making the less important policy judgments. The difference was that Reagan had a more structured ideological perspective. It shaped the contours of his administration's decision making more than did Ford's pragmatic views.

Nixon, too, was a delegator. In contrast to Ford and Reagan, however, he did not enjoy or encourage oral debate among his subordinates. Rather he preferred a system that produced option papers from which he could make judgments. Like Carter and Bush, he desired detailed written analyses and ranges of alternatives from which he could choose.

## STRATEGIES FOR POLICY MAKING

The organizational component is only one aspect of policy making. Presidents obviously need a mechanism to help them design and coordinate their program, but that mechanism alone cannot ensure their program's success. Policy must be strategically accomplished. External interests must be accommodated; agendas must be artfully constructed and packaged; and long-term national objectives must be maintained, despite the persistence of parochial perspectives and short-term goals.

### Accommodating External Forces

Changes within the political and institutional environment, the decentralization of power in Congress, growth of single-issue groups, and weakening of partisan coalitions have increased and diversified pressures on the presidency. This has affected the policy-making process in two principal ways. It has made it more sensitive to outside interests, and it has required that presidents devote more personal and institutional resources to the achievement of their domestic policy goals.

Prior to the 1970s the Bureau of the Budget and, to a lesser extent, the White House were relatively invulnerable to external groups seeking to influence their decisions. The Budget Bureau considered itself a presidential agency. It had only one principal constituent, the president. Civil servants, not political appointees, ran the process and made most of the decisions. They were expected to do so within the framework of the president's objectives but also on the basis of the merits of the issue.

Taking political factors into account was the job of senior presidential aides in the White House. They worked in a relatively closed environment. While leaders of the president's party, influential supporters, and friends could gain access, the general public, including most of the organized groups, were excluded. Congress and the bureaucracy were the principal turfs on which groups fought their political battles. The Bureau of the Budget and the White House were distanced from the fray.

This began to change in the 1970s. The reorganization of the Budget Bureau into the Office of Management and Budget and the creation of a number of political positions to oversee its operation, the increase in the size of the policy staffs in the White House and their growth in power and influence, and the need to mobilize interest groups behind the president's program all contributed to this increased receptivity to outside views and sensitivity to outside pressures. The reaction of Presidents Ford and Carter to Watergate, particularly to Nixon's closed presidency, provided further impetus to open the White House to public view and political influence.

Lobbyists, who themselves were increasing in number, began to contact administration officials directly in the OMB and the White House to try to affect their policy judgments. The White House, in turn, began to utilize interest group and community leaders in building coalitions for their programs. By the mid-1970s a separate office within the White House had been established to accomplish this objective. Titled public liaison, it became a primary link between the administration and interest group leaders.

Initially, the office functioned as a conduit, providing access for those outside the government who wished to affect administration policies. It also provided public relations opportunities for the president. Literally thousands of group representatives and community leaders have been invited to the White House to meet administration officials and hear them promote their programs. This practice has become part of the outreach efforts that administrations now regularly employ to build support for themselves and their programs. Professor Mark A. Peterson postulates that presidents have used interest groups to legitimize their position in office, to improve their political status, to build coalitions for their policy, and to extend representation and access to groups operating within the political environment.[12]

The strategies presidents have used to guide their relations with interest groups have varied with their particular goals. According to Peterson, Roosevelt mobilized groups to support his program; Johnson was more concerned with building a broad-based public consensus; Carter at first was interested in reaching out to those who lacked effective representation. He later, however, refocused his efforts toward groups that could more effectively help him get his policy initiatives through Congress. The Reagan administration also sought to build group support for its policy-making initiatives. It reached out to a variety of groups, both sympathetic and nonsympathetic to the administration's policy objectives, in order to cast Reagan and his leadership image in a more favorable light and to meet increasing group expectations of access to the administration and service from it. [13] Beginning with Reagan and continuing through Clinton, many presidential aides, not simply those in the public liaison office, have had regular and on-going contact with outside groups.

One potentially pernicious effect of the expansion of presidential–interest group activities has been the extension of "revolving door politics," the practice of public officials leaving the government, obtaining jobs in the private sector, and cashing in on their political contacts. The key to interest group influence is access. Those individuals who, by virtue of their personal acquaintances, knowledge, and experiences, can provide such access are extremely valuable to interest groups and will be well compensated for their ability to open doors, present positions, and potentially influence policy. Senior White House officials fall into this category. In one celebrated case, Michael Deaver, deputy chief of staff to Reagan during his first term, left the administration to form his own consulting–public relations firm. He was subsequently accused of violating a federal conflict-of-interest law that restricts the contacts former public officials may have with those with whom they worked for one year and prohibits forever their involvement on issues on which they worked while in government. Deaver was subsequently convicted of perjury after testifying about his private activities before Congress.

To avoid any appearance of impropriety, President Clinton requested that appointees in his administration take a pledge not to have contacts with those with whom they worked in the government for a period of five years after they leave public service.[14]

In addition to group outreach activities, the White House has expanded its communication with state and local governments and with party officials and political leaders around the country. A larger, more sophisticated White House communications operation has been created to market the president and his policy objectives more effectively with the general population. Beginning in the 1980s, more than one-third of the people who work in the White House have been involved in public relations activities of one type or another.

### Building a Policy Agenda

The changing institutional and political environment for policy has also affected the content of agendas. In recent years the scope of these agendas has become more modest while the policies within them have become more complex. Moreover, their promotion has become more closely tied to the cycle of presidential influence.

In the past, agendas tended to be laundry lists of proposals designed to appeal to as broad a segment of electoral supporters as possible. Franklin Roosevelt's New Deal, Truman's Fair Deal, Kennedy's New Frontier, Johnson's Great Society, even Nixon's New Federalism programs fit into this category. The depressed American economy of the 1930s, the increasing social consciousness of the 1960s, the democratizing of the nomination process in the 1970s, and the expansion of the electoral period during the past decade have all contributed to the demands for a large and diverse policy agenda.

The way in which presidents have formulated their domestic programs also contributed to the same end. By soliciting proposals from a variety of sources and established interests, presidents have generated multiple pressures on their own programs. The most effective way to deal with these pressures had been to accommodate them in packages that included something for almost everyone.

While these pressures have persisted and even increased, the president's ability to achieve them has diminished. Resources have become scarce; a huge national debt has developed. The government lacks the revenues to meet a plethora of policy demands. The system has become more pluralistic. Greater effort must be exerted to mobilize a majority coalition. This has increased the costs of domestic policy making for the president. More time, energy, and institutional resources have to be devoted to these activities.

One consequence of increasing costs and decreasing resources has been the need to limit items in the domestic agenda, prioritizing them more clearly and cycling them more effectively over the congressional calendar rather than overwhelming Congress with too many proposals too quickly. Another has been the need to package and promote the proposals in such a way as to maximize their public appeal. A third imperative for contemporary presidents is to avoid excessive involvement in the details of their administration's policy and maintain a longer-term national perspective.

LIMITING THE ITEMS.    The expansion of governmental activities has generated more groups with a stake in public policy. Today, there are more opinions to hear, more interests to balance, more agendas to combine. This has produced, in the words of Hugh Heclo, more "policy congestion."[15]

It has also increased the complexity of many issues with which contemporary administrations must deal. One policy decision affects another. Spheres of jurisdiction overlap. Distinctions between domestic and international concerns are no longer clear-cut.

The task for presidents and their aides is to sort out the relationships among the competing interests and complex issues and to integrate them into a comprehensive administrative policy. One way to do this has already been discussed—use an institutional mechanism that imposes a presidential perspective such as the Bureau of the Budget did prior to 1965 and the White House has done since then. Another tactic is to reduce the agenda to fewer critical items and bind them together in some fashion. The Reagan and, to a lesser extent, Clinton administrations have employed this latter strategy.

Upon taking office, both presidents tried to convert their campaign promises into carefully defined policy agendas. Reagan had two basic legislative initiatives: budget and tax reform; Clinton had three: economic stimulus, budget reduction, and health care reform. These items constituted each administration's principal legislative priorities for its first year in office.

Limiting items helps presidents set the pace and tone of public debate. It helps them focus public attention on certain presidential activities. This contributes to the perception that they are in command. It also enables them to concentrate resources behind their administration's priorities rather than have them dissipated in accordance with numerous wish lists that emanate from the Congress or the executive departments and agencies.

There is, of course, a negative side to limiting the agenda too much. Some people's expectations will not be satisfied. For the Reagan administration it was the social objectives of the conservatives that were largely abandoned. For the Clinton administration liberal and conservative Democrats each accused the administration of tilting against them. Another problem is that defeats will appear that much more serious if one of a few priorities is derailed as it was for Clinton when he failed to get his economic stimulus package through the Senate.

CYCLING POLITICAL ISSUES.    Another strategic consequence of the increased costs of domestic policy making is that an administration's priorities must be cycled over the course of the congressional calendar. Presidents cannot wait several months before making their initial proposals nor should they inundate Congress with them.

Moving quickly on the most controversial items is important for two reasons. Electoral cycles, department pressures, and public moods tend to decrease presidential influence over time. As members of Congress position themselves for the next election, as bureaucrats and their clientele begin to assert their claims on political appointees, as segments of the winning coalition become disillusioned, as the outparty begins to coalesce in opposition to the incumbent, it is more difficult for a president to achieve domestic policy goals. Moreover, presidential reputations are built early and tend to persist longer than does their ability to achieve policy successes.[16]

Carter found this out the hard way. He used his first six months in office to develop policies to implement his election promises. By the time these proposals were readied for Congress, Carter's honeymoon had ended and his policies got stuck in a legislative labyrinth.

The Reagan administration, in contrast, learned from the Carter experience. With his agenda in place prior to taking office, Reagan seized on his unexpectedly large electoral victory in 1980 to claim a mandate for his economic program and then moved quickly to obtain its enactment. Proposals that were developed later in the administration, such as the New Federalism and urban enterprise zone plans, met with considerably more congressional resistance. In general Reagan was less successful as his administration progressed. His congressional support declined even as his popularity increased.

Bill Clinton also learned from the Carter and Reagan experiences. He adjusted his legislative schedule and abandoned his campaign promise to introduce health care reform within the first 100 days of his administration. He delayed his health care proposals until September to avoid overwhelming Congress with too many complex issues and thereby diluting his administration's efforts to get its deficit reduction plan through Congress.

The dilemma presidents often face is that their influence tends to be greatest when their knowledge of substantive policy issues and how to win support for them is least. Not only do they not have sufficient time to educate themselves before making critical policy judgments, but they may not have time to develop innovative policy at all. According to Paul C. Light, declining influence requires presidents to look for available alternatives among existing options and take the first acceptable one.[17]

Declining influence may also require presidents to take advantage of items carried over on the legislative agenda from one Congress to the next. Backing proposals that already have garnered support in Congress and with the general public can enhance an administration's early legislative record although it obviously limits a president's personal impact on this legislation and the credit received from its enactment; it may also divert the congressional and public focus from other items that are higher priorities for the new president. Nonetheless, the opportunities for quick victories, the need to redeem campaign promises or platform planks on these pending, unresolved legislative issues, and the desire of a new president to placate groups in Congress who support the legislation are all inducements for the president to pursue this strategy rather than wipe the slate clean and begin anew. Thus Clinton announced that he supported and would approve legislation that the previous Congress enacted but his predecessor had vetoed—legislation requiring employers to provide for parental leave, requiring states to ease voter registration procedures, and permitting federal workers to become more involved in political activities.

The degree to which the ongoing legislative agenda limits the president's ability to set the public agenda for the country has been the subject of debate among political scientists. Charles O. Jones argues that a variety of factors affects presidential discretion: the election campaign, the range of policy alternatives being considered, and the political environment in which a president has to operate. Jones goes on to conclude that the greater the congruity between the president's agenda and the Congress's, the greater the likelihood for achieving major legislative successes. Jones points to the elections of 1964 and 1980 and to their legislative consequences to illustrate his point.[18]

Presidential discretion also varies with the type of issue, according to a study by Fengyan Shi. She postulates that presidents have more discretion on long-term issues than short-term ones and on ordinary (nonemergent) issues than on crisis and newly emergent ones.[19]

PACKAGING AND PROMOTING LEGISLATIVE PRIORITIES.    In addition to setting the agenda by deciding which items to include and when to include them, it is necessary to package them artfully. Presenting a few key proposals rather than a comprehensive set of policies reduces the number of instances in which supporters of the president can disagree, and presenting them as an either/or proposition lessens the chances that the president's proposal will be modified by others. The Reagan and Clinton experiences are instructive here. In 1981 Reagan presented Congress with a "take it or leave it" budget reconciliation plan. In 1993 Clinton gave Congress a third option with his budget reconciliation plan, declaring that if legislators did not like his proposed combination of spending cuts and tax increases they could change them. They did, jettisoning the president's proposed energy tax and increasing cuts in the Medicare program in the process. Moreover, Clinton's willingness to accept changes encouraged members of Congress to bargain up to the final vote whereas the Reagan strategy did not. Whether Clinton could have achieved a substantial deficit reduction plan had he not indicated his willingness to compromise, however, is questionable.

The fewer roll call votes on a legislative proposal, the easier it is for a president to concentrate resources and mobilize winning coalitions. Reagan successfully pursued this strategy in his 1981 and 1982 budget battles with the Democrats in Congress. Similarly, the packaging of the large personal and corporate income tax cut in 1981, the social security compromise in 1983, and the tax reform program in 1986 was key to their enactment into legislation.

Clinton adopted a similar strategy in 1993, but was less successful. In his State of the Union address he urged that his economic stimulus plan and budget deficit proposals be left intact. However, his failure to consult with or accept modifications from Republicans resulted in the defeat of the stimulus package by filibuster in the Senate. Clinton permitted amendments to the budget deficit plan and won, although barely, on the final vote.

To be successful, presidents must also promote their priorities within the Congress and among the general public. To gain congressional support, it is necessary to convince members of Congress that the proposed legislation is supported within their constituencies. Generating a constituency-based response is one way to achieve that objective. Clinton's prime-time televised speech in August 1993, a few days before the final vote on his deficit reduction plan, was designed to build such support and thus make it easier for Democrats to vote for legislation that included substantial tax increases. A similar public relations strategy was pursued successfully prior to the vote on the North American Free Trade Agreement in November 1993.

Showing the economic benefit for the constituency is another tactic that presidents use to win votes. In an effort to gain the support of New Jersey Senator Frank Lautenberg, up for reelection in 1994, the president announced that his budget legislation would create 75,000 new jobs in New Jersey; to gain the support of Senator Dennis DeConcini of Arizona, a state with a large elderly population, the president agreed to limit increased taxes on social security benefits. The president also met with and talked to numerous members of Congress prior to the final vote on this and other major legislation.

DISCERNING THE FOREST FROM THE TREES.    Constraints on time and energy suggest another lesson for contemporary presidents. They should not involve themselves too deeply in the details of decision making, although they must provide general policy guidance. Jimmy Carter is a case in point. Finding it difficult to delegate to others, he spent considerable time becoming an expert on the various policy issues in which he was interested or which came to his attention. At the beginning of his administration he read around four hundred pages of papers and memos a day! James Fallows, a former Carter speech writer, describes his boss as "the perfectionist accustomed to thinking that to do a job right you must do it yourself."[20] Fallows illustrated:

> He [Carter] would leave for a weekend at Camp David laden with thick briefing books, would pore over budget tables to check the arithmetic, and during his first six months in office, would personally review all requests to use the White House tennis court. . . . After six months had passed, Carter learned that this was ridiculous, as he learned about other details he would have to pass by if he was to use his time well. But his preference was still to try to do it all.[21]

Naturally, this prodigious effort took its toll, and Carter was eventually forced to cut back. Bill Clinton evidenced similar tendencies at the beginning of his presidency, personally examining policy issues and personnel selections in great detail.

In contrast to Carter and Clinton, Reagan took the opposite tack. While he articulated a strong ideological perspective, he left most of the details to senior White House and cabinet officials. This exposed him to the charge that he was manipulated by his staff and that he was overly dependent on key White House aides for the decisions he had to make, when he had to make them, and the range of options from which he had to choose. It also left him prey to his staff's misperceptions of what he wanted and its judgments of what was in his interest. The problems that developed in the White House national security staff and that culminated in the Iran–Contra affair demonstrate the dangers of a hands-off, disengaged approach to presidential staffing and decision making. (See Chapter 7 for a more detailed discussion of the Iran–Contra affair and its impact on presidential decision making.)

SUSTAINING A NATIONAL PERSPECTIVE.    Reagan's ideological perspective helped him tackle another policy-making problem that besets contemporary presidents—how to sustain a national perspective in the light of continuous parochial pressures that are exerted on almost every policy issue. Ideology provides a rationale for including (and excluding) certain items in a policy agenda and linking them to one another in a way that makes sense to partisan supporters. It helps transform an electoral coalition into a policy one. It is also useful in overcoming the tendencies that frequently lead executive officials to adopt views and advocate interests that are at variance with the president's.

The Reagan administration employed ideology in converting electoral promises into tangible policy goals. It also used ideology as a criterion for appointment. Cabinet and subcabinet officials were nominated in part because they shared the president's views. They were expected to impose those views on their agencies rather than the other way around.

Ideology, in short, can be a unifying tool. It can build support by simplifying and focusing. It can also give people a sense of where the president is coming from and going to. Predicting presidential reactions is useful for politicians in calculating their response to presidential requests and for the public in understanding the direction of the administration.

Ideological guidelines are not without their dangers, however. Rigid adherence to an ideological perspective makes compromise difficult. As it unites supporters so too can it unify opponents, thereby polarizing policy positions. It can blind adherents to the nuances of proposals and the need for adjustment and change. Pragmatic solutions may be disregarded. Policy is apt to be more precipitous and extreme. Continuity between administrations of differing ideological perspectives is more difficult to achieve.

On the other hand, lack of an overarching ideological or conceptual framework can produce the same problem within an administration. Critics have contended that policy inconsistencies in the Carter administration were due in part to this problem. Again as James Fallows observed:

> I came to think that Carter believes fifty things, but no one thing. He holds explicit, thorough positions on every issue under the sun, but he has no large view of the relations between them, no line indicating which goals (reducing unemployment? human rights?) will take precedence over which (inflation control? a SALT treaty?) when the goals conflict.[22]

The same criticism has been directed toward Clinton. In Reagan's case, however, the president's ideological perspective helped establish the goals and the initial programmatic components. The president subsequently deviated from these components when they appeared to be politically unattainable or economically or socially unfeasible.

MAINTAINING A LONG-RANGE VIEW.     Another problem related to promoting policy consistency is maintaining a long-range perspective. In making policy, everyday emergencies tend to drive out future planning. This limits the outlook of those involved in policy making to the short term and rarely beyond the next election.

Contemporary White Houses have attempted to design a longer-range domestic planning capability but without much success. In 1975 President Ford asked Vice President Rockefeller to provide leadership and direction for the establishment of social goals. However, Rockefeller's decision not to run for office one year later abruptly ended this effort. The Reagan administration's attempt to create a long-range policy-making capability in the form of a new office of planning and evaluation met with a similar fate. Charged with developing strategic plans for the president's agenda and schedule, the office fashioned a series of early blueprints that consisted of possible responses to international and national crises. As the administration got underway and confronted changing external conditions and public moods, the office's futuristic planning became less relevant to day-to-day decisions that had to be made, and the office was disbanded within two years.

## CONCLUSION

Presidents have become the nation's principal domestic policymakers. This role developed primarily in the twentieth century and largely as a consequence of social, economic, and political problems that required solutions by the federal government. With a national perspective, a large staff structure, and the ability to focus public attention and mobilize support, presidents have been placed in a position to propose policy and get it adopted. The electoral process has provided them with further incentives to do so. Congress, the executive, and the public look to them for policy leadership.

The mechanism necessary to accomplish this leadership took form over two decades. Initially the Budget Bureau provided the resources and managed the processes, with its senior civil servants working closely with the White House to develop, coordinate, and clear policy proposals emanating from the departments and agencies. Once presidents turned from departments and agencies to other sources for policy ideas, however, the budget agency's influence declined and the White House's increased.

Since the mid-1960s the president's chief policy aides have dominated the policy-making process. They, in turn, have depended on their assistants to monitor and integrate the input of others. The White House has also become more involved in building support for these priorities. Separate presidential offices charged with policy development and political liaison have now become established and institutionalized.

The development of these structures has enhanced the presidency's influence but not necessarily that of individual presidents. Although the goals and style of a president still shape domestic policy making, these individualized features cannot control a process that has become large and complex. Presidents are dependent on their staff for deciding when they should become involved, what options they should consider, and how those options are presented, articulated, and promoted inside and outside the government.

Changes within the political system have made the president's tasks more burdensome. Competing demands, complex issues, and confrontational politics have made it more difficult for the chief policymaker to design programs and obtain support for them. The dilemma presidents face is that expectations of their performance exceed resources at their disposal. This has affected strategies for policy making.

Today, to exert policy leadership presidents must accommodate external forces and mobilize them into a policy coalition. They must limit their priorities, cycling and carefully packaging and promoting them over the course of their administration. Finally, they must work to establish and maintain a long-term national perspective. It is important that they develop and move key parts of their legislative agenda early in their administration, not only because their chances for legislative success are better but because early successes enhance their reputation and increase the political capital they can use later on in their presidency. Addressing the national policy needs and contributing to the administration's political needs also serve the president's leadership needs.

These tasks are not easy. They require skillful personal and institutional leadership. Presidents cannot dictate policy outcomes but they can affect them. Their reputation, their subsequent achievements, and ultimately the fate of their presidency may hinge on how well they do so.

## NOTES

1. Franklin D. Roosevelt, "First Inaugural Address," March 4, 1933, as appears in the *Congressional Record*, 73rd Congress, Special Session, pp. 5–26.

2. Quoted in Richard E. Neustadt, "Presidency and Legislation: Planning the President's Program," *American Political Science Review* 49 (December 1955): 1015.

3. The one major exception was the creation of the social security program.

4. Paul C. Light, *The President's Agenda* (Baltimore: Johns Hopkins University Press, 1982), p. 217.

5. Richard L. Cole and Stephen J. Wayne, unpublished research.

6. Clark Clifford, quoted in Stephen J. Wayne, *The Legislative Presidency* (New York: Harper and Row, 1978), p. 104.

7. Lyndon B. Johnson, *The Vantage Point: Perspectives of the Presidency 1963–1969* (New York: Holt, Rinehart and Winston, 1971), pp. 326–27.

8. Richard P. Nathan, *The Plot That Failed* (New York: Wiley, 1975).

9. The council was not officially created until August 1993; however, it had met prior to that time. The White House claimed that an administrative oversight was responsible for the failure to formally establish the council at the outset of the Clinton presidency.

10. President Reagan did not like making decisions within the meeting itself because he did not want to upset those who opposed the position he took. After deciding on a course of action, Reagan would have his counselor, Edwin Meese, communicate the decision to the members of the council and oversee its implementation.

11. Ralph C. Bledsoe, "Policy Management in the Reagan Administration," in James P. Pfiffner and R. Gordon Hoxie, eds., *The Presidency in Transition* (New York: Center for the Study of the Presidency, 1989), pp. 60–61.

12. Mark A. Peterson, "The Presidency and Organized Interests: White House Patterns of Interest Group Liaison," *American Political Science Review* 86 (September 1992): 612–16.

13. Ibid., pp. 617–20.

14. According to the Clinton pledge, those officials who deal with foreign policy issues, such as trade, can never represent a foreign government or corporation after they leave the federal government.

15. Hugh Heclo, "One Executive Branch or Many?" in Anthony King, ed., *Both Ends of the Avenue* (Washington, D.C.: American Enterprise Institute, 1983), p. 32.

16. For a discussion of what strategies presidents should pursue to achieve their legislative policy objectives, see Mark A. Peterson, "Developing the President's Program: The President as a Strategic Player" (paper presented at the Annual Meeting of the Midwest Political Science Association, Chicago, March 1990); Cary Covington and Rhonda Kinney, "Presidential Agenda Setting Power, Attitudes Toward Risk, and Congressional Contexts: Accounting for Differences in Rates of Presidential Success in Congress" (paper presented at the Annual Meeting of the American Political Science Association, Washington, D.C., September 1991); and Patrick J. Fett, "Truth in Advertising: The Revelation of Presidential Legislative Priorities," *Western Political Quarterly* (Winter 1992): 895–920.

17. Light, *The President's Agenda*, p. 219.

18. Charles O. Jones, "Presidents and Agendas: Who Defines What for Whom?" in James P. Pfiffner, ed., *The Managerial Presidency* (Pacific Grove, Calif.: Brooks/Cole, 1991), pp. 197–213.

19. Fengyan Shi, "Agenda Setting: What Influence Do Presidents Actually Have?" (paper presented at the Annual Meeting of the American Political Science Association, Washington D.C., September 1993).

20. James Fallows, "The Passionless Presidency," *Atlantic*, May 1979, p. 38.

21. Ibid.

22. Ibid., p. 42.

## SELECTED READINGS

Bledsoe, Ralph C. "Policy Management in the Reagan Administration." In James P. Pfiffner and R. Gordon Hoxie, eds. *The Presidency in Transition*. New York: Center for the Study of the Presidency, 1989, pp. 54–61.

Edwards, George C., III, Steven A. Shull, and Norman C. Thomas, eds. *The Presidency and Public Policy-Making*. Pittsburgh: University of Pittsburgh Press, 1985.

Fett, Patrick J. "Truth in Advertising: The Revelation of Presidential Legislative Priorities." *Western Political Quarterly* (Winter 1992): 895–920.

Heclo, Hugh. "One Executive Branch or Many?" In Anthony King, ed. *Both Ends of the Avenue*. Washington, D.C.: American Enterprise Institute, 1983, pp. 26–58.

Jones, Charles O. "Presidents and Agendas: Who Defines What for Whom?" In James P. Pfiffner, ed. *The Managerial Presidency*. Pacific Grove, Calif.: Brooks/Cole, 1991, pp. 197–213.

LeLoup, Lance T., and Steven A. Shull. *Congress and the President: The Policy Connection*. Belmont, Calif.: Wadsworth, 1993.

Light, Paul C. *The President's Agenda*. Revised ed. Baltimore: Johns Hopkins University Press, 1991.

Peterson, Mark A. "The Presidency and Organized Interests: White House Patterns of Interest Group Liaison." *American Political Science Review* 86 (September 1992): 612–25.

Pfiffner, James P. *The Strategic Presidency: Hitting the Ground Running*. Chicago: Dorsey, 1988.

Wayne, Stephen J. *The Legislative Presidency*. New York: Harper and Row, 1978.

Wyszomirski, Margaret J. "A Domestic Policy Office: Presidential Office in Search of a Role." *Policy Studies Journal* 12 (June 1984): 705–18.

# 13

# Budgetary and Economic Policy Making

Presidents have always been concerned with the costs of government and the state of the economy, but that concern has never been greater than it is today. With a budget approaching $2 trillion, with a national debt in the range of $4 trillion, with a sizable budget deficit, with federal revenues tied to economic conditions, with the private sector increasingly sensitive to public expenditures, almost any substantive policy decision a president makes has significant budgetary and economic implications. Similarly, almost any major budget and economic decision has important political consequences.

Moreover, budgetary and economic decisions are interrelated. Budgetary problems, particularly deficits, are magnified by a weak economy and diminished by a strong one. A large and continuing budget deficit can have both long- and short-term effects on the economy, as can a surplus.

These factors make budgetary and economic policy making one of the most critical, complex, and persistent spheres for the exercise of presidential leadership. Like it or not, most things that presidents want to do cost money. Without sufficient financial resources they will be unable to achieve many of their most important policy objectives. But ironically *their* budgets are not theirs nor can they be theirs alone. Hampered by commitments made by their predecessors and by previous Congresses; obligated to pay interest on the national debt and meet the statutory requirements of other ongoing legislative programs; pressured to respond to natural disasters with emergency aid; and constrained by the need to maintain payrolls, continue research and development, and ensure the production of items, particularly in the area of defense, that are vital to the national security, presidents today exercise limited influence over how their budgets will be allocated. And to make matters worse, the influence that they do exert is subject to congressional modification in the form of budget resolutions and reconciliations. Similarly, the revenue side is also conditioned by previous and current legislation and also fluctuates with the economy. And all of these constraints have significant political consequences that further condition the behavior of elected officials, including the president.

So presidents are placed in a dilemma. They are expected to redeem their campaign pledges, meet the country's changing needs, and do so in a manner that is both economical and efficient. Yet they often lack the resources to achieve these objectives and the discretion to obtain those resources. Directing change under these circumstances is extremely difficult although it is not impossible, as Franklin Roosevelt and Ronald Reagan demonstrated at the outset of their administrations. Nonetheless, being a facilitator rather than a director tends to be the order of the day as far as budget and economic policy making are concerned.

This chapter will explore the president's leadership dilemma in a sphere that has become so associated with his popularity, his reelectability, his reputation, and, ultimately, his exercise of power: the federal budget and the national economy. Beginning with a historic overview of the executive budget, we will look at the development of a presidential role in budgeting. The involvement of executive branch and congressional units in budgetary decision making is also examined, as are the various stages in the executive and legislative phases of the process. Similarly, we explore the evolution of economic policy making and the participation of presidential and other executive branch offices in decision making within this sphere. Throughout we describe the forces that affect presidential action and limit presidential discretion. The concluding section summarizes the recent trends in budget and economic policy making.

## THE FEDERAL BUDGET

The budget is a document that forecasts revenue and estimates expenditures of the federal government. It does so for a fiscal year, a twelve-month period beginning October 1 and continuing through the following September 30. Since the primary purpose of the budget is to allocate limited funds, that allocation is, by definition, highly political. Competition for limited resources is inevitable. Priorities have to be established. The budget is an instrument that reflects those priorities in a very concrete way.

A presidential budget has been required since 1921. Prior to that time departments and agencies went directly to Congress for their appropriations. Their requests were compiled in a "Book of Estimates," but neither the president nor treasury secretary made any systematic attempt to coordinate total revenues, although they occasionally did modify some of the requests.[1] However, with revenues (primarily from custom duties) exceeding expenditures during most of the nineteenth century, the lack of centralized planning was not perceived to be much of a problem.

Expenditures rose at the end of the century and the beginning of the next, and modest surpluses turned into deficits. Concerned about them, Congress enacted legislation in 1905 to ensure that the government spent money prudently. It gave the president the statutory responsibility and authority to prevent the unwise and unnecessary expenditures of government funds.[2] The costs of World War I, however, vastly increased federal government expenditures, produced sizable budget deficits, and encouraged Congress to give the president budget authority. The Budget and Accounting Act of 1921 made the president responsible for an annual executive branch budget and established a bureau within the Department of the Treasury to handle these new presidential duties. Acting as a surrogate for the president, this bureau organized and ran a process that solicited yearly expenditure estimates from the departments and agencies, evaluated and adjusted them according to the president's goals, and finally combined them in a comprehensive executive budget. This budget review cycle has continued through the years although Congress's consideration of the budget has undergone significant change.

The federal budget, however, has also changed dramatically since the 1920s.[3] In its early years it was relatively small by contemporary standards, oriented toward the executive agencies, and utilized primarily as a vehicle for *controlling federal spending*. Since the primary object of the budget was to make the national government more economical, to eliminate the deficits, and to keep a lid on spending, federal outlays were substantially reduced during this initial period, 1921–1930.[4]

Total government expenditures were in the range of $2 billion to $3 billion. Most of the money went directly to the departments and agencies for the costs of running the government. There were relatively few public works projects that required direct funding.

The Great Depression of the 1930s had a major effect on the character of the budget. Increased demands for government intervention in the economy culminated in Franklin Roosevelt's New Deal programs. Followed by World War II and the Cold War, this larger governmental role greatly accelerated spending in domestic and defense areas. Fortunately, the economic recovery, beginning in the late 1940s and continuing through the 1950s, provided increased revenues for these greater expenditures. These developments not only expanded the size of the budget but also moved it into an *incremental* phase, one in which existing programs continued to be maintained with a budget that included an increment to cover increased costs.

During this phase, which reached its zenith in the 1960s, the budget highlighted new programs and supported existing ones. Agencies assumed that the costs of their ongoing programs would be met in addition to whatever priority legislation the president wished to introduce.

While the departments continued to administer their programs, more and more of the outlays went to third parties. Programs designed to help the invalid and the poor, senior citizens, veterans, and others provided direct payments to individuals from the treasury. Since the 1970s these so-called entitlement programs have consumed an ever-increasing proportion of government expenditures, expenditures that are not easily subject to presidential control. Today they constitute 46 percent of the total budget (see Figure 13-1).

The reason that entitlements are not under the president's control is that these programs and others like them legally entitle individuals to benefits as long as they meet stated eligibility requirements. These entitlements are independent of specific appropriations by Congress. In 1974, Congress decided to peg social security payments to the consumer price index, forsaking decision making even on the levels of benefits. The president also does not have the authority to change these payments; only an act of Congress can do so.

From the president's perspective, the sad fact is that a relatively small proportion of the total budget is subject to presidential control. Interest on the national debt, which constitutes about 14 percent of the total budget, must be met. Payments for agricultural commodities and government support programs are also required by law. Many of the costs of national defense, such as personnel, weapons systems, and ships and aircraft, are "big-ticket" items and cannot be reduced or eliminated without basic changes in security policy and/or significant cost to the taxpayer. When these expenditures and the entitlement programs are considered, the result is that presidents can exercise effective discretion over less than 25 percent of the total budget. Thus, presidents who

**Figure 13-1. The Federal Budget for Fiscal Year 1994**

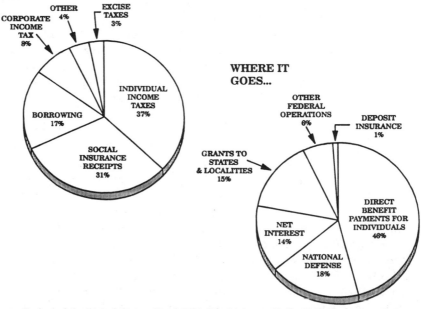

Source: *Budget of the United States, Fiscal 1994* (Washington, D.C.: U.S. Government Printing Office, 1993), p. 1.

wish to reduce government expenditures substantially have little leverage to do so, at least on their own.

The increasing proportion of the budget devoted to direct benefit payments to individuals has important effects. In addition to decreasing presidential influence on the budget, these payments have increased the political ramifications of budget decisions. Instead of primarily affecting departments and agencies, the budget now has a direct impact on many outside the government. As a consequence, outside constituencies composed of veterans, senior citizens, farmers, industry (such as defense contractors), labor, and others have organized to protect and extend their benefits. They regularly exert pressure on budget makers. This pressure makes it more difficult to use the budget as a device for controlling spending. By the late 1970s the budget demonstrated more of the presidency's weaknesses than its strengths; presidents were responsible for it yet controlled little of it.

In the 1980s the primary objective of presidential budgeting began to change. Seeds of this change were sown in the economic problems of the previous decade: the decline in the nation's productivity and its industrial competitiveness and the rise in inflation and unemployment, especially during the 1970s. These factors, along with a steadily increasing national debt and sizable deficits, led those inside and outside the government to question the wisdom of ever-increasing government expenditures within the domestic sphere, particularly when the economy was weak.

Upon taking office, President Reagan took the lead in reordering national priorities and used the budget to achieve his objectives. *Incremental* increases gave way to *decremental* adjustments. The proportion of the budget devoted to domestic discretionary spending was cut; entitlement programs such as social security were adjusted; money for defense was increased.

These changes affected the budget's orientation more than they affected overall outlays. Instead of distributing an expanding base of resources, the budget redistributed a declining one. This increased the competition and division among the agencies and outside groups concerned with "their" expenditures. With different interests and groups vying to protect and promote their own programs, a consensus supporting the budget was harder to achieve. Congress found it more difficult to enact budgetary policy, spending more time on budget matters and taking more votes on budget questions than it did in previous eras. Consideration of the budget drove other issues off the legislative calendar. This preoccupation has continued into the 1990s.

Presidents also had to devote more time and energy to their budget activities, not merely to formulating the budget but to obtaining congressional approval for it. As principal policymakers and coalition builders, they had little option. Their policy success and public approval were dependent, in large part, on their ability to get their budget proposals enacted into law.

Differing budget priorities and policy proposals characterized presidential–congressional relations during the last six years of the Reagan presidency and all of the Bush presidency. President Reagan and, to a lesser extent, President Bush wanted to maintain a relatively high level of defense expenditures and continue the level of personal and corporate income taxes that had been established in the early 1980s. To keep the budget relatively in balance, both presidents hoped to cut expenditures for domestic programs. Congress, however, was unwilling to do so, approving the bulk of their defense budgets but refusing to cut many of their proposals for decreasing domestic spending. Without a major increase in revenue, the result was readily predictable—a growing federal deficit. By the end of the Reagan administration, the yearly deficits had almost tripled the national debt. During the four years of the Bush administration they continued to rise at a rapid rate. When George Bush left office in 1992, the national debt exceeded $4 trillion, tripling over the twelve year period, 1980–1992. (See Table 13-1.) In the process the United States moved from being the world's greatest creditor nation to the world's largest debtor nation. The figures are startling, as Table 13–1 attests.

During this period Congress and the president repeatedly clashed over the importance of the debt, its real and potential impact on the economy, and how to deal with it. Each side blamed the other for the magnitude of the problem. Attempts to control deficit spending were largely unsuccessful.

In the 1980s Congress attempted to impose discipline on government spending by enacting legislation that automatically triggered cuts if expenditures exceeded revenues by a certain amount. The first of these legislative acts, the Balanced Budget and Emergency Deficit Control Act of 1985, known by the names of two of its sponsors, Senators Phil Gramm and Warren Rudman, required a balanced budget within five years of its passage (subsequently extended by further legislation to 1993), set specific deficit targets to be met over this period, and authorized automatic cuts in some domestic and most defense programs (except primarily those involving personnel) to bring the deficit to the required levels if the targets were not met. By authorizing automatic cuts, Congress was acknowledging its own inability to make tough and potentially unpopular political decisions.

The General Accounting Office (GAO) was originally given the responsibility to determine the size of these cuts after receiving estimates from the Office of Management and Budget (OMB) and the Congressional Budget Office (CBO). However, the Supreme Court determined that the GAO's role violated the constitutional principle of separation of powers by involving a congressional agency in executive decisions. Anticipating that the Court might place such an interpretation on the law, Congress provided an alternative mechanism in which a joint budget committee would receive the OMB and CBO reports and design legislation on which Congress would then vote to sequester the additional money.

Table 13-1. The National Debt (in billions)*

| Year | Current Dollars | Constant 1987 Dollarst | GDP | Interest on Debt Held by the Public as a Percent of Total Outlays |
|------|----------------|------------------------|-----|------------------------------------------------------------------|
| 1950 | 219.0 | 1,094.0 | 82.4 | 11.4 |
| 1955 | 226.6 | 1,001.4 | 58.9 | 7.6 |
| 1960 | 236.8 | 907.8 | 46.9 | 8.5 |
| 1965 | 260.8 | 922.1 | 38.9 | 8.1 |
| 1970 | 283.2 | 818.3 | 28.7 | 7.9 |
| 1975 | 394.7 | 829.6 | 26.1 | 7.5 |
| 1980 | 709.3 | 1,004.9 | 26.8 | 10.6 |
| 1981 | 784.8 | 1,009.2 | 26.5 | 12.1 |
| 1982 | 919.2 | 1,100.2 | 29.4 | 13.6 |
| 1983 | 1,131.0 | 1,229.8 | 34.1 | 13.8 |
| 1984 | 1,300.0 | 1,430.9 | 35.2 | 15.7 |
| 1985 | 1,499.4 | 1,589.7 | 37.8 | 16.2 |
| 1986 | 1,736.2 | 1,787.6 | 41.2 | 16.1 |
| 1987 | 1,888.1 | 1,888.1 | 42.4 | 16.0 |
| 1988 | 2,050.3 | 1,978.4 | 42.6 | 16.2 |
| 1989 | 2,189.3 | 2,021.5 | 42.3 | 16.5 |
| 1990 | 2,410.4 | 2,134.8 | 44.1 | 16.2 |
| 1991 | 2,687.9 | 2,282.4 | 47.7 | 16.2 |
| 1992 | 2,998.6 | 2,475.5 | 51.1 | 15.5 |
| 1993 estimate | 3,303.8 | 2,664.2 | 53.5 | 14.5 |
| 1994 estimate | 3,574.4 | 2,814.5 | 54.9 | 14.8 |
| 1995 estimate | 3,826.9 | 2,943.7 | 55.8 | 15.1 |
| 1996 estimate | 4,052.8 | 3,048.4 | 56.3 | 15.6 |
| 1997 estimate | 4,293.7 | 3,159.7 | 56.9 | 15.8 |
| 1998 estimate | 4,575.7 | 3,294.0 | 58.1 | 15.8 |

*Indicates debt held by the public.
†Debt in current dollars deflated by the GDP deflator with 1987 = 100.

Source: *Budget of the United States Government Fiscal 1994.* p. 32.

The legislation, however, did not achieve its objective. To stay within the targets prescribed by the law, Congress and the president devised a variety of accounting and reporting techniques that technically met the goals but actually evaded them. These included overly optimistic forecasts of revenue, underestimation of automatic government payments, the extension of expenditures into the next fiscal year, the pulling of revenues into the current year from the next one, and the enactment of supplemental spending bills not included in the Gramm–Rudman targets. The government even sold some of its assets to stay within the guidelines of the legislation. The need to bail out the savings and loan associations further aggravated the problem.

As a result real deficits continued to soar throughout the 1980s were projected to exceed $320 billion in the early 1990s. These large deficits created pressure on Congress and the president to try again to fix the problem. (Table 13-2 lists actual 'and estimated deficits from 1980 through 1998.)

After an extended series of meetings between representatives of the president and congressional leaders held behind closed doors in the spring of 1990, an agreement was reached to raise additional revenue and impose constraints on future government spending. Both aspects of the plan to save $500 billion over five years engendered controversy. The increase in revenue violated Bush's often-quoted campaign pledge not to raise taxes if he were elected in 1988. Conservatives within his own party were particularly unhappy and defiant. Democrats were critical as well, particularly with the projected savings that were to come from premium increases and deduction decreases in the Medicare program. Together these groups defeated the compromise, forcing the president and Congress to come up with a new package which a majority of the legislature and the president subsequently approved.

The Budget Enforcement Act of 1990 was designed to reduce the deficit by making Congress and the president more responsible for those parts of the budget they could control directly. It placed specific limits on discretionary spending, that is, spending that was not automatic, and set overall spending targets within broad categories. There was also a "pay-as-you-go" provision that required Congress to pay for the cost of

### Table 13-2.  U.S. Budget Deficits, 1980–1998

| Year | Deficit (in billions) |
|------|----------------------|
| 1980 | $ 73,835 |
| 1981 | 78,976 |
| 1982 | 127,989 |
| 1983 | 207,818 |
| 1984 | 185,388 |
| 1985 | 212,334 |
| 1986 | 221,245 |
| 1987 | 149,769 |
| 1988 | 155,187 |
| 1989 | 152,481 |
| 1990 | 221,384 |
| 1991 | 269,521 |
| 1992 | 290,398 |
| 1993* | 321,954 |
| 1994* | 264,055 |
| 1995* | 246,705 |
| 1996* | 211,706 |
| 1997* | 214,002 |
| 1998* | 250,439 |

*Estimate

Source: Historical Tables, *Budget of the U.S. Government Fiscal 1994*, p. 14.

any new program by obtaining savings from existing programs and to pay for any new tax reductions by obtaining additional revenues. The legislation shifted more enforcement responsibility from the Congress to the OMB and the president and also altered the schedule for the executive development and legislative consideration of the budget. (See Boxes 13-1 and 13-2 later in this chapter.)

Again, however, deficits persisted. One problem with the 1990 act was that it exempted unpredictable and uncontrollable expenditures such as foreign debt forgiveness, increases in U.S. contributions to the International Monetary Fund, and the expenses resulting from the Persian Gulf War. Additionally, the economic recession of 1991–1992 resulted in a shortfall of government revenues. With health care costs continuing to rise more rapidly than predicted, still more money required to bail out the savings and loan industry, and other national emergencies cropping up—such as Hurricane Andrew which devastated South Florida in 1991—large, unbalanced budgets remained a problem and became a major issue during the 1992 presidential election.

Candidates H. Ross Perot and Bill Clinton each blamed the Washington establishment for the problem and each proposed plans to deal with it. Clinton promised to reduce the deficit in half in four years. His deficit reduction plan, submitted to Congress in March 1993, featured both tax increases and spending cuts. Congress spent over five months debating Clinton's proposal, modifying it substantially before enacting the plan by the barest of margins in both houses. The bill provided for savings of $496 billion over five years, with $240 billion coming from revenue increases and $256 billion from spending cuts and caps. Subsequent forecasts put the total deficit reduction over $504 billion.

From the perspective of presidential leadership, the deficit problems and the political controversies that have resulted from them demonstrate the limitations of using the budget as an instrument of change. Not only are presidents constrained by their predecessors' commitments, existing legislation, and their campaign promises, but they are also subjected to institutional forces, constituency pressures, and economic fluctuations. Accommodation, not domination, describes presidential budgeting most of the time.

We now turn to the roles of the major participants in the process in an attempt to define more precisely their influence on budgetary policy.

## THE BUDGET MAKERS

### The President

Presidents bear the primary responsibility for the executive phase of the budget. Increasingly, they are also expected to play a major role in the legislative phase as well. In each area, they have limited influence, but in neither can they easily or effectively dictate the outcome.

There are various ways presidents can affect the executive budget. Their goals dictate its priorities and shape its initial guidelines; their policies determine the new big-item expenditures; their decisions resolve interagency disputes. They hear last-minute appeals and make final judgments on them. The budget presented to the Congress must meet with their approval.

In shaping the budget, presidents can get involved in detailed decision making, if they desire. Some have done so. Ford and Carter spent considerable time on budget matters. Nixon and Reagan did not. Nixon took little interest in the budget and delegated considerable authority to his budget director while Reagan took a slightly different tack. Interested in setting broad budget policy, he was content to establish priorities and make decisions on items brought to his attention. By leaving the detailed evaluation of agency estimates to officials in the Office of Management and Budget, and by avoiding details, Reagan distanced himself from internal and external pressures to spend. This made it easier for him to propose budgets with substantial cuts in domestic spending but not easier to mobilize support for those cuts in Congress.

George Bush and Bill Clinton were forced to assume a more active involvement in budget matters, particularly in the congressional phase of the process. Clinton did so immediately, substantially altering the budget outline his predecessor prepared. Bush did not; he modified Ronald Reagan's last budget only slightly. The reason that he only made modest changes has as much to do with the budgetary process as it did with his own priorities. The executive phase of that process takes almost nine months to complete. It is difficult to submit an entirely new budget in only two or three months in office.

### The Office of Management and Budget (OMB)

The OMB is the president's principal institutional entity that oversees the budgetary process. It was created as the Bureau of the Budget (BOB) in 1921 to "assemble, correlate, revise, reduce, or increase the estimates of the several departments or establishments."[5] Originally located in the Treasury Department, it was moved to the newly created Executive Office of the President in 1939, where it has remained ever since, although in 1970 its title was changed from the Bureau of the Budget to the Office of Management and Budget and its functions broadened to include management responsibilities.

Despite the fact that the Budget Bureau was housed in the Treasury Department for its first eighteen years, it functioned as an important, powerful, and independent presidential agency. During this early phase of its existence, the bureau exercised central oversight over the budget. It operated according to a standard rule that departmental estimates equal to or less than the previous year's were automatically approved, while estimates for more money had to receive the authorization of the budget director and, in some cases, even the president.

The objectives of promoting economical government and controlling spending contributed to the bureau's power. Since most of the outlays prior to the mid-1930s went to the executive departments and agencies, there was little interest in the budget outside the government. The lack of public visibility and external pressure worked to the bureau's advantage. Its decisions were final unless overruled by the president, an infrequent practice in those days. Executive agencies were forbidden to circumvent the process by going directly to Congress for funds.

As the budget expanded, so did the size and functions of the budget agency and the interest in its decisions. In the 1920s and the 1930s, the bureau consisted of fewer than forty-five employees.[6] New responsibilities generated by World War II and the clearance of legislative policy matters enlarged the staff to more than five hundred by 1949 and created an institutional memory upon which the White House grew increasingly to depend.[7] The budget for fiscal year 1994 provides for a staff size of approximately five hundred and fifty for the Office of Management and Budget.

Most of the people who worked in the bureau were civil servants. Initially, there were only two political appointees, the director and the deputy director. The latter, by tradition, was chosen from the ranks of the professionals who had worked their way up in the agency. As a consequence of its nonpartisan character, the Budget Bureau was particularly well suited to provide the president with "advice on the merits" as opposed to "advice on the politics." Moreover, its invulnerability to outside pressures, relative invisibility to the press, and accessibility to the president and his senior aides heightened its mystique and enhanced its clout.

Changes in the organization, influence, and roles of the BOB began to occur in the 1960s. These changes were a consequence of the increasing size of the White House staff, the increasing number of initiatives that emanated from it, and the increasing suspicion of the political loyalties of civil servants by new presidents and their staffs. Singularly and together, these factors decreased the agency's influence within the executive branch from 1961 through 1980. While it continued to run the budget review process and decide on routine budget matters, key issues became the more or less exclusive province of senior White House aides.

Changes in the character of the budget also worked to affect the bureau's role and ultimately its power. With less emphasis placed on limiting expenditures and more on highlighting programs, political policymakers, not career budget analysts, became the key players. With more requests emanating from the departments and agencies, budget review focused on the size of their increments rather than the merits of their existing programs. With an increasing percentage of the budget consisting of nondiscretionary spending, the Budget Bureau was limited in what it could cut and how much it could save. As a consequence of all these factors, the budget agency's influence declined while expenditures continued to expand. In the words of Allen Schick:

> Agencies became more vigorous (and successful) in pressing their claims for larger budget shares. The relationship (between the Budget Bureau and the executive agencies) became more a matter of bargaining, and less one in which high authority decided the outcome.[8]

Executive agencies acquired new allies and new bargaining chips in their efforts to maintain and increase spending. Outside groups, which benefited from the programs, supported agency requests on Capitol Hill, thereby creating an environment that made it difficult for the president to sustain cuts in these programs. Prior to the 1970s these external political pressures were felt indirectly by the bureau. After 1970 the budget agency itself became more directly subject to outside influences. Changes in the organization and orientation of the agency were primarily responsible for its increased sensitivity to political matters.

A reorganization in July 1970 gave the Budget Bureau its new name, Office of Management and Budget, a new structure, and more political appointees. Civil servants who had previously exercised policy judgments on budgetary and legislative matters were relegated to positions of lesser importance in the organizational hierarchy.

The politicization of the OMB has continued. Presidents Carter, Reagan, and Clinton added additional political positions and staffed them with people who shared their beliefs and perspectives. Today there are approximately three dozen senior political appointees in the top policy positions of the OMB.

The functions of the office also expanded during this period. Nixon and Ford used it to improve management techniques and evaluate existing programs. As noted previously, Carter set up a division within the agency to oversee reorganization efforts; Reagan used that office to increase oversight of executive regulations. He also used the OMB to achieve sizable cuts in domestic programs and to institute a series of management reforms. Bush gave his budget director, Richard Darman, considerable authority to negotiate agreements with Congress. Darman had the equivalent of cabinet rank and was an influential presidential adviser. Leon Panetta, Clinton's budget director, was a major lobbyist for the administration's deficit reduction plan during the summer of 1993.

In recent times the OMB's political sensitivities and its expanded functions have contributed to its influence. The willingness of presidents to use the agency to promote their objectives has worked to the same end. The OMB's clout in the process has increased, allowing it (in conjunction with the White House) to shift major allocations from agency to agency in accordance with the president's budget priorities. The extent that executive budgeting has become a top-down rather than bottom-up process has further contributed to the OMB's influence, particularly that of its top political appointees.

The OMB's ability to effect change does vary, however, over the course of an administration. In the beginning its institutional resources, particularly its access to information and expertise, are most valuable in overcoming departmental interests and congressional opposition to achieve new presidential goals. In the end its nay-saying abilities are apt to be most effective in maintaining the president's course.

How the Reagan administration obtained its 1981 budget cuts illustrates the advantage the OMB can give a president in his first year in office. In January 1981, before many of the departments were fully staffed and their secretaries had been fully briefed about their budget needs, the OMB proposed major reductions in domestic programs. Almost immediately, budget working groups were established. Composed of key White House personnel, budget officials, and appropriate department secretaries and their aides, the groups reviewed the proposed cuts and made recommendations to the president. In most cases the recommendations supported the cuts. Why? Reagan had stated his goals, the OMB had a near monopoly over budget information, and the composition of the groups was stacked against the departments. The secretaries were not in a position to advocate their departments' interests even if they wanted to do so.[9] The OMB also exerted considerable influence on policy making at the beginning of the Bush and Clinton administrations.

Over time, however, the advantages that the OMB can give a president decline. The inevitability of pressure to maintain existing benefits, the relatively small amount of discretionary spending, and the tendency of departments to develop their own constituency-oriented programs limit the OMB's ability to effect major change over the course of an administration.

### The Executive Departments and Agencies

While the OMB is the principal participant in the executive phase of the budgetary process, it is not the only one. In one way or another every single executive agency has an impact on the budget, mostly on its own.

Departments and agencies are asked to submit yearly estimates for their programs and operational costs. They are expected to defend these estimates before the OMB and the Congress. They may also have to appeal to the president if funding for a particular program is threatened.

Most agencies have a division that coordinates their budget preparation and another that facilitates their legislative activity. In deciding how much to request, agencies have limited discretion. A large percentage of their budget is required by existing legislation, either by formulas written into the law or by long-term commitments. Even within the discretionary portion there are presidential guidelines to follow, ceilings that cannot be exceeded, and administrative costs that must be met.

Nonetheless, the agencies have leeway when estimating their needs. They generally tend to request funds within an acceptable range but toward the top of that range, anticipating that the OMB will revise these requests downward. This expectation, in turn, contributes to their tendency to pad their estimates and the OMB's inclination to cut them.

In general, the agencies that are most aggressive in requesting funds for their programs enjoy the greatest political support (which permits them to be most aggressive).

Budget decisions of an agency frequently have impact beyond that agency. In the 1980s the large increase in defense expenditures came at the expense of discretionary domestic programs. Even within the Department of Defense, the intense rivalry among the army, navy, and air force has a major impact on how that department allocates its requests. In the 1990s the large decreases in defense spending precipitated even greater interservice rivalries to maintain their funds at as high a level as possible.

The president and his advisers establish the guidelines; the departments and agencies make their estimates; the OMB evaluates those estimates; but Congress has the last word. Box 13-1 indicates the major steps in the executive phase of the budgetary process.

### The Congress

The Constitution requires that the Congress appropriate all funds that the government spends and raise all revenues that it collects. Congress meets this requirement by the passage of separate appropriation bills and revenue measures. Prior to the Civil War one committee of each house drafted the legislation that raised and appropriated money. As the demands of government became greater, separate policy committees in each house handled their own appropriation. There was no comprehensive national budget, budget committees, or overall budget authority.

Following the passage of the Budget and Accounting Act of 1921, in which Congress required the president to present such a budget, the legislature centralized its own spending power in two appropriation committees, although it did permit its policy committees some authority to borrow, contract, and authorize legislation that obligated the government to additional expenditures.[10] The appropriation committees, however, did not consider the budget as a whole. Rather, using the president's executive estimates as guidelines, they drafted individual bills for the separate departments. In many instances, congressional appropriations did not match the president's budget estimates. Supplemental money bills, passed during the year, also magnified the difference between the president's requests and the appropriations made by Congress. The legislature's consideration of the budget was fragmented and highly political. Members could publicly support the president's goals yet push for exceptions for their own pet projects.

After several abortive attempts to pass a comprehensive budget rather than simply separate appropriation bills, Congress enacted legislation in 1974 that enabled it to do so. The Budget and Impoundment Control Act of that year established a congressional budget process, two congressional committees, and a Congressional Budget Office (CBO) to provide it with a budget capacity that rivaled the president's. The pro-

## BOX 13-1.    THE EXECUTIVE BUDGETARY PROCESS

There are four principal stages in the executive phase of the process. In the first, the overall guidelines of the budget are established. They are conditioned by the objectives of the president, the state of the economy, and the commitments of legislation, past and present. In the second stage, the departments and agencies prepare their estimates in accordance with these guidelines. Personnel from the Office of Management and Budget examine these estimates in a formal review process in the third stage. The fourth stage begins with the president being briefed by the budget director, hearing appeals from the department and agency heads, and making the final decisions. The budget is then printed and sent to Congress in late January or early February.

These stages of the budgetary process are detailed below.

| Approximate Times | Actions |
|---|---|
| | *Budget Policy Development* |
| **March, 1st year** | Senior economic advisers review the outlook for the current and future fiscal years; they predict effects on revenues and spending programs and report to the president. |
| **April–June** | The OMB conducts spring planning review sessions, exploring funding implications of major issues or programs that will be considered in the fall budget review. The OMB sets overall guidelines for the executive agency budget submissions and sends these, along with instructions on preparing their proposed budgets, to the agencies. |
| | *Agencies' Preparation of Proposed Budget* |
| **July–August** | Agencies develop their proposed budgets. |
| **September** | Agencies send their proposed budgets to the OMB by September 1 for the fiscal year that begins thirteen months later. Other executive branch agencies not subject to the OMB review process submit their budgets later in the fall. |
| | *OMB Review* |
| **September–October** | The OMB staff analyzes proposed budgets and holds hearings with agencies. |
| **October–November** | Economic advisers again review the outlook for the fiscal year that begins the next October. |

*(continued)*

**BOX 13-1.**    *(continued)*

The director holds agency-by-agency reviews at which agency requests and staff recommendations are considered and recommendations are made to the president. The legislative branch and the judiciary submit budget requests to the OMB. The OMB transmits the proposed budget and economic advisers' findings to the president. The OMB gives agencies their recommended budget levels—also known as "the mark."

*Presidential Decision*

**December**

The president reviews OMB recommendations and decides on totals for agencies and programs. Possible appeals by agencies to the president are made. The OMB prepares budget documents for transmittal to Congress.

**February, 1st Monday, 2nd year**

The president delivers a proposed budget to Congress. The OMB sends an "allowance letter" to each agency giving its total within the president's budget and also transmitting "planning numbers" for the next two fiscal years.

Source: The Office of Management and Budget, as amended and updated by the author.

cess set up a timetable for considering the budget; the committees were charged with drafting advisory and binding budget resolutions that the Congress could not exceed; and the CBO provided staff support for revenue and expenditure estimates.

While the Budget and Impoundment Control Act improved the capacity of Congress to consider a comprehensive budget, it did not force the legislature to abide by its own budget decisions. Separate appropriation bills still determined the actual expenditures; separate tax bills still determined the actual revenues. Thus, a gap between budget goals and appropriation and revenue measures was still possible, even probable. The 1974 act, however, did provide a procedure known as reconciliation by which Congress could direct its committees to legislate within the guidelines of its budget decisions. It was used for the first time in 1980.

Ronald Reagan took advantage of reconciliation in 1981 and 1982 by getting the Democratic House of Representatives to agree to a vote *with-*

*out* amendments on a binding budget resolution that reconciled the differences between its budget estimates, appropriation bills, and revenue measures. In this way he was able to achieve many of his policy objectives through the mechanism of a budget.

Today, a reconciliation provision is normally part of the binding budget resolution which Congress is supposed to enact in the spring of every year. It was the reconciliation compromise of August 1993 that finalized the deficit reduction plan that Clinton had outlined in his State of the Union address on February 17. The Clinton plan, which had been subject to considerable debate and modification in each house, required a conference committee to compromise the differences between the House and Senate versions of the bill. The compromise was then submitted for an up-or-down vote in each house. This procedure, which did not permit floor amendments or a Senate filibuster, enabled the president and congressional leaders to exert maximum pressure, which produced the razor-thin victories for the bill.[11]

The legislation on the budget enacted since the 1980s has not lessened the importance of presidential involvement in the congressional phase of the budgetary process. Rather, it has increased it. The president's critical assessments of the economy and the administration's targets for funding continue to provide the basis for initial deliberations by Congress. Over the course of the legislature's budget hearings, markup, and floor debate, presidents must adjust their projections and may modify requests. In fact, Congress requires a midyear update on July 15. At each stage presidential influence is important if the president's budget proposals are to prevail. Finally, if the deficit targets are not met, the sequestration process is triggered, and the president is forced to make cuts in many key federal programs. To avoid this, presidents need to work with Congress to reach mutually agreed-upon levels of spending.

The budget legislation, in short, has reinstituted a joint process in which both president and Congress have important roles to play. The process involves many people, requires many reports, and extends many months over the course of the legislative calendar. It is a difficult one, which is dependent on the need for compromise but is highly political and public, making compromise difficult to achieve in practice.

The need for institutional cooperation but the difficulty of obtaining it explains why presidents in recent times have been more successful in articulating their budgets than in getting them accepted without major modifications by Congress. Both institutions have their own agendas and their own constituencies. Even when the same party controls both institutions, these agendas and constituencies do not always or usually coincide. Clinton found this out in 1993 when he pursued his own deficit reduction plan only to meet opposition from conservatives within his own party as well as from his partisan political opponents.

With over half of the Senate and a fourth of the House serving on budget, appropriations, or revenue committees, the task of achieving a consensus is often herculean. It requires a great allocation of time and significant political and legislative skills, although these skills in and of themselves may not be sufficient.

Ronald Reagan is a good example of a president who effectively mobilized a major coalition to achieve many of his budget priorities during the first two years in office but had difficulty doing so thereafter. Reagan's initial success was a product of several factors: his public appeal, his administration's lobbying skills, and the unity of congressional Republicans in contrast to the disunity of congressional Democrats during that period. By 1983 he was in a much less favorable position with Congress. With his budgets ritually pronounced "dead on arrival," the president adopted a different tack, threatening to use his veto to deter Congress from enacting appropriation bills that exceeded his requests in the domestic sphere and fell short of his requests in the areas of defense and national security. (Box 13-2 lists the principal steps in the congressional budget process and the target dates for completing them.)

## PRESIDENTIAL LEADERSHIP AND THE BUDGET

Presidents have a leadership problem when it comes to the budget. That problem has been magnified in recent times by the persistence of sizable deficits and the accumulation of a huge national debt, both of which require bitter political medicine to improve. Were presidents able to dispense this medicine on their own, they might be able to do so in a way that was economically sound and politically viable. But they cannot because budgetary power is not centralized, budgetary responsibilities are shared, and budgetary commitments have already been made by previous legislative and executive actions.

All of this would not be so bad were it not for the expectation that presidents lead, that they design their own budgets, and incorporate within them their policy objectives. They are also expected to mobilize congressional and public support for their budget and oversee its implementation. Yet with limited political power even against recalcitrant members of their own party and practically none against their opponents, with limited persuasive power in the absence of a consensus or a crisis, and with limited time, energy, and knowledge to devote to this problem, they are at the mercy of a variety of forces, all of which they do not and cannot control.

Under the circumstances the budgetary process becomes a necessary evil for most presidents. It is the rare president who can use it to direct change. When this does occur, it is usually during the first year, following a change of administrations, and after an election in which economic and budgetary problems were the principal issues. The more likely result, however, is to use the budget as a facilitating tool, a starting point for political compromises and economic decisions that inevitably result from the give and take in a highly diverse representative system.

## BOX 13-2.    THE CONGRESSIONAL BUDGETARY PROCESS

The congressional phase of the process begins with the budget committees of each house considering the president's request. In stage two the committees report their targets for revenue and expenditures and Congress enacts an advisory budget resolution. During the third stage the authorization and appropriation committees begin to draft their legislation within the guidelines of the budget resolution. In the final stage Congress enacts a second budget resolution and has the power, if it desires, to reconcile differences among its revenue, appropriations, and budget committees.

These stages of the process are enumerated below:

| | |
|---|---|
| **February** | The first Monday of the month is the deadline for Congress to receive the president's budget. The Congressional Budget Office reports to budget committees on the president's budget. Budget committees hold hearings as background for a concurrent resolution. |
| **March** | Each standing committee sends its budget estimates to House and Senate budget committees. |
| **April 1** | The budget committees report a budget resolution to Congress. |
| **April 15** | Congress revises and enacts a concurrent resolution in which the House and Senate agree on budget targets for receipts, budget authorities, and outlays. |
| **May 15** | The House may consider individual appropriation bills. |
| **June 30** | The House completes action on annual appropriation bills. The Senate must complete action by October 1. |
| **July 15** | The OMB sends Congress an update of the president's February budget. |
| **June–September** | Authorization and appropriation bills are considered and adopted by both chambers of Congress. Congress must *reconcile* any changes in legislation it has enacted with its budget targets. |
| **August** | The OMB provides a "snapshot" of projected deficits. By August 15, the CBO issues its initial report on the projected deficit. By August 20, the OMB issues its initial report on the projected deficit and the president responds by issuing a sequestration order that reduces spending by the required amount to coincide with the budgetary spending limits. |

*(continued)*

---

**BOX 13-2.**    *(continued)*

**October 1**         The fiscal year begins. If Congress has not enacted
                      appropriation bills, it must enact a resolution to
                      continue spending at the current rate or some other
                      rate that coincides with the budget. Failure to do so
                      will deny money to the government and eventually
                      force its closure. By October 15, the president is-
                      sues his final sequestration order, which is effective
                      immediately. The comptroller general issues a com-
                      pliance report within thirty days of the president's
                      order.

---

The best presidents can do under these circumstances is to use the
budget as an instrument to achieve incremental change.

Whereas the legislation of the last two decades has increased the
president's need to be an active participant in congressional consideration of the budget, it has also reduced the executive's powers to control
spending deemed unwise or uneconomical. The 1974 Budget and Impoundment Control Act limited the president's impoundment authority,
that is, the ability to defer or rescind spending without congressional
consent. Under terms of the statute, a temporary deferral of spending
could have been overturned by either house of Congress; a permanent
deferral, known as a rescission, required the approval of both houses.
The Supreme Court subsequently ruled that a one-house veto was unconstitutional; the action of both legislative branches was necessary.
After President Reagan tried to use the deferral authority in the absence
of legislation, Congress enacted a law that limits presidential deferrals to
routine managerial decisions.

In the light of contemporary deficit problems and the difficulty that
Congress and the president have had resolving them, presidents have
requested authority to cut government spending in the form of a *line-item
veto*. Such a power would permit them to excise parts of appropriation
bills without negating the entire bill. Forty-three state governors present-
ly have this authority. In his 1986 State of the Union address, President
Reagan asked for this power. President Bush even claimed some of it,
declaring that thirty-one provisions of legislation enacted by Congress
and approved by him were unenforceable because they were unconstitutional. Bush's attorney general, however, disagreed with the president's interpretation, and the constitutional issue was never pursued.
President Clinton has also requested line-item veto power, discussing a
compromise with the Democratic leadership that would permit him to
defer or rescind spending subject to congressional disapproval.

## ECONOMIC POLICY MAKING

Presidents have been involved in the budget process since 1921, but not until the administration of Franklin Roosevelt in the 1930s have they been concerned on a regular basis with economic policy making. Prior to that time presidential activities were generally limited to initiating or supporting proposals to correct specific problems that had arisen within the economy. Theodore Roosevelt's trust busting and Woodrow Wilson's labor reforms are two examples of these early forms of presidential involvement.

The depth of the 1930s depression, the degree of public panic, and Herbert Hoover's resounding election defeat signaled the beginning of a more comprehensive presidential role in the economy. No longer could presidents enjoy the luxury of standing on the sidelines. Franklin Roosevelt's activism became the model for his Democratic successors. Even Republicans found that there was no turning back.

Congress expected and even required this involvement. The Employment Act of 1946 obligated the president to prime the economy to maximize employment and production. The Taft–Hartley Act of 1947 gave the president the power to intervene in labor–management disputes that threatened the nation's security and well-being. In each case Congress not only acknowledged an expanded presidential role but created mechanisms to help the executive fulfill it.

Every president since Roosevelt has strived to meet these expanded expectations. Their policies, however, have differed. Truman, Kennedy, and Reagan desired to lower taxes to stimulate economic growth. Clinton advocated investment tax credits to encourage business to modernize and expand. Eisenhower and Ford tried to achieve savings by cutting government spending while Bush tried to do so in a less painful way by cutting projected growth. Johnson obtained a surtax to help pay for the costs of the Vietnam War and his Great Society programs, while Nixon implemented wage and price controls to reduce inflation and stabilize the economy. Carter tried a variety of revenue and budget measures to deal with the high inflation and stagnant economy that plagued his presidency.

Differing fiscal approaches lay at the core of these presidential policies. A *fiscal* strategy is a plan to manipulate government revenue and expenditures to influence economic conditions. In contrast, a *monetary* approach regulates the supply of money to affect change. Presidents cannot affect monetary policy, generally the prerogative of the Federal Reserve Board, nearly as much as they can influence fiscal policy. However, even with fiscal policy, as pointed out previously, it is the Congress that enacts appropriations and revenue bills. Although presidents can influence the legislature's actions, they cannot control them.

Until the mid-1970s, fiscal strategies were predicated on Keynesian economics. John Maynard Keynes, an eminent British economist, argued that increases in government spending and reductions in government taxes would stimulate demand and invigorate the economy during periods of sluggish activity. The only trouble with adopting such a policy is that it also results in budget deficits. Keynes was not worried about these deficits, however, because he believed that in the long run a vibrant economy would generate greater revenues, reducing or eliminating the difference between expenditures and income. With the exception of Eisenhower, presidents Truman through Nixon subscribed to this belief.

An expanding economy coupled with relatively low unemployment and inflation during most of the 1950s and 1960s seemed to confirm the merits of the Keynesian approach. By the beginning of the 1970s, however, economic conditions began to change. Budget deficits increased, the rate of growth declined, and inflation rose dramatically throughout the decade. Keynesian economics did not contain satisfactory answers. Other theories began to command attention.

Monetarists, led by Professor Milton Friedman of the University of Chicago, contended that the supply of money was the key to sound economic growth, particularly to control the ravages of inflation. Increasing interest rates would reduce the amount of money in circulation, decreasing inflationary pressures and cooling the economy. Lowering interest rates, on the other hand, would have the opposite effect, stimulating demand and output by making borrowing cheaper and more money available. In periods of high inflation and an overheated economy, a tight money policy made sense. But when inflation was high and the economy stagnant, it did not. It was precisely this condition in the late 1970s that gave credence to still another economic strategy—supply-side economics.

The supply-side philosophy combined the Keynesian approach to generating demand with the monetarist's desire to regulate currency. Tax cuts stimulate spending while money supply controls inflation. Ronald Reagan, an advocate of this approach (and the first president to major in economics in college), sought to implement the fiscal component of this strategy as president. He proposed budgets that increased defense expenditures, cut domestic programs, and substantially reduced corporate and personal federal income taxes. Congress enacted the bulk of his requests to increase defense spending and cut taxes during his first two years in office, although he was forced to modify his tax stand in 1982 because of the need for additional revenues and the desirability of closing tax loopholes. Reagan pursued his supply-side policies throughout his presidency.

George Bush took a more pragmatic approach; he continued the general thrust of the Reagan program but moderated it where events and politics dictated. Like Reagan, Bush wished to minimize governmental interference in the private sector, maintain a strong defense, and keep taxes low. His desire to control the large budget deficit and have funds for domestic programs, however, forced him to accept a revenue increase as part of a compromise with congressional Democrats in 1990.

Bill Clinton has advocated policies that require a more active government role to stimulate the economy, spur investment, and shift priorities to the domestic sector. A key component of his economic program to reduce the deficit has been to raise taxes, but he has also accepted cuts in government spending, including caps on some entitlement programs such as Medicare and Medicaid.

The impact of Clinton's plan on the economy, or any president's for that measure, will be difficult to discern. So many factors that affect the economy and impact on the society lay beyond the president's control. Yet, presidents are held responsible for the state of economic affairs during their presidency. Carter's defeat in 1980 and, especially, Bush's in 1992 can be attributed to their perceived failure as economic policymakers. In both cases the public had no confidence that economic conditions would improve if they were to be reelected.

The issue is no longer whether presidents will be economic policymakers but what kind of economic policies will they make. To help them with these efforts, economic advisory mechanisms within the presidency have functioned since the 1940s to advise, coordinate, and implement economic policy.

## ECONOMIC POLICYMAKERS

### The Department of the Treasury

Most of the president's economic advisory structure has been established by Congress. The Treasury Department was the first executive branch agency to play a major role in the financial affairs of government. Charged with responsibility for collecting and dispersing federal funds, its functions have gradually expanded to include debt financing, import controls, and drug enforcement.

Representing the financial community, this department has exercised a conservative influence throughout the years on matters of economic policy. Its orientation is to promote stability and long-term growth.

The secretary's role as an economic adviser to the president has been enhanced in recent years by the emergence of international and domestic problems of particular concern to the department, such as stabilizing the value of the dollar in international financial markets, overseeing foreign investments of the United States, and conducting negotiations on the repayments of international loans. Similarly, within the domestic arena, tax policy and savings bank failures have thrust the Treasury Department into the center of political controversy. With no other presidential office or White House official charged with handling these matters, the secretary of the treasury has had to take the lead as adviser, coordinator, lobbyist, and spokesperson for the president. In this capacity the treasury secretary chaired the councils that fashioned and implemented major economic priorities in the Reagan and Bush administrations but not in the Clinton administration, although Treasury Secretary Lloyd Bentsen has been a prominent spokesman and advocate for the president's economic program.

### The Federal Reserve Board

The second oldest government agency concerned with economic policy is the Federal Reserve Board (known as the "Fed"). However, it is not a presidential agency. Created by legislation in 1913, its principal function is to regulate monetary policy. It does so by adjusting the discount rate that commercial banks must pay when they borrow money from one of the member banks in the Federal Reserve System. The percentage of deposits that commercial banks must maintain is also regulated by the Fed. A third way the Federal Reserve Board can affect the money supply is by requesting its regional banks to buy or sell government securities on the open market. It also intervenes on the international market to increase or decrease the value of the dollar in accordance with the needs of the American economy.

In theory, the Fed operates with considerable autonomy from the president and Congress. Its members, nominated by the president and appointed with the advice and consent of the Senate, serve for fourteen years. Its chair, designated by the president from members of the board of governors, has a four-year term that does not coincide with the president's. This increases the chair's independence.

However, the Fed does not operate in a vacuum. It must be concerned with the impact that the fiscal policies of the president and Congress have on the economy. The Fed regularly exchanges information about the nation's economy with other executive branch units, notably the Council of Economic Advisers and the Department of the Treasury.[12] Sensitive to political pressures, the Fed has tended to refrain from making visible policy decisions in election years.[13] In contrast, the decisions to raise interest rates, which are obviously less popular than those to lower them, are made more frequently in nonelection years.[14]

### The Council of Economic Advisers

The principal economic advisory units within the Executive Office of the President are the Council of Economic Advisers (CEA) and the Office of Management and Budget. Both have been established by statute. The Employment Act of 1946 created the CEA and charged it with advising the president on macroeconomic policy. This included analyzing economic conditions, forecasting trends, and preparing the president's annual economic report to Congress. In addition to providing the president with long-term advice, the council has become increasingly involved in short-term microeconomic issues such as trade policy, deregulation, even credit and housing programs. It has tried to avoid operational responsibilities and has for the most part succeeded.[15]

The council is small and specialized. It is composed of three members appointed by the president with the advice and consent of the Senate. They serve at the president's discretion. The council's chair, the principal link to the White House and to the president's other economic advisers, participates in high-level economic policy meetings, supervises the operation of the CEA and the preparation of its annual economic report, and occasionally has acted as an administration spokesperson on economic affairs.

The council is supported by a small staff, approximately ten to fifteen professionals, mostly economists, who come primarily from the academic community and stay for a few years before returning to their academic institutions. The constant turnover of professional staff on the council infuses it with new ideas but limits its institutional memory and organizational clout.[16] Members of the council are also drawn from academia and frequently have worked on the council's staff prior to their appointment. Most of those chairing the council have been university professors. Laura Tyson, who was appointed by Bill Clinton, is the first woman to hold this position.

The academic orientation of the council has made it less subject to outside pressures than other economic advisory units. As a consequence, when strong political pressures are exerted, the chair of the council can take a longer-term, less partisan perspective than can some of the president's other advisers. This was particularly evident during the third and fourth years of the Reagan presidency, when council chairman Martin Feldstein frequently disagreed with the administration's public position on interest rates and the deficit. After two years in office, Feldstein returned to his academic position, and there was some question whether another chair would be appointed. Reagan waited until after his 1984 reelection to do so.

In general, the council has declined in importance as economic policy has become more political and as the number of economic advisers to the president has proliferated. Nonetheless, the personal relationship of the chair and the president remains the key to the council's impact on economic policy making. Arthur Burns (Eisenhower), Walter Heller (Kennedy), and Alan Greenspan (Ford) were three chairmen who had their president's confidence and were able to exercise considerable influence on economic decisions. Others have not been as fortunate.

No longer enjoying the information advantage that it had when there were fewer economic policy units within the government and fewer economists to run them, the council's voice today is one among many. It has tended to deal primarily with microeconomic issues.

### The Office of Management and Budget

The OMB also performs economic advisory functions for the president. Not only does its director participate in the initial forecasts for revenue and expenditures as budget planning gets under way, but the director, deputy, and program associate directors continually analyze and evaluate the merits of department and agency requests. Revisions of the initial budget forecasts are also the responsibility of the OMB. Since the orientation of the budget director is toward the bottom line—the differences between expenditures and revenues—the director must be concerned with tax policy and other revenue-producing measures. The director regularly meets with the president's senior economic advisers.

## THE COORDINATION OF ECONOMIC ADVICE

In addition to using the Treasury Department, the Council of Economic Advisers, and the OMB in an advisory capacity, presidents have also concocted a number of other institutional arrangements for soliciting and coordinating recommendations and advice. The origins and organizations of these groups have varied.

Two political scientists, Erwin Hargrove and Michael Nelson, suggest that the pattern of economic advising since World War II can be described in stages.[17] In the first, 1946 to 1960, a broad, relatively unstructured relationship existed among the chair of the Council of Economic Advisers, the director of the Bureau of the Budget, and the secretaries of the treasury, commerce, and agriculture. These individuals, both collectively and individually, provided the president with advice, advocacy, and administration within the economic sphere.

Beginning in 1960 and continuing through the end of the Nixon administration, relationships among the president's primary economic advisers became more structured. A troika, consisting of the heads of three major advisory bodies—the Treasury Department, the OMB, and the CEA—met on a regular basis to coordinate policy. Within the group a rough division of authority emerged with the secretary of the treasury becoming the major spokesperson and revenue adviser, the chair of the council the principal forecaster and analyst, and the budget director the chief overseer of expenditures. Other cabinet secretaries, who had previously rendered economic advice, were generally excluded. This had the effect of reducing the impact of outside forces on the group and maximizing the range of presidential decisions.

The third phase of economic advising commenced in the 1970s. It is characterized by more participants, more external influences on policy judgments, and more formal advisory structures. With national economies more interdependent, foreign, defense, and national security affairs have greater impact on economic decisions and vice versa. As a consequence, the secretaries of state and defense, the president's national security adviser, and his special representative for trade negotiations all have legitimate concerns about the country's economic policy. Similarly, the explosion of federal programs in the 1960s, particularly entitlement programs, has created a large public constituency interested in and affected by economic decisions.

To cope with a policy-making process that has become more fragmentary, pluralistic, and political, recent administrations have had to devise mechanisms, consistent with their presidents' particular styles of decision making, that not only permit a range of views to be presented and interests to be accommodated, but also work to coordinate these concerns, to promote consensus, to maximize the president's discretion, and to ensure the effective implementation of his decisions.

Nixon initially appointed a Cabinet Committee on Economic Policy with himself as its chair. He quickly found, however, that the meetings consumed too much of his time and were not productive. Within a year he had abandoned this arrangement in favor of an advisory system in which he depended on a single aide—his treasury secretary—for information, expertise, and public relations.

Gerald Ford, who came to the presidency after spending many years in Congress, was more comfortable with a group of advisers debating policy. He established an Economic Policy Board (EPB). Consisting of practically the entire cabinet, the board was run by an executive committee composed of the president's chief economic advisers and those domestic department heads who had an ongoing interest in a range of broad economic issues. Meeting three to four times a week, this executive committee functioned as a policy forum and conduit. The president attended its sessions on an average of once a week. The EPB was supported by a staff structure tied to the office of the president's assistant for economic affairs, a new position Ford had created. The head of this office presented the board's recommendations to the president and saw that the president's decisions were properly executed.

During the Carter presidency a more informal economic policy group and advisory process emerged. While the group's composition was similar to Ford's EPB, Carter's organization lacked a staff back-up and a regular meeting schedule. Friction among its members, however, produced acrimonious debate and made coordination and consensus difficult. It also provided the president with multiple sources of information and expertise. Over time, Carter turned to key White House personnel, particularly domestic aide Stuart Eizenstat, for economic advice.

Presidents Reagan and Bush reverted to the Ford model although they did not resurrect the Economic Policy Board. Rather, they utilized their Cabinet Council on Economic Affairs as a forum for discussion, as a mechanism for providing recommendations, and as an institution for implementing presidential decisions. During the first term of the Reagan administration, the council met several times a week, with the president occasionally in attendance. It discussed a range of policy issues from budgets and taxes to foreign investment, strategic reserves, and banking institutions.[18] As the administration progressed and economic policy was established, meetings of the council became less frequent, as did the president's personal involvement in economic matters. Although Bush used a cabinet council to develop economic policy, he depended increasingly on his budget director and treasury secretary for advice as the recession persisted and deepened during 1991 and 1992.

Clinton created a National Economic Council, chaired by presidential adviser Robert Rubin, to develop, coordinate, lobby, and oversee the implementation of his economic program. The council met frequently during the administration's first six months in office to fashion the president's economic stimulus package and deficit reduction plan.

Presidents have considerable flexibility in establishing their own economic advisory system. How they do so relates to their personal style, their interest in economic matters, and the extent to which they wish to immerse themselves in the details of policy and make middle-level decisions. The advantage of the more formal advisory arrangement, such as the ones that Ford, Reagan, and Bush adopted, is that it relieved them of day-to-day decision making but still permitted them the opportunity to establish broad policy guidelines. In contrast, the more informal systems that Carter and, to a lesser extent, Clinton used maximize personal involvement, but also place greater decisional responsibilities on the president's shoulders.

## THE POLITICS OF ECONOMIC DECISION MAKING

Economic policy making has become more political, more pragmatic, and less stable. These changes have affected the advice the presidents receive as well as the accommodations they must make. They have also affected presidential involvement in economic matters.

The recommendation process is more sensitive to outside pressures from Congress, the bureaucracy, and organized interest groups, each of which has its own interests to protect and its own political axes to grind. Members of Congress must consider the economic impact on their constituencies, while department and agency heads must be responsive to their clientele, and organized groups must placate their supporters. To the extent that economic decisions require coalition building to become public policy, presidents must take these varied interests into account.

The politicization of economic decision making has made long-range planning more difficult. The election cycle must be considered when calculating the effect of policy change. Policymakers key recoveries to their own political benefit whenever possible.

Not only do short-run considerations such as elections tend to drive economic decisions, but they also enhance the pragmatic character of the decisions themselves. Presidents are more inclined to strive for what is politically feasible rather than what may be theoretically optimal or ideologically desirable. Perhaps this explains why presidents are more apt to pursue a policy of selective involvement in economic matters rather than to become a macromanager of the economy. This strategy has allowed them to claim credit for economic successes and share or, better still, avoid blame for economic failures.

The experience of the Reagan administration is a case in point. Coming into office with clear-cut views of how it wished to stimulate the economy, the administration was forced to compromise its initial budget and tax proposals in order to get them enacted into law.[19] The compromises became more extensive as the next presidential election approached and presidential influence in Congress declined. Pragmatic considerations, in short, muted the administration's ideological perspective but at the same time enhanced the chances for the passage of its legislative proposals. The Clinton administration provides another illustration of the need to be flexible, pragmatic, and willing to compromise if a presidential proposal is to be enacted into law.

The impact of politics on economic policy decisions has had another effect. It has made those decisions less stable over time. Unanticipated events and unintended consequences have forced presidents frequently to adjust their economic programs. President Ford was forced to abandon his Whip Inflation Now (WIN) program as economic conditions deteriorated and the country fell into a recession. President Carter had to recant a promise to provide taxpayers with a fifty-dollar rebate as the budget deficit soared. President Reagan had to support a large revenue increase one year after getting his massive tax cut through Congress. President Bush violated his "no new taxes" pledge in 1990, and President Clinton was not able to keep his campaign promise to cut middle-class taxes. The hopes and promises of candidates and the realities of governing often clash.

Another factor that contributes to fluctuations in economic policy is the economy itself. Although presidents are ritually blamed for unfavorable conditions and are expected to improve them, many events and situations are beyond their immediate control. Existing laws establish levels of revenue and high percentages of expenditures. Interest rates dictate the cost of government borrowing while cost-of-living adjustments (COLAs) automatically raise federal outlays. Presidents must meet these obligations. Over time they can try to change them, but change is not easy.

Similarly, international forces and events affect the American economy in ways that they did not prior to World War II. The rise in the price of imported oil in the mid-1970s contributed to the inflation in the United States at the end of the decade. The reindustrialization of Germany and Japan and the growth of new industries in Asia have adversely affected American competition in steel, shipbuilding, textile, and automobile manufacturing. The weakness and strength of the dollar affect the flow of trade and tourism, the stability of financial markets, and the ability of countries to meet their foreign debts. All of these factors have short- and long-term consequences. All of them interfere with presidential ability to manipulate the economy along the lines desired despite the fact that the chief executive is ritually blamed for the economy's poor performance and lauded for its success.

These external factors also affect the process of making economic decisions. They have made that process more complex. Because they have produced more people inside and outside the government who are interested in economic policy, more interests must be balanced, more coordination is necessary, more time must be devoted to economic affairs. The burdens on presidents and their advisers are greater; economic issues have more political impact; yet presidential control is more difficult to achieve. In no other policy area (except possibly the budget) are presidential limits more discernible. The increased complexity of the economic decision-making process compounds the president's leadership problem.

## CONCLUSION

Presidential responsibility has been enlarged in budgetary and economic spheres. That enlargement has been a product of need, statute, and precedent. Acknowledging its inability to fashion comprehensive budget and economic policy, Congress has required the president to do so. This requirement, coupled with the expanded role of the federal government, has forced presidents and their staffs to devote increasing resources to these activities.

It has not been easy. Expectations of presidential performance have grown, but the president's capacity to affect budgetary and economic matters has not kept pace. Much of the budget is dictated by existing law and policy commitments. Presidents can affect discretionary funding, but even here political pressures often undercut their efforts to reorder spending priorities and revenue measures. Similarly, within the economic sphere, myriad forces from within the country and abroad are not easily subject to the president's control. These factors mute presidential efforts to stimulate the economy, but at the same time make those efforts more important.

To help the president fulfill expectations of leadership within these areas, advisory mechanisms have developed and decision-making processes have evolved. The OMB continues to be the principal unit to provide the president with budget advice and oversee spending requests. However, the needs of the departments and agencies, the concerns of the House and Senate, and the interests of organized groups have involved many more participants in the budgetary and economic policy-making processes. This involvement has increased the complexity of these processes and has made them more political and less easily subject to presidential control. In both areas, power is decentralized and responsibility more difficult to pinpoint.

For presidents this has meant that they must devote more attention to economic matters (including the budget), they must weigh more factors in making critical judgments, and they must use more skills in articulating and shaping an administration position. For the presidency these changes have placed greater stress on the organizational mechanism that coordinates and integrates the policy decisions and builds support for them inside and outside the government. For budgetary policy they have made it more difficult to control expenditures, although Reagan has demonstrated that priorities can be reordered. For economic policy they have produced a short-term perspective with more variation within and between administrations, a policy that places more emphasis on political feasibility.

In short, presidential roles have increased but presidential influence has declined within the budgetary and economic spheres. Leadership is more difficult to exert. Presidents have less ability to control the factors that affect their judgments. Yet those judgments are increasingly expected to solve national problems and promote national prosperity. Directing change under normal conditions is difficult. Presidents need crises as action-forcing and coalition-building mechanisms to do so. This raises the stakes, delays solutions, and frequently shortens the time frame in which those solutions are developed and implemented. Mostly, the best presidents can do is facilitate. To do this effectively, they must devote more time to budgetary matters and selectively involve themselves in economic issues. They must coordinate support within the executive, build coalitions within Congress, balance interests, and maintain the confidence of the general public—a tall order to be sure.

## NOTES

1. For a discussion of the budgetary process during this early period, see Louis Fisher, *The Politics of Shared Power: Congress and the Executive* (Washington, D.C.: Congressional Quarterly, 1992), pp. 177–78.

2. The legislation, known as the Anti-Deficiency Act of 1905, has been cited as the statutory basis of the president's impoundment authority, that is, the president's power not to spend money appropriated by Congress if that expenditure would not be wise or prudent.

3. Our description of the evolution of the budget is based primarily on Allen Schick's discussion and analysis in his paper, "The Politics of Budgeting: Can Incrementalism Survive in a Decremental Age?" (paper presented at the Annual Meeting of the American Political Science Association, Denver, Colorado, September 1982).

4. In 1920 federal expenditures totaled $6.357 billion. By 1930 they had been reduced to $3.32 billion.

5. Louis Fisher, *Presidential Spending Power* (Princeton, N.J.: Princeton University Press, 1975), p. 35.

6. Larry Berman, *The Office of Management and Budget and the Presidency, 1921–1979* (Princeton, N.J.: Princeton University Press, 1979), p. 8.

7. Ibid., p. 102.

8. Schick, "The Politics of Budgeting," p. 7.

9. William Greider, "The Education of David Stockman," *Atlantic*, December 1981, pp. 33–34.

10. Fisher, *The Politics of Shared Power*, p. 183.

11. The House voted 218 to 216 in favor of the legislation on August 5, 1993. A 50–50 tie in the Senate one day later was broken by the vice president who cast the tie-breaking vote in favor of the legislation. No Republicans voted in favor of the bill.

12. James E. Anderson, "The President and Economic Policy: A Comparative View of Advisory Arrangements" (paper presented at the Annual Meeting of the American Political Science Association, Washington, D.C., August–September, 1991), p. 10.

13. John T. Woolley, *Monetary Politics: The Federal Reserve and the Politics of Monetary Policy* (New York: Cambridge University Press, 1984).

14. Ibid.

15. Political scientist James E. Anderson describes two instances, one in the Johnson administration and the other in the Carter administration, when the CEA got involved in the implementation of policies. In both cases it did so because the department and agencies were unable or unwilling to do so (Anderson, "The President and Economic Policy," p. 5).

16. Anderson, "The President and Economic Policy," p. 4.

17. Erwin C. Hargrove and Michael Nelson, *Presidents, Politics and Policy* (New York: Knopf, 1984), pp. 186–89.

18. Task forces operating at the subcabinet level supplemented the council's deliberations with working papers and in-depth studies. An executive secretary from the president's domestic policy office provided White House staff support and coordination (Murray L. Weidenbaum, "Economic Policymaking in the Reagan Administration," *Presidential Studies Quarterly* 12 [Winter 1982]: 95).

19. Hugh Heclo and Rudolph G. Penner, "Fiscal and Political Strategy in the Reagan Administration," in Fred I. Greenstein, ed., *The Reagan Presidency* (Baltimore: Johns Hopkins University Press, 1983); and Alan Schick, "How the Budget Was Won and Lost," in Norman J. Ornstein, ed., *President and Congress* (Washington, D.C.: American Enterprise Institute, 1982).

## SELECTED READINGS

Anderson, James E., and Jared E. Hazleton. *Managing Macroeconomic Policy: The Johnson Presidency*. Austin, Tex.: University of Texas Press, 1986.

Berman, Larry. *The Office of Management and Budget and the Presidency, 1921–1979*. Princeton, N.J.: Princeton University Press, 1979.

Genovese, Michael A. "The Presidency and Economic Management." *Congress and the Presidency* 14 (1987): 151–67.

Peterson, Paul E., and Mark Rom. "Lower Taxes, More Spending, and Budget Deficits." In Charles O. Jones, ed. *The Reagan Legacy*. Chatham, N.J.: Chatham House, 1988, pp. 213–40.

Pfiffner, James P., ed. *The President and Economic Policy*. Philadelphia: Institute for the Study of Human Issues, 1986.

Porter, Roger. *Presidential Decision Making: The Economic Policy Board*. Cambridge: Cambridge University Press, 1980.

Schick, Allen. *The Capacity to Budget*. Washington, D.C.: Urban Institute Press, 1990.

Shuman, Howard E. *Politics and the Budget: The Struggle Between the President and the Congress*. 3d ed. Englewood Cliffs, N.J.: Prentice-Hall, 1992.

Sloan, John W. "Economic Policymaking in the Johnson and Ford Administrations." *Presidential Studies Quarterly* 20 (Winter 1990): 111–25.

Stockman, David. *The Triumph of Politics*. New York: Harper and Row, 1986.

Tomkin, Shelley Lynne. "Reagan OMB's 'Congress Watchers.'" *The Bureaucrat* 16 (Summer 1987): 55–59.

Weidenbaum, Murray L. "Economic Policymaking in the Reagan Administration." *Presidential Studies Quarterly* 12 (Winter 1982): 95–99.

Weatherford, M. Stephen. "The Interplay of Ideology and Advice in Economic Policymaking: The Case of Political Business Cycles." *Journal of Politics* 49 (1987): 925–52.

Woolley, John T. *Monetary Politics: The Federal Reserve and the Politics of Monetary Policy.* New York: Cambridge University Press, 1984.

# 14

# Foreign and Defense Policy Making

Few would question the obligation of presidents to preserve and protect the nation. Few would deny them the constitutional and statutory authority to do so. Few would dispute their need to perform a variety of roles with the help of a responsive supporting staff. Still, the extent of presidents' powers, the scope of their roles, and the nature of their advisory systems have been subject to controversy.

These powers, those roles, and those advising systems all contribute to the president's leadership capacities and successes. Powers are essential. Traditionally, executives have enjoyed a broad prerogative in foreign affairs, a prerogative that expands during crises that threaten the interests and security of the country. That expansion, however, is limited in scope and time. One critical aspect of presidential leadership is how those limits are defined, both in legal and political terms.

Another component of the leadership equation in foreign affairs is the multiple roles presidents assume and the multiple forces that affect them. The roles derive from the Constitution, statute, and precedent. They have been more expansive in foreign affairs than in the domestic arena, but the president's leadership problem stems from the same basic root: Presidents do not control the environment in which they must operate nor do they exercise their responsibilities exclusively.

Congress is empowered to act in foreign affairs; an increasing array of interest groups plus private consultants and attorneys who represent foreign corporations and governments seek to influence foreign policy decisions, most of which have domestic implications. The mass media regularly report on and evaluate presidential actions in foreign affairs. Within the international arena the United States is one player among many. Its economy, its resources, its political and military positions are more interdependent with others than ever before. Moreover, presidents must deal with an increasing number of their own advisers who represent and present differing perspectives, organizations, and interests.

How all of these factors affect the president's capacity to lead in foreign affairs and shape foreign policy will be the subject of this chapter. First we describe the president's formal authority in theory and in practice. Next we turn to the expansion of the president's policy-making role, identifying the factors that have contributed to that expansion and the success presidents have had in achieving their policy goals. Changes in the international and domestic environment, particularly within the last decade, have complicated the president's task. We discuss those changes and their impact on presidential policy making within the context of the "two presidencies" thesis and then go on to describe and evaluate the advisory mechanisms that have been created to help the president coordinate, formulate, articulate, and implement foreign and defense policy. We conclude with a statement of how these factors singularly and together contribute to the kind of leadership a president can exert.

## CONSTITUTIONAL AND STATUTORY AUTHORITY

### The Original Design

The president's powers in foreign affairs and national defense have expanded significantly beyond their original design. The framers of the Constitution anticipated a policy-making role for the president, but they did not desire the executive to dominate that role. On the contrary, their fear that a president might pursue personal interests at the expense of the nation's welfare led them to divide and share policy-making responsibilities. Whether or not to go to war was to be the decision of Congress. The president had discretion to react in times of emergency to repel attacks but presumably not to initiate hostilities or in any other way establish permanent war policy. The expectation was that the Congress would do so. The president could, however, terminate hostilities.

Short of war, the executive was given considerable latitude in foreign affairs. The president could initiate treaties in conjunction with the Senate; their approval required the concurrence of two-thirds of the upper chamber. Similarly, the president could appoint ambassadors, but that too required the advice and consent of the Senate. The performance of the ceremonial duties of a head of state and the conduct of foreign policy were also seen as presidential responsibilities.

In performing these executive functions, presidents would inevitably make decisions that had policy implications. The framers did not fear this. They anticipated that Congress by virtue of its power to appropriate money, authorize programs, and regulate commerce would establish the contours of that policy and would be able to check presidential initiatives adequately.

### The Exercise of Powers

TREATY MAKING.    Treaty making was to be jointly exercised with the Senate. An incident that occurred early in the Washington administration, however, soured this arrangement and presaged the difficulties that the president would have in dealing with the upper chamber as both an advisory and consenting body. In August 1789, President Washington came to the Senate to request its advice on a treaty with Native Americans in western Georgia. Armed with thirteen questions prepared by his secretary of war, General Knox, Washington desired the Senate's guidance in the negotiations. Instead, he was treated to a long, discursive discussion that reached no conclusion. Forced to return two days later for what turned out to be insipid advice, Washington did not personally go back to the Senate for its counsel. Instead, he and his successors turned to their principal department heads for advice and to the Senate primarily for its consent as required by the Constitution.

The experience had a profound effect on presidential–senatorial relations. It discouraged the president from involving the Senate in the negotiation phase of treaty making. While some consultation continued, presidents began to do more on their own. Woodrow Wilson's refusal to consider senatorial opinion in the negotiations on the Treaty of Versailles represents one of the most flagrant examples of chief executive's going it alone.

Historically, the Senate has approved without modification about 70 percent of the approximately fifteen hundred treaties that have been submitted to it by the president since 1789. Only sixteen of those that have come to a vote have been voted down (the most famous probably being the Treaty of Versailles ending World War I and establishing the League of Nations). However, many other proposed treaties have been withdrawn by the president because of opposition in the Senate and thus have never come up for a vote. About one hundred and fifty have been withdrawn since World War II, including the SALT (strategic arms limitation talks) II treaty proposed by President Carter and withdrawn to protest the Soviet Union's armed presence in Afghanistan.

Not only can the Senate approve treaties without modification [as it did with the Intermediate Range Nuclear Forces Treaty (INF) Treaty with the Soviet Union in 1988] or reject them outright; it can also approve them with reservations or with amendments, thereby requiring changes or deletions. In early 1978 the Senate consented to two treaties dealing with the Panama Canal. It added a reservation to one of them stating that the United States had a right to use military force, if necessary, to keep the canal open. Sometimes these reservations, voiced in advance, can lead to modifications or side agreements in the negotiations on the treaty itself as they did with the North American Free Trade Agreement (NAFTA), which the Bush and Clinton administrations negotiated with Canada and Mexico.

From time to time the House of Representatives has also attempted to impose itself in the treaty-making process, but usually without success. Arguing that the Congress as a body is empowered to deal with foreign commerce, military affairs, war, and international policy, it has proposed legislation and used its appropriations authority to this end.

Both the president and the Senate have resisted the lower chamber's intrusion into their exclusive domain, however. When treaties require authorizing legislation or appropriations to be implemented as in the case of NAFTA, then the House will be involved as a coequal legislative body.

Whereas Senate consent is necessary for the ratification of treaties, it has not been considered essential for their termination. When President Carter ended a long-standing defense treaty with the Chinese Nationalists on Taiwan, he did not request the approval of the Senate. The legality of Carter's action, challenged by Senator Barry Goldwater, was upheld by a federal appellate court. The Supreme Court also concurred, although the justices split in their reasons for upholding the appellate court's decision.[1]

Presidents also have some discretion in their interpretation and reinterpretation of treaties. However, they cannot digress from the interpretation that they or their predecessors represented to the Senate during the treaty's ratification hearings. When amending the Intermediate-Range Nuclear Forces Treaty in 1988, the Senate declared that any digression from the "common understanding" of the treaty at the time of ratification would require joint action by Congress and the president by statute or by treaty.[2]

FORMULATING EXECUTIVE AGREEMENTS.    The need to obtain the Senate's consent has encouraged recent presidents to enter into executive agreements in order to avoid the formal treaty ratification process. The number of such agreements has mushroomed in recent years, as indicated in Table 14-1.

An executive agreement is concluded by the president on behalf of the United States with the head of government of another country. Unlike a treaty, it does not require a two-thirds vote of the Senate. Thus, when President Tyler failed to get the Senate to approve a treaty annexing Texas, he entered into an executive agreement to do so. Most executive agreements do not even need formal congressional approval, although some may require legislation to implement them. Such legislation is subject to a simple majority vote of both houses.

Unlike treaties, executive agreements do not supersede statutes. Otherwise, they are just as binding as treaties and have been used for such famous compacts as the destroyer bases deal with Great Britain in 1940, the Yalta and Potsdam agreements in 1945, and the Vietnam peace agreement of 1973.

Presidents have been careful in their choice of instruments for making international agreements. In recent years treaties have dealt with such diverse subjects as shrimp, the protection of Mexican archaeological artifacts, the dumping of wastes at sea, and the maintenance of lights in the Red Sea; executive agreements have also been used to end wars and to establish or expand military bases in other countries. In 1972, as a result of SALT, President Nixon signed a treaty limiting the defensive weapons of the Soviet Union and the United States and an executive

Table 14-1. Treaties and Executive Agreements Approved by the United
          States, 1789–1992

| Year | | Number of Treaties | Number of Executive Agreements |
|---|---|---|---|
| 1789–1839 | | 60 | 27 |
| 1839–1889 | | 215 | 238 |
| 1889–1929 | | 382 | 763 |
| 1930–1932 | | 49 | 41 |
| 1933–1944 | (F. Roosevelt) | 131 | 369 |
| 1945–1952 | (Truman) | 132 | 1,324 |
| 1953–1960 | (Eisenhower) | 89 | 1,834 |
| 1961–1963 | (Kennedy) | 36 | 813 |
| 1964–1968 | (Johnson) | 67 | 1,083 |
| 1969–1974 | (Nixon) | 93 | 1,317 |
| 1975–1976 | (Ford) | 26 | 666 |
| 1977–1980 | (Carter) | 79 | 1,476 |
| 1981–1988 | (Reagan) | 125 | 2,840 |
| 1989–1992 | (Bush) | 67 | 1,371 |

Note: Varying definitions of what comprises an executive agreement and its entry-into-force date make the above numbers approximate.

Source: Harold W. Stanley and Richard G. Niemi, *Vital Statistics on American Politics*, 4th ed. (Washington, D.C.: Congressional Quarterly, 1994), p. 280.

agreement limiting the offensive weapons of each country. Although most executive agreements are routine and deal with noncontroversial subjects such as food deliveries or customs enforcement, some implement important and controversial policies.

To influence executive agreements, Congress needs to know about them before they are finalized, while options are still available. Even more basic, it needs to know that the agreements even exist. In 1969 and 1970, the Senate Foreign Relations Committee discovered that Presidents Johnson and Nixon had covertly entered into a number of secret agreements with South Vietnam, South Korea, Thailand, Laos, Ethiopia, Spain, and other countries. In response to these actions Congress passed the Case Act of 1972, which requires the secretary of state to transmit to Congress within sixty days the text of any international agreement other than treaties to which the United States is a party. If presidents feel publication of an agreement would jeopardize national security, they may transmit the text only to members of the Senate Foreign Relations and House Foreign Affairs committees under an injunction of secrecy that only they (or their successors) may remove.

Presidents Nixon and Ford did not fully comply with the Case Act, however. Some agreements were not submitted to Congress and others were submitted after the sixty-day period. Consequently, in 1977 Congress passed legislation requiring any department or agency of the United States government that enters into any international agreement on behalf of the country to transmit the text to the State Department within twenty days of its signing. Neither of these two laws actually limits the president's power to act without Congress in defense and foreign affairs. Yet their passage indicates that Congress is increasingly unwilling to defer blindly to the president's judgment.

In addition to concluding a formal agreement, presidents have also engaged in a form of diplomacy that recognizes "understandings" with other countries. A case in point is the SALT II treaty. Although the Senate never approved it, the Reagan administration abided by most of its provisions (as did the Soviet Union). Similarly, the Carter administration continued to observe the SALT I treaty for three years after it expired. Short of enacting legislation that requires a specific action, Congress can do little to prevent the president from making a unilateral policy declaration in concert with the leaders of other governments.[3]

RECOGNIZING AND NOT RECOGNIZING COUNTRIES.    In addition to negotiating treaties and formulating executive agreements and understandings, presidents can initiate or terminate relations with other countries. The right of recognition has traditionally been considered a presidential responsibility. George Washington exercised it when he received Citizen Genet and thereby recognized the new French Republic in 1789. Presidents have even extended this to continuing to recognize a government that has been removed from power and to acknowledging the rights of a people who lack a state. Following the signing of an agreement between Israel and the Palestine Liberation Organization (PLO) at the White House on September 13, 1993, President Clinton indicated that the United States might grant formal recognition to the PLO if it renounced terrorism and recognized Israel's right to exist. The Senate has no role in this recognition process other than to consent to the choice of an American ambassador.

Recognizing countries can be controversial. In 1933 Franklin D. Roosevelt recognized the government of the Soviet Union, fifteen years after it was constituted and functioning. In 1979 Jimmy Carter extended recognition to the government that controlled mainland China, the People's Republic, following a period of thirty years of nonrecognition. In 1984 Ronald Reagan announced the resumption of formal diplomatic relations with the Vatican. Each of these actions provoked criticism about the merits of presidents' judgments, but not about their right to make them.

Presidents can also end relations. Before war ensues it is customary to sever relations with adversaries. Similarly, events short of war can also result in a disruption of diplomatic activity. The revolutionary activities of Cuba and Iran led Presidents Eisenhower and Carter to cut formal ties with these countries. However, some contact was maintained by an "interests section" that operated out of the embassy of a friendly country.

There are other actions that presidents can take to register their disapproval of the policies of other countries. Recalling an ambassador, instituting a trade embargo, reducing economic or military assistance, or

**President Clinton with Israeli Prime Minister Rabin and PLO Chairman Arafat at the signing of the Israel–PLO peace accord, September 13, 1993.** Reprinted by permission of The White House.

even categorizing a country as "terrorist," thereby denying it economic and military assistance or trade status as a most favored nation, are all devices that contemporary presidents have employed to sanction the actions of others. The Clinton administration labeled Sudan a terrorist country in 1993 after discovering a tie between two of its representatives at the United Nations and the terrorists who bombed the World Trade Center in New York City.

MAKING WAR.    The Constitution gives Congress the sole power to declare war, a power it has exercised only five times (in 1812, 1846, 1898, 1917, 1941). Such full-scale wars as those in Korea and Vietnam were not officially declared by Congress. In addition, presidents have employed a more limited use of force abroad without a declaration of war or statutory authority more than one hundred times. This presidential involvement of armed forces presents a conflict between constitutional theory and practice.

The roles as commander-in-chief, head of state, and head of government have undoubtedly contributed to the capacity of presidents to commit the nation to battle. Armed with a near monopoly of first-hand information, a potential for engaging public support, and an oath to provide for the common defense, they have used their prerogatives to broaden their constitutional powers. Jefferson ordered the navy and marines to retaliate against the Barbary pirates who threatened American shipping. Polk ordered the army into disputed territory with Mexico to protect Texas' claim to its borders. Lincoln instituted a blockade of the South and imposed other sanctions to put down the southern insurrection. Recent instances include the orders of President Eisenhower to send armed forces to Lebanon in 1958; of President Kennedy to blockade Cuba in 1962; of President Johnson to dispatch troops to the Dominican Republic in 1965; of President Nixon to bomb Cambodia in 1970; of President Ford to attack Cambodia in order to rescue the crew of the *Mayaguez* (a U.S. merchant ship seized by Cambodia in 1975); of President Carter to rescue the American hostages in Iran in 1980; of President Reagan to send an armed force to the Caribbean island of Grenada and marines to Lebanon in 1983 and to bomb Libya in 1986; of President Bush to send military forces to Panama in 1989 and the Persian Gulf in 1990–1991; and of President Clinton to bomb Iraq and to increase the size and armaments of American forces in Somalia.

Theoretically, Congress could have resisted many of these executive actions. In practice it has been unable and unwilling to do so. The House of Representatives condemned Polk, but only after the Mexican War had been concluded. Congress forced Nixon to end bombing in Cambodia, but only after that action had been carried on for more than two years. During periods of crisis, Congress finds it difficult, if not impossible, to oppose the president.

The Vietnam War, which stirred up deep dissent at home, was the last straw. In 1973 Congress passed the War Powers Resolution over President Nixon's veto. It requires that the president consult with Congress "in every possible instance" involving the use of American troops in hostile or potentially hostile situations. The president must report to Congress in writing within forty-eight hours after ordering U.S. armed forces into hostilities. More significantly, the military action must stop sixty days after the submission of this report unless Congress declares war, authorizes the use of force, extends the sixty-day period, or is unable to meet because of an attack upon the United States. At any time Congress can end the use of American armed forces by passing a concurrent resolution (which is not subject to a presidential veto).[4] The president may extend the use of force for thirty additional days if deemed necessary to protect departing American forces.

The law has aroused considerable debate about just what consultation means and whether the president could, in sixty days of hostilities, place the United States in a position from which Congress could not extract it. These issues were not resolved by the applications of the War Powers Resolution since its passage: the evacuations from Southeast Asia in April 1975, the rescue of the *Mayaquez* from Cambodia in May 1975, the attempted rescue of the hostages from Iran in 1980, the Grenada invasion of 1983, and the use of armed forces in the Persian Gulf in 1991.

In practically every administration there have been instances that could have fallen under the purview of the act but were not reported to Congress in accordance with its provisions. Why? What is the problem?

The issue is a constitutional one. Which institution, the presidency or Congress, has the right to commit armed forces to potential conflict? Presidents have believed that the War Powers Resolution unconstitutionally constricts their obligation to provide for the common defense by constraining their powers as commander-in-chief. Although they have not challenged the constitutionality of the legislation in court, they have narrowly interpreted its provisions, particularly its consultation and reporting requirements. Although President Bush claimed that he did not need Congress's approval to commit American troops in the Gulf, he did seek and receive congressional authorization to do so. In approving the legislation that Congress enacted authorizing the use of force in the Gulf, Bush said:

> As I made clear to congressional leaders at the outset, my request for congressional support did not, and my signing this resolution does not, constitute any change in the long-standing positions of the executive branch on either the President's constitutional authority to use the Armed Forces to defend vital U.S. interests or the constitutionality of the War Powers Resolution.[5]

Although Congress obviously disagrees with the interpretation that Bush and other presidents have given to the constitutionality of the War Powers Resolution, as a legislative body it has been reticent to impose the act's requirements on the president, much less start the clock running on the time limits contained in the legislation. Individual members, however, have raised and debated those issues with respect to specific presidential actions. In December 1990, fifty-four members of Congress took legal action against President Bush to require him to gain congressional approval before committing U.S. armed forces in the Persian Gulf.[6] Although the federal district court declared the request inappropriate because the president had not at that point committed troops to battle, the judge who heard the case rejected the broad claims of executive power that the administration put forth in arguing its position.[7]

Is the War Powers Resolution unworkable? Perhaps. Is it irrelevant? No. In theory it reasserts congressional authority while acknowledging expanded presidential powers; in practice, it does not prevent presidential initiatives but forces the president to consider the possibility that Congress, through action or inaction, could terminate those initiatives. This consideration presumably acts as a constraint on potentially unpopular presidential actions. However, the principal type of presidential initiatives that the War Powers Resolution seems designed to prevent, the long-term conventional limited wars similar to Korea and Vietnam, seem to be those that are least likely to occur if the political climate that has existed in the United States since the mid-1970s persists. If that climate were to change, the propensity of Congress to support military action begun by the president would probably increase as well. In general, the shorter the time frame and the quicker the needed response, the less Congress can play an effective role.

Although Congress is not likely to oppose presidential involvement in emergency situations that threaten the national security or adversely affect American interests abroad, its propensity for influencing presidential policy in nonemergency situations has increased. Congressional power to authorize conscription or maintain an all-volunteer military, to appropriate money for defense, even to affect the sales of arms has been greater in peacetime. Since the Vietnam War, presidents can no longer count on bipartisan support for all military actions, alliances, and aid. In 1981 President Reagan had to use all of his persuasive powers to keep Congress from preventing a sale of special reconnaissance aircraft known as AWACS (Airborne Warning and Control Systems) to Saudi Arabia. Later in his presidency, he was forced to modify or abandon other arms deals because they faced certain defeat in Congress.

Congress also intervened on the issue of whether to permit homosexuals to serve in the military. When President Clinton indicated his willingness to allow them to serve, members of Congress threatened legislation to undo any executive action. Hearings were held by the Senate Armed Services Committee and eventually a "Don't Ask; Don't Tell" compromise was reached among the president, the Department of Defense, and Congress.

COMMANDING THE MILITARY.    The powers of the president as commander-in-chief have also been expanded. The initial concept of this role was unclear. Did the framers of the Constitution vest the president with a title—civilian head of the military—or empower the office with operational authority? Over the years, presidents began to behave as if they had operational authority. Lincoln used the crisis of the Civil War to institute a series of military actions including a blockade of the South, the arrest of suspected traitors, activation of the state militia, establishment of military courts in areas of civil insurrection, and suspension of the writ of habeas corpus. Lincoln also got involved in the conduct of the war and the selection of field commanders.

Other presidents have also expanded the operational component of their commander-in-chief responsibilities. Franklin Roosevelt ordered the internment of persons of Japanese ancestry on the West Coast, chose the principal theaters of operations and points of invasion, and established a map room in the White House to keep abreast of developments during World War II. Harry Truman ordered the use of atomic weapons in that war, forbade American planes to cross the Chinese border during the Korean War, and dismissed his Pacific commander, Douglas MacArthur. John Kennedy personally monitored the Bay of Pigs invasion and the blockade of Cuba during the missile crisis. Lyndon Johnson approved strategic and tactical military decisions in Vietnam, including the bombing of targets and mining of ports, while Richard Nixon extended the bombing to Cambodia.

Ronald Reagan was a particularly active military commander. In addition to his commitment of American forces in Lebanon and Grenada and approving their military actions, he ordered the bombing of military targets in Libya, sent United States warships and personnel to Central America, and dispatched a naval force to the Persian Gulf. He was the first president in twenty-five years to review a war game conducted by the Defense Department and national security staff.

George Bush made crucial policy decisions to commit U.S. forces in Panama and the Gulf. He approved the plans of action submitted by the chairman of the Joint Chiefs of Staff Colin Powell, declared certain targets to be off limits, and indicated when hostilities should begin and end. He left combat strategy to his military commanders, however, and did not get involved in day-to-day tactical decisions. Similarly, Bill Clinton made the decision to bomb Iraq in retaliation for an attempt on the life of former President Bush when he was visiting Kuwait.

The destructiveness of nuclear weapons combined with their rapid deployment and delivery suggests that presidents can no longer leave war making solely to their military commanders. They must decide when and how to involve themselves. The ultimate responsibility for how war is to be conducted rests with the civilian commander, the president.

## THE EXPANSION OF A POLICY-MAKING ROLE

### Incentives for Presidential Leadership

The growth of the president's authority in foreign and military affairs has been the consequence of several factors: the increasing involvement of the United States within the international community; the public's desire for strong, personal leadership to direct that involvement; and the political ramifications of that leadership on the administration and its policy goals.

Since the end of World War II, the United States has been a dominant economic, military, and political power. It has tried to shape international developments, aiding its allies and resisting its adversaries, building its defenses yet promoting peaceful coexistence, fostering its interests yet supporting international cooperation. The industrial capacity, technological skills, and resource base of the United States were essential to the revitalization of the economies of countries in Western Europe and Asia following the destruction during World War II. The economic strength of the United States has also been an important source of technical, financial, and agricultural aid to the Third World, which needs the products and skills of an advanced technological society. The United States, in turn, has become increasingly dependent on the natural resources of developing countries, particularly those that produce energy. Today the economies of many nations, rich and poor, are more interdependent than ever before.

Resource dependency and economic interdependency have contributed to the incentives for American involvement as well as limited the control presidents have over foreign affairs. No longer can the United States afford to adopt an isolationist policy nor can the president avoid international policy, at least not for long. Held accountable for the performance of the domestic economy, a president has no choice but to tackle international problems as well.

The technological advances in armaments, particularly nuclear weapons, and the conflict situations in which the United States finds itself around the world have forced presidents to be continuously concerned about military preparedness, strategic planning, alliance building, and arms control. The vulnerability of all nations, the proliferation of nuclear weapons, and the persistence of armed conflict require the president to promote the common defense and peaceful coexistence at the same time.

Not only have world events forced the president to emphasize foreign and military affairs, but domestic political forces have also done so. The public looks to the president for leadership in times of crisis. A unifying figure, the president is the personification of state, the person around whom the country can rally.[8]

· In the short run, crisis situations may increase the public's approval of the president. When American hostages were seized in Iran in 1979, public approval of Carter's performance rose. Over time, when he was unable to obtain their release, his approval level declined. This suggests that in the long run the persistence of the crisis works to the president's disadvantage.

In addition to the short-run support that crises can generate, foreign policy leadership benefits the president in other respects. It contributes to the image of a strong national figure. This is particularly useful during reelection campaigns when strength, assertiveness, will, and direction are seen as most desirable presidential traits. The public wants to feel secure. People look to the president to satisfy that feeling. The nation's security in modern times has been a source of continuous concern and a recurring campaign issue.

The difficulties faced by presidents in formulating a policy agenda and in developing a consensus for it are not usually as arduous in foreign and military affairs as they are in domestic ones. Although partisanship has been increasingly evident in foreign and defense policy, presidential dependence on legislative enactments is still not as great as in the domestic area. Moreover, as the president's ability to effect domestic change decreases, the incentive to get involved in foreign affairs increases. Sometimes, however, too great an emphasis on foreign affairs can backfire, as it did for George Bush in 1991 and 1992. The public perceived that he devoted too much of his time and energy to foreign policy at the expense of domestic issues, particularly the economy. Yet, after Bill Clinton was elected to fix the economy and end government gridlock, he too found himself immersed in foreign policy issues.[9]

## Policy Goals and Presidential Success: The Two Presidencies Thesis

Are presidents more apt to be successful in crafting foreign policy than domestic policy? According to political scientist Aaron Wildavsky, they tend to be, particularly in the period from 1948 to 1964. In examining congressional action on presidential proposals during this period, Wildavsky found that presidents had significantly better records in foreign and defense policy than in domestic affairs. He concluded that there were actually two presidencies, one in foreign affairs and one in the domestic area:

> When refugees and immigration, which Congress considers primarily a domestic concern, are removed from the general foreign policy area, it is clear that Presidents prevail about 70 per cent of the time in defense and foreign policy, compared with 40 per cent in the domestic sphere.[10]

Wildavsky wrote in the mid-1960s after an era of bipartisanship in foreign affairs. He wrote after the emergence of the United States as a world power, after Presidents Roosevelt, Truman, Eisenhower, and Kennedy had established America's position as a leader of the Western world, container of communism, and promoter of international cooperation. He wrote before the Vietnam War.

The unpopularity of that war led to recriminations against the presidents who directed that effort and against the presidency itself. In an effort to deter future presidential action that lacked popular and congressional support, Congress passed a series of statutes such as the War Powers Resolution designed to constrain executive discretion in hostile or potentially hostile situations. As a consequence, presidents still retain the policy initiative, but Congress has improved its capacity to modify that initiative and to say no.

Political and institutional changes during the 1970s have contributed to a more assertive posture in foreign affairs by Congress. The domestic impact of foreign policy has become more pronounced, blurring the old distinction between foreign and domestic affairs and creating new incentives for legislative involvement. In fact, a new term, *intermestic*, has been coined to describe policy that has both foreign and domestic implications. Additionally, the increasing importance of such economic considerations as the budget deficit, corporate tax structure, and the value of the dollar on foreign policy issues and of such foreign policy issues as tariffs, trade, and immigration on domestic affairs have encouraged Congress to get involved and have made foreign policy subject to many of the same partisan pressures as domestic politics. The old adage that "politics stops at the water's edge" is no longer applicable for noncrisis situations.

With more committees and subcommittees dealing with international issues, more staff and better information facilities at their disposal, more foreign travel by legislators and their aides, more groups, governments, and individuals trying to affect policy judgments, members of Congress, individually and collectively, have become less disposed to acquiesce to the president's initiatives.

Congress affects foreign policy in a variety of ways. Its direct impact may be exercised through legislation. In addition to the Senate's confirmation of ambassadors and ratification of treaties, Congress enacts laws that regulate foreign commerce, military affairs, and international environmental matters. Although presidents usually take the initiative in proposing these laws, Congress can and does imprint its stamp. It passed laws that constrained President Reagan in his ability to support the Contras in Nicaragua and imposed sanctions against the white, apartheid government of South Africa against the wishes of the Reagan administration.

A legislative policy solution, however, is a clumsy and difficult tool for Congress to use. As political scientist James M. Lindsay wrote:

> Legislation almost by necessity is rigid, but diplomacy frequently requires flexibility. Congress acts slowly, but issues can change rapidly. In some cases, resorting to legislation may mean taking a sledgehammer to a problem that requires a scalpel. . . . In short, legislators often do not want to win, because they believe that legislated solutions will prove unwise or unworkable in practice.[11]

Thus Congress has generally delegated to the president considerable authority in foreign affairs because of its institutional incapacity to exercise that authority with the same dispatch, consistency, and national perspective as the president. At the same time, however, Congress has retained a check on how the president uses that delegated authority. For example, the Omnibus Trade and Competitiveness Act of 1988 gives the president authority to initiate a so-called "fast track" procedure for trade negotiations so long as neither the House nor Senate disapproves of the president's actions within ninety days. Similarly, Congress has institutionalized numerous reporting requirements into law, obligating the executive to inform Congress of actions or proposed actions that departments and agencies are considering. The CIA, for example, is required to inform the appropriate congressional committees of its covert operations.

In addition to these statutory requirements, Congress can also use the public arena to criticize presidential policy and try to change it. When President Reagan continued to back Philippine president Ferdinand Marcos after an election in which there were widespread allegations of fraud by his government, Senator Richard Lugar, chairman of the Senate Foreign Relations Committee and an observer of the elections, went on the Sunday morning talk shows to present the case against Marcos. He claimed the president was misinformed. The administration subsequently backed off its position.[12]

With presidential policy making subject to greater congressional scrutiny and influence, scholars have reexamined Wildavsky's "two presidencies" thesis. The results of that reexamination thus far have been mixed. In general, political scientists have found that presidents are still more likely to get their way on foreign affairs than on domestic issues, but they are also more likely to have Congress modify their proposals than in the past. One study of congressional compliance with presidential requests in foreign affairs found that Congress gave presidents all or part of what they wanted 65 percent of the time.[13]

Partisanship is also a factor that affects presidential success in Congress. When the White House and Congress are controlled by separate parties, Republican presidents have done better on "conflictual" foreign policy than domestic policy while Democratic presidents have not, according to a quantitative study by two political scientists, Richard Fleisher and Jon R. Bond.[14] There are several possible explanations for this finding. The authors contend that the congressional majority, the Democrats, support Republican presidents in foreign affairs because the Democrats share responsibility for governing.[15] Another possibility, suggests Professor Terry Sullivan, is that Republican foreign policy is more mainstream than Republican domestic policy.[16]

Although scholars may disagree on the "two presidencies" thesis, one conclusion is clear: Presidents have to work harder than in the past to achieve their foreign policy objectives. The days of a bipartisan consensus on most foreign policy issues are over.

The increasing interest and involvement of Congress in foreign policy decisions places presidents in a dilemma. How can they lead without followers? How can they be expected to make policy and be held accountable for it if they cannot be assured of its enactment? Presidents might desire to be strong policy leaders, but in normal times that leadership is often fragile. This is why they need a variety of policy experts and coalition builders to succeed. It is to that advisory mechanism that we now turn.

## THE DEVELOPMENT OF AN ADVISORY SYSTEM

### The Executive Departments

Throughout the nineteenth century and well into the twentieth, the secretary of state was the president's principal foreign policy adviser, providing information and advice as well as implementing policy decisions. In performing this role, the secretary has been assisted by a staff of career officials, who were organized primarily on the basis of five regional bureaus.

Over the years the State Department has become more specialized. Functional divisions dealing with economics and business, international organization, environmental and scientific affairs, and public and congressional relations have supplemented the political bureaus. Nonetheless, the department remains relatively small. Its 1994 budget of $2.6 billion pales by comparison to the Defense Department's $250.7 billion as does the size of its authorized work force (20,584 compared to over 1 million civilian employees and 1.6 million military for the Defense Department). One reason that the State Department has not grown dramatically as American involvement in world affairs has increased is that a variety of old and new agencies now also participate in international activities.

There is an intelligence community. Consisting of almost forty separate agencies, it is dominated by the Central Intelligence Agency, National Security Agency, and the Defense Intelligence Agency. There is a United States Information Agency (USIA), which operates libraries; sponsors cultural, scientific, and educational programs; coordinates press relations; and runs the Voice of America, a worldwide radio and television network. There is a special trade representative, an Arms Control and Disarmament Agency, and a National Aeronautics and Space Administration (NASA). Many of the principal executive departments also have international divisions and ongoing interests in international affairs. The State Department no longer enjoys a monopoly.

As noted in the previous chapter, a growing concern with international economic matters has hastened the development of an "economic complex," a set of institutions and individuals with interests and expertise in international economics.[17] These include the Departments of Treasury, State, Commerce, Agriculture, and Energy, the executive offices of the trade representative, the Council of Economic Advisers, the OMB, and the Fed. Congressional committees that regulate commerce, banking, agriculture, and foreign affairs are also part of this complex. Clinton has attempted to coordinate the executive units in a National Economic Council chaired by a senior presidential adviser.

The proliferation of agencies with international activities has presented presidents with several problems: how to balance competing perspectives and interests within their administration; how to coordinate and integrate policy advice; how to articulate policy with a single voice; and how to do all of this within their time frame without jeopardizing their goals or sacrificing their discretion in the decision-making process. The resolution of these problems has proved difficult. Solutions have varied with the style and goals of individual presidents and with the institutional needs of their office.

President Franklin Roosevelt relied primarily on his White House staff. Presidential aides provided liaison with the military and State

Department, acted as personal emissaries of the president to other governments, and funneled information and advice to Roosevelt. He, in turn, directed their activities.

Partially in reaction to the ad hoc nature of Roosevelt's advisory system and his reliance on personal aides rather than department heads, Congress enacted the National Security Act of 1947. This law, which combined the separate military departments into a single defense agency and established the Central Intelligence Agency, acknowledged presidential responsibilities within the national security sphere and provided a mechanism for meeting these responsibilities, the National Security Council (NSC).

### The National Security Council

The National Security Council consists of four statutory members: the president, vice president, secretary of state, and secretary of defense. It also includes a number of advisory members such as the director of the CIA, the chairman of the Joint Chiefs of Staff, the director of the Arms Control and Disarmament Agency, and other advisers that presidents have added from time to time.[18] Beginning with Truman, presidents provided it with staff support.

The council's charge is advisory but its mandate is broad: to help define goals and priorities; to coordinate and integrate domestic, foreign, and military policies; and to suggest specific courses of action—all within the national security sphere.

In the Truman presidency, the council functioned as a forum for discussion. Truman used it only sporadically until the Korean War, when he began meeting with it on a regular basis. During this period the council performed an important advisory role. President Eisenhower expanded this role, converting the NSC into a policy-making body. It operated as a planning board for developing general policy positions. A White House secretariat, headed by a special assistant to the president for national security affairs, helped provide organizational support.

As an advisory body the council reached its zenith during the 1950s. Eisenhower's penchant for using formal organizations to establish broad objectives meshed well with the capacity of the National Security Council to provide an integrated set of policy recommendations. Beginning with Kennedy, however, the council's policy-making function was eliminated and its advisory role declined. Although it continued to meet, often for symbolic purposes, its principal responsibilities were assumed by a special assistant to the president for national security affairs and his staff.

The NSC enjoyed a mild resurgence during the Reagan and Bush administrations. Functioning within a cabinet council system, it helped coordinate policy among the various agencies involved in national security issues. A major component of that job was to oversee the implementation of key presidential decisions. In doing so its staff provided coordination at the working-group level for various departments and agencies that were concerned with different aspects of national security policy. In the words of Colin Powell, the last national security adviser to hold office during the Reagan administration:

> We must make sure that all the relevant departments and agencies play their appropriate role in policy formulation. We must make sure that all pertinent facts and viewpoints are laid before the President. We must also make sure that no Cabinet official completes an "end run" around other NSC principals in pushing a policy line on which they too have legitimate concerns.[19]

The relative decline of the NSC's role as an advisory body has coincided with the development of a sizable staffing structure for the president's special assistant for national security affairs. Presidents have increasingly turned to that assistant for information, advice, and internal coordination.

### The Special Assistant for National Security Affairs

Kennedy was the first president to create the position of special assistant for national security affairs. His purpose was to integrate the growing diversity of executive branch perspectives and views and to do so without the burden of a large support system. Moreover, his preferred style of decision making was to interact with a few key aides rather than preside over a cabinet-like body.

Kennedy's involvement in the management of foreign and defense policy enhanced the role of his national security adviser at the expense of senior officials in the State and Defense departments. Power shifted from these departments to the White House. This shift continued and accelerated in subsequent administrations. Increasing reliance by presidents on their national security adviser enhanced the prestige and influence of the adviser and in the process produced tension with the secretary of state.

The national security office grew. The staff approached one hundred and fifty policy experts and supporting personnel by 1972. The reach of the president's assistant expanded. Not only was the person who held this position able to offer advice on a wider range of issues, but increasingly, that assistant was also able to act as the president's personal representative, negotiator, and spokesperson. Henry Kissinger, who served in this position during the Nixon and Ford administrations, performed all of these roles. In addition, he presided over an elaborate system of interagency committees that fortified his position and undercut that of the department heads. In this way he controlled the flow of information and ideas to the president. Traditional departmental interests were muted.

Kissinger's personal relationships, particularly with President Nixon, prevented others from circumventing his authority. Moreover, his "closed" style of operating, combined with Nixon's penchant to consult primarily, sometimes exclusively, with his national security adviser, reduced the influence of others. Secretary of State William Rogers was not even informed of the president's China initiative until it was under way. For all intents and purposes, the traditional policy functions of the secretary of state had been eclipsed. After Rogers resigned in 1972, Nixon made it official. He appointed Kissinger to head the State Department yet allowed him to continue in his national security position.

Ford disengaged the positions in 1974, appointing Kissinger's principal assistant, General Brent Scowcroft, to replace him. With this disengagement came a reversion of the adviser's responsibilities to those that were performed during the Kennedy period: briefing the president, acting as a liaison to the departments, and coordinating presidential responses after decisions had been made. This reduced role was short-lived, however. The Kissinger model was restored during the Carter administration by one of Kissinger's former students, Zbigniew Brzezinski. Assuming functions of adviser, advocate, and sometimes spokesman, Carter's assistant for national security affairs clashed frequently with Secretary of State Cyrus Vance.

While Brzezinski did not retain the elaborate substructure of standing committees and working groups that characterized the Kissinger operation, most important studies, option papers, and memos to the president were still routed through his office. Of his own role, Brzezinski stated:

> I work very closely with the President. I'm his adviser in foreign policy and security matters. And I'm the coordinator for him of all the work that comes for his decision from the State Department, from Defense and from the CIA. Finally, and expressly so, the President wishes me and my staff to help him play an innovative role, that is to say, to try to look beyond the problems of the immediate and help him define a larger and more distant sense of direction.[20]

Still another attempt to change the relationship among the president, his adviser, and the secretary of state occurred during the Reagan administration. Desiring to have the department heads play a larger role and to avoid the tension that had been created between the White House and other executive branch units, Reagan initially reduced the influence and visibility of his national security adviser and had him report to counselor Edwin Meese, the person who was charged with policy coordination in both domestic and national security affairs during the early years of the administration. Not only did this reduce the influence of the national security adviser, but it also reduced that of his staff. Power shifted to the State Department, but tension between it and the White House remained high. Fueled by clashing personalities, policy perspectives, and institutional interests, these tensions eventually led to the resignation of the secretary of state, Alexander Haig, and the upgrading of the White House national security operation under a new director and with new personnel. In all, Reagan had six national security advisers in eight years.

Turnover in the White House and specifically on the national security staff together with a lack of adequate presidential guidance and supervision contributed to the major foreign policy mishap of the Reagan administration, the Iran–Contra affair. The failure and unpopularity of the policy to sell arms to Iran in exchange for that country's help in obtaining the release of American hostages in Lebanon, combined with the illegal use of the profits from that arms sale to support the Contra forces fighting to overthrow the Nicaraguan government, prompted a reexamination of the role and procedures of the national security staff and its relationship to the president.

A presidential commission, headed by John Tower (former senator and Armed Services Committee chairman) and consisting of Edmund Muskie (a former senator and secretary of state during the Carter administration) and Brent Scowcroft (President Ford's and later President Bush's national security adviser), criticized the actions of several national security aides and the president's failure to supervise them. It recommended an end to the staff's participation in covert operations and a return to its principal functions of coordinating national security advice for the president, but it did not recommend structural or procedural changes in the staff's mode of operation. In accepting the commission's findings and recommendations, President Reagan issued a directive that gave the State and Defense department secretaries primary responsibility for foreign and defense affairs, subject to interagency review, within the national security policy process. The national security adviser was charged with making that process work on a daily basis as well as briefing the president and providing him with the information and advice necessary to make decisions and take actions.

Scowcroft assumed this less visible role after he was reappointed national security adviser by Bush. He stayed out of the public spotlight but continued to exercise considerable influence on presidential foreign policy making. He was a key adviser to the president during the Panama incursion and Persian Gulf War, a major architect of U.S. policy toward the Soviet Union both before and after its breakup, and a crisis manager and policy coordinator. Secretary of State James Baker played a more prominent role in designing foreign policy and reinstituting negotiations for a Middle East peace accord.

Clinton's national security adviser, Anthony Lake, has also maintained a low profile. He has operated behind the scenes as an adviser and coordinator, with Clinton's secretary of state, Warren Christopher, taking a more visible role as spokesman, adviser, and negotiator.

## ASSESSING THE ADVISORY SYSTEM

During the Cold War when national security matters were of prime concern, presidents tended to rely heavily on their national security advisers. This reliance allowed them to maximize their discretion, exercise more central control, act quickly and decisively, and do so in a manner that was consistent with their basic beliefs and their policy objectives. Naturally, presidents do not enjoy resistance to their policy from outside the administration, much less from within it (although the policy might benefit from such resistance). From presidents' perspectives reliance on *their* advisers minimizes this resistance and provides a more supportive environment for the achievement of these objectives.

There are several reasons why presidents tend to look inward when seeking advice. They know their White House advisers will be loyal and have only the administration's best interests in mind. In contrast, their department secretaries will have several constituents to consider: other governments, other departments, organized interest groups, and the department's own bureaucracy. Second, the national security assistant is more apt to be on the president's wavelength with a staff of policy experts chosen in large part because of their acceptable political and ideological views. The secretaries are supported by a cadre of civil servants (and in the case of defense, career military officials) who have survived precisely because they do not enunciate partisan views or see the world primarily in ideological terms. The national security adviser and staff can be ideological and partisan; the secretary of state must be pragmatic and diplomatic.

Moreover, the national security staff, unburdened by administrative responsibilities, can respond more rapidly and less visibly to presidential needs and requests, particularly emergencies. In contrast, the departments tend to move more slowly. They adhere to established procedures, utilize regular channels, and usually speak in carefully measured tones. Presidents often have become impatient with them and distrustful of them. Particularly fearful of leaks, some have even tried to avoid involving the departments entirely on very sensitive matters.

Not only does a White House office enjoy institutional advantages in responding to presidential needs, but the head of it also enjoys several personal advantages. He or she has better access to the president—including an office in the West Wing and a daily briefing—and fewer operational responsibilities, hence more time to focus on immediate problems that demand presidential decisions or actions. In contrast, the secretary of state must deal with a wider range of policy and administrative matters, including diplomatic and ceremonial functions.

It is easy to see why presidents have turned to their national security adviser. In addition to exercising more discretion within a supportive environment, they can more easily engage in top-down decision making and formulate policies that are consistent with their political beliefs and ideological convictions. Moreover, the policies themselves are apt to be more innovative and consist of fewer compromises than would result if a larger number of executive and legislative officials were involved. These advantages, however, are offset by several major disadvantages, which were noted in a report prepared for President Bush by the National Academy of Public Administration. The report said, in part:

The personal advice of the national security advisor, while not freighted with bureaucratic loads, is also less sensitive to the institutional apparatus necessary to build support and to implement policy decisions. Heavy reliance on informal processes may lead to inadequate communication and execution. . . . The departments provide greater institutional memory, continuity, professional experience, in-depth planning capability, and an orderly policy process. In negotiations with others, they also have the advantage of being once removed from the president so that mistakes are not likely to be as harmful, and changes of position can be made with less embarrassment to the president.[21]

As in other areas of policy, how presidents organize their national security advisory system ultimately depends on their own personality, policy goals, and institutional needs. There is no one right way to do it. As we have previously noted, style is an important influence on how presidents interact with their aides. Eisenhower thrived in group settings. Eliciting a team approach that emphasized consensus building from within, he set up a national security mechanism that provided internal coordination for a cabinet-based, advisory model. In contrast, Nixon's introverted personality, his secretive manner, and his need for power led him to adopt a hierarchical model in national security staffing. Jimmy Carter provided a third extreme. His desire to get involved in details, to evaluate a range of alternatives, but ultimately to make his own judgment caused him to utilize a variation of multiple advocacy—with undesirable consequences. His policy seemed to lack both direction and consistency.

A second component that affects the advisory structure is the goals themselves and the extent to which the president has made up his mind. Does he desire to reach a judgment or to exercise one he has reached? Lyndon Johnson's conviction about the Vietnam War and Bush's about the need to be firm in the Persian Gulf cast them in the role of advocates. As a consequence, they wanted (although perhaps did not benefit from) a system that supported their views. Both turned to their national security advisers to coordinate that system.

Having a strong ideological bent shapes decision making. Reagan desired an advisory system that would produce a policy consensus *within* his conceptual framework and a mechanism for implementing his basic goals but one that relieved him of day-to-day decisional responsibilities. In contrast, Carter opted for a structure that processed information without filtering it too much. What he wanted from his advisers were choices, not consensus.

Whereas style and goals explain differences in advisory systems, the institutional needs of the presidency have fostered some of the basic trends evident since the Eisenhower administration: the growth and specialization of a White House national security staffing structure, the increasing reliance on this structure by the president over the course of an administration, and the advisory and advocacy roles of the national security adviser that often conflict with the secretary of state.

In short, presidents have to be comfortable with the system and the system has to work. It needs to generate information and ideas, to organize and manage competing viewpoints, and to help define and achieve a president's basic goals. It should provide *continuity* in policy and promote the *integration* of policies. It should enable the president to exercise strong and steady leadership.

## CONCLUSION

The limited role that the framers of the Constitution envisioned for the president in foreign and military affairs has been expanded significantly. Today presidents are expected to take the policy-making initiative in both spheres. They are expected to oversee the conduct of war and diplomacy. They are also expected to perform the symbolic duties of chief of state and commander-in-chief.

Although presidential expectations have increased, the ability of the president to meet these expectations has declined, particularly since Vietnam. That decline is a product of several factors: the interdependence of the United States on the economies, resources, and security of other countries; the increasing impact of foreign policy decisions on domestic affairs; the proliferation of groups and governments trying to affect policy decisions; the more assertive role Congress has assumed; and the absence of a foreign policy consensus since the end of the Cold War. As a consequence, presidents have had to devote more time and increasing resources to the performance of their policy-making responsibilities. They have had to make greater efforts at coordination within the executive branch, at consensus building outside of it, and at gaining a congressional majority. In this sense, their needs in foreign and national security affairs are not much different than in the domestic arena, although expectations—their own, and those of the American public and foreign government leaders—seem to be greater.

With foreign and defense policy so important, presidents have turned increasingly to their national security staff for help. Established in 1960 and expanded in size and specialization since then, this internal White House mechanism has provided a cadre of loyal policy experts to help presidents with the everyday problems with which they have to deal. The national security staff functions primarily to inform and advise presidents and secondarily to handle their correspondence, speeches, and briefings. It has increased presidents' information, maximized their discretion, and created the capacity for rapid and decisive presidential responses. But, all of this has been achieved at some cost. Some administrations have experienced a great deal of tension between the White House and executive branch agencies.

Despite the increasing obstacles they face, presidents continue to emphasize foreign policy matters, particularly as their administrations progress. There are psychological, political, and policy reasons for doing so. As foreign policy leaders, they can act as unifying figures, overcome perceptions of partisanship, and work to achieve specific policy goals. Demonstrating leadership in this manner stands to increase their popularity, improve their reelectability, and enhance their place in history—all very desirable personal goals. Finally, there is that intangible but real desire to try to affect events, particularly to promote peace among nations. In international affairs, American presidents want and expect to be more than facilitators. They want and expect to be world leaders.

## NOTES

1. *Goldwater* v. *Carter*, 444 U.S. 996, 998 (1979).
2. Louis Fisher, *The Politics of Shared Power: Congress and the Executive* (Washington, D.C.: Congressional Quarterly, 1993), p. 156.
3. Fisher, *The Politics of Shared Power*, p. 157; Ryan J. Barilleaux, "Parallel Unilateral Policy Declarations: A New Device for Presidential Autonomy in Foreign Affairs," *Presidential Studies Quarterly* 17 (Winter 1987): 107–17.
4. The Supreme Court's legislative veto decision, *Immigration and Naturalization Service* v. *Chadha*, 462 U.S. 919 (1983), calls into legal question the use of concurrent resolutions as a means of restricting executive activity. Nonetheless, Congress has continued to delegate authority to the president subject to its approval or disapproval.
5. George Bush, *Weekly Compilation of Presidential Documents* 27 (January 14, 1991), p. 48.
6. *Dellums* v. *Bush*, 752 F. Supp. 1141 (D.D.C. 1990).
7. Fisher, *The Politics of Shared Power*, pp. 166–67.
8. Fred I. Greenstein, "Popular Images of the President," *American Journal of Psychiatry* 22 (1965): 523–29.
9. A computerized analysis by the president's scheduler of how Clinton spent his time during his first 100 days showed that foreign policy consumed approximately 25 percent of his working hours.
10. Aaron Wildavsky, "The Two Presidencies," in Aaron Wildavsky, ed., *Perspectives on the Presidency* (Boston: Little, Brown, 1975), p. 449.
11. James M. Lindsay, "Congress and Foreign Policy: Why the Hill Matters," *Political Science Quarterly* 107 (Winter 1992–1993): 612.
12. Herrick Smith, *The Power Game* (Ballantine Books: New York, 1988), pp. 43–44.
13. Ralph G. Carter, "Congressional Foreign Policy Behavior: Persistent Patterns of the Postwar Period," *Presidential Studies Quarterly* 16 (Spring 1986): 333–34.
14. Richard Fleisher and Jon R. Bond, "Are There Two Presidencies? Yes, But Only for Republicans," *Journal of Politics* 50 (August 1988): 747–67.
15. Ibid. pp. 762–65.
16. Terry Sullivan, "A Matter of Fact: The 'Two Presidencies' Thesis Revitalized," in Steven A. Shull, ed., *The Two Presidencies: A Quarter Century Assessment* (Chicago: Nelson Hall, 1991), pp. 154–55.
17. A good discussion of this complex and its components appears in I. M. Destler, "A Government Divided: The Security Complex and the Economic Complex" (paper delivered at the Annual Meeting of the American Political Science Association, Washington, D.C., August 1991).
18. Colin L. Powell, "The NSC System in the Last Two Years of the Reagan Administration," *Presidential Studies Quarterly, Proceedings* 6 (1989): 205.
19. Ibid., p. 206.
20. Zbigniew Brzezinski, quoted in Dom Bonafede, "Brzezinski—Stepping Out of His Backstage Role," *National Journal* 9 (October 15, 1977): 1596.
21. National Academy of Public Administration, *The Executive Presidency: Federal Management for the 1990s* (Washington, D.C.: National Academy of Public Administration, 1989), p. 10.

## SELECTED READINGS

Adler, David Gray. "The Constitution and Presidential Warmaking: The Enduring Debate." *Political Science Quarterly* 103 (1988): 1–36.

Barilleaux, Ryan J. "Parallel Unilateral Policy Declarations: A New Device for Presidential Autonomy in Foreign Affairs." *Presidential Studies Quarterly* 17 (1987): 107–17.

Berman, Larry. *Planning a Tragedy*. New York: Norton, 1982.

Berman, Larry, and Bruce W. Jentleson. "Bush and the Post–Cold War World: New Challenges for American Leadership." In Colin Campbell and Bert A. Rockman, eds. *The Bush Presidency: First Appraisals*. Chatham, N.J.: Chatham House, 1991, pp. 93–128.

Bock, Joseph G., and Duncan L. Clarke. "The National Security Assistant and the White House Staff: National Security Policy Decision Making and Domestic Political Considerations." *Presidential Studies Quarterly* 16 (1986): 258–79.

Destler, I. M. "Reagan and the World: An Awesome Stubbornness." In Charles O. Jones, ed. *The Reagan Legacy: Promise and Performance*. Chatham, N.J.: Chatham House, 1988, pp. 241–61.

Fisher, Louis. *The Politics of Shared Power: Congress and the Executive*. Washington, D.C.: Congressional Quarterly, 1993, pp. 145–76.

George, Alexander. *Presidential Decisionmaking in Foreign Policy: The Effective Use of Information and Advice*. Boulder, Colo.: Westview, 1981.

Kellerman, Barbara, and Ryan J. Barilleaux. *The President as World Leader*. New York: St. Martin's Press, 1991.

Koh, Harold Hongju. *The National Security Constitution: Sharing Power after the Iran–Contra Affair*. New Haven, Conn.: Yale University Press, 1990.

Lindsay, James M. "Congress and Foreign Policy: Why the Hill Matters." *Political Science Quarterly* 107 (Winter 1992–1993): 607–28.

Lord, Carnes. *The Presidency and the Management of National Security*. New York: Free Press, 1988.

Mann, Thomas E., ed. *A Question of Balance: The President, the Congress, and Foreign Policy*. Washington D.C.: Brookings Institution, 1990.

Mulcahy, Kevin V. "Presidents and the Administration of Foreign Policy: The New Role for the Vice President." *Presidential Studies Quarterly* 17 (1987): 119–31.

Rockman, Bert A. "America's Department of State: Irregular and Regular Syndromes of Policy Making." *American Political Science Review* 75 (1981): 911–27.

Rose, Richard, and Robert J. Thompson. "The President in a Changing International System." *Presidential Studies Quarterly* 21 (Fall 1990): 751–70.

Shull, Steven A. *The Two Presidencies*. Chicago: Nelson Hall, 1991.

# APPENDIX A

# Studying the Presidency

Although many people consider the presidency the most fascinating aspect of American politics, unfortunately it is not easy to research. This overview of studying the presidency is designed to alert students to the implications, both positive and negative, of adopting particular research approaches and methodologies. Armed with this awareness, researchers should be able better to understand the advantages and limitations of various research designs. They can then more knowledgeably construct one that best suits their needs.

## APPROACHES

There are many approaches to studying the presidency, ranging from concern with the constitutional authority of the office to dealing with the personality dynamics of a particular president. By *approaches* we mean orientations that guide researchers to ask certain questions and employ certain concepts rather than others. In this section we focus on four of the principal approaches employed by political scientists who study the presidency. The categories we use are neither mutually exclusive nor comprehensive. The goal here is not to create an ideal typology of scholarship on the presidency. Instead, it is to increase sensitivity to the implications of different approaches for what is studied, how a subject is investigated, and what types of conclusions may be reached. Similarly, our focus is on approaches per se rather than the works of individual authors or a comprehensive review of the literature.[1]

### Legal

The oldest approach to studying the presidency, what we shall term the legal perspective, concerns the president's formal powers. Legal researchers analyze the Constitution, laws, treaties, and legal precedents to understand the sources, scope, and use of the president's formal powers, including their legal limitations.[2] Because these have changed over time, the legal approach has a historical orientation.

With its emphasis on the historical development of the office and the checks and balances in the Constitution, the legal perspective also lends itself to discussion of the president's place in our system of government, both as it is and as scholars think it ought to be. Thus, there is often a clear prescriptive or normative element in these studies.

The range of issues involving presidential authority is great. Illustrations from the recent past include the right of the president to impound funds appropriated by Congress, the scope of the president's lawmaking power when he issues executive orders and proclamations, the president's authority to freeze federal hiring, the president's use of the pocket veto during brief congressional recesses, the constitutionality of the legislative veto, the role of the comptroller general in triggering budget reductions, the president's claims of a partial veto of "unconstitutional" provisions of statutes, and claims of executive privilege. Foreign policy issues have also reached the courts. These include the conduct of the Vietnam War by Presidents Johnson and Nixon without explicit congressional authorization, President Carter's termination of a defense treaty with Taiwan and his settlement of the Iranian assets and hostage issues, and, more generally, the president's use of executive agreements as substitutes for treaties.

Although the legal perspective has a deservedly honored place among American political scientists—the United States prides itself on the rule of law—it has its limitations. Most of what the president does cannot be explained through legal analysis. The Constitution, treaties, laws, and court decisions affect only a small portion of the president's behavior. Most of the president's relationships with the public, the Congress, the White House staff, and the bureaucracy do not easily fall within the purview of the legal perspective. Instead, this behavior can be understood only in terms of informal or extraconstitutional powers. Similarly, because the legal perspective is heavily government-centered, topics such as press coverage of the presidency, the public's evaluation of the president, and other relationships that involve nongovernmental actors are largely ignored.

Equally significant, the legal perspective, although it requires rigorous analysis, does not lend itself to explanation. Studies of the boundaries of appropriate behavior do not explain why actions occur within those boundaries or what their consequences are. Moreover, the heavy reliance on case studies by scholars employing this approach inevitably makes the basis of their generalizations somewhat tenuous.

Thus, although studies that adopt the legal perspective make important contributions to our understanding of American politics, they do not answer most of the questions that entice researchers to study the presidency. For answers to these questions, we must turn to alternative approaches.

### Institutional

A second basic approach to the study of the presidency focuses on it as an institution in which the president has certain roles and responsibilities and is involved in numerous structures and processes. Thus, the structure, functions, and operation of the presidency become the center of attention. These concerns are broad enough to include agencies such as the Office of Management and Budget and units in the White House such as the legislative liaison operation. Scholars following this approach can move beyond formal authority and investigate such topics as the formulation, coordination, promotion, and implementation of the president's legislative program, the president's relationships with the media and interest groups, or his decision-making processes.[3] Like the legal perspective, the institutional approach often traces the persistence and adaptation of organizations and processes over time. This gives much of the literature a historical perspective and also lends itself to evaluations of the success of institutional arrangements.

The institutional approach plays a crucial role in helping us to understand the presidency. Although at one time many institutional studies emphasized formal organizational structure and rules, such as organization charts of the White House or budgetary process procedures, in recent years the behavior of those involved in the operation of the presidency has received more attention. This has increased the utility of institutional research. It is, after all, necessary to collect empirical data about what political actors are doing before we can discuss the significance of their behavior, much less examine analytical questions of relationships such as those pertaining to influence. By seeking to identify patterns of behavior and studying interactions, such as those between the White House and the Congress, OMB, or the media, institutional research not only tells us what happens but, more significant, also helps us to understand *why* it happens. When scholars examine presidential efforts to influence the media, for example, they are looking at typical and potentially significant behavior that may explain patterns of media coverage of the White House.

The institutional approach has two principal limitations. First, description is often emphasized at the expense of explanation. We know a great deal more about how presidents have organized their White House staffs, for example, than about how these arrangements have affected the kinds of advice they have received. In other words, we know more about the process than about its consequences. This in turn provides a tenuous basis for the prescriptive aspect of some institutional research. We cannot have confidence in recommendations about presidential advisory systems, for example, until we understand their effects.

The second limitation of some institutional studies is that they may downplay or even ignore the significance of political skills, ideology, and personality in their emphasis on organizations and processes. Indeed, the implicit assumption that underlies the often extensive attention scholars devote to structures and processes is that they are very significant. Yet this assumption may not always be justified. It may be that the world view a president brings to the White House influences decisions more than the way the advisory system is organized. Similarly, ideology, party, and constituency views may be more important than the White House legislative liaison operation in influencing congressional votes on the president's program.

## Political Power

In the political power approach to the study of the presidency, researchers examine not institutions but the people within them and their relationships with each other.[4] These researchers view power as a function of personal politics rather than formal authority or position. They find the president operating in a pluralistic environment in which there are numerous actors with independent power bases and perspectives different from his. Thus, the president must marshal resources to persuade others to do as he wishes; a president cannot rely on expanding the institution's legal authority or adjusting its support mechanisms.

The president's need to exercise influence in several arenas leads those who follow the power perspective to adopt an expansive view of presidential politics that includes both governmental actors, such as the Congress, bureaucracy, and White House staff, and those outside of government, such as the public, the press, and interest groups. The dependent variables in studying presidential interactions (what authors are trying to explain) are many and may include congressional or public support for the president, presidential decisions, press coverage of the White House, bureaucratic policy implementation, or a set of policy options prepared by the bureaucracy for the president.[5] Because this approach does not assume presidential success or the smooth functioning of the presidency, the influence of bureaucratic politics and other organizational factors in the executive branch is as important to investigate as behavior in more openly adversarial institutions such as Congress.

Power is a concept that involves relationships between people, so this approach forces researchers to try to explain behavior and to seek to develop generalizations about it. Yet it also slights certain topics. The emphasis on relationships does not lead naturally to the investigation of the president's accountability, the limitations of the institution's legal powers, or the day-to-day operation of the presidency.

Some commentators are bothered by the top-down orientation of the power approach, that is, viewing the presidency from the perspective of the president.[6] They feel that this neglects the question of examining the presidency from the perspective of the American political system and that it carries the implicit assumption that the president should be the principal decision maker in American politics. These critics argue that such premises are too Machiavellian and that an evaluation of the goals and means of presidents must be added to analyses of power.

Others find exaggerated the depiction of the president's environment as basically confrontational, with conflicting interests of political actors creating centrifugal forces the president must try to overcome. Moreover, they claim that the heavy emphasis on power relationships may lead analysts to underestimate the importance of ideology or other influences on behavior.[7]

### Psychological

Perhaps the most fascinating and popular studies of the presidency are those that approach the topic from the perspective of psychological analysis. Some of these take the form of psychobiographies of presidents;[8] others are attempts to categorize presidents on the basis of selected personality dimensions.[9] They are all based on the premises that personality is a constant and that personality needs may be displaced onto political objects and become unconscious motivations for presidential behavior.

We need to take what goes on inside a person's head into account if we are to understand that person's behavior. A psychological perspective forces us to ask why presidents behave as they do and look beyond external factors, such as advisers, Congress, the media, and interest groups, for answers. If individual presidents were not strongly affected by their personalities, they would neither be very important nor merit much attention.

Psychological analysis also has a broader application to the study of the presidency. Presidents and their staffs view the world through cognitive processes that affect their perceptions of why people and nations behave as they do, how power is distributed, how the economy functions, and what the appropriate roles of government, presidents, and advisers are. Cognitive processes also screen and organize an enormous volume of information about the complex and uncertain environment in which presidents function. Objective reality, intellectual abilities, and personal interests and experiences merge with psychological needs (such as those to manage inconsistency and maintain self-esteem) to influence the decisions and policies that emerge from the White House. Cognitive processes simplify decision making and lessen stress, especially on complex and controversial policies such as the Vietnam War. Group dynamics may also influence decision making, limiting the appraisal of alternatives by group members. Efforts to sort out the impact of these factors are only in their early stages, but there is little question that we cannot claim to understand presidential decision making until those efforts succeed.[10]

Although psychological studies can sensitize us to important personality traits that influence presidential behavior, they are probably the most widely criticized writings on the presidency. A fundamental problem is that they often display a strong tendency toward reductionism; that is, they concentrate on personality to the exclusion of most other behavioral influences. As a result, they convey little information about the institution of the presidency or the relationships between psychological and institutional variables. Alternative explanations for behavior are rarely considered in psychological studies.

A related drawback is that psychological studies tend to stress the pathological aspects of a presidency. Scholars, like others, are drawn quite naturally to investigate problems. Their principal interest often becomes the relationship between the personality flaws of the president and what the author feels to be some of his most unfortunate actions in office. This reinforces the reductionist tendency because it is usually not difficult to find plausible parallels between psychological and decisional deficiencies.

The lack of systematic data is also a problem for psychological studies. It is difficult both to discern unconscious motivations or cognitive processes and to differentiate their effects from that of external factors. Often authors must rely upon biographical information of questionable validity about the behavior and environment of presidents, stretching back to their childhoods.

## Summary

The legal, institutional, power, and psychological approaches have advantages and disadvantages for the researcher. Each concerns a different aspect of the presidency and concentrates on certain variables at the expense of others. Those thinking of doing research on the presidency should carefully determine what it is they want to investigate *before* selecting an approach, because not all approaches will be relevant to answering their questions. Although the power and psychological approaches are stronger in their concern for explanation, the legal and institutional orientations are better at providing broad perspectives on the presidency. Selecting an approach is not the only decision one must make in building a research strategy, however. Appropriate methods must also be chosen.

## METHODS

Although political scientists have always been keenly interested in the American presidency, their progress in understanding it has been very slow. One reason for this is their reliance on methods that are either irrelevant or inappropriate to the task of examining the basic relationships in which the presidency is involved. This section examines some of the advantages and limitations of methods used by scholars to study the presidency. Throughout, we should remember that methods are not ends in themselves but techniques for examining research questions generated by the approaches discussed earlier.

### Traditional Methods

Studies of the presidency typically describe events, behavior, and personalities. Many are written by journalists or former executive branch officials who rely on their personal experiences. Unfortunately, such anecdotal material is generally subjective, fragmentary, and impressionistic. The commentary and reflections of insiders, whether participants or participant-observers, are limited by their own often rather narrow perspectives. For example, the memoirs of aides to Presidents Johnson and Nixon reveal very different perceptions of the president and his presidency. As Henry Kissinger writes about the Nixon White House staff:

> It is a truism that none of us really knew the inner man. More significant, each member of his entourage was acquainted with a slightly different Nixon subtly adjusted to the President's judgment of the aide or to his assessment of his interlocutor's background.[11]

Proximity to power may actually hinder rather than enhance an observer's perspective and breadth of view. The reflections of those who have served in government may be colored by the strong positions they advocated in office or a need to justify their decisions and behavior. Faulty memories further cloud such perceptions. Moreover, few insiders are trained to think in analytical terms of generalizations based on representative data and controls for alternative explanations. This is especially true of journalists.[12]

. Several examples illustrate the problem. One of the crucial decision points in America's involvement in fighting in Vietnam occurred during July 1965, when President Johnson committed the United States to large-scale combat operations. In his memoirs, Johnson goes to considerable lengths to show he considered very carefully all the alternatives available at the time.[13] One of his aide's detailed account of the dialogue between Johnson and some of his advisers shows the president probing deeply for answers, challenging the premises and factual bases of options, and playing the devil's advocate.[14] Other participants and scholars have also concluded that Johnson kept an open mind regarding U.S. intervention in Vietnam during their period.[15] Yet, other scholars and participants have concluded that this "debate" was really a charade, staged by the president to lend legitimacy to the decision he had already made.[16]

Another useful example, this one focusing on attributions of influence, is President Johnson's efforts at obtaining the support or at least the neutrality of the Senate Finance Committee chairman, Harry Byrd of Virginia, on the 1964 tax cut. Hubert Humphrey reported in his memoirs that Johnson cajoled Byrd into letting the tax bill out of committee, relying on Lady Bird's charm, liquor, and his own famous "treatment."[17] Presidential aide Jack Valenti tells a different story, however. He writes that the president obtained the senator's cooperation by promising to hold the budget under $100 billion.[18] Thus, we have two eyewitnesses reporting on two different tactics employed by the president and each attributing Senator Byrd's response to the presidential behavior that he observed.

To confuse matters further, Henry Hall Wilson, one of the president's congressional liaison aides, indicates that both eyewitnesses were wrong. According to Wilson, when the president proudly told his chief congressional liaison aide, Lawrence O'Brien, about his obtaining Byrd's agreement to begin hearings on the tax cut on December 7, O'Brien replied, "You didn't get a thing. I already had a commitment for the 7th."[19] In other words, according to O'Brien, Johnson's efforts were irrelevant and both eyewitnesses were wrong in attributing influence to him.

Even tapes of conversations in the Oval Office may be misleading. As Henry Kissinger explains with respect to the Watergate tapes:

> Anyone familiar with Nixon's way of talking could have no doubt he was sitting on a time bomb. His random, elliptical, occasionally emotional manner of conversation was bound to shock, and mislead, the historian. Nixon's indirect style of operation simply could not be gauged by an outsider. There was no way of telling what Nixon had put forward to test his interlocutor and what he meant to be taken seriously; and no outsider could distinguish a command that was to be followed from an emotional outburst that one was at liberty to ignore—perhaps was even expected to ignore.[20]

Problems also arise in studies employing traditional methods when authors make assertions about the behavior of the public. They often fail to look at available systematic data. For example, numerous authors premise analyses of the Reagan administration on the president's enjoying substantial support among the public. In reality, as we saw in Chapter 4, Reagan's average approval level was a quite ordinary 52 percent.[21]

Although insider accounts have limitations, they often contain useful insights that may guide more rigorous research. They also provide invaluable records of the perceptions of participants in the events of the presidency. As long as the researcher understands the limitations of these works and does not accept them at face value, they can be of considerable use.

Not all studies of the presidency that employ traditional methods are written by insiders. Many are written by scholars, based primarily on the observations of others.[22] As one might expect, a common criticism of the traditional literature on the presidency is that it appears to be the same presentation, repeated in slightly different versions. Although such studies may be useful syntheses of the conventional wisdom or present provocative insights about the presidency, they are more likely to suffer from the limitations of their data and add little to our understanding of the presidency.

## Quantitative Analyses

Research on the presidency, then, has often failed to meet the standards of contemporary political science, including the careful definition and measurement of concepts, the rigorous specification and testing of propositions, and the use of empirical theory to develop hypotheses and explain findings. This presents a striking irony: The single most important institution in American politics is the one that political scientists understand the least.

To increase our understanding of the presidency, we must move beyond the description of the institution and explain the behavior we observe, and we must seek to reach generalizations instead of being satisfied with discrete, often ad hoc analyses. Quantitative analysis can be an extremely useful tool in these endeavors.[23]

There have been three principal constraints on using quantitative analysis to study the presidency. The first, the frequent failure to pose analytical questions, has already been discussed. The second constraint has been the small number of presidents. Viewing the presidency as a set of relationships, however, helps to overcome this problem. Although the number of presidents may be few, many persons are involved in relationships with them, including the entire public, members of Congress, the federal bureaucracy, and world leaders. Because there are so many people interacting with the president, we are no longer inhibited by the small universe of presidents.

The third perceived constraint on the quantitative study of the presidency is lack of data. When we pose analytical questions, we are naturally led to search for data on the causes and consequences of presidential behavior. For example, we may ask what presidents want people to do. Among other things, they want support from the public, positive coverage from the media, votes for their programs from Congress, sound analysis from their advisers, and faithful policy implementation from the bureaucracy. Thus, we can look for data on these political actors, whose behavior is usually the dependent variable in our hypotheses—that is, what we are trying to explain. Similarly, we can seek data on independent variables—that is, causes of behavior toward the president, such as the determinants of public opinion, congressional support, and bureaucratic faithfulness.[24]

The proper use of quantitative analysis, like any other type of analysis, is predicated upon a close linkage between the methods selected and the theoretical arguments that underlie the hypotheses being tested. A statement that something causes something else to happen is an assertion, not a theoretical argument. A theoretical argument requires an emphasis on explanation of *why* two variables are related. Quantitative analysis is not an end in itself. Instead, it is a means of rigorously analyzing theoretically meaningful explanations of behavior.

Despite its utility for investigating a wide range of questions, quantitative analysis is not equally useful for studying all areas of the presidency. It is least useful where there is little change in the variables under study. If the focus of research is just one president and the researcher is concerned not with the president's interactions with others but with how factors such as the president's personality, ideas, values, attitudes, and ideology have influenced his decisions, then quantitative analysis will be of little help. These independent variables are unlikely to vary much during a president's term. Similarly, important elements in the president's environment, such as the federal system or the basic capitalist structure of its economy, change little over time. It is therefore difficult to employ quantitative analysis to gauge their influence on the presidency.

Quantitative analysis is also unlikely to be useful for the legal approach to studying the presidency. There are well-established techniques for interpreting the law, and scholars with this interest will continue to apply them.[25]

Normative questions and arguments have always occupied a substantial percentage of the presidency literature, and rightly so. Can quantitative analysis aid scholars in addressing these concerns? The answer is, partially. For example, to reach conclusions about whether the presidency is too powerful or not powerful enough (the central normative concern regarding the presidency) requires a three-part analysis. The first is an estimation of just how powerful the presidency is. Quantitative analysis can be of utility in measuring and explaining the power in the presidency in a wide range of relationships. For example, it can aid us in understanding the president's ability to influence Congress or the public.

The second step in answering the question of whether the presidency is too powerful or not powerful enough requires an analysis of the consequences of the power of the presidency. In other words, given the power of the presidency, what difference does it make? Are poor people likely to fare better under a weak or a powerful presidency, for example? Are civil rights and civil liberties more or less likely to be abused?

To answer rigorously these and similar questions requires that we correlate levels of power with policy consequences. This does not have to be done quantitatively, of course, but such analyses will be more convincing if we have empirical measurements of economic welfare, school integration, wiretapping, military interventions, and other possible consequences of presidential power as well as measures of mediating variables.

Quantitative analyses will be much less useful in the third part of the analysis: Do we judge the consequences of presidential power to be good or bad? Our evaluation of these consequences will be determined, of course, by our values. Nevertheless, it is important to remember that quantitative analysis can be very useful in helping us to arrive at the point where our values dominate our conclusions.

In short, quantitative analysis leads us to examine theoretical relationships, and it has considerable utility in testing and refining them. The question remains, however, whether quantitative analysis is useful for developing theories themselves, that is, basic conceptions of the relationships between variables.

Although quantitative studies cannot replace the sparks of creativity that lie behind conceptualizations, they may produce findings upon which syntheses may be built. Conversely, quantitative analysis may also produce findings contrary to the conventional wisdom and thus prod scholars into challenging dominant viewpoints. To this extent it may also be useful in theory building.

Quantitative analysis is not easy to do nor is there consensus on appropriate methods or measures. Inevitably, some authors will employ indicators that lack validity and reliability and tests that are inappropriate. Their conclusions are likely to be incorrect. In addition, findings can and should be refined as our indicators and tests are improved. In essence, quantitative analysis poses methodological problems precisely because it attempts to measure concepts and to test for relationships carefully. Studies that do not involve such concerns avoid methodological questions, but often at the expense of analytical richness.

## Case Studies

One of the most widely used methods for studying the presidency is the case study of an individual president, a presidential decision, or presidential involvement in a specific area of policy. The case study method offers the researcher several advantages. It is a manageable way to present a wide range of complex information about individual and collective behavior. Because scholars have typically found it difficult to generate quantitative data regarding the presidency, the narrative form often seems to be the only available choice.

Conversely, case studies are widely criticized on several grounds. First, they have been used more for descriptive than for analytical purposes, a failing not inherent in the case study. A more intractable problem is the idiosyncratic nature of case studies and the failure of authors to employ common analytical frameworks. This makes the accumulation of knowledge difficult because scholars often, in effect, talk past each other. In the words of a close student of case studies:

> The unique features of every case—personalities, external events and conditions, and organizational arrangements—virtually ensure that studies conducted without the use of an explicit analytical framework will not produce findings that can easily be related to existing knowledge or provide a basis for future studies.[26]

Naturally, reaching generalizations about the presidency on the basis of unrelated case studies is a hazardous task.

Despite these drawbacks, case studies can be very useful in increasing our understanding of the presidency. For example, analyzing case studies can serve as the basis for identifying problems in decision making[27] or in policy implementation.[28] These in turn may serve as the basis for recommendations to improve policy making. Case studies may also be used to test hypotheses or disconfirm theories, such as propositions about group dynamics drawn from social psychology.[29]

Some authors employ case studies to illustrate the importance of looking at aspects of the presidency that have received little scholarly attention, such as presidential influence over interest groups.[30] On a broader scale, Richard Neustadt used several case studies to help generate his influential model of presidential power.[31] Graham Allison used a case study of the Cuban missile crisis to illustrate three models of policy making.[32]

Writing a case study that has strong analytical content is difficult to do.[33] It requires considerable skill, creativity, and rigor because it is very easy to slip into a descriptive rather than an analytical gear. It is especially important to have an analytical framework in mind before one begins—to provide direction to data gathering and the line of argument. Those who embark on preparing case studies are wise to remind themselves of the pitfalls.

## CONCLUSION

Few topics in American politics are more interesting or more important to understand than the presidency. Researching the presidency is not a simple task, however. There are many reasons for this, including the small number of models to follow and the relative sparsity of research that has applied the approaches and methods of modern political science. But the obstacles to studying the presidency also present researchers with an opportunity. Few questions regarding the presidency are settled; there is plenty of room for committed and creative researchers to make important contributions to our understanding. The prospects for success will be enhanced if researchers realize the implications of the approaches and methods they employ and choose those that are best suited to shed light on the questions they wish to investigate.

## NOTES

1. For a more extensive discussion of approaches to studying the presidency, see Stephen J. Wayne, "Approaches," in George C. Edwards III and Stephen J. Wayne, eds., *Studying the Presidency* (Knoxville, Tenn.: University of Tennessee Press, 1983), pp. 17–49.

2. The classic work from the legal perspective is Edward S. Corwin's *The President: Office and Powers*, 4th rev. ed. (New York: New York University Press, 1957); an excellent more recent example is Louis Fisher, *Constitutional Conflict between Congress and the President*, 3rd rev. ed. (Lawrence, Kans.: University Press of Kansas, 1991).

3. See, for example, Stephen J. Wayne, *The Legislative Presidency* (New York: Harper and Row, 1978); Michael Baruch Grossman and Martha Joynt Kumar, *Portraying the President: The White House and the News Media* (Baltimore: Johns Hopkins University Press, 1981); Mark A. Peterson, "The Presidency and Organized Interests: White House Patterns of Interest Group Liaison," *American Political Science Review* 86 (September 1992): 612–25; and John P. Burke and Fred I. Greenstein, *How Presidents Test Reality* (Russell Sage Foundation, 1989).

4. The political power approach is best represented in Richard E. Neustadt, *Presidential Power and the Modern Presidents* (New York: Free Press, 1990).

5. See, for example, George C. Edwards III, *At the Margins: Presidential Leadership of Congress* (New Haven, Conn.: Yale University Press, 1989); *The Public Presidency* (New York: St. Martin's, 1983); and *Implementing Public Policy* (Washington, D.C.: Congressional Quarterly, 1980). Other examples of the political power approach include Fred I. Greenstein, *The Hidden-Hand Presidency* (New York: Basic Books, 1982); and Bert A. Rockman, *The Leadership Question* (New York: Praeger, 1984).

6. See Bruce Miroff, "Beyond Washington," *Society* 17 (July/August 1980): 66–72.

7. See Peter W. Sperlich, "Bargaining and Overload: An Essay on Presidential Power," in Aaron Wildavsky, ed., *The Presidency* (Boston: Little, Brown, 1969), pp. 168–92.

8. See, for example, Alexander L. George and Juliette L. George, *Woodrow Wilson and Colonel House: A Personality Study* (New York: Dover, 1964).

9. The most notable example is James David Barber's *The Presidential Character: Predicting Performance in the White House*, 4th ed. (Englewood Cliffs, N.J.: Prentice-Hall, 1992).

10. Some relevant studies include Alexander L. George, *Presidential Decisionmaking in Foreign Policy: The Effective Use of Information and Advice* (Boulder, Colo.: Westview, 1980); Bruce Buchanan, *The Presidential Experience: What the Office Does to the Man* (Englewood Cliffs, N.J.: Prentice-Hall, 1978); John D. Steinbruner, *The Cybernetic Theory of Decision* (Princeton, N.J.: Princeton University Press, 1974); Irving L. Janis, *Groupthink: Psychological Studies of Policy Decisions and Fiascoes*, 2nd ed. (Boston: Houghton Mifflin, 1982); and Richard E. Neustadt and Ernest R. May, *Thinking in Time* (New York: Free Press, 1986).

11. Henry Kissinger, *Years of Upheaval* (Boston: Little, Brown, 1982), p. 1182.

12. Excellent studies of the misperceptions of participants in presidential policy making include Richard E. Neustadt, *Alliance Politics* (New York: Columbia University, 1970); and Fred I. Greenstein and Richard H. Immerman, "What Did Eisenhower Tell Kennedy about Indochina? The Politics of Misperception," *Journal of American History* 79 (September 1992): 568–87.

13. Lyndon B. Johnson, *The Vantage Point: Perspectives of the Presidency, 1963–1969* (New York: Popular Library, 1971), pp. 144–53.

14. Jack Valenti, *A Very Human President* (New York: Norton, 1975), pp. 317–19, 358.

15. See George W. Ball, *The Past Has Another Pattern* (New York: Norton, 1982), p. 399; George McT. Kahin, *Intervention: How America Became Involved in Vietnam* (New York: Knopf, 1986), pp. 366–90.

16. Larry Berman, *Planning a Tragedy: The Americanization of the War in Vietnam* (New York: Norton, 1982), pp. 105–21; Chester Cooper, *The Lost Crusade: America in Vietnam* (Greenwich, Conn.: Dodd, Mead, 1970), pp. 284–85; U.S. Department of Defense, *United States–Vietnam Relations, 1945–1967*, vol. 3 (Washington, D.C.: U.S. Government Printing Office, 1971), p. 475.

17. Hubert H. Humphrey, *The Education of a Public Man: My Life and Politics* (Garden City, N.Y.: Doubleday, 1976), pp. 290–93.

18. Valenti, *A Very Human President*, pp. 196–97. See also Russell D. Renka, "Bargaining with Legislative Whales in the Kennedy and Johnson Administration" (paper presented at the Annual Meeting of the American Political Science Association, Washington, D.C., August 1980), p. 20.

19. Transcript, Henry Hall Wilson Oral History Interview, April 11, 1973, by Joe B. Frantz, p. 16, Lyndon B. Johnson Library.

20. Kissinger, *Years of Upheaval*, pp. 111–12.

21. See George C. Edwards III, *Presidential Approval* (Baltimore: Johns Hopkins University Press, 1990), p. 175.

22. See, for example, Richard Tanner Johnson, *Managing the White House* (New York: Harper and Row, 1974).

23. For a more extensive discussion of quantitative analysis of the presidency, see George C. Edwards III, "Quantitative Analysis," in Edwards and Wayne, eds., *Studying the Presidency*, pp. 99–124; and Gary King, "The Methodology of Presidency Research," in George C. Edwards III, Bert A. Rockman, and John H. Kessel, eds., *Researching the Presidency* (Pittsburgh: University of Pittsburgh Press, 1993), pp. 387–412.

24. Examples of quantitative studies of the presidency include Edwards, *Presidential Approval*; Samuel Kernell, *Going Public*, 2nd ed. (Washington, DC.: CQ Press, 1993); Jeffrey K. Tulis, *The Rhetorical Presidency* (Princeton, N.J.: Princeton University Press, 1987); Lee Sigelman, "Gauging the Public Response to Presidential Leadership," *Presidential Studies Quarterly* 10 (Summer 1980), pp. 427–33; Richard A. Brody, *Assessing the President: The Media, Elite Opinion, and Public Support* (Stanford, Calif.: Stanford University Press, 1991); Lyn Ragsdale, "The Politics of Presidential Speechmaking, 1949–1980," *American Political Science Review* 78 (December 1984): 971–84; Edwards, *At the Margins*; Jon R. Bond and Richard Fleisher, *The President in the Legislative Arena* (Chicago: University of Chicago Press, 1980); Darrell M. West, "Activists and Economic Policymaking in Congress," *American Journal of Political Science* 32 (August 1988): 662–80; John H. Kessel, *Presidential Parties* (Homewood, Ill.: Dorsey, 1984); Joel D. Aberbach and Bert A. Rockman, "Clashing Beliefs within the Executive Branch: The Nixon Administration Bureaucracy," *American Political Science Review* 70 (March 1976): 456–68; B. Dan Wood and James E. Anderson, "The Politics of U.S. Antitrust Regulation," *American Journal of Political Science* 37 (February 1993): 1–39; Richard Waterman and B. Dan Wood, "The Dynamics of Political Control of the Bureaucracy," *American Political Science Review* 85 (September 1991): 801–28; B. Dan Wood, "Principals, Bureaucrats, and Responsiveness in Clean Air Enforcement," *American Political Science Review* 82 (March 1988): 213–34.

25. For more on legal analysis of the presidency, see Louis Fisher, "Making Use of Legal Sources," in Edwards and Wayne, eds., *Studying the Presidency*, pp. 182–98.

26. Norman C. Thomas, "Case Studies," in Ibid., pp. 50–78.

27. See, for example, Alexander L. George, "The Case for Multiple Advocacy in Making Foreign Policy," *American Political Science Review* 66 (September 1972): 765–81; Burke and Greenstein, *How Presidents Test Reality*; and Ryan J. Barilleaux, *The President and Foreign Affairs* (New York: Praeger, 1985).

28. See, for example, Edwards, *Implementing Public Policy*.

29. See Janis, *Groupthink*.

30. See, for example, Bruce Miroff, "Presidential Leverage over Social Movements: The Johnson White House and Civil Rights," *Journal of Politics* 43 (February 1981): 2–23.

31. Neustadt, *Presidential Power*.

32. Graham T. Allison, *Essence of Decision: Explaining the Cuban Missile Crisis* (Boston: Little, Brown, 1971).

33. Recent examples of work focusing on a single president in an insightful and analytical fashion include Charles O. Jones, *The Trusteeship Presidency* (Baton Rouge, La.: Louisiana State University Press, 1988); and Erwin C. Hargrove, *Jimmy Carter as President* (Baton Rouge, La.: Louisiana State University Press, 1988).

## SELECTED READINGS

Edwards, George C., III, John H. Kessel, and Bert A. Rockman, eds., *Researching the Presidency*. Pittsburgh: University of Pittsburgh Press, 1993.

Edwards, George C., III, and Stephen J. Wayne, eds., *Studying the Presidency*. Knoxville, Tenn.: University of Tennessee Press, 1983.

# Nonelectoral Succession, Removal, and Tenure

The Constitution and statutes provide for contingencies that might require the selection, removal, or replacement of a president outside the normal electoral process. In addition to the provisions of Article 1 (Impeachment) and Article 2 (Impeachment and Succession), there have been three amendments (numbers 20, 22, and 25) and three laws concerning succession and term of office. This appendix will examine these contingency arrangements. It will also briefly describe the impeachment process and the two most serious attempts to remove a sitting president. The Constitution and statutes provide for methods of succession and removal.

## SUCCESSION

The principal reason for creating the vice presidency was to have a position from which the presidency would automatically be filled should it become vacant. Death, resignation, and impeachment constitute clear-cut situations in which this succession mechanism would work. Eight presidents have died in office and one has resigned. In each of the nine instances, the vice president became president.

One contingency the founders did not consider was temporary or permanent disability while in office. On a number of occasions, presidents have become disabled, unable to perform their duties and responsibilities. James Garfield, shot by a disappointed job seeker, lingered for almost three months before he died. More recently, Ronald Reagan was hospitalized twice, the first time following the attempt on his life and the other for an operation for cancer of the colon. During both hospital stays, he was unconscious for several hours and incapacitated for several months. Other presidents have also been incapacitated. Wilson suffered a stroke that disabled him for much of his last year in office, while Eisenhower's heart attack, ileitis operation, and minor stroke severely limited his presidential activities in 1955, 1956, and 1957 (see Chapter 8).

During none of these periods did vice presidents officially take over. In fact, Chester Arthur and Thomas Marshall, Garfield's and Wilson's vice presidents, respectively, avoided even the appearance of performing presidential duties for fear that their actions would be wrongfully construed. Vice President Richard Nixon did preside at cabinet meetings in Eisenhower's absence but did not assume the president's other responsibilities. Vice President George Bush, away from the capital at the time Reagan was shot, flew back to Washington immediately to be available if needed. However, to avoid any appearance of impropriety, he had his helicopter land at the vice president's residence even though he was scheduled to meet at the White House with senior presidential aides. By prearrangement with the vice president, President Reagan passed his powers and duties to Bush during the period when he was under the influence of anesthesia during his colon operation in 1985. He reassumed them when he declared himself able to do so several hours after his operation.

It was not until 1967 that procedures were established for the vice president to become acting president in the event of the president's disability. The Twenty-fifth Amendment to the Constitution permits the vice president to exercise the duties and powers of the presidency if the president declares in writing that he is unable to do so or if the vice president and a majority of the principal executive department heads reach that judgment. The president may resume office when he believes that he is able unless the vice president and a majority of the principal executive department heads object. In that case Congress must make the final determination. The procedures, however, are weighted in the president's favor. Unless Congress concurs in the judgment that the president is disabled, the president is entitled once again to exercise the duties and powers of the office.

Another important provision of this amendment provides for filling the vice presidency should it become vacant. Prior to 1967, it had been vacant sixteen times. The procedures permit the president to nominate a new vice president, who takes office upon confirmation by a majority of both houses of Congress. Gerald Ford and Nelson Rockefeller were the only two vice presidents who assumed office in this manner. Ford was nominated by President Nixon in 1973 upon the resignation of Spiro T. Agnew. After succeeding to the presidency upon Nixon's resignation, Ford nominated Rockefeller.

Although the presidency and vice presidency have never been vacant at the same time, Congress has provided for such a contingency should it arise by establishing a line of succession. The most recent succession law was enacted in 1947. It puts the Speaker of the House next in line to be followed by the president *pro tempore* of the Senate and the department heads in order of their seniority, beginning with the secretary of state. The provision for appointing a new vice president, however, makes it less likely that legislative and executive officials would ever succeed to the presidency, barring a catastrophe or an unlikely set of events that resulted in a president's death before a new vice presidential nomination could be made or confirmed.


## REMOVAL

In addition to providing for the president's replacement, the constitutional framers also thought it necessary to provide for the president's removal. They believed that it was too dangerous to wait for the electors' judgment in the case of a president who had abused the authority of the office. Impeachment was considered an extraordinary remedy but one that could be used against executive officials, including the president and vice president, who violated their public trust.

Article, 2, section 4, of the Constitution spells out the terms. The president, vice president, and other executive officials can be removed from office for treason, bribery, or other high crimes and misdemeanors. Precisely what actions would be considered impeachable offenses are left for Congress to determine.

The House of Representatives considers the charges against the president. If a majority of the House votes in favor of any of them, a trial is held in the Senate with the chief justice of the Supreme Court presiding. The House presents its case against the president. The latter, who may be represented by outside counsel, defends against the charges. A two-thirds vote of the Senate is required for conviction. A convicted president, who is removed from office, may still be subject to civil or criminal prosecution.

Only one president, Andrew Johnson, has ever been impeached. The incident that sparked his impeachment was Johnson's removal of Secretary of War Edwin Stanton. Congress had passed a law over Johnson's veto that required appointees to remain in office until the Senate approved their successor. Known as the Tenure of Office Act (1867), it permitted the president some discretion during a congressional recess but required the Senate's advice and consent after Congress reconvened. In the absence of senatorial approval, the office reverted to its previous occupant.

During a congressional recess, Johnson removed Stanton. The Senate refused to concur in the removal upon its return. Under the law, Stanton was entitled to his old job. However, the president once again removed him. Upon his removal for a second time, the House of Representatives passed a bill of impeachment against the president. The Senate trial lasted six weeks. In its first vote the Senate fell one short of the required two-thirds. A ten-day recess was called by those favoring Johnson's removal. Extensive lobbying ensued, but when the Senate reconvened, no one changed his vote. Johnson was acquitted. The Tenure of Office Act was subsequently repealed during the Cleveland administration.

A second attempt to impeach a sitting president occurred in 1973. When Richard Nixon dismissed Archibald Cox, the special prosecutor who had been investigating charges of administration wrongdoing in the Watergate affair, members of Congress called for Nixon's removal. The Judiciary Committee of the House of Representatives began hearings on the president's impeachment. During the course of these hearings, the committee subpoenaed tapes of conversations that the president had held with aides in the White House, conversations that had been secretly recorded by the president. Claiming that these were privileged communications, Nixon refused to deliver the tapes, although he did send edited transcripts of them to the House committee. Not satisfied with this response, the House took its case to court and won. The Supreme Court ordered Nixon to release the tapes. When he did so, they revealed his early knowledge of the break-in and his participation in the cover-up. This information heightened calls for the president's ouster.

The House Judiciary Committee approved three articles of impeachment against Nixon. It looked as if the full House would vote to impeach him and that the Senate would vote to convict him. Faced with the prospect of a long trial and probable conviction, Nixon resigned on August 9, 1974.

## TENURE

Electoral defeat and impeachment prematurely conclude a presidency—at least from the incumbent's perspective. Initially the Constitution imposed no limit on the number of times a president could be elected. Reeligibility was seen as a motive to good behavior. Beginning with Washington, however, an unofficial two-term limit was established. Franklin Roosevelt ended this precedent in 1940 when he ran for a third term and won.

Partially in reaction to Roosevelt's twelve years and one month as president, a Republican-controlled Congress passed and the states ratified the Twenty-second Amendment to the Constitution. It prevents any person from being elected to the office more than twice. Moreover, it limits to one election a president who has succeeded to the office and has served more than two years of his predecessor's term. Eisenhower was the first president to be subject to the provisions of the amendment, and Reagan was the second.

One of the consequences of this amendment is that it seems to weaken the president in the second term, particularly during the last two years in office. Not being able to run for the presidency again reduces a president's political power and lessens the capacity to mobilize public backing for the administration's programs and policies. On the other hand, it may improve the president's capacity to mobilize a bipartisan coalition because political motives may be less subject to suspicion if a president cannot seek reelection. This might result in a weaker domestic presidency but a stronger foreign policy one. It would certainly affect the incentives for policy making in each of these spheres.

# Provisions of the Constitution of the United States That Relate to the Presidency

## ARTICLE I

*Section 2.*

(3) [Representatives and direct Taxes[1] shall be apportioned among the several States which may be included within this Union, according to their respective Numbers, which shall be determined by adding to the whole Number of free Persons, including those bound to Service for a Term of Years, and excluding Indians not taxed, three fifths of all other Persons.][2] The actual Enumeration shall be made within three Years after the first Meeting of the Congress of the United States, and within every subsequent Term of ten Years, in such Manner as they shall by Law direct. The Number of Representatives shall not exceed one for every thirty Thousand, but each State shall have at Least one Representative; and until such enumeration shall be made, the State of New Hampshire shall be entitled to choose three, Massachusetts eight, Rhode-Island and Providence Plantations one, Connecticut five, New York six, New Jersey four, Pennsylvania eight, Delaware one, Maryland six, Virginia ten, North Carolina five, South Carolina five, and Georgia three.

(4) When vacancies happen in the Representation from any State, the Executive Authority thereof shall issue Writs of Election to fill such Vacancies.

(5) The House of Representatives shall choose their Speaker and other Officers; and shall have the sole Power of Impeachment.

*Section 3.*

(4) The Vice President of the United States shall be President of the Senate, but shall have no Vote, unless they be equally divided.

(5) The Senate shall choose their other Officers, and also a President pro tempore, in the Absence of the Vice President, or when he shall exercise the Office of President of the United States.

---

[1]The Sixteenth Amendment replaced this with respect to income taxes.
[2]Repealed by the Fourteenth Amendment.

(6) The Senate shall have the sole Power to try all Impeachements. When sitting for that Purpose, they shall be on Oath or Affirmation. When the President of the United States is tried, the Chief Justice shall preside: And no Person shall be convicted without the Concurrence of two thirds of the Members present.

(7) Judgment in Cases of Impeachment shall not extend further than to removal from Office, and disqualification to hold and enjoy any Office of honor, Trust or Profit under the United States: but the Party convicted shall nevertheless be liable and subject to Indictment, Trial, Judgment and Punishment according to Law.

*Section 7.*

(2) Every Bill which shall have passed the House of Representatives and the Senate, shall, before it become a Law, be presented to the President of the United States; If he approve he shall sign it, but if not he shall return it, with his Objections to that House in which it shall have originated, who shall enter the Objections at large on their Journal, and proceed to reconsider it. If after such Reconsideration two thirds of that House shall agree to pass the Bill, it shall be sent, together with Objections, to the other House, by which it shall likewise be reconsidered, and if approved by two thirds of that House, it shall become a Law. But in all such Cases the Votes of both Houses shall be determined by Yeas and Nays, and the Names of the Persons voting for and against the Bill shall be entered on the Journal of each House respectively. If any Bill shall not be re-turned by the President within ten Days (Sundays excepted) after it shall have been presented to him, the Same shall be a Law, in like Manner as if he had signed it, unless the Congress by their Adjournment prevent its Return, in which Case it shall not be a Law.

(3) Every Order, Resolution, or Vote to which the Concurrence of the Senate and House of Representatives may be necessary (except on a question of Adjournment) shall be presented to the President of the United States; and before the Same shall take Effect, shall be approved by him, or being disapproved by him, shall be repassed by two thirds of the Senate and House of Representatives, according to the Rules and Limitations prescribed in the Case of a Bill.

*Section 9.*

(2) The Privilege of the Writ of Habeas Corpus shall not be suspended, unless when in Cases of Rebellion or Invasion the public Safety may require it.

(8) No Title of Nobility shall be granted by the United States: And no Person holding any Office of Profit or Trust under them, shall, without the Consent of the Congress, accept of any present, Emolument, Office, or Title, of any kind whatever, from any King, Prince, or foreign State.

# ARTICLE II

*Section 1.*

(1) The executive Power shall be vested in a President of the United States of America. He shall hold his Office during the Term of four Years, and, together with the Vice President, chosen for the same Term, be elected, as follows:

(2) Each State shall appoint, in such Manner as the Legislature thereof may direct, a Number of Electors, equal to the whole Number of Senators and Representatives to which the State may be entitled in the Congress, but no Senator or Representative, or Person holding an Office of Trust or Profit under the United States, shall be appointed an Elector.

[The Electors shall meet in their respective States, and vote by Ballot for two persons, of whom one at least shall not be an Inhabitant of the same State with themselves. And they shall make a List of all the Persons voted for, and of the Number of Votes for each; which List they shall sign and certify, and transmit sealed to the Seat of the Government of the United States, directed to the President of the Senate. The President of the Senate shall, in the Presence of the Senate and House of Representatives, open all the Certificates, and the Votes shall then be counted. The Person having the greatest Number of Votes shall be the President, if such Number be a Majority of the whole Number of Electors appointed; and if there be more than one who have such Majority, and have an equal Number of Votes, then the House of Representatives shall immediately choose by Ballot one of them for President; and if no Person have a Majority, then from the five highest on the List the said House shall in like Manner choose the President. But in choosing the President, the Votes shall be taken by States, the Representation from each State having one Vote; A quorum for this purpose shall consist of a Member or Members from two thirds of the States, and a Majority of all the States shall be necessary to a Choice. In every Case, after the Choice of the President, the Person having the greatest Number of Votes of the Electors shall be the Vice President. But if there should remain two or more who have equal Votes, the Senate shall choose from them by Ballot the Vice President.][3]

(3) The Congress may determine the Time of choosing the Electors, and the Day on which they shall give their Votes; which Day shall be the same throughout the United States.

(4) No person except a natural born Citizen, or a Citizen of the United States, at the time of the Adoption of this Constitution, shall be eligible to the Office of President; neither shall any Person be eligible to that Office who shall not have attained to the Age of thirty-five Years, and been fourteen Years a Resident within the United States.

(5) In case of the Removal of the President from Office, or of his Death, Resignation, or Inability to discharge the Powers and Duties of the said Office, the same shall devolve on the Vice President, and the Congress may by Law provide for the Case of Removal, Death, Resignation or Inability; both of the President and Vice President, declaring what Officer shall then act as President, and such Officer shall act accordingly, until the Disability be removed, or a President shall be elected.[4]

(6) The President shall, at stated Times, receive for his Services, a Compensation, which shall neither be increased nor diminished during the Period for which he shall have been elected, and he shall not receive within that Period any other Emolument from the United States, or any of them.

(7) Before he enter on the Execution of his Office, he shall take the following Oath or Affirmation:—"I do solemnly swear (or affirm) that I will faithfully execute the Office of President of the United States, and will to the best of my Ability, preserve, protect and defend the Constitution of the United States."

*Section 2.*

(1) The President shall be Commander in Chief of the Army and Navy of the United States, and of the Militia of the several States, when called into the actual Service of the United States; he may require the Opinion in writing, of the

[3]This paragraph was superseded in 1804 by the Twelfth Amendment.
[4]Changed by the Twenty-fifth Amendment.

principal Officer in each of the executive Departments, upon any subject relating to the Duties of their respective Offices, and he shall have Power to Grant Reprieves and Pardons for Offenses against the United States, except in Cases of Impeachment.

(2) He shall have Power, by and with the Advice and Consent of the Senate, to make Treaties, provided two thirds of the Senators present concur; and he shall nominate, and by and with the Advice and Consent of the Senate, shall appoint Ambassadors, other public Ministers and Consuls, Judges of the supreme Court, and all other Officers of the United States, whose Appointments are not herein otherwise provided for, and which shall be established by Law: but the Congress may by Law vest the Appointment of such inferior Officers, as they think proper, in the President alone, in the Court of Law, or in the Heads of Departments.

(3) The President shall have Power to fill up all Vacancies that may happen during the Recess of the Senate, by granting Commissions which shall expire at the End of their next Session.

*Section 3.*

He shall from time to time give to the Congress Information of the State of the Union, and recommend to their Consideration such Measures as he shall judge necessary and expedient; he may, on extraordinary Occasions, convene both Houses, or either of them, and in Case of Disagreement between them, with Respect to the Time of Adjournment, he may adjourn them to such Time as he shall think proper; he shall receive Ambassadors and other public Ministers; he shall take Care that the Laws be faithfully executed, and shall Commission all the Officers of the United States.

*Section 4.*

The President, Vice President and all civil Officers of the United States, shall be removed from Office on Impeachment for, and Conviction of, Treason, Bribery, or other high Crimes and Misdemeanors.

## ARTICLE IV

*Section 4.*

The United States shall guarantee to every State in this Union a Republican Form of Government, and shall protect each of them against Invasion; and on Application of the Legislature, or of the Executive (when the Legislature cannot be convened) against domestic Violence.

## ARTICLE VI

(3) The Senators and Representatives before mentioned, and the Members of the several State Legislatures, and all executive and judicial Officers, both of the United States and of the several States, shall be bound by Oath or Affirmation, to support this Constitution; but no religious Test shall ever be required as a Qualification to any Office or public Trust under the United States.

## AMENDMENT XII[5]

The Electors shall meet in their respective states and vote by ballot for President and Vice President, one of whom, at least, shall not be an inhabitant of

[5]Adopted in 1804.

the same state with themselves; they shall name in their ballots the person voted for as President, and in distinct ballots the person voted for as Vice President, and they shall make distinct lists of persons voted for as President, and of all persons voted for as Vice President, and of the number of votes for each, which lists they shall sign and certify, and transmit sealed to the seat of the government of the United States, directed to the President of the Senate;—The President of the Senate shall, in presence of the Senate and House of Representatives, open all the certificates and the votes shall then be counted;—The person having the greatest number of votes for President, shall be the President, if such number be a majority of the whole number of Electors appointed; and if no person have such majority, then from the persons having the highest numbers not exceeding three on the list of those voted for as President, the House of Representatives shall choose immediately, by ballot, the President. But in choosing the President, the votes shall be taken by states, the representation from each state having one vote; a quorum for this purpose shall consist of a member or members from two thirds of the states, and a majority of all the states shall be necessary to a choice. [And if the House of Representatives shall not choose a President whenever the right of choice shall devolve upon them, before the fourth day of March next following, then the Vice President shall act as President, as in the case of the death or other constitutional disability of the President.][6]—The person having the greatest number of votes as Vice President, shall be the Vice President, if such number be a majority of the whole number of Electors appointed, and if no person have a majority, then from the two highest numbers on the list, the Senate shall choose the Vice President; a quorum for the purpose shall consist of two thirds of the whole number of Senators, and a majority of the whole number shall be necessary to a choice. But no person constitutionally ineligible to the office of President shall be eligible to that of Vice President of the United States.

# AMENDMENT XV[7]

*Section 1.*
The right of citizens of the United States to vote shall not be denied or abridged by the United States or by any State on account of race, color, or previous condition of servitude.
*Section 2.*
The Congress shall have power to enforce this article by appropriate legislation.

# AMENDMENT XIX[8]

The right of citizens of the United States to vote shall not be denied or abridged by the United States or by any State on account of sex.
Congress shall have power to enforce this article by appropriate legislation.

---

[6]Superseded by the Twentieth Amendment, section 3.
[7]Adopted in 1870.
[8]Adopted in 1920.

## AMENDMENT XX[9]

*Section 1.*

The terms of the President and Vice President shall end at noon on the 20th day of January, and the terms of Senators and Representatives at noon on the 3rd day of January, of the years in which such terms would have ended if this article had not been ratified; and the terms of their successors shall then begin.

*Section 2.*

The Congress shall assemble at least once in every year, and such meeting shall begin at noon on the 3rd day of January, unless they shall by law appoint a different day.

*Section 3.*

If, at the time fixed for the beginning of the term of the President, the President elect shall have died, the Vice President elect shall become President. If a President shall not have been chosen before the time fixed for the beginning of his term, or if the President elect shall have failed to qualify, then the Vice President elect shall act as a President until a President shall have qualified; and the Congress may by law provide for the case wherein neither a President elect nor a Vice President elect shall have qualified, declaring who shall then act as President, or the manner in which one who is to act shall be selected, and such person shall act accordingly until a President or Vice President shall have qualified.

*Section 4.*

The Congress may by law provide for the case of the death of any of the persons from whom the House of Representatives may choose a President whenever the right of choice shall have devolved upon them, and for the case of the death of any of the persons from whom the Senate may choose a Vice President whenever the right of choice shall have devolved upon them.

*Section 5.*

Sections 1 and 2 shall take effect on the 15th day of October following the ratification of this article.

*Section 6.*

This article shall be inoperative unless it shall have been ratified as an amendment to the Constitution by the legislatures of three fourths of the several States within seven years from the date of its submission.

## AMENDMENT XXII[10]

*Section 1.*

No person shall be elected to the office of the President more than twice, and no person who has held the office of President, or acted as President, for more than two years of a term to which some other person was elected President shall be elected to the office of the President more than once. But this Article shall not apply to any person holding the office of President when this Article was proposed by the Congress, and shall not prevent any person who may be

[9]Adopted in 1933.
[10]Adopted in 1951.

holding the office of President, or acting as President, during the term within which this Article becomes operative from holding the office of President or acting as President during the remainder of such term.

Section 2.

This article shall be inoperative unless it shall have been ratified as an amendment to the Constitution by the legislatures of three fourths of the several States within seven years from the date of its submission to the States by the Congress.

# AMENDMENT XXIII[11]

Section 1.

The District constituting the seat of Government of the United States shall appoint in such manner as the Congress may direct:

A number of electors of President and Vice President equal to the whole number of Senators and Representatives in Congress to which the District would be entitled if it were a State, but in no event more than the least populous State; they shall be in addition to those appointed by the States, but they shall be considered, for the purposes of the election of President and Vice President, to be electors appointed by a State; and they shall meet in the District and perform such duties as provided by the twelfth article of amendment.

Section 2.

The Congress shall have power to enforce this article by appropriate legislation.

# AMENDMENT XXIV[12]

Section 1.

The right of citizens of the United States to vote in any primary or other election for President or Vice President, for electors for President or Vice President, or for Senator or Representative in Congress, shall not be denied or abridged by the United States or any state by reasons of failure to pay any poll tax or other tax.

Section 2.

The Congress shall have power to enforce this article by appropriate legislation.

# AMENDMENT XXV[13]

Section 1.

In case of the removal of the President from office or of his death or resignation, the Vice President shall become President.

[11]Adopted in 1961.
[12]Adopted in 1964.
[13]Adopted in 1967.

*Section 2.*

Whenever there is a vacancy in the office of the Vice President, the President shall nominate a Vice President who shall take office upon confirmation by a majority vote of both Houses of Congress.

*Section 3.*

Whenever the President transmits to the President pro tempore of the Senate and the Speaker of the House of Representatives his written declaration that he is unable to discharge the powers and duties of his office, and until he transmits to them a written declaration to the contrary, such powers and duties shall be discharged by the Vice President as Acting President.

*Section 4.*

Whenever the Vice President and a majority of either the principal officers of the Executive departments or of such other body as Congress may by law provide, transmit to the President pro tempore of the Senate and the Speaker of the House of Representatives their written declaration that the President is unable to discharge the powers and duties of his office, the Vice President shall immediately assume the powers and duties of the office as Acting President.

Thereafter, when the President transmits to the President pro tempore of the Senate and the Speaker of the House of Representatives his written declaration that no inability exists, he shall resume the powers and duties of his office unless the Vice President and a majority of either the principal officers of the executive departments or of such other body as Congress may by law provide, transmit within four days to the President pro tempore of the Senate and the Speaker of the House of Representatives their written declaration that the President is unable to discharge the powers and duties of his office. Thereupon Congress shall decide the issue, assembling within forty-eight hours for that purpose if not in session. If the Congress, within twenty-one days after receipt of the latter written declaration, or, if Congress is not in session, within twenty-one days after Congress is required to assemble, determines by two thirds vote of both houses that the President is unable to discharge the powers and duties of his office, the Vice President shall continue to discharge the same as Acting President; otherwise, the President shall resume the powers and duties of his office.

# AMENDMENT XXVI[14]

*Section 1.*

The right of citizens of the United States, who are 18 years of age or older, to vote shall not be denied or abridged by the United States or any state on account of age.

*Section 2.*

The Congress shall have power to enforce this article by appropriate legislation.

[14]Adopted in 1971.

# Index

# About the Authors

*George C. Edwards III* (Ph.D., University of Wisconsin) is Distinguished Professor of Political Science at Texas A&M University and director of The Center for Presidential Studies. He also holds the Jordan Professorship in Liberal Arts and is involved in the development of the George Bush Presidential Library. Edwards is one of the nation's leading scholars of the presidency and has written or edited fifteen books on American politics and public policy making, including *Researching the Presidency* (1993), *Presidential Approval* (1990), *At the Margins: Presidential Leadership of Congress* (1989), and *National Security and the U.S. Constitution* (1988). He is coauthor of *Government in America* (1994), an introductory text.

*Stephen J. Wayne* (Ph.D., Columbia University) is a professor of government and the head of the American Government Section at Georgetown University. An author of numerous professional articles, book reviews, book chapters, and encyclopedia articles, he has also published several books, including *The Road to the White House, 1992* (St. Martin's, 1992), *The Quest for National Office* (St. Martin's, 1992; edited with Clyde Wilcox), and the forthcoming *The Politics of American Government* (St. Martin's, 1995). He is also Advisory Editor in Political Science to McGraw-Hill's College Division and a series editor for M. E. Sharpe. Professor Wayne makes frequent media appearances and is widely quoted as an analyst on elections and the presidency. He has lectured extensively at colleges and universities in the United States and abroad.

Professors Edwards and Wayne are coeditors of *Studying the Presidency* (1983) and were leaders in the National Academy of Public Administration's Presidential Transition Project (1988), providing advice to the new president. Both have served as president of the Presidency Research Section of the American Political Science Association.